Less managing. More teaching. Greater learning.

 INSTRUCTORS...

Would you like your **students** to show up for class **more prepared**?
(Let's face it, class is much more fun if everyone is engaged and prepared...)

Want an **easy way to assign** homework online and track student **progress**?
(Less time grading means more time teaching...)

Want an **instant view** of student or class performance? *(No more wondering if students understand...)*

Need to **collect data and generate reports** required for administration or accreditation? *(Say goodbye to manually tracking student learning outcomes...)*

Want to **record and post your lectures** for students to view online?

 With **McGraw-Hill's *Connect*® Plus Finance,**

INSTRUCTORS GET:

- Simple **assignment management**, allowing you to spend more time teaching.
- **Auto-graded** assignments, quizzes, and tests.
- **Detailed Visual Reporting** where student and section results can be viewed and analyzed.
- Sophisticated **online testing** capability.
- A **filtering and reporting** function that allows you to easily assign and report on materials that are correlated to accreditation standards, learning outcomes, and Bloom's taxonomy.
- An easy-to-use **lecture capture** tool.
- The option to **upload course documents** for student access.

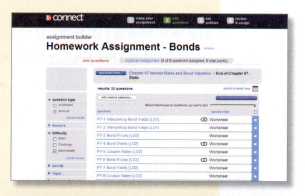

Want an online, **searchable version** of your textbook?

Wish your textbook could be **available online** while you're doing your assignments?

 ### *Connect® Plus Finance* eBook

If you choose to use *Connect® Plus Finance*, you have an affordable and searchable online version of your book integrated with your other online tools.

Connect® Plus Finance eBook offers features like:

- Topic search
- Direct links from assignments
- Adjustable text size
- Jump to page number
- Print by section

 Want to get more **value** from your textbook purchase?

Think learning finance should be a bit more **interesting**?

 ### Check out the STUDENT RESOURCES section under the *Connect®* Library tab.

Here you'll find a wealth of resources designed to help you achieve your goals in the course. Every student has different needs, so explore the STUDENT RESOURCES to find the materials best suited to you.

personal finance

building your future

The McGraw-Hill/Irwin Series in Finance, Insurance and Real Estate

Stephen A. Ross Franco Modigliani Professor of Finance and Economics
Sloan School of Management Massachusetts Institute of Technology Consulting Editor

FINANCIAL MANAGEMENT

Block, Hirt, and Danielsen
Foundations of Financial Management
Fourteenth Edition

Brealey, Myers, and Allen
Principles of Corporate Finance
Tenth Edition

Brealey, Myers, and Allen
Principles of Corporate Finance, Concise
Second Edition

Brealey, Myers, and Marcus
Fundamentals of Corporate Finance
Seventh Edition

Brooks
FinGame Online 5.0

Bruner
Case Studies in Finance: Managing for Corporate Value Creation
Sixth Edition

Cornett, Adair, and Nofsinger
Finance: Applications and Theory
Second Edition

Cornett, Adair, and Nofsinger
M: Finance
First Edition

DeMello
Cases in Finance
Second Edition

Grinblatt (Editor)
Stephen A. Ross, Mentor: Influence through Generations

Grinblatt and Titman
Financial Markets and Corporate Strategy
Second Edition

Higgins
Analysis for Financial Management
Tenth Edition

Kellison
Theory of Interest
Third Edition

Ross, Westerfield, and Jaffe
Corporate Finance
Ninth Edition

Ross, Westerfield, Jaffe, and Jordan
Corporate Finance: Core Principles and Applications
Third Edition

Ross, Westerfield, and Jordan
Essentials of Corporate Finance
Seventh Edition

Ross, Westerfield, and Jordan
Fundamentals of Corporate Finance
Tenth Edition

Shefrin
Behavioral Corporate Finance: Decisions that Create Value
First Edition

White
Financial Analysis with an Electronic Calculator
Sixth Edition

INVESTMENTS

Bodie, Kane, and Marcus
Essentials of Investments
Eighth Edition

Bodie, Kane, and Marcus
Investments
Ninth Edition

Hirt and Block
Fundamentals of Investment Management
Tenth Edition

Hirschey and Nofsinger
Investments: Analysis and Behavior
Second Edition

Jordan and Miller
Fundamentals of Investments: Valuation and Management
Sixth Edition

Stewart, Piros, and Heisler
Running Money: Professional Portfolio Management
First Edition

Sundaram and Das
Derivatives: Principles and Practice
First Edition

FINANCIAL INSTITUTIONS AND MARKETS

Rose and Hudgins
Bank Management and Financial Services
Ninth Edition

Rose and Marquis
Financial Institutions and Markets
Eleventh Edition

Saunders and Cornett
Financial Institutions Management: A Risk Management Approach
Seventh Edition

Saunders and Cornett
Financial Markets and Institutions
Fifth Edition

INTERNATIONAL FINANCE

Eun and Resnick
International Financial Management
Sixth Edition

Robin
International Corporate Finance
First Edition

REAL ESTATE

Brueggeman and Fisher
Real Estate Finance and Investments
Fourteenth Edition

Ling and Archer
Real Estate Principles: A Value Approach
Third Edition

FINANCIAL PLANNING AND INSURANCE

Allen, Melone, Rosenbloom, and Mahoney
Retirement Plans: 401(k)s, IRAs, and Other Deferred Compensation Approaches
Tenth Edition

Altfest
Personal Financial Planning
First Edition

Harrington and Niehaus
Risk Management and Insurance
Second Edition

Kapoor, Dlabay, and Hughes
Focus on Personal Finance: An Active Approach to Help You Develop Successful Financial Skills
Third Edition

Kapoor, Dlabay, and Hughes
Personal Finance
Tenth Edition

Walker and Walker
Personal Finance: Building Your Future
First Edition

personal finance

building your future

Robert B. Walker
Mount Mercy University

Kristy P. Walker
University of Iowa

personal finance
building your future

VICE PRESIDENT AND EDITOR-IN-CHIEF: **BRENT GORDON**

PUBLISHER: **DOUGLAS REINER**

EXECUTIVE EDITOR: **MICHELE JANICEK**

EXECUTIVE DIRECTOR OF DEVELOPMENT: **ANN TORBERT**

DEVELOPMENT EDITOR II: **JENNIFER LOHN**

VICE PRESIDENT AND DIRECTOR OF MARKETING: **ROBIN J. ZWETTLER**

MARKETING DIRECTOR: **BRAD PARKINS**

EXECUTIVE MARKETING MANAGER: **MELISSA S. CAUGHLIN**

VICE PRESIDENT OF EDITING, DESIGN, AND PRODUCTION: **SESHA BOLISETTY**

SENIOR PROJECT MANAGER: **DIANE L. NOWACZYK**

SENIOR BUYER: **MICHAEL R. MCCORMICK**

COVER AND INTERIOR DESIGNER: **MATT DIAMOND**

SENIOR PHOTO RESEARCH COORDINATOR: **KERI JOHNSON**

PHOTO RESEARCHER: **ALLISON GRIMES**

SENIOR MEDIA PROJECT MANAGER: **SUSAN LOMBARDI**

MEDIA PROJECT MANAGER: **ALPANA JOLLY, HURIX SYSTEMS PVT. LTD.**

COVER IMAGE: **© GETTY IMAGES**

TYPEFACE: **10/12 MINION PRO REGULAR**

COMPOSITOR: **LASERWORDS PRIVATE LIMITED**

PRINTER: **QUAD/GRAPHICS**

PERSONAL FINANCE: BUILDING YOUR FUTURE

Published by McGraw-Hill/Irwin, a business unit of The McGraw-Hill Companies, Inc., 1221 Avenue of the Americas, New York, NY, 10020. Copyright © 2013 by The McGraw-Hill Companies, Inc. All rights reserved. Printed in the United States of America. No part of this publication may be reproduced or distributed in any form or by any means, or stored in a database or retrieval system, without the prior written consent of The McGraw-Hill Companies, Inc., including, but not limited to, in any network or other electronic storage or transmission, or broadcast for distance learning.

Some ancillaries, including electronic and print components, may not be available to customers outside the United States.

This book is printed on acid-free paper.

1 2 3 4 5 6 7 8 9 0 QDB/QDB 1 0 9 8 7 6 5 4 3 2

ISBN 978-0-07-353065-9
MHID 0-07-353065-4

Library of Congress Cataloging-in-Publication Data

Walker, Robert B.
    Personal finance : building your future / Robert B. Walker, Kristy P. Walker. — 1st ed.
        p. cm. — (The McGraw-Hill/Irwin series in finance, insurance and real estate)
    Includes index.
    ISBN-13: 978-0-07-353065-9 (alk. paper)
    ISBN-10: 0-07-353065-4 (alk. paper)
    1. Finance, Personal. I. Walker, Kristy P. II. Title.
HG179.W3124 2013
332.024—dc23

2011036669

www.mhhe.com

dedication

We dedicate this textbook to our children, Nate, Erin, and Clay, who always make us proud.

about the authors

Robert B. Walker (Bob) is the Business Department Chair at Mount Mercy University, where he teaches both undergraduate and graduate students. He received his bachelor's degree in philosophy from Miami University, an MBA from the University of Iowa, and a PhD from Iowa State University. He spent 18 years working in community banks before starting his own consulting practice. During this time, he was the Executive Director of the East Central Iowa Chapter of the American Institute of Banking, a division of the American Bankers Association. He taught nine years at Kirkwood Community College as Banking and Finance Coordinator before becoming Department Chair at Mount Mercy University. Professor Walker served on the Associates Degree Board of Commissioners for the Accreditation Council for Business Schools & Programs (ACBSP) and was actively involved in Kirkwood Community College's initial ACBSP accreditation. He was a Sam M. Walton fellow at Kirkwood Community College, starting the school's Students in Free Enterprise (SIFE) team and is currently lead Sam M. Walton Fellow for Mount Mercy's SIFE team.

Kristy P. Walker is the Director of Clinical Applications and Associate Director of the Department of Health Care Information Systems at the University of Iowa Hospitals and Clinics. She received her bachelor's degree in computer science and an MBA from the University of Iowa. She has contributed to a number of publications, including the *Journal of American Medical Record Association* and proceedings from the Health Information and Management Systems Society (HIMSS) and the American Medical Informatics Association (AMIA). She currently serves on the State of Iowa Electronic Health Information Advisory Council. In the past, she served on the Iowa Health Information Technology Plan Task Force and as a lecturer for the University of Iowa.

preface

This new book offers students a comprehensive and engaging treatment of personal finance, while incorporating unique themes, an application-driven pedagogy, and a definitive action plan. Unlike other texts on the market, it offers a frank and timely discussion of living within one's means and incorporating personal values and priorities into a personal financial plan. The intent is to help readers set priorities that guide their financal decisions, rather than the other way around. This book establishes a path toward financial freedom that is less about accumulating wealth and more about building a future tailored to individual goals.

Before we began writing this text, we accumulated and analyzed data from a publisher-sponsored survey about the challenges, goals and themes, topic coverage, and other needs of finance professors nationwide in personal finance courses. We then used this information to build a book and package that directly address those needs and desires. We are very excited to bring you a fresh outlook on personal finance. This text teaches the fundamentals of living within one's means, the principles of voluntary simplicity, the importance of looking to your values to set goals, the need for persistence in reaching your financial goals, and the importance of becoming financially independent.

GOALS AND THEMES

As we began to write, and throughout the development of the book, we focused on three main goals and themes: responsible financial decision making, alignment of personal and financial goals, and the importance of maintaining a personal financial plan.

Responsible Financial Decision-Making

Almost every personal finance instructor has the same central goal: to help students establish financial literacy so they can take and keep control of their finances. Before they can develop their own financial plan, however, it is crucial that students understand the key terms, concepts, and principles of financial planning. To address that need, the text offers a

Making $ense

1.1 What determines your money personality?

1.2 How do you take control over spending?

1.3 When is enough *enough?*

continuing case

Throughout the text, the continuing case scenario at the end of the chapter will involve lessons encountered by the housemates of 906 East College Street. All of the residents are either current students or recent graduates. Leigh, Blake, and Nicole are siblings. Their parents bought the home, which is close to campus, as an investment when Leigh started at the university her freshman year. The following profiles describe each of the housemates and their intermediate-term goals. For each housemate, identify a SMART short-term goal that supports his or her success in achieving an intermediate goal.

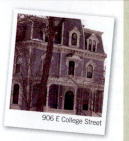

906 E College Street

comprehensive table of contents and pedagogical features, providing students with the foundation they need to make responsible financial decisions. Extensive assessment tools built right into the book keep students on the right track toward mastering the material. The central goal is to make this material relevant and easy to master so that students can take control of their finances and be responsible decision makers.

To help students learn how to make responsible choices with their finances, the textbook includes:

▶ **Learning Objectives** that shape the organization and goals of each chapter. These objectives link to individual sections of the book and are referenced in the review and assessment materials, allowing instructors to assign the most important concepts in personal finance in a deliberate and complete fashion and test students' mastery of that content.

▶ **Concept checks** in the Making $ense boxes at the end of each section that test students' retention of key content.

▶ Quality end-of-chapter **concept questions** and **quantitative practice problems,** along with a **running case** for concept application, that allow additional opportunities for assessment and review.

Alignment of Personal and Financial Goals

Financial success means different things to individuals with different priorities. *Personal Finance* recognizes this fact and sets itself apart from the field by helping students direct their finances according to *their* goals. Many personal finance books presuppose maximized wealth accumulation as the students' outright goal. While maximizing wealth may well be in the long-term interests of many, not everyone is going to be wealthy—nor is everyone motivated by the pursuit of wealth. By recognizing that students need, want, and are fulfilled by different things, this book encourages students to take a closer look at their own lives and priorities as they set their financial plans and to consider the opportunity costs of their decisions in terms of both their financial *and* their personal goals.

 Budget: A mathmatical confirmation of your suspicions. 🟣

—A.A. LATIMER

> "Any intelligent fool can make things bigger, more complex, and more violent. It takes a touch of genius—and a lot of courage—to move in the opposite direction."
>
> —E.F. SCHUMACHER

Similarly, the text examines the value of *mindful spending*. "Going green" may originally have been meant only as a reference to preserving the environment, but it has come to encompass the growing tendency in all aspects of our lives to reuse materials, reduce waste, and increase long-term sustainability. This text applies these same principles to personal finance, emphasizing the importance of *living within one's means* by living simply, reducing consumption, and budgeting for a long-term, sustainable financial plan.

To help students understand the running theme of aligning financial and personal goals, the textbook includes:

▶ **Financial Fitness/Stopping Little Leaks** boxes that give creative and, in some cases, eye-opening tips about how cutting down on small, unnecessary spending can lead to big savings.

▶ An online **Every Penny Counts spending journal** and instructions for using it effectively.

Maintaining a Personal Financial Plan

We encourage readers throughout the book to actively assess their relationship with money by including in every section examples relevant to students' lives and plans. Through ample opportunities to actively apply the concepts to their own financial decisions, by the end of the course, students will have laid the foundation for their own successful personal financial plan. In this way, the text teaches students to make and review financial plans as a lifelong habit.

This goal of building a personal financial plan is emphasized by the model: *Learn. Plan & Act. Evaluate.* (LPAE). Every chapter summary presents this model to help make explicit for students how they can apply the chapter's topics and concepts in their own lives. Students *learn* the concepts of personal finance by reading the text and studying the material. They *plan* by leveraging this knowledge and building a personal financial plan. They *act* by executing the plan

financialfitness:
STOPPING LITTLE LEAKS

Simple Savings While You Sleep

There are lots of little things you can do to save almost unconsciously. For example, investing in a programmable thermostat that turns off your air conditioning or furnace while you are gone during the day or while you sleep can save you $15 per month. In turn, you can automatically deposit that $15 into a high-interest savings account.

and by using critical thinking skills to continually assess whether their plan is working and what adjustments need to be made. Finally, they are asked to *evaluate* how their plan fits in with their financial and personal goals. In this way, personal finance comes to life for the students, making it accessible and easily applicable to their own lives.

To help students engage in building their personal financial plan, the textbook includes:

▶ Chapter-by-chapter updates of the **LPAE** theme.

> **LEARN** - bulleted summaries of the topics students have studied and the objectives achieved.

> **PLAN & ACT** - a checklist of action items for students to do while setting up their financial plan.

> **EVALUATE** - questions that help students analyze the effectiveness of their plan.

▶ An online **Goal Tracker** at the end of each chapter. This feature helps students create their own financial plan and align their personal goals with their finances.

Learn. | Plan & Act. | Evaluate.

LEARN. This chapter explored your relationship with money, your vision for your future, and your goals given your financial stage in life. You were exposed to the concept of voluntary simplicity—where more money may not always be better—and the idea that there comes a time when enough is enough. One of the best reasons for studying personal finance is to avoid the nightmares that lack of control and lack of direction bring. Finally, you learned how to create SMART goals to reach your vision of the future.

Work Sheet: Goals		Response				
1.7	SMART Short-Term Goal:					
1.7	SMART Intermediate Goal:					
1.7	SMART Short-Term Goal:					
Work Sheet: Evaluation		Response	Short-Term Goal Tracking (Y/N)	Intermediate Goal Tracking (Y/N)	Long-Term Goal Tracking (Y/N)	If not, identify plan as to how to get back on track:
2.1	Estimated Cost of Goals:					
2.2	Saving Plan for Goals:					
	Goal Tracker (Date):	__/__/__				
Work Sheet: Evaluation		Response	Short-Term Goal Tracking (Y/N)	Intermediate Goal Tracking (Y/N)	Long-Term Goal Tracking (Y/N)	If not, identify plan as to how to get back on track:
3.2	Budget support of goal:					
	Goal Tracker (Date):	__/__/__				
Work Sheet: Evaluation		Response	Short-Term Goal Tracking (Y/N)	Intermediate Goal Tracking (Y/N)	Long-Term Goal Tracking (Y/N)	If not, identify plan as to how to get back on track:
4.1	Financial Instrument supporting goal:					
	Goal Tracker (Date):	__/__/__				

> "The only reason a great many American families don't own an elephant is that they have never been offered an elephant for a dollar down and easy weekly payments."
>
> —MAD MAGAZINE

Worksheet 13.1 - The Social Science of the Stock Market

(1) Review the top news stories over the past few weeks and consider the impact they have had on the market (Dow).

(2) After completing Worksheet 13.1, what characteristics or patterns do you see?

(3) How does this observation impact your decisions as to what type of stock to buy or sell and when?

Date	Event	Impact on the Dow

◀ **Worksheets,** highlighted at the end of each chapter (and available in full on the Online Learning Center at www.mhhe.com/walkerpf1e), that show students step-by-step how to get financial aspects of their lives under control. For example, in Chapter 5, a chapter on credit cards, one of the accompanying worksheets guides students through how to access a credit report, follow up on inaccuracies, and develop action plans to improve their overall score.

> ❝I am having an out of money experience.❞
>
> —AUTHOR UNKNOWN

COURSE CHALLENGES

Our market research, conversations with colleagues, and personal experiences in the classroom converged on two persistent course challenges: (1) how to engage students in the material, and (2) how to reach students who lack the computational skills needed to solve financial problems. We designed the book to address both of those challenges.

Engaging Students

One of the biggest challenges instructors say they face when teaching personal finance is keeping students engaged and interested in the material. Students may be interested in areas of personal finance that affect them *right now*, such as credit card debt, financing an education, and buying a car that they want. Unfortunately, their enthusiasm often wanes as the conversation turns to topics that may seem irrelevant to their current lives, such as investing or estate planning.

To help students become and stay engaged with the variety of personal finance topics in the course, the textbook includes:

- ▶ **Chapter-opening scenarios** that make the topics real and relatable to student readers. Personal finance is, well, personal. The chapter-opening scenarios lay the groundwork for the importance of the chapter topic by sharing the stories of real people. These stories illuminate how financial planning (or the lack of) affects people differently depending on their age and life situation.

- ▶ **In the News** boxes, which incorporate **current events** into the text.

- ▶ **QR codes,** which enable students to use their smartphones to access relevant, updated content about current events or chapter quizzes directly from the Walker website.

- ▶ **Examples of real-life situations** to reinforce concepts and lessons. These examples are taken from current events, hypothetical situations, and actual experiences.

◀ Clay, age 14, high school freshman, a dollar in hand for each thousand in savings

Power of Compounding

Each year since birth, Clay received $1,000 from his grandparents for his birthday. As a high school senior "I decided to keep my birthday money in savings instead of using it for college expenses. The

---

IN THE NEWS

Scan here for more information on the latest events "In the News"

New status symbol: Family mission statements

Mission statements are moving from the boardroom to the family room. A growing number of multimillionaires and billionaires, hoping to stave off costly feuds, are drawing up family mission statements—lofty treatises filled with words like "legacy," "values," and "stewardship" that aim

Mission statements are surging in popularity, along with the number of rich people who are passing down wealth in hopes of creating family dynasties. There are now 4.5 million U.S. households with investable assets of $1 million or more. Since so many of today's wealthy are entrepre-

a one-sentence statement written by a wealthy couple. It said, "We want our capital to allow our children and their children to be able to find their passion and pursue it with excellence." "What they were saying with the mission statement was 'Don't worry about whether you can earn a living if that gets in the way of you being the best painter or teacher or poet.' It was about self-realization, not spending." Glenn Kurlander, managing director of Citi Private Bank's family wealth advisory services, helped craft a six-page statement that

---

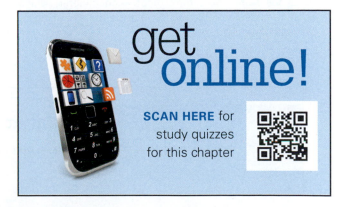

get online!

SCAN HERE for study quizzes for this chapter

QR Code is a registered trademark of DENSO WAVE INCORPORATED.

- **You're the Expert cases,** which are extended problems that put students in hypothetical situations and then ask them to lay out a financial plan and solve problems.

- **Interesting quotes** about finance, such as those you see here in the preface. Our students have enjoyed the quotes over the years and have demonstrated their enthusiasm by sharing new ones with us.

- **Live and interactive media** through the authors' blog (www.frugalfunandfinancialfitness.blogspot.com) and Twitter account (@frugalfinances). Through these resources, students can access additional articles, tips, and thoughts about finance directly from the authors.

- **Financial Fitness** boxes, which provide additional interesting and useful tips and information about different aspects of financial planning.

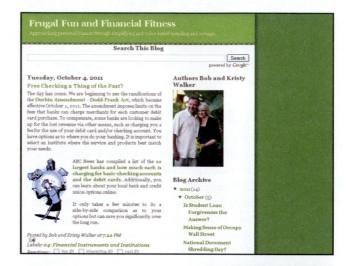

Solving Financial Problems

A second challenge of this course, especially for the increasing number of personal finance students who are not finance majors, is learning how to apply mathematical equations in order to solve financial problems. To address this challenge, the text incorporates strategies and tools to help students master the math in personal finance:

- A detailed explanation of **time value of money** early in the book (Chapter 2). This allows students time to learn the concept and then move on to applying it throughout the course, in different areas of personal finance.

- **Doing the Math** boxes throughout each chapter, which present example problems that require the use of financial calculations to solve.

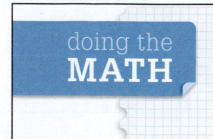

doing the
MATH

2.2 Future Value of a Lump Sum

Example: *You received $20,000 when you turned 16 and decided to invest it for five years at 4% interest. How much will that $20,000 be worth when you turn 21?*

1. Calculate using the long-hand method.

2. Calculate using the reference table method.

ORGANIZATION OF CHAPTERS

The nationwide survey of finance professors also helped determine the text's key topics, how much coverage each topic requires, and where each topic fits best in a typical course. The book's organization, described below, provides a comprehensive and logically sequenced approach to personal finance that aligns with the goals of varying types of personal finance programs. Where coverage strays from most other books on the market, we explain our reasoning below.

Section One: MONEY $ MONEY $ MONEY

This section emphasizes that personal financial success is more easily achieved when the student's spending and saving plans are aligned with his or her overall values and goals. Values, vision, mission, and goals established in Chapter 1 serve as a guide when evaluating options in subsequent chapters. We discuss the time value of money early in the book, so students have a solid understanding of savings, investing, and opportunity cost. The student's record of every penny spent in Chapter 3 teaches the student to: (1) get control of spending, (2) set a realistic budget based on spending needs, and (3) determine whether his or her spending reflects personal values and priorities.

Section Two: CREDIT MANAGEMENT

This section is particularly relevant given the financial crisis that began in 2008. We decided it was a good idea to spend time discussing not only the importance of avoiding debt, but also the steps involved in debt management. Due to the current recession, many Americans are faced with the task of lowering their personal debt load. We provide specific strategies for how to dig out of debt, while also emphasizing that debt is created over time and that it may take time, discipline, and sacrifice to get one's finances back in order. We also examine bankruptcy and the foreclosure process so that there is an understanding of the debtor's rights and responsibilities during the process.

Section Three: LIMITING YOUR LIABILITY

Section Three covers the topics of taxes and insurance. Insurance is important in securing our investments and assets. This unit encourages saving money by being a wise consumer of insurance and taking advantage of tax deductions and incentive plans that minimize tax liability.

Section Four: WEALTH ACCUMULATION

This section first covers investment basics and then moves into mutual funds and stocks and bonds. We cover mutual funds first for a couple of reasons: (1) More people invest in mutual funds than in individual stocks and bonds; and (2) finance majors will have specific classes to cover the details of stocks, bonds, derivatives, options, and other financial instruments. General studies majors probably do not need such detailed information, and it may be more confusing than helpful for them. We also spend time covering real estate investments in this unit. Many people during the early 2000s thought real estate investment was a way to amass a quick fortune. We discuss how the real estate bust in 2008–2009 cost many people their life savings and forced them into bankruptcy.

Section Five: PERPETUAL PAYOFFS

The final section examines retirement, estate planning, and charitable giving, tying back to the book's theme of values-based personal finance and purposeful living. We conclude by talking about a sustainable lifestyle and by coaching students to continually re-evaluate where they are in their financial plans and whether they are still on track to meet their goals.

SUPPLEMENTS

Personal Finance comes with an innovative, engaging, and complete set of instructional resources to improve the classroom experience of both students and teachers.

Online Learning Center (OLC): www.mhhe.com/walkerpf1e

The **Online Learning Center (OLC)** contains access to web-based study tools and instructor resources created just for this book. OLCs can be delivered in many ways: through the textbook website, through a course management system like Blackboard, or through McGraw-Hill's *Connect*®. Ask your McGraw-Hill sales representative for more details.

For Instructors

The **Instructor Edition of the OLC** holds all supplementary material, including the following resources:

- The *Instructor's Manual,* prepared by the authors, includes discussion starters, teaching tips, projects, supplementary links and resources, and insights into the prepared lecture material that comes with the book. It also supplies lecture outlines, supplementary activities, answers to concept checks, and end-of-chapter questions, cases, and problems.

- The *Test Bank,* also prepared by the authors, consists of more than 1,100 true-false, multiple-choice, and essay questions. Each question is correlated to a specific learning objective, topic, level of difficulty, Bloom's taxonomy category, and AACSB standard. Instructors can use these tags to filter questions easily and accurately and to find and select material for tests.

- *Computerized Testing Software – McGraw-Hill's EZ Test* is a flexible and easy-to-use electronic testing program. The program allows instructors to create tests from book-specific items. It accommodates a wide range of question types, and instructors may add their own questions. Instructors can create multiple versions of the test, and any test can be exported for use with course management systems. EZ Test Online gives you a place to easily administer your EZ Test-created exams and quizzes online. The program is available for Windows and Macintosh environments.

- *Chapter PowerPoint® Presentations,* created by the authors, offer clear, concise, and interactive ways of presenting material to students. These may be edited and customized for best use in the classroom.

For Students

The **Student Edition of the OLC** contains a great variety of tools for students to gain experience in hands-on personal finance:

- *Self-Study Quizzes* consist of 10 to 15 self-grading multiple-choice questions covering the key topics in the chapter.

- *Worksheets* give students practice in tracking spending, setting budgets, shopping for insurance, and the like.

- *GoalTracker* helps students think through and record their goals and helps them realize those goals as they learn the concepts of personal financial planning.

- *Current Events Blog,* updated regularly by the authors, engages students in understanding the importance of personal finance and applying the concepts of planning in a real-life context (http://frugalfunandfinancialfitness .blogspot.com).

McGraw-Hill's Connect® Finance

You may package your text with a variety of other learning tools that are available to your students, including McGraw-Hill's *Connect® Finance.*

Less Managing, More Teaching, Greater Learning McGraw-Hill *Connect® Finance* is an online assignment and assessment solution that connects students with the tools and resources they will need to achieve success. *Connect®* helps prepare students for their future by enabling faster learning, more efficient studying, and higher retention of knowledge.

McGraw-Hill Connect® Finance Features *Connect® Finance* offers a number of powerful tools and features to make managing assignments easier, so faculty can spend more time teaching. With *Connect® Finance,* students can engage with their coursework anytime and anywhere, making the learning process more accessible and efficient. *Connect® Finance* offers you the features described below.

Simple assignment management With *Connect® Finance,* creating assignments is easier than ever, so you can spend more time teaching and less time managing. The assignment-management function enables you to:

- Create and deliver assignments easily with selectable end-of-chapter questions and test bank items.

- Streamline lesson planning, student progress reporting, and assignment grading to make classroom management more efficient than ever.

- Go paperless with the eBook and online submission and grading of student assignments.

Smart grading When it comes to studying, time is precious. *Connect® Finance* helps students learn more efficiently by providing feedback and practice material when they need it, where they need it. When it comes to teaching, your time is also precious. The grading function enables you to:

- Have assignments scored automatically, giving students immediate feedback on their work and side-by-side comparisons with correct answers.

- Access and review each response; also, manually change grades or leave comments for your students to review.

- Reinforce classroom concepts with practice tests and instant quizzes.

Instructor library The *Connect® Finance* Instructor Library is your repository for additional resources to improve student engagement in and out of class. You can select and use any asset from the library that enhances your lecture.

Student study center The *Connect® Finance* Student Study Center is the place for students to access additional resources. The Student Study Center:

▶ Offers students quick access to lectures, practice materials, eBooks, and more.

▶ Provides instant practice material and study questions, easily accessible on the go.

Student progress tracking *Connect® Finance* keeps instructors informed about how each student, section, and class is performing, allowing for more productive use of lecture and office hours. The progress-tracking function enables you to:

▶ View scored work immediately and track individual or group performance with assignment and grade reports.

▶ Access an instant view of student or class performance relative to learning objectives.

Lecture capture through Tegrity Campus For an additional charge, Lecture Capture offers new ways for students to focus on the in-class discussion, knowing they can revisit important topics later. Captured lectures can be delivered through *Connect* or separately. See below for more details.

McGraw-Hill Connect® Plus Finance McGraw-Hill reinvents the textbook learning experience for the modern student with *Connect® Plus Finance*. A seamless integration of an eBook and *Connect® Finance*, *Connect® Plus Finance* provides all of the *Connect® Finance* features plus the following:

▶ An integrated eBook, allowing for anytime, anywhere access to the textbook.

▶ Dynamic links between the problems or questions you assign to your students and the location in the eBook where that problem or question is covered.

▶ A powerful search function to pinpoint and connect key concepts in a snap.

In short, *Connect® Finance* offers you and your students powerful tools and features that optimize your time and energies, enabling you to focus on course content, teaching, and student learning. *Connect® Finance* also offers a wealth of content resources for both instructors and students. This state-of-the-art, thoroughly tested system supports you in preparing students for the world that awaits.

For more information about *Connect®*, go to www.mcgrawhillconnect.com, or contact your local McGraw-Hill sales representative.

 **Tegrity Campus: Lectures 24/7**

Tegrity Campus is a service that makes class time available 24/7 by automatically capturing every lecture in a searchable format for students to review when they study and complete assignments. With a simple one-click stand-and-stop process, you capture all computer screens and corresponding audio. Students can replay any part of any class with easy-to-use browser-based viewing on a PC or Mac.

Educators know that the more students can see, hear, and experience class resources, the better they learn. In fact, studies prove it. With Tegrity Campus, students quickly recall key moments by using Tegrity Campus's unique search feature. This search helps students efficiently find what they need, when they need it, across an entire semester of class recordings. Help turn all your students' study time into learning moments immediately supported by your lecture.

To learn more about Tegrity watch a two-minute flash demo at http://tegritycampus.mhhe.com.

Blackboard and McGraw-Hill

The Best of Both Worlds
www.domorenow.com

McGraw-Hill Higher Education and Blackboard have teamed up. What does this mean for you?

1. **Your life, simplified.** Now you and your students can access McGraw-Hill's Connect® and Create™ right from within your Blackboard course—all with one single sign-on. Say goodbye to the days of logging in to multiple applications.

2. **Deep integration of content and tools.** Not only do you get single sign-on with Connect® and Create™, you also get deep integration of McGraw-Hill content and content engines right in Blackboard. Whether you're choosing a book for your course or building Connect® assignments, all the tools you need are right where you want them—inside of Blackboard.

3. **Seamless Gradebooks.** Are you tired of keeping multiple gradebooks and manually synchronizing grades into

Blackboard? We thought so. When a student completes an integrated Connect® assignment, the grade for that assignment automatically (and instantly) feeds your Blackboard grade center.

4. **A solution for everyone.** Whether your institution is already using Blackboard or you just want to try Blackboard on your own, we have a solution for you. McGraw-Hill and Blackboard can now offer you easy access to industry leading technology and content, whether your campus hosts it, or we do. Be sure to ask your local McGraw-Hill representative for details.

McGraw-Hill Customer Care Contact Information

At McGraw-Hill, we understand that getting the most from new technology can be challenging. That's why our services don't stop after you purchase our products. You can e-mail our Product Specialists 24 hours a day to get product-training online. Or you can search our knowledge bank of Frequently Asked Questions on our support website. For Customer Support, call 800-331-5094, e-mail hmsupport@mcgraw-hill.com, or visit www.mhhe.com/support. One of our Technical Support Analysts will be able to assist you in a timely fashion.

ASSURANCE OF LEARNING READY

Assurance of learning is an important element of many accreditation standards. *Personal Finance* is designed specifically to support your assurance of learning initiatives. Each chapter in the book begins with a list of numbered learning objectives which appear throughout the chapter, as well as in the end-of-chapter materials. Every test bank question is also linked to one of these objectives, in addition to level of difficulty, topic area, Bloom's taxonomy level, and AACSB skill area. You can use our test bank software, *EZ Test* and *EZ Test Online,* and *Connect®,* McGraw-Hill's online homework solution, to search the test bank by these and other categories, providing an engine with which to make the collection and presentation of Assurance of Learning data simple and easy.

AACSB STATEMENT

The McGraw-Hill Companies is a proud corporate member of AACSB International. Understanding the importance and value of AACSB Accreditation, *Personal Finance* recognizes the curricula guidelines detailed in the AACSB standards for business accreditation by connecting selected questions in the test bank to the general knowledge and skill guidelines found in the AACSB standards.

The statements contained in *Personal Finance* are provided only as a guide for the users of this text. The AACSB leaves content coverage and assessment within the purview of individual schools, the mission of the school, and the faculty. While *Personal Finance* and the teaching package make no claim of any specific AACSB qualification or evaluation, we have, within the test bank, labeled selected questions according to the six general knowledge and skills areas.

ACKNOWLEDGMENTS

We would like to thank the following reviewers for their time and feedback. Their help has sincerely made the text stronger and provided balance. For this, we are extremely grateful.

Angel Alexander	Bala Maniam
Brenda Anthony	John Marcis
Michael Araujo	Mario Mastrandrea
Sean Basford	Diane Masuo
Pam Bennett	Robert McCalla
Ross Blankenship	Jamshid Mehran
Karin Bonding	Jim Meir
Walter Boyle	Tammi Metz
Craig Bythewood	Dianne Morrison
Ron Camp	Pattabiraman Neelakantan
Peter Chen	Thomas O'Keefe
Margaret (Meg) Clark	Dan Oglevee
Fernando Conde	Diana Parker
Barbara Connolly	Martina Peng
Nirmalendu Debnath	Lori Radulovich
Beth Deinert	Andreas Rauterkus
Susan Feinberg	Greg Richey
Chuck Finnell	Andrew Salcido
Elizabeth Fletcher	Lawrence Schuffman
Roy Fletcher	Patricia Shaw-Crabb
Paula Freston	Michael Slates
David Fricke	Martin Spechler
Wayne Gawlik	Edith Strickland
Terri Gonzales	Sven Thommesen
Judith Griffin	Steve Tolbert
Jana Hosmer	Lilian Nnenna Ukadike
Sandra Huston	Shafi Ullah
Seonah Kendall	Randall Valentine
Jim Keys	Dick Verrone
Lee Kitchen	Rubina Vohra
Juannae Landry	Andy Whitman
Jeff Livingston	Walt Woerheide
Thomas Lynch	Bruce Xiao

We also would like to thank McGraw-Hill/Irwin for taking a chance on new authors and having faith in our abilities, especially Michele Janicek, Elizabeth Hughes, Jennifer Lohn, Melissa Caughlin, Diane Nowaczyk, Ann Torbert, Bradley Woodrum, Johnna Barto, and all of the other editors, production staff, and marketing staff we have had the pleasure of working with. We most certainly could never have accomplished this journey without them.

No thanks would be complete without acknowledging our family and friends, who have been patient with us as we have stepped out from time to time over the past two years to work on this project; to our children for agreeing to read and provide feedback on the chapters (yes, we talk finance at home too!); to Ila Zimmerman for her assistance with the ever-changing tax laws; and to Jen McCarthy and Dean and Sabrina Awe in helping with the test bank. We could not, and would not, have done it without you.

Robert B. Walker
Kristy P. Walker

NOTE TO STUDENTS

Have you ever considered what life would be like without keeping up with the Joneses, buying on credit, paying for it over time, and getting into perma-debt? Over Bob's 18 years in the banking industry, and then teaching personal finance, he knew that our collective habits of over-spending and under-saving would eventually catch up with us. He often wondered how much growth and prosperity we saw in the '90s and 2000s was financed by credit.

We witnessed the results of over-spending in the fall of 2008 with the fall of Lehman Brothers and the beginning of our current financial crisis. During this time of conventional wisdom being upended, he kept looking for a textbook that he could teach from that emphasized value-based spending, savings, and investing, and successfully debunked the myth that money and the accumulation of material things will make you happy.

As a couple, living with our own financial challenges and watching our children grow, we thought we could offer a new perspective on personal finance: one that emphasizes spending, saving, and investing in accordance with your own personal values. Our fundamental philosophy is that money does not provide happiness. Spending, saving, and investing in accordance with your individual values and goals, and using money wisely as a resource (and not an end in itself) can reduce stress and lead to happiness. You *can* do well and do good at the same time. There is nothing more rewarding than watching students grow and achieve their goals, and that served as powerful motivation for us to write this book.

This book is not only about personal finance, but also about personal happiness and pursuing your passions. It has lessons that can be followed for a lifetime to help you achieve personal financial success.

Thank you for purchasing this book, and we wish you the best of luck as you use this book to better understand your finances and your goals. We invite you to follow us on Twitter (@FrugalFinances) and on our blog (http://frugalfunandfinancialfitness.blogspot.com) to keep current with the changing financial landscape as it relates to the principles of this text and to continue the conversation. We are here to help and hope that, in our small way, we can help you find as much happiness and fulfillment as we have found by living simply and in line with what is most important to us.

Happy Finances!

Bob and Kristy

brief
contents

section one
MONEY $ MONEY $ MONEY $ 2
chapter 1 Money Matters: Values, Vision, Mission, and You 2
chapter 2 Time Value of Money 28
chapter 3 Planning and Budgeting 52
chapter 4 Financial Instruments and Institutions 78

section two
CREDIT MANAGEMENT 108
chapter 5 Consumer Credit: Credit Cards and Student Loans 108
chapter 6 Credit Bureau Reports and Identity Theft 136
chapter 7 Auto and Home Loans 162
chapter 8 Debt, Foreclosure, and Bankruptcy 192

section three
LIMITING YOUR LIABILITY 220
chapter 9 Tax Management 220
chapter 10 Insurance: Covering Your Assets 246

section four
WEALTH ACCUMULATION 276
chapter 11 Investment Basics 276
chapter 12 Mutual Funds 296
chapter 13 Stocks 322
chapter 14 Bonds 348
chapter 15 Real Estate Investments 374

section five
PERPETUAL PAYOFFS 394
chapter 16 Retirement and Estate Planning 394
chapter 17 Financial Planning for Life 420

contents

PREFACE IX

section one
MONEY $ MONEY $ MONEY $ 2

CHAPTER 1   MONEY MATTERS: VALUES, VISION, MISSION, AND YOU 2
GOAL SETTING 4

1.1 PERSONAL RELATIONSHIPS WITH MONEY 4
   Step 1: Understanding Your Perception of Financials 5
   Step 2: Identifying Your Values 5

1.2 FINANCIAL INDEPENDENCE, LITERACY, AND PLANNING 8
   Step 3: Assessing Methods for Achievement 8
   Financial Literacy 9
   Options to Financial Independence 11
   Financial Life Stages 12

1.3 VISION, MISSION, AND GOALS 14
   Step 4: Creating a Vision for Your Future 14
   Step 5: Establishing Your Mission 14
   Step 6: Setting Your Goals 15

1.4 CAREER CHOICES, MONEY, AND HAPPINESS 17
   What Makes You Happy? 17
   Career and Education Choices 18
   Information on Careers 18
   Learn. Plan & Act. Evaluate. 19

CHAPTER 2   TIME VALUE OF MONEY 28
POWER OF COMPOUNDING 30

2.1 WHAT GIVES MONEY VALUE 30

2.2 POWER OF COMPOUNDING 30
   Compounding Interest 31
   Making Compounding Work for You 32
   Pay Yourself First 35

2.3 THE TIME VALUE OF MONEY 35
   Future Value of a Lump Sum 35
   Present Value of a Lump Sum 37
   Future Value of an Annuity 39
   Present Value of an Annuity 41
   Calculating Loan Payments 44
   Learn. Plan & Act. Evaluate. 45

CHAPTER 3   PLANNING AND BUDGETING 52
BUDGETING FROM THE BEGINNING 54

3.1 ANALYZING YOUR SPENDING HABITS: EVERY PENNY COUNTS 54
   Step 1: Keep a Spending Journal 55
   Step 2: Understand Elements of Personal Financial Statements 56
   Step 3: Create a Personal Cash Flow Statement 59

3.2 OPPORTUNITY COST 60

3.3 WAYS TO SAVE MONEY AND LIVE WITHIN YOUR MEANS 63
   Pay Yourself First 63
   Cash Allocations to Budgeted Buckets 63
   Stopping Little Leaks and Making Big Adjustments 64
   Sustainable Consumption 65

3.4 REALISTIC BUDGET BUILDING 66
   Building Your Budget 67
   Reviewing and Revising Your Budget 67
   Learn. Plan & Act. Evaluate. 70

CHAPTER 4   FINANCIAL INSTRUMENTS AND INSTITUTIONS 78

EXPENSIVE LESSONS 80

4.1 ALIGNING FINANCIAL INSTRUMENTS WITH LIFE STAGES 80
Dependent Life Stage (Age <16) 80
Independent Life Stage (Age 16–24) 82
Early Family Life Stage (Age 25–40) 84
Empty Nest Life Stage (Age 41–65) 85
Retirement Life Stage (Age 66+) 86

4.2 CHECKING AND SHARE DRAFT ACCOUNTS 88
The Negotiable Instrument 88
Balancing Your Checking Account 89
Types of Checking Accounts 92
ATM and Debit Cards 93
Overdraft Protection 93

4.3 FINDING THE RIGHT FINANCIAL INSTITUTION 94
Financial Institutions 94
Insured Savings 95
Convenience 95
Products and Services 96
Cost 96
Learn. Plan & Act. Evaluate. 99

section two
CREDIT MANAGEMENT 108

CHAPTER 5   CONSUMER CREDIT: CREDIT CARDS AND STUDENT LOANS 108

CREDIT CARD LESSONS 110

5.1 BASICS OF CREDIT AND INTEREST RATES 110
Credit Options 111
Applying for Credit 112
The Five Cs of the Credit Decision 113
Risk and Interest Rates 116

5.2 UNDERSTANDING CREDIT CARDS 116
The Advantages and Disadvantages of Credit Cards 116
Credit Limits 117
Grace Periods 117
Interest Rates 117
Charges and Fees 118
Choosing a Credit Card 120

5.3 STUDENT LOANS 122
Federal Student Loans to Students 122
Federal Student Loans to Parents 122
Private Student Loans 122
Repaying Student Loans 123
Calculating Payments 124

5.4 COSTLY CASH 125
Payday Loans 125
Title Loans 127
Rent-to-Own 128
Considering the Alternatives 128
Learn. Plan & Act. Evaluate. 129

CHAPTER 6   CREDIT BUREAU REPORTS AND IDENTITY THEFT 136

THE PERFECT CREDIT SCORE 138

6.1 ESTABLISHING CREDIT 138

6.2 READING CREDIT REPORTS 139
Credit Reporting Agencies 139
Credit Card Purchases 140

6.3 DERIVING THE CREDIT SCORE 141
FICO Score Range 142
FICO Score Variables 142

6.4 IMPROVING YOUR CREDIT SCORE 144
Accessing Your Credit Report 144
Strengthening Your Credit Report 145

6.5 CORRECTING ERRORS ON YOUR CREDIT REPORT 147
Reporting Errors 147
Identifying Missing Accounts 148
Expunging Negative Information 148

6.6 SAFEGUARDING AGAINST IDENTITY THEFT 149
Defining Identity Theft 149
Strategies to Protect Your Identity 150
Victim of Identity Theft 151

6.7 FINANCIAL LIFE STAGES OF DEBT MANAGEMENT 152
Learn. Plan & Act. Evaluate. 153

CHAPTER 7 AUTO AND HOME LOANS 162

THE CAR DECISION 164

7.1 THE AUTO PURCHASE 164
Step 1: Analyze Needs versus Wants 164
Step 2: Determine What You Can Afford 165
Step 3: Do Your Homework 165
Step 4: Comparison Shop 168
Step 5: Negotiate the Deal 168
Step 6: Shop for Financing 168
Step 7: Close the Deal 168
Step 8: Complete After-Sale Activities 169

7.2 HOME OWNERSHIP 170
Rent vs. Buy 170
Life Stages and Home Ownership 172

7.3 BUYING A HOME 174
Selection Criteria 174
The Role of the Real Estate Broker 174
The Purchase Price 175
Refinancing Your Home 179

7.4 HOME EQUITY LOANS 181
Types of Home Equity Loans 181
Comparison Shopping 182
Disadvantages of Second Mortgages 182
Learn. Plan & Act. Evaluate. 183

CHAPTER 8 DEBT, FORECLOSURE, AND BANKRUPTCY 192

EMERGENCY FUND START 194

8.1 EARLY WARNING SIGNS OF FINANCIAL TROUBLE 194
Forewarnings 194
Emergency Fund Refuge 196

8.2 STOPPING LITTLE LEAKS 196
Necessary versus Nonessential Spending 196
Trimming Expenses 197

8.3 DIGGING OUT OF DEBT 199
Steps to Digging Out of Debt 199
Managing Past Credit Card Debt 201

8.4 FORECLOSURE 203
Avoiding Foreclosure 204
The Foreclosure Process 206

8.5 INS AND OUTS OF BANKRUPTCY 208
Types of Bankruptcy 208
Counseling and Education Requirements 208
Consequences of Bankruptcy 208
Life after Bankruptcy 211
Learn. Plan & Act. Evaluate. 212

section three
LIMITING YOUR LIABILITY 220

CHAPTER 9 TAX MANAGEMENT 220

TAX REALITY 222

9.1 TYPES OF TAXES 222
Principles of Progressive and Regressive Taxes 222

9.2 FILING TAXES 227
Tax-Filing Basics 227
Using Tax Forms 229
Tax Audits 230

9.3 TAX RATES 232
Marginal Income Tax Rates 232
Average Tax Rate 232
Alternative Minimum Tax (AMT) 232
Comprehending Capital Gains 233

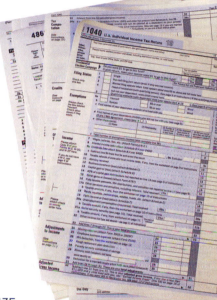

9.4 STRATEGIES TO MINIMIZE YOUR TAX LIABILITY 235
Exemptions and Deductions 235
Itemizing 236
Lowering Taxable Income 237
Tax Credits 240
Learn. Plan & Act. Evaluate. 240

CHAPTER 10 INSURANCE: COVERING YOUR ASSETS 246

HEALTH INSURANCE: EXPENSIVE BUT WORTH EVERY PENNY 248

10.1 THE IMPORTANCE OF INSURANCE 248
Insurance Basics 248
Selecting an Insurance Company 248
Knowing the Terms of the Policy 248

10.2 AUTO INSURANCE 249
Liability Auto Insurance 250
Full Coverage Auto Insurance 250
Lowering Your Costs 252

10.3 HOMEOWNER'S AND RENTER'S INSURANCE 252
  Home Insurance Basics 252
  Insuring Your Personal Property 253
  Lowering Your Costs 255

10.4 HEALTH INSURANCE 255
  Health Insurance Basics 255
  Health Insurance Options 256
  Lowering Your Costs 258

10.5 DISABILITY AND LONG-TERM CARE
    INSURANCE 259
  Advance Directives 259
  Disability Insurance 259
  Long-Term Care Insurance 261
  Lowering Your Costs 262

10.6 LIFE INSURANCE 262
  Types of Life Insurance 263
  Recommended Amount of Life Insurance 264
  Personal Finance Life Stages 264
  Lowering Your Costs 266
  Learn. Plan & Act. Evaluate. 266

section four
WEALTH ACCUMULATION 276

CHAPTER 11   INVESTMENT BASICS 276
INVESTMENT STRATEGIES 278

11.1 SAVINGS VERSUS INVESTMENTS 278
  Impact of Inflation on Savings 278
  Risk of Investing 279

11.2 RISK AND RETURN 280
  Default or Credit Risk 280
  Interest Rate Risk 280
  Market Risk 281
  Liquidity Risk 282
  Analyzing Your Risk Tolerance 282

11.3 THE INVESTMENT PYRAMID 283
  Base: No-Risk, Known-Return Investments 283

Tier I: Low-Risk, Low-Return Investments 284
Tier II: Intermediate-Risk, Intermediate-Return
  Investments 284
Tier III: High-Risk, High-Return Investments 284

11.4 DIVERSIFICATION OF ASSETS 284
  Why Diversify? 284
  Targeted and Automatic Asset-Allocation Mutual
    Funds 284

11.5 PORTFOLIO EVALUATION 285
  Maintaining Balance 285
  Life Stages and Investments 286
  Learn. Plan & Act. Evaluate. 289

CHAPTER 12   MUTUAL FUNDS 296
INVESTMENT SEED MONEY 298

12.1 MUTUAL FUND BASICS 298
  History of Mutual Funds 298
  Mutual Fund Regulation 299
  Costs and Fees of Mutual Funds 299

12.2 TYPES OF MUTUAL FUNDS 299
  Actively Managed Mutual Funds 301
  Index Market Funds 301
  Exchange-Traded Funds (ETFs) 301
  Equity Mutual Funds 301
  Bond Mutual Funds 303
  Money Market Mutual Funds 303
  Other Specialized Funds 304

12.3 BENEFITS AND RISKS OF MUTUAL FUNDS 304
  Benefits 304
  Risks 308

12.4 COSTS AND CLASSES OF MUTUAL FUNDS 308
  Finding the Mutual Fund Price 309
  Mutual Fund Costs 309
  Share Classes 311

12.5 CHOOSING AND BUYING A MUTUAL FUND 312
  Investment Strategies 312
  Where to Buy Mutual Funds 315
  Learn. Plan & Act. Evaluate. 316

CHAPTER 13   STOCKS 322
STARTING IN STOCKS 324

13.1 STOCK BASICS 324
  Private and Public Companies 324
  Types of Stock 325
  Stock Exchanges 325

13.2 STOCK EVALUATION 327
  Expectations 327
  The Market and Indexes 328
  Comparison of Indexes 329
  Stock Quotes 329

13.3 COMPANY
EVALUATION 334
  Research 334

MARKET	2.997	+	0.43
GRVT	1.442	+	0.96
AAPR	6.883	-	1.02
G&D	4.690	+	0.36
COOC	5.014	+	0.2
RIBB	0.653	+	0.

INDEX 100   5,898.07

1d 1w 1m 3m 6m 1y

Dec A'10 Aug Dec A'11 - Quotes delayed by 15 minutes

INDEX 100   5,898 +83.21 (1.43%)
1d 1w 1m 3m 6m 1y 2y

6091
5609
5172
4645
3456
2104

Dec A'10 Aug Dec A'11 - Quotes delayed by 15 minutes

13.4 BUYING AND SELLING STOCKS 336
Types of Brokers 336
Types of Trades 336
Investment Clubs 338
Buying Stock Directly 339
Personal Finance Life Stages and Stock Ownership 340
Learn. Plan & Act. Evaluate. 341

CHAPTER 14   BONDS 349
BURIED TREASURE 350

14.1 BOND BASICS 350
What Are Bonds? 350
How Do Bonds Work? 350

14.2 TYPES OF BONDS 353
United States Savings Bonds 353
Treasury Bonds, Bills, Notes, and TIPS 353
Municipal Bonds 353
Corporate Bonds 355

14.3 BOND EVALUATION 356
Bond Ratings 357
Researching Bonds 357
Bond Value 359

14.4 BENEFITS AND RISKS OF BONDS 361
Benefits 362
Risks 362

14.5 BUYING BONDS 364
Strategy 364
Where to Buy 365
Learn. Plan & Act. Evaluate. 366

CHAPTER 15   REAL ESTATE
INVESTMENTS 374
LONG-TERM GAINS 376

15.1 REAL ESTATE BASICS 376
Types of Real Estate Investments 376
Measuring Return on Investment 377

15.2 RENTAL PROPERTY 378
Advantages of Rental Property 378
Disadvantages of Rental Property 379
Landlordship 380
Shared Ownerships 382
Temporary Rentals 383

15.3 REAL ESTATE INVESTMENT TRUSTS 384
How to Invest in REITs 384
How to Avoid Scams 385

15.4 FLIPPING REAL ESTATE 386
Measuring Your ROI on Flipping 386
Steps to Successful Flipping 386
Flipping Land 389
Learn. Plan & Act. Evaluate. 389

section five
PERPETUAL PAYOFFS   394

CHAPTER 16   RETIREMENT AND ESTATE
PLANNING 394
TRADE-OFFS 396

16.1 RETIREMENT PLANNING 396
Company Savings Plans 396
Simplified Employee Pension Plans 398
Individual Retirement Accounts 398

Social Security 399
Life Stages of Retirement Planning 401

16.2 ESTATE PLANNING 404
Wills 404
Trusts 406
Power of Attorney 407
Advance Directives 407

16.3 CHARITABLE GIVING 408
Selections 408
Impact on Taxes 408
Learn. Plan & Act. Evaluate. 410

**CHAPTER 17   FINANCIAL PLANNING FOR
                LIFE 420**

FOUNDATION-SETTING 422

17.1 BALANCE 422

17.2 SUSTAINABILITY 423
Frugality 424
Focus on Goals 424

17.3 REASSESSMENTS 425
Monthly Budget Review 425
Annual Budget Review 425
Other Financial Reassessments 426
Learn. Plan & Act. Evaluate. 427

APPENDIX A: FINANCIAL TABLES 429

APPENDIX B: LIMITED SOLUTIONS 438

GLOSSARY 457

CREDITS 463

INDEX 465

personal finance

building your future

"What's money? A man is a success if he gets up in the morning and gets to bed at night, and in between he does what he wants to."

—BOB DYLAN, *Singer songwriter (1941–)*

chapter  one

money matters: values, vision, mission, and you

The first step to understanding why we spend money is to learn about our money personalities. If you received a $600 stimulus check, would you hit the mall to buy a large luxury item with the rebate as a down payment? Or would you pay off bills? Perhaps you would treat yourself to a small necessity and then bank the majority of the windfall.

Think about your current financial situation and your spending habits. Do they reflect your desired lifestyle and goals? Like Ashley, who you will meet in the chapter opener on the next page, you will learn about your relationship with money. To increase happiness, sometimes less may be more; think about the point where enough is enough. Studying this chapter will help you lay the foundation for a financial plan that is guided by your personal mission statement and incorporates your goals. Using the online worksheets that accompany the text, you will outline your values, vision, and mission statement to help you navigate your overall financial plan. ■

LEARNING OBJECTIVES

After reading this chapter, you should be able to:

LO 1-1 Evaluate your spending and saving habits and define what financial success means to you.

LO 1-2 Develop a plan for engaging in fiscally responsible, goal-based spending and saving.

LO 1-3 Align your financial plan with your personal goals.

LO 1-4 Explore the different career choices that fit your personal mission statement and established goals.

Goal Setting

Ashley, a sophomore at a mid-size public college, recently developed her values, vision, and mission statements and used them to set her short-term, intermediate, and long-term goals: "I thought I was living my life according to my values, but until I used the mind maps and built my mission statement, I really had no idea if I was living out my mission. It was hard to express my mission statement so that it said what I wanted it to say about me, my priorities, and my goals. The whole process helped clarify for me what I want to do and where I want to go. Setting my short-term, intermediate, and long-term financial goals helped me decide how I'm going to spend and save my money. I feel like I have my money working for me now, not the other way around."

1.1 PERSONAL RELATIONSHIPS WITH MONEY

■ ■ **LO 1-1** Evaluate your spending and saving habits and define what financial success means to you.

A **financial plan** is a goal-based activity that incorporates your future income plan *(career goals)*, budget plan

Understanding your relationship with money.

(spending goals), investment plan *(gaining assets goals)*, insurance plan *(protection goals)*, and estate plan *(giving goals)*. In the process of developing a personal financial plan, you very well may discover your passion and a sense of purpose. By aligning your actions with your values,

> "He that is of the opinion money will do everything may well be suspected of doing everything for money."
>
> —BEN FRANKLIN *(1706–1790)*

you will reduce clutter in your life and gain control over your time and money. Money is simply a resource, a commodity. To truly be in control of money is to be in a position where you are in balance with your priorities. The following sections lay out the steps to creating a foundation for your financial plan.

Step 1: Understanding Your Perception of Financials

Money can influence your attitudes and behavior. Not having enough money is stressful. Having a lot of money can cause others to be envious. If you had a lot more money than your friends, would they expect you to always pay? Would you feel like they were taking advantage of your wealth? How does having more money impact your level of happiness? As shown in Figure 1.1 below, the first step in the financial journey is to assess your current relationship with money. To do so, take the Money Relationship Quiz in Figure 1.2 on the next page.

your relationship with money Count up the number of times you circled A, B, C, D, and E statements. If you mostly circled:

A: You value money for the security it provides.

B: You want a lot of material items, and you want them now.

C: Money helps you feel important.

D: Money is a resource to get the things you need or want.

E: You are not concerned with money; there is no reason to worry about it.

Are you surprised by the assessment? Knowing how you feel about money is the key to understanding your spending, savings, and investment habits. Aligning money spending and saving habits with your overall priorities and life goals allows you to maintain a sense of control, direction, and purpose with your financial life.

To understand why you do what you do, you need to uncover your **money personality** (online Worksheet

financial plan
goal-based activity related to future income, spending, investment, protection, and giving

money personality
style and habits of money management

personal values
those things that are most important to you and to which you must be true to lead a happy and fulfilled life

1.1). Similar to personality traits, our money personalities are part nurture and part nature. They are made of a combination of values, how we were raised, and our parents' traits. Your money personality determines, in part, how you deal with money and finances.

Some people enjoy knowing where every penny is spent and are very aware of their financial condition. Other people never balance their checkbooks and will take the bank's word for their balance. These people are more likely to have overdraft fees with their checking account and over-limit fees on their credit cards, and they are likely to spend more money on transaction fees and other charges than the first group. For some people, image or "keeping up with the Joneses" is important. Others are oblivious to material trends. These are just a few extreme ways people interact with money and their personal finances.

Step 2: Identifying Your Values

Personal values are unique to you and influence your actions and decision making. Personal values develop early in life and are influenced by family, religion, social groups, and culture. If how you are living your life does not coincide with your personal values, you will be in conflict. As shown in Figure 1.3 on the next page, identifying your values is the second step in setting the foundation of your financial plan. If you understand what you value, you can make better decisions and choices to reduce inner conflict. Knowing your values can help you create a financial plan that fits well; as a result, you will be more successful in adhering to the plan.

values-driven financial planning Taking time to think about what you value will help guide you in creating an overall financial plan. Online Worksheet 1.2, "Clarifying Values," will help unearth your personal values.

▼ **FIGURE 1.1**

Setting the foundation of your financial plan, step 1

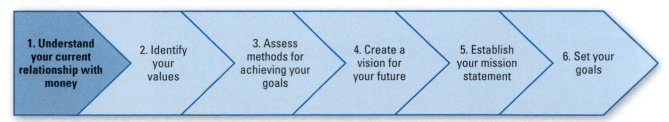

1. Understand your current relationship with money   2. Identify your values   3. Assess methods for achieving your goals   4. Create a vision for your future   5. Establish your mission statement   6. Set your goals

voluntary simplicity
a simplified lifestyle, where unvalued consumption and clutter are reduced

frugal
avoiding waste; to be resourceful when fulfilling one's need for goods and services

enough
point at which increased spending has a diminishing rate of fulfillment

▼ **FIGURE** 1.2

Money relationship quiz

In order to self-assess your relationship with money, circle the statements that best describe you:

  A. It's a good feeling to have money in my wallet.

  B. No one can ever really have enough money.

  C. Clothing should look expensive.

  B. You cannot live without credit.

  D. There are a lot of things more important than money.

  E. Keeping track of every dollar would drive me crazy.

  A. It is important to record every dollar you spend.

  C. Money and prestige go hand in hand.

  E. A person can get along without a savings account.

  D. It is easy to have fun with simple things that do not cost much money.

  A. Money should only be spent for necessities.

  C. I want nothing but the very best.

  E. If I just wait, my money problems will take care of themselves.

  D. Money does not buy happiness.

  B. It would be easy to spend $5,000 in just a couple of days.

  A. I shop around to find the best price.

  E. If I need money, it will come from somewhere.

  A. I will not buy anything unless I have enough money for it.

  C. If I am going to buy something, I am going to buy the best option of it.

  B. I will never buy something used, always brand new.

  D. A lot of money would be nice, but I do not really need it.

  E. I never make plans about money.

Source: Money Relationship Quiz extracted from "Money Talks," ANR Publication 8272. © 2007 by the Regents of the University of California Division of Agriculture and Natural Resources.

By identifying your priorities and building a financial plan focused on supporting those priorities, you will increase your probability of success. Your perspective will change from one of negativity (I'm making a sacrifice) to one of positive gratification (I'm investing in things I care about). Let's look at some of the methods we can use to achieve our goals.

trade-offs **Voluntary simplicity** is selecting a simplified lifestyle and reducing unvalued consumption in order to focus energy on other priorities. People choose this lifestyle for many reasons, such as to: live more environmentally friendly; increase quality time with friends and family; reduce stress; and improve health, spirituality, and frugality.

To be **frugal** is to be resourceful when fulfilling needs for goods and services, perhaps using already owned items or doing things yourself. It is to be penny-wise and practice restraint in how you consume goods and services. It is the epitome of Benjamin Franklin's adage, "Waste not, want not."

enough Between frugal and excessive is the balance point of *enough*. Joe Dominguez and Vicki Robin in *Your Money or Your Life* (1992) describe the relationship between consumer purchasing and consumer fulfillment as one of diminishing returns after reaching enough. As shown in Figure 1.4, you receive fulfillment on money spent to survive. Fulfillment increases, but at a decreasing rate until **enough** purchases of luxuries. Once *enough* is reached, fulfillment decreases with increased spending.

A simple example would be buying a pair of shoes. The first pair is out of necessity. Other shoes may serve different purposes (i.e., working out, dressing up, going to the beach, shoveling snow), but if one continues to acquire more shoes, each new pair brings about less fulfillment. At a certain point, a person may not have room for any more shoes, may not find the ones wanted because there are so many, or may not find satisfaction in an additional pair. In fact, one more pair of shoes

▼ **FIGURE** 1.3

Setting the foundation of your financial plan, step 2

1. Understand your current relationship with money
2. **Identify your values**
3. Assess methods for achieving your goals
4. Create a vision for your future
5. Establish your mission statement
6. Set your goals

▼ FIGURE 1.4

Defining enough

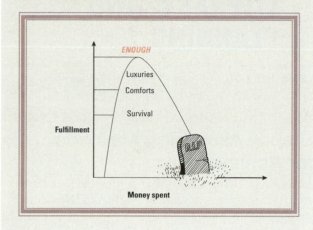

Purchases beyond *enough* do not increase happiness.

Source: J. Dominguez and V. Robin, *Your Money or Your Life,* Rev. Ed. (New York, NY: Penguin Books, 1999).

can bring about *more* problems. With decisions based on your values, mission, and goals, you decide when enough is *your* enough.

allocations What you do with your money is a reflection of your priorities. Financial experts recommend saving at least 10% of your income for retirement and an emergency fund. Saving 10% and living on 90% is referred to as the **90-10 rule** and demonstrates a value of retirement and financial security.

A cousin of the 90-10 rule is the **80-10-10 rule**, which reflects a value for community responsibility as well as retirement and financial security. It is living on 80% of your income, saving 10%, and giving away 10%. Whether giving to the Arbor Society to plant more trees or to a local food bank to help those in need, the goal of this rule is to start the habit of saving and giving.

A plan of action to go from 100-0 to 90-10 or to 80-10-10 can begin with incremental increases and gradual adjustments. If aiming for an 80-10-10 financial plan, start off by living on 98% of your income, saving 1%, and giving 1%. The following year, increase savings and giving by 1% each. Keep this pattern up, and over a 10-year adjustment period, an 80-10-10 goal can be achieved.

To be successful at saving, you need to pay yourself first. To make this habit as painless as possible, establish automatic transfers or withdrawals from a paycheck or checking account into a savings or investment account. Many investment companies will establish an investment account by setting up an automatic transfer of $50 each month. Transfers from checking to savings can be set up for any amount and

scheduled to occur on the same day of each month. Many charities, nonprofit foundations, and religious organizations are able to establish automatic payment from your checking account. By establishing automatic transfers and withdrawals, you are placing your savings and giving goals on the same level as paying your bills. You are making a commitment to your values and priorities.

personal financial success What is your definition of **personal financial success**? Is it having millions of dollars in the bank? Is it being able to drive a new sports car or travel the world? Or is financial success just having enough money to cover your basic needs?

The wealthiest Americans include Bill Gates, Warren Buffett, and Donald Trump. Each is well known for his business and financial success. Likewise, each one has different personal priorities and has chosen different ways to use his wealth. Warren Buffet has lectured that money and material wealth do *not* bring happiness. For all but the very few, there will always be someone with more money, more toys, more material goods, a bigger house, and a bigger boat. You have to determine your own definition of financial success. Section 1.3 will walk you through how to establish financial goals based on your personal values, vision, and mission.

financialfitness:
STOPPING LITTLE LEAKS

Stress Management

To escape the stress of everyday life, you may be tempted to go shopping. Items purchased during these "escape" moments are not necessarily items you highly value or include on your priority list. Counter any urge to indulge in "retail therapy"—shopping to improve one's mood. Next time you are feeling down, go for a run, a bike ride, or a brisk walk. You will get an exercise-induced endorphin boost and the feeling will cost you nothing.

financialfitness:
NUMBERS GAME

Trade-offs

Consider your values and the costs involved when either both adults of a household work outside the home or one adult works long hours and overtime. Costs can include: daycare; clothing; commuting; food bought at the workplace or a restaurant; escape entertainment; and the cost of decompressing. It brings in extra income, but it also increases expenses and stress. It is important to strike a good balance.

There are different ways to get to financial independence.

1.2 FINANCIAL INDEPENDENCE, LITERACY, AND PLANNING

■ ■ **LO 1-2**   Develop a plan for engaging in fiscally responsible, goal-based spending and saving.

Step 3: Assessing Methods for Achievement

As shown in Figure 1.5, step 3 in setting the foundation of your financial plan involves assessing methods for achieving your goals. A popular financial goal is to achieve financial independence. For some people, this may be the definition of financial success. **Financial independence** is when passive income exceeds expenditures (see Figure 1.6). This is a simple concept that, when understood, can influence decision making on every purchase. Do you really want to spend all your money on "wants" of today? Or do you want to invest some of it and save to reach financial independence sooner? Once you achieve financial independence, you do not have to work for income, but can choose whether or not to work and how to spend your time and energy.

Passive income is money received from investments and savings. It is, as the Internal Revenue Service (IRS) states, **non-earned income**. It is the income received from money and investments that are working for you. Passive income can be from stock dividends, interest from bank investments, money from rental property, or other investments. Many people do not achieve financial independence

financialfitness:
JUST THE FACTS

Control

Money (or the lack thereof) is among the biggest stress inducers. We worry more about money than about our marriages or our health. Reduce money as a stress point by taking control through planning and budgeting.

Setting the foundation of your financial plan, step 3

▼ **FIGURE** 1.6

Financial independence

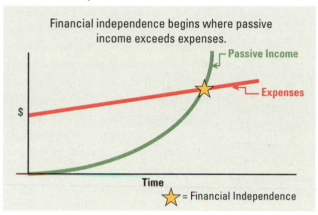

Financial independence begins where passive income exceeds expenses.

▼ **FIGURE** 1.7

Controlling the timeline to financial independence

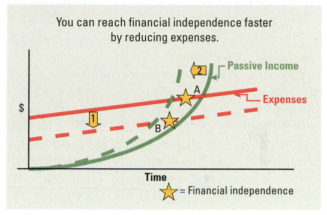

You can reach financial independence faster by reducing expenses.

until late in life, after years of putting money into savings or in retirement accounts and relying on Social Security as part of their passive income.

Figure 1.7 illustrates the relationship between passive income, expenses, and financial independence. To reach financial independence sooner: (1) reduce your expenses and live more frugally; (2) increase your savings and/ or invest more money sooner; or (3) do both. However, increasing the return on savings and investing usually increases risk.

Many baby boomers who wanted to decrease their time to financial independence invested their retirement savings in high-risk, high-return stocks. This plan played out well until the financial crisis of 2008 caused the stock market to decrease 54% in value, which decreased the amount of passive income received from retirement investments. Those who were planning to retire that year faced tough decisions about when and how to retire. Many had to choose between postponing retirement or reducing expenses and living on less money to gain their financial independence. A basic understanding of financial products and diversifying investments across the products can help reduce these types of risks. (This topic is covered in more detail in Chapter 11, "Investment Basics.")

Financial Literacy

Financial literacy is the ability to understand finances, as well as an understanding of the risks and potential rewards of financial investments and the types of financial products

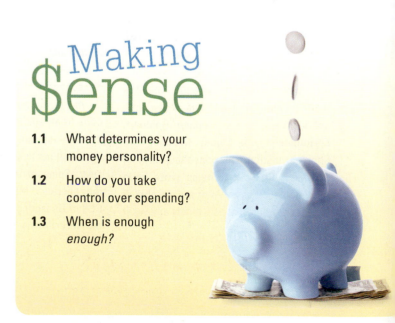

$ense Making

1.1 What determines your money personality?

1.2 How do you take control over spending?

1.3 When is enough *enough?*

Scan here for more information on the latest events "In the News"

New status symbol: Family mission statements

Mission statements are moving from the boardroom to the family room. A growing number of multimillionaires and billionaires, hoping to stave off costly feuds, are drawing up family mission statements—lofty treatises filled with words like "legacy," "values," and "stewardship" that aim to carry rich families (and their fortunes) safely through the ages. These statements, also known as "family constitutions," "strategic plans," or "family codes of conduct," can range in length from a single sentence to 10 pages. They give a clan's proclamations on everything from inheritance and philanthropy to religion, education, and the purpose of wealth. Some even define what constitutes "the family" (i.e., in-laws sometimes don't count).

The goal of mission statements is to help keep the peace in affluent families. By agreeing on a basic set of principles, families hope to avoid lawsuits between relatives about money. They also hope to draw up moral guides for future generations, so that kids and grandkids will inherit values as well as wealth. "The family mission statement is a chance for the family to think through what are their guiding principles and values that define them," says Stephen Goldbart, co-founder of the Money, Meaning and Choices Institute, a consulting firm in Kentfield, Calif., that helps write such documents. "It says 'What are we about? What is our purpose as a family and what drives us forward?'"

Mission statements are surging in popularity, along with the number of rich people who are passing down wealth in hopes of creating family dynasties. There are now 4.5 million U.S. households with investable assets of $1 million or more. Since so many of today's wealthy are entrepreneurs or executives, they're transferring their obsession with strategic visions and micromanagement to their families. Money, Meaning and Choices says its mission statement business has more than doubled over the past five years and that it now works on at least one a week. Relative Solutions, a New Jersey-based advisory firm, says its mission-statement business has also surged. "Family mission statements have become very trendy," says Lee Hausner, a family-wealth psychologist and co-founder of IFF Advisors in Irvine, Calif., which also is doing a brisk trade in mission statements. The cost of hiring an adviser to create a statement can run from $15,000 to $100,000, advisers say.

Yet, some caution that getting family members to agree on a mission statement can create the very tensions they are supposed to diffuse. . . . "The problem is, you have so many families who have gone from rags to riches and how do you pass values through a series of generations and not just the money," Mr. George says. Some of the best statements are the shortest. Maria Elena Lagomasino, CEO of Genspring Family Offices, a wealth advisory firm in Palm Beach, Fla., cites a one-sentence statement written by a wealthy couple. It said, "We want our capital to allow our children and their children to be able to find their passion and pursue it with excellence." "What they were saying with the mission statement was 'Don't worry about whether you can earn a living if that gets in the way of you being the best painter or teacher or poet.' It was about self-realization, not spending." Glenn Kurlander, managing director of Citi Private Bank's family wealth advisory services, helped craft a six-page statement that quotes Sir Thomas Browne and Alexander Pope. It begins with a five-point plan for the family to, among other things, "value compassion, honesty, integrity, passion and engagement," and to be "secure in the knowledge that our financial capital cannot change our fundamental individual and family identity."

Family mission statements aren't entirely new. John D. Rockefeller Jr. had his motto inscribed on a stone tablet facing Rockefeller Center. It reads, in part, "I believe that every right implies a responsibility; every opportunity, an obligation; every possession, a duty. . . ."

ROBERT FRANK, *The Wall Street Journal,* The Wealth Report, October 12, 2007. Reprinted with permission.

Questions

1 What are the benefits for a family that comes together to create a mission statement?

2 How does a mission statement help define your inner compass?

and services available to help you achieve your goals. From the time you get your first job, you can invest in a retirement plan, and at your first full-time job, you may need to make decisions regarding your **401(k) retirement plan**. Making wise personal finance decisions is *your* responsibility. No one is going to be more concerned about your financial welfare than you.

There are thousands of different investment opportunities. How do you know you picked the right one to meet your investment objectives? Even if you get assistance from a certified financial planner, who can you trust? You have to know enough to protect your assets. On March 12, 2009, prominent investment manager Bernie Madoff pled guilty to an 11-count criminal charge, admitting to defrauding thousands of investors with total losses estimated to be over $64.8 billion. Mr. Madoff had the confidence of many nonprofit foundations who invested millions with him, trusting they were making sound investments. This goes to show that even people who should know about investments can make poor decisions about who to trust.

No one but you can control your spending and make on-the-spot financial decisions that reflect your values. This book will not make you a certified financial planner, but it will give you enough knowledge to understand the realm of personal finance and help you make wise decisions for yourself.

Options to Financial Independence

Financial literacy is the key to achieving financial independence. There are a number of avenues to reach your goals sooner, rather than later.

downshifting One way to financial independence is to reduce your expenditures via deliberately **downshifting**, or cutting back. It can involve trying to maintain the same lifestyle spending less money, living frugally, or taking on a new lifestyle–requiring prioritization, an adjustment in values, and a totally different mind-set. People decide to downshift for a variety of reasons. Some want to escape job stress, while others downshift because of a life-changing experience, health problems, or a crisis in the family.

---

doing the MATH

1.1 Financial Independence

You are thinking about retiring. You currently live off $120,000/year. Your investment projections payout according to the graph:

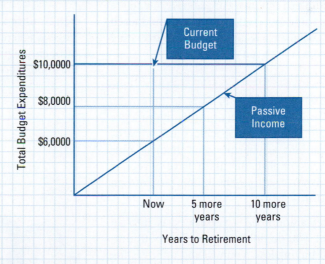

1. To retire now, you need to downsize by how much a month?

2. If you put off retirement for five years, what could you afford for an annual budget?

3. If you plan to maintain your current lifestyle, how long will you need to keep working until your retirement income accommodates your current budget?

dollar cost averaging
investing a fixed dollar amount at regular intervals

investment account
outlay of money into a bank or stock with the objective of making a profit

personal financial plan
strategy to improve current financial situation based on an analysis of your liabilities, cash flow, savings, investments, and long-term accumulation plans

financial life stages
general periods throughout a lifetime representing different financial challenges and needs

financialfitness:
STOPPING LITTLE LEAKS

Resources

Voluntary simplification, downshifting, and frugal living can sometimes call for a creative response to make do with what's on hand. The website www.choosingvoluntarysimplicity.com is a helpful resource for those interested in a more in-depth exploration of downshifting and frugal lifestyle ideas.

augmenting income

At the other extreme, instead of lowering expenses, you might get a second job to increase income and live the lifestyle you desire without debt. Perform an honest and real inventory of your skills and your ability to create value. Take a look at what you are currently doing and look for untapped areas. For example, if you are knowledgeable in a trade or a craft, maybe you could teach a class at night. If socializing is up your alley, bartending once a week can provide both fun and cash.

investing to achieve greater passive income

One way to develop passive income is to start an automatic investment plan. **Dollar cost averaging** is the practice of investing or saving money at specific times, regardless of market conditions or your personal financial outlook. One way to accomplish this is to have a regular amount deducted from every paycheck and put into an **investment account**.

By depositing a set amount on a regular basis into an investment account, you do not have to worry about timing the market and buying low. You will end up investing some money at low prices and some at high prices, but what is important is that you will be consistently paying yourself first. In doing so, your savings will grow. The magic of compound interest (see Chapter 2) will ensure the invested money is working hard for you. You can trim expenses without making big sacrifices and put the savings directly into investment savings. A little here and

little there and before you know it, you will be financially independent.

financial planning

To reach your personal financial goals, you need to have a **personal financial plan**. Based on an analysis of what you owe *(liabilities)*, the money you have coming in and out *(cash flow)*, and your savings and investments, a good financial plan will provide a strategy to improve your financial situation. A personal financial plan helps you to be in control of your finances by being proactive in making decisions and by anticipating expected increases and/or decreases in income and expenses. A good financial plan lets you think about the future and make purposeful decisions that reflect your values and vision. A plan helps you create a road map to financial success. You probably would not go on a vacation without using a map or GPS (or both) to reach your destination. Likewise, having a financial plan helps you reach your *financial destination*.

Financial Life Stages

As shown in Figure 1.8, there are different **financial life stages** that represent the general financial situations that people experience throughout their lifetime. Your current financial life stage impacts your financial plan.

dependent life stage (age <16)

The Dependent Life Stage is where you first learn about money management through a regular allowance. This is the time to learn about the importance of savings, giving, and budgeted spending.

Different life stages come with different financial needs.

Values instilled at this age will have a lasting effect on your money makeup. Peers also have a great influence on spending habits during this time period. Family members dedicating funds toward a college savings plan can be crucial at this early stage.

independent life stage (age 16–24) The Independent Life Stage is characterized by the beginnings of financial independence and responsibility. Before this stage, you may have had only a savings account, and a first checking account typically marks an early milestone. At the Independent Life Stage, you are earning money, but your earnings are low and usually from only part-time or summer employment. You should be saving all you can for college, a car, or a home down payment. You don't have money to waste, and your parents may still be supporting you. If you are in this stage, it is beneficial to shop for deals, look for free checking with overdraft protection, start retirement savings as soon as you have earned income, track your spending, determine your values and goals, exhibit those goals in your spending, and start your financial plan.

early family life stage (age 25–40) The beginning of the Early Family Life Stage is when you start your profession and truly live independently outside of school and without assistance from parents. With your full-time job, you may have a company-matched retirement plan. You will have to make retirement investment decisions for your company-sponsored plan as well as continue to invest in your retirement savings. You may be saving to buy your first house, get married, start a family, go back to school to get

an advanced degree, or invest in your children's future college. You will be making more money so you should start investing to save 6–10 months' income in an emergency fund savings account. Your expenses also will increase. You should be continually tracking your spending and investing to make sure they are in alignment with your (and your partner's, if applicable) values, vision, and mission.

empty nest life stage (age 41–65) At this point in life, your children have moved out of the house and you have reduced expenses. Possibly, your house is paid off and you are at the height of your career, making more money than ever before. You will be investing more money and looking for more conservative investments to reduce the risk of your retirement accounts losing value in the short run. You also will need to begin to plan for retirement. Continue to check where you spend every penny to make sure you are in alignment with your values, vision, and goals.

retirement life stage (age 66+) The final stage occurs when you have retired from your career and reached financial independence. You can choose to work if you want or you may volunteer your time and expertise to help others. You are truly able to pursue your passions. At

▼ **FIGURE 1.8**

Personal finance life stages

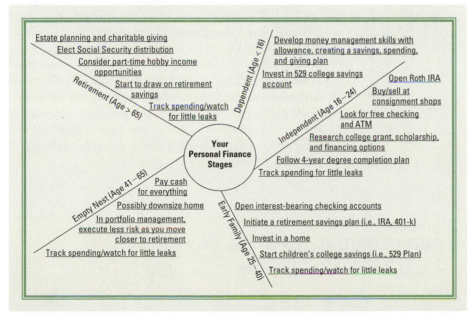

this stage, you start to draw on your retirement savings. Still, continue to track your spending to make certain it reflects your values and your financial plan.

financial fitness:
JUST THE FACTS

Longer, Healthier Life

How do you spend less and live longer? Americans spend only 10.4% of their disposable income on food, less than half of what a typical family spent in 1929. In any given day, the typical person can cut two-thirds of the fat, shave 700 calories, and save at least $7 a day, or more than $2,500 a year, by selecting healthy food options compared to eating processed fast food or "cheap" junk food. If you eat healthfully, you will lose weight, save money, and live a longer, healthier life.

$ Making $ense

1.4 What is passive income?

1.5 What are the strategies to reaching financial independence sooner?

1.6 What are the benefits of dollar cost averaging?

1.7 What is the purpose of a financial plan?

1.3 VISION, MISSION, AND GOALS

■ ■ **LO 1-3** Align your financial plan with your personal goals.

Step 4: Creating a Vision for Your Future

To know where you want to go, you need to have a vision of the destination. A vision statement defines a sense of purpose and paints a picture of the future. Your vision will tie directly into your long-term goals. Your vision of the future is just like the destination on a road trip. Your financial plan is the road map to get you on the journey to your financial future. As shown in Figure 1.9, step 4 of setting the foundation for your financial plan involves creating a vision for your future.

A vision might be what you picture yourself doing in retirement. For example, a vision statement might be: "When I'm 65 years old I will be retired and living in a home in Breckenridge, Colorado, where all my kids and grandkids will come and play." As you create your vision of the future, be sure it is in alignment with your priorities. Reflect back on your values and ask yourself how the vision fits the values. Use online Worksheet 1.3 to write your vision statement.

Step 5: Establishing Your Mission

What is your personal mission? A mission is a purpose of being. Using your values and vision of the future, create a **personal mission statement**. As shown in Figure 1.10, this is step 5 of setting the foundation of your financial plan. Your mission statement should reflect what you want to be known for and the vision of where you want to be. It will help you clarify priorities and keep you motivated. Your personal mission statement should reflect your strengths *(the things you do best)*, passions *(the things you enjoy doing)*, gifts *(the things you do naturally well without effort)*, and stakeholders *(those who have helped you and those who you have helped)*. A simple example can be found in Figure 1.11.

> " If you can dream it, you can do it.
> —*WALT DISNEY (1901–1966)*

▼ **FIGURE** 1.9

Setting the foundation of your financial plan, step 4

▼ **FIGURE** 1.10

Setting the foundation of your financial plan, step 5

▼ **FIGURE** 1.11

A simple example of a value-, vision-driven mission statement

Once you have drafted a mission statement, edit it so it can fit on the back of a business card. Keep it simple. Keep it understandable. Try to make it motivational. Memorize it. Being able to refer back to a personal mission statement will help you maintain focus and direction as you process the lessons in the coming chapters.

Step 6: Setting Your Goals

So far you have established your values, created a vision, and written a mission statement. You now should have a better idea of where you want to go. Now is the time to create the path to your personal and financial destination. Your goals will help create action plans which will build a road to success. As shown in Figure 1.12 on the next page, setting your goals is the final step in setting the foundation of your financial plan.

Without a deadline, a goal is just a dream. Goals can be divided into three major time periods: **Long-term goals** take more than five years to attain; **intermediate goals** are attained in one to five years; and **short-term goals** may be reached in less than one year. Refer back to Figure 1.8,

▼ FIGURE 1.12

Setting the foundation of your financial plan, step 6

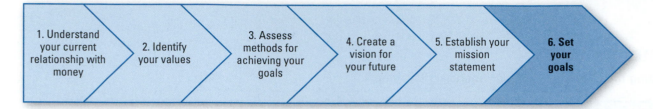

1. Understand your current relationship with money
2. Identify your values
3. Assess methods for achieving your goals
4. Create a vision for your future
5. Establish your mission statement
6. **Set your goals**

▼ FIGURE 1.13

Example: a mind-map of long-term goals

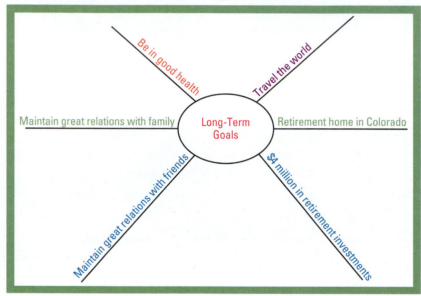

Personal Finance Life Stages (p. 13). What kinds of goals do you want to accomplish next year? In five years? In ten years? Long-term goals should be similar to your vision statement. To determine your long-term goals, ask yourself the following: What would you do if you were handed a $1,000,000 check? Be as specific as possible and visualize what it would feel like to accomplish those goals. Use Worksheet 1.5 to create your long-term goals, like those shown in Figure 1.13.

Intermediate goals are the steps in the next one to five years that need to be accomplished in order to reach long-term or lifetime goals. Select one long-term goal and put it in the center of your mind-map. What goals need to be accomplished in the next one to five years in order to reach that long-term goal? Use Worksheet 1.5 to create intermediate-term goals, like those shown in Figure 1.14.

▼ FIGURE 1.14

Example: a mind-map of intermediate-term goals

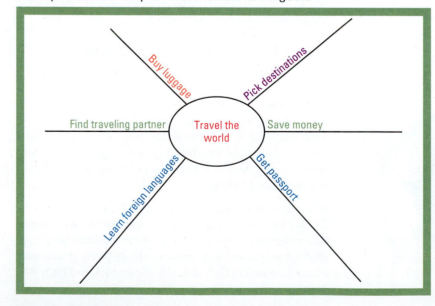

Finally, develop short-term goals. Select one intermediate goal and place it in the center of your mind-map. What goals need to be accomplished this year in order to achieve that intermediate goal? Use Worksheet 1.5 to outline short-term goals, like those shown in Figure 1.15.

You have just taken long-term goals and broken them down into steps that can be achieved daily. To be most successful, goals need to be **SMART**:

S – Specific

M – Measurable

A – Attainable

R – Realistic

T – Time-bound, having a specific end date and timeline.

Example: a mind-map of short-term goals

SMART goal
objective that is Specific, Measurable, Achievable, Realistic, and Timely

leads to improved performance and goal attainment. Use this same philosophy in goal setting. If the goal is not obtained, analyze the situation for what went right and what you can do differently the next time. There is no changing the past, but you can impact your future. Use online Worksheet 1.6 to review your goals and revise them as needed to make them SMART goals.

1.4 CAREER CHOICES, MONEY, AND HAPPINESS

■■ **LO 1-4** Explore the different career choices that fit your personal mission statement and established goals.

What Makes You Happy?

What makes someone happy is very personal and therefore hard to define. According to Sonja Lyubomirsky (2008), genes (50%), circumstances (10%), and intentional activity (40%) determine happiness.[1] That is, attitude and self-directed behavior make up 40% of happiness. A study of the

The more *specific* the goals, the more likely they will be achieved. If the goal is to purchase a new car, know what make, model, color, interior, and options the car will have and how to pay for it. Goals need to be *measurable.* "Saving more money" is not a measurable goal. How much money is "more"? If a goal is to save more money, make it SMART by setting out to save $1 a day or $7 a week. At the end of the day, evaluate if you saved $1.

Attainable and *realistic* goals are the reality checks to see if the goal can be accomplished. Can you save $1 a day? Goals are meant to motivate, inspire, and stretch you to reach beyond normal capacity. Goals should be achieved 80–90% of the time. If you are achieving your goals 100% of the time, the goals may not be challenging enough. If you are attaining your goals only 60% of the time, the goals may not be realistic.

T is for *time-bound,* having a specific end date for reaching the goal. In the example above, the goal of saving $1 a day is a SMART goal, but what happens if $1 isn't saved? Some people will add the unmet goals of one day to the following day. However, if these unachieved goals accumulate, the goal soon becomes increasingly difficult and eventually unattainable.

If a goal is not reached in the allotted time, reevaluate the goal. Was the goal truly achievable and realistic? It might have been at the time it was set, but circumstances may have changed. Continually reevaluate your goals to make sure they are realistic and attainable.

Most sporting events have specific time frames; a winner is determined at the end of the competition. Following the game, individuals evaluate their performance and determine what went well and what they need to do differently in the next competition. This continual improvement philosophy

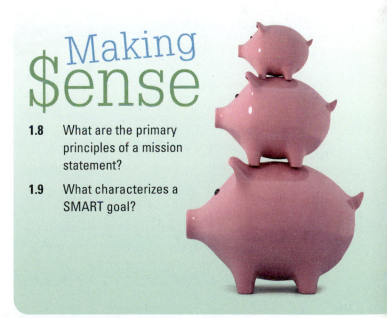

Making $ense

1.8 What are the primary principles of a mission statement?

1.9 What characterizes a SMART goal?

[1]S. Lyubomirsky, *The How of Happiness: A Scientific Approach to Getting the Life You Want* (New York, NY: Penguin Press, 2008).

wealthiest Americans, those making over $10 million a year, showed their happiness was just slightly higher than blue-collar workers and office staff.[2] Money only makes you happy if:

- You have more than everyone else in your tribe

- You use it to do good and are responsible with your money

- You have enough to survive

For all but one of us in the world, there always will be someone richer. Happiness is more dependent on your *attitude* toward money and life and how much you feel in control of your life and money. Deciding when enough is enough is a major factor in happiness. Your sense of fulfillment decreases in proportion to the amount of money spent after reaching your *enough* point.

You are in control of your finances when you see money as a resource, use money according to your values, and do not spend more than you make. There will always be more things to buy, but a conscious decision to be happy with what you have can help determine 40% of your happiness. You also can achieve a feeling of accomplishment by having your

> " It is pretty hard to tell what does bring happiness; poverty and wealth have both failed. "
>
> —KIN HUBBARD, *American journalist (1868–1930)*

money work for you (rather than having to work for the money) and by using it in accordance with your values (rather than in conflict with your values).

Career and Education Choices

How did you choose a major? Did you look up what people were making in a specific field and pick that major so as to achieve a specific salary? Are you still undeclared? What major would you select if money were not an issue? What careers would best match your values, interests, and talents?

In Denmark, the salaries are very similar for different professions. The government (via taxes) takes care of health care and retirement. Denmark has been classified as a "post consumerism" society, meaning that it is not as important for individuals to have a lot of material items. It also has been declared to be the "Happiest Place on Earth," according to a 2006 BBC article.[3]

What do the Danes know? They know and apply the theory that money can't buy happiness. Frederick Hertzburg, author of *The Motivation to Work* (1959), contends that once a person has enough money to meet basic needs, money is not a motivator. The Danes are given the opportunity to pursue their passions with enough money to meet their needs. To be happy, choose a career where you can pursue your passions, in line with your values, with enough money to cover your needs, and learn to live within your means.

Information on Careers

With your values, vision, and mission statement in mind, you can research a career many different ways. The U.S. Bureau of Labor Statistics publishes an *Occupational Outlook Handbook* describing a multitude of careers. For each career, it has sections on the nature of the work, the required training and other qualifications, current employment, the job outlook, and earnings. This is a good place to start researching a career.

Internships and job shadowing provide an opportunity to get a feel for the culture and the true working environment of different careers. Internships can be paid or unpaid and are usually for the period of a semester or a summer. Book research can only go so far in describing the career and the work; it does not provide much information on the culture of the working environment.

College career centers have different survey tools to help students define their passions and talents. The centers also

financialfitness:
STOPPING LITTLE LEAKS

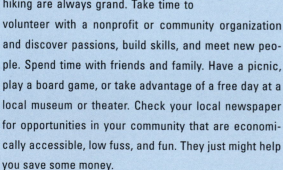

Happiness Via Leisure

Leisure can be both frugal and fun. Take advantage of free festivals or music in the park. Take a walk or ride on the bike trails, or float down a river in an inner tube. Picnics and hiking are always grand. Take time to volunteer with a nonprofit or community organization and discover passions, build skills, and meet new people. Spend time with friends and family. Have a picnic, play a board game, or take advantage of a free day at a local museum or theater. Check your local newspaper for opportunities in your community that are economically accessible, low fuss, and fun. They just might help you save some money.

---

[2] E. Diener, J. Horwitz, and R. A. Emmonds, "Happiness of the Very Wealthy," *Social Indicators Research* 16, pp. 263–74.
[3] BBC News, July 28, 2006, retrieved from http://news.bbc.co.uk/2/hi/5224306.stm.

get online!

SCAN HERE for study quizzes for this chapter

have information about different career options and connections to establish a job shadowing experience. The person/job fit can make work a joy or drudgery. When work has meaning and is in step with your values, vision, and mission, it can be a joy.

Collectively, the sections in this chapter should help you establish the foundation on which to build a personal financial plan that will incorporate your values, vision, mission, and goals. ■

> " Vision without action is a daydream. Action without vision is a nightmare. "
> —JAPANESE PROVERB

Making $ense

1.10 What drives your ability to be happy?

1.11 Identify the relationship between career and happiness.

1.12 Where can you find information on career options?

Learn. Plan & Act. Evaluate.

➡ **LEARN.** This chapter explored your relationship with money, your vision for your future, and your goals given your financial stage in life. You were exposed to the concept of voluntary simplicity—where more money may not always be better—and the idea that there comes a time when enough is enough. One of the best reasons for studying personal finance is to avoid the nightmares that lack of control and lack of direction bring. Finally, you learned how to create SMART goals to reach your vision of the future.

SUMMARY

■ ■ **LO 1-1** Evaluate your spending and saving habits, and define what financial success means to you.

Knowing how you feel about money is the first step to understanding your spending, savings, and investment habits. The second step is to identify your personal values, which provide direction as to where to spend your time and money. As money is spent, fulfillment increases until it reaches the point where enough is *enough*. Once this point is reached, fulfillment decreases as spending continues to increase. The 90-10 and 80-10-10 rules identify allocations toward values for community responsibility, retirement, and financial security. Determine your own definition of financial success. Money and material wealth do not bring happiness. Personal financial success involves achieving financial goals based on your personal values, vision, and mission.

■ ■ **LO 1-2** Develop a plan for engaging in fiscally responsible, goal-based spending and saving.

Financial literacy is key to achieving financial goals. It is the ability to understand finances, know the risks and potential rewards of investments, and identify which financial products and services best meet your needs. Financially literate people know enough to protect their assets, understand the realm of personal finance options, and make wise decisions. There are a number of avenues to reach your goals sooner rather than later, including downshifting, augmenting your income, and investing to achieve greater passive income. Financial planning consists of an income plan (job and career goals), a spending plan (a budget of expenses and future spending), an investment plan (gaining assets), a protection plan (insurance), and a giving plan (estate planning). Your life stage has an impact on your financial plans. The stages include: Dependent Life Stage (Age 16 and under); Independent Life Stage (Age 16–24); Early Family Life Stage (Age 25–40); Empty Nest Life Stage (Age 41–65); and Retirement Life Stage (Age 66 and over).

■ ■ **LO 1-3** Align your financial plan with your personal goals.

To know where to go, you need a vision of your destination. A vision statement defines a sense of purpose and a picture of the future. A mission statement is a written statement about your purpose for being. Using your values and your vision of the future, create a personal mission statement to give clarity to your priorities and motivation. Once you establish your values, vision, and mission statement, create a path to your personal and financial destinations via goal setting. Goals provide action plans. Long-term goals are greater than five years; intermediate goals can be attained in one to five years; and short-term goals are reached in less than one year. Goals need to be SMART: Specific, Measurable, Attainable, Realistic, and Time-bound, having a specific end date and timeline.

■ ■ **LO 1-4** Explore the different career choices that fit your personal mission statement and established goals.

By seeing money as a resource, allocating money to priorities, and not spending more than you make, you are in control of your finances. You can achieve a feeling of accomplishment by having money work for you. To be happy, choose a career where you can pursue your passions, in line with your values, with enough money to cover your needs, and learn to live within your means.

⟳ **PLAN & ACT.** Your financial plan (goals) should be aligned with your values and vision. In the words of Dr. Vance Havner, "The vision must be followed by the venture. It is not enough to stare up the steps—we must step up the stairs." [4] Climbing the stairs takes discipline, conscious thought, and action. A daily action plan that works toward achieving goals is the staircase to success. Your Plan & Act to-do list is as follows:

☐ Take the Money Relationship quiz (Worksheet 1.1).

☐ Identify your personal values (Worksheet 1.2).

☐ Clarify the most significant values with decisions on a career choice (Worksheet 1.3).

☐ Draft a personal mission statement (Worksheet 1.4).

[4]Havner (1901–1986) was a very popular "revivalist" and Bible conference speaker and authored more than 30 books of sermons and devotionals.

☐ Establish long-term, intermediate, and short-term goals (Worksheet 1.5).

☐ Ensure your goals incorporate SMART goal criteria (Worksheet 1.6).

⊜ EVALUATE.

After completing the Plan & Act to-do list, you will have a foundation on which to build a personal financial plan that incorporates your values, vision, mission, and goals. Do you feel your mission statement is a good fit? A mission statement can give you guidance when dealing with a difficult decision. As you encounter detours along life's journey, be sure to take time to reflect and re-evaluate your goals and objectives based on your priorities at your given stage in life.

» GoalTracker

In your online supplements, open the GoalTracker spreadsheet and log your goals from Worksheet 1.6. Over the course of this text, continue to revisit these goals, applying lessons learned from each chapter to help assess how you are tracking on your goals.

key terms

401(k) Retirement Plan	Financial Literacy	Passive Income
80-10-10 Rule	Financial Plan	Personal Financial Plan
90-10 Rule	Frugal	Personal Financial Success
Dollar Cost Averaging	Intermediate Goal	Personal Mission Statement
Downshifting	Investment Account	Personal Values
Enough	Long-Term Goal	Short-Term Goal
Financial Independence	Money Personality	SMART Goal
Financial Life Stages	Non-Earned Income	Voluntary Simplicity

self-test questions

1. Which of the following is *not* a strong driver of your spending and saving habits? *(LO 1-1)*

    a. Your values
    b. How you were raised
    c. Your parents' traits
    d. Weather

2. At what point is enough *enough?* *(LO 1-1)*

    a. Fulfillment is increasing at a decreasing rate.
    b. Fulfillment begins to decrease with increased spending.
    c. Fulfillment increases at a decreasing speed.
    d. Fulfillment increases at an increasing rate.

3. Which are not motivators to selecting a path of "Voluntary Simplicity"? *(LO 1-1)*

    a. Living more environmentally friendly
    b. Increasing quality time, reducing stress, and improving health
    c. Frugality
    d. Confusion

4. What additional contribution explains the difference between the 90-10 Rule and the 80-10-10 Rule? *(LO 1-1)*

    a. Community responsibility
    b. Retirement
    c. Financial security
    d. Return on investment

5. When is financial independence achieved? *(LO 1-2)*

    a. Expenditures are no longer a concern
    b. Passive income exceeds expenditures
    c. Expenditures are equal to non-earned income
    d. Passive income is greater than non-earned income

6. What differentiates passive income from non-earned income? *(LO 1-2)*

    a. Passive income is earned income.
    b. Non-earned income is income that does not have to be filed on income taxes.
    c. Non-earned income is the value of bartered services or goods.
    d. There is no difference.

7. Which is *not* an example of passive income? *(LO 1-2)*

   a. Interest payment from a savings account
   b. Stock dividend payment
   c. Tips
   d. Rental income

8. Which is *not* a component of building a successful personal financial plan? *(LO 1-2)*

   a. Spending plan
   b. Development plan
   c. Protection plan
   d. Giving plan

9. Which is *not* one of the personal finance life stages? *(LO 1-2)*

   a. Early family
   b. Retirement
   c. Independent
   d. Development

10. Which is *not* characteristic of a SMART goal? *(LO 1-3)*

    a. Specific
    b. Meaningful
    c. Attainable
    d. Realistic

11. Which is *not* the purpose of a mission statement? *(LO 1-3)*

    a. To reflect what you want to be known for
    b. To provide a vision of where you want to be
    c. To serve as a Facebook profile statement
    d. To provide a compass

12. Which statement correctly matches a time frame with goals? *(LO 1-3)*

    a. Long-term goals are greater than five years.
    b. Intermediate goals should be reached within the year.
    c. Short-term goals should be reached this semester.
    d. Goals should be met within three months.

13. Why do goals need to be specific? *(LO 1-3)*

    a. To know what to aim for
    b. Because people are more likely to achieve them
    c. To enable you to define achievement
    d. All of the above

14. Why do goals need a timeline? *(LO 1-3)*

    a. Establishing an endpoint is the first step in building a plan to achieve a goal
    b. It gives priority to achieving a goal over a given period of time
    c. Both
    d. Neither

15. What resources can be helpful when researching a career? *(LO 1-4)*

    a. Inquire about opportunities for internships
    b. Job shadow a professional in the career for a day
    c. Visit your college career center
    d. All of the above

16. According to Sonja Lyubomirsky, what percent of control do you have over your own happiness? *(LO 1-4)*

    a. 25%
    b. 40%
    c. 66%
    d. 100%

17. In which case will money *not* lead to happiness? *(LO 1-4)*

    a. You have more than everyone else in your tribe
    b. You have enough to buy everything you desire
    c. You use it to do good and are responsible with your money
    d. You have enough to survive

18. When researching career options, what will you *not* find in the *Occupational Outlook Handbook*? *(LO 1-4)*

    a. Nature of the work
    b. Qualifications
    c. Job outlook
    d. Occupational employment hazards

problems

1. If your goal budget was to follow the 90-10 rule, and you were bringing home about $2,000/month, how would your check be allocated over the course of the year? *(LO 1-1)*

2. For the past year, you made $58,000. To see if you were following the 80-10-10 rule, what amount and where would you see your income dispersed over the past year? *(LO 1-1)*

3. You are a fresh graduate with a new salary of $4,700 a month. You estimate you will be paying about 20% toward taxes. How much should you put in your savings each month? *(LO 1-1)*

4. You are starting a brand new job with a salary of $70,000. One third (33%) will go toward taxes (state, local, federal, and social security). Following the 90-10 rule, what is the most you should budget for monthly living expenses? *(LO 1-1)*

5. You currently follow the 90-10 rule. You decide you want to gradually shift to the 80-10-10 rule over the next 20 years, at a steady rate. What percentage of your income will you be budgeting incrementally each year for giving? *(LO 1-1)*

6. If you are able to save $1,000/month, following the 90-10 rule, what is your annual take-home income? *(LO 1-1)*

7. You are closing in on retirement. You are concerned you will not have built up enough in your savings over the next five years. You currently give $6,000/year to charity. If you change the allocation of your giving from 10 to 2%, how much will you still be giving each year? *(LO 1-1)*

1. Abby is a recent graduate who landed a great engineering job. Given the economic downturn and the pressure to run a lean shop, a number of more experienced veteran staff members have been downsized. As a result, a significant amount of responsibility and hours have fallen to her. She has been successful, but it has involved working 12 hours a day for 6–7 days each week for the past three months with no end in sight. She is fast approaching burnout, but to move to another job in the current market would be risky. (LO 1-1, LO 1-2)

   a. What steps would you recommend that Abby take to sort out her dilemma?
   b. List three pros and cons for two of her options.
   c. What would you suggest she do?

2. Eric's uncle left him a trust fund that will provide him $50,000/year for the next 20 years. He is a 28-year-old bachelor making a salary of $4,200/month, with a condo payment, fees, and utilities totaling $1,750/month. He also has a car payment, gas costs, and maintenance expenses averaging $600/month. Clothing, eating out, and other expenses vary greatly depending on how active his social life is that month. He has managed to steer clear of any credit card debt, but he has not started putting away money toward any long-term goals and he is living paycheck to paycheck. (LO 1-2)

   a. With his current windfall, how close is Eric to reaching financial independence?
   b. What are two options Eric has for achieving financial independence?
   c. Does Eric have the option of quitting his current job?
   d. If Eric were to quit his job, what would he have to do to maintain financial independence over the long-run?

3. Issie is a new high school graduate. She is excited about the field of nursing, loves international travel, and enjoys meeting people. She thinks the Peace Corps would be a great adventure while she is still single and young. Research the Peace Corps (www.peacecorp.gov) and Doctors Without Borders (www.doctorswithoutborders.org). Step through the process of creating short-term, intermediate, and long-term goals that will carry Issie through her Independent Life Stage. (LO 1-3)

worksheets

Find the worksheets online at www.mhhe.com/walkerpf1e

1.1 MONEY PERSONALITY

Work through Worksheet 1.1 to self-test your relationship with money.

	In order to self-assess your relationship with money, circle the statements below that best describe your outlook.
A	It's a good feeling to have money in my wallet.
B	No one can ever really have enough money.
C	Clothing should look expensive.
B	You can't live without credit.
D	There are a lot of things more important than money.
E	Keeping track of every dollar would drive me crazy.
A	It's important to record every dollar you spend.
C	Money and prestige go hand in hand.
E	A person can get along without a savings account.
D	It's easy to have fun with simple things that do not cost much money.
A	Money should only be spent for necessities.
C	I want nothing but the very best.
E	If I just wait, my money problems will take care of themselves.
D	Money doesn't buy happiness.
B	It would be easy to spend $5,000 in just a couple of days.
A	I shop around to find the best price.
E	If I need money, it will come from somewhere.
A	I won't buy anything unless I have enough money for it.
C	If I am going to buy something, I am going to buy the best option of it.
B	I will never buy something used, always brand new.
D	A lot of money would be nice, but I don't really need it.
E	I never make plans about money.
	Count up the number of times you circled A, B, C, D and E statements. If you mostly circled:
	A: You value money for the security it provides.
	B: You want a lot of material items and you want them now.
	C: Money helps you feel important.
	D: Money is a resource to get the things you need or want.
	E: You are not concerned with money, there is no reason to worry about it.
	How does this statement reflect your relationship with money? Give a specific example:
	How does this statement *not* reflect your relationship with money? Give a specific example:

1.2 CLARIFYING VALUES

Complete Worksheet 1.2 to help you reach a better understanding of your most significant values when making decisions on a career choice.

Personal Values and Career Selection		High (H)	Med (M)	Low (L)
Accomplishment	Sense of having done something well			
Competence	Feeling of being effective			
Contentment	Peace of mind			
Contribution	Being part of and adding value to a larger enterprise			
Creativity	Creative in some form or medium			
Culture	Interest in art, music, and literature			
Economic security	Regular income			
Enjoyment	Lots of fun and laughs			
Esteem	Making an impact and gaining admiration			
Experience	Having a lot of experience on the job			
Family	Supportive of time with family, balance of time commitment			
Fitness	Keeping in good physical condition			
Flexibility	Being able to do what you want to do when you want to do it			
Friendship	Having close friends around			
Honesty	Being able to say what you think			
Integrity	Being clear and consistent in dealing with others			
Personal growth	Continuing to learn			
Popularity	Being liked by most people			
Power	Control and influence over others			
Religion	Practicing strong religious beliefs			
Risk-taking	Opportunities to speculate, gamble, take chances			
Security	Freedom from anxiety about the future			
Self-confidence	Activity confirms the value of your contribution			
Stability	Solid, lasting experience; having a predictable place			
Status	Prestige and being looked up to			
Strong convictions	Firm principles			
Teamwork	Being part of an effective team			
Technical excellence	Being at the forefront of technical development			
Uniqueness	Nonconforming			
Wealth	Making as much money as possible			
Winning	First in a competitive situation			

1.3 VISION STATEMENT

Create a vision statement using Worksheet 1.3.

Create a vision statement. Your vision statement should define your sense of purpose and paint a picture of your future. Reflect back on your values and ask yourself how your vision fits in with your values. Do you need to change your vision to fit your values, or do you need to change your values to fit your vision?

My vision of my future in 10, 20, and 30 years looks like this:
It relates most strongly with my values of:

1.4 MISSION STATEMENT

Use the two websites in Worksheet 1.4 to help you develop your mission statement.

Use these two websites to help you develop your mission statement:
Ø Franklin Covey Institute: www.franklincovey.com/msb/
Ø Nightingale Conant: www.nightingale.com/mission_statement.aspx
Combine the two and develop a personal mission statement that accurately describes your purpose of being. Make sure it reflects your values and vision.
1
2

1.5 GOALS

Use the mind maps in Worksheet 1.5 to create long-term, intermediate, and short-term goals, bearing in mind what you already have identified as your values and your personal mission statement.

1. Long-Term Goals: Identify one long term goal (> 5 years out):
2. Intermediate Goals (1-5 years): Write a long-term goal in the center of the mind map. On the spokes, write up to four intermediate goals that you need to achieve in the next 1-5 years to get closer to your long-term goal.
3. Intermediate Goals (1-5 years): Write a long-term goal in the center of the mind map. On the spokes, write up to four intermediate goals that you need to achieve in the next 1-5 years to get closer to your long-term goal.

1.6 SMART GOALS

In Worksheet 1.6, review your long-term, intermediate, and short-term goals and make them into SMART goals.

Review your long-, intermediate, and short-term goals and make them into SMART goals.
S – Specific
M – Measurable
A – Attainable
R – Realistic
T – Time, having a specific end date and timeline
SMART Long-Term Goals:
SMART Intermediate Goals:
SMART Short-Term Goals:

Throughout the text, the continuing case scenario at the end of the chapter will involve lessons encountered by the housemates of 906 East College Street. All of the residents are either current students or recent graduates. Leigh, Blake, and Nicole are siblings. Their parents bought the home, which is close to campus, as an investment when Leigh started at the university her freshman year. The following profiles describe each of the housemates and their intermediate-term goals. For each housemate, identify a SMART short-term goal that supports his or her success in achieving an intermediate goal.

906 E College Street

Housemate	Profile	Intermediate Goal
Leigh	Graduate, art teacher, oldest sister. Works part-time at the local co-op for the discount, sells artwork at the local farmer's market, bikes to work. Vegetarian, loves to garden, and has four egg-laying backyard hens.	*Intermediate Goal:* Backpack through Europe for a summer in five years
Blake	Junior, business student, brother. Expected to someday come back to work in the family business, but first he would like to try a career on Wall Street.	*Intermediate Goal:* Hawaiian Iron Man triathlon in five years
Nicole	Freshman, pre-nursing for the moment, youngest sister.	*Intermediate Goal:* Graduate in four years
Karri	Fifth-year student, communications major. Loves shoes and high fashion, chocolate and wine, and the Big Apple.	*Intermediate Goal:* Anchor the evening news for a local television network
Peter	Graduate from Culinary Art School, sous chef. Did an internship in Tokyo, would love someday to go back and visit. Originally from Colorado, wants to summit all of the state's 14,000-foot peaks someday.	*Intermediate Goal:* Open his own sushi restaurant in three years
Brett	Second-year med student, focused on emergency medicine. Interested in someday seeing the world via volunteerism for Doctors Without Borders.	*Intermediate Goal:* Complete med school and residency with as little debt as possible
Jen	Freshman at the community college, undecided major. Very social, fastest texter in high school graduating class.	*Intermediate Goal:* Pick a major, transfer to the university after two years, graduate with a bachelor's degree in four years
Jack	Recent graduate in general studies. Currently tending bar part-time, no benefits. Would like to advocate for paintball as an Olympic sport.	*Intermediate Goal:* Decide on a career and avoid moving back in with mom and dad

"Americans are getting stronger. Twenty years ago, it took two people to carry ten dollars worth of groceries. Today, a five-year old could do it.

—HENRY YOUNG, *English comedian (1908–1998)*

time value of money

In this chapter, you will learn what gives currency value and how it is distributed throughout the United States. You will also learn money has a defined value when you spend it today (present value), but through the power of compound interest, it will have a different value (future value) if it is not spent until a future date. You will be taught how to calculate the future value of today's lump sum of money as well as the future value of a steady stream of investment. Additionally, you will learn the present value of lump sums against the future value of an investment. ■

LEARNING OBJECTIVES

After reading this chapter, you should be able to:

LO 2-1 Explain what gives paper currency value and how the Federal Reserve Bank manages its distribution.

LO 2-2 Differentiate between simple and compound interest rates and calculate annual percentage yields and the value of paying yourself first.

LO 2-3 Calculate the future and present value of lump sums and annuities in order to know what amount to put aside to meet financial goals.

◄ Clay, age 14, high school freshman, a dollar in hand for each thousand in savings

Power of Compounding

Each year since birth, Clay received $1,000 from his grandparents for his birthday. As a high school senior, "I decided to keep my birthday money in savings instead of using it for college expenses. The $17,000 that my grandparents have given me over the years now totals more than $30,000. If at all possible, I am going to keep the money to invest. I have a goal of becoming a millionaire before my older brother. I know that keeping it all in the money market account and continuing to add just the $1,000 gift money each year from my grandparents will help me reach my goal to become a millionaire when I'm in my 50s."

2.1 WHAT GIVES MONEY VALUE

■■ **LO 2-1** Explain what gives paper currency value and how the Federal Reserve Bank manages its distribution.

What gives money value? If you have studied the microeconomics of supply and demand, you know that something in limited supply and high demand has value. It is the same with paper currency. There is a limited supply and a relatively high demand. The dollar is a form of currency that you can exchange for other things of value like food, gas, clothing, and rent (or you can save it where it will have stored value).

Paper money is backed by the full faith and credit of the United States government and the Federal Reserve Bank. Pull out a dollar bill from your wallet and you will see the words "Federal Reserve Note" printed at the top in the center of the bill. Paper money is printed by the Bureau of Engraving and Printing in Washington, D.C., and Fort Worth, Texas. The bureau supplies the Federal Reserve Bank with Federal Reserve notes (paper money). Money is continually printed to replace mutilated currency. Coins are minted by the United States Mint. Currently only Philadelphia and Denver produce coins for circulation. The United States Mint supplies coins to the Federal Reserve Bank, which in turn supplies coins to local banks and credit unions. This is how money starts out. Now you need to learn how to make it grow.

2.2 THE POWER OF COMPOUNDING

■■ **LO 2-2** Differentiate between simple and compound interest rates and calculate annual percentage yields and the value of paying yourself first.

How can you increase the value of your money? If you put your money in a tin can and bury it in your backyard, your dollar will not grow or multiply. When you need the money, you will have relatively the same amount you put in, assuming you can find it and it has not decomposed. However, you can also choose to save or invest that money where it can earn some type of return, based on the risk of the investment.

If Ben Franklin deposited $20 for you 250 years ago and it earned a 5% rate of interest compounded annually, how much money would you have today? What if it earned an 8% return? Or a 10% return? Figure 2.1 illustrates how compound interest impacts value with time.

["The mint makes it first, it is up
to you to make it last."
—ERROL FLYNN, *Australian actor (1909–1959)*]

Compounding Interest

If you put $100 in a savings account at a local bank, you will earn interest on the savings. For example, assume the savings account is earning a generous 12% **annual percentage rate (APR)**. At the end of one year from the time of depositing the $100, you will have earned $12 in interest, or 12% of the deposited amount. Your total account balance would be $112 at the end of the year. At the end of second year, your account balance would be $124, of which $12 was the interest earned over the second year. This is using *simple* interest, where interest is paid annually.

Compounding is where interest is added to the initial deposit and you begin to earn interest on interest. For example, if the interest is compounded quarterly, an interest payment is added to your account four times a year. To compute a quarterly rate, divide the annual interest rate by 4. For example,

12% annually ÷ 4 time periods = 3% per quarter

Next, calculate your **annual percentage yield (APY)**, which is how much total interest is earned in a year. The annual percentage yield shows the effective interest rate, which takes into account the effects of compounding. Assume you deposit $1,000 for one year in an account that pays 12% interest compounded quarterly. For the first quarter, you earn 3% on your deposit ($1,000 × 3% = $30 in interest). This $30 is added to your deposit, so for the second quarter, interest is earned on the account balance of $1,030. To calculate the next interest payment, you multiply the new balance by 3% ($1,030 × .03 = $30.90 in interest). At the end of six months, you have a new balance of $1,060.90 and have earned $60.90 in interest on the original deposit of $1,000.

For the next time period, you would perform the same calculation with the new balance ($1060.90 × 3% =

$31.83 in interest). For the last period, the balance of $1,092.73 × 3% = $32.78 in interest. At the end of the year, you would end up earning a total of $125.51 in interest. Your yield (what you actually earned) on your deposit of $1,000 at 12% percent compounded quarterly would be $125.51, a percentage yield of 12.55% (125.51/1,000). The more frequently your interest is compounded, the higher your yield.

The formula to calculate annual percentage yield (APY) is:

$$APY = (1 + r/n)^n - 1$$

Making $ense

2.1 What gives the U.S. dollar currency value?

2.2 How does the role of the Bureau of Engraving and Printing differ from that of the United States Mint?

▼ **FIGURE 2.1**

The value of $20 over 250 years

@10% = $446,000,000,000

@ 8% = $4,500,000,000

@ 5% = $4,000,000

2.1 Simple Interest, Compound Interest, and APY

Simple Interest on $1,000 @ 12%

Deposit of $1,000 on Jan 1 . . .

$1,000 + (1,000 × .12) = $1,120 *Resulting balance on Dec. 31*

Compound Interest Quarterly on $1,000 @ 12%

12% ÷ 4 time periods = 3% per quarter

Deposit of $1,000 on Jan 1 . . .

$1,000.00 + (**1,000.00** × **.03**) = 1,000.00 + 30.00 = $1,030.00

$1,030.00 + (**1,030.00** × **.03**) = 1,030.00 + 30.90 = $1,060.90

$1,060.90 + (**1,060.90** × **.03**) = 1,060.90 + 31.83 = $1,092.73

$1,092.73 + (**1,092.73** × **.03**) = 1,092.73 + 32.78 = **$1,125.51** *Resulting balance on Dec 31*

30.00 + 30.90 + 31.83 + 32.78 = **$125.51 Annual Yield**

125.51/1,000 = 12.55% APY

1. What would be the value difference on earned interest for $10,000 at 12% simple interest versus 12% interest compounded monthly over the course of one year?

2. What would be the APY earned on $10,000 at 12% interest compounded monthly over the course of one year?

where

> r = the stated annual interest rate, and
> n = the number of times the interest payment is compounded per year

Using the information in the nearby *Doing the Math* example,

$$\text{APY} = [1 + (0.12/4)]^4 - 1$$

Yields at this 12% rate are as follows:

compounded annually	12.00%
compounded semiannually	12.36%
compounded quarterly	12.55%
compounded monthly	12.68%
compounded daily	12.75%

As of December 19, 1991, the Truth in Savings Act requires banks to disclose the fees, the annual percentage rate (APR), and the annual percentage yield (APY) on interest-bearing accounts so consumers can more fairly compare account options. In our example, an interest-bearing account at 12% APR, compounded daily, yields a 12.75% APY. Before the Truth in Savings Act, banks would advertise their rates but not their yields. An interest-bearing account advertised at 12.5% with simple interest would actually earn less interest than an account with an APR of 12% with interest compounded daily (12.75% APY). The Truth in Savings Act helped eliminate investor confusion with compounding interest and the related yields.

You work hard for your money, and you want your money to work hard for you. Compounding interest helps your money work for you. With this concept in mind, would you rather have $1,000 today or $1,000 a year from now? If you had that money today, you could invest it. At the end of one year with a 12.75% APY you would have $1,127.50, an earnings of $127.50. Understanding interest helps you to grasp the concept of **time value of money**: A dollar today is worth more than a dollar tomorrow.

Making Compounding Work for You

As Albert Einstein stated, "The most powerful force in the universe is compound interest." For this force to work for you, it takes *discipline* to deposit money and *time* for the force to work. Consider the following example of three different college students; Wild Willie, Smart Sam, and Dedicated Dave (see Figure 2.2).

Wild Willie liked to have fun and lived a carefree life during college. He would spend his money on the things he wanted, when he wanted them. Like water through a sieve, money in his wallet ran out as fast as he put it in. From the age of 19–29, he spent all he made, not worrying about retirement until he turned 30.

Smart Sam also liked to have fun, but he had a future orientation toward retirement. He made it a priority to pay himself first by setting aside money for retirement from the age 19–29. He put off temptations of immediate gratification in support of future financial security. However, after age 29, he decided to stop making contributions.

Dedicated Dave is a lot like Smart Sam, but he decided to continue his contributions until retirement. It is obvious Dedicated Dave would have more in his retirement fund than either Wild Willie or Smart Sam. All three decided to work until age 69 so they all had 50 years until retirement. If they each put in $2,000 per year in the years that they contribute, Dedicated Dave will have contributed $104,000 to retirement, Wild Willie will have contributed $84,000, and Smart Sam will have deposited $20,000. Who will have more money at retirement? The answer can be found in Figure 2.3 on the next page.

It may surprise you, but due to compounding, Smart Sam will have more money than Wild Willie, even though Wild Willie deposited $60,000 more money into a retirement fund. At age 70, all three got together to see how much they had. They all had received 10% interest for the entire 50 years of investing. Dedicated Dave stated that he had a nest egg of $2,820,859 through the dedication of paying himself first and making a commitment to his retirement.

Wild Willie talked about all the fun he had in college and how he, like Dedicated Dave, became committed to saving, but started 10 years behind Dave. Wild Willie was pleased to announce that his nest egg had accumulated to $1,075,274 from his original investment of $84,000.

Smart Sam stated how he made a few sacrifices in college and deposited only $20,000 in 10 years starting from age 19. Willie and Dave both wondered how much he accumulated. Sam sheepishly stated that his $20,000 had turned into $1,745,585, which was over $670,000 more than Willie, even though Willie contributed $60,000 more than Sam.

time value of money where a dollar now is worth more than a dollar in the future, even after adjusting for inflation, because a dollar now can earn interest

▼ FIGURE 2.2

Wild Willie, Smart Sam, and Dedicated Dave

When they were young, Willie, Sam, and Dave had slightly different investment strategies. When they retired, they had largely different results.

Source: University of Iowa.

financialfitness:
ACTION ITEM

APR vs. APY

APR is the annual rate of interest without taking into account the compounding of interest within that year. Alternatively, APY (annual percentage yield) does take into account the effects of intra-year compounding. This subtle difference can significantly affect the amount of interest accumulated in a savings account. When shopping around for a bank account, make sure to compare APY, minimum balances, and fees. The website www.bankrate.com is an objective, comprehensive, and free online resource for researching national and local options.

▼ FIGURE 2.3

Wild Willie-Smart Sam-Dedicated Dave investment matrix

Age	Smart Sam	Deposited	Wild Willie	Deposited	Dedicated Dave	Deposited
19	$2,000.00	$2,000.00			$2,000.00	$2,000.00
20	$4,200.00	$2,000.00			$4,200.00	$2,000.00
21	$6,620.00	$2,000.00			$6,620.00	$2,000.00
22	$9,282.00	$2,000.00			$9,282.00	$2,000.00
23	$12,210.20	$2,000.00			$12,210.20	$2,000.00
24	$15,431.22	$2,000.00			$15,431.22	$2,000.00
25	$18,974.34	$2,000.00			$18,974.34	$2,000.00
26	$22,871.78	$2,000.00			$22,871.78	$2,000.00
27	$27,158.95	$2,000.00			$27,158.95	$2,000.00
28	$31,874.85	$2,000.00			$31,874.85	$2,000.00
29	$35,062.33		$2,000.00	$2,000.00	$37,062.33	$2,000.00
30	$38,568.57		$4,200.00	$2,000.00	$42,768.57	$2,000.00
31	$42,425.42		$6,620.00	$2,000.00	$49,045.42	$2,000.00
32	$46,667.97		$9,282.00	$2,000.00	$55,949.97	$2,000.00
33	$51,334.76		$12,210.20	$2,000.00	$63,544.96	$2,000.00
34	$56,468.24		$15,431.22	$2,000.00	$71,899.46	$2,000.00
35	$62,115.06		$18,974.34	$2,000.00	$81,089.41	$2,000.00
36	$68,326.57		$22,871.78	$2,000.00	$91,198.35	$2,000.00
37	$75,159.23		$27,158.95	$2,000.00	$102,318.18	$2,000.00
38	$82,675.15		$31,874.85	$2,000.00	$114,550.00	$2,000.00
39	$90,942.66		$37,062.33	$2,000.00	$128,005.00	$2,000.00
40	$100,036.93		$42,768.57	$2,000.00	$142,805.50	$2,000.00
41	$110,040.62		$49,045.42	$2,000.00	$159,086.05	$2,000.00
42	$121,044.69		$55,949.97	$2,000.00	$176,994.65	$2,000.00
43	$133,149.16		$63,544.96	$2,000.00	$196,694.12	$2,000.00
44	$146,464.07		$71,899.46	$2,000.00	$218,363.53	$2,000.00
45	$161,110.48		$81,089.41	$2,000.00	$242,199.88	$2,000.00
46	$177,221.53		$91,198.35	$2,000.00	$268,419.87	$2,000.00
47	$194,943.68		$102,318.18	$2,000.00	$297,261.86	$2,000.00
48	$214,438.05		$114,550.00	$2,000.00	$328,988.05	$2,000.00
49	$235,881.85		$128,005.00	$2,000.00	$363,886.85	$2,000.00
50	$259,470.04		$142,805.50	$2,000.00	$402,275.53	$2,000.00
51	$285,417.04		$159,086.05	$2,000.00	$444,503.09	$2,000.00
52	$313,958.74		$176,994.65	$2,000.00	$490,953.40	$2,000.00
53	$345,354.62		$196,694.12	$2,000.00	$542,048.74	$2,000.00
54	$379,890.08		$218,363.53	$2,000.00	$598,253.61	$2,000.00
55	$417,879.09		$242,199.88	$2,000.00	$660,078.97	$2,000.00
56	$459,667.00		$268,419.87	$2,000.00	$728,086.87	$2,000.00
57	$505,633.70		$297,261.86	$2,000.00	$802,895.56	$2,000.00
58	$556,197.07		$328,988.05	$2,000.00	$885,185.11	$2,000.00
59	$611,816.77		$363,886.85	$2,000.00	$975,703.62	$2,000.00
60	$672,998.45		$402,275.53	$2,000.00	$1,075,273.98	$2,000.00
61	$740,298.29		$444,503.09	$2,000.00	$1,184,801.38	$2,000.00
62	$814,328.12		$490,953.40	$2,000.00	$1,305,281.52	$2,000.00
63	$895,760.94		$542,048.74	$2,000.00	$1,437,809.67	$2,000.00
64	$985,337.03		$598,253.61	$2,000.00	$1,583,590.64	$2,000.00
65	$1,083,870.73		$660,078.97	$2,000.00	$1,743,949.71	$2,000.00
66	$1,192,257.81		$728,086.87	$2,000.00	$1,920,344.68	$2,000.00
67	$1,311,483.59		$802,895.56	$2,000.00	$2,114,379.14	$2,000.00
68	$1,442,631.95		$885,185.11	$2,000.00	$2,327,817.06	$2,000.00
69	$1,586,895.14		$975,703.62	$2,000.00	$2,562,598.76	$2,000.00
70	**$1,745,584.65**		**$1,075,273.98**	$2,000.00	**$2,820,858.64**	$2,000.00
Amount Invested at 10%	**$20,000.00**			**$84,000.00**		**$104,000.00**

After dinner, all three agreed with Albert Einstein that compound interest is the most powerful force in the universe. Willie, in hindsight, wished he had saved $2,000 a year for retirement when he turned 19. That would have been only $166.67 a month, or $38.46 a week, or $5.48 a day.

Pay Yourself First

The secret to accumulating wealth, saving for retirement, or becoming a millionaire (if you so desire) is to start early and to regularly pay yourself first. Automatic withdrawals and transfers can simplify the process. You can establish an automatic bank transfer for any amount of money to go from checking to savings. Many mutual funds and investment companies will allow you to open an account with an automatic transfer of $50. The challenge with a bank transfer is that the money is very easy to access. If you invest in a mutual fund or investment account, the money is a little harder to access and you will have to think twice before withdrawing it. For compounding to work, you have to leave the money alone to watch it grow. We will learn more about mutual funds and investment accounts in Unit 4, Wealth Accumulation.

2.3 THE TIME VALUE OF MONEY

■■ **LO 2-3** Calculate the future and present value of lump sums and annuities in order to know what amount to put aside to meet financial goals.

As you are learning, money has a defined value when you spend it today (**present value**), but it will have a different

Money not spent today can have a different future value.

Making $ense

2.3 How do you calculate the annual percentage yield (APY)?

2.4 Why is it better to put a little into your savings each month when you are young rather than wait until you are older, even though the amount you put away each month may be less?

value (**future value**) if it isn't spent until a future date. The question is, How do you calculate the future value of your investment or savings?

There are three methods to calculate value. You could: (1) calculate it long-hand as illustrated earlier in the chapter, (2) use a financial calculator, or (3) use the tables provided in the appendix to this text. With these methods, you can find:

- The *future value* of an amount invested today
- The *present value* of an amount you will receive in the future
- The *future value* of an amount you deposit annually
- The *present value* of an amount if you make annual payments

The time value of money is most commonly applied to two types of cash flows: a single dollar amount (referred to as a **lump sum**) and an **annuity** (a stream of equal payments that are received or paid at equal intervals over time).

Future Value of a Lump Sum

The first and easiest concept is the future value of a single lump sum amount. As an example, suppose that at the time of your birth your rich aunt deposited $10,000 for you into an account earning 5% annually. How much money would you have on your 18th birthday? How much money would you have when you turn 30? How much would you have by the time you retire at age 65?

future value (FV), long-hand method

We can calculate the future value of money by using the formula

$$FV = PV\,(1 + i)^n$$

where

FV = Future value
PV = Present value
i = Interest rate
n = Number of periods

$FV = PV\,(1 + i)^n$
$FV = \$10{,}000\,(1 + 0.05)^{18}$
$FV = \$10{,}000\,(1.05)^{18}$
$FV = \$10{,}000\,(2.406619)$
$FV = \$24{,}066.19$ on your 18th birthday

$FV = PV\,(1 + i)^n$
$FV = \$10{,}000\,(1 + 0.05)^{30}$
$FV = \$10{,}000\,(1.05)^{30}$
$FV = \$10{,}000\,(4.321942)$
$FV = \$43{,}219.42$ on your 30th birthday

$FV = PV\,(1 + i)^n$
$FV = \$10{,}000\,(1 + 0.05)^{65}$
$FV = \$10{,}000\,(1.05)^{65}$
$FV = \$10{,}000\,(23.839901)$
$FV = \$238{,}399.01$ on your 65th birthday

future value (FV), reference table method

You can also use the future value interest factor (FVIF) table (Figure 2.4) to easily calculate the future amount. To do so, you would use the formula below and the corresponding factor from the FV table found in the interest rate (i) column and the number of time periods (n) row:

$FV = PV\,(FVIF_{i,n})$
$FV = \$10{,}000\,(FVIF_{5,18})$
$FV = \$10{,}000\,(2.4066)$
$FV = \$24{,}066.00$ on your 18th birthday

$FV = PV\,(FVIF_{i,n})$
$FV = \$10{,}000\,(FVIF_{5,30})$
$FV = \$10{,}000\,(4.3219)$
$FV = \$43{,}219.00$ on your 30th birthday

As you can see, the answers differ slightly due to rounding.

The FVIF table is a simple Excel table with the formula of compounding (the interest of this period multiplied by balance of last period) embedded in each cell. The result in each cell (for a given time period and a given interest rate) assumes the original beginning balance is $1. Note that as the time periods and interest rates increase, the future balance result cell also increases. This result cell is known as the **future value interest factor (FVIF)**. Finding the factor for the selected time period and interest rate for $1, and then multiplying that factor by the actual beginning balance, gives you the future value of your current lump sum. The full FVIF table can be found in Appendix A. The actual Excel document can be found online in the "Factors" document.

future value (FV), financial calculator method

You can also use a financial calculator to find the future value of an amount (Figure 2.5). All financial calculators have the buttons N (number of time periods), I/YR (interest rate per year), PV (present value), PMT (payment), and FV (future value).

Continuing with the same problem, if you were using a financial calculator to find out how much you would have in 65 years, you would press 65, N (number of time periods); 5, I/YR; (interest rate per year); −10,000, PV (present value—a *negative* value because it is a deposit); and 0, PMT (payment). When you press the FV (future value) key, $238,399.01 will show up on your screen, the same number we got when we used the formula $FV = PV\,(1 + i)^n$. See Figure 2.6.

Using financial calculators is useful when calculating odd interest rates, long periods of time, or figures involving monthly payments. If your interest rate changed from 5 to 7.38% in this example, you would use the same calculator keys but change the interest rate number (see Figure 2.7). When you press the FV key, $1,023,342.42 will show up on your screen, the same number you would get using the formula $FV = PV\,(1 + i)^n$.

$FV = PV\,(1 + i)^n$
$FV = \$10{,}000\,(1 + 0.0738)^{65}$
$FV = \$10{,}000\,(1.0738)^{65}$
$FV = \$10{,}000\,(102.334242)$
$FV = \$1{,}023{,}342.42$

 The most powerful force in the universe is compound interest. 99

—ALBERT EINSTEIN *(1879–1955)*

▼ FIGURE 2.4

Future value of $1 invested today at the end of *n* periods (Future Value Interest Factor (FVIF) Table)

Period	1%	2%	3%	4%	5%
1	1.0100	1.0200	1.0300	1.0400	1.0500
2	1.0201	1.0404	1.0609	1.0816	1.1025
3	1.0303	1.0612	1.0927	1.1249	1.1576
4	1.0406	1.0824	1.1255	1.1699	1.2155
5	1.0510	1.1041	1.1593	1.2167	1.2763
6	1.0615	1.1262	1.1941	1.2653	1.3401
7	1.0721	1.1487	1.2299	1.3159	1.4071
8	1.0829	1.1717	1.2668	1.3686	1.4775
9	1.0937	1.1951	1.3048	1.4233	1.5513
10	1.1046	1.2190	1.3439	1.4802	1.6289
11	1.1157	1.2434	1.3842	1.5395	1.7103
12	1.1268	1.2682	1.4258	1.6010	1.7959
13	1.1381	1.2936	1.4685	1.6651	1.8856
14	1.1495	1.3195	1.5126	1.7317	1.9799
15	1.1610	1.3459	1.5580	1.8009	2.0789
16	1.1726	1.3728	1.6047	1.8730	2.1829
17	1.1843	1.4002	1.6528	1.9479	2.2920
18	1.1961	1.4282	1.7024	2.0258	2.4066

Snippet of FVIF table, full table in Appendix A.
Factor used if interest rate (i) = 5% and periods (n) = 18.

▼ FIGURE 2.5

Financial calculator keys

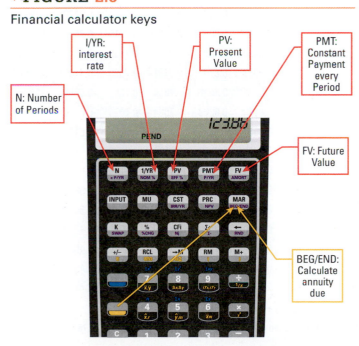

▼ FIGURE 2.6

Future value example

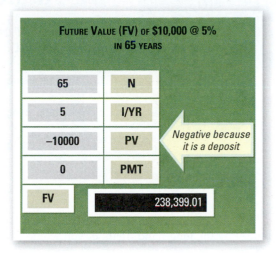

▼ FIGURE 2.7

Future value example

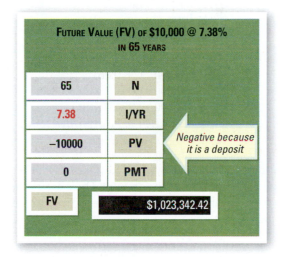

Present Value of a Lump Sum

Now you want to know how much money you would have to deposit today to have a specific amount in the future. This process is known as **discounting**. You are discounting the future value to the present value in today's dollars. Say you just had your first child and you ask your parents (the child's grandparents) to put money in a college savings account. You would like your child to have $10,000 from each set of grandparents when your child turns 18. How much would each set of grandparents have to deposit today to grow to $10,000 over the next 18 years, assuming a 6% interest rate compounded annually (simple interest)?

2.2 Future Value of a Lump Sum

You received $20,000 when you turned 16 and decided to invest it for five years at 4% interest. How much will that $20,000 be worth when you turn 21?

1. Calculate using the long-hand method.

2. Calculate using the reference table method.

3. Calculate using a financial calculator.

present value (PV), long-hand method To calculate the amount by the long-hand method, you would use the formula

$$PV = FV/(1 + i)^n$$

where

PV = Present value
FV = Future value
 i = Interest rate
 n = Number of time periods

$PV = FV/(1 + i)^n$
$PV = \$10,000/(1 + 0.06)^{18}$
$PV = \$10,000/(1.06)^{18}$
$PV = \$10,000/(2.854337451)$
$PV = \$3,503.44$ *to be deposited today*

present value (PV), reference table method You can also use the present value interest factor (PVIF) table in Figure 2.8 to calculate the amount. Once again, the factor is found in the interest rate column (i) and number of time periods (n) row.

$PV = FV (PVIF_{i,n})$
$PV = \$10,000 (PVIF_{6,18})$
$PV = \$10,000 (.3503)$
$PV = \$3,503.00$ *to be deposited today*

As you can see, there is a rounding difference of $0.44 when using the tables versus the formula in this example.

The PVIF table is a simple Excel table with the formula of compounding (the interest of this period divided by 1 and multiplied by balance of last period) embedded in each cell. The result reflected assumes an original future balance of $1. Note that as the time periods and interest rates increase, the present value result cell decreases. This result cell is known as the **present value interest factor (PVIF)**. Finding the factor for the selected time period and interest rate for $1, and then multiplying that factor by the

actual future balance gives you the present value of your future lump sum. The PVIF table can be found in Appendix A. The actual Excel document can be found online in the "Factors" document.

present value (PV), financial calculator method You can also use a financial calculator to figure the present value of a lump sum. You would use the same

▼ **FIGURE 2.8**

Present value of $1 to be received at the end of n periods (Present Value Interest Factor [PVIF])

Period	1%	2%	3%	4%	5%	6%
1	0.9901	0.9804	0.9709	0.9615	0.9524	0.9434
2	0.9803	0.9612	0.9426	0.9246	0.9070	0.8900
3	0.9706	0.9423	0.9151	0.8890	0.8638	0.8396
4	0.9610	0.9238	0.8885	0.8548	0.8227	0.7921
5	0.9515	0.9057	0.8626	0.8219	0.7835	0.7473
6	0.9420	0.8880	0.8375	0.7903	0.7462	0.7050
7	0.9327	0.8706	0.8131	0.7599	0.7107	0.6651
8	0.9235	0.8535	0.7894	0.7307	0.6768	0.6274
9	0.9143	0.8368	0.7664	0.7026	0.6446	0.5919
10	0.9053	0.8203	0.7441	0.6756	0.6139	0.5584
11	0.8963	0.8043	0.7224	0.6496	0.5847	0.5268
12	0.8874	0.7885	0.7014	0.6246	0.5568	0.4970
13	0.8787	0.7730	0.6810	0.6006	0.5303	0.4688
14	0.8700	0.7579	0.6611	0.5775	0.5051	0.4423
15	0.8613	0.7430	0.6419	0.5553	0.4810	0.4173
16	0.8528	0.7284	0.6232	0.5339	0.4581	0.3936
17	0.8444	0.7142	0.6050	0.5134	0.4363	0.3714
18	0.8360	0.7002	0.5874	0.4936	0.4155	0.3503

Snippet of PVIF table, full table in Appendix A.

Factor used if interest rate (i) = 6% and periods (n) = 18.

keys as in our earlier example, but now you would input the future value and solve for the present value: 18, N (number of time periods); 6, I/YR (interest rate per year); 10000, FV (future value); and 0, PMT (payment). When you press the PV key, −$3,503.44 will show up on your screen, the same number we got using the formula $PV = FV/(1 + i)^n$. Because it is a negative cash flow, money going out, the number is negative. See Figure 2.9.

Future Value of an Annuity

Your parents want to contribute to your child's education, but instead of a lump sum payment of $3,500, they plan to contribute $500 each year for 18 years. How much money from your parents would your child have in his or her educational fund after 18 years at 6% interest compounded annually? This is an example of an annuity.

An **ordinary annuity** is a stream of equal payments that occurs at the *end* of a period. An **annuity due** is a stream of equal payments that occurs at the *beginning* of a period. When calculating the future value of an annuity, it is always helpful to draw a timeline with the payments. Figure 2.10 shows the timeline of an ordinary annuity and Figure 2.11 on the next page shows the timeline of cash flows for an annuity due. When we use the word *annuity* in finance, we assume it refers to an ordinary annuity.

future value of an annuity (FVA), long-hand method

There are many ways to calculate the future value of an annuity. Using the long-hand method, you can calculate the interest earned starting in period 1 (for an ordinary annuity) or period 0 (for an annuity due), add the interest to the principal, and then add the next payment and calculate the interest. This process is repeated until the number of payments is complete. Consider the following ordinary annuity example using a payment stream of $500:

$500 × 1.06 = $530.00 (*value at the end of period 1*)
$530 + $500 = $1030 × 1.06 = $1,091.80 (*value at the end of period 2*)
$1,091.80 + $500 = $1,591.80 × 1.06 = $1,687.31 (*value at the end of period 3*)

This is a long, tedious process that could lead to input errors. The formula to calculate the future value of an ordinary annuity is:

$$FVA = PMT \{[(1 + i)^n - 1] / i\}$$

where

FVA = Future value of an annuity
PMT = Payment

▼ FIGURE 2.9

Present value example

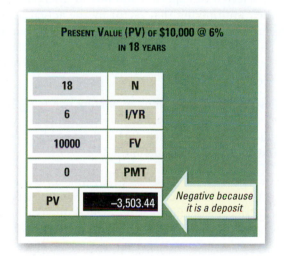

PRESENT VALUE (PV) OF $10,000 @ 6% IN 18 YEARS

18	N
6	I/YR
10000	FV
0	PMT
PV	−3,503.44

Negative because it is a deposit

▼ FIGURE 2.10

Ordinary annuity payments start at the end of the first period

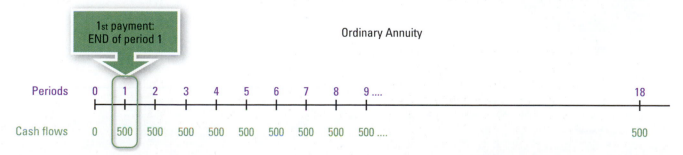

2.3 Present Value of a Lump Sum

You are 16 and know you need $100,000 when you turn 22 (in six years) to pay for medical school. In order to have enough savings at that point, how much must you deposit in a college fund today, assuming a 4% simple interest rate?

1. Calculate using the long-hand method.

2. Calculate using the reference table method.

3. Calculate using a financial calculator.

i = Interest rate
n = Number of time periods

In our example above, PMT = $500, i = .06, and n = 18:

$$FVA = \$500\{[(1 + 0.06)^{18} - 1] / 0.06\}$$
$$FVA = \$500\{[(1.06)^{18} - 1] / 0.06\}$$
$$FVA = \$500[(2.853396 - 1) / 0.06]$$
$$FVA = \$500(1.8543396 / 0.06)$$
$$FVA = \$500(30.90566)$$
$$\textbf{FVA = \$15,452.83 } \textit{total amount funded}$$

future value of an annuity (FVA), reference table method You can also calculate the future value of an annuity by using the future value interest factor of an annuity (FVIFA) table (see Figure 2.12). The table for 6% interest for 18 years gives you the factor of 30.906.

$$FVA = PMT \times FVIFA_{i, n}$$
$$FVA = \$500 \times 30.906$$
$$\textbf{FVA = \$15,453.00 } \textit{total amount funded}$$

As you can see, our answer using the FVIFA table is slightly different due to rounding.

The FVIFA table is a simple Excel table with the formula of compounding embedded in each cell. The result in each cell (for a given time period and interest rate) assumes an original beginning balance of $1. Note that as the time periods and interest rates increase, the future balance result cell also increases. This result cell is known as the **future value interest factor of an annuity (FVIFA)**. Finding the factor for the selected time period and rate of interest for $1 and then multiplying that factor by the actual beginning balance gives you the future value of an annuity. The FVIFA table can be found in Appendix A. The actual Excel document can be found online in the "Factors" document.

As illustrated in this section, an annuity due is identical to an ordinary annuity, except the payments occur at the beginning of a period instead of at the end of a period. Each payment occurs one period earlier.

future value of an annuity (FVA), financial calculator method To calculate the future value of an annuity due, calculate the future value of an ordinary annuity by using the formula FVA = PMT $\{[(1 + i)^n - 1] / i\}$ (or

▼ FIGURE 2.11

Annuity due payments start at the beginning of the first period; the total number of payments is one plus that of an ordinary annuity

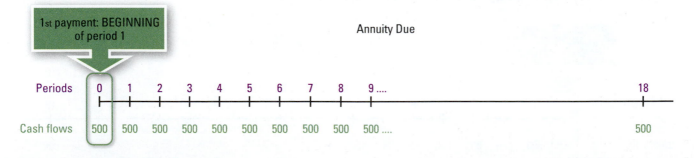

▼ FIGURE 2.12

Future value of an annuity of $1 per period at the end of *n* periods (future value interest factor of an annuity [FVIFA])

Period	1%	2%	3%	4%	5%	6%
1	1.000	1.000	1.000	1.000	1.000	1.000
2	2.010	2.020	2.030	2.040	2.050	2.060
3	3.030	3.060	3.091	3.122	3.153	3.184
4	4.060	4.122	4.184	4.246	4.310	4.375
5	5.101	5.204	5.309	5.416	5.526	5.637
6	6.152	6.308	6.468	6.633	6.802	6.975
7	7.214	7.434	7.662	7.898	8.142	8.394
8	8.286	8.583	8.892	9.214	9.549	9.897
9	9.369	9.755	10.159	10.583	11.027	11.491
10	10.462	10.950	11.464	12.006	12.578	13.181
11	11.567	12.169	12.808	13.486	14.207	14.972
12	12.683	13.412	14.192	15.026	15.917	16.870
13	13.809	14.680	15.618	16.627	17.713	18.882
14	14.947	15.974	17.086	18.292	19.599	21.015
15	16.097	17.293	18.599	20.024	21.579	23.276
16	17.258	18.639	20.157	21.825	23.657	25.673
17	18.430	20.012	21.762	23.698	25.840	28.213
18	19.615	21.412	23.414	25.645	28.132	30.906

Snippet of FVIFA table, full table in Appendix A.
Factor used if interest rate (i) = 6% and periods (n) = 18.

the FVA table) and multiply it by 1 plus the interest rate $(1 + i)$ since the payments come at the beginning of the period.

$$FVAd = FVA(1 + i)$$

where

FVAd = Future value of an annuity due
FVA = Future value of an ordinary annuity
i = Interest rate per period

In our example, the value of an annuity due would be:

FVAd = FVA(1 + i)
FVAd = $15,453.00(1 + 0.06)
FVAd = $15,453.00(1.06)
FVAd = $16,308.18 *funded*

When calculating the future value of an ordinary annuity or an annuity due using a financial calculator, it is important to make sure the calculator is set for payments at the beginning of a period for an annuity due, or at the end

of the period for an ordinary annuity. A financial calculator will have a "BEG/END" key. When you press this key, the display will show "BEGIN" when it is set to calculate an annuity due (see the financial calculator in Figure 2.5).

To use a financial calculator for an ordinary annuity in the current example, first clear everything in the calculator's memory and make sure the calculator is set for payments at the end of the period. Next, press: 18, N (number of time periods); 6, I/YR (interest rate per year); and −500, PMT (a negative number because it is a payment). When you press the FV key, $15,452.83 will show up on your screen, the same number we got using the formula FVA = PMT {[(1 + i)^n − 1] / i}. See Figure 2.13.

future value interest factor of an annuity (FVIFA) factor multiplied by the annuity (payment) to determine the amount in the account at a future date

Present Value of an Annuity

You want to be able to retire at age 65 with an income stream of $100,000 a year for the next 20 years. You think you will earn a 5% return on your money. How much money will you need to save before you retire? An ordinary annuity will help you to achieve your goal.

present value of an annuity (PVA), long-hand method
The formula to calculate the present value of an ordinary annuity is

$$PVA = PMT (\{1 − [1 / (1 + i)^n]\} / i)$$

▼ FIGURE 2.13

Future value of ordinary annuity example

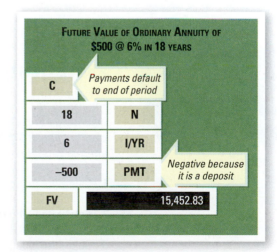

The value of an annuity can add to a comfortable retirement.

where

$$PVA = \text{Present value of annuity}$$
$$PMT = \text{Payment}$$
$$i = \text{Interest rate per period}$$
$$n = \text{Number of periods}$$

In our example we would use the following:

$$PVA = \$100,000\ (\{1 - [1\,/\,(1 + 0.05)^{20}]\}\,/\,0.05)$$
$$PVA = \$100,000\ (\{1 - [1\,/\,(1.05)^{20}]\}\,/\,0.05)$$

$$PVA = \$100,000\ \{[1 - (1\,/\,2.653294)]\,/\,0.05\}$$
$$PVA = \$100,000\ [(1 - .37689)\,/\,0.05]$$
$$PVA = \$100,000\ (.623111\,/\,0.05)$$
$$PVA = \$100,000\ (12.4622103)$$
$$\mathbf{PVA = \$1,246,221.03}\ \textit{needed in retirement savings}$$

present value of an annuity (PVA), reference table method   You can also use the present value interest factor of an annuity table (see Figure 2.14). Using the table, you would calculate the following:

2.4 Future Value of an Annuity

You are 16 and know you need $100,000 when you turn 22 to pay for medical school, but instead of making a lump sum payment into a savings account, your parents plan to deposit $15,000 each year into an ordinary annuity account with a 4% simple interest rate. How close to your goal will this get you?

1. Calculate using the long-hand method.

2. Calculate using the reference table method.

3. Calculate using a financial calculator.

Present value of an annuity of $1 per period for *n* periods (present value interest factor of an annuity [PVIFA])

Period	1%	2%	3%	4%	5%
1	0.990	0.980	0.971	0.962	0.952
2	1.970	1.942	1.913	1.886	1.859
3	2.941	2.884	2.829	2.775	2.723
4	3.902	3.808	3.717	3.630	3.546
5	4.853	4.713	4.580	4.452	4.329
6	5.795	5.601	5.417	5.242	5.076
7	6.728	6.472	6.230	6.002	5.786
8	7.652	7.325	7.020	6.733	6.463
9	8.566	8.162	7.786	7.435	7.108
10	9.471	8.983	8.530	8.111	7.722
11	10.368	9.787	9.253	8.760	8.306
12	11.255	10.575	9.954	9.385	8.863
13	12.134	11.348	10.635	9.986	9.394
14	13.004	12.106	11.296	10.563	9.899
15	13.865	12.849	11.938	11.118	10.380
16	14.718	13.578	12.561	11.652	10.838
17	15.562	14.292	13.166	12.166	11.274
18	16.398	14.992	13.754	12.659	11.690
19	17.226	15.678	14.324	13.134	12.085
20	18.046	16.351	14.877	13.590	12.462

Snippet of PVIFA table, full table in Appendix A.

Factor used if interest rate (*i*) = 5% and periods (*n*) = 20.

$PVA = PMT \times PVA_{i,\,n}$
$PVA = \$100{,}000 \times PVA_{5,\,20}$
$PVA = \$100{,}000 \times 12.462$
PVA = \$1,246,200.00 *needed in retirement savings*

The PVIFA table is a simple Excel table with the present value of an annuity formula embedded in each cell. The result in each cell (for a given time period and interest rate) assumes the original beginning balance is $1. Note that as the periods and interest rates increase, the future balance result cell also increases. This result cell is known as the **present value interest factor of an annuity (PVIFA)**. First find the factor for the selected time period and interest rate for $1 and then multiply that factor by the actual beginning balance to get the present value of an annuity. The PVIFA table can be found in Appendix A. The actual Excel document can be found online in the "Factors" document.

financialfitness:
STOPPING LITTLE LEAKS

Automatically on Time

Pay your bills automatically and on time. Online banking supports setting up automatic withdrawal to the payee on the exact day the bill is due, leaving your funds earning interest in your account for as long as possible, plus you cut down on the cost of the check, envelope, and stamp. Setting up your monthly bills for automatic payment saves you time as well as guarding against accidental late fees.

doing the
MATH

2.5 **Present Value of an Annuity**

Your budgeted expenses while in medical school will be $40,000 each year for three years. At 4% simple interest, how much money will you need to save before the start of med school if using an ordinary annuity to fund expenses?

1. Calculate using the long-hand method.

2. Calculate using the reference table method.

3. Calculate using a financial calculator.

present value of an annuity (PVA), financial calculator method As you can see, the formula has greater accuracy. If you use a financial calculator, make sure your payments are set for the end of the period and not the beginning and make sure everything is cleared from the memory of the calculator. For our example, input 20, N (number of time periods); 5, I/YR (interest rate per year); and −100000, PMT (a negative number because it will be your payment). When you press the PV key, $1,246,221.03 will show up on your screen, the same number we got using the formula PVA = PMT ({1 − [1 / (1 + i)^n]} / i). See Figure 2.15.

Calculating Loan Payments

Suppose you want to buy a car and need to know how much your payments will be. You can use the present value interest factor of an annuity to calculate loan payments. The first step is to solve for the payment factor, and then you can solve for the payment. Use the present value of an ordinary annuity formula to solve for the payment factor:

$$\mathbf{PVA = PMT\ (\{1 - [1 / (1 + \it{i})^{\it{n}}]\} / \it{i})}$$

where

$$PVA = \text{Present value of an ordinary annuity}$$
$$PMT = \text{Payment}$$
$$i = \text{Interest rate per period}$$
$$n = \text{Number of periods}$$

If you are financing $15,000 at 6% interest for three years, making annual payments, you know the following:

$$PVA = 15,000$$
$$i = .06$$
$$n = 3$$

> Though no one can go back and make a brand new start, anyone can start from now and make a brand new ending.
>
> —AUTHOR UNKNOWN

Using the formula, your equation would be:

$$15,000 = PMT\ (\{1 - [1/(1 + .06)^3]\}/.06)$$
$$15,000 = PMT\ \{[1 - (1/1.06^3)]/.06\}$$
$$15,000 = PMT\ \{[1 - (1/1.191016)]/.06\}$$
$$15,000 = PMT\ [(1 - .839619)/.06]$$
$$15,000 = PMT\ (.160381/.06)$$
$$15,000 = PMT\ (2.67301)$$

Next, solve for PMT by dividing both sides by 2.67301:

$$15,000/2.67301 = PMT\ (2.67301)/2.67301$$

and your answer is:

$$\mathbf{5,611.65 = PMT}$$

To pay off your $15,000 loan in three equal payments over three years at 6% interest, you would need to make payments of $5,611.65.

Using the tables, your formula would be:

$$PVA = PMT\ (PVIFA_{i,n})$$
$$15,000 = PMT\ (2.673)$$
$$\mathbf{5,611.67 = PMT}$$

When using a financial calculator, be sure you are using one payment per year. You would input 15,000, PV (present value of car); 3, N (number of annual payments); and 6, I/YR (interest rate). Solve for PMT and your answer is 5,611.65. See Figure 2.16.

If you want to know your monthly payments using the formula or the tables, divide your interest rate by 12 (for 12 months in a year). Now your number of payments total 36 (36 months in three years). For the above example, we find the following:

▼ **FIGURE 2.15**

Present value of annuity (PVA) example

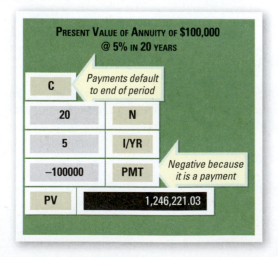

▼ **FIGURE 2.16**

Annual payment example

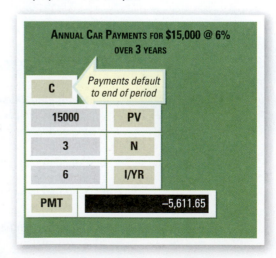

$$PVA = 15,000$$
$$i = .06/12 = 0.005$$
$$n = 36$$
$$PMT = ?$$

Using the formula, your equation would be:

$$15,000 = PMT\ (\{1 - [1/(1 + .005)^{36}]\}/.005)$$
$$15,000 = PMT\ \{[1 - (1/1.005)^{36}]/.005\}$$
$$15,000 = PMT\ \{[1 - (1/1.19668)]/.005\}$$
$$15,000 = PMT\ [(1 - .835645)/.005]$$
$$15,000 = PMT\ (.164355/.005)$$
$$15,000 = PMT\ (32.8710)$$
$$\mathbf{456.33 = PMT}$$

Using the tables, you would have to refer to a more detailed table or extrapolate to find the factor. The interest rate i would be 0.5% and the number of payments n would be 36. Obviously, it is easier to use the formula or a financial calculator. Extrapolating, you would find $PVIFA_{5,36}$ equals 32.871.

$$PVA = PMT\ (PVIFA_{i,n})$$
$$15,000 = PMT\ (32.871)$$
$$456.33 = PMT$$

▼ **FIGURE 2.17**

Annual payment example

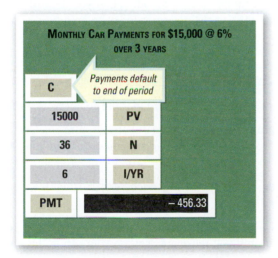

When using a financial calculator, make sure you are using 12 payments per year. For our example, input 15,000, PV (present value of car); 36, N (number of payments); and 6, I/YR (interest rate). Solve for PMT and your answer is 456.33. See Figure 2.17. ■

Learn. ⟩ Plan & Act. ⟩ Evaluate.

➡ **LEARN.** You now know that U.S. currency comes from the Bureau of Engraving and Printing and the United States Mint. You also know a little about what gives currency value. You learned that, through the compounding of interest, you can make your money grow. You also learned to discern between annual percentage rate (APR) and annual percentage yield (APY) when shopping for savings account options. Finally, you learned how to use formulas to compute present and future values of lump sums and annuities.

■ ■ **LO 2-1** Explain what gives paper currency value and how the Federal Reserve Bank manages its distribution.

Money is a form of currency you can exchange for other things of value like food, gas, clothing, or rent. Or you can save it where it will have stored value. Paper money is backed by the full faith and credit of the United States government and the Federal Reserve Bank.

■ ■ **LO 2-2** Differentiate between simple and compound interest rates and calculate annual percentage yields and the value of paying yourself first.

Money not invested will lose value over time. Money earns value via compound interest. Compounding is where interest is added to the initial deposit and you begin to earn interest on interest. The annual percentage yield (APY) shows the interest rate taking into account the effects of compounding. Banks must disclose both the annual percentage rate (APR) and the annual percentage yield (APY) on interest-bearing accounts so consumers can make fair comparisons. Understanding interest helps you to grasp the concept of time value of money (the idea that a dollar today is worth more than a dollar tomorrow). The secret to accumulating wealth is to pay yourself first and to start early. Automatic withdrawals and transfers take some of the pain and thought out of paying yourself first.

■ ■ **LO 2-3** Calculate the future and present value of lump sums and annuities in order to know what amount to put aside to meet financial goals.

Money has a defined value if spent today, but it will have a different value if it isn't spent until a future date. Value can be calculated long-hand or by using a financial calculator, a spreadsheet, or financial tables. With these tools, you can calculate the future value of an amount invested today (future value of a lump sum), the present value of an amount you will receive in the future (present value of a lump sum), the future value of amounts that you deposit annually (future value of an annuity/ordinary annuity), or the present value of an amount if you make annual payments (present value of an annuity/ordinary annuity).

➲ PLAN & ACT. Your Plan & Act to-do list is as follows:

☐ You outlined your goals in Chapter 1. Now assess the cost of those goals (Worksheet 2.1).

☐ Review your options for designating current savings to a specific future goal and calculate how much money you need to deposit annually to support that term-goal (Worksheet 2.2).

☐ Calculate how much you need to set aside in savings each year, starting now, to reach your retirement goal (Worksheet 2.3).

☐ Consider starting a "Dedicated Dave" automatic deposit account by putting $5 per day into savings. Not drawing from it until you retire puts you on your way to becoming a millionaire.

➲ EVALUATE. Think back to your goals outlined in Chapter 1. The formulas in this chapter can help you assess your options as you work toward saving to support those goals. As you continue to work through the chapters and find more opportunities to save, remember how much more powerful it is to save even a little now as opposed to waiting until later in life to start saving.

›› GoalTracker

After completing Worksheet 2.1, open your online GoalTracker to record the estimated costs and saving plans of your SMART goals. Assess how you are achieving the stated goals. If you are not on track, give thought to what steps you should take to get back on schedule.

Annual Percentage Rate (APR)

Annual Percentage Yield (APY)

Annuity

Annuity Due

Compounding

Discounting

Future Value

Future Value Interest Factor (FVIF)

Future Value Interest Factor of an Annuity (FVIFA)

Lump Sum

Ordinary Annuity

Present Value

Present Value Interest Factor (PVIF)

Present Value Interest Factor of an Annuity (PVIFA)

Time Value of Money

self-test questions

1. What gives paper money value? *(LO 2-1)*

   a. Gold in the U.S. Treasury
   b. Supply and demand
   c. The Bureau of Engraving and Printing
   d. The United States Mint

2. Why does the Bureau of Engraving and Printing print new money each year? *(LO 2-1)*

   a. To help the U.S. economy
   b. To replace mutilated currency
   c. To keep pace with population growth
   d. Inflation

3. Why is it better to save a little each month for a far-off retirement goal than to wait until five years into your first job post-graduation? *(LO 2-2)*

   a. The magic of compounding grows money at an increasing rate the longer it is saved.
   b. If you don't start early, you never will.
   c. You are likely to be taxed less when first employed as you are typically working at an entry level wage or salary.
   d. It is not any better to start five years earlier.

4. If you are given a 10% interest rate, compounded quarterly, what formula will you use to compute the APY? *(LO 2-2)*

   a. $(1 + 4/10)^{10} - 1$
   b. $(1 + 10/4)^{4} - 1$
   c. $(1 + 4/10)^{4} - 1$
   d. $(1 + 10/4)^{10} - 1$

5. What formula would you use to calculate the annual percentage yield on an account that pays 6% interest compounded quarterly? *(LO 2-2)*

   a. $(1 + .4/.06)^{4} - 1$
   b. $(1 + .06/4)^{4} - 1$
   c. $(1 + .06/4)^{6} - 1$
   d. $(1 + .4/.06)^{6} - 1$

6. You decide to deposit your high school graduation money gift of $1,000 into a savings account. *(LO 2-3)*

   a. What formula would you use to compute its worth when you graduate from college in four years?
      (1) $PV (1 + i)^{n}$
      (2) $FV (1 - i)^{n}$
      (3) $FV (1 + n)^{i}$
      (4) $FV (1 - n)^{i}$

   b. If you decided to use the reference table method and wanted to know the value of your deposit in four years, what factor would you use if your deposit was earning a 3% interest rate annually?
      (1) 0.8885
      (2) 1.1255
      (3) 4.1836
      (4) 3.7171

   c. Using a calculator, which values would you use to solve for FV?
      (1) N = 4; I/YR = 3; PV = 1000; PMT = 0
      (2) N = 4; I/YR = 3; PV = 0; PMT = 10000
      (3) N = 4; I/YR = 3; PV = −1000; PMT = 0
      (4) N = 4; I/YR = 3; PV = 0; PMT = −1000

   d. What would be the value of the gift money upon graduation from college?
      (1) $1,418.36
      (2) $1,888.50
      (3) $1,371.71
      (4) $1,125.50

7. You plan to go away on a cruise for your five-year anniversary. You estimate that the trip will cost about $10,000. *(LO 2-3)*

   a. What formula would you use to determine how much of your wedding gift money to place in savings today to have enough for the cruise in five years?
      (1) $FV/(1 - i)^{n}$
      (2) $FV/(1 + n)^{i}$
      (3) $FV/(1 - n)^{i}$
      (4) $FV/(1 + i)^{n}$

b. If you decided to compute the value using the reference table method, what factor would you use if you were earning a 4% interest rate annually?
  (1) 0.8219
  (2) 0.54163
  (3) 1.2167
  (4) 4.4518

c. If using a calculator, which values would you use to solve for PV?
  (1) $N = 5$; $I/YR = 4$; $FV = 10000$; $PMT = 0$
  (2) $N = 5$; $I/YR = 4$; $FV = -10000$; $PMT = 0$
  (3) $N = 5$; $I/YR = 4$; $FV = 0$; $PMT = 10000$
  (4) $N = 5$; $I/YR = 4$; $FV = 0$; $PMT = -10000$

d. How much of the gift money should you deposit today to have enough in savings to pay for the anniversary cruise?
  (1) $8,219
  (2) $5,416
  (3) $12,167
  (4) $4,451

8. You get a $12,000 bonus annually. You plan to save it for your first home down payment in three years. *(LO 2-3)*

a. Which formula will you use to determine how much you will have for a down payment?
  (1) $PMT(\{1-[1/(1 + i)^n]\}/i)$
  (2) $PMT\{[(1 + i)^n - 1]/i\}$
  (3) $PMT\{[(1 - i)^n - 1]/i\}$
  (4) $PMT[(1/1 + i)^n/i]$

b. If you decided to compute the value using the reference table method, what factor would you use if you were earning a 3% interest rate annually?
  (1) 3.0909
  (2) 2.8286
  (3) 0.9151
  (4) 1.0927

c. Using a calculator, which values would you use to solve for FV?
  (1) $N = 3$; $I/YR = 3$; $PV = 12000$; $PMT = 0$
  (2) $N = 3$; $I/YR = 3$; $PV = 0$; $PMT = 12000$
  (3) $N = 3$; $I/YR = 3$; $PV = -12000$; $PMT = 0$
  (4) $N = 3$; $I/YR = 3$; $PV = 0$; $PMT = -12000$

d. How much will you have as a down payment in three years?
  (1) $38,828.60
  (2) $36,915.10
  (3) $37,090.80
  (4) $37,092.70

9. You have a long-term goal to take a leave of absence to travel around the world on a three-year adventure. *(LO 2-3)*

a. Which formula would you use to calculate how much needs to be saved before you can cover the annual expenditure of $100,000 per year on this adventure?
  (1) $PMT(\{1-[1/(1 + i)^n]\}/i)$
  (2) $PMT\{[(1 - i)^n - 1]/i\}$
  (3) $PMT\{[(1 + i)^n - 1]/i\}$
  (4) $PMT[(1/1 + i)^n/i]$

b. Using the reference table method, what factor would you use if you were earning a 3% interest rate annually?
  (1) 2.8286
  (2) 3.0909
  (3) 0.9151
  (4) 1.0927

c. Using a calculator, which values would you use?
  (1) $N = 3$; $I/YR = 3$; $PMT = 100000$
  (2) $N = 3$; $I/YR = 3$; $PMT = -300000$
  (3) $N = 3$; $I/YR = 3$; $PMT = 300000$
  (4) $N = 3$; $I/YR = 3$; $PMT = -100000$

d. How much savings will you need prior to your leave of absence?
  (1) $282,850
  (2) $309,090
  (3) $274,530
  (4) $327,810

problems

1. What is the APY of a 4% interest rate, compounded annually? *(LO 2-2)*

2. What is the APY of a 6% interest rate, compounded quarterly? *(LO 2-2)*

3. Your parents gave you $1,000 for your sweet 16th birthday. You want to deposit it in a CD account that is earning 6% annually. Calculate how much your gift will be worth when you graduate from college on your 22nd birthday using the following methods: *(LO 2-3)*
  a. Long-hand formula
  b. Reference table
  c. Financial calculator

4. You plan to buy a boat in 10 years for no more than $25,000. If interest rates are running 5% annually, calculate how much you need to put away each year using the following methods: *(LO 2-3)*
  a. Long-hand formula
  b. Reference table
  c. Financial calculator

5. You plan to contribute $1,200 each year to your nephew's college education. He will graduate from high school in 10 years. Interest rates are 6%. Calculate how much money you should have saved for him by the time he is ready to go to college using the following methods: *(LO 2-3)*
  a. Reference table
  b. Financial calculator

6. You are about to set sail on your long-term goal of sailing the seven seas over a seven-year period. You anticipate expenses to run $300,000 per year and that you will be earning 3% interest on your savings. Calculate how much you will need in savings to cover the cost of the adventure using the following methods: *(LO 2-3)*
    a. Reference table
    b. Financial calculator

7. You deposit $7,000 of your high school graduation gift money into a savings account. How much will it be worth when you graduate from med school in seven years if interest rates are: *(LO 2-3)*
    a. 3%?
    b. 5%?
    c. 6%?

you're the expert

1. Each year on his child's birthday, Ben puts $100 into a savings account that earns 5% annually. *(LO 2-3)*

    a. How much will the child have at age 65?
    b. What would the outcome have been had Ben started the savings account on the day of the child's birth versus the end of the child's first year?
    c. What accounts for the difference?

2. Kip and Kay are about to get married and are looking for an apartment. Kay very much wants a nice downtown location in the social center of the city. Kip would prefer a cheaper location, so they are able to still set aside some savings each month in a money market account. Kay believes getting settled requires so many start-up costs that a monthly savings account can wait for a few years until both of their salaries have increased. How would you suggest they resolve their differences? How would you lay out the numbers to present your recommendation? *(LO2-2)*

3. Jerry and Dee have different opinions on how to save money. Jerry likes to have the highest possible amount withheld from his paycheck for their income taxes. That way, he knows he will not come up short, and he loves getting a big tax refund each spring. When the refund comes, he deposits it into savings; he feels that this is a less painful way to save. Dee prefers to calculate monthly tax withholdings closer to the actual amount owed. Jerry and Dee received an $8,000 tax refund check this year. *(LO 2-2, LO 2-3)*

    a. What is the cost of Jerry's method of saving vs. Dee's if the account they are depositing the money in has an APY of 5.4%?
    b. What if they were to deposit $666.66 monthly into a savings account that pays 3% interest compounded monthly?
    c. What is the difference if their account earns 6% APR compounded monthly?

4. Wanda wants to take some time off in five years to backpack through Europe for three months. She estimates her trip expenses for the three months in today's dollars will be approximately $20,000. *(LO 2-3)*

    a. If inflation is running 2% a year, what should her financial savings goal be to support the trip?
    b. Wanda could make a one-time deposit today in a savings account that earns 5% interest over the period. How much would she have to deposit today to support the trip?
    c. If Wanda is starting with a zero savings balance for her trip, how much will she have to put away each month in her savings account if it offers an APY of 4%?

Find the worksheets online at www.mhhe.com/walkerpf1e

worksheets

2.1 COST OF LONG-, INTERMEDIATE, AND SHORT-TERM GOALS

Go to Worksheet 2.1 and calculate the cost of one long-term SMART goal, one intermediate SMART goal, and one short-term SMART goal from Worksheet 1.6.

2.1 Select one SMART long-term, one intermediate, and one short-term goal from Chapter 1 Worksheet 1.6 and estimate the cost of each.	
SMART Long-Term Goal:	Cost
SMART Intermediate Goal:	Cost
SMART Short-Term Goal:	Cost

2.2 COST PER MONTH OF SAVING FOR GOALS

In Worksheet 2.2, log your options for designating current savings to specific future goals and calculate how much money must be deposited annually to support your selected long-term, intermediate, and short-term goals.

2.2 Review your options to designate current savings to specific future goals and calculate how much money you need to deposit annually to support your long-term, intermediate, and short-term goals.	
Saving Plan for Long-Term Goal:	Cost/Month
Saving Plan for Intermediate Goal:	Cost/Month
Saving Plan for Short-Term Goal:	Cost/Month

2.3 SAVING FOR THE GOAL OF RETIREMENT

Review your long-term goals from Chapter 1. Is there a set age when you would like to retire? Complete Worksheet 2.3 based on this desired age for retirement.

2.3 Look at your long-term goals from Chapter 1. Is there a set age that you want to retire? Complete the following worksheet based on your desired age for retirement.	
Number of years from retirement:	
Desired amount in retirement savings:	
Given a 5% annual interest rate, use the FVIFA table or formula to calculate how much money you need to save per year:	
Given a 7% annual interest rate, use the FVIFA table or formula to calculate how much money you need to save per year:	
Given a 10% annual interest rate, use the FVIFA table or formula to calculate how much money you need to save per year:	
Plan of action, given these findings:	

Leigh, Blake, and Nicole's grandparents were over to the house visiting for brunch. After sharing the story of Wild Willie, Smart Sam, and Dedicated Dave, the grandparents offered each grandchild a gift of $10,000 if they can present a financially responsible plan for how to use the gift. In light of their intermediate-term goals, what plans would you recommend Leigh, Blake, and Nicole offer?

The other housemates, upon hearing the story, decided they would begin to set aside $20 each week to put toward savings. Keeping in mind the intermediate goals of each housemate and checking www.bankrate.com for the current options in today's market, create a savings plan for each member of the household (i.e., lump sum, annuities, what they would put away and when, and what each option would deliver in savings in the end).

A summary of the housemates' goals can be found in the first Continuing Case problem on page 27.

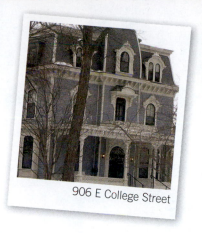

906 E College Street

> **"**Before buying anything, it is well to ask if one could do without it.**"**
>
> —JOHN LUBBOCK, *English banker and politician (1834–1913)*

chapter three

planning and budgeting

How much do you spend on little expenses? Do you know where the money that disappears from your wallet goes? When you get credit card bills, are you surprised by how much you have charged and what little you have to show for it? If this is the way you feel, you are not alone. In this chapter, you will learn how to construct a budget and plan for savings. ▇

LEARNING OBJECTIVES

After reading this chapter, you should be able to:

LO 3-1 Analyze your spending habits by using tools such as spending journals and balance sheets.

LO 3-2 Estimate the opportunity costs of your purchases.

LO 3-3 Identify methods of saving money.

LO 3-4 Construct a realistic budget that reflects your priorities and provides a means of protection from overspending.

◀ Leslie, age 25, master's degree student, nursing major at a large public college, with her fiancé, Nate

Budgeting from the Beginning

Leslie is a 25-year-old recent graduate, working on a master's degree. She and her fiancé, Nate, decided they wanted to start their life together debt-free and in control of their spending. After getting engaged, they sat down and looked at their values and priorities and then established their budget.

"Before we set a budget, money would just fly out of our checking accounts and we would always be left at the end of the month living on Ramen Noodles and hot dogs. Now that we have a budget, we enjoy our time more. We don't have to worry about running short of money each month. We have paid off the vast majority of our debt, which leaves a lot more in our savings. We want to start out on the right foot, not bringing a lot of debt into our marriage. We don't want to worry about unexpected emergencies; we know the stress that running short on money can create. We want to make sure we are well-practiced at sticking to a budget so we can kick off our marriage being financially secure."

3.1 ANALYZING YOUR SPENDING HABITS: EVERY PENNY COUNTS

■■ **LO 3-1** Analyze your spending habits by using tools such as spending journals and balance sheets.

Do you know where all your money goes? It may sound overwhelming to track every penny, but it is the best way

When dealing with your financial future, every penny counts.

to control spending and be sure your money is working for you. If you want to lose weight, write down everything you eat and review it; if you want more time in your day, log what you are doing every hour and analyze the little leaks of time wasted. Likewise, if you want to save money, keep a money journal and record where you spend every penny. When you track spending, you become more aware of what you are buying and how much it costs. You begin to think about the value of what you are buying before you spend.

For your money journal to be effective, you must be disciplined and keep track of *all* of your spending for at least one month. You must write down where you spend every penny—from candy and gum to gas and phone bills. The more diligent you are, the greater the insight you will gain as to your spending habits. Items you should record during the one-month time period include your expenses for

3.1 Little Leak Tally

Calculate the daily, weekly, yearly, and decade costs of something you buy almost every day:

Item:_____ @ cost of _____.

_____ daily cost × 7 = _____ weekly cost

_____ weekly cost × 52 = _____ yearly cost

_____ yearly cost × 10 = _____ decade cost

What would you do with the money if someone handed you a check for this amount today?

---

rent, utilities, cell phone, gas, entertainment, and so on. You might surprise yourself as to where you spend money. Here are some examples of how little expenses add up:

Buying two soda pops a day in a vending machine:

$$\$1.25 \times 2 = \$2.50/day$$
$$\$2.50 \times 5 \text{ days} = \$12.50/week$$
$$\$12.50 \times 4 \text{ weeks} = \$50.00/month$$
$$\$12.50 \times 52 \text{ weeks} = \$650.00/year$$
$$\$650.00 \times 10 \text{ years} = \$6,500.00/decade$$

Buying a snack from the vending machine:

$$\$1.00/day \times 5 \text{ days} = \$5.00/week$$
$$\$5.00 \times 4 \text{ weeks} = \$20.00/month$$
$$\$5.00 \times 52 \text{ weeks} = \$260.00/year$$
$$\$260.00 \times 10 \text{ years} = \$2,600.00/decade$$

Buying one magazine a week:

$$\$5.00/week \times 4 \text{ weeks} = \$20.00/month$$
$$\$5.00/week \times 52 \text{ weeks} = \$260.00/year$$
$$\$260.00 \times 10 \text{ years} = \$2,600.00/decade$$

Going out Saturday evening:

$$\$50.00/week \times 4 \text{ weeks} = \$200.00/month$$
$$\$50.00/week \times 52 \text{ weeks} = \$2,600.00/year$$
$$\$2,600.00 \times 10 \text{ years} = \$26,000.00/decade$$

Paying for parking tickets:

$$\$10.00/week \times 4 \text{ weeks} = \$40.00/month$$
$$\$10.00/week \times 52 \text{ weeks} = \$520.00/year$$
$$\$520.00 \times 10 \text{ years} = \$5,200.00/decade$$

Buying cigarettes:

$$\$5.00/day \times 7 \text{ days} = \$35.00/week$$
$$\$35.00/week \times 4 \text{ weeks} = \$140.00/month$$
$$\$35.00/week \times 52 \text{ weeks} = \$1,820.00/year$$
$$\$1,820.00 \times 10 \text{ years} = \$18,200.00/decade$$
$$\$1,820.00 \times 55 \text{ years} = \$100,100.00/lifetime$$

By analyzing your daily spending, you can calculate weekly costs. Use the format provided in *Doing the Math* 3.1 to gauge the monthly and yearly costs of one of your expenses.

Before being able to create a savings and spending plan, you need to figure out how much money is coming in and what expenditures are going out. You can get a perspective of your current financial situation by following three steps: (1) keep a spending journal, (2) understand the elements of personal financial statements, and (3) create a personal cash flow statement (see Figure 3.1 on the next page).

Step 1: Keep a Spending Journal

To help you keep track of your money, as soon as you spend any money—cash, credit card, debit card—enter it in a spending journal. At the end of the day, take five minutes to input entries into the "Every Penny Counts" online spreadsheet. The spreadsheet will total monthly expenditures for you. You also might consider using one of the popular personal financial software products, such as Quicken (www.quicken .com) or www.mint.com to keep track of your spending, savings, earnings, investing, and giving. Worksheet 3.1 includes

---

["Small leaks can sink a mighty ship."]

—BEN FRANKLIN (1706–1790)

12 months of spreadsheets so you can identify the trend of your spending habits over the course of a full year (see Figure 3.2 for an example).

Use your "Every Penny Counts" spreadsheet to keep track of your expenses for at least three months. Why three months? Think about the extraordinary expenses over the course of a single semester. If this is the fall semester, you may have to plan for holiday shopping or traveling home for Thanksgiving and winter break, both of which will increase your expenses during those months. You might be able to compensate for these extra expenses by working over winter break or using money you receive as a gift. Spring semester may include a spring break trip. If you plan to travel, you will need to save and budget for your getaway.

Whether you are newly responsible for your own spending or if you have been on your own for years, it is important to track your daily spending. By making minor changes in your spending, you can stop the small leaks, and your ship can stay afloat without major adjustments to your lifestyle.

Step 2: Understand the Elements of Personal Financial Statements

To know where you are going, you have to know where you have been. Your **personal financial statement** is an accounting of what you have to show for your spending—what you own and what you owe. Also known as a balance sheet, this is a snapshot or a picture of your financial condition as of a specific date and time. It is derived by listing all the items of value that you own (your *assets*) and all the claims against those assets (your *liabilities*). See Figure 3.3 on page 58 for an example of a personal financial statement.

assets An **asset** is an item of value that you own. On your balance sheet, list your assets from the most liquid to the least liquid. **Liquidity** refers to how quickly an asset can be turned into cash without a substantial loss in value. To complete a balance sheet, first add up your cash and any money in checking accounts, savings accounts, and certificates of deposit. *Cash* is currency as well as the money in your checking account that you can withdraw on demand. Your savings account can be withdrawn in most cases without notifying a bank. Depending on when you opened your account and when you deposited checks into your account, you may have limited access to your money (this is discussed in more detail in Chapter 4).

Next on your balance sheet, list any money owed to you and the cash value of any life insurance (not the face value). The **cash value** is the amount you would receive if you were to cancel your policy. Some life insurance policies have a cash value if held for a given time period. The **face value** of the life insurance policy is the amount of money the beneficiary would receive if you were to die. (Insurance will be discussed in more detail in Chapter 10.)

Your personal property assets include your clothing, furniture, bicycles, and so on. On a balance sheet, these items should be valued at "resale" prices. The laptop computer you just purchased for $1,000 may sell for only $100 at a garage sale. Be realistic when evaluating your personal property, valuing it at "garage sale" prices. When we talk about insurance in Chapter 10, you will want to do a household

financialfitness:
ACTION ITEM

Making Money

If you had a job at home over the summer, see if you can work a few hours during your break to help carry you through the rest of the school year. If you are headed home, this is a great time to look for a new summer job or paid internship. With an internship, not only might you get paid, but you gain valuable experience in your field of study.

▼ **FIGURE 3.1**

Steps to gaining perspective on your financial situation

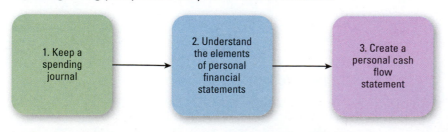

▼ FIGURE 3.2

Sample every penny counts worksheet

Every Penny Counts Diary: Month 3
Days of the Month

Daily Expenses	DAY 1	DAY 2	DAY 3	DAY 4	DAY 5	DAY 6	DAY 7
Breakfast	$3.54	$4.00					
Snacks	$3.75						
Gasoline/Oil	$30.00						
Laundry/Dry Cleaning							
Parking	$2.25	$2.25					
Newspaper/Magazine							
Other							
Lunch	$7.07	$5.00					
Snacks/Pop							
Beauty/Barber		$18.00					
Books							
Cigarettes/Alcohol							
Clothing/Shoes							
Gifts	$10.00						
Household (cleaning supplies, etc.)							
Groceries	$27.00						
Gym							
Dates							
Movie/Theatre	$16.00						
Nightclub/Bar							
Video Rental		$4.00					
Other Entertainment							
Other 1							
Other 2							
Other 3							
Grand Total for the Day	$99.61	$33.25	$0.00	$0.00	$0.00	$0.00	$0.00

Monthly Fixed Expenses	Total
Rent/Mortgage	$300.00
Second Mortgage	
Utilities	$75.00
Student Loan	
Cable TV	
Newspaper	
Telephone (Land line)	
Telephone Long Distance	
Cell Phone	$75.00
Internet Connection	
Child Care	
Health Insurance	
Medical Expenses	
Prescriptions	
Credit Card #1	
Total Monthly Expenses	$450.00

Total Daily Expenses	$132.86
Total Monthly Expenses	$450.00
Grand Total Expenses for Month (total daily expenses + total monthly expenses) =	$582.86
Net Take-home Pay for Month	
Pay Period 1	$800.00
Pay Period 2	
Pay Period 3	
Total Net Take-home Pay for Month	$800.00

"The Big Picture" (net take-home pay - grand total expenses for month)	$217.14

Every Penny Counts Diary Totals

	Total Daily Expenses	Total Monthly Expenses	Total Daily plus Monthly Expenses	Total Net Take-home Pay	"The Big Picture" (net take-home pay -grand total for month)
Month 1	$704.86	$450.00	$1,154.86	$1,700.02	$545.16
Month 2	$899.00	$450.00	$1,349.00	$1,672.62	$323.62
Month 3	$722.45	$450.00	$1,172.45	$1,823.54	$651.09
Total	$2,326.31	$1,350.00	$3,676.31	$5,196.18	$1,519.87

> " Too many people spend money they haven't earned, to buy things they don't want, to impress people they don't like. "
>
> —Will Smith, actor
> *(September 25, 1968–)*

▼ FIGURE 3.3

Sample personal balance sheet

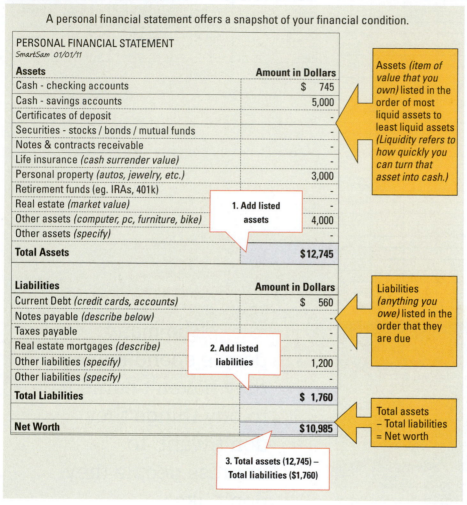

A personal financial statement offers a snapshot of your financial condition.

PERSONAL FINANCIAL STATEMENT
SmartSam 01/01/11

Assets	Amount in Dollars
Cash - checking accounts	$ 745
Cash - savings accounts	5,000
Certificates of deposit	-
Securities - stocks / bonds / mutual funds	-
Notes & contracts receivable	-
Life insurance *(cash surrender value)*	-
Personal property *(autos, jewelry, etc.)*	3,000
Retirement funds (eg. IRAs, 401k)	-
Real estate *(market value)*	-
Other assets *(computer, pc, furniture, bike)*	4,000
Other assets *(specify)*	-
Total Assets	**$12,745**

1. Add listed assets

Liabilities	Amount in Dollars
Current Debt *(credit cards, accounts)*	$ 560
Notes payable *(describe below)*	-
Taxes payable	-
Real estate mortgages *(describe)*	-
Other liabilities *(specify)*	1,200
Other liabilities *(specify)*	-
Total Liabilities	**$ 1,760**
Net Worth	**$10,985**

2. Add listed liabilities

3. Total assets (12,745) − Total liabilities ($1,760)

Assets *(item of value that you own)* listed in the order of most liquid assets to least liquid assets *(Liquidity refers to how quickly you can turn that asset into cash.)*

Liabilities *(anything you owe)* listed in the order that they are due

Total assets − Total liabilities = Net worth

annual statement in January for the previous year. Most savings and investment institutions support a web portal where you should be able to log on at any time and check the fund balance.

If you own real estate, it also is listed as an asset. However, your mortgage is listed as a liability. To determine the value of real estate, look at similar properties that have sold recently. A realtor can provide an opinion on the value of your house. If you really want to know the value of your real estate, you can pay for an appraisal. The cost of an appraisal for a single family dwelling can cost $600 or more. Other assets that should be listed separately are specific items of value, like baseball card collections, jewelry, antiques, and so on.

liabilities A **liability** is a debt that you owe. On a balance sheet, liabilities are listed in the order in which they are due. Any current liabilities are liabilities due within one year. First, list the total amount owed to credit card companies. This is the outstanding balance that has not yet been paid. Next, list the balance of any outstanding loans. This includes loans from parents, friends, and financial institutions—such as automobile loans. Your real estate loans (or mortgages) are what you owe on real estate. Next, list any student loans outstanding. Finally, list any other liabilities.

net worth Your **net worth** is the difference between what you own and what you owe. Your personal financial statement (or balance sheet) should balance, so that Assets − Liabilities = Net worth. One of the ways to look at a balance sheet is to view it as a score card. Are you achieving the financial goals you want to achieve and are they reflected in your net worth total?

Your net worth will vary greatly across your life stages. For example, before starting college, you might have a positive net worth. Once in college, depending on how much you need to borrow, you could easily fall into a negative net worth. During this time, you are investing in your education and your future; however, a balance sheet does not list educational attainment as an asset.

inventory and determine the replacement cost of your assets. However, you do not want to have your replacement cost on your balance sheet.

If you have an automobile, enter its value in the asset section of the balance sheet. List the value of the automobile at the private sale or average retail price. The market value of an automobile can be found at www.nada.com, www.kbb.com, or www.edmonds.com. Note the condition of the automobile to come up with a fair market value. If you have a loan outstanding on an automobile, the amount of the loan will be listed as a liability.

Any retirement funds you may have are also listed as assets. You can find the balances of your retirement funds from the financial companies managing those funds. You should receive statements at least quarterly, as well as an

personal cash flow statement measures your cash inflows and outflows in order to show your net cash flow for a specific time period

cash inflow cash coming in (i.e., salary, gifts, and interest income)

cash outflow cash going out (i.e., rent, utilities, and groceries)

net cash flow cash inflows minus cash outflows for a specific time period

Step 3: Create a Personal Cash Flow Statement

A **personal cash flow statement** measures your **cash inflows** and **outflows** in order to show your net cash flow for a specific period of time. The main sources of cash inflows are salary or wages and interest from savings and investments. Cash outflows are all of your expenses or money spent (e.g., rent, tuition, books, food, car lease, dining out). Your **net cash flow** is simply your cash inflows minus your cash outflows (see Figure 3.4 on the next page for an example). A positive net cash flow (also known as being "in the black") means you have earned more than

The cash value of the assets on your balance sheet may not be the same as what you paid for them.

financialfitness:
ACTION ITEM

Annual Assessment

Every January, compile an annual balance sheet as of December 31st of the previous year. Why December 31st? Your bank, mutual funds, stocks, retirement funds, and so on will mail you your end-of-year balances. It makes compiling your balance sheet easy. It is a good time to see if you have gained or lost money over the previous 12 months.

Making $ense

3.1 What value does a spending journal have?

3.2 What are the elements of a personal financial statement?

3.3 Define net worth.

3.4 How often should you compile a balance sheet?

you have spent, and you have some money left over from that period. A negative net cash flow (also known as being "in the red") means you are spending more money than you receive.

If you currently have a negative cash flow or you want to increase your positive net cash flow, you need to assess your spending habits and adjust them as necessary. Using a personal financial statement can help you see how your spending habits are impacting your net worth.

Sample personal cash flow statement

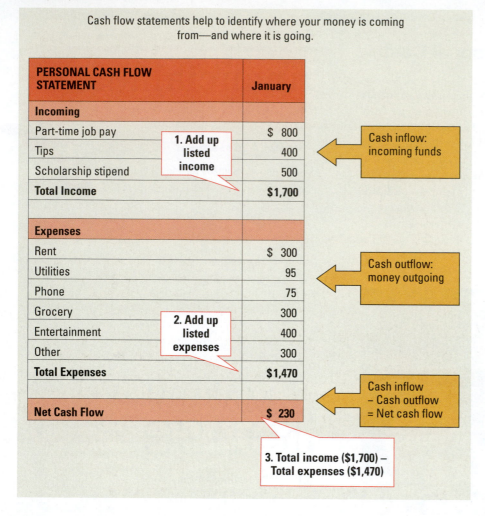

Cash flow statements help to identify where your money is coming from—and where it is going.

PERSONAL CASH FLOW STATEMENT	January
Incoming	
Part-time job pay	$ 800
Tips	400
Scholarship stipend	500
Total Income	**$1,700**
Expenses	
Rent	$ 300
Utilities	95
Phone	75
Grocery	300
Entertainment	400
Other	300
Total Expenses	**$1,470**
Net Cash Flow	**$ 230**

1. Add up listed income

2. Add up listed expenses

Cash inflow: incoming funds

Cash outflow: money outgoing

Cash inflow – Cash outflow = Net cash flow

3. Total income ($1,700) – Total expenses ($1,470)

It is typically easier to monitor your income. If you work, all you have to do is log your paychecks. It is harder to keep track of your spending. However, by tracking where you spend every penny, you will become a better manager of a finite resource—your money.

Monitoring your net cash flow from a cash flow statement can help you increase your net worth (see Figure 3.5). If you have a positive net cash flow in a given period, you can put that money into savings (assets) or pay off liabilities. In this way, you will grow your net worth.

3.2 OPPORTUNITY COST

■ ■ **LO 3-2** Estimate the opportunity costs of your purchases.

Every penny you spend is a penny you did not save to spend elsewhere for something you really want. This may sound simple, yet how many times have you bought little things like snacks without thinking about the expense and then, when it comes to the big items you really want, like concert tickets, you don't have the money? By keeping track of every penny, you can stop these little leaks and redirect the money to your bigger goals. As a result, you will feel more in control of your money and your life. You will feel good about the decisions you make to spend, save, invest, or donate your money.

Many people cannot wait for something they want. As a result, they often choose to buy on credit instead of saving for an item. When you buy on credit, you are making future obligations of your income. You may have your iPad, Droid, or big screen television today, but you will have to pay for it with your future earnings.

Opportunity cost is the cost of an alternative that must be forgone in order to pursue another option. For example, the opportunity cost of eating out versus packing your lunch can save you $5 a day. The opportunity cost of lunch out on a daily basis is $5 a day which could have been invested over time, leading to hundreds of thousands of dollars (recall the example of Smart Sam in Chapter 2). The choice is yours as to what opportunity you will pursue.

The opportunity cost of going to college is the money you would have earned if you had worked instead. On one hand, you lose four years of salary while getting your degree. On the other hand, thanks to your education, you hope to earn more during your career to offset the lost wages. Is it worth it to go to college and pursue a degree?

The answer is an overwhelming yes! The median annual earnings for full-time workers age 25 and older in 2009 were $8,805 higher for someone with an associate's degree compared to a high school degree, and $19,550 higher for someone with a bachelor's degree compared to a high school degree (see Figure 3.6 on page 62).

It can be difficult to take opportunity costs into account, but it is worth doing in order to reach your goals.

Figure 3.7 on the next page indicates the unemployment rate and the median dollars earned in 2009 by degree. As you can see, it pays to earn a degree.

Furthermore, there is an economic motivation to earn your bachelor's degree in four years rather than five or six years. From an opportunity cost standpoint, you will be spending an extra $20,000–$40,000 per year for the education compared to earning an extra $25,000–$65,000 per year in salary once you graduate. That one extra year of college costs you between $45,000 and $105,000. Here the opportunity cost is high. On the other hand, if you can graduate a year early, you gain that opportunity cost. See the nearby *Doing the Math* example to calculate how much an extra year at school would cost you.

The goal of keeping track of your spending is not to judge where you spend your money, but to increase your awareness of your personal cash flow. Review your "Every Penny Counts" online spreadsheet (Worksheet 3.1). Do your spending habits align with your goals? For example, it is easy to say you don't want to be in debt, but if you realize that you eat out three or four nights of the week and pay with your credit card, then your habits and goals are not aligned. How much could you save by not eating out? Could that money be used to reduce your debt or saved for a special purchase?

▼ **FIGURE 3.5**

Personal cash flow and net cash totals

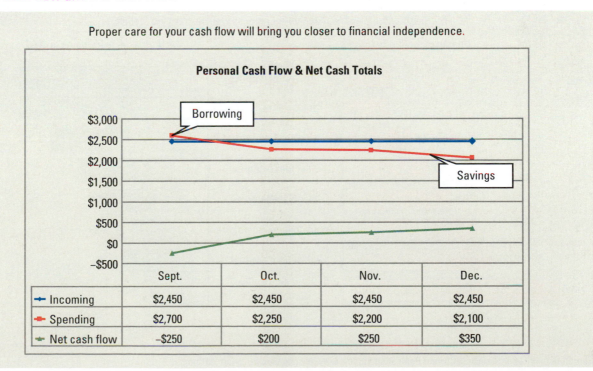

Proper care for your cash flow will bring you closer to financial independence.

Personal Cash Flow & Net Cash Totals

	Sept.	Oct.	Nov.	Dec.
Incoming	$2,450	$2,450	$2,450	$2,450
Spending	$2,700	$2,250	$2,200	$2,100
Net cash flow	–$250	$200	$250	$350

> ❝ He that wants money, means, and content is without three good friends. ❞
>
> —WILLIAM SHAKESPEARE (1564–1616)

▼ **FIGURE** 3.6

Median annual earnings by education degree (2009)

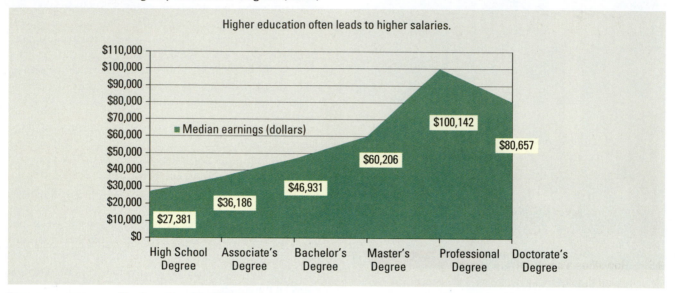

Source: www.census.gov/hhes/www/cpstables/032010/perinc/new03_001.htm

▼ **FIGURE** 3.7

Unemployment rates and median weekly earnings by degree for full-time and salary workers age 25+

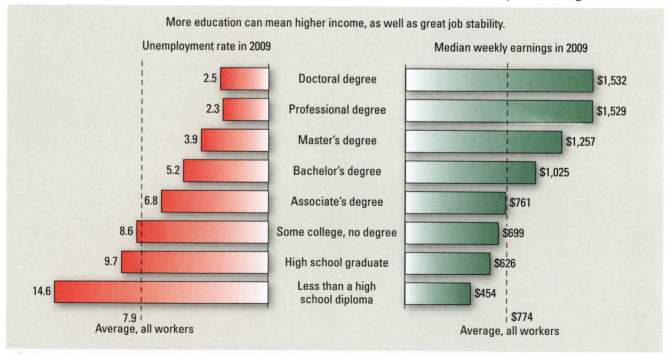

Source: Bureau of Labor Statistics, Current Population Survey, www.bls.gov/emp/ep_chart_001.htm.

3.2 Your Opportunity Cost

Calculate the opportunity cost of one extra year of college:

Tuition, room, board, books, fees, spending money   _____

Plus your estimated salary upon graduation   +_____

Equals opportunity cost of one extra year of college   =_____

Is it worth it to you to work extra hours, take fewer credits, and graduate in five years, or would you be better off to not work a part-time job, take extra classes, and get an extra student loan to graduate sooner?

Making $ense

3.5 How does a small leak sink a budget?

3.6 What is the opportunity cost of completing college in five years versus four years?

3.3 WAYS TO SAVE MONEY AND LIVE WITHIN YOUR MEANS

■■ **LO 3-3** Identify methods of saving money.

You have had the opportunity to examine your spending habits by writing down where you spend every penny. Do your spending and savings habits match your personal goals and the vision of where you want to be in five to ten years? Or do you need to make changes in order to live within your means and save money?

Budgets are easy to make but hard to follow. It is easy to overspend using your debit or credit card, although using these cards makes it easy to track where you have spent your money. Studies show people spend less when they use cash. Using cash to buy everything can save you money, but without your "Every Penny Counts" journal handy, it may be more difficult to track where you are spending your cash. Let's look at some ways to help you achieve your goals.

Pay Yourself First

If you create a budget and tell yourself you will save what is left over at the end of the month, you will not save much. In fact, some months you will not save anything, because you had unexpected expenses. If you want to save money, the most important lesson to learn is to pay yourself first. You need to treat these payments into your savings and investment accounts as if they were bills you would never consider not paying. Make paying *yourself* part of your budget.

By breaking down your savings goals into monthly, weekly, or even daily amounts, saving can seem less daunting. To save $1,200 a year, you would need to save $100 a month, or $23.80 a week, or $3.29 a day. By packing your lunch or eating dinner at home you can save at least that amount.

Let's look at some other possible methods for keeping a budget and saving money.

Cash Allocations to Budgeted Buckets

An easy and old form of sticking to a budget is to have envelopes for every category in your budget. Using this method, you have separate envelopes for groceries, rent, utilities, gas, entertainment, dining, insurance, and so on. For each paycheck, you put the cash you have budgeted into the corresponding envelopes. When you go to the grocery store,

financialfitness:
STOPPING LITTLE LEAKS

Curbing Calling Cost

There are lots of little ways to save money. Think about how much you spend on cell phone minutes each year. Curb this expense by shifting some of those minutes to an alternative inexpensive or free Internet phone calling service (e.g., www.Skype.com/Calls, www.google.com/talk/, etc.). These options also support group conversations, web cam calls, and sharing photos.

break at SeaWorld with the money left over. It was a great family vacation on a limited budget; they got to do everything they wanted based on their priorities and goals and spent quality family time together. The envelope system worked for them.

Stopping Little Leaks and Making Big Adjustments

In reviewing your journal of how and when you have spent money, look for little leaks—little changes that can make a big difference in your spending without forcing major changes in your lifestyle. If you can stop those little leaks, you can see your money working for you.

If stopping the little leaks is not enough to achieve your financial goals, you may need to make some more drastic changes. There are two sides to the earning/living equation: income and outgo. You may need to increase your income or reduce your expenditures or both. Do you need to reorganize your loans, credit cards, and other expenditures? Do you need to take in a roommate and share

you take that envelope with you. This method allows you to easily check how much money you have for the rest of the month by counting the money in the envelopes. You might also store your clipped coupons in the grocery envelope so you have them with you when you go grocery shopping. This is a great way for roommates to share expenses for food, rent, and utilities. The money is in the envelope when the bill comes due.

One caveat: You will need to resist the temptation to borrow from one envelope when another envelope runs out. It is easy to start down this slippery slope, moving seemingly small amounts of money from one envelope to another. It is critical to just say "no" when you feel that temptation. Once you start, it is hard to come back.

One spring break, a family went camping along the gulf coast of Texas. They put their spending money for the week in an envelope and shared how much money was in the envelope. On the vacation, they stopped in San Antonio. San Antonio has a Six Flags amusement park and a SeaWorld attraction and the kids wanted to do both. The decision was made to go to Six Flags before reaching the coast. If there was enough money left over from the week, they agreed to swing back to SeaWorld on the way home. This was a great family exercise to make everyone aware of priorities, the opportunity costs involved, and limited resources. During the week, the parents wanted to go out for dinner on more than one occasion. The kids strongly persuaded them to eat at the campsite to save money. After coming to a mutual agreement, they spent family time at the campsite each evening during dinner. They ended spring

financialfitness:
STOPPING LITTLE LEAKS

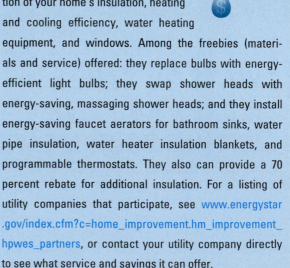

Energy Star Savings

Many utility companies offer energy inspection audits that can include free energy-saving improvements. They provide a report of the condition of your home's insulation, heating and cooling efficiency, water heating equipment, and windows. Among the freebies (materials and service) offered: they replace bulbs with energy-efficient light bulbs; they swap shower heads with energy-saving, massaging shower heads; and they install energy-saving faucet aerators for bathroom sinks, water pipe insulation, water heater insulation blankets, and programmable thermostats. They also can provide a 70 percent rebate for additional insulation. For a listing of utility companies that participate, see www.energystar.gov/index.cfm?c=home_improvement.hm_improvement_hpwes_partners, or contact your utility company directly to see what service and savings it can offer.

expenses? Or do you need to find a better paying job or take on a second job? Keep in mind there are opportunity costs involved.

In the beginning of the chapter, you read about Leslie and Nate's goal of going into marriage debt-free. When they tracked their spending, they discovered they were spending over $800 a month on dining out. By realizing this fact and making small changes, like eating more meals at home, they were able to achieve their goal of getting out of debt. That little change made a big difference in their overall financial health.

Sustainable Consumption

Another means to saving money is to maintain a mode of sustainable consumption, that is, not spending more than you make. You can achieve sustainable consumption through simplification, understanding the difference between need and want, and aligning your spending with your priorities. It is both good for your wallet and the environment. It is being conscientious about not being wasteful.

Some examples of sustainable consumption are: turning off lights when you leave a room; unplugging lamps or small appliances that rarely get use; adjusting your thermostat to use less energy while you are gone during the day and are asleep at night; purchasing new appliances with energy savings and efficiency in mind; and buying local or growing your own vegetables and herbs. Other acts of sustainable consumption could include taking an automotive course and learning to work on your own vehicle or doing your own home repairs. Or it could involve hosting a game night playing "retro" board games with your friends instead of going out on the town for an evening.

> " Art is the elimination of the unnecessary. "
>
> —PABLO PICASSO (1881–1973)

Although such frugality may not be appropriate for everyone, remember: Every financial decision has an opportunity cost and a benefit. When making a financial decision, you should think about how the opportunity cost and the benefit balance—and whether the decision falls in line with your overarching goals and priorities.

Penny-pinching is fine, but it won't save the profligate

Sometimes I read about ways to pinch pennies and I feel good. We turn off lights, often buy in bulk, use compact fluorescent light bulbs and put tap water in our reusable bottles instead of buying disposable ones: *A pat on the back*. Then I read another list and realize there are some things I just don't want to do. I don't make my own cleaning supplies. I am pretty hopeless about remembering coupons. I rarely wash out baggies: *A kick in the pants.*

It turns out there are a million ways to save small amounts of money, and not all of them are going to fit all of us. I know some people who have elaborate coupon systems that work well for them, but it's just not something I want to spend time on. I do use every rewards card I can, though, to rack up points toward a free movie ticket, meal, or flight. I'm not saying my choices make sense. I'm simply saying that saving is as individual as spending.

And perhaps, despite common wisdom, the small ways to save don't really help us. They can even hurt us by fooling us into believing we are making genuine financial changes when we're not. "We've read so much about economizing—here's how to clip a coupon and save 10 to 20%," said Jeff Yeager, who wrote *The Ultimate Cheapskate's Road Map to True Riches* (Broadway Books, 2008). "But what we're missing is the golden epiphany of the time—not can we save, but what do we need?" Cutting out the little stuff, what's known as the latte factor, "works on paper, but not necessarily in reality," said Mr. Yeager, who also runs the website ultimatecheapskate.com. "It's analogous to the easy weight-loss plans—that you can save in a quick and painless way." If we're living way beyond our means, drinking a little less coffee may make us feel as if we're doing something, but we're really avoiding making the more challenging decisions. Rather, we need to focus on the big choices in life, like buying a smaller house or downsizing the one we have now. Or living at home during college so we don't run up debt and then moving out when we graduate (rather than, as seems to be increasingly necessary, moving back in with the parents after college). *I can see these issues are important to think about and even act on. But can we start a bit smaller?*

. . . How about this idea, which is a common one, but worth repeating? Eat out much less. Forty-five percent of the average family's food budget is spent on meals prepared outside the house (that includes fast food). Imagine how much we can save by eating at home. I don't have to imagine it. I know. That's one of the things we cut back on last year, and it has made a difference. But notice, I said cut back. We haven't eliminated it altogether. There are times when a Chinese takeout or a restaurant dinner is just what we need. . . . "The key is satisfied spending." That is, don't just spend out of habit, but because it's something you really want. For instance, many people eat lunch out almost every day. It may be because they enjoy the food, but part of it is the activity surrounding the meal—getting outside and socializing. So try to do that in a cheaper way. Instead of going to a restaurant, buy some fresh lunch options at a grocery store. Then meet with friends and eat outside or in the work cafeteria. . . . There are some more ideas I picked up. They may not help you climb out of a deep financial hole, but if you just need to trim your budget slightly, they're worth considering

ALINA TUGEND, "Penny-Pinching Is Fine, but It Won't Save the Profligate," *The New York Times,* April 23, 2010. Reprinted with permission.

Questions

1 What is your opinion about the "latte factor"?

2 Where do you find balance between focusing on the little factors versus the big factors?

3.4 REALISTIC BUDGET BUILDING

■ ■ **LO 3-4** Construct a realistic budget that reflects your priorities and provides a means of protection from overspending.

What is a **budget**? A budget is nothing more than a plan of how you are going to spend and save your money. Businesses create income and expense statements to allocate financial resources in order to achieve strategic objectives. You should run your own spending and savings like a business. How do you want to allocate your financial resources? What goals are important to you and where will you reduce your spending (increase your savings) to achieve your goals?

Building Your Budget

By writing down where you spend every penny, you can observe your own spending habits. After the first month, you can project your spending and earnings for the next 12 months. Your next goal is to project times when you know you will have extraordinary expenses and income changes, in order to maintain a positive cash flow.

Think about your spending cycles throughout the year. At the beginning of each semester, you have the additional expenses of paying tuition and buying books. In December you might have the expense of buying gifts. As well, you might receive money as a gift. You may work more hours over school breaks or you may plan to travel. All of this can be projected in your budget.

Each spending and savings decision should tie to your goals and the opportunity cost involved. What are you forgoing now in order to achieve something later? Every spending and earning decision has an opportunity cost associated with it. Your budget should reflect your values so you can allocate your resources the way you want and maintain control over your money. See Figure 3.8 on the next page for an example of a budget.

Use the following steps to build your own budget:

- **Step 1:** Record your *income* and when you receive it.

- **Step 2:** List all your *fixed payments* and the dates on which they are due. This includes your rent, utilities, cell phone, car insurance, and so on.

- **Step 3:** List all of your *variable monthly expenses.* Variable expenses include gasoline, groceries, dining out, entertainment, and so on. Reflect back on your money journal and your last month of spending. How much did you spend on groceries, dining out, vending machine snacks, or movies?

- **Step 4:** The last section of the budget worksheet includes your *extraordinary expenses* or the things you don't think about much. Estimate how much you spend on car repairs, gifts given to others, home repairs, pet expenses, books, and so on. With repair expenses, estimate what you think these costs will be over a year and then budget that amount proportionally every month. For example, if you estimate you will spend $1,200 for car repairs and maintenance for the year, then set aside $100 a month for auto repairs. You do not know when you will need new brakes, a new water pump, or new wiper blades. By putting a little aside each month in your budget, you will have the money when repairs and maintenance are needed. You are now being proactive in managing your finances, rather than reactive.

Some people get in financial trouble because they are *reactive* in their finances. They do not set aside money each month to take care of repairs, emergencies, or even the holidays. Some fall back on the use of credit cards to cover variability in monthly expenses. In doing so, they find themselves paying a penalty of 10 to 39 percent in interest to the credit card companies to carry expenses over to the next month. This is the price for not planning. By properly budgeting and planning, you can avoid using your credit cards and the cost of credit card interest.

Reviewing and Revising Your Budget

You want your budget to be a realistic forecast of your income and spending. Through weekly assessments, your budget will continually improve. So set aside some time each week to tally up what you have spent and compare it to your budget. How did you do? Did you spend more or less than you budgeted? This is a good time to look at your **budget variances**, or where your income and spending differ from your budget.

$Making $ense

3.7 What are the principles behind paying yourself first?

3.8 List methods for saving money.

3.9 Identify methods for staying on a budget.

3.10 Define sustainable consumption.

financialfitness:
STOPPING LITTLE LEAKS

Cheap Trips

Student travel discount cards offer discounts on accommodations, food, and transportation when traveling nationally or internationally. Check out STA Travel (www.statravel.com/) or International Student Travel Confederation, ISTC (www.istc.org).

Budget spreadsheet template

This budget template can be an excellent start for building a budget of your own.

Personal budget

	Jan	Feb	March	April	May	June	July	Aug	Sept	Oct	Nov	Dec
INCOME												
Wages	0.00	0.00	0.00	0.00	0.00	0.00	0.00	0.00	0.00	0.00	0.00	0.00
Tips												
Interest/dividends	0.00	0.00	0.00	0.00	0.00	0.00	0.00	0.00	0.00	0.00	0.00	0.00
Miscellaneous	0.00	0.00	0.00	0.00	0.00	0.00	0.00	0.00	0.00	0.00	0.00	0.00
Income totals	0.00	0.00	0.00	0.00	0.00	0.00	0.00	0.00	0.00	0.00	0.00	0.00
EXPENSES												
Home												
Mortgage/rent	0.00	0.00	0.00	0.00	0.00	0.00	0.00	0.00	0.00	0.00	0.00	0.00
Utilities	0.00	0.00	0.00	0.00	0.00	0.00	0.00	0.00	0.00	0.00	0.00	0.00
Telephone	0.00	0.00	0.00	0.00	0.00	0.00	0.00	0.00	0.00	0.00	0.00	0.00
Home repairs	0.00	0.00	0.00	0.00	0.00	0.00	0.00	0.00	0.00	0.00	0.00	0.00
Home totals	0.00	0.00	0.00	0.00	0.00	0.00	0.00	0.00	0.00	0.00	0.00	0.00
Daily living												
Groceries	0.00	0.00	0.00	0.00	0.00	0.00	0.00	0.00	0.00	0.00	0.00	0.00
Drycleaning	0.00	0.00	0.00	0.00	0.00	0.00	0.00	0.00	0.00	0.00	0.00	0.00
Dining out	0.00	0.00	0.00	0.00	0.00	0.00	0.00	0.00	0.00	0.00	0.00	0.00
Daily living totals	0.00	0.00	0.00	0.00	0.00	0.00	0.00	0.00	0.00	0.00	0.00	0.00
Transportation												
Gas/fuel	0.00	0.00	0.00	0.00	0.00	0.00	0.00	0.00	0.00	0.00	0.00	0.00
Insurance	0.00	0.00	0.00	0.00	0.00	0.00	0.00	0.00	0.00	0.00	0.00	0.00
Repairs	0.00	0.00	0.00	0.00	0.00	0.00	0.00	0.00	0.00	0.00	0.00	0.00
Car wash/detailing services	0.00	0.00	0.00	0.00	0.00	0.00	0.00	0.00	0.00	0.00	0.00	0.00
Parking	0.00	0.00	0.00	0.00	0.00	0.00	0.00	0.00	0.00	0.00	0.00	0.00
Public transportation	0.00	0.00	0.00	0.00	0.00	0.00	0.00	0.00	0.00	0.00	0.00	0.00
Transportation totals	0.00	0.00	0.00	0.00	0.00	0.00	0.00	0.00	0.00	0.00	0.00	0.00
Entertainment												
Cable TV	0.00	0.00	0.00	0.00	0.00	0.00	0.00	0.00	0.00	0.00	0.00	0.00
Internet												
Video/DVD rentals	0.00	0.00	0.00	0.00	0.00	0.00	0.00	0.00	0.00	0.00	0.00	0.00
Movies/plays	0.00	0.00	0.00	0.00	0.00	0.00	0.00	0.00	0.00	0.00	0.00	0.00
Concerts/clubs	0.00	0.00	0.00	0.00	0.00	0.00	0.00	0.00	0.00	0.00	0.00	0.00
Entertainment totals	0.00	0.00	0.00	0.00	0.00	0.00	0.00	0.00	0.00	0.00	0.00	0.00
Health												
Health club dues	0.00	0.00	0.00	0.00	0.00	0.00	0.00	0.00	0.00	0.00	0.00	0.00
Insurance	0.00	0.00	0.00	0.00	0.00	0.00	0.00	0.00	0.00	0.00	0.00	0.00
Prescriptions	0.00	0.00	0.00	0.00	0.00	0.00	0.00	0.00	0.00	0.00	0.00	0.00
Over-the-counter drugs	0.00	0.00	0.00	0.00	0.00	0.00	0.00	0.00	0.00	0.00	0.00	0.00
Co-payments/out-of-pocket	0.00	0.00	0.00	0.00	0.00	0.00	0.00	0.00	0.00	0.00	0.00	0.00
Veterinarians/pet medicines	0.00	0.00	0.00	0.00	0.00	0.00	0.00	0.00	0.00	0.00	0.00	0.00
Life insurance	0.00	0.00	0.00	0.00	0.00	0.00	0.00	0.00	0.00	0.00	0.00	0.00
Health totals	0.00	0.00	0.00	0.00	0.00	0.00	0.00	0.00	0.00	0.00	0.00	0.00
Vacations												
Plane fare	0.00	0.00	0.00	0.00	0.00	0.00	0.00	0.00	0.00	0.00	0.00	0.00
Accommodations	0.00	0.00	0.00	0.00	0.00	0.00	0.00	0.00	0.00	0.00	0.00	0.00
Food	0.00	0.00	0.00	0.00	0.00	0.00	0.00	0.00	0.00	0.00	0.00	0.00
Souvenirs	0.00	0.00	0.00	0.00	0.00	0.00	0.00	0.00	0.00	0.00	0.00	0.00
Rental car	0.00	0.00	0.00	0.00	0.00	0.00	0.00	0.00	0.00	0.00	0.00	0.00
Vacations totals	0.00	0.00	0.00	0.00	0.00	0.00	0.00	0.00	0.00	0.00	0.00	0.00
School												
Tuition	0.00	0.00	0.00	0.00	0.00	0.00	0.00	0.00	0.00	0.00	0.00	0.00
Lab Fees	0.00	0.00	0.00	0.00	0.00	0.00	0.00	0.00	0.00	0.00	0.00	0.00
Other Fees	0.00	0.00	0.00	0.00	0.00	0.00	0.00	0.00	0.00	0.00	0.00	0.00
Books	0.00	0.00	0.00	0.00	0.00	0.00	0.00	0.00	0.00	0.00	0.00	0.00
School totals	0.00	0.00	0.00	0.00	0.00	0.00	0.00	0.00	0.00	0.00	0.00	0.00
Dues/subscriptions												
Magazines	0.00	0.00	0.00	0.00	0.00	0.00	0.00	0.00	0.00	0.00	0.00	0.00
Newspapers	0.00	0.00	0.00	0.00	0.00	0.00	0.00	0.00	0.00	0.00	0.00	0.00
Internet connection	0.00	0.00	0.00	0.00	0.00	0.00	0.00	0.00	0.00	0.00	0.00	0.00
Public radio	0.00	0.00	0.00	0.00	0.00	0.00	0.00	0.00	0.00	0.00	0.00	0.00
Public television	0.00	0.00	0.00	0.00	0.00	0.00	0.00	0.00	0.00	0.00	0.00	0.00
Religious organizations	0.00	0.00	0.00	0.00	0.00	0.00	0.00	0.00	0.00	0.00	0.00	0.00
Charity	0.00	0.00	0.00	0.00	0.00	0.00	0.00	0.00	0.00	0.00	0.00	0.00
Dues/subscription totals	0.00	0.00	0.00	0.00	0.00	0.00	0.00	0.00	0.00	0.00	0.00	0.00
Personal												
Clothing	0.00	0.00	0.00	0.00	0.00	0.00	0.00	0.00	0.00	0.00	0.00	0.00
Gifts	0.00	0.00	0.00	0.00	0.00	0.00	0.00	0.00	0.00	0.00	0.00	0.00
Salon/barber	0.00	0.00	0.00	0.00	0.00	0.00	0.00	0.00	0.00	0.00	0.00	0.00
Books	0.00	0.00	0.00	0.00	0.00	0.00	0.00	0.00	0.00	0.00	0.00	0.00
Music (CDs, etc.)	0.00	0.00	0.00	0.00	0.00	0.00	0.00	0.00	0.00	0.00	0.00	0.00
Personal totals	0.00	0.00	0.00	0.00	0.00	0.00	0.00	0.00	0.00	0.00	0.00	0.00
Financial obligations												
Long-term savings	0.00	0.00	0.00	0.00	0.00	0.00	0.00	0.00	0.00	0.00	0.00	0.00
Retirement (401[k], Roth IRA)	0.00	0.00	0.00	0.00	0.00	0.00	0.00	0.00	0.00	0.00	0.00	0.00
Credit card payments	0.00	0.00	0.00	0.00	0.00	0.00	0.00	0.00	0.00	0.00	0.00	0.00
Income tax (additional)	0.00	0.00	0.00	0.00	0.00	0.00	0.00	0.00	0.00	0.00	0.00	0.00
Other obligations	0.00	0.00	0.00	0.00	0.00	0.00	0.00	0.00	0.00	0.00	0.00	0.00
Financial obligation totals	0.00	0.00	0.00	0.00	0.00	0.00	0.00	0.00	0.00	0.00	0.00	0.00
Misc. payments												
Other	0.00	0.00	0.00	0.00	0.00	0.00	0.00	0.00	0.00	0.00	0.00	0.00
Other	0.00	0.00	0.00	0.00	0.00	0.00	0.00	0.00	0.00	0.00	0.00	0.00
Other	0.00	0.00	0.00	0.00	0.00	0.00	0.00	0.00	0.00	0.00	0.00	0.00
Other	0.00	0.00	0.00	0.00	0.00	0.00	0.00	0.00	0.00	0.00	0.00	0.00
Other	0.00	0.00	0.00	0.00	0.00	0.00	0.00	0.00	0.00	0.00	0.00	0.00
Misc. payments totals	0.00	0.00	0.00	0.00	0.00	0.00	0.00	0.00	0.00	0.00	0.00	0.00
Total expenses	0.00	0.00	0.00	0.00	0.00	0.00	0.00	0.00	0.00	0.00	0.00	0.00
Cash short/extra	0.00	0.00	0.00	0.00	0.00	0.00	0.00	0.00	0.00	0.00	0.00	0.00

Source: Microsoft Template.

> I'm living so far beyond my income that we may almost be said to be living apart.
>
> —E.E. CUMMINGS, *Poet (1894–1962)*

Consider the following ideas to help you successfully review and revise your budget:

- Set aside 30 minutes a week to focus on the budget.

- Walk through every line of the budget and think about what went well and what you will do differently next time. If you overspent, move money from the emergency fund to cover the shortage or strategize how to make up the difference.

- Forget past mistakes. What's done is done. You cannot change the past, but you can impact the future. As you start out, your budget will not be perfect, but it will improve with time.

- Plan next month's budget before the month arrives. Make your spending and investing decisions before you receive your money.

- Remember to always pay yourself first.

- Celebrate when you make it a week on your budget.

If other people are involved in your finances, a weekly budget meeting provides a great opportunity to discuss the past and the future. The objective of a weekly meeting is to keep everyone focused on the long-term financial goals and motivated to achieve those goals. This meeting could take a few hours the first time, so set aside a time when you will be uninterrupted.

In establishing a household budget meeting, determine who will take on the role of the accountant, the person who inputs and keeps track of income and expenses. This should be the person who likes to balance the checkbook and is detail-oriented. The accountant should provide *budget reports* of actual income and spending. Quicken and www.mint.com are common software programs that can

financialfitness:
NUMBERS GAME

Holiday Cash

If you celebrate the holidays with gifts, some banks offer "Holiday Club" accounts, where you can regularly deposit money into an account that does not allow you to make withdrawals. This is sometimes called *smoothing*, or spreading an annual expense over the course of the year. The bank will then send you a check before Thanksgiving so you can take advantage of all the sales on "Black Friday" (the Friday after Thanksgiving)—the busiest shopping day of the year.

help with this reporting; however, all you need is paper and a pencil to create a spreadsheet.

Even though only one person will take on the role of the accountant, it is important to establish a budget together. In establishing a budget, everyone has input and ownership in the budget process. The important part of the creation of a budget is to do it together, having an open and honest conversation about future financial decisions and goals. The accountant has no more say in the budget than the other parties involved.

doing the MATH

3.3 Budgeting for Variability

Estimate your variable yearly expenses:

(_____)/12 months = (_____), the amount to set aside each month to cover future anticipated expenses

How much should you be saving to put toward variable expenses on a weekly basis?

financialfitness:
JUST THE FACTS

Money and Stress

Money and stress are closely linked. A lot of unnecessary spending comes from a desire to feel comfort or fill an emotional need. Spending achieves a temporary boost, followed by an even deeper sense of dread. Spending money does not satisfy your emotional needs, and you have wasted hard-earned funds on frivolous things instead of putting it to use in alignment with your longer-term goals. Stress also makes you tired and hungry, causing you to get less done (and by extension make less money) and eat more food (which also costs money). If the stress is left unchecked, serious medical problems can result. The next time you feel stressed, try going for a walk or just sitting outside for awhile. Spend time identifying the causes of your stress and addressing your problems in a proactive manner. You will feel much better—and save a lot of money.

Making $ense

3.11 What are the components of a budget?

3.12 How does a budget help control spending?

3.13 What are the benefits of a weekly budget meeting?

After you establish your budget, establish a time for your weekly review. The focus of this weekly meeting should be the budget, not things in the past. By focusing on the budget, you can open up lines of communication, take away the emotion tied to money, and plan for the future. ■

Learn. Plan & Act. Evaluate.

➡ **LEARN.** At the start of this book, you identified your goals and values and created a personal mission statement. Over the course of this chapter, you began a daily log of your spending, and you learned how to compile a personal balance sheet and a cash flow statement. With these assessment tools, you have a good footing and know where you currently sit financially. Lastly, you learned how to project a budget that incorporates not only current inflows and outflows, but also makes allocations to items aligned with your personal mission statement and objectives.

SUMMARY

■ ■ **LO 3-1** Analyze your spending habits by using tools such as spending journals and balance sheets.

To really know where your money goes, track every penny you spend. From preparing a daily journal of your spending, calculate weekly, monthly, and yearly costs. By making minor changes in spending, you can stop the little leaks. Your personal financial statement is an account of what you have to show for all your spending and who you owe, as well as your net worth. A personal cash flow statement measures your cash inflows and outflows. Using a personal financial statement helps raise awareness of how your spending habits impact your net worth. Monitoring net cash flow from a cash flow statement can help you increase your net worth.

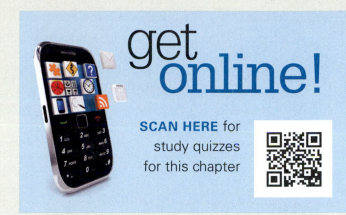

SCAN HERE for study quizzes for this chapter

■ ■ **LO 3-2** Estimate the opportunity costs of your purchases.

Every penny you spend is a penny you cannot spend somewhere else for something you really want or need. By keeping track of every penny, you can stop these little leaks and redirect the money to your bigger goals. Opportunity cost is the cost of an alternative that must be forgone in order to pursue another option.

■ ■ **LO 3-3** Identify methods of saving money.

Remember to pay yourself first by making payments into savings and investment accounts as if they were bills you would never skip. Make saving easy by setting up automatic transfers out of your paycheck or checking account and into your savings and investments. You can achieve sustainable consumption through simplification and understanding the difference between a need and a want. Every financial decision has an opportunity cost and a benefit. When making a financial decision, think about how the opportunity cost and the benefit balance out and whether the decision falls in line with your overarching goals and values.

■ ■ **LO 3-4** Construct a realistic budget that reflects your priorities and provides a means of protection from overspending.

A budget is a plan of how you are going to save and spend your money. Your goal is to project those times when you are likely to have extraordinary expenses and when your income will change, in order to maintain a positive cash flow. Every spending and earning decision has an opportunity cost associated with it. Your budget should reflect your values so you can allocate your resources the way you want and maintain control over your money. It is important to set aside time each week to review your budget.

⟳ **PLAN & ACT.** A budget and a daily spending journal are tools that will help you stay on the path of successfully managing your resources and being in control of your money and your time. You should not only track spending, but also log ideas on how to be thrifty as you come across them. Make positive notes to yourself when you successfully ward off an impulse purchase or come up with a creative "upcycling" solution to meet a need. As you spend, keep asking yourself about the opportunity cost of the purchase and remember the reasons to save for larger purchases. Use your journal as an opportunity to compliment yourself on a daily basis for staying on track with your budget and making incremental steps toward a savings goal. A daily assessment of where you are and where you want to be will help you succeed in meeting your goals. Your Plan & Act to do list is as follows:

☐ Keep a journal of your daily spending (Online file "Every Penny Counts" Journal).

☐ Create a personal balance sheet (Worksheet 3.1).

☐ Construct a cash flow statement (Worksheet 3.2).

☐ Draft a budget (Worksheet 3.3).

☐ Schedule weekly budget reviews.

☐ Set up an automatic transfer from your paycheck or checking account into your savings.

⊃ **EVALUATE.** Refer back to your goals in Chapter 1 and compare them to where you are spending your money. When you look at your bank statement, you are examining your spending priorities. From your "Every Penny Counts" worksheet, list your categories of spending from highest to lowest. What have you learned about your spending habits? Are there areas where you really did not intend to spend money? How will you change your spending for the next week? Do you feel your spending reflects your priorities? Little changes in your behavior (without changing your lifestyle) can make a big difference in your saving and spending habits.

» GoalTracker

Once you create a budget, you will have a tool to evaluate your monthly spending and savings. Have you allocated appropriate spending and savings to support your goals from Chapter 1? Following the completion of Worksheet 3.2, open the online GoalTracker to make notes on how your budget supports your SMART goals. Assess how you are achieving the stated goals. If you are not doing well, give some thought as to what steps you should take to get back on track.

key terms

Asset	Cash Outflow	Net Cash Flow
Balance Sheet	Cash Value (of Life Insurance)	Net Worth
Budget	Face Value (of Life Insurance)	Opportunity Cost
Budget Variance	Liability	Personal Cash Flow Statement
Cash Inflow	Liquidity	Personal Financial Statement

self-test questions

1. What value does a spending journal bring? *(LO 3-1)*

   a. It provides an opportunity to analyze where you may be wasting money.
   b. It provides you a base whereby you can create a budget.
   c. It provides insight into your spending habits.
   d. All of the above

2. What is the equation for a balance sheet? *(LO 3-1)*

   a. Balance sheet − Net worth = Assets
   b. Assets + Liabilities = Net worth
   c. Assets − Liabilities = Net worth
   d. Income − Expenses = Net worth

3. Which one of the following is *not* an asset? *(LO 3-1)*

   a. A bicycle
   b. A jar full of saved coins from loose change
   c. A car loan
   d. An IOU from your roommate

4. Which one of the following is *not* a liability? *(LO 3-1)*

   a. A credit card balance
   b. A car loan

   c. A student loan
   d. An ATM Card

5. When is your cash flow "in the red"? *(LO 3-1)*

   a. Income > Spending
   b. Spending > Income
   c. Net cash flow > Income − Spending
   d. Net cash flow > Spending − Income

6. Define opportunity cost. *(LO 3-2)*

   a. The money it costs to take advantage of an opportunity
   b. The cost of an alternative that must be forgone in order to pursue a certain action
   c. Payment for an opportunity
   d. The cost of opportunities to purchase necessities

7. Identify a strategy to spend less and earn more. *(LO 3-3)*

   a. Pay yourself first
   b. Automatically transfer savings and investments out of your paycheck or checking account
   c. Break down your savings goals into monthly, weekly, and daily amounts
   d. All of the above

8. What are some strategies for keeping to a budget? *(LO 3-4)*

   a. Weekly budget meetings
   b. Envelopes
   c. Bargain shopping and coupon clipping
   d. All of the above

9. What is discussed at a budget meeting? *(LO 3-4)*

   a. Evaluation of what mistakes were made
   b. Assignment of who should be recorder for the month

   c. Assessment of what changes need to be made to next month's budget based on actual variances
   d. Strategizing as to how to "Rob Peter to Pay Paul"

10. What do you use for a foundation to build a budget? *(LO 3-4)*

   a. Age appropriate examples from www.mint.com
   b. A spending journal
   c. A Microsoft budget template
   d. Your neighbor's spending

problems

1. If you buy a bag of chips and a soda every Monday through Friday from a vending machine (at $1.00 per bag and $1.25 per pop), how much do you spend on the vending machine munchies over the course of a year? *(LO 3-1)*

2. What is your net cash flow if you had a total income last month of $2,000 but your expenses totaled $2,500, $500 of which was covered by your credit card? *(LO 3-1)*

3. If the median income for someone with an associate's degree is $9,100 higher annually than for someone with a high school degree, and the total cost of schooling for the two years costs $20,000, at what point does the investment in the education break even? *(LO 3-2)*

4. If you wanted to have $5,000 saved up by the end of the year, what amount would you need to save on a monthly basis? A weekly basis? A daily basis? *(LO 3-3)*

5. If you go out for lunch Monday through Friday between classes and spend between $7 and $11 for each meal, how much do you spend over the course of a 16-week semester? *(LO 3-4)*

6. If you make four to five trips home during the school year and plane tickets cost between $300 and $400 per trip, how much should you budget on a monthly basis to cover this variable cost? *(LO 3-4)*

7. You estimate that next year you will need to buy new tires for your car at a cost of $500. This is in addition to the typical maintenance costs, which have been between $400 and $600 in previous years. If you get paid every other week, how much should you budget out of each paycheck to cover the estimated yearly variable expense of car repairs? *(LO 3-4)*

you're the expert

1. Ben has $2,000 and $2,333 in his checking and savings accounts, respectively. He lives in a dorm room and drives a 1999 Honda Accord four-door Dx with 120,000 miles. He owns the latest Xbox video games and has a high-powered computer and stereo worth $2,500. Other than a $4,000 student loan, he is debt-free. Create a personal financial statement in order to calculate Ben's net worth. Given that Ben is currently a student, do you have concerns regarding his current net worth? Why or why not? *(LO 3-1)*

2. Jerry is preparing to go to college in the fall and is worried about expenses. He has $189 in his checking account, $2,500 in his savings account, and a CD account for $5,000 that matures September 1. He owes his brother $75 for a joint gift in which he participated. His parents are able to send him $1,000 each month, but room, board, and tuition

   will run $1,800 per month. He is unsure of his book expenses.

   a. Prepare Jerry's personal financial balance sheet statement. What is his current net worth? *(LO 3-1)*
   b. Will he be able to focus his time on school or will he need to subsidize his expenses by getting a job or a student loan? To assess his choices, create his cash flow statement. Does he have a positive or a negative cash flow? *(LO 3-1)*
   c. What are the risks he incurs by taking fewer credits each year so he can more easily handle a part-time job to offset his living expenses? *(LO 3-2)*
   d. Suggest some alternatives. *(LO 3-3)*

3. Rachael is in her senior year at college and is taking a summer and one semester to do a six-month internship in recreational services. The resort where she is interning is providing room, breakfast, and lunch during the five days a week she works, as well as a small

stipend of $250/week after taxes. This will be her only source of income over the next six months. Rachael's living expenses include her cell phone at $65/month, groceries at about $25–35/week, clothing at $100/month, haircuts at $20/month, and approximately $50/week for recreation. Complete a cash flow statement for Rachael and answer the following questions.

a. What is Rachael's total cash inflow? *(LO 3-1)*
b. What is Rachael's total cash outflow? *(LO 3-1)*
c. What is Rachael's net cash flow? *(LO 3-1)*
d. Rachael would like to have at least $1,000 saved up at the end of her internship to go on an all-inclusive vacation trip to Mexico in January with her friends before returning for her last semester of classes. Prepare a monthly budget that will help her achieve that goal. *(LO 3-4)*

e. In the second month of her internship, Rachael dropped her cell phone in the sink and it is not insured. She would love to get a Droid with a data plan. A new phone will cost her $200 and the monthly plan will be $65/month. How can she adjust her budget to achieve the short-term goal of a new phone and data plan as well as the long-term goal of saving enough money for her trip to Mexico? *(LO 3-2, LO 3-3)*

f. Show how the adjustments in (e) will alter her budget from the second month onward. *(LO 3-4)*

worksheets

Find the worksheets online at www.mhhe.com/walkerpf1e

3.1   PERSONAL FINANCIAL STATEMENT

Create your personal financial statement using Worksheet 3.1.

3.1 PERSONAL FINANCIAL STATEMENT (BALANCE SHEET)

[Date]

Assets	Amount in Dollars
Cash — checking accounts	$ -
Cash — savings accounts	-
Certificates of deposit	-
Securities — stocks / bonds / mutual funds	-
Notes & contracts receivable	-
Life insurance (cash surrender value)	-
Personal property (furniture, computer)	-
Automobile (market value)	-
Retirement funds (i.e., IRA, 401[k])	-
Real estate (market value)	-
Other assets (specify)	-
	-
	-
Total Assets	

Liabilities	Amount in Dollars
Credit cards	$ -
Loans (auto and others)	
Student loans	
Notes payable (describe below)	-
Real estate mortgages (describe)	-
Other liabilities (specify)	-
	-
Total Liabilities	
Net Worth	

3.2 CASH FLOW STATEMENT

Create your personal cash flow statement using Worksheet 3.2.

3.2 Cash Flow Statement (College)

Monthly Income

Item	Amount
Estimated monthly net income	
Financial aid award(s)	
Other income	
Total	**$0.00**

Monthly Expenses

Item	Amount
Rent	
Utilities	
Cell phone	
Groceries	
Auto expenses	
Student loans	
Other loans	
Credit cards	
Insurance	
Laundry	
Haircuts	
Medical expenses	
Entertainment	
Miscellaneous	
Total	**$0.00**
Net Cash Flow	**$0.00**

Semester Expenses

Item	Amount
Tuition	
Lab fees	
Other fees	
Books	
Deposits	
Transportation	
Total	**$0.00**

Discretionary Income

Item	Amount
Monthly income	$0.00
Monthly expenses	$0.00
Semester expenses	$0.00
Difference	**$0.00**

3.3 PERSONAL BUDGET

Create your personal budget using Worksheet 3.3.

Personal budget

	Jan	Feb	March	April	May	June	July	Aug	Sept	Oct	Nov	Dec	Year
INCOME													
Wages	0.00	0.00	0.00	0.00	0.00	0.00	0.00	0.00	0.00	0.00	0.00	0.00	0.00
Tips													
Interest/dividends	0.00	0.00	0.00	0.00	0.00	0.00	0.00	0.00	0.00	0.00	0.00	0.00	0.00
Miscellaneous	0.00	0.00	0.00	0.00	0.00	0.00	0.00	0.00	0.00	0.00	0.00	0.00	0.00
Income totals	0.00	0.00	0.00	0.00	0.00	0.00	0.00	0.00	0.00	0.00	0.00	0.00	0.00
EXPENSES													
Home													
Mortgage/rent	0.00	0.00	0.00	0.00	0.00	0.00	0.00	0.00	0.00	0.00	0.00	0.00	0.00
Utilities	0.00	0.00	0.00	0.00	0.00	0.00	0.00	0.00	0.00	0.00	0.00	0.00	0.00
Telephone	0.00	0.00	0.00	0.00	0.00	0.00	0.00	0.00	0.00	0.00	0.00	0.00	0.00
Home repairs	0.00	0.00	0.00	0.00	0.00	0.00	0.00	0.00	0.00	0.00	0.00	0.00	0.00
Home totals	0.00	0.00	0.00	0.00	0.00	0.00	0.00	0.00	0.00	0.00	0.00	0.00	0.00
Daily living													
Groceries	0.00	0.00	0.00	0.00	0.00	0.00	0.00	0.00	0.00	0.00	0.00	0.00	0.00
Drycleaning	0.00	0.00	0.00	0.00	0.00	0.00	0.00	0.00	0.00	0.00	0.00	0.00	0.00
Dining out	0.00	0.00	0.00	0.00	0.00	0.00	0.00	0.00	0.00	0.00	0.00	0.00	0.00
Daily living totals	0.00	0.00	0.00	0.00	0.00	0.00	0.00	0.00	0.00	0.00	0.00	0.00	0.00
Transportation													
Gas/fuel	0.00	0.00	0.00	0.00	0.00	0.00	0.00	0.00	0.00	0.00	0.00	0.00	0.00
Insurance	0.00	0.00	0.00	0.00	0.00	0.00	0.00	0.00	0.00	0.00	0.00	0.00	0.00
Repairs	0.00	0.00	0.00	0.00	0.00	0.00	0.00	0.00	0.00	0.00	0.00	0.00	0.00
Car wash/detailing services	0.00	0.00	0.00	0.00	0.00	0.00	0.00	0.00	0.00	0.00	0.00	0.00	0.00
Parking	0.00	0.00	0.00	0.00	0.00	0.00	0.00	0.00	0.00	0.00	0.00	0.00	0.00
Public transportation	0.00	0.00	0.00	0.00	0.00	0.00	0.00	0.00	0.00	0.00	0.00	0.00	0.00
Transportation totals	0.00	0.00	0.00	0.00	0.00	0.00	0.00	0.00	0.00	0.00	0.00	0.00	0.00
Entertainment													
Cable TV	0.00	0.00	0.00	0.00	0.00	0.00	0.00	0.00	0.00	0.00	0.00	0.00	0.00
Internet													
Video/DVD rentals	0.00	0.00	0.00	0.00	0.00	0.00	0.00	0.00	0.00	0.00	0.00	0.00	0.00
Movies/plays	0.00	0.00	0.00	0.00	0.00	0.00	0.00	0.00	0.00	0.00	0.00	0.00	0.00
Concerts/clubs	0.00	0.00	0.00	0.00	0.00	0.00	0.00	0.00	0.00	0.00	0.00	0.00	0.00
Entertainment totals	0.00	0.00	0.00	0.00	0.00	0.00	0.00	0.00	0.00	0.00	0.00	0.00	0.00

906 E College Street

In the last chapter, after the grandparents visited, the housemates discussed putting at least $20/month toward their savings. In order to achieve this goal, they decide they need to come up with a spending and savings plan. Previously, everyone fended for themselves, with the majority of meals eaten out. They discuss that one way they can cut back on expenses is to start making more meals at home. They agree that each housemate will make three dinners a month. For the meals in which they are responsible, they will buy the groceries. The meals-at-home dates will be decided at the start of each month. Other monthly expenses will be divided equally among the housemates: utilities $250, Internet/cable $150, and water/garbage $100.

Build Jack's monthly budget, taking into consideration that he works four nights a week bartending, where he averages $100 in tips and $49 in wages each night. He pays $350 a month in rent. He believes each meal that he makes for his housemates will cost him $40. He spends about $20 each week on other groceries, $75 per month on his paintball hobby, $50 per week on entertainment, and $200 each month on clothing and incidentals. He is thinking about going back to school, so he would like to start putting money toward that goal, as well as $20 each month toward long-term savings and $75 per month into a third savings account to cover monthly variable expenses and emergencies.

A summary of the housemates' goals can be found in the first Continuing Case problem on page 27.

1. Create a cash flow statement to assess how much money would be available for savings.

2. Create a monthly budget for Jack.

3. How much money could Jack reasonably save for college each month?

"Money speaks sense in a language all nations understand. "

—APHRA BEHN, *The Rover (1640–1689)*

chapter four

financial instruments and institutions

Throughout your life, your banking and finance needs will change. In this chapter, you will learn which financial instruments are commonly used in the different life stages. Savings and checking accounts are the foundation instruments, and learning to manage your checking account well is essential to staying financially responsible on a month-by-month basis. ▪

LEARNING OBJECTIVES

After reading this chapter, you should be able to:

LO 4-1 Identify which bank products are the best fit for different personal finance life stages.

LO 4-2 Use and efficiently manage checking and share draft accounts.

LO 4-3 Assess financial institutions and accounts to determine which ones best meet your needs.

Expensive Lessons

Now a customer service representative, Amanda learned a lot about managing personal finances as a college freshman. She says, "I wasn't quite prepared for all the responsibilities of living away from home: apartment living, college class schedules, a budget, and the nuances of managing a checking account. The first month, I made a number of $5 and $10 ATM withdrawals over the course of a weekend that ended up costing me $25 each. I would have greatly benefited by getting a checking account when I was 16 to learn the mechanics of managing the account and to be disciplined in monitoring the balance. The first month on my own with a checking account came with an expensive lesson. I highly recommend that people work with a checking account while they are still in high school and living at home before having to take on the responsibilities of managing their living expenses as well."

4.1 ALIGNING FINANCIAL INSTRUMENTS WITH LIFE STAGES

■ ■ **LO 4-1** Identify which bank products are the best fit for different personal finance life stages.

Financial instruments are tools for helping you achieve your goals and making your life easier. In Chapter 1 we discussed the five different life stages in personal finance: dependent, independent, early family, empty nest, and retirement. Depending on one's life stage, one's financial needs are constantly changing. In this section we will examine various bank products and how they target the different personal finance life stages.

Dependent Life Stage (Age <16)

From birth up to the age of 16, you are not likely to be earning money from an employer, but you may be receiving money through gifts, an allowance, and/or odd jobs. During the Dependent Life Stage, many different financial instruments are available to help you accumulate wealth and achieve your goals (see Figure 4.1). The three bank products that best meet one's personal finance needs during this stage are savings accounts, college savings plans, and certificates of deposit.

savings accounts Everyone should get a savings account as soon as possible. A savings account accumulates wealth for purchases later in life, such as a bicycle, a car, or college tuition. Savings accounts offer access to money, earn interest on deposits, and provide a safe place to put your money.

A savings account helps a person save money. Some accounts have limits on third party withdrawals (checks, debit payments, and automatic payments). Most savings accounts pay interest on balances. Some accounts may have tiered rates where you earn a higher interest rate for maintaining a larger balance in the account. Different financial institutions may compound interest monthly, quarterly, semiannually, or annually. In comparing different savings accounts, you need to look at the fees for ATM withdrawals, the minimum balance to earn interest, any transaction fees, and the annual percentage yield (APY).

There is usually no limit on in-person withdrawals; however, consult your financial institution for details. Financial institutions reserve the right to require up to a seven-day notice for withdrawals from a savings account, although this is rarely exercised. Be sure to read the financial disclosure document carefully before opening an account.

529 plans or college savings plans A **529 plan** is an account—technically called a *qualified tuition plan*—designed to encourage saving for future college expenses. The 529 plan gets its name from Section 529 of the Internal Revenue Code. Individual states determine which 529 plans are offered and who manages the 529 plan. There are two types of 529 plans: prepaid tuition plans and college savings plans. States can choose to offer a prepaid tuition plan, which allows investors to prepay tuition in current dollars, or a college savings plan. See Figure 4.2 for a comparison of the two plans.

All 50 states and the District of Columbia sponsor at least one type of 529 plan. In addition, some private colleges and universities sponsor a prepaid tuition plan. College savings plans allow account holders to establish an account for the student (the beneficiary) to pay for qualified college expenses. The college savings plans are usually managed by a mutual fund company and offer many different investment options as well as state tax advantages.

certificates of deposit Certificates of deposit (CDs), or *time deposits,* are instruments that require the investor to deposit a specific sum of money that is then held until a designated time in the future. Most common time periods range from 3 to 60 months (five years). Financial institutions usually pay a higher rate of interest for longer time periods. These rates are normally higher than savings or checking account interest rates.

529 plan
funds set aside for post-secondary education expenses

certificate of deposit (CD)
an instrument issued by a bank that guarantees the payment of a fixed interest rate for holding a sum of money until a designated time in the future

▼ **FIGURE** 4.1

Financial instruments introduced at the Dependent Life Stage

Savings accounts
529 plans/college savings plans
Certificates of deposit

Dependent Life Stage (Age <16)

▼ **FIGURE** 4.2

A comparison of prepaid tuition and college savings plans

Prepaid Tuition Plan	College Savings Plan
Locks in tuition prices at eligible public and private colleges and universities.	No lock on college costs.
All plans cover tuition and mandatory fees only. Some plans allow you to purchase a room and board option or use excess tuition credits for other qualified expenses.	Covers all "qualified higher education expenses," including: • Tuition • Room & board • Mandatory fees • Books, computers (if required)
Most establish lump sum and installment payments prior to purchase based on the age of the beneficiary and the number of years of college tuition purchased.	Many plans have contribution limits in excess of $200,000.
Many state plans are guaranteed or backed by the state.	No state guarantee. Most investment options are subject to market risk. Your investment may make no profit or even decline in value.
Most plans have an age/grade limit for the beneficiary.	No age limits. Open to adults and children.
Most state plans require either the owner or the beneficiary of the plan to be a state resident.	No residency requirement. However, nonresidents may only be able to purchase some plans through financial advisers or brokers.
Most plans have a limited enrollment period.	Enrollment is open all year.

Source: Smart Saving for College, FINRA.

> "There are three faithful friends—an old wife, an old dog, and ready money."
>
> —BEN FRANKLIN *(1706–1790)*

financialfitness:
JUST THE FACTS

Tuition Dollars

Research 529 plans by going to www.collegesavings.org, where you can find the different types of investments and investment providers. Investments can range from safe to risky with a wide range of projected returns. The closer you are to using the funds, the less risk you should have in your 529 plan.

Certificates of deposit usually require a minimum opening amount, commonly ranging from $500 to $1,000. Many CDs have a fixed rate of interest, and there are usually substantial penalties for cashing in the CD early. These penalties can range from the equivalent of one month to one year of interest that you would have otherwise earned.

Certificates of deposit are good investment instruments for establishing a solid savings foundation. If you know you will not need to use the money for a given time frame, investing in a CD is a safe way to earn interest in the meantime. For example, if you have $5,000 in your savings account that you are going to use in two years for college, a safe investment would be to put that money into a 24-month certificate of deposit.

Independent Life Stage (Age 16–24)

At 16, you can get a job and a driver's license and take responsibility for some of your expenses. Sixteen is a good age to start managing your personal finances. You should already have a savings account and you might have some certificates of deposit. At this stage you may want to add some additional financial instruments, such as a checking account with an ATM card, an individual retirement account, and perhaps a credit card. You also may need to take out loans for education and/or transportation. Other financial instrument options to consider during this personal finance life stage are listed in Figure 4.3.

checking accounts The next financial instrument you need is a **checking account**. A checking account is an account that allows the holder to write checks against funds deposited in the account. In Section 4.2 we will explore checking and share draft accounts, including how to write a check (and what makes it a *negotiable instrument*), how to balance your checking account, types of checking accounts (as well as *ATM* and *debit cards*), and overdraft protection. You will use a checking account throughout your financial life stages. Failing to pay close attention to the checks you write and the withdrawals you make will get you into serious trouble.

electronic (Internet) banking and bill payment services As you become liable for more bills and use your checking account more often, you will want to have access to your account through electronic banking and bill payment services. Electronic banking allows you to check your account balances, make loan payments, transfer money from one account to another, and look at your bank statements from

▼ **FIGURE 4.3**

Financial instrument options introduced during the Independent Life Stage

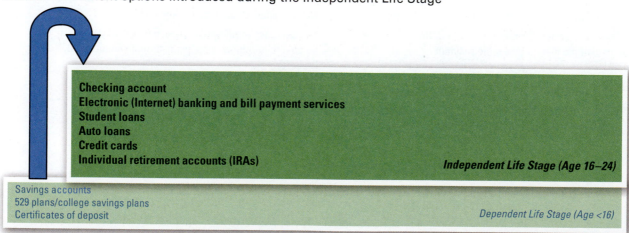

Checking account
Electronic (Internet) banking and bill payment services
Student loans
Auto loans
Credit cards
Individual retirement accounts (IRAs)

Independent Life Stage (Age 16–24)

Savings accounts
529 plans/college savings plans
Certificates of deposit

Dependent Life Stage (Age <16)

Paying bills online can save you time and money.

the comfort of your own home via the Internet and your computer. There are usually no charges for this service from your bank. Many electronic banking services allow you to download your bank statements, see what checks have cleared, and import this information directly into a money management software tool (such as Quicken or www.mint.com).

Bill payment services allow you to pay your bills electronically through your home computer and are usually associated with your bank's electronic banking system. These systems eliminate the need to write checks, buy stamps, and mail bills. By setting up automatic bill payments, you are authorizing the bank to transfer money electronically from your checking account to the bill you specify. Many of your bills can also be paid electronically from the payee company's website, where you can authorize the company to withdraw a specified amount from your bank account on specified dates.

student loans

At the time you attend college, you may not have saved enough money to cover all of your college expenses; therefore, you may need to borrow money. There are three major categories of student loans: (1) federal student loans, which are made directly to the student; (2) federal student loans, which are made to the parents; and (3) private student loans, which may be made to either the student or the parents. We will cover student loans in more depth in Chapter 5.

auto loans

During the Independent Life Stage, you most likely will take out your first auto loan to purchase an automobile or motorcycle. A bank, credit union, or finance company will let you borrow money to purchase a vehicle. When you borrow money to purchase a vehicle, the bank will use the vehicle as **collateral** to secure the loan. If you do not pay your loan on time, the bank has the right to take the vehicle and sell it, with the proceeds going toward the remaining balance of your loan. We will cover auto loans in greater detail in Chapter 7.

individual retirement accounts (Roth and traditional IRAs)

It is never too early to start saving and planning for retirement. Once you have a paying job where you receive a tax form, you can be like Smart Sam and Dedicated Dave in Chapter 2 and start making contributions into an **individual retirement account (IRA)**.

The Internal Revenue Service (IRS) requires that you have earned income before you can contribute to an IRA. Earned income includes all the taxable income and wages you receive from working either for yourself or for a business. If you are working your way through high school or college and/or have a summer job, you can contribute to an IRA.

Contributions to a *traditional IRA* reduce your taxable income and are known as "pretax" contributions. The money you contribute grows **tax-deferred**. With a traditional IRA, you pay taxes on the money you withdraw in the year you withdraw the money. Contributions to a *Roth IRA* are made after you pay taxes on your income. The money you contribute grows tax-free and withdrawals are usually tax-free, unlike the traditional IRA. There are income limits and restrictions on who can contribute to an IRA, as well as a maximum amount you can contribute per year. You cannot withdraw money from an IRA without penalty until you reach the age of 59½. We will discuss retirement accounts in more detail in Chapter 16.

credit cards During the Independent Life Stage, you are likely to receive your first credit card. Credit cards are like debit cards, except that instead of transferring money directly out of your checking account, as with a debit transaction, with each credit card transaction you are actually borrowing money from a bank. The bank then issues a statement when the money has to be repaid. Credit cards allow you to buy now and pay later. The issuing bank must approve you in order for you to receive a credit card. Once approved, the bank issues a *revolving line of credit,* for example $1,000, where you can charge up to $1,000 to be repaid. The bank will charge interest on the outstanding portion if you do not repay the complete amount when billed for your purchases. Credit cards are useful financial tools; however, it is very easy to overspend with a credit card. Chapter 5 will cover credit cards in greater detail.

Early Family Life Stage (Age 25–40)

In the Early Family Life Stage, you will build on your previous accounts from the Dependent and Independent Life Stages. Additionally, you most likely will add a 401(k) retirement plan, a mortgage loan, a second mortgage, a home equity line of credit, investment accounts, and—if you have children or are considering going to graduate school—a 529 plan. Also, you may be financially secure enough to consider making other investments. The financial instrument options introduced at this personal finance life stage are listed in Figure 4.4.

401(k) plan Starting a career as a full-time employee, you may be offered an opportunity to participate in a **401(k) plan**. A 401(k) plan is an employer-sponsored retirement plan and is similar in many ways to a traditional IRA. Employees choose a percentage of their salary to contribute to the 401(k) plan. This contribution is pretax; therefore, it reduces the taxable salary of the employee and the 401(k) grows tax-deferred. The employee cannot withdraw from his or her 401(k) plan until age 59½ without penalty. All withdrawals are taxable.

Many employers match their employees' contributions up to a specified amount. As an example, your employer might match your contributions up to 6%. If you contribute 6% of your salary to the 401(k), the employer also will contribute 6% of your salary, making the total contribution 12% of your salary. If you choose to contribute only 4% of your salary, the employer also will contribute only 4%. In this case, you will miss out on 2% of the employer match, and, additionally, your 401(k) will not grow as fast. Chapter 11, "Investment Basics," and Chapter 16, "Retirement and Estate Planning," cover 401(k) plans in more detail.

▼ **FIGURE 4.4**

Financial instrument options introduced at the Early Family Life Stage

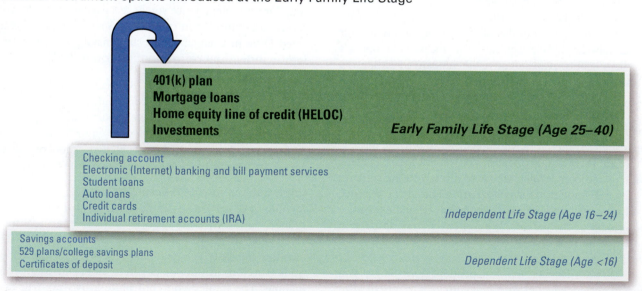

401(k) plan
Mortgage loans
Home equity line of credit (HELOC)
Investments
Early Family Life Stage (Age 25–40)

Checking account
Electronic (Internet) banking and bill payment services
Student loans
Auto loans
Credit cards
Individual retirement accounts (IRA)
Independent Life Stage (Age 16–24)

Savings accounts
529 plans/college savings plans
Certificates of deposit
Dependent Life Stage (Age <16)

mortgage loans As you establish yourself in your career and life, you might want to buy a home. **Mortgage** loans are designed to allow you to borrow 80% or more of the value of a house and pay it back over a period of up to 30 years. There are three main types of mortgages: (1) *fixed rate*, in which the interest rate is fixed for the life of the loan; (2) *adjustable rate*, in which the interest rate on the mortgage can be adjusted every one, three, five, or seven years, depending on the interest rate adjustment period selected; and (3) *balloon* , in which the rate is fixed and the entire loan comes due in three, five, or seven years, depending on the term selected. Mortgage loan payments can be made over a period of 10 to 30 years.

Mortgage loans are secured by the house or *real property*. If you default on the loan, the mortgage holder (usually a bank) can foreclose on the property and sell it to recover the amount owed on the loan. **Foreclosure** is the legal process where the lender can seize and sell the property as stipulated in the terms of the mortgage contract. It is usually the lender's last option because of the time and expense involved in the foreclosure process. Chapter 7 covers mortgage loans in more detail.

home equity loans and home equity lines of credit Home equity loans and home equity lines of credit (HELOC) are loans secured by the equity in your house. **Home equity** is the value of the house minus any loans secured by the house. For example, say your house is worth $150,000 and you have $80,000 left to pay on your mortgage. If you do not have any other loans against your house, your home equity is $70,000 ($150,000 − $80,000 = $70,000). If you borrow against that $70,000, the lender will place a second mortgage against your home, using your house as collateral. Home equity loans are also referred to as *second mortgage loans*. If you do not pay on your home equity loan, that lender can foreclose on your house, just like the lender with the primary mortgage. Home equity loans can help to finance home repairs, remodeling, or any major purchase. A traditional home equity loan has a fixed rate, fixed payment, and a fixed maturity date.

A **home equity line of credit (HELOC)** is a line of credit secured by a mortgage on a home and is similar to a credit card. If you receive a $30,000 HELOC, the lender will place a mortgage against your house for $30,000. If you need money, you can advance yourself money by writing a check on the HELOC account. You are normally only charged interest on the amount you borrow. You do have to make minimum payments, but the amount you pay back is available for you to borrow again. Home equity loans

financialfitness:
NUMBERS GAME

Right-Sizing, Safe-Sizing

Over a million homes were lost to foreclosure in 2008. In July 2009, the number of foreclosures reached an all-time high: one in every 355 homes nationwide received default notices, auction notices, or were seized by creditors. Losing your home to an auction block is devastating. The lesson learned from the real-estate bust is to take a hard look at what you call home. *Right-size* your dream home to be sure it is your "Home, Sweet Home"—not a source of panic, struggle, and despair.

and lines of credit are covered in more detail in Chapter 7, "Auto and Home Loans."

investments As you begin to make more money than you spend and have a good foundation in savings, you will want to consider different investments that could offer a higher return than a savings account or a certificate of deposit. Investments usually carry some risk that you could lose part or all of your investment, but they also offer higher potential returns for taking that risk. Investments hopefully provide a way for your money to grow faster than the rate of inflation, thereby increasing your wealth.

Investments can range from stocks, bonds, mutual funds, and real estate to derivatives, futures, options, and reverse default swaps. Section 4 covers basic investments in more detail. This book does not cover derivatives, futures, options, and reverse default swaps, as they are covered in more advanced classes in finance. Reverse default swaps are complicated investment vehicles and were among the leading contributors to the 2008 financial crisis.

Empty Nest Life Stage (Age 41–65)

As the kids leave the house for college or start life on their own, you reach the Empty Nest Life Stage. In this stage you are generally reaching the top of your earnings capacity

reverse mortgage

a loan secured by the value of one's home whereby the homeowner receives either a monthly or a lump sum from the lender; the loan is paid in full from the proceeds of the sale of the house when the homeowner dies or moves out of the house

and have fewer payments than ever before. You may have paid the house off, and you may no longer have any car payments because you can pay cash for your automobiles.

In this life stage, you may be using all of the accounts previously mentioned (see Figure 4.5). You may use a mortgage loan to purchase a vacation or retirement home. You may decide to establish a 529 plan for your grandchildren or use a 529 plan to further your own education.

You will continue to have savings, certificates of deposit, IRAs, and 401(k) plans; and now you may have the financial ability to contribute much more to your investments. Section 4, Wealth Accumulation, covers different investments and investment strategies for this stage in more detail.

Retirement Life Stage (Age 66+)

The Retirement Life Stage is when you reach financial independence. You no longer need to work for money and you are free to retire from your primary occupation. While you may continue to work, it will not be about the money, but about your passion to do what you have always wanted to do. You may be able to afford the time to volunteer for Habitat for Humanity or to help out at your local school or church. You may want to spend your time pursuing a sport or hobby.

In this stage of life, you will have to select when to take payment on your Social Security. You may be offsetting your retirement with withdrawals from your 401(k), IRA accounts, and other investments. You may find you need to increase your income from these sources. If you own your home and there are no liens on it, you may consider using a reverse mortgage (see Figure 4.6).

A **reverse mortgage** is a loan to a homeowner that uses the house as collateral and disperses the proceeds from the loan to the homeowner either monthly or in a lump sum. Instead of payments to the bank, in this type of loan the bank advances loan proceeds to the individual. The loan is paid off from the sale of the house when the homeowner dies or moves out of the house. All the interest on the loan is added to the lien and is paid off with the sale of the home.

▼ **FIGURE** 4.5

Financial instrument options extended through the Empty Nest Life Stage

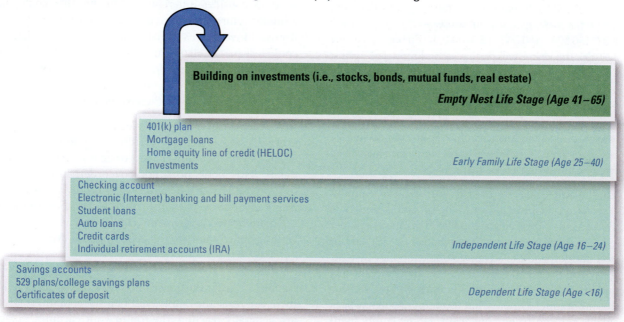

Building on investments (i.e., stocks, bonds, mutual funds, real estate)

Empty Nest Life Stage (Age 41–65)

401(k) plan
Mortgage loans
Home equity line of credit (HELOC)
Investments

Early Family Life Stage (Age 25–40)

Checking account
Electronic (Internet) banking and bill payment services
Student loans
Auto loans
Credit cards
Individual retirement accounts (IRA)

Independent Life Stage (Age 16–24)

Savings accounts
529 plans/college savings plans
Certificates of deposit

Dependent Life Stage (Age <16)

Financial instrument options introduced at the Retirement Life Stage

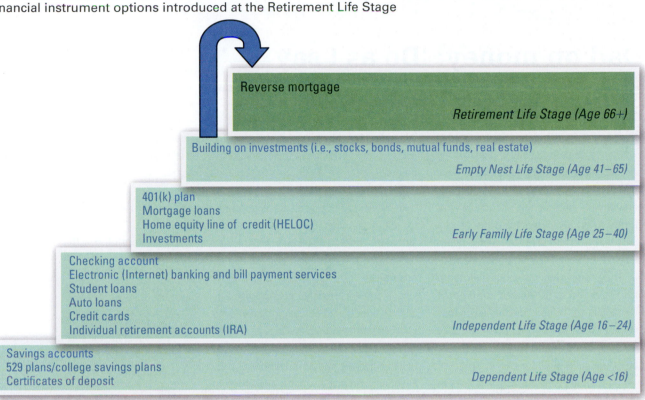

Reverse mortgage

Retirement Life Stage (Age 66+)

Building on investments (i.e., stocks, bonds, mutual funds, real estate)

Empty Nest Life Stage (Age 41–65)

401(k) plan
Mortgage loans
Home equity line of credit (HELOC)
Investments

Early Family Life Stage (Age 25–40)

Checking account
Electronic (Internet) banking and bill payment services
Student loans
Auto loans
Credit cards
Individual retirement accounts (IRA)

Independent Life Stage (Age 16–24)

Savings accounts
529 plans/college savings plans
Certificates of deposit

Dependent Life Stage (Age <16)

Being comfortable during retirement is important, and requires plenty of advance planning.

Making $ense

4.1 At what personal finance life stage should you start a savings plan for college?

4.2 What type of financial instrument encourages saving for future college expenses?

4.3 Which time deposits usually pay a higher rate of interest when you agree to deposit your money for a longer time period?

4.4 Explain how a home equity line of credit (HELOC) works.

Dad on money: 'Do as I say . . .'

Over the span of a lifetime, we learn more about saving and investing from personal experience than from any expert. In my case, the most formative experiences have been the lessons learned by watching my parents with their money, especially later in their lives. My parents are the first to admit that when it comes to handling their money, they haven't been great role models. They rarely thought about their long-term finances and allowed credit-card bills to pile up. When regular paychecks stopped, they were trapped, especially later in life when it became harder for my dad to land a new job. . . .

. . . It's one thing to lose a job when you're younger, but as you age the prejudices against hiring older workers make it harder to land a job. And frankly, the older you get, the pickier you are about what you

want to do. Eventually, my father landed in real estate, where he had a knack for spotting good investment opportunities for others.

It was his contrarian eye for real estate that provided the biggest positive lesson for me. In the late 1990s, real estate was still moribund and the stock market was booming. But my father helped me see an opportunity to be an owner and a landlord in a quiet Brooklyn neighborhood. A decade later it paid off both for me and my children far better than any mutual fund.

In the meantime, my parents continued to be hamstrung by their credit-card debts. Eventually, my sister, Debby, and I were in a position to help dig them out. Today, they live with my sister and help take care of her young children. In many ways, the lessons I've learned from my parents are pretty

basic. But they're the foundation on which more complicated financial thinking can be built. "Plan far ahead," my parents say. "A 10-year plan is of no avail. A 20-year plan is insufficient. A 50-year plan is what you need, and ignore the 'charge it' and 'cash it in' impulse. Teach your children to do the same."

TOM LAURICELLA, "Dad on Money: 'Do as I Say . . .'", *The Wall Street Journal*, June 20, 2010. Reprinted with permission.

Questions

1 What financial instrument could the parents have tapped that might have provided for a better outcome?

2 What take-away lessons does this article provide you as it relates to the first four chapters of this textbook?

Reverse mortgages allow you to tap the equity in your home, so you can live a more comfortable retirement and still remain in your home without making payments. However, there are usually high up-front costs associated with reverse mortgages. Alternatives to reverse mortgages would be to sell the house and move into a less expensive residence or to take a home equity line of credit (HELOC) on the residence and use the funds as needed. You should weigh all the options before choosing to enter into a reverse mortgage.

4.2 CHECKING AND SHARE DRAFT ACCOUNTS

■ ■ **LO 4-2** Use and efficiently manage checking and share draft accounts.

Formally known as demand accounts, *checking accounts* and *share draft accounts* are two of the most commonly

used financial instruments. At a **commercial bank**, your checking account is referred to as a **demand deposit account**. At a **credit union**, it is referred to as a **share draft account**. The demand deposit account really describes your account's intended purpose. You can deposit money and then "demand" that it be withdrawn or given to another party through a written check, draft, debit card, or electronic payment. These are known as third party transactions. The share draft account is a demand account at a credit union.

The Negotiable Instrument

When you think about it, checks are amazing instruments. A check is a written order for a bank to pay a specific sum of money from your account to another party. Checks are **negotiable instruments**, which means another person can cash, or negotiate, the check. That person can also transfer the rights to another person, who can cash it, deposit it, or negotiate it to another person, who can access your account for the specific sum of money.

A negotiable instrument, defined in the Uniform Commercial Code under Article 3, has to be dated, payable for a specific amount of money, signed by the person who owns the account, and payable to someone or some company. As you can see in Figure 4.7, there is a place for you to enter:

1. The date

2. An unconditional order to pay

3. A specific sum of money, and

4. Your signature

As shown in Figure 4.7, a check will also include the bank's routing number (ABA check routing number) as well as the account number. Here are a few pointers to avoid having your check altered from how you wrote it:

- In the currency box, put a dollar sign ($) in front of the amount to prevent people from changing your check from $500 to $1,500.

- The written amount is the legal amount. To keep someone from altering the check, always start to write out the amount on the far left-hand side of the check, and then draw a line so no one can alter the amount.

- The memo line is for your own records so you can remember why you wrote the check.

- Always date and sign the check.

Once you have written a check, made a deposit, taken money out of an ATM, or used your debit card, it is very important to record the transaction in your check register or with your money management program (e.g., Quicken or www.mint.com). Failure to record your transactions can lead to inaccurate records and overdraft fees—the charges banks assess for taking out more money than you have. These overdraft fees can be greater than $30 per overdraft item.

Balancing Your Checking Account

Every month your financial institution will send you a statement summarizing your checking or share draft

▼ FIGURE 4.7

Example of a written check

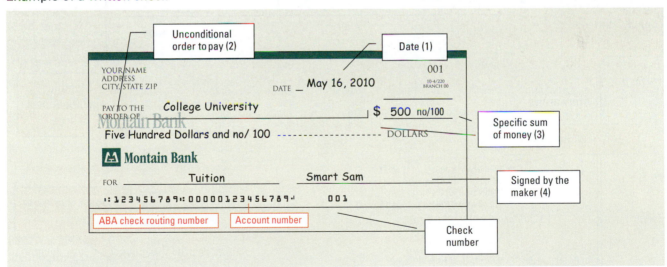

—Countless first-time checking account users

account activity. This statement (see Figure 4.8) will show your beginning balance and any check, ATM, and debit card transactions. It also will show any deposits to your account as well as your ending balance. You can use this information to balance your checking account. Always check for errors or evidence of identity theft.

keeping track of your transactions

To keep track of the deposits you make and the checks you write, as well as any debit card and ATM withdrawals and fees charged by your bank, you will need to record these transactions in your check register. For each transaction, always record the type, date, and amount of the transaction and maintain a running balance (see Figure 4.9, Steps 1–3).

reconciling your checking account

Reconcile your checking account every month to be certain there are no errors. Begin by marking every checking account register item that appears on your statement. If there is an item on your statement that is not listed in your check register, determine if it is accurate. If the item is correct, add it in your check register. If the item is incorrect, call your financial institution to have it investigated.

The steps to reconciling your checking account are as follows:

1. Mark every checking account register item that appears on your statement. If there is an item on your statement that is not listed in your check register, determine if it

▼ **FIGURE 4.8**

Sample checking account statement

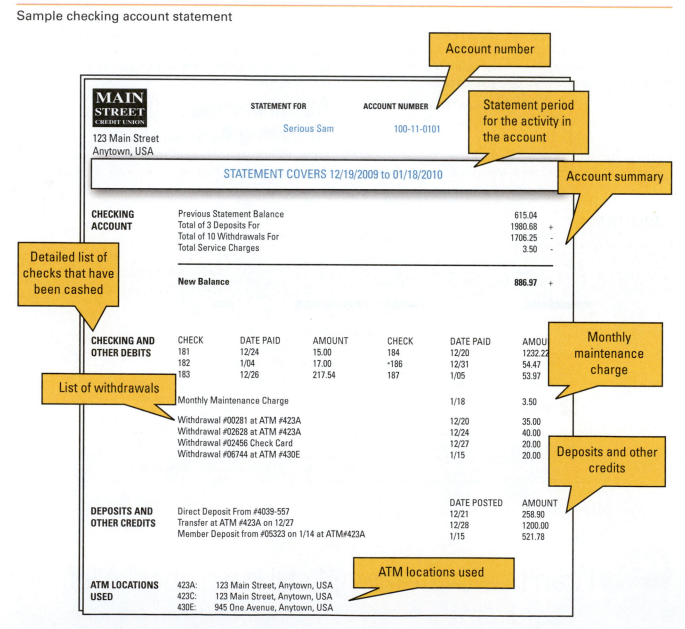

Sample checking account register

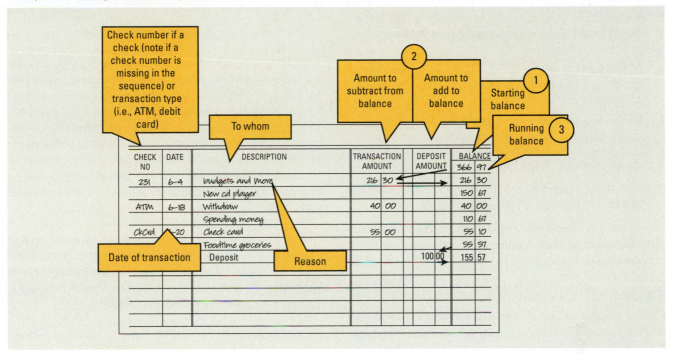

doing the
MATH

4.1 Keeping Track of Your Checks

You opened a checking account with a $500 deposit on the 1st of the month. The only other transactions are one check written for a textbook ($117) and a $50 ATM withdrawal, both of which took place on the 25th.

Number or Code	Date	Transaction Description	Payment Amount	√	Fee	Deposit Amount	Balance

What is your account's current balance?

is accurate. If the item is correct, add it in your check register. If the item is incorrect, call your financial institution to have it investigated.

2. Your monthly statement should include a reconciliation worksheet. Enter the ending balance shown on your statement (see Figure 4.10).

3. List the deposits and other credits that are in your checking account register but not listed on your statement. Add these to your ending balance.

4. List the checks, ATM withdrawals, fees, and other debits in your checking account register that are not listed on the statement. Subtract these from your balance in Step 3 to get your new ending balance.

5. Write the ending balance in your checking account register.

Maintaining a checkbook register and reconciling your checking account each month will help keep you from overdrawing your account.

Types of Checking Accounts

Checking accounts provide versatility in how to pay people and businesses. Checking accounts can save you money by not having to purchase money orders or cashier's checks or wire money. However, checking accounts can cost a lot of money in overdraft fees and other charges if you write checks in excess of the balance in the account. Therefore, it's important to closely examine how you are going to use a checking account and discuss your requirements with an

account service representative at your local financial institution. Shopping around at other banks or credit unions will help you find the best account to meet your needs. Let's look at some common types of checking accounts to help determine which account might be best for you.

basic checking Basic checking is the no-frills account for someone without a large balance who needs to pay bills by check or electronic bill payment. To avoid monthly maintenance fees, you might need to have your paycheck directly deposited into the account or maintain a minimum balance. You are also generally limited in the number of checks you can write and/or the number of ATM transactions you are allowed per month. If you exceed that number, there will be a fee for each item in excess of your limit.

free checking Free checking has no monthly service charge or per-item fee regardless of your balance. With some free checking accounts, you cannot have overdraft protection. Be very aware of all the fees that could apply if you are opening a free checking account.

interest-bearing checking Interest-bearing checking accounts pay interest on your balance; however, you usually have to meet many requirements for the bank to pay that interest. Some of the requirements include: keeping a high minimum balance (over $1,000), having your paycheck directly deposited, and using your debit card as a credit card (non-PIN transactions) a minimum number of

▼ FIGURE 4.10

Sample checking account reconciliation worksheet

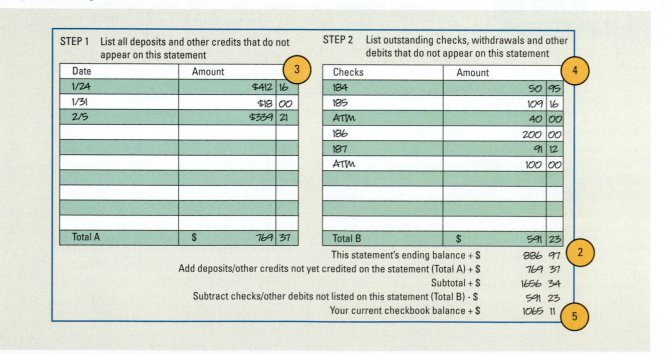

STEP 1 List all deposits and other credits that do not appear on this statement ③

Date	Amount	
1/24	$412	16
1/31	$18	00
2/5	$339	21
Total A	$ 769	37

STEP 2 List outstanding checks, withdrawals and other debits that do not appear on this statement ④

Checks	Amount	
184	50	95
185	109	16
ATM	40	00
186	200	00
187	91	12
ATM	100	00
Total B	$ 591	23

This statement's ending balance + $ 886 97 ②
Add deposits/other credits not yet credited on the statement (Total A) + $ 769 37
Subtotal + $ 1656 34
Subtract checks/other debits not listed on this statement (Total B) - $ 591 23
Your current checkbook balance + $ 1065 11 ⑤

times per month. Again, be very aware of all the fees and requirements before opening up this type of account.

ATM and Debit Cards

Automated teller machine (ATM) cards are also known as *bank cards* or *cash cards*. Issued by a bank or credit union, they link directly to a checking, share draft, and/or savings account. ATM cards *do not* carry a credit card logo, like Visa or MasterCard, and they must be used with a personal identification number (PIN). These cards can be used at ATMs to withdraw cash, to transfer money between two accounts associated with the card (checking and savings), and to make deposits. ATM cards are also accepted by many businesses with the necessary PIN pads. ATM cards are giving way to the more popular debit card.

Debit cards are rapidly taking the place of checks, cash, and ATM cards. These cards carry a credit card logo, like Visa or MasterCard, and are tied to checking or share draft accounts. With your authorization (using a PIN number), they can be used at a retailer to transfer funds from your account to the merchant's account. Debit cards also can be used to take money out of an ATM.

Without using a PIN number, you can also use the debit card like a check, transferring money from your account to the retailer's account for the amount purchased. Using the card without a PIN number is also similar to using a credit card, in that you have to sign for transactions above a specific dollar amount. Unlike a credit card, where the use of the card means you are borrowing money to be repaid later, a debit card transfers the money directly out of your checking account. One caveat: If you don't record every transaction in your check register, you can quickly overdraw your account.

Overdraft Protection

Just in case you make a math mistake, for example, add instead of subtract or forget to write down an ATM withdrawal, debit card transaction, or check, you will want to have overdraft protection. Overdraft protection will either transfer money from a savings account to a checking account or advance money from a line of credit loan to cover an overdraft. You usually have to pay fees and/or interest, but these fees are less than the overdraft fee itself. Overdraft protection benefits you in three ways:

1. *It can save you money in overdraft fees and merchant fees.* As we mentioned, the bank may charge anywhere from $20 to $50 for a single overdraft. In addition, it is not uncommon for the business to which you have

doing the MATH

4.2 Reconciling a Checking Account

You need to reconcile a brand new checking account opened with a $500 deposit on the 1st of the month. The only transactions have been one check written for a textbook for $117 and one $50 ATM withdrawal, both of which took place on the 25th. Neither transaction appears on your statement, which only shows the opening deposit of $500 as well as a $500 ending balance.

Step 1: List all deposits and other credits that do not appear on this statement			Step 2: List outstanding checks, withdrawals, and other debits that do not appear on this statement	
Date	Amount		Checks	Amount
Total A	$		Total B	$
This statement's ending balance: Add deposits/other credits not yet on this statement (Total A)				
Subtotal: Subtract checks/other debits not listed on this statement (Total B)				
Your current checking account balance				

In reconciling your account, what should you show as a balance?

financialfitness:

JUST THE FACTS

Checking ChexSystems

ChexSystems is a check verification service and a credit reporting agency that collects and distributes information to banks on people who have bounced a check or cheated a bank in some way. Approximately 80% of banks and credit unions subscribe to ChexSystems as a way to protect themselves from people who open checking accounts and write bad checks. Negative information is maintained for up to five years. You can receive your ChexSystem report once a year at www.consumerdebit.com/consumerinfo/us/en/chexsystems/report/index.htm. You can also find out more information at the ChexSystems website (www.consumerdebit.com) or at the bankrate.com website (www.bankrate.com/finance/checking/chexsystems.aspx).

$ense Making

4.5 How does an ATM card differ from a debit card?

4.6 Why is it important to maintain a check register?

4.7 Why do you need to reconcile your check register with your bank statement each month?

4.8 What advantages does overdraft protection provide?

written the check to charge you $30 or more for writing a bad check.

2. *Overdraft protection can save your reputation.* Anyone can make a mistake, but you don't want to get a reputation for writing bad checks and have your checks refused by businesses. If you have too many overdrafts, the bank or credit union will actually close your account and report you to ChexSystems. This also makes it difficult to open another checking account with a different financial institution.

3. *It can save you time.* It takes time to contact your bank and the business or person to whom you wrote the check. It takes time to find the mistake in your checking account. It takes time to ask for a loan from family, friends, or a bank to cover your overdraft.

4.3 FINDING THE RIGHT FINANCIAL INSTITUTION

■■ **LO 4-3** Assess financial institutions and accounts to determine which ones best meet your needs.

There are many things to consider when choosing a financial institution. You have to decide what factors are important and then choose the financial institution that best meets your needs. For most people, the most important features to consider are convenience, products and services, and cost.

Financial Institutions

There are three major classifications of financial institutions: commercial banks, credit unions, and savings and loan associations. They serve as **financial intermediaries**, accepting money for deposits and then lending out the money to others.

commercial banks Commercial banks come in all sizes, from very large banks to smaller community banks. They are owned by stockholders and are in business to make money for their stockholders.

The largest banks in the United States are Bank of America, Wells Fargo, JPMorgan Chase, and Citibank. These banks have many branch locations throughout the United States and offer a large number of products and services. Many of these large banks have central decision making for loans and therefore are not as flexible in their lending practices as local community banks. The largest banks also have ATMs throughout the United States. If you travel a lot, you might consider it advantageous to bank with one of the larger banks.

By contrast, community banks are usually locally owned by families or community member stockholders who live in the area. They may not have the latest and greatest in technology or the largest lineup of products or services, but they usually make their loan decisions locally.

credit unions Credit unions are financial cooperatives originally established for people who have a "common bond." The typical common bond is place of employment. For example, all of the employees and students at the University of Iowa can form a credit union where only employees or students and family members of the University of Iowa can conduct business. With this common bond, there are no stockholders, but it is considered a *member owned,* not-for-profit institution. The depositors of a credit union, considered members, receive dividends based on the amount of money in an account rather than interest on their deposit accounts. Being not-for-profit institutions, credit unions, in most states, do not have to pay federal or state income taxes. This allows credit unions to offer higher interest rates and lower loan rates and to take greater risk on loans than commercial banks.

Many credit unions have recently become "community" credit unions, allowing anyone who lives in the market area to become a member. Thus, community credit unions have dropped the common bond requirement, other than living in the market area. For example, to be a member of the University of Iowa Community Credit Union (www.uiccu.org), you have to: (1) live or work in one of 15 counties in Iowa, (2) be a relative of a current member, or (3) be a former student or alumnus of the University of Iowa. Credit unions offer many of the same products as banks and are competitive in pricing.

savings institutions Savings institutions are also referred to as savings and loan associations (S&L), thrift institutions, and savings banks. They were originally designed for offering savings accounts and providing mortgage loans for homeowners. S&Ls were deregulated in the 1980s, which allowed them to make consumer and commercial loans and offer products and services similar to commercial banks.

Savings institutions are for-profit companies owned by stockholders, like commercial banks. Most savings institutions are locally owned and serve a small market area, like community banks.

Insured Savings

Savings accounts at banks are insured for up to $250,000, based on ownership by the Federal Deposit Insurance Corporation (FDIC); likewise, savings accounts at credit unions are also insured for up to $250,000, based on ownership by the National Credit Union Share Insurance Fund (NCUSIF), an arm of the National Credit Union Administration (NCUA). This means that if a bank or credit union goes bankrupt, the FDIC or the NCUA will take over the financial institution and pay out the deposits up to $250,000 based on ownership.

financial intermediaries financial institutions that accept money for deposits and then lend the money to others

This $250,000 insurance ceiling on accounts is effective through December 31, 2013. On January 1, 2014, the standard insurance amount will return to $100,000 per depositor for all account categories except for IRAs and other specified retirement accounts, which will remain at $250,000 per depositor. This temporary increase of FDIC and NCUA insurance was authorized through the Emergency Economic Stabilization Act of 2008. For more specific information, contact your financial institution or visit www.ncua.gov or www.fdic.gov. Look for the FDIC sign (see Figure 4.11) or the NCUA sign (see Figure 4.12 on the next page) on the outside of the financial institution to make sure your account is insured.

Convenience

Before computer banking and direct deposit, people received actual paychecks from their employers. To make

> ## A bank is a place that will lend you money if you can prove that you don't need it.
> —BOB HOPE, *American comedian and actor (1903–2003)*

a deposit or a withdrawal, they had to make a trip to the bank. As a result, the major criteria for selecting a bank usually included: (1) the nearness of the bank to one's place of employment or home, and (2) its hours of operation. Today banking has become more convenient, with online banking, electronic bill pay, ATM and debit cards, automatic withdrawals to pay bills, and the automatic deposit of paychecks.

Now many people only go into a bank to open an account and to deposit their loose change. To be where customers are, many banks have opened satellite offices in grocery stores. We now define convenience as 24-hour online banking, call centers where you can talk to a customer service representative 24/7, accessible ATM machines, and the ability to use any ATM machine without a fee. You may actually be banking with your home bank, hundreds of miles away from your school, and have full access to your account via electronic banking.

Convenience in banking may be as close as your cell phone. If you have a smartphone, you may be able to download applications to track your spending and have access to online banking to pay bills, check balances, and make transfers. Check to see if you have access to your financial institution via your phone.

▼ **FIGURE 4.11**

Logo identifying a bank or savings institution insured by the FDIC

Source: www.FDIC.gov

▼ **FIGURE 4.12**

Logo identifying a credit unit insured by the NCUA

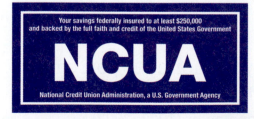

Source: www.NCUA.gov

Products and Service

As we saw earlier in the chapter, different financial instruments may be more appropriate depending on one's particular life stage. While institutions may have many similar offerings, one institution might pay a higher rate of interest while another might allow more checks and debits out of a checking account without a fee. When shopping around for a bank, compare the products that will best fit your financial needs. (See Worksheet 4.3 for help in comparing your options.) To compare the products and services offered by the banks you are considering, create a table that lists the products and services for each banking option. This enables you to do a side-by-side comparison, as well as rank each option based upon how well they meet your needs. You can then more easily choose the institution that best satisfies the majority of your priority needs (see Figure 4.13).

For most people, service has become the most important factor for selecting a financial institution. An important consideration is to find a bank that will lend you money. All financial institutions will accept deposits, but there is a possibility they may not lend you money. The personal service you receive and the bankers you know are important factors when it comes to borrowing money.

Some financial institutions offer private banking to customers who have substantial investments, net worth, and income. These customers receive a **private banker** whose job is to know these customers and take care of all their financial needs. Banks identify these customers as some of their most valuable and profitable clients, so the financial institution goes above and beyond to provide exceptional customer service to them.

No matter what your life stage, it is good to get to know your financial service provider so you can get the personal service you deserve. Banking has become a very competitive industry and financial institutions are always looking for new customers and ways to better serve existing customers. Take time to go in to your financial institution and build a relationship with a customer service representative and/or loan officer.

Cost

Everyone wants to get a fair deal on prices and no one likes to pay extra fees. However, you should realize that financial institutions need to cover their costs and make money to stay in business. Thus, financial institutions have to increase their fees to make up for declining profits in interest income. You wouldn't expect to go into a grocery store, fill up your cart, and walk out the door without paying. Likewise, you should expect to pay for the financial products and services you use. Nevertheless, you should be aware of a few important fees in order to minimize charges on your accounts.

Product and service comparison checklist example

Service/Product	Priority Rank (Hi = 1; Lo = 10)	FI 1: Rank (Best =1)	FI 1 Score (Priority Rank × FI 1 Rank)	FI 2: Rank (Best = 1)	FI 2 Score (Priority Rank × FI 2 Rank)
Hours/Evenings/Weekends	10	1	10	1	10
Locations	9	1	9	2	18
Fees/Minimum balance	1	1	1	2	2
Fees/ATM usage	2	1	2	1	2
Interest rate—savings	4	2	8	1	4
Interest rate—checking	3	2	6	1	3
Interest rate—home loans	7	2	14	1	7
Interest rate—auto loans	6	2	12	1	6
Visa/MasterCard available/Annual fee	5	1	5	2	10
Safety deposit box rates	8	1	8	1	8
Total Scores (lowest score best fit)			**75**		**70**

minimum balance Many financial institutions require a minimum balance in an account to avoid monthly maintenance fees. Monthly maintenance fees are charges to cover some of the overhead the bank has, such as the cost of maintaining statements. Check with your financial institution about the minimum required balance to avoid fees, as well as the minimum required balance to earn interest. Keeping your account above the minimum balance can save you money.

transaction costs Financial institutions can impose fees based on the number of transactions on an account. You can incur ATM fees if you exceed a maximum number of withdrawals or if you use an ATM machine not owned by or affiliated with your financial institution. You may be able to avoid the ATM withdrawal fees by getting cash back from a debit card purchase at a retailer.

Financial institutions impose check fees when you purchase your checks. They also may charge a fee when you write checks or you may be limited on the number of checks you can write without a fee. Be aware of the number of checks you write in order to minimize these fees. Financial institutions will offer to order checks for you when opening an account; however, you may be able to order less expensive checks from other sources.

overdraft fees An overdraft can cost up to $50 or more. Some of this fee goes to cover the cost of the overdraft, but the majority of the cost is a punitive charge to keep people

financialfitness:
STOPPING LITTLE LEAKS

Beware of Teaser Rates

When shopping around for the best place to keep your money, be wary of institutions offering teaser rates (i.e., a low rate for the first two months, then dramatically increasing interest rates and/or fees thereafter). You want to pick a bank with good service and products that will give you better returns in the long run (not just two months).

financialfitness:
ACTION ITEM

Deciding Who Pays

When you use a debit card and your PIN number at a retailer, the financial institution pays a small fee to the retailer. When you use a debit card as a credit card and sign for the transaction, the retailer has to pay a small fee to the bank. Every time you use a debit card, you get to decide who pays the cost of the transaction, either the retailer or the bank.

get online!

SCAN HERE for study quizzes for this chapter

Making $ense

4.9 How is a credit union different from a commercial bank or savings and loan?

4.10 What financial competitive edge does a credit union have over a commercial bank or savings and loan?

4.11 Why might you select a small community bank over a national commercial bank?

4.12 What advantage does a large national bank have over a small community bank or credit union?

4.13 What criteria would you use to select a financial institution?

from overdrawing their account. The American banking system works because people trust that checks are good and that they will receive the money indicated on a written check. To help reduce overdraft fees, you might want to establish overdraft protection with your bank. Some financial institutions charge fees for automatic overdraft transfers from savings to checking and/or charge fees and interest for overdraft protection advances from a line of credit.

other fees Check with your financial institution for a list of their fees. When opening an account, the financial institution provides a disclosure of all possible fees. Here is a sampling of the possible fees you may encounter:

- **Stop payment fee:** If a check is lost or stolen, you may want to stop the payment of that check. By calling the financial institution, they can place a stop payment on the check for a fee. However, be prepared to pay a fee of $25 or more to place a stop on a check. You will have to go in to the bank to sign a stop payment request.

- **ATM/Debit card replacement fee:** This fee is the cost to replace a lost, stolen, or damaged ATM/debit card.

- **Coin counting fee:** Most banks will only charge noncustomers to count coins.

- **Deposited item returned:** This fee is charged when a deposited check has to be returned because the person who wrote you the check did not have enough money in his or her account to cover the check.

- **Inactive account fee:** If the account is not active for a specific period of time, a financial institution may charge a fee for not using your account.

- **Money order/cashier checks:** There is a charge to issue a money order or cashier's check. These instruments can take the place of a personal check; because they require the funds to be prepaid, they are a more trusted form of payment than a personal check.

- **Teller fee:** There may be a charge to see a teller in person. If the account is designed for most transactions to be online or via ATM or phone, you may be limited to the number of times you can use a teller to conduct transactions. ■

["Not investing is a surefire way to fail to accumulate the wealth necessary to ensure a sound financial future. Compound interest is a miracle. Time is your friend."]

—JOHN C. BOGLE, *Vanguard Group founder (1929–)*

⮕ LEARN.
In this chapter you learned about several financial products and services, including their features and benefits and how they relate to the personal finance life stages introduced in Chapter 1. You also learned about demand deposit accounts and how to balance a checking account. Finally, you learned about the three major types of financial institutions and how to evaluate which one is best for you.

SUMMARY

■ ■ **LO 4-1** Identify which bank products are the best fit for different personal finance life stages.

The Dependent Life Stage usually involves savings accounts, 529 plans, and certificates of deposit (CDs). At the Independent Stage, individuals explore checking/share draft accounts, electronic (Internet) banking, bill payment services, and possibly college student loans and auto loans. Once you have a paying job, you can start an individual retirement account (IRA) and get a credit card. In the Early Family Stage, you may add a 401(k) retirement plan, mortgage loan, second mortgage, home equity line of credit, and investment accounts; if you have children or are considering going to graduate school, you will want to have a 529 plan. The Empty Nest Stage is typically when your earnings peak; you have fewer payments and are able to contribute much more to your investments. At the Retirement Life Stage, you should no longer need to work for money and should be prepared for Social Security payments. You may be making withdrawals from 401(k) plans, IRA accounts, and investments.

■ ■ **LO 4-2** Use and efficiently manage checking and share draft accounts.

Checking accounts from commercial banks and share draft accounts from credit unions are known as demand deposit accounts; the movement of funds in and out of these accounts occurs via checks, ATM cards, debit cards, and online banking web portals. Record the transactions in a check register and reconcile the account balance once a month to avoid inaccurate records and overdrafts.

■ ■ **LO 4-3** Assess financial institutions and accounts to determine which ones best meet your needs.

There are three major types of financial institutions: commercial banks, credit unions, and savings institutions. Commercial banks specialize in making loans to businesses. Savings institutions specialize in mortgage loans and credit unions offer services to people with a common bond. Stockholders own banks and savings institutions, which are for-profit corporations. Credit unions are member-owned, not-for-profit, cooperative financial institutions—the depositors are the members. Credit unions do not pay federal income tax; therefore, they offer higher deposit rates, lower loan rates, and have the ability to take more risk in lending.

⮕ PLAN & ACT.
As you continue down the road to financial independence and financial freedom, it is important to plan for your future financial needs.

☐ Create a timeline of your goals and match them with the appropriate financial instruments (Worksheet 4.1).

☐ Bring your check register up-to-date (Worksheet 4.2).

☐ Reconcile your check register (Worksheet 4.2).

☐ Evaluate your local financial institutions to assess the best option for you (Worksheet 4.3).

→ EVALUATE. Are you in the right financial institution to meet your current and future needs? Reflect back on your goals from Chapter 1 and decide when you think you will need a vehicle loan, a mortgage loan, or your next student loan. Make sure these goals are reflected in the Goals/Financial Life Stages Itinerary that you create using Worksheet 4.1.

›› GoalTracker

Open your online **GoalTracker** to make notes as to which of the financial instruments support your goals. Assess how you are tracking your progress toward achieving your stated goals. If you are not on track, give thought to what steps you should take to get back on track.

key terms

Automated Teller Machine (ATM)

Certificate of Deposit (CD)

Checking Account

Collateral

Commercial Bank

Credit Union

Debit Card

Demand Deposit Account

Financial Intermediaries

529 Plan

Foreclosure

401(k) Plan

Home Equity

Home Equity Line of Credit (HELOC)

Individual Retirement Account (IRA)

Mortgage

Negotiable Instruments

Private Banker

Reverse Mortgage

Share Draft Account

self-test questions

1. In which life stage should you explore the following financial instruments? *(LO 4-1)*

    a. Savings account
       (1) Dependent
       (2) Independent
       (3) Early Family
       (4) Empty Nest
       (5) Retirement

    b. Home equity line of credit
       (1) Dependent
       (2) Independent
       (3) Early Family
       (4) Empty Nest
       (5) Retirement

    c. Reverse mortgage
       (1) Dependent
       (2) Independent
       (3) Early Family
       (4) Empty Nest
       (5) Retirement

    d. Student loan
       (1) Dependent
       (2) Independent
       (3) Early Family
       (4) Empty Nest
       (5) Retirement

    e. Auto loan
       (1) Dependent
       (2) Independent
       (3) Early Family
       (4) Empty Nest
       (5) Retirement

    f. 401(k) Plan
       (1) Dependent
       (2) Independent
       (3) Early Family
       (4) Empty Nest
       (5) Retirement

    g. Mortgage
       (1) Dependent
       (2) Independent
       (3) Early Family
       (4) Empty Nest
       (5) Retirement

    h. 529 Plan
       (1) Dependent
       (2) Independent
       (3) Early Family
       (4) Empty Nest
       (5) Retirement

i. Certificate of Deposit
   (1) Dependent
   (2) Independent
   (3) Early Family
   (4) Empty Nest
   (5) Retirement
j. Credit Card
   (1) Dependent
   (2) Independent
   (3) Early Family
   (4) Empty Nest
   (5) Retirement

2. The FDIC and NCUA normally insure deposits up to what amount? (LO 4-1)

   a. $100,000
   b. $250,000
   c. $500,000
   d. $1,000,000

3. What is the difference between a debit card and a credit card? (LO 4-2)

   a. A debit card takes money out of your checking account, whereas a credit card extends credit to you when you use it.
   b. Debit cards may be used only in the United States.
   c. Credit cards always have fees attached, whereas debit cards do not.
   d. You can use your debit card only at ATM machines and you can use your credit card only for purchases.

4. From the list below, choose which tool(s) can help you manage your checking account. (LO 4-2)

   a. A check register
   b. Computer programs such as Quicken
   c. Online websites like www.mint.com
   d. All of the above

5. Which of the following methods can you use to move money out of a demand deposit account? (LO 4-2)

   a. Check
   b. ATM
   c. Automatic transfer
   d. All of the above

6. How do you know that your savings account money is insured? (LO 4-3)

   a. A Federal Deposit Insurance Corporation (FDIC) sign
   b. A National Credit Union Share Insurance Fund (NCUSIF) sign
   c. A National Credit Union Administration (NCUA) sign
   d. All banks and credit unions are insured

7. From the list below, choose which factor(s) you should consider when selecting a bank. (LO 4-3)

   a. ATM locations and interest rates
   b. Account and services offered and fees associated with those accounts and services
   c. A knowledgeable and friendly staff
   d. All of the above

8. What are the differences between banks and credit unions? (LO 4-3)

   a. Banks pay federal income tax and credit unions do not.
   b. Banks are owned by stockholders and credit unions are owned by members.
   c. Credit unions offer share draft accounts and banks offer checking accounts for their demand deposit accounts.
   d. All of the above

9. You have $238,095 in a savings account, earning 5% APY with interest paid monthly. How long can you let it sit before you need to move at least some of the funds into another account to be sure that it is secure? (LO 4-3)

   a. Three months
   b. Six months
   c. One year
   d. One year and one month

problems

1. You are now 80 years old and, unfortunately, you have outlived your retirement fund. You do own a lovely home valued at $200,000. Your Social Security is about $3,000/month short to cover your expenses. You are considering a reverse mortgage so you can stay in your home. The terms would include a financing fee of $10,000 and interest of 10%. List the pros and cons of taking on a reverse mortgage. What would be an alternative? (LO 4-1)

2. You want to open a checking account with a $500 deposit. You estimate you will write 10 checks a month

and use an ATM from other banks about twice a week. Bank A charges $1 per check if you drop under a minimum balance of $100, but you can use another bank's ATM without a fee. Bank B has free checking but charges $1 each time you use another bank's ATM. Calculate the difference in fees between the two banks over the course of one year for the following scenarios: (LO 4-2)
   a. Your balance slips below $100 every other month.
   b. Your balance slips below $100 every other month, but you are now able to pay a bill online each month, dropping the number of checks you have

to write to nine monthly. You also find you are only using the other bank's ATM about once a week.

   c. You maintain a minimum balance of $500, write three checks a week, and use another bank's ATM only about once a month.

3. You have $1,000 in a savings account and your checking account requires an $800 balance. You are earning 1% on your savings account. If you go below an $800 balance on your checking account, you incur a $5 fee that month. What is the difference between the interest you earn on your savings account and the fee you pay on your checking account each month if you drop below your minimum? *(LO 4-2)*

4. You have $500 in a share draft account. You earn 4% interest, compounded monthly. You have set up your account so that your annuity payment of $1,000 is deposited on the first of each month. You don't need to use the funds at this time so you have made no withdrawals. After one year, what is the share draft account's balance? *(LO 4-3)*

5. At the end of the month, you have only $10 left in your checking account. You deposit your $200 paycheck from your part-time waitressing job, but the restaurant is not doing well and your paycheck bounces. Your bank holds you accountable and charges you $50 for depositing a bad check. What is the balance of your checking account after attempting to deposit your bad paycheck? *(LO 4-3)*

6. You opened up a new account that pays 4% interest on the average balance of the account for the month but charges 25 cents for every transaction. What is your break-even point (number of transactions) if your average balance is $500? *(LO 4-3)*

you're the expert

1. Aunt Emma passed away and the family is together listening to the reading of her will. Sheila, a freshman in college, has just learned that she and her brothers (the younger brother is 10 and the older brother has just graduated from college and started his first job) will each receive $40,000. Sheila has expenses covered for her first year of school but not years 2–4. What recommendations do you have for Sheila and her two brothers? Using your college's estimated cost, how would you suggest Sheila use her inheritance to cover her tuition, room and board, books, and fees for the next three years? (You can find your college's estimated cost from your college's website, financial aid office, or admissions office.) *(LO 4-1)*

2. Jerry is celebrating the birth of his first child and both sets of grandparents want to set aside money to go toward the newborn's college fund. What options would you recommend to them and why? *(LO 4-1)*

3. Audrey has a new checking account, and she wants to complete the check register for the month. She started with a balance of $1,500 and wrote a check (#1001) on 8/22 at U Books for $378.21 for this semester's books. She used her debit card once on the 25th to withdraw $25 to pay for pizza and have cash for the week. On the 29th, she used her card for $36.81 of groceries, and on 9/3, she used the card to fill up on gas for $45. She also deposited her last paycheck of $425.92 on 9/18. *(LO 4-2)*

   a. Use the sample register below to show what her register looks like.

Number or Code	Date	Transaction Description	Payment Amount	√	Fee	Deposit Amount	Balance

b. Audrey's bank statement on 9/18 reads as follows:

Checking Account			Previous Statement Balance on 8/19/09			1500.00
			Total of 0 deposits for			0.00
			Total of 5 withdrawals for			497.02
			Total service charges			3.50
			New balance on 9/18			999.48
Checks and Other Debits		Check	Date Paid	Amount		
		1000	9/1	12.00		
		1001	8/22	378.21		
				Monthly maintenance charge	9/18	3.50
				ATM withdrawal 123 Main	8/25	25.00
				Good Foods	8/29	36.81
				Gas Plus	9/3	45.00

Use the bank statement above to reconcile the check register that follows.

Step 1: List all deposits and other credits that do not appear on this statement.			Step 2: List outstanding checks, withdrawals, and other debits that do not appear on this statement.	
Date	Amount		Checks	Amount
Total A	$		Total B	$
This statement's ending balance				
Add deposits/other credits not yet on this statement (Total A)				
Subtotal				
Subtract checks/other debits not listed on this statement (Total B)				
Your current checking account balance				

c. Go back to (a) and make any adjustments needed in order to complete the reconciliation.

4. Don, a recent graduate, has his first job and has opened a checking account with a local bank. He asked a lot of questions about checking account fees and debit card fees before deciding on this bank. When he returned from his first international trip, he was surprised to see numerous fees on his credit card and bank statements. He called the bank and was told they recently added service charges on international transactions involving their checking and debit cards. When he protested that this information was not shared with him when he opened the account two months ago, the bank responded they notified him in the disclosure statement when he opened his account. In looking back at the statement, he sees the bank indeed provided the disclosure. What are some of his options? *(LO 4-3)*

4.1 TIMELINES, GOALS, AND FINANCIAL INSTRUMENTS

1. Using Worksheet 4.1, record your goals, the dates by which you hope to achieve those goals, and the financial instruments you will use to achieve them. (LO 4-2)

2. Keep Worksheet 4.1 on file and use it as a roadmap for selecting the appropriate financial instruments to reach your goals. (LO 4-2)

Goals/Financial Life Stages Itinerary

Dependant Life Stage (Age <16)	Institution	Goal
Savings Account		
Certificate of Deposit		

Independent Life Stage (Age 16-24)	Institution	Goal
Savings Account		
Certificate of Deposit		
Electronic Banking / Bill Payment Service		
Student Loans		
Auto Loans		
Individual Retirement Accounts		
Credit Cards		

Early Family Life Stage (Age 25-40)	Institution	Goal
Savings Account		
Certificate of Deposit		
Electronic Payment / Bill Payment Service		
Student Loans		
Auto Loans		
Individual Retirement Accounts		
Credit Cards		
529 Plan		
401(k) Plan		
Mortgage Loans		
Home Equity Line of Credit		
Investments		

Empty Nest Life Stage (Age 41-65)	Institution	Goal
Savings Account		
Certificate of Deposit		
Electronic Banking / Bill Payment Service		
Auto Loans		
Individual Retirement Accounts		
Credit Cards		
401(k) Plans		

4.2 MAINTAINING A CHECK REGISTER

1. Complete your own check register for this month using either Worksheet 4.2 or the register in your checkbook. (LO 4-2)

Number or Code	Date	Transaction Description	Payment Amount	V	Fee	Deposit Amount	Balance

2. Next, find your last bank statement and reconcile your check register *(LO 4-2)*.

Step 1: List all				Step 2: List	
Date	Amount	Payee		Checks	Amount
Total A	$			Total B	$
This statement's ending balance					
Add deposits/ other credits not yet listed on this statement					
Subtotal					
Subtract checks/ other debits not deducted on this statement					
Your current checking account					

4.3 FINANCIAL INSTITUTION SCORE CARD

Worksheet 4.3 will help you evaluate financial institutions and identify which one is the best fit for you. *(LO 4-3)*

1. In the Priority Rank Column (the pink squares), rank the listed banking services in sequence of importance to you, with 1 being the most important and 10 being the least important.

2. Select up to three financial institutions in your community to evaluate. Try to include a commercial bank, a savings institution, and a credit union in your analysis.

3. Evaluate the financial institutions with respect to the 10 services/products listed on the worksheet. For each service/product item, rank the financial institutions from 1 to 3, with 1 being the best. Enter the rank in the FI's Rank squares (yellow).

4. Score each FI service/product comparative ranking by multiplying Priority and Rank. (For each row, **Priority Rank** × **FI Rank** = **FI Score**)

5. Total each of the FI Score columns (green). The financial institution with the lowest score is the one whose products and service offerings best fit your needs.

Service/Product	Priority Rank (Hi=1; Lo=10)	FI 1: Rank (Best = 1)	FI 1 Score (Priority Rank*FI1 Rank)	FI 2: Rank (Best = 1)	FI 2 Score (Priority Rank*FI2 Rank)	FI 3: Rank (Best = 1)	FI 3 Score (Priority Rank*FI3 Rank)
Hours/Evenings/Weekends							
Locations							
Fees/Minimum balance							
Fees/ATM usage							
Interest rate — savings							
Interest rate — checking							
Interest rate — home loans							
Interest rate — auto loans							
Is there a Visa or Mastercard available? Is there a fee?							
Safety deposit box rates							
Total Scores *(lowest score is best fit)*							

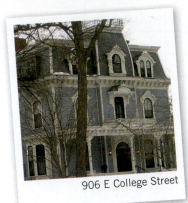

906 E College Street

Nicole still has her checking account with her hometown bank and the ATM fees are killing her. Jack banks at the local credit union, which has 10 ATMs around town and allows unlimited use of these; however, it charges for withdrawals from other bank-owned ATMs. Peter banks at a large national bank with ATMs all over the country. He likes his bank because he travels back to Colorado frequently, and he can typically find his bank's ATMs when he travels; however, there are only three of his bank's ATMs in this town. Leigh banks at a locally owned bank which has purchased some of her artwork. She likes banking with them because they gave her a car loan when she was a new teacher and didn't have a long salary history; as a result, she feels very comfortable with the personal service they provide.

Jen is also still banking with her hometown bank. She plans to spend the summer in an internship at a resort in Florida and then will be back in town in the fall. Since she doesn't plan on returning to her hometown during the summer break, she thinks it is time to change banks as well.

All of the banks used by the roommates have similar accounts and fees.

A summary of the housemates' goals can be found in the first Continuing Case problem on page 27.

1. Whose bank would you suggest Nicole switch her checking account to and why?

2. Whose bank would you suggest Jen switch her checking account to and why?

> **"** Growing up is that slow, painful transition from praying that your face will clear to praying that your check will clear. **"**
>
> —UNKNOWN

consumer credit: credit cards and student loans

According to the Federal Reserve Report of June 2010, on average, 43% of U.S. families spend $1.22 for each dollar earned. According to MSN.com and CardWeb.com, only 40% of active credit card accounts are paid off monthly and 3% of credit card accounts are past due by 30 days or more each month. Starting in the fall of 2009, overall household debt has been on the rise, but actual credit card usage has shown a gradual decline. Since the start of the financial crisis in 2008, lenders and companies have begun shedding credit card customers who they believe are at risk of default. Additionally, consumers have reduced the amount of debt they carry due to concerns over the current economy.

The use of credit has both advantages and disadvantages. Using credit allows you to purchase items ranging from a house to a car to an MP3 player—before you actually have the money. However, using credit gives someone else control over your future income. Before undertaking any credit, it is important to know your options and understand the responsibilities and cost of the debt. It is equally important to learn how lenders make credit decisions. When you choose to take on debt, make time to research the different credit options and always read the fine print. In this chapter, you will learn what credit is and what goes into a credit decision for consumer loans. You will learn about the benefits and drawbacks of credit cards as well as finance options for education. You also will learn about the hazards of predatory lending and rent-to-own schemes. ■

LEARNING OBJECTIVES

After reading this chapter, you should be able to:

LO 5-1 Explain the responsibilities, importance, and cost of credit as well as the options available for accessing credit.

LO 5-2 Evaluate the features, benefits, and disadvantages of many different types of credit cards.

LO 5-3 Describe the mechanics of obtaining and repaying student loans.

LO 5-4 Assess the drawbacks and benefits of payday loans, title loans, and rent-to-own credit options and identify alternatives.

Dee, age 32, computer science college graduate, clinical application manager

Credit Card Lessons

Dee, now a 32-year-old single mother, started using credit cards right out of college. She was never taught money management by her parents and never had conversations with them regarding credit cards. "I thought I could handle it; I was a college graduate, for goodness sakes. I kept thinking that I would pay the balance off the next month, but then the next month came and I needed to pay the utility bills first. It was too easy to use the card to get by until the next payday.

"Every year, I would use the tax refund to catch up and pay off any debt. Over the years, I learned that the best way to stay out of credit card trouble is simply not to use them. I now pay cash or use a debit card for all purchases. If I don't have the cash then I don't buy it. I finally am in control of my spending and do not have this overwhelming dread of how to tackle a mountain of debt which I can hardly remember accumulating. Credit cards are a temptation to overspend, and I am much happier living without them."

5.1 BASICS OF CREDIT AND INTEREST RATES

■■ **LO 5-1** Explain the responsibilities, importance, and cost of credit as well as the options available for accessing credit.

Credit is a convenient way to buy things now and pay for them later. According to the Federal Reserve Bank, as of June 2010, the total amount of American consumer debt

totaled $2.42 trillion. In February 2010, the Nielson Report reported that the average outstanding credit card debt (for households with credit cards) was $15,788. Why is this so high? The answer is the strong temptation of instant gratification: the opportunity to buy now and pay later.

When you use credit, you are borrowing the money from someone or some company that will require repayment at a later date, usually with interest. Interest is the cost of borrowing the money and is usually calculated as a percentage of the money you owe. The more money you borrow, the more interest you will pay. The longer the period you borrow the money, the more interest you will pay. The more money you pay someone else in interest, the less money you have for your own goals.

Before taking on credit, you should have a good understanding of the cost of borrowing money and the impact of that cost. The more money you pay in interest, the closer someone else is to their next million—and the farther away you are from yours. Before you decide to use credit you need to decide who it is you want to make into a millionaire first: you or the lender.

Credit can help you achieve your goal of owning a house or car, if used wisely.

Credit Options

Before applying for a credit card or a loan, examine your current budget and determine the amount of payments you can comfortably afford. If you finance $30,000 for your new Jeep for four years at 7% interest, your payments will be over $700 per month. Even stretching to five years, your payments will be almost $600 per month. Can you afford to buy the new Jeep Grand Cherokee or would financing $10,000 for a used car at 7% for four years ($240 per month) be a better fit for your budget?

Before using credit, you need to look at your monthly budget and decide how much you can afford to repay each month. Ultimately, you are deciding where you want your money to go: to you or to the creditor. Any time you decide to use credit instead of cash, you are making the decision to give a portion of your future income to someone else in the form of interest and principal paid.

Once you decide how much you can afford to repay and are willing to spend, you need to decide where to borrow the money. You have a considerable number of options, including general credit cards, retail consumer credit cards, banks, credit unions, savings institutions, and finance companies. Figure 5.1 introduces and compares these options.

general purpose credit cards The major general purpose credit card companies are Discover, Visa, MasterCard, and American Express. Except for Discover, these companies are recognized worldwide, although not all are accepted everywhere. It is up to the merchant to decide if it wants to accept credit cards and which credit cards it will accept. General purpose credit card companies make money by charging the cardholders fees and interest on unpaid balances. They also charge merchants a percentage of sales based on the number and volume of sales.

General purpose cards can be either unsecured or secured. A **secured credit card** requires a security deposit equaling the credit limit of the credit card. If the issuing company does not receive payments, it can receive its money by cashing in the security deposit. These cards are useful for people just starting to build or rebuild their credit history. To research secured credit card options and review a list of 10 questions you should ask yourself before getting a secured credit card, go to www.bankrate.com.

An **unsecured credit card** is just that—unsecured. The credit card company allows you to borrow money based on your promise to repay it. This promise is made when you sign the application or loan document. Unsecured loans also are known as **signature loans** because you guarantee repayment based on your signature.

General purpose credit card companies also issue premium cards. Premium cards (gold, platinum, and titanium) offer higher credit limits and have extra features such as travel insurance or extended product warranties. Some general purpose credit card companies also offer rewards to consumers for using the card. Common reward programs are airline miles and rebates (cash back).

Most credit cards are **revolving lines of credit**. These cards specify a certain credit amount that you can borrow; this is referred to as your credit line. Suppose your credit limit is $1,000 and you charge $300. You have used up $300 of your credit line, leaving $700 more to be used. After you receive your statement, let's say you pay $200. This payment applies to your outstanding balance, and now your outstanding balance is $100 and you have access to $900 to charge on your credit card. You are charged interest only on the amount borrowed, not on the amount of your credit line.

store credit cards Many major retail stores, such as Best Buy, Lowe's, Target, and Macy's, offer their own in-house credit cards. These types of credit cards are known as proprietary or retail credit cards. Merchants entice you to use their card by offering discounts if you apply for their card or 0% interest on major purchases over a 3- to 36-month time period if you use their credit

credit a contractual agreement in which a borrower receives something of value now and agrees to repay the lender at some date in the future, generally with interest

secured credit card a credit card linked to a savings account where the lender may claim the funds in the account in the event that payments are not made

unsecured credit card a credit card without collateral, where repayment is based on your promise to repay the borrowed amount

signature loans unsecured loans, where guarantee of payment is based on your word (your signature on the written agreement)

revolving lines of credit you can take and repay funds at will

▼ **FIGURE** 5.1

Characteristics of different credit options

	General Purpose Credit Cards	Retail Credit Cards	Depository Institutions	Payday Loans
Ease of Approval	Med	Med	Low	High
Interest Rate	Med-high	Med-high	Low	Very high
Needed Credit Score	Med-high	Low-med	High	Very low
Types of Purchases	Meals/Gas/Clothing	Appliances/Clothing	Major purchases (house/auto)	Last resort emergency fund

5.1 Revolving Line of Credit Example (0% APR)

Fill in the blanks below based on a $1,000 revolving line of credit with the outlaid charge and payment history.

Credit Limit: $_____

  1.) Charge: $300

Available Credit: $_____ How much more I can borrow: $_____

I owe: $_____

  2.) Payment: $200

Available Credit: $_____ How much more I can borrow: $_____

I owe: $_____

  3.) Payment: $100

Available Credit: $_____ How much more I can borrow: $_____

I owe: $_____

card. Retail stores encourage usage of their own credit cards to avoid paying a transaction fee to the general purpose credit card companies. Store credit cards may have less stringent credit standards because these stores want you to purchase merchandise from them.

depository institutions Banks, credit unions, or savings institutions have the most stringent credit standards for making a loan. Many financial institutions will not make loans for under $1,000 because of the paperwork and time involved. These financial institutions can issue either (1) a line of credit, which is similar to a credit card with no fixed payment, or (2) a fixed-term loan, where you know the amount of each payment and when the loan is due. Depository institutions make their money by lending out depositors' money at a higher rate of interest. The difference between the interest rate banks pay a depositor and the interest rate they charge a borrower is known as the **interest rate spread**.

finance companies Finance companies borrow money from banks or investors or use their own money to provide loans and leases to their customers. Some finance companies specialize in specific types of business loans: manufactured housing, furniture stores, or car dealerships. Many of the automobile manufacturers have their own finance companies to assist in consumer financing in the sale of their vehicles. Ford Motor Credit, General Motors Acceptance Corporation (GMAC), and Toyota Motor Credit are examples of finance companies owned by auto manufacturers.

Other finance companies help people who do not have stellar credit. These loans typically involve higher costs than loans offered by depository institutions (either through their interest rates and/or fees). The higher cost is to compensate the lender for the risk of making the credit available. Examples of this type of credit are rent-to-own arrangements, payday loans, and title loans (covered in Section 5.4).

Applying for Credit

A credit application is the first step in getting a loan or a credit card. The application will ask you to provide the information listed in Figure 5.2. If you are applying for credit with another person, either in a joint credit

financialfitness:
STOPPING LITTLE LEAKS

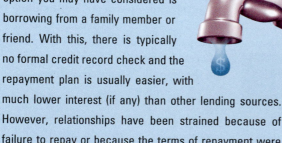

Promising Promissory Note

One low- or no-interest borrowing option you may have considered is borrowing from a family member or friend. With this, there is typically no formal credit record check and the repayment plan is usually easier, with much lower interest (if any) than other lending sources. However, relationships have been strained because of failure to repay or because the terms of repayment were not clear. If you borrow from friends or family, clarify the details up front. You can download blank promissory notes from www.nolo.ocm that are legal and binding, or you can request a blank template from your local bank.

application or as a cosigner, he or she will need to provide the same required information on the application as well.

The Five Cs of the Credit Decision

Lenders decide to whom they will grant credit cards and loans based on the five Cs of credit. That is, they evaluate your *character* (will you be responsible and repay the loan?), your *capacity* (do you have enough income minus your expenses to pay the loan?), your *collateral* (do you have something of value to secure the loan?), your *capital* (your net worth—if things go badly, do you have other assets that could be sold to pay the loan?), and *conditions* (the economic conditions for specific industries).

character Character and capacity are the most important Cs of the credit decision. The only way lenders can assess your character and know if you will follow through on your commitment to repay the loan is a credit report and a credit score. Financial institutions believe the best predictor of your future behavior is your past performance. If you have not used credit responsibly in the past, the lender will assume you will not do so in the future. Likewise, if you have a good track record of responsible credit use, the lender will assume you will be responsible in the future. Lenders also look for signs of stability, for example, length of time at one residence, with one employer, or in the same line of business.

With local banks and credit unions, it is important for your banker to know you and know your character to help support the loan decision. Local bankers are active members in the community, partly to make connections and get to know people. If your banker knows you, he or she might have the flexibility to deviate from credit scores in making the loan decision. This benefits both you and the financial institution. The banker knows you and can vouch for your character and you know the banker, who you can call whenever you have financial question or need a loan.

If you do not have a credit history and the lender does not know you, you may need a **cosigner**. This individual also signs your credit application and loan documents, thereby committing to step in and make payments on your behalf if you do not make payments on the loan when due. With a cosigner, the loan decision is based on your and your cosigner's character, capacity, collateral, capital, and conditions. All credit cards now require a cosigner if you are under the age of 21 and you cannot show proof of enough income to repay the debt.

capacity Capacity is your ability to repay debt based on your income and other obligations. This is often evaluated using the **debt-to-income ratio**. Your debt-to-income ratio is the total of your monthly recurring debt payments divided by your monthly gross income. The standard measurement is the *28/36 rule*: Your monthly house payment or rent (including taxes and insurance) should be no greater than 28% of your monthly gross income and all your debts should be no more than 36% of your income. If your debt-to-income ratio is above 36%, you

interest rate spread the difference between the interest rate of deposits and the interest rate of loans

cosigner another person who signs your loan and assumes equal responsibility for repayment

capacity ability to repay debt based on income and other obligations

debt-to-income ratio monthly recurring debt payments divided by monthly gross income

▼ **FIGURE** 5.2

Requested information on a credit application

Demographics
- Name, birth date, current and previous address, social security number, phone number, and other personal identifying information.

Income
- Current income and employer, employment and salary history. Some applications require a copy of your latest pay stub or tax return to verify your income. You are not required to include child support or separate maintenance payments or government support you receive; however, if you do list it as income, the creditor must include that income when looking at your total income.

Assets and Liabilities
- Assets and your obligations to others. You may have to list only your checking, savings, and investment accounts and your outstanding loans and credit cards. However, they may ask for a complete balance sheet, detailing all of your assets, liabilities, and net worth. This information will be used to see if you have the capital to repay the loan or credit card.

Contacts
- Identification and contact information of nearest relative not living with you. If you skip out on the loan, the collectors will call your nearest relative in order to try to locate you.

Attest and Authorization
- Signature on the credit application stating that everything on the application is true and correct and authorizing the lender to request a credit report from a credit bureau.

Revolving lines of credit, like revolving doors, can be easy to get into but hard to get out of.

financialfitness:
NUMBERS GAME

Debt Ratio Limits

In recent years, debt-to-income ratios have increased to as much as 31% (nonhousing) and 43% (overall), according to the Federal Housing Administration (FHA). Financial difficulties hit when one's total debt load, including one's home mortgage, is in the 40% range, leaving only 60% of gross income for taxes, utilities, food, clothing, and entertainment. At 45%, you can keep your head above water only if you watch every penny. A total debt load of 50% or more of your monthly gross income will sink you in debt. Life is more manageable if your monthly debt payments (excluding your housing payment) do not exceed 20% of your monthly gross income.

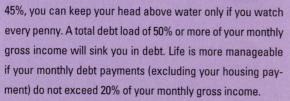

may incur higher interest rates because you are at a higher risk for defaulting on your debt obligation.

The example worksheet in Figure 5.3 calculates your non-housing capacity as well as your overall total debt-to-income ratio (the total of all income sources divided by all non-housing debt payments). Lenders rate the resulting debt-to-income ratio as follows:

< 10%	Great shape
10%–20%	Good credit risk
20–35%	Questionable credit risk
> 36%	High credit risk

In the sample debt-to-income worksheet in Figure 5.3, $320 (all nonhousing monthly debt payments) divided by $3,400 (the total of all monthly income sources) equals a nonhousing debt-to-income ratio of 9%, which lenders consider to be great credit shape.

Next, enter your housing payment to see the housing and overall debt-to-income ratios. Remember that your goal is to keep your monthly housing payment at or less than 28% of your gross income and maintain an overall debt-to-income ratio at or less than 36%.

collateral **Collateral** is an asset of value pledged against a loan. If you cannot make the loan payment, the lender can take possession of the item and sell it to repay the loan. Common sources of collateral are vehicles, stocks, bonds, and certificates of deposit.

For most auto loans, the vehicle serves as the collateral or security interest. When buying a car, you are generally required to provide a down payment of 10–20% of the purchase price so the security interest is always greater than the loan balance. The lender will place a lien on the vehicle by taking possession of the title and filing the necessary paperwork at the county courthouse. If you fail to repay the loan, the lender can **repossess** (take possession of) the vehicle and sell it. If the vehicle sells for more than the loan value and recovery cost, you will receive a refund. If the vehicle sells for less than the loan value and recovery cost, you will owe the difference.

If certificates of deposit, stocks, or bonds secure the loan and serve as collateral and the loan is not repaid, the securities are sold and the proceeds go to repay the loan. Since the value of stocks and bonds can vary, lenders want the value of the stocks and bonds to be much greater than the amount of the loan. If a loan is taken out to purchase stocks or bonds and those same stocks or bonds are used to secure the loan, it is considered a **margin loan**; in this case, the Federal Reserve Bank requires that the loan be no greater than 50% of the value of the stocks or bonds. This can cause problems when stock prices plummet, as they did in 2008 and 2009. When this happens, borrowers have to either sell their stocks to repay the loan, pay down their loans to keep a 50% ratio, or add more collateral to secure the loan.

capital Capital is your net worth, or your assets minus your liabilities. The risk of defaulting on your credit obligation decreases as your net worth increases. A higher net worth provides you the option of selling items of value to repay the loan if income decreases and you are unable to make required payments.

conditions *Conditions* refers to the economic conditions of the industry in which the borrower is employed. For example, during the financial crisis of 2008–2009, autoworkers and suppliers were uncertain about their futures as Chrysler and General Motors declared bankruptcy. The risk of making loans to autoworkers increased because of the uncertainty of their future income. Because they were at risk of being laid off, lenders could not be certain these borrowers would have the capacity to repay their credit obligations.

▼ **FIGURE 5.3**

Sample debt-to-income ratio calculation worksheet

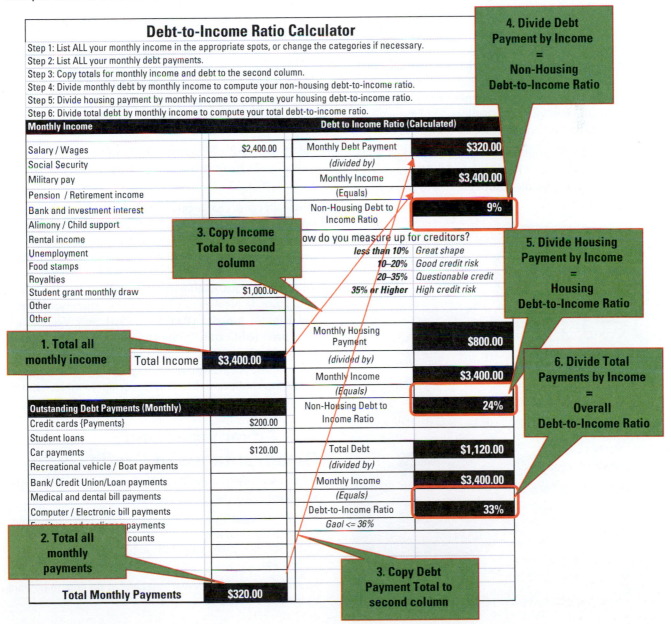

> ## "The only reason a great many American families don't own an elephant is that they have never been offered an elephant for a dollar down and easy weekly payments."
> —*MAD Magazine*

Risk and Interest Rates

When you borrow money, you usually do not get the loan for free. Of course, there are some special car loans and credit cards that offer 0% financing for a specific time period. We will evaluate these offers later in this chapter to see if they are a good deal. For now, let's assume you are charged interest on the amount you borrow. What determines the interest rate you will be charged?

The first factor is the cost of money. A bank pays its depositors interest in order to attract deposits. If the average interest rate to attract depositors is 3%, the cost of money to the bank is 3%. The bank's largest source of income is interest from lending money. Usually banks like to have a 3–4% interest spread. Therefore, if the bank's cost of money is 3%, then its best loan rate for a low-risk customer will be 6–7%.

A borrower who does not have a stellar credit history has a higher risk of default. Therefore, the lender wants compensation for taking on the additional risk to make a loan.

Depending on the borrower's risk rating on the five Cs of credit, the loan interest rate could be higher. It is not uncommon for credit card rates to be 12–18% or higher based on the risk of the applicant and how much, if any, collateral is securing the loan. This is because credit cards usually are unsecured; in most cases, if you declare bankruptcy, the credit card company loses the money you owe it. The rule of thumb is: "The higher the risk, the higher the rate." Your interest rate depends on the risk that you will not repay the lender.

5.2 UNDERSTANDING CREDIT CARDS

■ ■ **LO 5-2** Evaluate the features, benefits, and disadvantages of many different types of credit cards.

Originally called charge cards, credit cards have been around since the 1920s. They were first issued by department stores, gas stations, and hotel chains to increase the convenience of travel and reduce the amount of cash consumers would have to carry with them. Diners Club started the trend of credit cards in the 1950s, issuing the first card that was good at 27 restaurants in New York City. In 1958, American Express and Bank of America (BankAmericard, now Visa) issued their first credit cards. In the United States, the four most popular cards are Visa, MasterCard, Discover, and American Express. Today, with the average household owing over $15,000 in credit card debt, it is important to understand all aspects of the credit card.

The Advantages and Disadvantages of Credit Cards

When used wisely, a credit card offers many benefits. Some advantages to consider are the following:

- *Arbitration.* If there is a disagreement regarding a purchase, you can alert your credit card company to remove the charge from your bill until the issue has been resolved.
- *Automatic bill payments.* You can set up bills to be paid via your credit card.

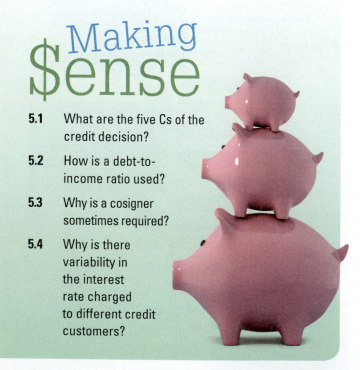

Making $ense

5.1 What are the five Cs of the credit decision?

5.2 How is a debt-to-income ratio used?

5.3 Why is a cosigner sometimes required?

5.4 Why is there variability in the interest rate charged to different credit customers?

- *Identity theft safeguards.* You will not be held responsible for any charges on your account that are not yours if they are reported within 60 days of your statement.

- *Credit builder.* If you pay off your balance in a timely manner and use only 10% of your credit limit, it helps to lift your credit score. Credit information is used by employers, insurance companies, and landlords, so it pays to be vigilant.

- *Extended warranties.* Some credit cards will double any manufacturer's warranty for free.

- *Interest-free loans.* If you pay your bill in full every month, you are essentially getting an interest-free loan on every purchase you charge.

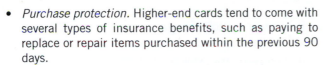

It is important to weigh credit decisions carefully.

- *Purchase protection.* Higher-end cards tend to come with several types of insurance benefits, such as paying to replace or repair items purchased within the previous 90 days.

- *Rental car coverage.* Credit cards often can fill in the gaps of what is typically not covered by your auto insurance, covering deductibles and charges such as "loss of use" that are not part of an auto insurer's plan.

- *Rewards.* Using credit cards can pay off in the form of free plane tickets, free hotel stays, or cash back and discount deals.

The overarching disadvantage to credit cards is that they make it too easy to spend money you don't have. Those not-so-big purchases add up quickly over the span of a month, and you end up with a balance higher than you can pay in full. Carrying a balance adds significant dollars to purchases bought with credit. At the end of each month, interest accrues on the balance, which pushes you further into debt.

Credit cards have advantages, but it is important to exercise discipline when using them. Maintain control and charge only what you can pay for in full and on time each month, if at all possible.

Credit Limits

The lender issuing the credit card sets a limit on the amount you can charge. Credit card companies use a set of complex matrixes to determine your limit, based on your credit score, net income, debt-to-income ratio, disposable income, and default risk. The best way to increase your credit limit is to pay your credit card bill on time all the time. Then you can call and ask for an increase in your credit limit. Try never

to carry a balance of more than 30% of your unsecured credit card limit. Anything greater flags you as a lending risk. Of course, if you are using a secured general purpose credit card, your credit limit will depend on the amount of your security deposit.

Grace Periods

A grace period is the amount of time you have to pay your bill in full before finance charges are activated. Grace periods are set by the credit card companies and range from no grace period to 28 days. Most credit cards offer a 21–25 day grace period, which usually applies to new purchases only. Grace periods generally do not apply to cash advances and balance transfers; for these transactions, interest charges start immediately. If you do not pay your entire balance when it is due, new purchases may not be eligible for a grace period. In this case, you will be charged interest as soon as you make a purchase.

Interest Rates

Lenders determine interest rates on credit cards using the same factors they use for establishing credit card limits. They use complex matrixes based on your credit score, debt-to-income ratio, and default risk. It is important that you understand how credit card companies calculate and apply these complicated rates.

A single credit card can have multiple interest rates. General use cards may have one rate for purchases, a different rate for balance transfers, and another rate for cash advances. Credit cards may have an introductory rate for a limited time period, which then changes when the introductory period ends. If you miss a payment or are late with payments, credit cards have a default rate that can be 29% or higher.

Interest rates can be fixed or variable. Even if you have a *fixed rate,* your interest rate can change at the discretion of the credit card company as long as it notifies you as stated in its disclosure. *Variable interest rates* can change if the benchmark rate changes. Most interest rate disclosures on credit card statements are difficult and complicated to understand. However, it is important to comb through the fine print to be aware of possible fees and what activities can adversely impact your interest rate.

The finance charge on your outstanding balance may be calculated over one or two billing cycles or using a number of different methods, such as the adjusted balance, the average daily balance, or the minimum finance charge method.

adjusted balance method. The adjusted balance method is advantageous for cardholders. Payments or credits received during the current billing period are subtracted from the balance at the end of the previous billing period. Purchases made during the billing period are not included. This method gives you until the end of the billing cycle to pay the balance and avoid interest charges.

average daily balance method. The most common calculation method, the average daily balance method, credits your balance with any payments or refunds each morning in the billing period. Under some plans, any new purchases are also added. At the end of the billing cycle, the credit card company adds the daily balances and divides by the number of days in the billing period to get the "average daily balance."

minimum finance charge. If your calculated finance charge is below your minimum finance charge, the credit card company will charge you the minimum finance charge. As an example, if your minimum finance charge

Charges and Fees

In addition to interest rates, special fees and finance charges complicate the cost of a credit card. It is wise to know about these charges before using your credit card.

finance charges The finance charge is the total cost of borrowing on your credit card, including interest and fees.

---

doing the MATH

5.2 Credit Card Calculation Comparisons at 24% APR (2%/MONTH)

Your previous credit card balance was $200, on 1/15 you charged an iPod for $300, and your end-of-month balance was $500. The following month, you made a payment of only $105 and then charged $500 on 2/14 to purchase an iPad.

a) What is your new balance at the end of the month if interest is calculated based on the adjusted balance method*?

b) What is your new balance at the end of the leap year month if interest is calculated based on the average daily balance**?

c) What is your new minimum payment due***?

*__Adjusted Balance Method__ Interest Payment for Period: 2% * 200 = **$4**

**__Average Daily Balance Method__ Interest Payment for Period: ($200*14 days) + ($500*14 days)/28 days = $350*2% = $7

***__Minimum Finance Charge__ (of $5) Minimum payment for Adjusted Balance Method = $5 (minimum finance charge), for Average Daily Balance Method = $7

is $5 and your calculated finance charge is $1, you will be charged the $5 minimum finance charge.

fees Fees are a major source of income for credit card companies and can cost you a lot of money if you are not careful. Figure 5.4 lists some of the most common fees to look for.

zero percent deals Are "0% for six months" offers really good deals? For major purchases, some retail credit cards will offer deals with no payments and no interest for a specific time period. With some of these offers, the lender merely defers the interest if you do not pay off the balance in the allotted time period. In other words, the interest is calculated like a regular credit card but is not added to your balance until after the specified time period. If you pay off your balance in time, no interest is added to your balance. If not, the accrued interest is added—which could amount to hundreds of dollars in interest.

credit costs As a result of the Truth-in-Lending Act (1969), lenders must disclose the finance charge and the annual percentage rate (APR). The finance charge is the total cost of the loan, inclusive of interest costs, service charges, credit-related insurance costs, or appraisal fees. The **annual percentage rate (APR)** is the yearly cost of borrowing the money, inclusive of all interest costs and other fees. As discussed in Chapter 2, the APR is the percentage cost of the loan on a yearly basis, which makes it easier to compare options regardless of the amount you borrow or how long the period of the repayment plan extends. When calculating your monthly fees and charges, remember to divide the APR by 12 months to find the monthly interest rate.

errors on your statement Credit card companies are known to make errors on statements. In July 2009, due to a programming error, a Texas man was charged $23,148,855,308,184,500 for a dinner at a local restaurant

financialfitness:
JUST THE FACTS

Credit Card Penalties

Not monitoring your credit card statements can cost you. Many credit card users don't realize when they are charged a new higher "penalty" interest rate, which typically is double the regular rate. Financially troubled credit card borrowers often owe more in penalty fees and interest charges than for purchases or cash advances.

▼ **FIGURE 5.4**

Credit card fees

Annual fee	• Can be charged once a year or each month and is the fee the credit card companies charge you for having the card.
Cash advance fee	• Can be two separate fees, a flat fee for the cash advance (for example, $5.00) no matter the amount of the cash advance and a percentage fee for the cash advance (for example, 3%). If you were to take a $500 cash advance, you would be charged a $5.00 flat fee plus a $15 percentage fee, a total of $20.00.
Late-payment fees	• Assessed if your minimum payment arrives at the credit card company after the due date. Late payment fees can range from $15 – $39 or more. Your interest rate may also change to the default interest rate if you are late in paying your credit card.
Over-limit fees	• Assessed if your credit card balance exceeds your credit limit. This could occur if you use your credit card and go over the credit limit before your payment reaches the credit card company. Over-limit fees can range from $15 – $39 or more, depending on your credit card company.
Return-item fees	• Charged if your payment is returned to the credit card company for any reason. Your payment could be returned by your bank for insufficient funds, holds on your account, or stop payments.
Balance transfer fee	• Percentage fee charged when moving the balance from one credit card to another. This fee can range from 1% – 5% of the transferred amount. Credit card companies commonly encourage balance transfers by offering 0% for six months, but they do not mention the transfer fee exception in the fine print. If you were to transfer $1,000 from one card to another to get 0% for six months, you would be charged $50 if your credit card has a 5% transfer fee.
Other fees	• Detailed in the fine print on the disclosure of the credit card application. These disclosures are sent to you by mail and will be included with your monthly credit card statement any time there is a change in a policy. Most credit card customers do not read the disclosures and then are suprised when their interest rates, fees, or polices change.

financialfitness:
STOPPING LITTLE LEAKS

Leaving Credit Cards at Home

According to a study by Dunn and Bradstreet, credit card users spend 12 to 18% more when using credit instead of cash. When you use cash, you have a stronger appreciation for your spending, as well as a heightened awareness that the money is a limited resource. Psychologically, it's more difficult to empty your wallet of all your cash and therefore you spend less. When shopping, leave the plastic at home. Take the budgeted amount you intend to spend with you in cash.

financialfitness:
JUST THE FACTS

Credit Card Tips

Visit the following websites for good tips on managing your credit cards:

Consumers Union: Top 10 Credit Card Traps
www.creditcardreform.org/credit_card_tips.html
Consumers Union: Credit Card Tips
www.creditcardreform.org/credit_card_tips.html

---

and assessed an overdraft fee. The bank removed the charge and the overdraft fee after he brought it to the bank's attention. Errors are not always so glaring, so check your statement carefully. If you find an error on your statement, you should call the credit card company immediately and then follow up your phone call with a written letter. According to the Fair Credit Billing Act, you should:

1. Contact the credit card company in writing within 60 days of the date that appears on the statement which contains the error.

2. Send the letter to the *billing inquiries* address on your statement.

3. Include your name, account number, and the date and a description of the disputed charge and why you think it is an error. Include copies of any documents supporting your argument.

4. Keep a copy for your own records. The credit card company will investigate your complaint and if the charge is found to be in error, you will not have to pay any interest on the disputed amount.

Choosing a Credit Card

Worksheet 5.2 (see the online supplement and the Worksheets section at the end of this chapter) can help you evaluate the different credit card features and decide which ones

are important to you. Before completing the worksheet, think about how you are going to use the credit card. If you plan to pay your balance in full, all the time, then the most important features for you are the grace period and any other fees associated with the card. The interest rate is not important because you plan to always pay the balance in full. On the other hand, if you are going to carry a balance on your account, you will want to know the interest rate as well as how the finance charges are calculated and what fees are associated with the card. Figure 5.5 provides some tips for managing your credit card.

financialfitness:
STOPPING LITTLE LEAKS

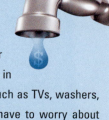

Cash Purchase Discounts

Using your credit card costs the retailer in fees. Work this to your advantage by shopping with cash. Walking into a retail store with the cash you have to allocate toward your big item purchase can be effective in negotiating a lower price for items such as TVs, washers, and dryers. Additionally, you won't have to worry about overspending or missing the credit card payment date.

Tips for keeping your credit card rates and fees low

Select card wisely	• Don't start out with a credit card that offers poor terms if you qualify for better ones. Don't fall for the "pre-approved" credit cards that come to you in the mail as they may not offer the lowest fees and interest rates.
Pay on time	• After you charge, pay by or before the due date. While one late payment won't result in massive credit damage, you will be assessed a fee and your interest rate can increase, not only on this account, but possibly on others that you have as well.
Maintain balance < 30% of credit limit	• Ideally, you should not carry a balance on your credit cards. If you do, make sure that amount is less than 30% of your credit line. Anything greater and your creditor may consider you a lending risk and increase your interest rate.
Look out for new fees	• Scan monthly statements for additional fees and read mail regarding adjustment notices. Credit card companies will sometimes slip in small monthly fees.
Be judicious about all your activity	• Credit card companies are constantly evaluating the risks and costs of funding. If they see that a customer is not paying other household bills on time or is applying for a number of new accounts, they may up your rate.
Complain if rates or fees increase	• If your fees and interest rates do spike without you doing anything to warrant the change, call your creditor and politely ask that it be returned to its previous rate. If you have a better offer from a different creditor, ask that they match it. Always ask that they seal the deal in writing.

financialfitness:
ACTION ITEM

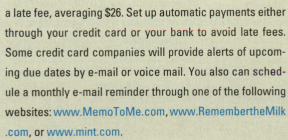

Automating Credit Payments

Consumer Action's 2008 Credit Card Survey reports that 95% of credit cards tack on a late fee, averaging $26. Set up automatic payments either through your credit card or your bank to avoid late fees. Some credit card companies will provide alerts of upcoming due dates by e-mail or voice mail. You also can schedule a monthly e-mail reminder through one of the following websites: www.MemoToMe.com, www.RemembertheMilk.com, or www.mint.com.

Making $ense

5.5 To maintain a high credit rating, what is the most you should carry as a balance on a credit card?

5.6 What are some things you can do to help keep your credit card interest rate and fees low?

5.7 What should you watch for on 0% credit offerings?

5.8 What steps can you take to remedy an error on your credit card statement?

5.3 STUDENT LOANS

■ ■ **LO 5-3** Describe the mechanics of obtaining and repaying student loans.

Another type of unsecured credit is student loans. Funds from a student loan should be used to pay for education-related expenses, such as college tuition, room and board, or textbooks. Many of these loans, including the Perkins Loan and the Stafford Loan, are offered to students at a low interest rate. In general, students do not need to pay back these loans until the end of a grace period, which usually begins after they have completed their education. There are three major categories of student loans: (1) federal student loans made directly to the student; (2) federal student loans made to the parents; and (3) private student loans made to students or parents.

To apply for any federal student aid, you must complete a free application for federal student aid (FAFSA). Many colleges, universities, and scholarship applications require you to complete the FAFSA. You can access the FAFSA from www.fafsa .ed.gov. The FAFSA tries to determine financial need. Once the federal government assesses your financial need, it can determine your eligibility for federal loans and grants.

Federal Student Loans to Students

Federal student loans are low-interest loans for students. They are used to help pay for the cost of education after high school. These loans can be either subsidized by the federal government or unsubsidized. Figure 5.6 offers a comparison of subsidized versus unsubsidized federal student loans. Guaranteed by the United States Department of Education, these loans offer a grace period of six months after you graduate (or become a less-than-half-time student without graduating) before you must start making payments.

There is a limit to the amount students can borrow, based on their year in college, their major, and their tax filing status. Graduate students and students who have been declared independent by the IRS have higher loan limits. Federal student loans to students include Perkins Loans, Stafford Loans, Federal Family Education Loans, Ford Federal Direct Student Loans, and Federal Direct Student Loan Program consolidation loans.

Federal Student Loans to Parents

Parents can borrow money to help their dependents attend college through PLUS loans (an acronym for

" If you think education is expensive, try ignorance. "

—DEREK BOK, *president of Harvard University, 1971–1990 (1930–)*

It is true that education is an investment in your future. As with any other investment, it is important to make informed financial decisions.

"Parent Loan for Undergraduate Students"). Parents are responsible for repaying these loans and can borrow much more than students can. The amount parents can borrow is usually enough to cover any shortfall in the cost of education.

PLUS loans made to parents after July 1, 2008, include the option of beginning repayments either 60 days after the loan is fully dispersed or six months after the dependent student graduates or is no longer enrolled at least on a half-time basis. PLUS loans have a higher interest rate than federal loans issued to students and, like unsubsidized federal student loans, the interest accrues immediately. Graduate students may now apply for and receive PLUS loans, commonly referred to as Grad PLUS loans.

Private Student Loans

Private student loans are not guaranteed by a government agency and are made directly to the student or the parents of the student by banks and finance companies. Private

Subsidized vs. unsubsidized federal student loans

Subsidized $10,000 Federal Student Loan	Unsubsidized $10,000 Federal Student Loan
Amount borrowed = $10,000	Amount borrowed = $10,000
Accrued interest = $1,500	Accrued interest = $1,500
Interest paid by government while in school and maintaining half-time status or greater = $1,500	Interest paid by government while in school and maintaining half-time status or greater = $0
Amount due upon graduation or going below half-time status = $10,000	Amount due upon graduation or going below half-time status = $11,500
Payments deferred for 6 months after graduation or going below half-time student status	Payments deferred for 6 months after graduation or going below half-time student status

student loans generally have higher fees and interest rates than those loans guaranteed by a government agency. Private student loans have two features that distinguish them from government student loans: (1) they do not require a FAFSA, and (2) the funds are disbursed directly to the borrower. In comparison, government student loans require a FAFSA and disburse the funds directly to the educational institution.

Repaying Student Loans

Once you graduate, it will be time to start repaying your student loans. There are a few options to consider before you decide how to make your payments.

student loan consolidation and refinancing As a result of loans being disbursed each semester, you may find you have multiple loans at multiple rates. To consolidate the loans into one amount with a common rate, you must apply for consolidation with one of the lenders. Refinancing typically means reduced monthly payments with a longer repayment period—usually at a lower interest rate. If you have federal student loans and private loans, the interest rates will most likely vary greatly; therefore, they will need to be refinanced separately as you cannot combine federal and private student loan debt.

deferment Deferring the repayment of a loan postpones repayment of the principal for a specific period of time. Deferment is typically granted for people who: (1) continue to be enrolled in school; (2) are disabled and undergoing some type of rehabilitation; or (3) have left school and are either unemployed or are able to display a marked financial hardship. For subsidized loans, no interest accrues during this time. For private loans, interest will accrue and will be recapitalized (added to the loan balance), thus increasing the size of the loan.

financialfitness:
STOPPING LITTLE LEAKS

Shopping Student Loans

Federally guaranteed loans should always be the first place you look when borrowing for your college education. Generally, the interest rate will be lower and the repayment terms will be more flexible than private student loans. Examine all of your options and carefully read the disclosures before deciding on a loan. Your school's financial aid office can provide more information on student loans and help you make the right decision. Helpful websites for financial aid and student loans include:

Federal Student Aid: www.studentaid.ed.gov or www.federalstudentaid.ed.gov

FAFSA: www.fafsa.edu.gov

Sallie Mae Student Loans: www.salliemae.com

Federal Direct Loans: www.ed.gov/directloan/

Bankrate Student Loans: www.bankrate.com/student-loans.aspx

forbearance Those individuals without an approved reason for deferment, but who are still unable to pay, may be granted forbearance. During this period, payments can be postponed or reduced, but interest will continue to accrue. Interest is not subsidized during a forbearance period because it is viewed as a voluntary postponement by the debtor. As a result, those granted forbearance continue to be responsible for the additional interest accrued while payments to the principal are not being made. Forbearance typically is granted in twelve-month intervals, but it can be as short as three- or six-month intervals.

alternate payment options As with any debt, there are always options based on an individual's specific circumstances. Federal lenders are typically easier to work with than private lenders. For federal lenders the options include: extended repayment; graduated repayment; income sensitive repayment; income contingent repayment; and income-based repayment. For more information on these options, it is best to contact your lender and ask about what each of them can do for you. As with a deferment or forbearance, it is extremely important to contact your lender to discuss

amortization

the process of reducing debt through regular installment payments of principal and interest that will result in the payoff of a loan at its maturity

usury law

state laws specifying the maximum legal interest rate at which loans can be made

predatory lending

the act of lending money at an unreasonably high interest rate, making repayment excessively difficult or impossible for the borrower

these options while your account is in good standing.

Calculating Payments

To calculate your loan payments, use the formulas discussed in Section 2.3 of Chapter 2. Recall the formula for the present value of an annuity:

$$PVA = PMT \left(\{1 - [1/(1+i)^n]\}/i\right)$$

where

PVA = Present value of an annuity
PMT = Payment
i = Interest rate per period
n = Number of periods

If you are financing $1,000 at 12% interest annually (or 1% monthly) for one year and making monthly payments, you know the following:

$$PVA = \$1,000$$
$$i = .01$$
$$n = 12$$

Using the formula, your equation would be as follows:

$$\$1,000 = PMT \left(\{1 - [1/(1+.01)^{12}]\}/.01\right)$$
$$\$1,000 = PMT \{[1 - (1/1.01^{12})]/.01\}$$
$$\$1,000 = PMT \{[1 - (1/1.126825)]/.01\}$$
$$\$1,000 = PMT \left(1 - 0.887449\right)/.01$$
$$\$1,000 = PMT\ 0.112551/.01$$
$$\$1,000 = PMT\ 11.25508$$

Next, solve for PMT by dividing both sides by 11.25508

$$\$1,000/11.25508 = PMT\ [11.25508]/11.25508$$

financialfitness:
JUST THE FACTS

Default Interest Rates

If you neglect to pay your student loans, you will accrue penalties, fees, and interest. Your account  will eventually adjust to a default rate, and it will continue to accrue interest until action is taken. The process and rates for each type of loan vary. For more information, visit the Federal Financial Aid website: www.finaid.org/loans/default.phtml.

and your answer is:

$$PMT = \$88.84879$$

To pay off your $1,000 loan in 12 equal payments over one year at 1% monthly interest, you would make monthly payments of $88.85.

To calculate the monthly payments using the present value interest factor of an annuity (PVIFA) table (Appendix A), your formula would be:

$$PVA = PMT\ (PVIFA_{1,12})\ \text{(see Appendix A)}$$
$$1,000 = PMT\ (11.255)$$
$$\mathbf{88.85 = PMT}$$

To calculate the monthly payments using a financial calculator, you would input 1,000, PV (present value of loan); 12, N (number of monthly payments); and 1, I/YR (monthly interest rate). Solving for PMT, your answer would be –88.85. See Figure 5.7.

doing the MATH

5.3 Student Loan Payments Example

Over the course of four years, you took out four different loans of $10,000. You believe you may be able to consolidate the loans and make one payment each month over the next 10 years, at 6% interest.

1. Use the online amortization calculator (Figure 5.8) to calculate the monthly payment.

2. Using a financial calculator, what is your computed monthly payment?

3. Go to http://www.amortization-calc.com/ to input your number and print out a copy of your student loan amortization table.

Monthly payments calculator example

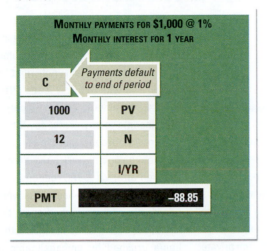

5.9 How do subsidized student loans compare to unsubsidized student loans?

5.10 What options do you have for managing the repayment of your student loans?

amortization tables **Amortization** is the process of reducing debt through regular installment payments of principal and interest that will result in the payoff of a loan at its maturity. To determine what portion of each payment is going toward paying the principal and what portion is going toward paying the interest on your loan, you can create an amortization table using Excel. See Figure 5.8 for an example of an amortization table for a 12-month, $1,000 loan at 12% interest and monthly payments. An amortization table calculator is included on the website accompanying this text or you can find an online amortization table calculator at www .amortization-calc.com.

▼ **FIGURE** 5.8

Example of an amortization table for a 12-month, $1,000 loan at 12% APR

Amortization Table

Loan Amount	$1,000.00			
Annual Interest Rate	12	(whole number)		
Payments per Year	12			
Number of Payments	12			
Payment Amount	$88.85			

Payment Number	Beginning Principal Amount	Interest Paid	Principal Paid	Ending Principal Balance
1	$1,000.00	$10.00	$78.85	$921.15
2	921.15	9.21	79.64	841.51
3	841.51	8.42	80.43	761.08
4	761.08	7.61	81.24	679.84
5	679.84	6.80	82.05	597.79
6	597.79	5.98	82.87	514.92
7	514.92	5.15	83.70	431.22
8	431.22	4.31	84.54	346.68
9	346.63	3.47	85.38	261.30
10	261.30	2.61	86.24	175.07
11	175.07	1.75	87.10	87.97
12	87.97	0.88	87.97	0.00

5.4 COSTLY CASH

■ ■ **LO 5-4** Assess the drawbacks and benefits of payday loans, title loans, and rent-to-own credit options and identify alternatives.

Payday loans, cash advance loans, check advance loans, post-dated check loans, or deferred deposit loans flaunt their services in ads on the radio, television, and Internet as easy cash for an emergency situation. These small, short-term, high-rate loans by check cashers, finance companies, and others come at a very high price. These lenders are in a different category than credit card companies or banks and work around **usury laws**. These companies are in the business of what often is referred to as **predatory lending,** charging their clients triple digit annual percentage rates (APRs). It's not an exaggeration to see 250% (and higher) APRs on these loans, yet only a handful of states have passed strict laws prohibiting these exorbitant percentage rates.

Payday Loans

For payday loans, you write the payday lender a personal check for the amount you want to borrow plus the fee for the

Scan here for more information on the latest events "In the News"

Student loan overhaul approved by Congress

Ending one of the fiercest lobbying fights in Washington, Congress voted Thursday to force commercial banks out of the federal student loan market, cutting off billions of dollars in profits in a sweeping restructuring of financial-aid programs and redirecting most of the money to new education initiatives. The vote was 56 to 43 in the Senate and 220 to 207 in the House, with Republicans unanimously opposed in both chambers.

Since the bank-based loan program began in 1965, commercial banks like Sallie Mae and Nelnet have received guaranteed federal subsidies to lend money to students, with the government assuming nearly all the risk. Democrats have long denounced the program, saying it fattened the bottom line for banks at the expense of students and taxpayers . . . Democrats celebrated the legislation, a centerpiece of President Obama's education agenda, as a far-reaching overhaul of federal financial aid, providing a huge infusion of money to the Pell grant program and offering new help to lower-income graduates in getting out from under crushing student debt. Congressional allies of the student-loan

industry attacked the overhaul as an overreaching government takeover. The legislation substitutes an expanded direct-lending program by the government for the bank-based program, directing $36 billion over 10 years to Pell grants, for students from low-income families. Although private banks will no longer be allowed to make student loans with federal money, many will continue to earn income by servicing those loans.

The Congressional Budget Office said the direct-lending approach would save taxpayers about $61 billion over 10 years. Roughly $40 billion of the savings will be redirected to higher education. Education programs will get an additional $10 billion from the health care package. The bill includes some landmark changes, like automatic increases, tied to inflation, in the maximum Pell grant award. But for individual students, the increase in the maximum Pell grant—to $5,900 in 2019-20 from $5,550 for the 2010-11 school year—is minuscule, compared with the steep, inexorable rise in tuition for public and private colleges alike. And because college costs are rising so quickly, the maximum Pell grant now covers only about a third of the average cost of attending a public university, compared with three-quarters in the 1970s, when the program began. So each year, more students graduate with debt of more than $20,000.

The legislation will make it easier to pay back student loans, by reducing the share

of income that a graduate must devote to loan payments and by accelerating loan forgiveness—but not right away. Those who take out new loans after July 1, 2014, will have to devote 10 percent of their income to payments, down from the current 15 percent, and those who keep up their payments will have their loans forgiven after 20 years, reduced from the current 25. "Income-based repayment is a fantastic addition to the Senate bill that will allow over a million students to avoid being crushed by unmanageable levels of debt," said Rich Williams, a higher-education advocate at the U.S. Public Interest Research Group. With the new legislation, students will have to take out their loans through their college's financial aid office, instead of using a private bank.

In lobbying fiercely against the overhaul, the private banks argued that it would eliminate jobs, even though the government will hire many of the same banks on a contract basis to service the loans and perform other back-office administration. Furthermore, the banks said that with the government as the only lender, students would not get the same level of service.

DAVID M. HERSZENHORN and TAMAR LEWIN, "Student Loan Overhaul Approved by Congress," *The New York Times*, March 25, 2010. Reprinted with permission.

Questions

1 What is your position on the student loan overhaul?

2 What economic impact do you believe it will have in the short run? In the long run?

loan. The payday lender gives you the amount of the check less the fee and agrees to hold your check until your next payday. Fees on these loans may be a percentage of what you want to borrow or may be based on an incremental scale (e.g., for every $100 borrowed, there is a $15 fee). The payday lender also will allow you to **roll over** the loan (extend it past your next payday) for an additional fee. Each time you roll over the loan, the lender charges a fee. The Federal Truth in Lending Act treats payday loans like other types of credit, so the lenders must disclose the cost of the loan. Payday lenders must give you the finance charge (a dollar amount) and the annual percentage rate (APR) in writing before you sign for the loan. Payday loans are expensive credit. How expensive?

calculating the payday loan cost Let's say you need to borrow $100 for two weeks for car repairs. You write a personal check to the lender for $115 (or agree to an electronic debit from your account on your next payday), with $15 being the fee to borrow the money. The payday lender agrees to hold your check until your next payday. When that day comes, either you pay the lender (or he debits your checking account for $115), or you roll over the loan and are charged $15 more to extend the financing for 14 more days. The cost of the initial $100 loan is a $15 finance charge, which computes to an annual percentage rate of 391% (365 days in yr /14 days × $15 = 391% APR). If you take the full month to pay back the $100, your finance charge for the use of $100 for 28 days climbs to $30.

Title Loans

Title loans offer you cash from the lender if you sign over the title of your paid-for car to secure the loan. Typically, these loans are for no more than 25% of the value of your car and are due back in full in 30 days. There is no credit check and only minimal income verification. If you fail to pay back the loan in 30 days, you could lose your car. If the title loan lender sells the car for less than the balance due, you still owe money and you no longer have a car to get to and from work. By federal law, title loan lenders have to disclose their interest rates in terms of the annual percentage rate. If you have to get a title loan, make sure the lender doesn't quote the monthly percentage rate. For example, a monthly percentage rate of 25% is equivalent to a 300% APR.

calculating the title loan cost In addition to high interest, title loans usually include a number of fees that add up quickly. These can include processing fees, document fees, late fees, origination fees, lien fees, and even mandatory roadside assistance fees.

doing the MATH

5.4 Payday Loan Example

You took out a 14-day, $200 loan for a fee of $20. You were unable to pay it back for two months and elected to roll over the loan.

14-Day loan amount:	$200
Initial loan fee:	$20
Balance owed:	$220
14-Day extension (roll over):	$20
Balance owed:	$240
14-Day extension (roll over):	$20
Balance owed:	$260
14-Day extension (roll over):	$20
Balance owed:	$280

The cost of the two-month loan of $200 comes at a cost of $80.

1. What is the cost of the $200 loan if you need a third month before you can finally pay?

2. What is the annual percentage rate of the payday loan?

These lenders also give you the option of interest-only payments for a set period of time. In these cases, the loans are usually set up for a longer period of time (compared to the typical 30 days) and allow you to make interest-only payments either monthly or bimonthly. These types of payments are called "balloon payments"—you pay the interest of the loan each month and, at the end of the term, you owe the full amount of the loan.

The terms of these loans are crafted to keep you in a cycle of debt and bring you to the verge of repossession. Not being able to pay off the initial loan and then renewing it the next month costs you even more money in interest, on top of the original amount you initially borrowed. If you cannot pay back the loan, the title loan lender will sell your car and use the proceeds to pay off the balance of the loan as well as any expenses associated with the repossession.

Rent-to-Own

The Federal Trade Commission (FTC) continues to investigate the rent-to-own industry because its effective interest rates average over 1800%. People rent items they think they cannot afford because they are looking only at the weekly cost. For example, a rent-to-own washer for $19 per week for 90 weeks totals $1,710, whereas a new washer at a retail store costs half that amount. Even better, by saving $19 for just 12 weeks, you could easily purchase a used floor model. Short-term thinking sets you up for being taken advantage of by predatory lenders.

Considering the Alternatives

Before you decide to take out a payday loan or a title loan or shop at a rent-to-own outlet, consider your alternatives. Figure 5.9 lists some options for you to evaluate.

The bottom line on payday loans, title loans, and rent-to-own arrangements: Try to find an alternative. If you must use payday or title loans, borrow only as much as you can afford to pay with your next paycheck, with enough left over to make it to next payday. ■

financialfitness:
JUST THE FACTS

Predatory Lending Practices

Payday loans and title loans are illegal in just a few states. Websites sponsored by nonprofit organizations that provide helpful information about understanding and dealing with predatory lending practices include the Center for Responsible Lending (www.responsiblelending.org/payday-lending/) and the Consumer Federation of America (/www.consumerfed.org/topics.cfm?section=Finance&topic=Credit%20and%20Debt).

▼ **FIGURE** 5.9

Alternatives to payday loans, title loans, and rent-to-own arrangements

Contact a credit union or small loan company and ask about a personal loan.
- Some banks offer short-term loans for small amounts at competitive rates.

Look into a cash advance on a credit card.
- It may have a lower interest rate than other sources of funds. Make sure you check out the terms and compare all available offers.

Shop for the credit offer with the lowest cost (APR).
- Compare the APR and the finance charge, which includes loan fees, interest, and other credit costs.

Contact creditors and ask for more time to make the payments or to temporarily pay only a portion of the loan or just the interest.
- Many are willing to work with consumers who they believe are acting in good faith. They may offer an extension on your bills. Evaluate what the charges would be for the extension (e.g., a late charge, an additional finance charge, or a higher interest rate).

Ask your bank about its overdraft protection on your checking account.
- Find out the terms of the overdraft protection, what it costs and what it covers, and if it is available to you.

See if you can get a paycheck cash advance from your employer or emergency community assistance or borrow from friends or family.

financialfitness:

Predatory Prey

A 2004 study by the Consumer Federation of America found that 75% of the interviewed borrowers of title loans had to give the lender a copy of their car keys. In some cases, lenders started the car to make sure it ran and took pictures of the car prior to the applicant filling out a loan application form. An Arizona title loan company installs GPS systems in the cars, so it can track the cars and shut them off remotely if it doesn't receive payment on time. If you can't pay, these lenders will come looking for you and your car.

Making $ense

5.11 Why is a payday or title loan considered predatory lending?

5.12 What are the disadvantages of rent-to-own contracts?

5.13 What are the alternatives to a payday or title loan?

Learn. > Plan & Act. > Evaluate.

➡️ **LEARN.** In this chapter, you learned about credit and what impacts the credit decision for consumer loans. You learned about the benefits and drawbacks of credit cards and finance options for education. You also learned about the hazards of predatory lending and rent-to-own schemes.

SUMMARY

■ ■ **LO 5-1** Explain the responsibilities, importance, and cost of credit as well as the options available for accessing credit.

Before applying for a credit card or a loan, examine your current budget and determine what type of payments you can comfortably afford. A total debt-to-income ratio of 36% or higher, including housing payments, makes you a high credit risk. All commercial lenders require a loan application before issuing a loan. Lenders make decisions on who receives credit cards and loans based on the five Cs of credit (character, capacity, collateral, capital, and conditions). Higher risk loans may require a cosigner and demand a higher interest rate.

■ ■ **LO 5-2** Evaluate the features, benefits, and disadvantages of many different types of credit cards.

Credit cards offer a complicated matrix of fees and features that vary greatly. In addition, the terms and conditions can change after you have the card. Types of cards range from general purpose cards to retail cards with special offerings, such as secured premiums and rewards. Look at all the features, including the grace period, the interest rate, and the cost of fees and charges, and choose a credit card based on how you plan to use it. Follow the steps laid out by the Fair Credit Billing Act to remedy any errors on your statement. Monitor your monthly statements and watch your credit limit closely to retain a low interest rate and low fees.

■ ■ **LO 5-3** Describe the mechanics of obtaining and repaying student loans.

There are three major categories of student loans: (1) federal student loans made directly to the student; (2) federal student loans made to the parents; and (3) private student loans made to students

or parents. To apply for any federal student aid, you must complete a free application for federal student aid (FAFSA). Upon graduation, prepare to start repaying your student loans. Important options include loan consolidation and refinancing, deferment, forbearance, and alternate payment options. Use the PVA formulas to calculate your loan payments. An amortization table can help you calculate how much of each payment goes toward the principal and the interest.

■ ■ **LO 5-4** Assess the drawbacks and benefits of payday loans, title loans, and rent-to-own credit options and identify alternatives.

Payday and title loans are small, short-term, high-rate loans. Rent-to-own outlets typically charge 1800% interest. These lenders are in a different category than credit card companies or banks and work around usury laws, charging triple-to-quadruple-digit annual percentage rates (APRs) and exorbitant fees. The terms of these loans are crafted to make it easy to roll over the loan and keep you in a cycle of debt; for title loans, the risk of repossession is extremely high.

➡ PLAN & ACT.

This chapter provides the planning tools for knowing how much debt you can responsibly take on and how to evaluate which credit options are appropriate for you. Your Plan & Act to-do list is as follows:

☐ Calculate your debt-to-income ratio (Worksheet 5.1).

☐ Compare your credit cards to assess which one best meets your needs (Worksheet 5.2).

☐ Set up your credit cards to be paid automatically, online.

➡ EVALUATE.

Take time to review your credit card disclosures to be aware of all possible fees and interest rates. Whatever financial situation you are in, avoid predatory lenders at all costs. Use Worksheet 5.1 to assess how much debt you can take on. Does your debt-to-income ratio adhere to the standard 28/36 rule? Is your non-mortgage/rent debt payment under 20%? If not, what steps can you take to get it there?

From Worksheet 5.2, which credit card is the best match for your needs? Can you reduce the number of credit cards you own? Schedule and perform annual reviews of your credit cards to reassess your credit needs and to see if you can renegotiate a lower interest rate with the credit card companies.

›› GoalTracker

Visit your online GoalTracker to log how you are doing on your SMART goals. Reflect on your current debt-to-income ratio standings. If you are not on target, log ideas on how you can get there.

key terms

Amortization	Collateral	Interest Rate Spread
Annual Percentage Rate (APR)	Cosigner	Margin Loan
Capacity	Credit	Predatory Lending
Capital	Debt-to-Income Ratio	Repossess

Revolving Lines of Credit

Roll Over

Secured Credit Card

Signature Loans

Unsecured Credit Card

Usury Laws

1. Why does a credit application request contact information for your next-of-kin relative who does not share a residence with you? *(LO 5-1)*

   a. Marketing ploy
   b. Cosigner
   c. Default payment contact if you skip out on payment
   d. To see if you are related to anyone in the company

2. You want to buy a car, and your gross annual income is $25,000. *(LO 5-1)*

   a. At 15% of your monthly income, how much of a loan payment can you make?
      (1) $425
      (2) $350
      (3) $312.50
      (4) $350.12
   b. To keep the total payment under 36% of your monthly income, how much money do you have left for rent and other debt obligations?
      (1) $450.37
      (2) $437.50
      (3) $537.40
      (4) $540.50

3. The average interest rate on deposit accounts is 3% for five-year certificates of deposit. A low-risk customer, with a nearly zero default risk, comes into the bank and wants to purchase a car and finance it over five years. What is the interest rate this customer can expect to pay on the loan, assuming the bank wants a 4% spread? *(LO 5-1)*

   a. 5%
   b. 6%
   c. 7%
   d. 8%

4. On a 0% revolving credit account with a $1,000 line of credit, you charged $300 for a new iPod, $40 for a night out, and $80 for concert tickets. You also made a $200 payment. You started with no charges against your account. What is your available credit? *(LO 5-1)*

   a. $220
   b. $780
   c. $870
   d. $1,000

5. Which of the factors below does *not* impact the variability of the credit card interest rate between applicants? *(LO 5-1)*

   a. Credit risk of applicant
   b. The 5 Cs of credit

   c. Amount of time at present employer
   d. Relationship of cosigner

6. Which of the features below is *not* an advantage to a credit card? *(LO 5-2)*

   a. Arbitration
   b. Easy bill payments
   c. Identity theft safeguards
   d. Credit builder

7. Which credit card finance calculation method is most advantageous to the card holder? *(LO 5-2)*

   a. Adjusted balance method
   b. Average daily balance method
   c. Two-cycle balance
   d. Previous billing cycles

8. Which of the fees below is *not* typically related to the credit card? *(LO 5-2)*

   a. Annual fee
   b. Cash advance fee
   c. Late-payment fee
   d. Over-limit fee
   e. Return-item fee
   f. Electronic payment fee
   g. Balance transfer fee

9. How does a subsidized federal student loan differ from an unsubsidized one? *(LO 5-3)*

   a. The applicant is required to demonstrate financial need.
   b. Interest on the loan is accrued.
   c. The government pays the interest while the student is in school.
   d. Payments are deferred for six months after graduation.
   e. All of the above

10. What loans can parents and graduate students receive to help pay for college expenses? *(LO 5-3)*

    a. PLUS loans
    b. Direct loans
    c. Sallie Mae loans
    d. All of the above

problems

1. You had a $1,000 balance last month after your payment on your credit card. You charged one pair of shoes on the 10th for $100. Your card has a minimum finance charge fee of $5 per month and an APR of 12%. What is your total balance due this period if the card's fees are calculated via the adjusted balance method? *(LO 5-2)*

2. You have a credit card balance of $10. You have made no charges this past month. Your card has a minimum finance charge fee of $5 per month and an APR of 12%. What is your total balance due this period if the card's fees are calculated via the average daily balance method? *(LO 5-2)*

3. You have no balance on your card, nor did you use it last month. Your card has a minimum finance charge fee of $5 per month and an APR of 12%. What is your new balance? *(LO 5-2)*

4. What are your monthly payments on the $10,000 student loan you are now ready to pay back, if the payments will be spread over the next 10 years with a 6% APR? *(LO 5-3)*

5. For a $10,000 student loan with a 6% APR, how much of the payment will go toward the principal and how much will go toward paying interest for each of the first six payments? *(LO 5-3)*

6. What was the APR on a $1,000 payday loan taken out for 30 days if your repayment on the loan cost you $1,050? *(LO 5-4)*

7. The charge on your rent-to-own washer is $25 per month. After 36 months, you get to keep the washer. How much does the washing machine end up costing you? *(LO 5-4)*

you're the expert

1. Frank is 21 and has his first credit card with a monthly APR of 1.5%. He went on a shopping spree the first month and now has a $1,000 balance. Budget-wise, it would be nice if he could just pay the minimum payment of $40 each month until he graduates in five months. *(LO 5-1)*

   a. How much of the $40 payment goes toward interest and what percentage goes toward reducing the principal?
   b. What is Frank's APR (annual percentage rate)?
   c. Frank missed two payments and his default rate of 36% APR kicks in. What is his monthly percentage rate now? *(LO 5-2)*

2. Anna needs $100 in cash to go home for the weekend and all she has is a credit card. Her cash advance fee is $10 and the credit card company charges a 3% fee. She decides to get a cash advance. *(LO 5-2)*

   a. How much will the cash advance cost her?
   b. What is the true cost of the $100 (as a percentage of the original $100)?
   c. If it takes her one year to pay off the cash advance and the credit card company charges 18% APR, how much will Anna end up paying in interest and fees for her $100 cash advance?

3. Rocco recently graduated and his student loans will come due in six months. Over the course of four years in college, he took out a student loan at the beginning of each school year. The first three were government subsidized and the fourth was an unsubsidized student loan. He has a job lined up as a financial planner. He knows that until he builds his customer base, he will have a lower, entry-level salary. *(LO 5-3)*

   a. What should Rocco do with his student loans and what payment option should he choose?
   b. What should Rocco do with his student loans if he decides to go back to get his master's degree in two years?

4. Leigh's parents are in an auto accident and she needs quick money to fly home. She doesn't have enough in her account to pay for the $800 plane ticket, nor does she own a credit card. She hastily makes the decision to stop in at a title loan office. She gives them the title of her car as collateral to secure her 30-day loan of $1,000 at an interest rate of 18%. She has a processing fee of $50 and a mandatory roadside service fee of $75. Her parents end up being hospitalized for three months. Leigh, tending to matters at home, extends the short-term loan twice more, paying only the interest for the first three months. However, the fees repeat with each rollover. At the end of three months, her parents are home from the hospital and she shares her financial situation with them. *(LO 5-4)*

   a. If they choose to pay off the loan in full after three months, what will the loan actually end up costing?
   b. What is the resulting APR?
   c. Does Leigh have any other alternatives at this point?
   d. What would have been an alternative option for funding the airline ticket on such short notice?

5.1 DEBT-TO-INCOME RATIO CALCULATIONS

Use the online debt-to-income ratio calculator to compute your debt-to-income ratios. Where do you fall? If you are not where you want to be, are there action items that you can follow up on to improve your debt-to-income ratio?

Monthly Income		Debt to Income Ratio (Calculated)	
Salary / Wages		Monthly Debt Payment	$0.00
Social Security		(divided by)	
Military Pay		Monthly Income	$0.00
Pension / Retirement Income		(equals)	
Bank and Investment Interest		Non-housing Debt-to-Income Ratio	#DIV/0!
Alimony / Child Support			
Rental Income		**How do you measure up for creditors?**	
Unemployment		less than 10% Great Shape	
Food Stamps		10 - 20% Good Credit Risk	
Royalties		20 - 35% Questionable Credit	
Student Grant Monthly Draw		35% or Higher High Credit Risk	
Other			
Other			
		Monthly Housing Payment	$0.00
		(divided by)	
Total Income	**$0.00**	Monthly Income	$0.00
		(equals)	
		Non-housing Debt-to-Income Ratio	#DIV/0!
Outstanding Debt Payments (Monthly)			
Credit Card {Payments		Total Debt	$0.00
Student Loans		(divided by)	
Car Payments		Monthly Income	$0.00
Recreational Vehicle / Boat Payments		(equals)	
Bank/ Credit Union/Loan payments		Debt-to-Income Ratio	#DIV/0!
Medical Dental Bill Payments		Goal <= 36%	
Computer / Electronic Bill Payments			
Furniture and Appliance Payments			
Other Credit Loans or Accounts			
Other Debt Payments			
Other Debt Payments			
Total Monthly Payments	**$0.00**		

5.2 CREDIT CARD SCORECARD

This worksheet will help you evaluate different credit card features to determine which card is the best fit for you.

1. In the Priority Rank column (pink squares), rank the listed features in sequence of importance, with 1 being the most important and 24 being the least. Give consideration to how you plan to use the card and how you plan to make payments.

2. Select three credit cards to evaluate. For each feature, rank the card from 1–3, with 1 being the best. Enter the rank in the CC# Rank columns (in yellow).

3. Score each credit card feature's comparative ranking by multiplying Priority and Rank. (For each row, **Priority Rank** × **CC# Rank** = **CC# Score**.)

4. Total each credit card score column (in green). The lowest score is your best fit.

Credit Card Features	Priority Rank	CC 1: Rank	CC 1 Score (Priority Rank*CC1 Rank)*	CC 2: Rank	CC 2 Score (Priority Rank*CC2 Rank)*	CC 3: Rank	CC 3 Score (Priority Rank*CC3 Rank)*
APR: purchases			0		0		0
APR: cash advances			0		0		0
APR : balance transfers			0		0		0
APR if you pay late			0		0		0
Interest rate: fixed, variable, or tiered			0		0		0
Grace period: balance paid off			0		0		0
Grace period: carry a balance			0		0		0
Grace period for cash advances			0		0		0
Finance charge calculation: 1 or 2 cycles			0		0		0
Finance charge calculation: include/exclude new purchases			0		0		0
Finance charge calculation: average or adjusted			0		0		0
Minimum finance charge			0		0		0
Fee: annual			0		0		0
Fee: late payment			0		0		0
Fee: over credit limit			0		0		0
Fee: set-up			0		0		0
Cash advance: transaction fee			0		0		0
Cash advance limits			0		0		0
Credit limit amount			0		0		0
Secured/regular/premium card			0		0		0
Feature: rebates			0		0		0
Feature: frequent flier miles			0		0		0
Feature: insurance			0		0		0
Feature: other			0		0		0
Total Scores		0		0		0	

continuing case

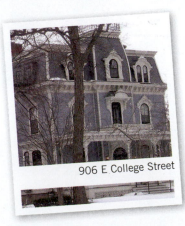

906 E College Street

In his senior year, Jack took a spring break trip to Daytona Beach with his friends. He had not saved up for the trip, so he financed it with his brand new credit card. He had the time of his life, giving no thought to all to the items he charged as the week unfolded: jet skiing, parasailing, lavish evenings out, and a tattoo. The following month, he was appalled to realize his charges came to a total of $2,700.

Jack is in no position to pay off this debt. He has been paying the $120 minimum payment each month. The card's interest rate is a 21% APR. Although he has barely used his card, the balance seems to be growing. For Jack, this credit card has come to symbolize his spring break week in Florida: out of control.

On top of the credit card, Jack's student loans are coming due. He had four different federal student loans over the course of his undergraduate years, all at different interest rates. He is considering taking graduate classes as one option to defer payment of his student loans.

A summary of the housemates' goals can be found in the first Continuing Case problem on page 27.

1. Given his situation, what advice do you have for Jack regarding his credit card debt?

2. What advice do you have for Jack regarding his student loans?

> "That money talks I'll not deny, I heard it once:
> It said, 'Goodbye.'"
>
> —RICHARD ARMOUR *(1906–1989)*

credit bureau reports and identity theft

s a credit score of zero a good thing or a bad thing?

The one disadvantage of a zero credit score is that if you have an unexpected need to borrow money in the future, it will be difficult to do so without a credit record. Establishing a credit history and credit score will allow you to borrow money to buy things now and pay for the items over time with future earnings.

During the different stages of your life, you may need to rely on credit to purchase a car, help pay for your college education, buy furniture or clothes,

pay for travel or entertainment, or buy a house. If you need credit to make the purchase, your credit score will help lenders determine your creditworthiness. Your credit score is an asset you should maintain and protect. The higher your score, the more access you will have to credit, the lower the interest you will be charged on loans, and the more money you will save. ■

LEARNING OBJECTIVES

After reading this chapter, you should be able to:

LO 6-1 Examine the importance of credit and understand how to establish personal credit.

LO 6-2 Describe the information on a credit report.

LO 6-3 Summarize how a FICO credit score is calculated.

LO 6-4 Identify strategies to improve your FICO credit score.

LO 6-5 Explore options for correcting errors on your credit report.

LO 6-6 Analyze how identity theft occurs and determine strategies to protect yourself against it.

LO 6-7 Recognize credit risks and learn about debt management steps you can employ at pivotal points during your financial life stages.

◄ Brian and Alicia, parents of three

The Perfect Credit Score

Brian and his wife, Alicia, have a distinctive attitude toward credit scores. He says, "We know couples who compete with one another as to who has the highest credit score. My wife and I believe that the perfect score is a zero. We pay cash or use our debit card for everything and don't have any credit cards. We have an emergency fund to keep us from having a credit card or credit line for emergencies. Having open lines of credit and competing for a high credit score is playing with fire and is a ticket to uncontrollable debt. By living within our means and having the priority of a debt-free life, we are able to pay cash for everything we purchase, which has given us a great sense of financial freedom and control."

6.1 ESTABLISHING CREDIT

■ ■ **LO 6-1** Examine the importance of credit and understand how to establish personal credit.

Perhaps a credit card application in the mail or an on-the-spot offer of a "free gift" has lured you into signing up for a credit card. A week later, the new credit card comes to you in the mail. To see if this card really works, you buy the new pair of shoes you have been wanting. You have told yourself you will *always* pay off the full amount of the credit card when the bill comes. However, the bill doesn't come for four weeks and in the meantime, you have charged eight meals, two more pairs of shoes, an MP3 player, and 48 new MP3s. You are shocked to see that your bill is over $500.

Although you told yourself you would *always* pay the balance each month, $500 is more money than you can afford to pay. The credit card company only requests a minimum payment of $10 and you think you can at least double that payment and then pay off the balance with holiday money after the end of the first semester. You have not considered the interest you will be paying on the balance.

Congratulations! You have just fallen into debt. The credit card company's hope is that you will continue to be in debt and therefore, continue to pay the 18%-plus interest on the borrowed money. Credit card companies don't want you to pay off the balance in full. They want you to remain in **perma-debt**, where you never get out of debt. They want you to think that it is easy to use your card and just make the minimum payments. Now the "free" T-shirt is the most expensive thing you own because of the interest you are paying.

Credit card companies are willing to issue credit cards to college students because they are a good credit risk—even if they have never had any credit in the past. They know students are smart and after graduation they will get good jobs. They also know that if students get over their heads in debt, most parents will bail them out (after a lecture).

The Credit CARD Act of 2009 requires consumers under age 21 to show evidence of enough income to make payments or have an adult cosigner in order to receive a credit card in his or her own name. The act also prohibits credit card companies from inducing college students to apply for credit cards by offering free gifts (T-shirts, M&Ms, sports bags) on campus. Credit card companies can offer these incentives only if they are at least 1,000 feet off campus.

If you have fallen into debt and think you might be in perma-debt, this chapter will help you create a path out

[**"My problem lies in reconciling my gross habits with my net income."**]

—ERROL FLYNN, *Australian film actor (1909–1959)*

of debt. If you have yet to receive your first credit card or loan, this chapter will help you understand how to build and maintain an outstanding credit history that will open doors to purchasing the house, car, or other items you want. By maintaining an outstanding credit history, you will save money by receiving low interest rates on future loans because you have proven yourself to be a good credit risk.

Debt is an important resource to tap at different points in your life. Therefore, it is important to establish a credit history to demonstrate responsibility with credit. When it comes time to purchase your first car or home and you plan to pay for it by taking out a loan, creditors will want to know how you have handled credit in the past. If you have no track record, the unknown will make it more difficult for you to get a loan. The simplest, most common form of debt is a credit card. Creditors believe the best predictor of future behavior is past performance. To establish a credit record, apply for a credit card. Use it wisely. For the months you select to use it, pay it off on time and in full.

6.2 READING CREDIT REPORTS

■ ■ **LO 6-2**   Describe the information on a credit report.

If you have established credit, you have a credit record financial institutions can access to see if you are a good

credit risk. Your credit report and credit score can open up doors when it comes time to borrow money, or they can keep you from getting the loan you want. The consequences of not knowing your credit score could prevent you from achieving your financial goals. Therefore, you should obtain your credit report and check it every four months. Your credit report and credit score are valuable assets you should protect and verify.

Credit Reporting Agencies

In the United States, there are three national credit reporting agencies: TransUnion (www.transunion.com), Equifax (www.equifax.com), and Experian (www.experian.com). These agencies provide a service of gathering credit information from banks, credit unions, credit card companies, and finance companies about businesses and individuals and then reporting that information when requested by businesses or individuals. Any time you apply for credit, the person issuing that credit can request a credit bureau report. Your credit report and credit score are a reflection on your credit-worthiness based on your past use of credit.

Your credit report not only contains information on how you have handled credit in the past, but it also contains personal information about you. It contains your name, current address, previous addresses, year of birth, current employer, and previous employers. It also contains

$Making $ense

6.1   What is perma-debt?

6.2   Why is it important to establish a credit record?

6.3   How do you establish a credit record?

information from public records, such as a bankruptcy or tax lien, unpaid child support, and any monetary judgments. Your credit report also includes a record of any recent inquiries into your credit report, as well as your past and current loans, credit cards, and your payment history regarding those obligations.

All three credit reporting agencies have different formats for both their paper and online reports. However, all of

4. *Date last reported* shows when the creditor last reported credit information to the credit bureau and when the credit bureau last updated your credit report for the specific creditor.

5. *Credit limit or original amount and high balance* indicate whether or not you have used all of your credit. Lenders tend to look at this as the possible maximum debt you could have if you used all of your credit cards.

> ## "If you think nobody cares if you're alive, try missing a couple of car payments."
>
> —EARL WILSON, *Major League baseball pitcher (1934–2005)*

these reports contain similar information about your credit history. Figure 6.1 shows a sample section of a credit report. Note the following items:

1. *Account* includes the name, address, phone number, and account number identifying who extended you the credit.

2. *Type, terms, and monthly payments* displays whether the credit is fixed term with fixed payments, like a car loan, or whether it is revolving credit, like a credit card.

3. *Date opened* indicates how long the account has been open. The longer your account has been open, the better your credit score.

financialfitness:
JUST THE FACTS

Credit History Impact

You may have guessed that bank and credit card companies view credit reports, but so do cell phone companies, utilities, insurance agents, potential landlords, and employers. Depending on your credit history, you may be required to place a larger security deposit on your apartment or make higher insurance payments. You may not be able to get the apartment you want or a decent cell phone contract. You may not get hired. A high credit score is an indication of being highly responsible and trustworthy.

6. *Recent balance and required payment* show the amount you owe as of your last statement and your minimum payment due.

7. *Comments* provides a place where you or the creditor can include notes about your account. The creditor might place a comment as to the date on which an account was closed and by whom. For example, "closed 12/1/2011 by consumer" indicates that you closed out the account. "Closed 12/1/2011 by creditor" indicates that the creditor closed the account. Closing the account at your request is much better for your credit score than having an account closed by the creditor. If you pay off your car loan as agreed, it will just show the date closed with a zero balance. You can place comments at the end of a credit report, explaining any of your payment history. For example, if you were in a car accident and were unable to work and got behind on your payments, but are now caught up, you might want to place a comment explaining your situation.

8. *Payment history* indicates how you have made payments in the past. Note the payment history key in Figure 6.1. A track record of *Paid* or *Pays as Agreed* represents how responsible you are with credit and is the strong driver of your credit score.

Credit Card Purchases

A key part of your credit history is how you have used credit cards. To improve your FICO credit score (discussed in more detail in the next section), do not use more than 10% of your credit limit when making purchases. People with the best credit have a utilization rate of no more than 7%. A 30% usage is a red flag. If your credit utilization is 50% or more of your credit limit, you are significantly hurting your credit score according to the FICO '08 scoring model adopted in May 2008.

Credit card purchases are easy to track. As a result, data mining to get insight into consumer habits is big

▼ FIGURE 6.1

Sample credit report account detail

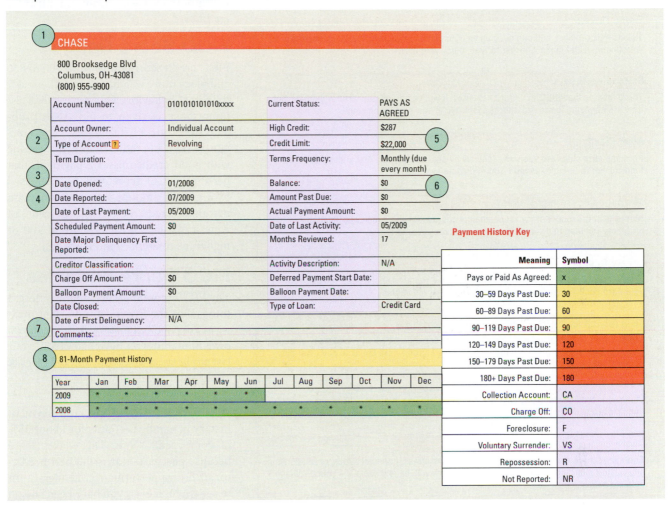

① **CHASE**		
800 Brooksedge Blvd Columbus, OH-43081 (800) 955-9900		

Account Number:	0101010101010xxxx	Current Status:	PAYS AS AGREED
Account Owner:	Individual Account	High Credit:	$287
Type of Account ?:	Revolving	Credit Limit:	$22,000
Term Duration:		Terms Frequency:	Monthly (due every month)
Date Opened:	01/2008	Balance:	$0
Date Reported:	07/2009	Amount Past Due:	$0
Date of Last Payment:	05/2009	Actual Payment Amount:	$0
Scheduled Payment Amount:	$0	Date of Last Activity:	05/2009
Date Major Delinquency First Reported:		Months Reviewed:	17
Creditor Classification:		Activity Description:	N/A
Charge Off Amount:	$0	Deferred Payment Start Date:	
Balloon Payment Amount:	$0	Balloon Payment Date:	
Date Closed:		Type of Loan:	Credit Card
Date of First Delinquency:	N/A		
Comments:			

(Callouts: ② ③ ④ ⑤ ⑥ ⑦)

Payment History Key

Meaning	Symbol
Pays or Paid As Agreed:	x
30–59 Days Past Due:	30
60–89 Days Past Due:	60
90–119 Days Past Due:	90
120–149 Days Past Due:	120
150–179 Days Past Due:	150
180+ Days Past Due:	180
Collection Account:	CA
Charge Off:	CO
Foreclosure:	F
Voluntary Surrender:	VS
Repossession:	R
Not Reported:	NR

⑧ **81-Month Payment History**

Year	Jan	Feb	Mar	Apr	May	Jun	Jul	Aug	Sep	Oct	Nov	Dec
2009	*	*	*	*	*	*						
2008	*	*	*	*	*	*	*	*	*	*	*	*

Source: www.equifax.com

business. Credit card companies get paid for sharing your purchasing records with third party agencies. Figure 6.2 on the next page provides a list of the top 8 items that you should think twice about before paying by credit card, according to marketplace.org.

6.3 DERIVING THE CREDIT SCORE

■ ■ **LO 6-3** Summarize how a FICO credit score is calculated.

Multiple sets of mathematical formulas are used to calculate your credit score. Bill Fair, an engineer, and Earl Isaac, a mathematician, founded Fair Isaac Corporation in

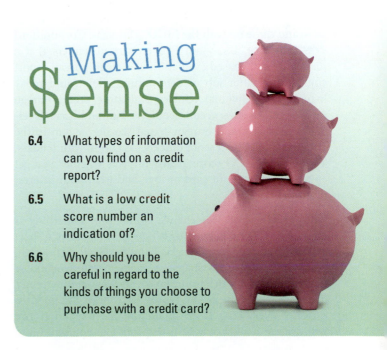

Making $ense

6.4 What types of information can you find on a credit report?

6.5 What is a low credit score number an indication of?

6.6 Why should you be careful in regard to the kinds of things you choose to purchase with a credit card?

▼ FIGURE 6.2

Things to avoid paying for by credit card

Traffic Tickets

- Tickets look reckless and can push up your insurance rates, which could put a strain on your finances and make it harder for you to pay your bills.

Retreading Tires

- This indicates that you can't afford new tires. If you've bought new tires in the past, but now are choosing to retread, this can look like things are turning south.

Adult Playthings

- Porn and strip clubs are seen as escapism by card companies. And guess what they're thinking you're trying to escape from? Financial worries.

Marriage Counseling/ Therapy

- Money is at the root of many psychological and relationship problems. Relationship problems can lead to divorce. Divorce can destroy your finances.

Lottery Tickets

- Lottery tickets or trips to Las Vegas don't reflect a sound financial plan. You don't want your card company to think you're irresponsible or a gambler.

Cash Advances

- Credit-card companies promote these products because they bring in loads in interest charges. But tapping your card for cash or using a credit-card check to pay other bills doesn't look good.

Income Taxes

- Using your credit card to pay your taxes raises a red flag. It could indicate your debts and bills are overwhelming you.

Booze

- Springing for too many drinks may be a sign of job stress, financial stress, or relationship stress. And charging booze several times in a row will make it seem like your bar binge was not a fluke.

Source: http://marketplace.publicradio.org/display/web/2009/07/08/pm

1956 and came up with the **FICO** (Fair Isaac Corporation) **credit score**. Isaac and Fair convinced lenders that a mathematically based evaluation of a credit bureau report could do a better job of determining who would repay loans than individual lenders evaluating credit bureau reports and making credit decisions. Fair and Isaac developed the first credit bureau–based scoring system in the 1980s and the FICO score quickly caught on with lenders. Today, your FICO score greatly impacts whether you get approved for a credit card or loan and what your interest rate will be.

Your credit score can change every time something is reported to a credit bureau. Whereas your balance sheet is a snapshot of your assets, liabilities, and net worth, your credit score is a snapshot of your creditworthiness as determined by the information in your credit report. Over 100 different credit scores have been designed to measure everything from predicting the likelihood you will declare bankruptcy to how profitable you will be to

a credit card company. The FICO score is designed to measure the likelihood that a borrower will default on a loan or credit card.

FICO Score Range

FICO credit scores range from 300 to 850 and place more weight on recent behavior than past behavior. This means that less importance is given to old credit problems over time. FICO also is set up to recognize signs of credit trouble. If someone with good credit misses a payment, that person's FICO score will be decreased by a greater amount than someone with marginal credit. Over 50 percent of Americans have a FICO score of 700 or higher (as referenced in Figure 6.3)

FICO Score Variables

The FICO score measures many different things, but the five most important measures are payment history, how much you owe, how long you have had credit, your last application for credit, and the types of credit you have used.

your payment history Your payment history generally accounts for about 35% of your credit score. This makes sense because past behavior is the best predictor of future performance. Lenders want to see when, if ever, you have been late on payments, how late you have been, and how often you have been late. Late payments that occurred two years ago will have less influence on your credit score than late payments that happened two months ago. Being 30 days late once is not nearly as bad as being 60, 90, or 120 days late. The more days you let your bills go unpaid, the more it hurts your credit score. Being late on a payment only once hurts your credit score less than being late on multiple accounts multiple times.

how much you owe How much you owe accounts for about 30% of your FICO credit score. FICO looks at both your *revolving* credit (credit cards and lines of credit) and your *installment* credit (car loans and mortgage loans). With revolving credit, FICO compares how much you owe to what is available for you to borrow. The closer you come to maxing out your credit card, the higher the probability that you will default on your obligations. Lenders like to see you use no more than 30% of your available credit. For example, if you have a credit card with a $1,000 limit, you should charge no more than $300 dollars.

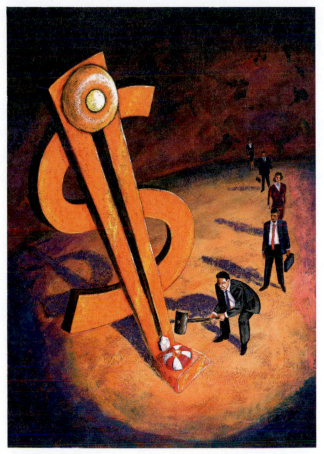

How do you score?

Your FICO score is also affected by how many of your accounts have outstanding balances. A larger number of accounts with balances can be an indicator of higher risk default due to over-extension. With installment credit, how much you have borrowed and how much you have paid back affects your FICO score. For example, if you borrowed $15,000 to buy a car and have paid back $5,000 without being late on any of your payments, you have shown an ability to manage and repay your debts.

length of credit history The length of your credit history accounts for about 15% of your FICO score. In general, the longer you have had a credit account, the better your FICO score. FICO considers your oldest account, your newest account, and the average age of all of your accounts. Closing out an account you have had for a long time, even if you don't use it, could hurt your FICO score.

recent applications for new credit New credit and applications for new credit account for about 10% of your FICO score. If you recently opened up many new credit accounts, you represent a higher risk of default. Your FICO score also looks at how many recent requests for credit you have made. Inquiries remain on your credit report for two years and FICO scores only consider the past 12 months. If you are shopping for auto loan rates and every bank pulls a credit bureau report on you, your credit score could go down.

types of credit in use The types of credit you presently use account for about 10% of your FICO score. Your FICO score improves with a mix of both revolving and installment credit. By using both revolving and installment credit, you demonstrate responsibility in managing your credit and show low credit risk. All of the information found in your credit report helps drive your credit score (see Figure 6.4).

FICO credit score
a credit score method that reflects your credit risk based on a snapshot of your credit report at a particular point in time

▼ **FIGURE** 6.3

National distribution of FICO scores

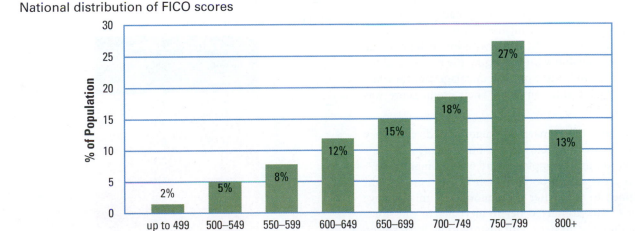

Source: www.myfico.com/crediteducation (7/21/2009).

"" Poverty often deprives a man of all spirit and virtue;
it is hard for an empty bag to stand upright. ""
—BEN FRANKLIN (1706–1790)

▼ FIGURE 6.4

Activities that drive your FICO score

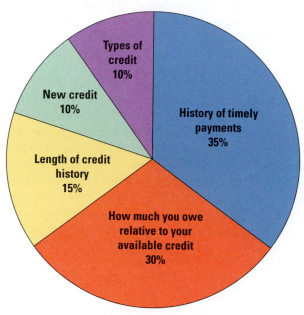

the resulting FICO number A FICO credit score above 800 is considered excellent, above 700 is good, above 650 is fair, and a score *under* 600 is poor (see Figure 6.5).

Sometimes the credit history of one person can affect the credit score of another. This is often the case when a married couple has joint accounts. Sue and Ward had been married for 20 years. They had two children, a home, two cars, a small business, a number of rental properties, and four credit cards with low balances. Sue had taken responsibility for managing the money and the payments over the course of their marriage and they had always made payments on time. Their credit score was very good at 750.

Unfortunately, their marriage deteriorated and they agreed to divorce and close their business. During this period, Ward was not employed and was not making payments on a car still in both of their names. Sue's credit score dipped to 600. After three months of missed payments, the bank contacted her to alert her to the situation. Sue didn't want her credit history to be hurt, so she took responsibility to bring the loan current while she pressured Ward to trade the car for a used model in his

name. The bank placed a comment in her credit report. Sue continued to manage her money carefully, paying her bills on time and paying the balance of her credit cards each month. As the missed payments continued to age on her credit file, they had less impact on her score and her credit score rose to a stellar 800.

Because your FICO score is based on your credit report, reviewing your credit report and correcting any errors are vital tasks to ensure your credit score reflects your creditworthiness.

6.4 IMPROVING YOUR CREDIT SCORE

■ ■ **LO 6-4** Identify strategies to improve your FICO credit score.

The first step to improving your credit score is to know where you currently stand. So let's explore how to obtain your credit report.

Accessing Your Credit Report

The only place from which to safely receive a free copy of your credit report is the government-sanctioned Central

▼ FIGURE 6.5

FICO score classifications

FICO Credit Score	
Excellent	850
	800
Good	750
	700
Fair	650
Poor	600
	550
	450
	400
	350
	300

financialfitness:
NUMBERS GAME

Poor Credit Score Cost

Your FICO score is a big factor in determining the interest rate you will be awarded on your mortgage loan. Examples shown in the table below are from September 2010 on a $200,000, 30-year mortgage. The difference between an excellent and a fair FICO score will cost you more than $36,000 in interest paid.*

Your FICO Score (range)	Your APR	Total Interest Paid
800–850 (excellent)	4.606%	$369,364
700–799 (good)	4.783%	$377,021
650–699 (fair)	4.997%	$386,381
300–649 (poor)	5.427%	$405,515

*Using calculator from www.bankrate.com.

Making $ense

6.7 What does the FICO score predict?

6.8 What is considered a good FICO score?

6.9 What are the five most important indicators that impact the FICO score?

Source Annual Credit Report Request Service at www.annualcreditreport.com. Other sites will provide you with a free credit report if you sign up for their credit protection or credit review service. For example, if you go to www.freecreditreport.com for your "free" credit report, you will have to sign up for a membership in Triple Advantage Credit Monitoring, which costs $14.95 per month. According to its website, you have nine days after enrollment to cancel your membership during your free trial membership. Your "free" credit report will end up costing you $179.40 annually if you don't cancel the membership.

At www.annualcreditreport.com, you can view your credit report from each of the three credit reporting agencies once a year. As you review your credit report, check for errors. According to a CBS news report (2004), as many as 80% of credit reports contain errors, and 25% include serious errors that could affect one's credit score. In 2007, *Consumer Reports* reported that individuals find 13 million inaccuracies in their credit reports each year. Since your credit score reflects what is in your credit report, you need to be sure that your credit report accurately reflects your information and only your information. We will discuss how to correct errors in your credit report in the next section.

Strengthening Your Credit Report

Your credit score takes a long time to build and improve, but it requires only a short time to fall. Let's look at some specific strategies you can employ to improve your credit score.

pay your bills on time Since your payment history makes up over 30% of your credit score, you cannot afford to make any late payments. Here are some tips to help you continually make payments on time.

- Write the check or go online to pay your bill as soon as you get your statement. If you are using an online bill payer service, you can pick the date the payment will be sent to the creditor.

- Go to the creditor's website to pay the bill or enroll in automatic bill payment. Many creditors' websites allow you to pay your bill online, deducting the money from your checking account. You can also choose the date on which the money will be withdrawn from your account. If you sign up for automatic bill payment, be sure to record the payment in your check register.

- Contact your bank for automatic payments for all of your loans. Look at your budget to be sure the payments are timed to coincide with when you will have money in your account. When you apply for a loan, you can choose your payment date. Make sure the payment date is timed to coincide with when you get paid.

keep credit card balances low The second largest impact on your credit score is the amount of credit you use compared to the amount of credit you have available. Use only a third or less of the credit available on your lines of credit and credit cards. To improve your credit score, you

financialfitness:
ACTION ITEM

Report Access

By establishing the Central Source Annual Credit Report Request Service, Congress has made it easier for you to get your credit reports and credit scores from the three national credit reporting agencies. Through the www.annualcreditreport.com website you can either: (1) complete a request form online, (2) call to request a form at 1-877-322-8228, or (3) mail a copy of a written request (available from the site as Worksheet 6.1 at the end of this chapter). As a helpful reminder, put three recurring annual appointments on your calendar or phone to check your credit report (staggering the start dates by four months), with each one being one of the three national credit reporting agencies so it is easy to remember which report is due to be requested (e.g., January: TransUnion; May: Equifax; and September: Experian).

financialfitness:
STOPPING LITTLE LEAKS

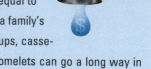

Waste Not, Want Not

According to research by the University of Arizona's Garbage Project, the average household throws away at least 470 pounds of food, equal to 14% of the food brought into a family's home. Using leftovers for soups, casseroles, crockpot meals, or in omelets can go a long way in trimming your food expenses.

---

may want to pay down those credit cards that are closest to their credit limit first.

pay off debt vs. transferring the balance
Even though those offers for "zero interest for six months on balance transfers" sound great, do not move your money around. There is usually a transaction fee of a few percentage points on the amount you transfer and opening new accounts can lower your credit score. The temptation to continue using the existing credit card will just result in more debt as well as more avenues of debt to juggle.

limit the number of new credit accounts
Do not be tempted by all the credit card offers you get. You should have no more than two major credit cards. At the checkout lane, the store associate will ask if you would like to save 10% today by opening a store credit card. If you want to improve your credit score, just say no. You could end up paying

> ❝ Always taking out of the pot, and never putting in, one will soon come to the bottom. ❞
> —BEN FRANKLIN *(1706–1790)*

more in interest on other loans and credit cards than you save on the 10% of your purchase because that new credit card will lower your credit score. It is also difficult to stay on top of multiple credit cards. The more cards you have, the more likely you are to accidentally miss a payment or not realize how large your overall debt has grown. When things are hectic, it becomes too easy for the situation to get out of control.

catch up on missed payments
If you are in a hole and behind on payments, catch up on your payments as soon as possible. Stop using credit and contact your creditors to establish a repayment plan. It will take a long time to rebuild your credit score, but it is best to start the rebuilding as soon as possible.

credit counseling
There are no quick fixes to repairing your credit report. *Consumer Reports* (2007) cautions against using companies that offer to repair your credit report. Many of these companies charge fees and promise great results like cutting the amount of debt you owe in half. Be wary of offers that seem too good to be true. Many of these companies are fraudulent and exist to take advantage of people in desperate situations. The National Foundation of Credit Counseling (www.nfcc.org) is a well-regarded nonprofit organization you can contact for guidance if you need help managing your debt.

All of these little things will make a positive improvement in your credit

Making $ense

6.10 Where can you securely check your credit report and credit score?

6.11 Why is it important to check your credit report?

6.12 What can you do to improve your credit score?

score. Your credit score is a reflection of your financial responsibility in using credit. With an outstanding score, you will save money in lower interest rates, insurance rates, and deposit requirements. Take the time and effort necessary to get your credit score above 800, and be one of the 13% of Americans who have an exceptional credit score.

6.5 CORRECTING ERRORS ON YOUR CREDIT REPORT

■ **LO 6-5** Explore options for correcting errors on your credit report.

Through the Fair Credit Reporting Act, you have the option of contesting any errors you discover on your credit report. Correcting these errors may involve reporting the errors, identifying missing accounts, or expunging negative information.

Reporting Errors

To report an error discovered on your credit report, contact the credit bureau in writing and state what information you believe to be incorrect. Include copies of all documents supporting your position and enclose a copy of the credit bureau report, with the referenced error highlighted. For a sample dispute letter showing how to approach the credit bureau, see Figure 6.6 on the next

page. Send your letter by certified mail with return receipt requested so you have documentation that the credit bureau has received your letter. Finally, be sure to keep the original documentation and a copy of your letter as a reference in the event the error is not corrected.

The credit bureau must investigate the error within 30 days unless it considers your dispute frivolous. Following its investigation, the credit bureau will forward the relevant information about the error to the organization that provided the alleged misinformation. That organization must investigate and review the claim and then report its results to the credit bureau. If the information in your report is found to be in error, the organization must notify all three credit bureaus of the needed correction to your credit record.

The credit bureau must give you the results of the investigation in writing as well as a free copy of your credit report if the dispute results in a change to your report. This free report does not count as your free annual credit report. You can request that the credit bureau send notices to anyone who has received a copy of your credit report in the past six months, along with an explanation of the error. You also can request that a corrected credit report be sent to anyone who received a copy of your credit report for employment purposes in the past two years. If the investigation does not resolve the error, you can write a statement explaining the error, which will be included in your credit report.

Identifying Missing Accounts

You can also add accounts to your credit report if they are missing. Not all companies report to the three credit bureaus. To add accounts, you will need to write the credit

Date
Your Name
Your Address, City, State, Zip Code

Complaint Department
Name of Company
Address
City, State, Zip Code

Dear Sir or Madam:

I am writing to dispute the following information in my file. I have circled the items I dispute on the attached copy of the report I received.

This item (identify item(s) disputed by name of source, such as creditors or tax court, and identify type of item, such as credit account, judgement, etc.) is (inaccurate or incomplete) because (describe what is inaccurate or incomplete and why). I am requesting that the item be removed (or request another specific change) to correct the information.

Enclosed are copies of (use this sentence if applicable and describe any enclosed documentation, such as payment records and court documents) supporting my position. Please reinvestigate this (these) matter(s) and (delete or correct) the disputed item(s) as soon as possible.

Sincerly,
Your name

Enclosures: (List what you are enclosing.)

Source: Federal Trade Commission.

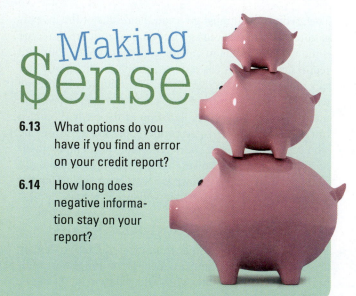

Making $ense

6.13 What options do you have if you find an error on your credit report?

6.14 How long does negative information stay on your report?

bureau and ask for the account in question to be added. For a fee, the credit bureau can verify an account and add it to your credit report, even though it is not required to do so.

Expunging Negative Information

Only time will clear up your credit file if negative information is accurate. Negative information stays on your credit report for seven years and bankruptcy information remains for ten years. Unpaid judgments can be reported for seven years or until the statute of limitations runs out, whichever is longer. There is no time limitation on reporting information about criminal convictions.

The Federal Trade Commission provides a wealth of information about credit reports, identity theft, and consumer-related trade issues at its website, www.ftc.gov. It also provides information for keeping your credit report safe and secure. Your credit report and credit score open doors to allow you to borrow money for the things you

Recommended websites related to credit reports

Federal Trade Commission (FTC)	www.ftc.gov
Experian Credit Bureau	www.experian.com
TransUnion Credit Bureau	www.transunion.com
Equifax Credit Bureau	www.equifax.com
Social Security Administration	www.ssa.gov

want. On the other hand, they can also keep you from getting loans, jobs, insurance, and apartments. Take the time to examine your credit report and correct any errors. Figure 6.7 provides a list of online references to assist you in examining your credit report and correcting any errors you discover.

6.6 SAFEGUARDING AGAINST IDENTITY THEFT

■ ■ **LO 6-6** Analyze how identity theft occurs and determine strategies to protect yourself against it.

When you have worked hard to build a good credit history and a good FICO credit score, the last thing you want is for someone to steal your identity and ruin your credit. Therefore, you should understand the ramifications of identity theft and know how to protect yourself.

Defining Identity Theft

Identity theft occurs when someone steals your personal information to commit theft or fraud. This type of theft occurs when someone uses your name, Social Security number, or checking, savings, or credit card account number to make unauthorized purchases, apply for new credit cards and loans, or make withdrawals or write checks from your account. Once they have the information they are looking for, identity thieves can ruin your credit rating and your personal reputation. Many types of identity theft can be prevented. One method is to continually check the accuracy of personal documents and promptly deal with any discrepancies.

The most common form of identity theft is the unauthorized use of your credit or debit card or checks to make purchases or withdrawals from your account. The less common but more damaging aspect of identity fraud is when a thief uses your personal information to obtain credit and open bank accounts. If they open these accounts in a different address, you may not know the fraud is occurring until you review your credit file or collectors come looking for you to pay a

loan in your name that you did not take out.

According to the Federal Trade Commission, as many as 9 million people are victims of identity theft annually, costing businesses over $50 billion each year. Consumers spend over $5 billion annually to undo what identity thieves have done.

Federal laws have been established to limit your liability, but identity theft still costs you time and money. Your liability is limited to $50 if someone steals and uses your credit card. It is different with bank debit or ATM cards. In this case, you must report the fraud to the bank within two days of discovering the transaction or you could lose up to $500 or the entire amount.

As such, it is very important to review your credit card and bank statements as soon as you receive them to check for fraudulent transactions. Many credit card companies and banks provide free online access to statements. Reviewing your statements online is a good habit to get into to avoid becoming a victim of identity theft. Some credit card companies phone their card holders to check authorization when unusually large amounts are charged against their accounts.

identity theft
the crime of obtaining the personal or financial information of another person and assuming that person's name or identity in order to make transactions or purchases

Watch where you swipe your card to avoid identity theft.

Identity theft can happen to anyone; identity thieves do not check your income statement before taking your identity.

Strategies to Protect Your Identity

Even if you do everything right to protect your identity, thieves have been known to steal victims' identities from banks, department stores, and even from the federal and state governments. However, there are steps you can take to reduce your risk.

check your financial statements To limit the amount a thief can get, check all of your financial statements for accuracy as soon as you receive them. This includes monthly credit card, banking, investment, and brokerage statements. If there are any errors or inaccuracies, report them immediately to the institution that issued the statement. Contact information is always printed on the statement. Follow up all phone calls with a written letter for documentation purposes.

monitor your credit report As discussed in Section 6.4, it is important to request a copy of your credit report from www.annualcreditreport.com. This is the only site where you can go to request a free credit report. All three credit bureaus also provide credit reports, at a cost, if you sign up for their fraud protection or credit monitoring service, but it is far from free.

don't give out personal information Unless you initiated the transaction, don't give out any personal information over the telephone, Internet, or on paper. Many places now require only the last four digits of your Social Security number to verify your identity. If you receive e-mails or phone calls asking for this information, identity thieves are **phishing** for information so they can steal your identity. Financial institutions and credit card companies will never e-mail or call you to request passwords, Social Security numbers, or your mother's maiden name for "verification" purposes.

buy a shredder Shred bank statements, financial statements, credit card statements, credit card applications, or any other documents containing personal information that an identity thief might use. Identity thieves look through trash to gain personal information they can use to commit fraud. Shredding documents can reduce the risk of having your identity stolen.

empty your wallet Do not carry more cards than you need. Keep your Social Security card and your passport locked in a safe or safe deposit box at a financial institution. You should carry your state-issued ID and your school ID, but you may not want to carry a credit card unless you think you will need it. If it is not with you, keep it locked up in a safe place.

lock it up Lock up your purse, backpack, or wallet at all times when these items are not physically with you. Do not make it tempting for a person to reach inside your purse, wallet, or backpack and steal your credit cards, school ID, or driver's license. This includes locking up important information while at home, work, and school. Make a list of all your credit card numbers and their customer service phone numbers and keep it in a safe, secure place you can access if your cards are lost or stolen. If your cards are stolen by an identity thief, they will be used right away. Therefore, contact your credit card companies immediately if you know your cards are missing. Quick action on your part can reduce the damage an identity thief can do and may aid the police in his or her capture and prosecution.

protect your mail Identity thieves can steal mail from your home or apartment to gain personal information. Consider using a post office box or a locked mailbox for incoming mail. If you do not utilize an electronic payment system, always drop off payment envelopes in a postal mailbox or deposit your mail at a post office.

practice good cell phone security Never discuss personal financial information on a cell phone or cordless phone. Identity thieves can intercept the phone call or overhear personal information necessary to steal your identity.

secure your computer Only deal with reputable websites when purchasing anything from the Internet. Identity thieves can create fake websites to gain personal information. Log off and quit your browser when you are finished visiting online bank sites, credit card sites, your e-mail account, or any other site on a public computer. If you don't, the next user on the computer could gain personal information and make transactions on your behalf. Never pay bills or conduct financial transactions on public computers. Keep your firewalls, virus protection, and spyware protection up to date to prevent hackers and identity thieves from gaining access to your computer. Unplug your Internet connection and turn off your wireless antenna when you are not using the Internet. Hackers cannot access your computer if they don't have a way in.

Change your passwords at least every 90 days. Passwords should be at least eight characters long and include both letters and numbers and they should never follow a pattern. Do not make your password your phone number or any other piece of information that could be easily derived by someone else. Finally, do not write your password on any credit, ATM, or debit card or on a piece of paper in your wallet or on your desk.

protect your PIN Be aware of people looking over your shoulder when you use an ATM or enter your PIN number. By learning your PIN number, an identity thief will have immediate access to your account, so always shield the PIN pad when entering this information.

watch out for skimming **Skimming** is when an identity thief steals the information from your credit card by swiping it through a processing machine that gathers the information. Be watchful of what the cashier does with your card when you hand it to him or her; swipes on multiple machines could be happening. At restaurants, where they take your card out of sight, make sure you feel the establishment is trustworthy, or else pay in cash. Check your statement carefully when it includes multiple charges made during a big vacation; fraudulent charges can easily slip by undetected.

freeze your credit report To safeguard against unauthorized access to your credit report, you can place a freeze on access to your credit report by contacting all three of the credit bureau agencies. A freeze prevents creditors, lenders, and services from accessing your credit report without your approval. A freeze on your credit report can cost money, however, depending on your state laws. Check with each credit bureau for specific information on how to place a freeze and the cost involved.

If you choose to freeze your credit bureau report and you would like to authorize a business to access your report, you can request a temporary lift or removal of the freeze. However, it can take up to three business days to process the request, so you will need to plan ahead.

Although it is no guarantee, your constant vigilance in protecting your information can reduce the chance that your identity will be stolen. Make it difficult for identity thieves to gain access to your personal information and always check your credit report at least once a year.

Victim of Identity Theft

If you are a victim of identity theft, you will need to take the following steps to restore your credit standing:

Step 1: Contact one of the three major credit bureaus and then follow up in writing. Additionally, place a fraud alert on your credit report. The credit bureau is required to contact the other two agencies to place a fraud alert on your credit file. The fraud alert is good for 90 days and can be extended to seven years if you provide the credit bureau with an *identity theft report.*

Step 2: Obtain copies of your credit report from all three companies. Examine them closely for errors or fraud.

Step 3: Contact the local police and file a report. Obtain a copy of the police report and the report number. Creditors will want a copy of the police report to clear your credit.

Step 4: Contact all of your creditors to alert them of the fraud and close the accounts in which the fraud occurred. Follow up all phone calls to your creditors with written letters and retain copies for your own records.

Step 5: File a complaint with the Federal Trade Commission at www.ftc.gov/idtheft or by phone at 1-877-IDTHEFT (438-4338).

Step 6: Place a freeze on your credit reports at all three credit bureaus.

Step 7: Continue to monitor your credit bureau reports for future identity theft.

These steps take time and have associated costs; however, they can help you limit the amount of financial damage that can transpire once you realize you have become a victim of identity theft.

financialfitness:
ACTION ITEM

Identify Theft Protection

Visit the Federal Trade Commission at www.ftc.gov/idtheft for a more in-depth exploration of identity theft, how to protect yourself, and steps to take if you should find yourself a victim.

$Making $ense

6.15 What constitutes identity theft?

6.16 What actions can you take to protect yourself against identity theft?

6.17 What steps should you take if you become a victim of identity theft?

Scan here for more information on the latest events "In the News"

Stolen Facebook accounts for sale

Researchers at VeriSign's iDefense division tracking the digital underworld say bogus and stolen accounts on Facebook are now on sale in high volume on the black market. During several weeks in February, iDefense tracked an effort to sell log-in data for 1.5 million Facebook accounts on several online criminal marketplaces, including one called Carder .su. That hacker, who used the screen name "kirllos" and appears to deal only in Facebook accounts, offered to sell bundles of 1,000 accounts with 10 or fewer friends for $25 and with more than 10 friends for $45, says Rick Howard, iDefense's director of cyber intelligence. The case points to a significant expansion in the illicit market for social networking accounts from Eastern Europe to the United States, he said . . .

Criminals steal log-in data for Facebook accounts, typically with "phishing" techniques that trick users into disclosing their passwords or with malware that logs keystrokes. They then use the accounts to send spam, distribute malicious programs and run identity and other fraud. Facebook accounts are attractive because of the higher level of trust on the site than

exists in the broader Internet. People are required to use their real names and tend to connect primarily with people they know. As a result, they are more likely to believe a fraudulent message or click on a dubious link on a friend's wall or an e-mail message. Moreover, the accounts allow criminals to mine profiles of victims and their friends for personal information like birth dates, addresses, phone numbers, mothers' maiden names, pets' names and other tidbits that can be used in identity theft.

Last summer, Eileen Sheldon's Facebook account was hacked and used to send messages to about 20 friends claiming she was stranded in Britain without a passport and needed money. Ms. Sheldon, who lives in California, had recently been living in London, and one friend, believing the ruse, wired about $100 to the thieves. Other friends smelled a fraud and warned Ms. Sheldon, who quickly reported the problem to Facebook. She does not know how her password was stolen . . .

Many users are eager to amass friends and accept friend requests from people they do not know, even though Facebook

discourages it. Facebook says it has sophisticated systems to defeat fake accounts, including tools for flagging them when they are created so they can be investigated. This allows Facebook to "disable them before the bad guys get very far," a spokesman, Simon Axten, said. Facebook also monitors for unusual activity that is associated with fake accounts, like many friend requests in a short period of time and high rates of friend requests that are ignored. It also investigates reports of suspicious users. The relatively low asking prices for the Facebook accounts point to the fact that Facebook accounts do not translate into instant profit. "The people that buy these things are going to have to do more work to make money," Mr. Axten said.

RIVA RICHMOND, "Stolen Facebook Accounts for Sale," *The New York Times*, May 2, 2010. Reprinted with permission.

Questions

1 What concerns are raised by this article?

2 Will this information change how you personally manage your Facebook account?

6.7 FINANCIAL LIFE STAGES OF DEBT MANAGEMENT

■ ■ **LO 6-7** Recognize credit risks and learn about debt management steps you can employ at pivotal points during your financial life stages.

Debt is a tool to be used wisely, responsibly, and carefully throughout your life. Responsible use of debt can allow you to buy the car or house you want and have low interest rates on all of your loans and credit cards. Irresponsible use of debt can lead you to default on your payments and have a lower credit score, resulting in higher interest rates and the possibility of not qualifying for a future loan.

dependent life stage As a minor you can neither legally sign a contract nor obtain a credit card. If you cannot establish credit, you cannot create debt. If you are under 18 years old, you should feel lucky that you don't have to worry yet.

independent life stage At this stage, you are starting on the journey to build your credit file. After age 18, you might apply for and receive a credit card. If you are under 21, you will have to show proof of income or have a cosigner on your credit application. Be very careful how you use it. Your credit limit is not your money to spend, but money to borrow; therefore, you must repay it. With your first credit card, your credit report is starting to build. It is important to always make your payments on time and not use more than 30% of your credit line. Review every financial statement you receive carefully, looking for errors and any irregularities. Budget your spending so you can repay the entire credit card balance every month.

As your credit report builds, be very careful with your personal information. Never give out your Social Security number or log-in or password information. Be careful what financial information you carry on your person. Begin monitoring your credit bureau reports from www.annualcreditreport.com and be on the lookout for errors. Contact the credit bureaus if you notice any problems or inaccuracies on your credit report. Continue working to build your credit score.

young family life stage Strive to get your credit score above 800 before you purchase a home. This will lower your interest rate and speed up the credit approval process. Maintain a constant watch over your credit report and credit score to protect them. Shred everything with personal information on it and lock up your credit cards, Social Security cards, and passports when not in use. Keep a list of all your credit card numbers and their contact information in case your cards are lost or stolen.

Making $ense

6.18 What are the side effects of irresponsible use of debt?

6.19 What steps can you take to build your credit rating as you enter the independent life stage?

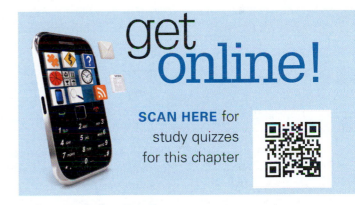

get online!

SCAN HERE for study quizzes for this chapter

empty nest and retirement stages Continue to monitor your credit report and protect your personal information so you don't become a victim of identity fraud. ■

Learn. ▶ Plan & Act. ▶ Evaluate.

➡ **LEARN.** In this chapter you learned how to read a credit report, build your credit history, and increase your credit score. You also learned about how to protect your personal information to reduce the risk of someone stealing your identity and what to do if identity theft happens to you.

SUMMARY

■■ **LO 6-1** Examine the importance of credit and understand how to establish personal credit.

To establish a positive credit record, always make payments on time and pay the balance in full whenever possible. To start a credit record, apply for a credit card; this is the simplest, most common form of debt. It is important to establish a credit history so you can demonstrate responsibility with credit and be considered a good credit risk (that is, have a strong credit score). This will be important down the road when you apply for your first car or home loan.

■ ■ LO 6-2 Describe the information on a credit report.

There are three national credit reporting agencies: TransUnion, Equifax, and Experian. Credit reports provide a reflection of your creditworthiness based on your past use of credit. Information on the credit report includes: credit account name, address, phone number and account number; date opened and last reported; type, terms, and monthly payments; credit limit or original amount and high balance; recent balance and required payment, as well as payment history; and comments. The report also tracks types of credit card purchases and makes assessments as to credit risks based on purchasing habits. This information is used to derive your credit score, which is a number used to indicate your credit risk and trustworthiness.

■ ■ LO 6-3 Summarize how a FICO credit score is calculated.

In the 1980s, Bill Fair and Earl Isaac developed a scoring algorithm, the FICO (Fair Isaac Corporation) credit score, which is used to predict the likelihood that a borrower will repay his or her debt in full and on time. FICO credit scores range from 300 to 850 and place more weight on recent behavior than past behavior. Over 50 percent of Americans have a score of 700 or higher. The five most important measures used by the FICO score are: payment history, amount owed, how long you have had credit, your last application for credit, and the types of credit used.

■ ■ LO 6-4 Identify strategies to improve your FICO credit score.

The only way to receive a free copy of your credit report is through the government-sanctioned Central Source Annual Credit Report Request Service, at www.annualcreditreport.com. Check your credit report every four months for errors and address any inaccuracies. To improve your credit score, never miss a payment and pay your bills on time; if you carry a balance, keep your credit card balances under one-third of your credit limit, pay off outstanding balances, and never transfer a balance between cards. Limit the number of new credit accounts you open.

■ ■ LO 6-5 Explore options for correcting errors on your credit report.

The Fair Credit Reporting Act allows you to correct errors discovered on your credit report. To report an error, provide clear documentation of the error to all the agencies and the creditor who made the error and be patient. Once the error has been corrected, request that a new report be provided to all of the parties who received the erroneous report. Negative information and bankruptcy information stay on your credit report for 7 and 10 years, respectively, and there is no time limitation on criminal conviction information.

■ ■ LO 6-6 Analyze how identity theft occurs and determine strategies to protect yourself against it.

Identity theft occurs when someone uses your name, Social Security number, checking account number, savings account number, or credit card account number to make unauthorized purchases, apply for new credit cards and loans, or make unauthorized withdrawals or write checks from your account. Strategies to reduce the risk of identity theft include: (1) checking your financial statements; (2) monitoring your credit report on a regular basis; (3) not giving out personal information over the phone if you did not initiate the call; (4) never sharing personal information on a wireless or cell phone; (5) shredding any papers that include financial information; (6) not carrying unnecessary credit cards or personal information on your person; (7) keeping credit cards, your Social Security card, and your passport locked up when not in use; (8) exercising good computer security habits; (9) protecting your incoming and outgoing mail; (10) being on the watch for skimming; and (11) covering the keypad when using your PIN number in public.

■ ■ **LO 6-7** Recognize credit risks and learn about debt management steps you can employ at pivotal points during your financial life stages.

Debt is a tool to be used wisely, responsibly, and carefully throughout your life. Enter into responsible use of debt during the Independent Life Stage. Demonstrating responsibility with credit at an early age will position you well for utilizing debt to acquire the things you will need later in the Young Family Life Stage, such as your first home. It will also allow you to obtain credit at the lowest interest rate possible. Irresponsible use of debt can lead you to default on your obligations and thus lower your credit score, resulting in higher interest rates, the possibility of not qualifying for a future loan, and the devastation of perma-debt. During the Empty Nest and Retirement Stages, debt management may no longer be an issue, but you will need to continue to monitor your credit report and protect your personal information.

⇨ PLAN & ACT. Your personal financial plan should now include
active monitoring of your credit score. Your Plan & Act to-do list is as follows:

☐ Review your credit report from www.annualcreditreport.com (Web Activity 6.1).

☐ Add notes to your calendar to remind yourself to review your credit report every four months.

☐ Select strategies for increasing or protecting your credit score.

⇨ EVALUATE. Evaluate a current copy of your credit report to confirm
its accuracy.

›› GoalTracker

Assess what steps you can take to strengthen your credit score. Log your findings in your online **GoalTracker.**

---

key terms

FICO Credit Score   Perma-debt   Skimming
Identity Theft   Phishing

---

self-test questions

1. To receive a credit card if you are under 21 you must: *(LO 6-1)*

   a. Have a cosigner

   b. Show evidence you have enough income to cover payments

   c. Both a and b

   d. Either a or b

2. Perma-debt occurs when: *(LO 6-1)*

   a. You pay off your credit card balance in full every billing cycle

   b. You transfer your credit card balance to receive 0% interest or a new card

   c. You receive your first credit card

   d. You never pay off your credit card balance in full

3. Where can you go to receive free credit reports from TransUnion, Equifax, and Experian? *(LO 6-2)*

   a. www.FreeCreditReport.com
   b. www.AnnualCreditReport.com
   c. www.MyCreditReport.com
   d. Directly from the sites www.equifax.com, www.transunion.com, and www.experian.com

4. In reviewing the payment history section of your credit report, you notice that there is a "30" recorded in the box for this past January. What does this mean? *(LO 6-2)*

   a. The previous 30 months were paid as agreed.
   b. Your payment was 30 days late in January.
   c. $30 is your minimum payment for the month of January.
   d. You had a balance of $30 on that card in January.

5. You're preparing for a good friend's bachelor party and need to pick up gag gifts, party favors, and the beverages for the evening. How should you pay for the items? *(LO 6-2)*

   a. Cash
   b. Check
   c. Debit card
   d. Credit card

6. What is the most important thing for you to do to improve your FICO credit score? *(LO 6-3)*

   a. Never borrow money or apply for credit.
   b. Apply for every credit card you can, but never use them.
   c. Pay all of your bills on time.
   d. Stay in perma-debt with balances of 95% of your credit limit.

7. Your FICO score can range from: *(LO 6-3)*

   a. 300–850
   b. 0–850
   c. 0–1,000
   d. 300–1,000

8. Your credit score can change: *(LO 6-3)*

   a. Only on your birthday
   b. When you check your credit report
   c. Every time something is reported to a credit bureau
   d. Both b and c

9. The five most important factors that affect your FICO score are: *(LO 6-3)*

   a. Your age, income, payment history, types of credit you use, and how much you owe
   b. Your payment history, how much you owe, how long you have had credit, your last application for credit, and the types of credit you use
   c. How much you owe, your income, your payment history, your age, and how long you have had credit
   d. Your payment history, how much you owe, how long you have had credit, types of credit you use, and your income

10. How often should you check your credit report? *(LO 6-4)*

    a. Once a year
    b. Monthly
    c. Three times a year
    d. Four times a year

11. To improve your credit score, you should use what percentage of your available credit? *(LO 6-4)*

    a. Only 10%
    b. Only 30%
    c. Only 50%
    d. Only 75%

12. Through what act do you have the right to contest errors, add missing accounts, or expunge negative information from your credit report? *(LO 6-5)*

    a. Fair Credit Reporting Act
    b. Fair Expunge Act
    c. Fair Credit Expunge Act
    d. Fair Lending Act

13. If you find an error on your credit report you should: *(LO 6-5)*

    a. Call the credit bureau and the creditor
    b. Contact the credit bureau and creditor by writing a dispute letter
    c. Not worry as the creditor and the credit bureau will catch the mistake
    d. Contact the Federal Trade Commission (FTC)

14. Identity theft: *(LO 6-6)*

    a. Most likely will never happen to you
    b. Victimizes as many as 9 million people a year
    c. Is reported every time it happens
    d. Only happens to the rich

15. What is the most common form of identity theft? *(LO 6-6)*

    a. Unauthorized use of a credit card, debit card, or check
    b. Use of another person's personal information to obtain credit
    c. Use of another person's personal information to obtain a job
    d. Use of another person's personal information to travel to another country

16. In which life stage is credit usually first used? *(LO 6-7)*

    a. Dependent
    b. Independent
    c. Young Family
    d. Empty Nest
    e. Retirement

17. At what financial life stage should you start monitoring your credit bureau report? *(LO 6-7)*

    a. Dependent
    b. Independent
    c. Young Family
    d. Empty Nest
    e. Retirement

Refer to the diagram below to answer problems 1 and 2.

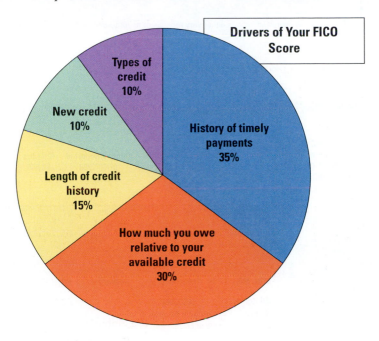

Drivers of Your FICO Score

- History of timely payments 35%
- How much you owe relative to your available credit 30%
- Length of credit history 15%
- New credit 10%
- Types of credit 10%

1. You are looking to improve your credit score quickly. To make the most progress, which two areas should you concentrate on first? *(LO 6-3)*

2. If 850 is a perfect FICO score and you have no new credit but are perfect in all other categories, what would you estimate your FICO score to be? *(LO 6-3)*

3. If your credit card limit is $15,000 and lenders like to see you using no more than 30% of your available credit, what is the most you should charge? *(LO 6-3)*

4. Your card has a limit of $20,000. You currently have used 90% of your credit limit. To improve your credit score, how much should you pay down on your balance? *(LO 6-4)*

5. Your card has a limit of $1,000. You plan to go on a honeymoon in one year and want to use the credit card as a back-up. You plan to request your limit to be raised after three months of charging only the following: $150 in month 1; $200 in month 2; and $199 in month 3. Each month you have paid the balance in full. What average percentage of your credit limit did you use each month? *(LO 6-4)*

6. List 10 things you can do to protect yourself against identity theft. *(LO 6-6)*

7. What are the steps you should take if you discover that your wallet with your ID, Social Security card, and all your credit cards has been stolen? *(LO 6-6)*

1. You put an ad on Craigslist for a third roommate. You ask the applicant for a copy of his credit report. Reading this report, are you comfortable taking this individual on as a roommate? Why or why not? *(LO 6-1, LO 6-4)*

Equifax Credit Report

Applicant Information

Name:	PAT SM
SSN:	633-37-2
Address:	Main St
	Small T

Fraud Indicators

This SSN may be invalid - it was either very recently or never issued by the Social Security Administration.

Tradelines

Applicant Information

Name:	PAT SM
AKA:	
SSN:	633-37-2
Date of Birth:	04/20/19
Current Address:	Main St
	Small T
Former Address:	Main S
	Small T
Former Address:	Main St
	Small T

Consumer Statements

Date Report
09/02/200

Name/Kind of Business	Type/Terms	ECOA	Opened/Reported	Balance	Limit	Past Due
HORMEL CR Credit Unions	Installment	Individual	07/08/1988 11/09/2003	$9,545	$10,000	
Status: 1: Pays account as agreed						
CIBC NB	Revolving	Joint	8/11/2000	$0		$600
All Banks			11/7/2009			
Status: 1: Pays account as agreed						
CIBC NB	Installment	Individual	8/1/2000	$0		$10,000
All Banks	000010M		12/1/2009			
Status: 1: Pays account as agreed						
Comment: Line of credit						
CIBC NB	Revolving	Individual	8/9/2000	$0		$1,000
All Banks			12/7/2009			
Status: 1: Pays account as agreed						
Comment: Paid account /zero balance						
Narrative: Line of credit						
PINCTY FCU Credit Unions	Installment	Individual	3/4/2002 12/2/2009	$0		$0
Status: 1: Pays account as agreed						

GMAC Auto Fina
Status: 1

WASHM
Mortgag
Status: 1

EQUIFAX
All Bank
Status: 1

JCP/MC
Sales Fin
Status: 1

	Balance	Limit	Past Due	Balance
Creditor Totals:		$34,227	$61,243	$0

2. You have just made it through your last semester of school. Classes were challenging, so you had to cut back on the number of hours at your part-time job. As a result, you were not able to keep up with your bills for the last two months prior to graduation. To help ease the situation, you applied for a new card and transferred the balance of your existing two cards, avoiding the necessity to make a payment for either of those cards that month. The following month, you were short on grocery and gas money, but your new card was at its limit so you ended up using both of your old cards you had initially planned to cancel. You also incurred a number of expenses getting ready to move following graduation. Additionally, you needed a whole new professional wardrobe and took advantage of a department store's discount offer by opening an account. You are now ready to start your first post-graduation job in a new town. You are horrified to learn that your application to rent a condo in the ideal location has been turned down due to your credit report.

a. What things did you do in the last three months that hurt your credit score? *(LO 6-3)*

b. What actions can you take to improve your credit report? *(LO 6-4)*

3. You discover your old cell phone company has listed an outstanding balance for $19.00 dating back to

May 16 when you ended your contract with them. You know that at the time you closed the account, you had overpaid the previous month and they had issued you a check for $19.00.

a. List the steps you need to follow to remedy your credit report. *(LO 6-5)*

b. Provide a copy of the dispute letter you need to write. *(LO 6-5)*

6.1   ACCESSING YOUR CREDIT REPORT (Web Activity)

The following is a copy of the PDF from Central Source Annual Credit Report Request Service. Visit the site of www.annualcreditreport.com online and request access to your free credit report. Following a review of your report, identify action items you can follow up with to improve your score. *(LO 6-5, LO 6-6)*

EQUIFAX®   experian®   TransUnion®

Annual Credit Report Request Form

You have the right to get a free copy of your credit file disclosure, commonly called a credit report, once every 12 months, from each of the nationwide consumer credit reporting companies - Equifax, Experian and TransUnion.

For instant access to your free credit report, visit www.annualcreditreport.com.

For more information on obtaining your free credit report, visit www.annualcreditreport.com or call 877-322-8228.

Use this form if you prefer to write to request your credit report from any, or all, of the nationwide consumer credit reporting companies. The following information is required to process your request. **Omission of any information may delay your request.**

Once complete, fold (do not staple or tape), place into a #10 envelope, affix required postage and mail to:
Annual Credit Report Request Service P.O. Box 105281 Atlanta, GA 30348-5281.

Please use a Black or Blue Pen and write your responses in PRINTED CAPITAL LETTERS without touching the sides of the boxes like the examples listed below:

A B C D E F G H I J K L M N O P Q R S T U V W X Y Z   0 1 2 3 4 5 6 7 8 9

Social Security Number:

Date of Birth:
Month / Day / Year

------- Fold Here -------   ------- Fold Here -------

First Name   **M.I.**

Last Name   **JR, SR, III, etc.**

Current Mailing Address:

House Number   **Street Name**

Apartment Number / Private Mailbox   **For Puerto Rico Only: Print Urbanization Name**

City   **State** **ZipCode**

Previous Mailing Address (complete only if at current mailing address for less than two years):

House Number   **Street Name**

------- Fold Here -------   ------- Fold Here -------

Apartment Number / Private Mailbox   **For Puerto Rico Only: Print Urbanization Name**

City   **State** **ZipCode**

Shade Circle Like This → ●

Not Like This → ⊗ ∅

I want a credit report from (shade each that you would like to receive):
○ Equifax
○ Experian
○ TransUnion

○ Shade here if, for security reasons, you want your credit report to include no more than the last four digits of your Social Security Number.

31238

If additional information is needed to process your request, the consumer credit reporting company will contact you by mail.

Your request will be processed within 15 days of receipt and then mailed to you.

Copyright 2004, Central Source LLC

906 E. College Street

Brett, being a second-year med student and over 21 years old, is constantly receiving credit card applications in the mail. He recently applied for and received a Visa card with a $30,000 credit limit. So far, he has been able to get through school without taking out any student loans, but money is getting tight. He worries about the next tuition payment and how to afford the next school break. He has been highly stressed and feels he needs to reward himself by getting out of town. Brett is also concerned about identify theft. This semester there was a security breach of a student file. Although he is unaware of any identity theft from the breach, he has a heightened concern about becoming a target of identity theft.

1. What advice would you provide Brett for his upcoming school break?

2. If he should head out of town, what advice would you offer to help him protect his identity?

A summary of the housemates' goals can be found in the first Continuing Case problem on page 27.

"Money alone sets all the world in motion."
—PUBLIUS SYRUS, *Maxim 656 (42 BC)*

section two

chapter seven

auto and home loans

Your car and home are among the largest purchases you will ever make. You will likely fund these purchases by taking out a loan. In this chapter, you will become familiar with auto loans and mortgages. ■

LEARNING OBJECTIVES

After reading this chapter, you should be able to:

LO 7-1 Recognize how to get the best deal when purchasing a car, compare purchase versus lease options, and gain an understanding of the loan approval process.

LO 7-2 Compare buying versus renting a home and evaluate which stage in life is best to make this investment.

LO 7-3 Describe the steps involved in purchasing a home, including financing options, and discuss the mortgage refinancing decision.

LO 7-4 Explain how home equity loans are used and describe the precautions that need to be taken when using them.

◀ Richie, age 22, graduate student at a small private university

The Car Decision

Richie moved out of his home state to attend graduate school. He said: "I decided on a university 500 miles from home. I didn't think Nell (the name of his car) was up to the long-distance trips, so I started looking for a newer-model used car. I really wanted a new car, but with still being a student, it would have been more than I could afford. I asked my father for advice, and I was surprised how much he knew about cars. When we found a used car I liked, I used the Internet to make sure I was getting a good buy. My dad helped me negotiate the deal. It was hard to say goodbye to Nell, but Belle (the name of the new car) is beautiful. I know she will make the 500 mile trips with ease, and I will save money with better gas mileage."

7.1 THE AUTO PURCHASE

■ ■ **LO 7-1** Recognize how to get the best deal when purchasing a car, compare purchase versus lease options, and gain an understanding of the loan approval process.

Most of us contemplate buying a car at some point in our lives. A car loses value with time, so you don't want to find yourself paying for a car you can no longer use. Any purchase spanning multiple years is a big decision. Before committing yourself to the long-term debt and payments involved in an auto purchase, you need to investigate all aspects of why you want it, what purposes it will serve, and how you will use it. In the sections that follow (outlined in Figure 7.1), we will walk through the steps involved in the auto purchase process.

Step 1: Analyze Needs versus Wants

The first step in the auto buying process involves having a clear understanding of what kind of vehicle you *want* versus what kind of vehicle you *need*. Do you need something reliable because you travel hundreds of miles to visit your family, or do you just need to get across town and around your neighborhood? Do you need something that gets great gas mileage or do you need something with a lot of power to pull your boat?

For many people, their vehicle represents an extension of their personal image and personality. As you watch commercials advertising cars and trucks, note how the ads focus on image. Driving a hybrid says you are green, progressive, and environmentally friendly. Jeep has long capitalized on the image of go-anywhere, do-anything independence in its advertisements.

Identifying your needs is the first step in selecting a vehicle. Needs are different from wants. You may *need* basic transportation to get to and from school, but you really *want* a four-door Jeep Wrangler Unlimited because you think it is cool and it makes you look great. You really don't need four-wheel drive, as you rarely go off road while going back and forth from your apartment to school. The Jeep gas mileage isn't the greatest either. To make the best decision, try to come to grips with what you need versus what you want. You can begin by considering the following:

- How much cargo do you carry?
- What type of driving experience do you want?
- How does the climate where you live impact what you need? Do you need snow tires or air conditioning?
- Are you looking for speed, acceleration, and handling, or fuel economy?
- Do you prefer manual or automatic transmission?

> "In less enlightened times, the best way to impress women was to own a hot car. But women wised up and realized it was better to buy their own hot cars so they wouldn't have to ride around with jerks."
>
> —SCOTT ADAMS, *Dilbert creator (1957–)*

A purchase to be proud of!

▼ **FIGURE 7.1**

The auto purchase process

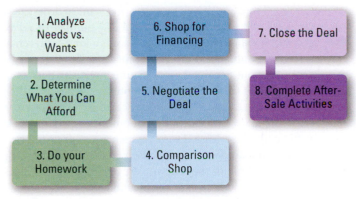

1. Analyze Needs vs. Wants
2. Determine What You Can Afford
3. Do your Homework
4. Comparison Shop
5. Negotiate the Deal
6. Shop for Financing
7. Close the Deal
8. Complete After-Sale Activities

- How important is a GPS or an entertainment system?
- Do you need two-wheel drive, all-wheel drive, or four-wheel drive?

Step 2: Determine What You Can Afford

Ideally, you want to pay cash for all of your vehicles. For many of us, that is not a possibility yet. Two factors determine if you can afford a vehicle: the down payment and the monthly payment. Many lenders require a 20% down payment to finance the purchase of a vehicle. Assuming this scenario, if you buy a $20,000 car, you will need $4,000 for the down payment plus enough for registration fees and taxes.

Keep in mind that you need to calculate how much you can afford and still keep your overall debt-to-income ratio at 36% or less (as discussed in Chapter 5). To determine how much you can afford to pay, multiply your monthly gross income by 36% to determine the limit of how much can be put to service your debt each month. Subtract all your

monthly debt obligations, including the possible monthly car payments, from this value. If you have a positive balance, then you can afford the payment amount for a new car. Your monthly payment is dependent on the number of months you finance your vehicle, the amount financed, and the interest rate.

Step 3: Do Your Homework

Now that you know what you can afford, it is time to do some serious homework. It helps to study financing options, pricing, service and maintenance requirements, and insurance. Fortunately, there are plenty of good resources online to assist you. See the Financial Fitness box on the next page for several useful online references.

used cars A car is an investment that rarely appreciates in value. Most new cars depreciate 35% to 40% in the first three years of ownership. This makes it less expensive to purchase a used car than a new car. Many cars today last well over 100,000 miles with regular maintenance. If you are unsure about buying a used vehicle, ask for transferable dealer warranties. When you buy a used car, you may be getting a deal by not taking a big hit on depreciation—or you may be buying someone else's troubles. If you are buying a used car, it is imperative that you have an independent mechanic put the car on a lift and check it out. This will cost around $100, but it can save you thousands if the car you are about to purchase is ready to break down. When researching online, review the dependability and reliability of the car.

new cars There are benefits to buying a new car, even though it loses value the moment it leaves the dealership. In buying a new car, you might be able to get a lower interest rate than a used car, and you also may be

With used cars, it is important to know exactly what you're getting.

7.1 Calculate Affordable Monthly Auto Payments

To calculate how large an auto payment you can afford, multiply your monthly income by 0.36 (% of income is the limit of what should be allocated to servicing debt). Then subtract your current monthly debt payments. The result is the maximum monthly auto (and insurance) payments you can afford. To calculate your affordable auto payment:

Your total monthly income: (_____) × 0.36 =	(_____)
Subtract other debt	− (_____)
Affordable Auto Payment:	= (_____)

financialfitness:
ACTION ITEM

Researching the Decision

When selling or buying an automobile, it is important to do your homework. The following online references can be helpful when making a car purchase decision:

Consumer Reports	www.consumerreports.org
Edmunds	www.edmunds.com
National Automobile Dealers Association	www.nada.com
Kiplinger Car Guide	www.kiplinger.com
J.D. Power and Associates	www.jdpower.com
MotorTrend Magazine	www.motortrend.com
AutoWeek Magazine	www.autoweek.com
Kelley Blue Book	www.kbb.com
CARFAX	www.carfax.com
Federal Trade Commission	www.ftc.gov

eligible for dealer and government rebates and incentives. Many auto dealers have rebates for new college graduates and those who are active in the military. Check the manufacturer's website for up-to-date information on incentive offers. With a new vehicle, you usually have a 36-month, 36,000-mile warranty. These warranties can amount to reduced maintenance costs compared to a used vehicle. New vehicles also come with the latest safety features, which can lower insurance costs. Finally, with a new car you know

with greater certainty that the car has not been driven and is in perfect condition, free from dings and scratches.

leases Leases work well for those who want to drive a new car every two to three years, drive a low number of miles, and take good care of their car. A lease is a long-term rental agreement with a limit on the number of miles that can be driven without penalty. Leases require a security deposit at the signing of the lease and then monthly payments. At the end of the lease term, you return the car. You do not own the car, but you do have the option of purchasing your vehicle at the end of the lease. Lease payments are almost always lower than loan payments because you are paying only for the depreciation for the time you are driving the car. Leases also usually include an early termination charge; if you don't like the car and want another, it will cost you extra money.

If you plan to drive a lot of miles or like keeping your car for a long time, a lease is not for you. Purchasing a new car is more expensive than leasing, but only until the car is paid off. Then the miles you drive are cheap. Also, when a lease expires, you may face the possibly difficult decision of either buying the car or entering into a new lease agreement, at a possibly greater cost. Carefully consider the options and examine all the pros, cons, and fine print before making your decision. Figure 7.2 outlines the comparative differences between leasing and owning.

See Figure 7.3 for a comparison of the costs involved in a lease versus buy decision.

price Cars and houses, the two highest-priced items you will buy, are two purchases for which you typically can negotiate the price. New cars have a sticker on the window listing the options and the Manufacturer Suggested Retail Price (MSRP). That is *not* the dealer's cost. *Consumer Reports* (www.consumerreports.org) offers a service that provides a new-car price report that shows the dealer cost, dealer incentives, and amounts retained for dealer profit

Leasing vs. buying

	LEASING	BUYING
Car ownership	You do not own the car but get to use it for the duration of the lease	You own the car
Up-front costs	Up-front costs include the first month's payment, a refundable security deposit, a capitalized cost reduction (like a down payment), taxes, registration, and other fees/charges	Up-front costs include the cash price or a down payment, taxes, registration, and other fees/charges
Monthly payments	Monthly lease payments are usually lower than monthly loan payments because you are paying only for the vehicle's depreciation during the lease term, plus rent charges (like interest), taxes, and fees	Monthly loan payments are usually higher than monthly lease payments because you are paying for the entire purchase price of the vehicle, plus interest and other finance charges, taxes, and fees
Early termination	You are responsible for any early termination charges if you end the lease early	You are responsible for any pay-off amount if you end the loan early
Vehicle return	You return the car at the end of the lease, paying any end-of-lease costs	You own the car; it is not necessary to return it
Future value	A leased vehicle has no future value because you do not own it	The vehicle will have fair market value when you trade or sell it
Mileage	Most leases limit the number of miles (often 12,000–15,000 per year) you can drive. If you negotiate a higher mileage limit, plan to pay a higher monthly payment. You will also pay charges for exceeding the limits at the time you return the automobile	There is no limit to the number of miles you may drive
Excessive wear	Most leases limit wear during the lease term. Exceeding these limits is an extra charge at the time you return the car	There are no limits or charges for excessive wear
End of term	At the end of the lease (typically 2–4 years), you may have a new payment either to finance the purchase of the existing car or to lease another car	At the end of the loan term (typically 4–6 years), you have no further loan payments

▼ **FIGURE** 7.3

Cost of leasing vs. buying: an automobile comparison

What are the costs involved in a decision to lease vs. buy a 2010 Honda Civic sedan valued at $15,000?

LEASING		PURCHASING	
		Cost of Vehicle	$15,000
Security Deposit	$500	Down Payment	$3,000
Monthly Lease Payments $220 * 36 months	$7,920	Monthly Loan Payments at 0% for 36 months = $334	$12,000
End of Lease Changes (if applicable)	$500		
Total Cost of Lease	**$8,920**	**Total Cost to Buy**	**$15,000**
Value of Asset after 3 years	**$0**	**Value of Asset after 3 years**	**$9,600**

and the MSRP. Kelley Blue Book (www.kbb.com) and National Auto Dealers Association (www.nada.com) also provide pricing information on new and used cars. Knowing the price or value of a car gives you an advantage when negotiating a final sales price.

reliability and service records The reliability of vehicles is rated by *Consumer Reports*, J.D. Power and Associates, and auto magazines. (You can access these reports online or at your local library.) Predicted reliability is based on past performance and can provide you with knowledge of how the vehicle is likely to hold up. Some new-car purchases include suggested maintenance schedules so you can better estimate the cost of ownership.

CarFax provides a service to help protect buyers of used cars. Using vehicle identification numbers (VINs), CarFax offers reports on specific used vehicles. It checks to see if the vehicle has been in a severe accident or in a flood, if it is a lemon, if the airbags have been deployed, how many owners the vehicle has had, and if it has been a rental or fleet car. It might also include service records if they have been forwarded to CarFax (www.carfax.com).

insurance cost Insurance cost is something a lot of people fail to consider when purchasing a new vehicle. You might have had only liability insurance on your old, paid-for car. If you have a loan on the vehicle, the lender will require full coverage insurance. Check with your insurance agent to find out the insurance cost of your new car and use that new figure in your budget. We will go into more detail regarding auto insurance in Chapter 10.

Step 4: Comparison Shop

Car dealers might try to get you to rush your decision by telling you someone else is looking at the vehicle you are interested in buying. If the vehicle you want sells before you make an offer, the dealer will usually work with you to find a similar one. So, take the time to do your research before you make a decision.

test drive Once you have narrowed down your list and know which vehicle you would like to purchase, stop in at a local dealer for a test drive to see how well it fits you. On the test drive, check the acceleration, braking, cornering, engine noise, hill-climbing ability, and passing acceleration. These are aspects of the car that can be discovered only by taking it for a test drive. Once you have driven the car and are satisfied with your decision, you will need to decide where you will buy the vehicle.

car dealerships Local car dealerships are the most common place to buy new and used vehicles. The advantage of buying from a dealership is that it may offer financing, extended warranties, and a shop for car repairs. Local dealers are established in the community. If something goes wrong with the car, you know where to find them.

private sales In private sales, you deal directly with the current owner of the vehicle. You may have found the car by seeing a "for sale" sign in the car's window or a listing in your local newspaper or you may have searched the Internet and found it on eBay or Craigslist. Before you purchase the vehicle, you will need to check the VIN, registration, and title to be sure the person selling the car is the actual owner. Ask for all maintenance records and get a CarFax report. When you buy the car and close the deal, you will want to be sure you have a clean title, free from any bank liens. To verify this, you may need to meet the seller at his or her bank to pay off the loan before the title is released. If the title is held by a non-local bank, you may have to send a cashier's check to the lender to pay off the loan and release the title.

Step 5: Negotiate the Deal

After doing all your homework and taking the car for a test drive, it is time to make an offer. If you are buying a new car, you know the MSRP (sticker price) and you have done your

homework on the price the dealer paid for the car. If you are buying a used car, you have done your research and know the stated value of the car from Kelley Blue Book (KBB), National Auto Dealers Association (NADA), and/or *Consumer Reports*. This puts you on a level playing field with the dealer or seller before you make the offer. Acceptable offers for new cars range from 2% to 5% above the dealer cost. This provides the dealer with enough profit to stay in business and make a little money. Private sellers may have more flexibility in accepting lower prices, depending on what is owed on the car and how quickly they need the money.

trade-in Trading in your old car for a newer car is a convenient way to conduct business. There is no worry or hassle about selling the old car to a private individual, and if your old car is not paid for, you won't be making two car payments until the older car is sold. However, dealers make a lot of money from selling trade-ins and this can complicate the transaction. The less the dealer credits you for a trade-in, the more he will make in the resale. Go to www.nada.com or www.kbb.com and do some research to get an idea of what your old car is worth, so you make certain you benefit fairly from the trade-in.

Step 6: Shop for Financing

If you decide to finance your vehicle, the rate you receive will be determined by your credit history and credit score, the term of the loan, the amount of your down payment, and the value of any collateral.

banks and credit unions Before negotiating with a car dealer, visit a local financial institution to see about prequalifying for a loan. Provide the details of what you want to buy and your down payment, and your banker will perform a credit investigation and tell you your rate and payments on the car. Then, when you go to the auto dealer, you will already know what you qualify for and what your rate and payments will be. This does not lock you into the financing through your financial institution; however, it serves as a useful point of reference. Keep in mind that credit unions, being not-for-profit and member-owned, sometimes have the best loan rates in town.

dealer financing Dealers generally will offer to find financing for your new purchase. Auto dealers sometimes offer 0% loans for up to 72 months to entice consumers to make the purchase. Many of these deals also include a cash discount if you do not take advantage of the 0% financing. To calculate the advantage of the 0% offer, you will need to compare the opportunity cost of the 0% financing to the cash discount (see Figure 7.4).

Step 7: Close the Deal

Many dealerships employ a finance and insurance (F&I) salesperson along with the car salesperson. The F&I person's job is to find financing for you and to offer you

Decision matrix for 0% financing

Example: You are purchasing a car for $20,000. The dealer is offering a $20,000 loan with 0% financing over five years or a $2,000 cash discount.				
Car Dealer Loan of 0% for $20,000 for 5 years *(60 month)*	vs.	Bank Loan of 4.5% for $18,000 for 5 years *(60 month)*	vs.	Credit Union Loan of 4% for $18,000 for 5 years *(60 month)*
20,000/60 = 333.33		PV = 18,000, FV = 0, I/YR = 4.5, N = 60		PV = 18,000, FV = 0, I/YR = 4, N = 60
Monthly Payments: $333.33		Monthly Payments: $335.57		Monthly Payments: $331.50
Comparison of Total Cost of Options (over 5 years)				
$20,000.00	vs.	$20,134.46	vs.	**$19,189.84**

insurance while generating a profit for the dealership. After the price has been agreed upon, the salesperson will take you over to the F&I person if you do not have financing. You can skip this step by arranging your own financing.

The F&I person will also try to sell you extras—extended warranties, extra insurance, GAP, credit life insurance, credit disability insurance, rust proofing, undercoating, fabric protection, and paint sealant—as a way to increase the profit for the dealership. You will have to decide if these offers are desirable. Remember, the F&I salesperson is making a commission on everything he or she sells.

Step 8: Complete After-Sale Activities

You have closed the deal and signed the paperwork and now you are ready to drive your car home. Before you take it off the lot, do a thorough walk around the exterior and look closely through the interior. If there are any scratches, dings, or marks, make sure you get the dealer to take care of them. If they cannot fix your car on the spot, have the dealer put in writing the work that will be performed. Call your insurance agent and make sure you have insurance coverage before you drive the car off the lot. You will have a temporary license on

> "One half of knowing what you want is knowing what you must give up before you get it."
>
> —Sidney Howard, *American playwright and screenwriter (1891–1939)*

Doing your homework up front can make driving your new car off the lot a pleasure.

Making $ense

7.1 How do you determine how large an auto payment you can afford?

7.2 What are the advantages of leasing (rather than buying) an automobile?

7.3 Why are "0% interest" and "$0 down" offers not always the best deals?

the car if you buy it from a dealer. If you buy the car from an individual, you will need to transfer the title and buy new license plates at your county courthouse or department of motor vehicles (DMV). Finally, enjoy your new ride!

7.2 HOME OWNERSHIP

■ ■ **LO 7-2** Compare buying versus renting a home and evaluate which stage in life is best to make this investment.

In this section we will consider renting versus buying a house, mortgage lending practices, types of mortgage loans, second mortgages, home equity lines of credit, the process of foreclosures, and what to do if your property is about to be foreclosed upon. A **mortgage** is the legal document used to allow a lender to use real property as collateral. If a borrower fails to pay on a home loan that is secured by a mortgage, the lender can evict the borrower from the house and resell the property to pay off the loan. This process is known as *foreclosure*.

Rent vs. Buy

Your lifestyle and personal choices will determine whether you become a homeowner or remain a renter. If you live in a downtown, metropolitan area, your only options may be to rent or buy a condominium. Many apartment complexes have turned into condominiums to allow renters the opportunity to become homeowners. When you rent, you sign a lease that states the terms of the rental agreement, such as the amount of rent to be paid, late fees if the rent is not paid on time, the amount of the security deposit, and the length of the contract.

These wheels will get you where you need to go—and get you past "Go"!

renting When you are out of college and in your first job, renting might be the most logical choice. You may not know how long you will be in a city before you get transferred, and you may not have any money saved for a down payment. Renting usually costs less, does not require your time for maintenance, and allows you the ability to move easily, either at the end of the lease or by terminating the lease early. If you do not like performing your own maintenance or doing yard work, renting might be your best choice. Maintaining a house takes time and money. Early termination of a lease usually involves a penalty fee, but you may be able to sublease the apartment. A **sublease** involves transferring the rental agreement from you, the current tenant, to a new tenant.

By renting a home, you will have more free time to do other things you enjoy. Buying a home is a major decision and it decreases liquidity. Figure 7.5 lists the advantages and disadvantages of renting.

buying For many, home ownership is part of the American dream. Some of the advantages of home ownership include the increase in equity and tax incentives.

▼ **FIGURE 7.5**

Advantages and disadvantages of renting

Advantages of Renting	Disadvantages of Renting
You can move easily at the end of the lease without a termination fee, or pay a termination fee if you move during the lease; much faster than selling a house	If the value of the property goes up, you will not share in that gain and you will never gain equity
Someone else is responsible for all the repairs; all you have to do is call the apartment manager	Rent might increase when the lease is up
No unexpected repair bills	Limited ability to personalize your living space
No property tax	No tax advantages
No homeowners association fees	Many rules to obey
No homeowners insurance, just renters insurance on the contents of the apartment	Landlord can make inspections
No risk of losing money on your investment if the housing market declines	May not be able to have pets
Low initial cost	
May not have to pay utilities	

financialfitness:
STOPPING LITTLE LEAKS

Paths to a Down Payment

To save money for a down payment on a home, consider temporary alternative living situations. Offer to split the cost with a close relative or family member in sharing their home. Consider a group living environment. If you have a home with an empty room, consider renting it out to another person who needs short-term, temporary housing. The extra money will help on the down payment for your next home.

increase in equity The increase in equity means you will eventually own your own home when you pay off your mortgage. This does not mean living without any home expenses. You will still have to pay property taxes and insurance, as well as maintenance and home repair expenses, but you will no longer have a mortgage on the house.

Most homes maintain or increase in value in the long term. As you pay down your mortgage and your house appreciates (we hope), the equity in your home will grow. **Equity** is the difference between the value of what you own and what you owe. As your equity increases, so does your net worth. You can use the equity in your home to secure other loans, as we will discuss later in this chapter.

tax advantages The U.S. government encourages home ownership through tax incentives. Generally, if you itemize your deductions, the interest you pay on your primary and secondary mortgages is tax deductible. If you pay points at your closing to get a better interest rate, they also may be deductible on your taxes. The real estate taxes and property taxes you pay your local government are also deductible on your taxes.

When you sell a house, you might have capital gains, that is, you may have made a profit by selling the house for more than what you paid for it. When this increase comes from an investment, like stocks, you are required to pay capital gains tax. However, home sales are exempt from capital gains tax if (1) you have lived in the house for two of the last five years and (2) the capital gains are less than $250,000 for a single person or $500,000 for a married couple.

personal ownership Personalizing your own space and making a house a home is very important to many people. If you own your home, you do not need to ask the landlord for permission to paint the walls, and there is no worry about damage deposits. Carefully weigh the benefits and disadvantages of renting versus homeownership to decide which is better for you given your particular situation and life stage (see Figure 7.6).

The New York Times hosts an interactive graph that can help you compare the costs of renting versus buying and determine how long you need to stay in one location in order for buying to be the better option (see Figure 7.7 on the next page). It's important to remember a home purchase is typically a long-term decision.

mortgage
a legal document used to allow a lender to use real property as collateral

sublease
the transfer of a lease agreement to a new tenant

equity
the difference between what is owned and what is owed

▼ FIGURE 7.6

Advantages and disadvantages of buying a home

Advantages of Buying a Home	Disadvantages of Buying a Home
Gain equity as you pay down the mortgage	Increased monthly expenses, larger monthly payment, larger utility bills, and property care costs
The value of the house may increase	The value of your house may decrease
Can personalize your living space	Takes longer to sell and could delay a move
Eventually live payment-free	Generally a larger initial investment (the down payment)
Can provide tax advantages on the interest and property taxes you pay	Opportunity cost: You could invest your down payment in something else that might have a better return
Capital gains exclusion if you have lived in your house for at least two of the past five years before selling	If you don't pay your mortgage, the bank could foreclose on you, and you could be without a home
Can get second mortgage home equity loans	Unknown maintenance cost—things break and you have to fix them or pay someone else to fix them
	Closing costs

Interactive comparative costs of buying versus renting

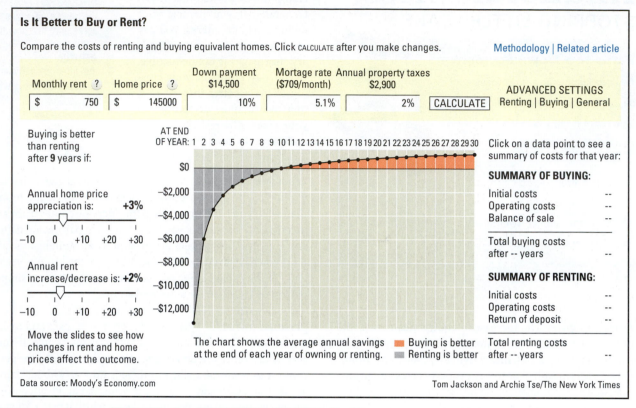

Is It Better to Buy or Rent?

Compare the costs of renting and buying equivalent homes. Click CALCULATE after you make changes.   Methodology | Related article

Monthly rent ?	Home price ?	Down payment $14,500	Mortage rate ($709/month)	Annual property taxes $2,900		ADVANCED SETTINGS Renting	Buying	General
$ 750	$ 145000	10%	5.1%	2%	CALCULATE	

Buying is better than renting after **9** years if:

Annual home price appreciation is: **+3%**
-10   0   +10   +20   +30

Annual rent increase/decrease is: **+2%**
-10   0   +10   +20   +30

Move the slides to see how changes in rent and home prices affect the outcome.

AT END OF YEAR: 1 2 3 4 5 6 7 8 9 10 11 12 13 14 15 16 17 18 19 20 21 22 23 24 25 26 27 28 29 30

$0
-$2,000
-$4,000
-$6,000
-$8,000
-$10,000
-$12,000

The chart shows the average annual savings at the end of each year of owning or renting.   ■ Buying is better   ■ Renting is better

Click on a data point to see a summary of costs for that year:

SUMMARY OF BUYING:

Initial costs	--
Operating costs	--
Balance of sale	--
Total buying costs after -- years	--

SUMMARY OF RENTING:

Initial costs	--
Operating costs	--
Return of deposit	--
Total renting costs after -- years	--

Data source: Moody's Economy.com   Tom Jackson and Archie Tse/The New York Times

Source: www.nytimes.com/2007/04/10/business/2007_BUYRENT_GRAPHIC.html?_r=1#

financialfitness:
STOPPING LITTLE LEAKS

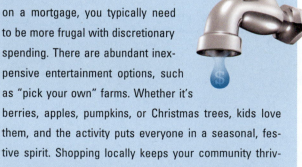

Savings from Home

When making the decision to take on a mortgage, you typically need to be more frugal with discretionary spending. There are abundant inexpensive entertainment options, such as "pick your own" farms. Whether it's berries, apples, pumpkins, or Christmas trees, kids love them, and the activity puts everyone in a seasonal, festive spirit. Shopping locally keeps your community thriving, which is important in keeping value in your home. Shopping close to home also increases the green factor as fewer resources are consumed in bringing food to the table.

Life Stages and Home Ownership

Most people buy their first home in the Early Family Life Stage, after finishing their education and starting their career. A first home most likely will be a "starter" home—an entrance into home ownership. This might be a condominium, a zero lot line (duplex), or a small single family dwelling. These homes are usually less expensive and require a relatively small down payment.

Some people remain in their original home until they have paid off the mortgage, perhaps making upgrades over the years. However, you might want a larger home, with more bedrooms and a larger lot. You may be one of those who see a larger house as the welcome ticket to suburbia. You may be concerned about the public schools and community services. If you decide to move, you can use the equity (the value of the house beyond any amounts still owed) from your first house as a down payment for the second house. You might also use a home equity loan to purchase an automobile, remodel your home, or finance college expenses.

Later in the Early Family Life Stage or perhaps early in the Empty Nest Life Stage, you might want to trade up to a

It is important to review and understand all of the fine print on your mortgage.

third home. This might be the house of your dreams, now that you have enough equity in your home and enough income to support the larger payments.

Empty Nesters sometimes buy a vacation home or a home for retirement. Empty Nesters are usually at the top of their earnings potential and have fewer bills, giving them a high discretionary income. A vacation home also might be seen as an investment at this life stage; Empty Nesters can make money by renting the home or selling it when its value increases. Empty Nesters who have successfully managed their finances can pay off their home and "burn their mortgage," a symbol of freedom from home loan payments.

During the Retirement Life Stage, you might downsize into a smaller home, with everything handicap-accessible and on one floor. You may choose to pay for this house in cash, using the equity from the sale of your previous home. In this life stage you also might decide to use a reverse mortgage, as discussed in Chapter 4, to increase your liquidity and have more cash to spend.

Of course, these benchmarks will not hold true for everyone. You may decide home ownership is not right for you and choose to rent all of your life.

Making $ense

7.4 What are the advantages of renting?

7.5 What are the advantages of buying your own home?

7.6 When does it make more financial sense to buy than rent?

 Nor need we power or splendour, wide hall or lordly dome; the good, the true, the tender, these form the wealth of home. "

—SARAH J. HALE, *American writer (1788–1879)*

7.3 BUYING A HOME

■■ **LO 7-3** Describe the steps involved in purchasing a home, including financing options, and discuss the mortgage refinancing decision.

If you someday want to own a home, make sure you are buying it because it's truly where you want to live—and not simply an investment or an asset that you hope will appreciate in value over time. Homeownership provides stability in location and payment as well as tax benefits. Once you determine you are ready for homeownership, the next step is the selection process.

Selection Criteria

Buying a home is an important investment and should be undertaken only after much thought and careful research. Let's look at some of the criteria to consider when making a selection.

price Target a home that reasonably meets your budget; that is, make sure you can afford the down payment, the monthly mortgage payments, the insurance, the taxes, and the maintenance costs. A good rule of thumb is that your home price should be no more than two times your total gross annual household income and all of your monthly household debt payments should be no more than 36% of your total monthly gross income.

location Convenience of location in relation to both work and play is important. Is public transportation an option? If you have to commute a long distance each day, it will impact

your overall budget as well as your time. Additionally, location has a huge impact on the resale value. Make sure the surrounding property and homes are consistent in value with the purchase price and investment you plan for your the home.

maintenance New homes and well-constructed homes will have lower repair expenses. A home with a large yard will require more work and money than a small yard or no yard. You will want to allocate a certain percentage of your budget to home maintenance.

school systems The reputation of the school system also drives the value of your home. Even if you don't have children, this will be an important criterion when it comes to reselling your asset.

insurance The cost of insurance impacts your budget; the more expensive the home, the more costly the insurance. Additionally, if the home is in a high-risk area, such as a flood plain, your insurance cost will be greater.

taxes Property taxes vary greatly from one location to the next. Annual property taxes are based on the county-assessed value of the home and include city, school, and other taxes.

homeowners associations Some homes are part of a homeowners association that assesses fees. You will need to add these expenses to your budget and include them in the overall cost of owning the home.

resale value A home is a large asset. You want it to appreciate in value over the time of your ownership. Two key drivers to keeping and adding value to the property are proper maintenance of the home and a desirable location.

> " People are living longer than ever before, a phenomenon undoubtedly made necessary by the 30-year mortgage. "
> —DOUG LARSON, *American newspaper columnist (1926–)*

A home is a place you can feel safe and secure, whatever else is happening around you—and can be a wise investment also.

The Role of the Real Estate Broker

A real estate broker (agent) links buyers with sellers, works for the seller, and is paid a commission on the sale of the property. The commission ranges between 3% and 7% of the selling price of the home and is divided between the listing agent and the selling agent. The *listing* agent is the agent that the seller chooses to advertise the house. The listing agent will help you determine the listing price based on recent sales of similar property. Your agent will list your house on the multiple listing service (MLS) so other real estate agents can see it is for sale. He or she also will place a "For Sale" sign in your yard and may schedule "open houses" where the public is invited to come and view your house during specific hours. The listing agent also will inform you when prospective buyers will be shown the house.

If you are looking for a house, a real estate broker can help you determine your borrowing capacity, identify your financing options, and help you find a lender. The agent can tell you about the location of schools, shopping, and churches—as well as inform you about taxes, utilities, zoning, and future plans for the community. Finally, the broker can recommend companies that will conduct inspections for such things as termites, dry rot, asbestos, faulty structure, roof condition, or radon gas.

If you buy the house, your agent is considered the *selling* agent and receives one-half of the commission. In some cases, the real estate broker is both the listing agent and the selling agent and receives the full commission.

selling without a real estate agent

With commissions of 3–7%, many sellers try to sell their homes without a real estate agent. If you choose this route, you can market your house in a number of ways, including newspapers, Craigslist, flyers, a sign in your yard, or word of mouth. Keep in mind that you will have to arrange all of the showings and show the house yourself. There are websites to help you and they do so by charging a fee. One such site is www.forsalebyowner.com. These websites will charge either a monthly fee or a one-time fee for their service. If you are selling your house without a real estate broker, you will have to do all the paperwork or pay an attorney to do so. In taking on the task of selling your home yourself, you could expose yourself to liability issues and fail to maximize your home price.

The Purchase Price

The actual purchase price of a home should take into consideration both the *one-time costs* on the day of the purchase, such as the down payment and closing fees, as well as the *ongoing monthly costs* for the life of the mortgage, which includes your monthly payments, taxes, and insurance costs.

affordable down payment

Most lenders will require 20% of the purchase price as a down payment when you buy a home. This is to protect the lender from loss if you fail to repay your mortgage and the lender has to foreclose on your house. If you put less than 20% down, the lender may require you to purchase **private mortgage insurance (PMI)**. PMI pays the lender if the lender forecloses on your home and its sale does not cover the mortgage and the cost to foreclose. You usually can request to have PMI dropped from the payments once your **loan to value (LTV) ratio** is 80% or less, either as a result of the house appreciating in value or you paying down the mortgage.

affordable monthly mortgage payments

You have found a house, you have saved the down payment, and now it is time to get a loan to buy the house. You can check mortgage loan rates at your local financial institution, in the newspaper, or online at www.bankrate.com and other similar websites. You also can calculate your monthly payment by searching online for "mortgage loan calculators." Keep in mind that these calculators provide only the interest and principal payment amount. They do not include the cost of insurance or taxes for the property.

To calculate the insurance payments, contact an insurance agent. Your local county and/or city assessor's office can confirm how much you will owe in real estate taxes. Property taxes are typically due once or twice a year and are payable to the county and/or city assessor. Many assessors list the property by address online so you can search for the assessed property value and taxes.

private mortgage insurance (PMI) insurance for the lender if it needs to foreclose on the home and the sale of the home does not cover the mortgage and the cost of the foreclosure

loan to value (LTV) ratio ratio expressing the amount of a first mortgage lien as a percentage of the total appraised value of real property

financialfitness:
STOPPING LITTLE LEAKS

Saving for the Down Payment

Saving for the down payment of your first home can seem like a monumental task. Ways to save for a down payment include:

—Set up an automatic transfer from your paycheck to a savings account designated for your down payment.

—Get a second or part-time job and save the money for a down payment.

—Save your tax refund.

—Sell unwanted items on eBay or have a garage sale.

—When you get a raise, save the raise and live off your current income.

—Ask for a gift or loan from your parents for part of your down payment.

There are many options available to finance your home purchase. Depending on the amount of the loan, common mortgages last from 10 to 30 years in length. Mortgage loans include fixed-rate/fixed-term loans; adjustable-rate mortgages (ARMs); and balloon-payment mortgages.

fixed-rate/ fixed-term mortgages When interest rates are low, it is good to lock in your interest rate with a **fixed-rate/fixed-term mortgage**. The bank that initiates the loan receives an origination fee and may receive fees for servicing the loan, but the loan is then sold to investors, who take on the risk. The Federal National Mortgage Association (FNMA, "Fannie Mae") and the Federal Home Loan Mortgage Corporation (FHLMC, "Freddie Mac") are government-sponsored enterprises organized to purchase mortgages to help make home ownership affordable. The benefit of a fixed-rate/fixed-term mortgage is that you know how much the mortgage interest and principal payments will be for the life of the loan.

adjustable-rate mortgages (ARMs) **Adjustable-rate mortgages (ARMs)** are home loans in which the rate and payments can change based on the terms of the loan. Unlike the fixed-rate/fixed-term mortgages sold on the secondary market, many banks keep ARM loans "in house." These loans adjust to the current interest rate every adjustment period, protecting the bank from interest-rate risk.

ARM loans are advantageous in many ways. Since the loan is not sold on the secondary market, the closing costs are usually less and the credit criteria may be less stringent. ARMs also can be advantageous in certain conditions: when interest rates are high and you think rates will decrease; when you plan to be in the home for only the initial adjustment period; if your credit is not particularly good; or if you do not have 20% of the purchase price for a down payment. Before choosing an adjustable-rate mortgage, you should understand the properties listed in Figure 7.8.

A word of warning: Before the housing/financial crisis that began in 2008, many people purchased homes using adjustable-rate mortgages and based their payment expectations on their introductory or teaser rates. Some speculated they could sell their home for a healthy profit before the introductory rate expired and then purchase another one. During this time, many homes were doubling in purchase price in just two to five years. When the housing and financial crises hit, the housing market crashed and houses lost value, with some falling to only 50 to 75% of the initial purchase price. Those whose introductory mortgage rates expired at this time could not afford to sell their homes for a loss and could not afford the payments at the new, higher rates. Those who were taking risks and speculating on housing prices lost. Learn this lesson well: Homes are for living in and not for purchasing and flipping for profit.

balloon-payment mortgages **Balloon-payment mortgages** are fixed-rate loans for a short period of time whose monthly payments are amortized over a longer time period

financialfitness:
NUMBERS GAME

Delicate Balance

In 2010, Republicans pressed for legislation to stop the losses at Fannie Mae and Freddie Mac (government-sponsored enterprises that buy up and repackage mortgages to keep loan prices stable). Fannie and Freddie have incurred more than $150 billion in losses since the burst of the housing bubble. Some Republicans argue the time has come to end Fannie Mae and Freddie Mac's taxpayer-backed "slush fund" and to require the agencies to operate on a level, competitive playing field with other lending institutions. However, analysts from both sides of the aisle contend the proposal would destabilize the entire housing market: pushing mortgage prices up, pulling support from low- and middle-income Americans, and further crippling housing recovery goals.

Properties of an Adjustable-Rate Mortgage (ARM)

Introductory Rate
- Teaser rate for the first adjustment period. This rate may be at or even below the index rate to entice people to finance their home with an adjustable rate mortgage.

Adjustment Period
- Length of time between rate adjustment periods. Common adjustment periods are 1, 3, 5, 7, and 10 years. If you had a 3-year adjustment period, you would have the introductory rate for the first three years and then your rate would adjust to the index rate plus the margin. Your rate and payment change every three years, based on the index rate.

Amortization
- Term of the loan; your payments are calculated based on the total term of the loan left using the rate of the current period.

Index Rate
- Published rate that your loan rate is tied to. The index rate may be the one-year Treasury bill rate, LIBOR (London Interbank Offered Rate), or the Wall Street Journal Prime rate.

Margin
- Interest rate charged over your index rate. For example, your rate at your adjustment interval may be the one-year Treasury bill rate plus 2%.

Adjustment Period Cap
- Maximum amount that the rate may increase at any given adjustment period.

Lifetime Rate Cap
- Maximum rate of your ARM.

Floor
- Lowest rate you will be charged.

than the loan. When the loan comes due, the remaining balance of the loan is due. For example, suppose you have a seven-year balloon with a 30-year amortization at 6% interest. Your payments are calculated over a 30-year time period at the 6% interest, with the entire loan coming due after seven years. When the loan comes due, you can refinance the remaining balance. Like ARMs, balloon-payment mortgages are usually kept in-house at local banks and not sold on the secondary market. These types of loans are advantageous when rates are high and you know you will not be in the home longer than the term of the balloon payment.

Figure 7.9, on the next page, provides some mortgage options and a description of the types of borrowers generally best served by each mortgage type.

closing costs The down payment and closing costs are due after the seller accepts the offer for the home and at the time of the **closing**. During the closing, the title for the home is transferred to the buyer, and the seller is paid in full. Closing cost fees—including fees for the loan application,

origination, points, appraisal, home inspection, and title search—can add up very quickly. An itemized list of closing costs includes:

Loan Application Fee: A charge for preparing the application, typically ranging from $75 to $300.

Loan Origination Fee: Usually a 1% charge of the amount of the mortgage loan. Some lenders may offer a different origination fee for acceptance of a different interest rate.

Points: Fees paid up front to the lender in exchange for a lower interest rate on a mortgage loan, typically between 1% to 2% of the amount of the mortgage loan. Called **points**, one point equals one percentage point of a loan. For example, a lender may advertise 5.25% with no points and 5% with one point. You are essentially buying down your interest rate by paying a percentage fee up front.

Appraisal Fee: An appraisal is an estimate of the market value of the home and is used to protect the lender's interests. The appraisal fee typically runs between $350 and $700.

Home Inspection: Some lenders require a home inspection, such as pest, structure condition, septic system, or water tests. Inspections typically cost from $175 to $350.

Title Search: A title search ensures that the property is owned by the seller. Costs vary from $175 to $900.

financialfitness:
JUST THE FACTS

Credit Score Impact

If your credit rating is below 600, lenders see you as having a higher risk of defaulting on a loan. Rather than succumbing to the temptation of utilizing subprime, high interest rates, it is better to wait for a period of time and build up your credit score before applying for a loan to refinance your home.

Mortgage map

Mortgage Type	Loan Characteristics	Appropriate for Borrowers Who:
Fixed-term/fixed-rate mortgage (30, 20, 15, 10 years)	Interest rate and monthly payments remain the same for the entire term of the loan	-Plan to own >10 years; like total payment stability
10/1 year **adjustable-rate mortgage**	Interest rate and monthly payments are the same for 10 years. In year 11, the interest rate adjusts every year, so payment is subject to change every year for the remainder of the loan	-Plan to own >10 years; like initial payment stability, can accept later changes OR - Plan to move < = 10 years, but want the loan to remain in force if plans change
7/23 (2-Step) or 30 due in 7 **fixed mortgage**	Interest rate and monthly payments are the same for 7 years. Conversion option: In year 8, the interest rate is adjusted to reflect prevailing rates; the resulting payment is the same for the remainder of the loan	-Plan to own >10 years; can tolerate one payment adjustment OR -Plan to move within 7 years; want the loan to remain in force if plans change
7/1 year **adjustable-rate mortgage**	Interest rate and monthly payments are the same for 7 years; starting in year 8, the interest rate adjusts every year, so payment is subject to change every year for the remainder of the loan	-Plan to own >7 years; like initial payment stability, can accept later changes OR -Plan to move < = 7 years; want the loan to remain in force if plans change
7 year **balloon mortgage**	Interest rate and monthly payments are the same for 7 years; at the end of 7 years, the loan is due in full. Borrower must refinance into a new loan at prevailing interest rates	-Plan to own >7 years; are willing to refinance at market rates OR - Plan to move < = 7 years; like payment stability
5/25 (2-Step) or 30 due in 5 **fixed mortgage**	Interest rate and monthly payments are the same for 5 years; conversion option: In year 6, the interest rate adjusts to reflect prevailing rates. The resulting payment will remain the same for the remainder of the loan	-Plan to own >5 years; can tolerate one payment adjustment OR - Plan to move < = 5 years; want loan to remain in force if plans change
5/5 & 5/1 year **adjustable-rate mortgages**	Interest rate and monthly payments are the same for 5 years; in year 6, the interest rate adjusts every 5 years (for 5/5 ARM) and every year (for 5/1 ARM)	-Plan to own >5 years; like initial payment stability, can accept later changes OR - Plan to move < = 5 years; want loan to remain in force in case plans change
5 year **balloon mortgage**	Interest rate and monthly payments are the same for 5 years; at the end of 5 years, the loan is due in full. Borrower must refinance into a new loan at the prevailing interest rates	-Plan to own >5 years; are willing to refinance at prevailing market rates OR - Plan to move within 5 years; like payment stability
3/3 & 3/1 year **adjustable-rate mortgages**	Interest rate and monthly payments are the same for 3 years; in year 4, the interest rate adjusts every 3 years (for 3/3 ARM) and every year (for 3/1 ARM)	-Plan to own >3 years; like initial payment stability, can accept later changes OR - Plan to move < = 3 years; want loan to remain in force if plans change
1 year **adjustable-rate mortgage**	The interest rate is adjusted every year, so monthly payment is subject to change every year for the entire 30-year loan term	-Want lowest rate possible; willing to accept yearly payment changes OR - Cannot qualify at higher rate programs

Source: www.interest.com/content/firsttime/whichmtge.asp

Sample estimate of closing costs and fees

Closing Cost Item	Estimate for $150,000 house	
	5% down payment	20% down payment
Down payment	$7,500	$30,000
Application fee	$75–$300	$75–$300
Loan origination fee (1 to 1.5% of loan)	$1,200–$1,800	$1,452–$2,137
Points (0%–3%)	$0–$4,500	$0–$3,600
Appraisal fee	$350–$700	$350–$700
Inspection fee	$175–$350	$175–$350
PMI	$125–$250	—
Title search	$175–$900	$700–$900
Total closing fees	$2,325–$8,800	$2,752–$7,987

See Figure 7.10 for the total estimated closing costs and fees for a $150,000 home.

the good faith estimate The Real Estate Settlement Procedures Act (RESPA) requires your mortgage lender to give you a *good faith estimate* of all your closing costs within three business days of submitting your application for a loan, whether you are purchasing or refinancing the home. This estimate includes your total finance charge and the annual percentage rate (APR). This APR is likely to be higher than the stated contract interest rate on your mortgage because it takes into account discount points, mortgage insurance, and certain other fees that add to the cost of your loan.

finance shopping Think about settlement fees before submitting a purchase offer. Remember: Many fees and charges are negotiable. When shopping among several lenders and brokers, use a mortgage shopping worksheet like the one shown in Figure 7.11 on the next page to compare costs.

Refinancing Your Home

As interest rates fluctuate over time, you may benefit from refinancing your home at a lower rate. If you have an ARM, you may want to lock in the rate to be more secure about what your future payments will be over the life of the loan. When refinancing your home, you still have the one-time cost of closing fees. How do you calculate the break-even period?

Use the step-by-step "Refinance Break-Even Worksheet" in *Doing the Math* 7.2, below, to get a ballpark estimate of how much time must pass before you recover your refinancing costs and begin to benefit from a lower mortgage rate.

doing the MATH

7.2 Refinance Break-Even Worksheet

You have a $200,000, 30-year fixed-rate mortgage at 5% and a current loan at 6%. The fees for the new loan are $2,500, paid in cash at closing.

1. Current monthly mortgage payment	$1,199
2. Subtract proposed new monthly payment	($1,073)
3. Equals monthly savings	$126
4. Subtract your tax rate from 1 (e.g., 1 − 0.28 = 0.72)	0.72
5. Multiply your monthly savings (#3) by your after-tax rate (#4)	126 × 0.72
6. Equals after-tax savings	$91
7. New loan's total fees and closing costs	$2,500
8. Divide total costs by new monthly after-tax savings (from #6)	$2,500/91
9. Equals number of months it will take to recover refinancing costs	27 months

Based on these calculations, it would be beneficial to refinance only if you plan to stay in the home for more than 27 months.

1. Where is the break-even point if the the fixed-rate mortgage drops to 4% with a new monthly payment of $955/month?

Sample mortgage shopping worksheet

Mortgage Shopping Worksheet	Lender:		Lender:	
	Mortgage 1	**Mortgage 2**	**Mortgage 1**	**Mortgage 2**
Mortgage: fixed-rate, adjustable-rate, conventional, FHA				
Minimum down payment required				
Loan term (length of loan)				
Contract interest rate				
Annual percentage rate (APR)				
Points (may be called loan discount points)				
Monthly PMI premiums				
How long must you keep PMI?				
Monthly payment (*principal, interest, PMI*)				
Application fee or loan processing fee				
Origination fee or underwriting fee				
Lender fee or funding fee				
Appraisal fee				
Document preparation and recording fees				
Credit report and other fees				
Title search/Title insurance				
Surveys and home inspections				
Total closing/Settlement cost estimates				
Other Questions and Considerations				
Are any fees or costs negotiable?				
Is there a prepayment penalty?				
How long does the penalty period last?				
Are extra principal payments allowed?				
Is the lock-in agreement in writing?				
Is there a fee to lock in?				
When does the lock-in occur?				
How long will the lock-in last?				
If the rate drops before closing, can I lock in at a lower rate?				
Is credit life insurance a condition of the loan?				
If the Loan Is an Adjustable-Rate Mortgage				
What is the initial rate?				
What is the maximum the rate could be next year?				
What are the rate and payment caps each year and for the life of the loan?				
How often does the rate change?				
What index will the lender use?				
What margin will the lender add to the index?				
How much does the credit life insurance cost?				

Making $ense

7.7 What selection criteria should you use when buying a home?

7.8 What role does a realtor have in brokering the sale of a home?

7.9 What types of mortgage loans are available and how do they differ?

7.10 What up-front costs should you expect to pay at the time of closing?

7.11 When does it make sense to refinance your home?

7.4 HOME EQUITY LOANS

■ ■ **LO 7-4** Explain how home equity loans are used and describe the precautions that need to be taken when using them.

In a home equity loan, the homeowner borrows on the paid value of the property. In simple terms, it is another mortgage on your home—a loan secured against your property, sometimes referred to as a second mortgage. The term *second* indicates the loan does not have priority in case you default on payments. Your first mortgage has priority and will be paid before any funds go toward the second mortgage. Second mortgages are higher risk and therefore have a higher interest rate than first mortgages.

Individuals typically use home equity loans when they need money for a major purchase or expense. They may not have unlimited credit on their credit cards and their other assets may not be as liquid. Traditionally, home equity loans were used to fund home improvements such as remodels and additions or to assist with the purchase of a second home. Over the past decade, it has become more common to use a home equity loan for consumer spending such as buying a new car, paying for college, or for debt consolidation.

Types of Home Equity Loans

Lending institutions offer a variety of home equity loans: home equity lines of credit (HELOC), fixed-rate/fixed-term loans, and balloon-payment loans.

home equity line of credit (HELOC) A home equity line of credit (HELOC) is like a secured credit card in which the collateral is the equity of your home. The bank places a second mortgage against your home for the maximum amount you can borrow, which is your credit limit. You pay interest only on the amount of money you use from your line of credit, similar to a credit card. If you use the money on your line of credit, you have to make minimum payments, which is also similar to a credit card. The interest rate on a HELOC is variable, based on an index plus a margin, which is similar to an adjustable-rate mortgage. However, the interest rate on a HELOC can adjust more frequently.

Generally, you gain access to your line of credit by writing a check or making a transfer from your credit line to your checking account. However, some banks are now issuing secured home equity *credit cards*. It can be very dangerous, however, to have such easy access to the equity of your home.

The advantages to a home equity line of credit are the ease of access to the equity of your home and tax incentives. With a HELOC, you apply only once for the loan and can use it for any expenses. Your available credit can increase or decrease depending on your outstanding balance. As you pay off the HELOC, you have more credit available to use.

The other major advantage of any home equity loan is the tax advantage. In most cases, the interest you pay on an equity loan (second mortgage) is deductible on your income tax if you itemize your deductions. This deduction is phased out if your income is high enough that you are subject to the alternative minimum tax (AMT). We will discuss the AMT more in Chapter 9. This tax advantage reduces the effective interest rate and makes equity loans more attractive to borrowers than credit cards and traditional auto loans.

fixed-rate/fixed-term loan Fixed-rate/fixed-term equity loans are popular when financing home improvements or an automobile. Like a traditional auto loan, these loans have a fixed payment for a specific time frame, usually two to seven years, with a fixed interest rate. Besides the tax advantage of the interest you pay, there is the advantage of knowing when the loan will be paid off and what the payments will be. When

> ❝ **Never spend your money before you have it.** ❞
> —THOMAS JEFFERSON, *U.S. president (1743–1826)*

using the equity in your home to finance a car, the bank will not place a lien on your car and will not hold the title of your car as collateral. Instead of using your car as collateral, the bank will use the equity of your home.

balloon-payment loan If you are making a major purchase like a motor home or a boat, you may want to stretch the payments over 10 or 15 years, while using the equity of your home as collateral. Banks are willing to do this using balloon-payment loans.

You may finance your boat with an amortization over 15 years, with a fixed rate and fixed payments for the first five years and a balloon payment of the remaining balance due at the end of the fifth year. At that time, you will have to either pay off the loan or refinance the balance of the loan at the current interest rate. This could change your payment amount. The bank is willing to do this because of the collateral pledged (your house) and because it protects the bank from interest rate risks. The advantage to you is you get to buy what you want with low payments over a longer period of time, in addition to enjoying an income tax advantage.

Comparison Shopping

In evaluating the different types of loans, you need to investigate various lenders. How do they differ regarding interest rates and payments, terms of the loan, points, fees, penalties, and credit insurance? Look at the monthly payments. Use the APR to compare one loan with another. Is the interest rate fixed or variable? If variable, how often and by how much can it change? What are the terms of the loan? Investigate the length of time given to repay the loan and the type of loan. Is it a line of credit, fixed rate, or variable rate? If variable, how much and how often can it change? Evaluate what you will need to pay in points and fees. As with a home loan, one point equals 1% of the loan amount (1 point on a $10,000 loan is $100). Generally, the higher the points, the lower the interest rate on the loan will be. Traditional financial institutions normally charge between 1 and 3% of the loan amount in points and fees. Ask about the penalties for late or missed payments and for paying off or refinancing the loan early.

Loan packages can require insurance, such as credit life, disability, or unemployment insurance, but in most cases this is optional. Depending on the type of policy, credit insurance can cover some or all of your payments if you can't make them. However, credit insurance can be a bad deal for you, the buyer, especially if the premiums are collected up-front at the closing and financed as part of the loan. If you are required to have insurance on your loan, shop around for the best rate and premiums.

After you have answers to these questions, start negotiating with more than one lender. Don't be afraid to make lenders and brokers compete for your business by letting them know you are shopping for the best deal. Ask each lender to lower the points, fees, or interest rate. And ask each to meet—or beat—the terms of the other lenders. Utilize the same mortgage shopping worksheet that you used when shopping for the original mortgage. (See Figure 7.11 on page 180). You can also use Worksheet 7.3 (online).

Disadvantages of Second Mortgages

The main disadvantage of a second mortgage is the added risk of losing your home. Make sure your intended use of the funds is worth this serious risk.

A home equity loan for the purpose of debt consolidation is not always a good idea. The interest rate on a home equity loan may be lower than that of a credit card, but if you fail to pay on your credit card you still have your home. Typically, a second mortgage involves hefty fees. Depending on how much you need and how long you'll need it, a second mortgage may not work for you simply because of the fees.

Many consumers have used home equity to pay off debt. If your credit card rate is two or more times that of a home equity loan interest rate, it can be tempting. If you are making payments on multiple credit cards, it's likely that the combined payments for these cards are higher than

Making $ense

7.12 What kinds of home equity loans exist?

7.13 How do people typically use a home equity loan?

7.14 How do you comparison-shop for a home equity loan?

7.15 What precaution do you need to take if you choose to use a home equity loan for debt consolidation purposes?

what you would pay in a single home equity loan payment. And in most cases, interest paid on a home equity loan is tax deductible, the same as mortgage interest.

However, home equity loans don't eliminate debt. For a fee, you have shifted multiple high-interest debts to one low-interest account. But if you fail to change the habits that led you into debt in the first place, you will likely accumulate even more debt in the long run and put your home at risk. If you take out a home equity loan for the purpose of consolidating your credit cards, then it is important to avoid credit cards completely until you have repaid your home equity loan.

Remember, you are using home equity (which is debt secured by your property) to pay down credit card debt (which is unsecured debt). If something goes wrong, you could lose your home. ■

Learn. ▶ Plan & Act. ▶ Evaluate.

➡ LEARN. This chapter examined the steps involved in the purchase of a car and the advantages and drawbacks of home loans and renting. The federal government promotes home ownership by supporting long-term loans through government agencies like FNMA and by providing income tax incentives through the deduction of mortgage interest on your itemized income tax return. The chapter also explored three different types of home equity loans, along with the advantages and disadvantages of using the equity in your home to finance other purchases.

SUMMARY

■ ■ **LO 7-1** Recognize how to get the best deal when purchasing a car, compare purchase versus lease options, and gain an understanding of the loan approval process.

Distinguish needs from wants when making the decision to purchase a car. Play close attention to your debt-to-income ratio. When determining what you can afford, include the cost of insurance and maintenance. Options to consider in determining the price you can afford include used vs. new and leasing vs. owning. Financing options include banks, credit unions, and dealerships. After the purchase, keep your vehicle well-maintained and keep service records to help it retain value for a future sale or trade-in.

■ ■ **LO 7-2** Compare buying versus renting a home and evaluate which stage in life is best to make this investment.

Based on your current life stage and lifestyle, renting may be a better option than home ownership. If buying a house, plan on living there at least two years so any profit you make at the time of resale is exempt from capital gains tax and so that any increase in the value of your house might be enough to cover the cost of your real estate agent and your loan, as well as moving expenses.

■ ■ **LO 7-3** Describe the steps involved in purchasing a home, including financing options, and discuss the mortgage refinancing decision.

Loan fees for buying or refinancing a home can cost thousands of dollars and are collected at the closing. There are a variety of financing options, including fixed-rate/fixed-term mortgages, variable-rate mortgages, and balloon-payment mortgages. The best option depends on your life stage, how long you plan to own the home, and your current financial condition.

■ ■ **LO 7-4** Explain how home equity loans are used and describe the precautions that need to be taken when using them.

In a home equity loan, the homeowner borrows on the paid value of the property. Lending institutions offer home equity loans in the form of a line of credit or a loan with

a fixed or variable rate. In evaluating home equity loan options, compare the interest rate, payment options, term of the loan, points, fees, penalties, and insurance. The main disadvantage of second mortgages is the added risk of losing your home. Taking out a home equity loan for the purpose of debt consolidation means you are using home equity (debt secured by the property) to pay down credit card debt (unsecured debt). If you are unable to make your loan payments, you can lose your home. For financial security, avoid credit cards and other consumer debt completely until the home equity loan has been paid off.

➡ PLAN & ACT. Using the information

from this chapter, you are now able to plan when, how, and if you will buy a car or a house. Your Plan & Act to-do list is as follows:

- ☐ Assess purchase versus lease options for your next auto purchase (Worksheet 7.1).
- ☐ If you own or lease a car, review your auto maintenance recommendations to confirm you are taking care of this asset.
- ☐ Create an online log to maintain your auto maintenance records (Worksheet 7.2).
- ☐ Decide whether your lifestyle today is better suited to renting or buying a home. Use the online calculator illustrated in Figure 7.7 to help make this determination.

➡ EVALUATE. Review your automotive needs; if you need or want a new

vehicle, start researching to find out what vehicle is best for you. If buying a first home is in your future, start saving today for the down payment. How do these auto and home decisions fit in terms of your overall goals?

›› GoalTracker

Log on to your online **GoalTracker** to assess the impact that these decisions have on your goals and timelines. Track overall how you are doing on your short-, mid-, and long-term goals.

key terms

Adjustable-Rate Mortgage (ARM)	Fixed-Rate/Fixed-Term Loan	Private Mortgage Insurance (PMI)
Balloon-Payment Mortgage	Loan to Value (LTV) Ratio	Sublease
Closing	Mortgage	
Equity	Points	

1. The first step in buying an automobile is to: *(LO 7-1)*
   a. Look online at cars for sale
   b. Analyze your needs and wants
   c. Calculate your debt-to-income ratio
   d. Watch television ads to determine current car deals that are being offered

2. Your debt-to-income ratio should be no higher than: *(LO 7-1)*
   a. 16%
   b. 28%
   c. 36%
   d. 42%

3. Many venders require what percentage down payment when purchasing a car? *(LO 7-1)*
   a. 0%
   b. 10%
   c. 20%
   d. 30%

4. To get a fair and honest review of a car's reliability and dependability, you should go to or ask: *(LO 7-1)*
   a. www.consumerreports.com
   b. The dealer
   c. Maker's website (e.g., www.ford.com)
   d. People driving that type of car

5. In the first three years, the average new car depreciates: *(LO 7-1)*
   a. 5–10%
   b. 10–20%
   c. 20–30%
   d. 35–40%

6. The benefits of buying a new car include the: *(LO 7-1)*
   a. Warranty
   b. Rebates
   c. Dealer incentives
   d. Safety features
   e. All of the above

7. You should lease a new car if you: *(LO 7-1)*
   a. Drive lots of miles
   b. Plan on keeping your car for a long time
   c. Want a new car every 2–3 years
   d. Want to own a car

8. When buying a new car, you should: *(LO 7-1)*
   a. Expect to pay the window sticker price
   b. Research the dealer cost and negotiate to get the lowest price
   c. Expect to pay more than the window sticker price
   d. Offer the dealer $5,000 less than the window sticker price

9. Insurance cost for a new vehicle: *(LO 7-1)*
   a. Should always be considered before making a purchase
   b. Is not important because insurance is not expensive
   c. Should include only liability insurance
   d. Is paid by the seller of the vehicle

10. When financing a vehicle you should: *(LO 7-1)*
    a. Use dealer financing because it is always the best rate
    b. Use your local bank or credit union because they are familiar with you
    c. Use a credit union because it always has the best rate
    d. Shop banks, credit unions, and dealer financing for the best rate

11. It is always better to take 0% financing over a cash rebate. *(LO 7-1)*
    a. True
    b. False

12. Renting a place to live: *(LO 7-2)*
    a. Is never a good idea if you are going to live there for more than three years
    b. Is not a good idea after college
    c. Is always better than buying a house
    d. Can be the better decision for some people

13. Buying a home: *(LO 7-2)*
    a. Should be done as soon as you can afford to make the payments
    b. Saves you money and time, compared to renting
    c. Provides you with tax advantages if you itemize on your income tax
    d. Is not a good investment because property values might go down

14. When buying a house, you should consider: *(LO 7-3)*
    a. Price and location
    b. Maintenance cost and property taxes
    c. School system and insurance cost
    d. Homeowners association fees and resale value
    e. All of the above

15. Realtors and real estate agents: *(LO 7-3)*
    a. Should never be trusted because they are paid only when the house sells
    b. Can help you make the best decision when purchasing real property
    c. Get paid a salary
    d. Can sell only houses and property they personally list

16. PMI stands for: *(LO 7-3)*

   a. payments, maintenance, insurance
   b. principal, maturity, interest
   c. property, materials, instructions
   d. private mortgage insurance

17. To avoid paying PMI, you are required to have a ____ down payment. *(LO 7-3)*

   a. 5%
   b. 10%
   c. 15%
   d. 20%

18. A fixed-rate/fixed-term mortgage loan is good if: *(LO 7-3)*

   a. Rates are low
   b. You plan to own your home longer than five years
   c. You want to be sure your mortgage payment doesn't change
   d. All of the above

19. Adjustable-rate mortgage loans are good if: *(LO 7-3)*

   a. Rates are high
   b. You plan to own the home for fewer than five years
   c. You are comfortable with your mortgage payment changing
   d. All of the above

20. The closing costs of a mortgage loan are: *(LO 7-3)*

   a. The same at every financial institution
   b. Normally paid by the buyer and are in addition to the down payment
   c. Not that much and should not be considered in deciding to buy a house
   d. Paid along with taxes on April 15th every year

21. You should refinance your home: *(LO 7-3)*

   a. Every time interest rates drop
   b. If you are going to move within six months
   c. Only if you plan to say in your home long enough to recover your closing cost expenses
   d. Every five years

22. Home equity loans are: *(LO 7-4)*

   a. Used only for repairs and upgrades on your primary residence
   b. Secured by a second mortgage against your home
   c. Only for people who own their homes outright and no longer have a mortgage
   d. Rare and most banks do not like making them

23. Home equity lines of credit: *(LO 7-4)*

   a. Should be used like a credit card
   b. Can be dangerous since they provide easy access to the equity of your home
   c. Are not advisable
   d. Provide no tax incentive

24. In evaluating equity loans, you should look at: *(LO 7-4)*

   a. Interest rates and payment amounts
   b. The term of the loan and penalties
   c. Points and fees
   d. All of the above

25. The biggest disadvantage of a home equity loan is: *(LO 7-4)*

   a. A possible tax refund on the interest paid
   b. You could lose your home if you do not make payments
   c. You have to pay fees, points, and closing costs to get the loan
   d. You have to have equity in a home to get a home equity loan

problems

1. You just graduated and accepted the job of your dreams. You will be making $4,000 a month and renting an apartment that will cost you $950 a month. You have no other debt. *(LO 7-1)*
   a. What amount can you afford for a car payment?
   b. What amount can you afford for a car payment if you also have a student loan payment of $250 a month and credit card payments of $200 a month?
   c. What could you do if you wanted to buy a more expensive car?

2. You pick out a new car and the dealer is offering 0% interest for 60 months or a $4,000 cash-back bonus. Your negotiated price is $25,000. Your credit union is currently offering a special 3.5% for 60-month car loans. What should you do and why? Show your work. *(LO 7-1)*

3. You are ready to purchase your first home. Your annual salary is $42,000. You have been able to save $15,000 for a down payment, and the only debt you currently owe is your student loan with a payment of $150 a month and your car payment of $350 a month. *(LO 7-2)*
   a. Given your current situation, how much can you afford for a house payment?
   b. If you no longer have a car payment, what monthly mortgage payment could you qualify for, given your outstanding credit history?

4. What is the loan payment on a 30-year, fixed-rate/fixed-term mortgage loan of $100,000 at 8%? *(LO 7-3)*

5. You are looking to finance your home. The bank is offering a three-year ARM (adjustable-rate mortgage) with an introductory rate of 3.5%. It has a 3%

adjustment cap per adjustment period, with an 8% lifetime adjustment. The rate is 4% over the one year LIBOR rate, which is currently 1.25%. *(LO 7-3)*

   a. What will your interest rate be after three years if the LIBOR rate does not change?

   b. In three years, what is the maximum interest rate you could be charged?

   c. If LIBOR increases 1% per year for the next 10 years, up to 11.25%, what is the maximum interest rate you will pay? When will that rate take effect?

6. You are financing a home for $100,000. The loan is a fixed-rate loan of 5%. Complete the following table to compare monthly payments and overall interest for the four different maturity periods shown. *(LO 7-3)*

Maturity Period	Monthly Payment	Total Interest Paid
10 years		
15 years		
20 years		
30 years		

7. You are selling your house and you think it will sell for $275,000. You talk to a real estate agent who is willing to list your house for $279,900. His fee is 7%. You currently owe $175,000 on your home. *(LO 7-3, LO 7-4)*

   a. How much will the real estate agent's fee be if you get a full price offer?

   b. How much will it be if you accept an offer for $275,000?

   c. After you pay off your existing mortgage, how much money will you have for a down payment on your next house in (a) and (b)? Assume you continue to use the same real estate agent.

   d. If you sell the house on your own for $275,000, how much money will you have for a down payment on your next house?

   e. If the buyer wants you to pay closing costs of $3500, how much money will you have for a down payment on your next house in (a), (b), and (d)?

   f. You decide not to sell your house but to remodel and put on an addition. What is the equity in your house?

   g. The bank will let you borrow 90% of the appraised value of your house, which appraises at $275,000. What is the maximum home equity loan you can get?

you're the expert

1. Tanner is 18 years old and has received a full scholarship to play soccer in college. He has been working at the local grocery store since he was 16—part-time during the school year and full-time over the summer. Tanner has just found the car of his dreams. He has negotiated his best deal with the car dealer, and the "on-the-road" price, including tax, title, and license, is $21,500. He has $12,000 saved up, but he will need some of that money for college. His parents have been saving money for his college as well. *(LO 7-1)*

   a. What things does Tanner need to consider before purchasing the car?

   b. What are his options for buying the car?

   c. Tanner goes to his local banker (a friend of the family for 20 years) and asks for a loan. What item is the banker going to look at to make the loan decision? What options will the banker present to Tanner for purchasing the car and why?

2. Harold and Maud just graduated from college, got married, and are starting their first jobs in Chicago. Harold is a school teacher and Maud is a marketing representative for the Chicago Blackhawks hockey team. Harold is making $32,000 a year and because he is working in special education, his student loans are forgiven. Maud is making $28,500 and is paying $200 a month in student loans. They both drive 10-year-old cars and have only the furniture they had in college. Both are working downtown, and they are looking for a place to live.

a. What are the benefits and drawbacks of renting downtown, renting outside of Chicago, or buying a small house or condominium? What would you recommend for Harold and Maud? *(LO 7-2)*

b. Harold and Maud decide to buy a house because that is what their parents did and what they encouraged them to do. List the selection criteria they should use to find the perfect location and house to purchase. *(LO 7-3)*

c. Harold and Maud decide to buy a two-bedroom condominium, located a 75-minute drive (without traffic jams) or a 30-minute train ride from their work. They are looking at financing options for their first mortgage. For their first home loan, what would you recommend for them and why, given their life stage? Besides the down payment, what other expenses will they occur? *(LO 7-3)*

d. Harold and Maud have been in their condominium for two years and rates have dropped 2%. They are expecting their first child in six months. What should Harold and Maud consider before they decide to refinance? What would you advise Harold and Maud to do? *(LO 7-3)*

e. Fifteen years go by and Harold and Maud now have three children—14, 12, and 4 years old. Harold is now principal of the school where he started teaching, and Maud is now the director of sales and promotion for the Chicago Bears. They sold the condominium and have been living in their current house for 13 years. They would like to move to a bigger house in the same school district. Advise Harold and Maud on their options for selling their home, the fees associated with a sale, the pros and cons of using a realtor versus selling the home on their own, and real estate loans they should consider. Harold and Maud would like this home to be the last home they live in while they finish their careers in Chicago and get their children through college. *(LO 7-4)*

3. Jewel's offer of $150,000 for her first home has been accepted. She will make a down payment of 10%. Applied to the loan amount will be the bank's loan-origination fee of 1% of the loan and a charge of 1.5 points. Other fees include a $50 loan-application fee, a $300 appraisal fee, and $250 for a title search and insurance. How much cash will Jewel need at the closing? Will she need private mortgage insurance (PMI)? *(LO 7-3)*

4. Jamal is considering taking out a home equity loan to cover the expenses of remodeling his home. He is doing much of the work himself on weekends over the course of the summer. He estimates the cost will range between $10,000 and $12,000. His bank offers two home equity loan options: a variable-rate Line of Credit (LOC) at 5% that will adjust annually or a fixed-rate loan for three years at 6%. He can afford $400 a month in payments, and the payment on his fixed-rate loan for $12,000 would be $364.06. *(LO 7-4)*

a. If interest rates go up 1% per year, which loan is Jamal's best option and why?

b. If interest rates go up 1.5% per year, which loan is Jamal's best option and why?

worksheets

Find the worksheets online at www.mhhe.com/walkerpf1e

7.1 BUY VS. LEASE

Complete the worksheet to assess the total cost and value of the option to buy versus lease.

Research options for your next vehicle on **www.edmunds.com**. Complete the worksheet below to assess the total cost and value of the option to buy versus lease.

Vehicle Make/Model/Year: _____

LEASING		PURCHASING	
		Cost of vehicle	
Security deposit		Down payment	
Monthly lease payments of ____ * ____ months =		Monthly loan payments of $_____ at ___ % for _____ months =	
End of lease charges (if applicable)			
Total cost of lease		Total cost to buy	
Value of asset after ___ years		Value of asset after ___ years	

7.2 AUTO MAINTENANCE

If you own or lease a vehicle, collect your maintenance records and record them in your online ledger. Passing this on to the next owner will help in resale value as the buyer will have a higher confidence that you have taken care of the vehicle.

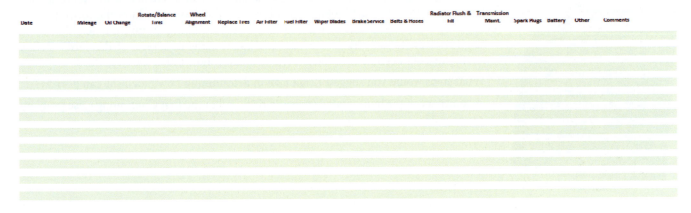

Date	Mileage	Oil Change	Rotate/Balance Tires	Wheel Alignment	Replace Tires	Air Filter	Fuel Filter	Wiper Blades	Brake Service	Belts & Hoses	Radiator Flush & Fill	Transmission Maint.	Spark Plugs	Battery	Other	Comments

7.3 HOME EQUITY

Comparison-shop for a home equity loan using the following worksheet.

Compare answers to these questions	Lender A	Lender B	Lender C	My Current Home Mortgage
Monthly mortgage payments				
Cost of credit (APR)				
Cost of borrowing (interest rate)				
If variable interest rate:				
How often				
By how much				
Points to be paid				
Fees to be paid				
Application or loan processing fee				
Origination or underwriting fee				
Lender or funding fee				
Appraisal fee				
Document preparation and recording fees				
Broker fees				
Application fees refundable?				
Years to repay				
Installment loan or a line of credit?				
Balloon payment				
Total closing costs				
Penalty for late or missed payments/Payoff				
Affordable?				

906 E College Street

Leigh is getting tired of living in the house and sharing a kitchen with everyone. She decides it is time to start looking for a house to purchase. She likes the town and the neighborhood, so she doesn't want to move far. In walking around the neighborhood, Leigh notices "for sale by owner" and real estate signs in several of the yards. Before talking to a banker and a realtor, she wants to know how much she can afford.

What steps would you suggest Leigh take in determining how much she can borrow?

A summary of the housemates' goals can be found in the first Continuing Case problem on page 27.

> **"** Just pretending to be rich keeps some people poor. **"**
>
> —ANONYMOUS

debt, foreclosure, and bankruptcy

Today, many people are only one major expense away from bankruptcy and financial hardship. Debt may come on gradually, but it can easily pile up to the point where you cannot see over the mound. Digging out of debt is like losing weight: For people who are overweight, the extra 50 pounds didn't happen overnight. It comes from consuming more calories than expended over a long time period. Likewise, by spending more than you make, you are piling up a mountain of debt. Just like losing weight, shedding that mountain of debt requires a plan, discipline, time, and hard work. In the event that you are unsuccessful in applying these methods, you should understand the processes of foreclosure and bankruptcy—your final options for becoming debt-free. ■

LEARNING OBJECTIVES

After reading this chapter, you should be able to:

LO 8-1 Examine the early warning signs of financial trouble and learn how to avoid mistakes that can lead to financial crisis.

LO 8-2 Discover how little changes in your spending habits can make a big difference in your financial well-being.

LO 8-3 Create a workable plan to become debt-free and in control of your finances.

LO 8-4 Describe options for protecting your credit if at risk of foreclosure.

LO 8-5 Identify when bankruptcy is a viable option and know the consequences and how to restore your credit afterward.

◀ Abe, age 22, bioengineering graduate student; Brandy, age 23, first-year pediatric inpatient nurse

Emergency Fund Start

Brandy had never been in debt until she got married. Her husband Abe had a credit card he used for getting ready for school and an outstanding loan for a car that kept breaking down. Even though they had not paid off the car, it needed a frustrating amount of repairs. Their budget allowed for only minimum payments on their credit card, and they weren't making any headway on its balance. They finally resolved they would put every extra penny toward the credit card to pay it off. They sold Abe's car and put the payments for the car loan and maintenance toward paying off the credit card debt.

During this time, Abe was still in school and they were living paycheck-to-paycheck, with no emergency fund to protect them from unplanned expenses. Not wanting to fall back into credit card debt again, they started putting $25 into a savings account each week. It slowly grew to an eventual $1,000. Now, whenever they need to use the account, they make it a priority to build it back to their $1,000 minimum balance. They feel better making payments to themselves and earning interest on the money rather than paying a credit card company interest and fees. Having a clear sense of their priorities and being able to discern needs from wants has helped them to make tough financial decisions together.

8.1 EARLY WARNING SIGNS OF FINANCIAL TROUBLE

■ ■ **LO 8-1** Examine the early warning signs of financial trouble and learn how to avoid mistakes that can lead to financial crisis.

As we discussed in Chapter 5, credit card companies make it easy to borrow and tempting to make just the minimum payment. Doing so is like eating a bag of chips from the vending machine every afternoon; at first it doesn't show on your waistline, but then the scale shows an increase in weight and your clothes become tighter. Noticing your debts are piling up is more difficult to recognize, though.

Forewarnings

Many people were not prepared for the economic downturn of 2008–2009 and had no emergency fund. During this time, credit card debt ballooned rapidly, especially in parts of the nation where the economy was particularly weak, suggesting people turned to their credit cards just to cover daily expenses. In 2010 and 2011, national unemployment continued to be grim; moreover, job loss

For most, financial trouble doesn't come without warning.

> ["Think what you do when you run into debt; you give another person power over your liberty."]
>
> —BEN FRANKLIN *(1706–1790)*

resulted in the loss of health insurance and added stress for many people, which turned into medical bills.

How is your fiscal health? Figure 8.1 lists some warning signs of which you should be aware; these signs may indicate that you are on the path to financial illness, out-of-control spending, and possibly, financial disaster.

The checklist in online Worksheet 8.1 can help you identify whether you exhibit any of the early warning signs of financial problems. If you are unable to make minimum payments or unable to make loan payments, or if you are getting calls from bill collectors, then you are beyond the early warning signs of credit trouble and into the red-flag zone (see Figure 8.2).

▼ **FIGURE** 8.1

Yellow-flag warnings

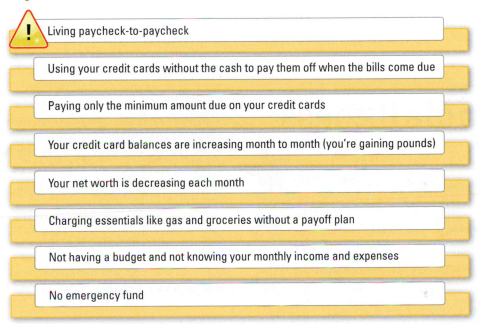

▼ **FIGURE** 8.2

Red-flag warnings

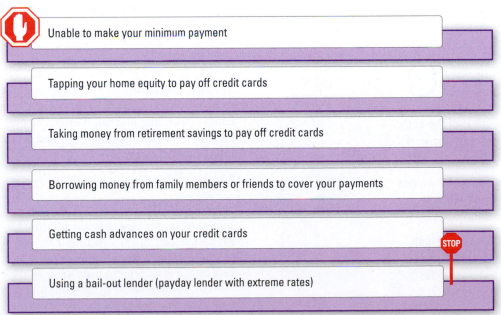

The best way to avoid a crisis is to take control. If you want to stay in physical shape and remain in good health, you work out and have a plan and goals. Likewise, to avoid a financial crisis, you must develop a plan to stay in good *fiscal* shape.

Emergency Fund Refuge

It is vital to have at least $1,000 in an emergency fund. Once you establish that minimum emergency fund, your next goal should be to save at least six months' income in the emergency account. Even if you think you have a secure job, companies can reorganize and eliminate job positions without notice. Other emergencies, like major auto repairs, medical bills, or family crises, could also require you to

dip into your emergency fund. Establishing an emergency fund takes discipline and hard work, but it will give you peace of mind and freedom.

Recall that in Chapter 3 you logged your spending habits and created balance sheets, income statements, and a budget. A study of your spending journal should shed light on little leaks in your personal spending. Review your balance sheet. You may have a negative net worth right now because of student loans and college expenses. Education is an investment in your future, but you still need a plan in place to repay your student loans.

A study of your past spending and savings habits can help you pinpoint opportunities for changing your financial patterns in order to achieve your financial goals. Worksheet 8.2 (online) helps you review your financial past and assess how much of an emergency fund you need. You cannot change the past, but you can act in the present and affect the future. Changing habits is not easy. It takes a goal and discipline to achieve success. Writing goals that reflect your values and vision and working with a partner or a budget buddy help hold you accountable and increase your chances for success.

Living debt-free requires *saving* for the items you want. Credit companies have made it easy to buy now and pay later, but becoming rich has one simple rule: *Spend less than you make, and save or invest the rest.* Just like eating fewer calories than you burn helps you lose weight, following this fiscal rule will increase your net worth and help you reach your financial goals.

financial fitness:
ACTION ITEM

Evaluating Spending

Need help evaluating your spending? Track your spending patterns using the free service provided by www.Wesabe.com. To begin, you enter your accounts to organize your spending into different categories. Wesabe then helps you pinpoint areas where you could improve and offers feedback from other Wesabe users—while keeping your identity and personal information confidential.

8.2 STOPPING LITTLE LEAKS

■ ■ **LO 8-2** Discover how little changes in your spending habits can make a big difference in your financial well-being.

The first and easiest step to achieving financial success is to stop little leaks. If you have not kept up an "every penny counts" spending journal, it might be time to begin. Start logging where every penny goes and decide which expenditures are necessary.

Necessary versus Nonessential Spending

You need to pay rent, pay for utilities, buy food, and put gas in the car. But do you *need* to stop for coffee every morning or buy a drink from a vending machine? We need very little, yet we tend to *want* a lot. To dig out of debt, you need to separate needs from wants and spend money only on needs. The fastest way to get debt-free is to put wants on hold until everything is paid off. Use Worksheet 8.3 on

Making $ense

8.1 What are some of the early warning signs of financial trouble?

8.2 What are some of the signs of out-of-control credit card spending?

8.3 What is the one question you need to ask yourself each time you consider taking on more debt?

financialfitness:
ACTION ITEM

Gas Savings

The Internet offers a wealth of thrifty ideas to save on everyday spending. One example is www.gasbuddy.com. Enter your zip code and you will be connected to a network of websites that pinpoint which gas stations near you charge the lowest and highest prices. Plan your next fill-up accordingly.

financialfitness:
STOPPING LITTLE LEAKS

Food Savings

Consider the following ways to save on essentials like groceries, beyond using coupons.

— Purchase fresh fruits and vegetables in bags rather than individually. You'll pay roughly half the price.

— Don't buy nongrocery items at the supermarket. Health and beauty goods are usually cheaper at mass-market retailers.

— Opt for frozen seafood over fresh. Vacuum-packaged salmon, flounder, and tilapia fillets and bags of frozen shrimp cost 20–40% less than their counterparts at the fresh fish counter. (Most "fresh" fish has been previously frozen during transport.)

— Buy ground beef and chicken breasts in bulk or family-size packages and save 20% on ground beef and 50% on chicken per pound.

— Look for an item's cost per unit (CPU). It's listed on the shelf sticker next to the price. The CPU makes it easier to compare an item's cost per pound or ounce.

— Buy generics. They almost always are cheaper and taste tests have found consumers typically cannot distinguish the name brand from the generic product.

the website to help sort out your needs (the essential) from your wants (the nonessential).

Trimming Expenses

After identifying necessary expenditures, see where you can trim back on even these expenses. Take a more frugal approach, avoid waste, and be resourceful. Ask yourself questions such as these:

1. Can I move to a less expensive apartment or house? Can I refinance my mortgage?

2. Can I save money on gas, or give up a car altogether? If my family has multiple cars, can we get by with just one?

3. Can I get a better price on insurance? (Call around and make sure you are getting the best price you can. Consider taking a higher deductible.)

4. Can I drop a land line and either use only my mobile phone or save money by calling over the Internet with services such as Skype?

5. Can I live without cable or satellite TV?

6. Can I cut down on my utility bills?

7. Can I cut down on eating out? Take sack lunches? Buy food in bulk? Start using coupons?

Even for your essential expenditures, such as housing and food, there may be opportunities to cut back and save

money. With this extra cash flow from stopping leaks, start a savings account. Have money directly deposited into this separate savings account so you do not miss it. This is the concept of paying yourself first. The deposit into your savings account is as important as all your other bills.

Regularly paying yourself first is a lifelong habit for developing financial security. Stopping the little leaks will make

> ## "It is easier to make money than to save it; one is exertion, the other self-denial."
>
> —THOMAS HALLIBURTON, *Canadian author (1796–1865)*

it less painful to start saving. With this habit in place, you will barely miss the money you are saving, and your increasing net worth will make it all worthwhile.

Your savings will serve as an emergency fund for the unexpected (e.g., unforeseen car repairs, emergency family travel, or unexpected health bills). You may want to establish an emergency fund in a different bank, where it is more difficult to gain access or make a transfer. If you physically have to go to the bank for access, you will have to think twice about using the money in an emergency

account. Overly convenient emergency funds are tempting to "borrow" from when it is not an emergency. Once you start dipping into the emergency fund for nonemergencies, it soon disappears.

To build your emergency fund fast, you could hold a garage sale or sell some of your possessions on eBay or Craigslist or you could get a second job. Like Brandy and Abe in the chapter opener, you need to have a minimum of $1,000 for unexpected expenses in order to avoid using credit cards. This is the first step in your commitment to digging out of debt. If you have to use some of the $1,000 emergency fund, pay it back as soon as possible.

tips for stopping little leaks Thousands of everyday changes can help you stop the little leaks. Financial Fitness boxes throughout this book suggest ways to stop those little leaks. Be creative: Try each day to identify a new habit to take on or a little thing you can do to be thrifty. The trick is to find ways to spend less but still enjoy yourself. You need to keep it fun, or it will be difficult to stick with. Here are some additional tips for stopping the little leaks:

Cut coupons; look for sale items; make a list and only buy necessities. Plan out a menu for the week when the grocery stores send out their weekly advertisements. When grocery shopping, take with you only the amount of cash you have budgeted for your shopping trip. Take a calculator so you know when you hit the limit and buy only things on the list. Cut or print coupons only for items you need and normally buy.

Make shopping harder. Delete bookmarked shopping sites from the computer. Gather up your catalogs and then call the toll-free numbers for each and ask to be removed from their mailing lists, or go to www.catalogchoice.org, a free service that helps you unsubscribe from catalogs.

Change your everyday habits. Plot out the most risk-free routes to and from work and for daily errands. If lattes are a weakness, give a wide berth to expensive coffee shops. If clothes are a passion, steer clear of trendy boutiques.

Cut out convenience foods. Use reusable bottles to drink water throughout the day instead of buying bottles of water or soda pop from a vending machine. Take baby carrots, fruit, almonds, or other healthy snacks to work or school instead of buying snacks. This not only saves money, but you will be eating more healthfully.

Pack your lunch. Packing a lunch can save $5 or more every day, and you will probably eat better. Recruiting friends to do the same will give you a solid support network.

Return unwanted purchases. Make sure everything is returnable and always keep the tags and receipts for at least two weeks. This gives you plenty of time to cool off after the thrill of the purchase to see if the item is a need or a want, and it provides time for you to reevaluate the opportunity cost of the purchase.

Avoid the malls when bored or depressed. Avoid the temptation to shop when you are in a down mood. If you go to the

financialfitness:
STOPPING LITTLE LEAKS

Literary Savings

Save on book money by using www .PaperBackSwap.com. Membership is free. Members exchange books with each other, with the only cost being postage. The idea is "mail a book—get a book." Every time you mail a book to another member, you can request one for yourself. If you own an e-reader, many titles that are old enough to be in the public domain can be downloaded at no cost. Better yet, make a trip to your local library for some free reading—provided you return your books on time!

Making
$ense

8.4 What does it mean to be frugal?

8.5 Why is it important to pay yourself first?

mall, you are likely to buy something. Go for a walk or a run if you are having a bad day, but not to the mall.

Consider voluntary simplicity. Does your life reflect your values, and is your money working the way you want it to? You can search your local library for books on voluntary simplicity and simple living. This philosophy encourages cutting out the complexity (and therefore the cost) of things that are not a priority to you. A good place to start is with *Your Money or Your Life,* by Joe Dominguez and Vicki Robin (Penguin), which shows how living simply can be the path to financial independence.

8.3 DIGGING OUT OF DEBT

■ ■ **LO 8-3** Create a workable plan to become debt-free and in control of your finances.

You may find yourself in debt as a result of poor spending and saving habits. You may still be paying for things consumed long ago or no longer used. Digging out of debt takes time and it requires a change in spending and saving habits.

Steps to Digging Out of Debt

Escaping debt requires discipline and sacrifice. You are breaking old habits and changing your lifestyle. The Every Penny Counts journal helps you think about the opportunity cost of buying anything. Every penny you spend on something is one less penny you can put toward paying off your debts. Penny by penny, you can get out of debt by following the steps listed in Figure 8.3.

stop using credit cards In a study from Sloan School of Management at MIT,[1] Drazen Prelec and Duncan Simester found that people who paid by credit card were willing to spend on average between 59% to 113% more on sporting event tickets and banners then those paying with cash. According to another study,[2] when McDonald's started allowing credit card purchases, the average purchase went from $4.50 to $7.00. Using a credit card not only enables you to spend money you don't have, it desensitizes you to your budget boundaries as well.

The first step to digging out of debt is to stop using credit cards and loans and start paying for everything with cash. Take scissors and cut up your unnecessary credit cards or run them through a shredder. Break the habit of using credit cards and the cycle of credit card dependence. Establish an emergency fund so you do not use credit cards for that purpose.

create a realistic budget and use the envelope system Create a realistic budget and stick with it. In Chapter 3, you used the Every Penny Counts spending journal to come up with a realistic budget based on your previous spending. You also learned about the envelope system of budgeting. Using this system, you can actually see how much is left to spend in each area of your budget at all times. Make an envelope for every category in your budget. When you get paid, put the cash budgeted for each category in its appropriate envelope. Refer back to Chapter 3 for details on budgeting. Your primary goal each month should be to spend less than you earn and stay within your budget. If you do this consistently, your financial situation will improve.

exercise the "10 seconds" and "month-end" holds Whenever you pick up an item while shopping, hold it for 10 seconds. Ask yourself if you really need it. Contemplate if the money spent on this item would be better spent somewhere else. Chances are you will almost always put the unnecessary item back on the shelf, and you will be happy you did not

▼ **FIGURE 8.3**

Steps to digging out of debt

7. Increase your income
6. Make payments on time
5. Pay off debt
4. Don't buy things you cannot afford
3. Exercise the "ten seconds" and "month-end" holds
2. Create a realistic budget and use the envelope system
1. Stop using credit cards

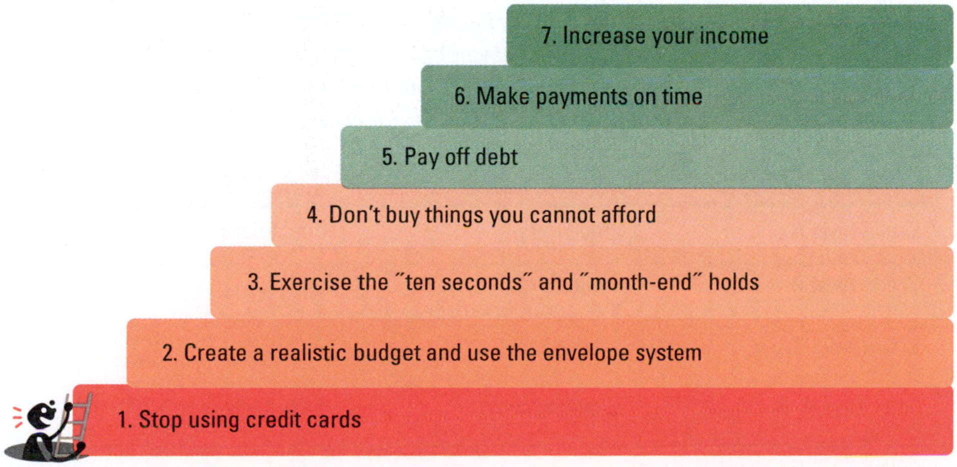

[1] Prelec, D. and Simester, D. "Always Leave Home Without It: A Further Investigation of the Credit-Card Effect on Willingness to Pay." Sloan School of Management, MIT, 2000.

[2] Shapiro, A. "Why We Spend More Using Credit Versus Cash," July 3, 2008, www.npr.org/templates/transcript/transcript.php?storyId=92178034.

waste money on something unnecessary. When tempted by an *expensive* and nonessential item, force yourself to wait until the end of the month and give it consideration when reviewing your budget. If you still remember you want the item and have the budget to afford it, then go back and buy the item. This tactic will help ward off impulsive decisions to buy expensive items and keep you from buying things you cannot afford.

don't buy what you cannot afford Forcing yourself to pay cash for everything will help you buy only the things you can afford. When considering an expensive object, think of your take-home hourly wage. Is having the

object worth that many hours of work to you? Looking at purchases in this way can help curb impulsive buying.

pay off debt To start digging out of debt, focus on the goal of paying it off. There are two schools of thought when it comes to paying off your debts. One is to pay the debt with the highest interest rate first and the other is to pay the debt with the smallest balance first.

The reasoning behind paying off the debt with the highest interest rate first is that the higher the interest rate, the more money you are paying in interest. Therefore, if you pay off your highest interest debts first, you will save more money. The downside to this method is that it may take a long time before that initial debt is paid off, and you may become discouraged and think that getting out of debt is an impossible task.

Paying off your smallest debts first helps you build momentum to pay off other debts. You succeed sooner in paying off one debt, which can provide you with a good feeling and the motivation to continue paying off your other debts. Once your smallest debt is paid off, apply what you were paying on that debt to your next smallest debt, building the amount of money you are applying to your debts until they are all paid off. The downside to this method is that you will pay more money in interest. Use an online calculator such as the one described in the Financial Fitness box to calculate how long it will take to pay off your current debts. Use Worksheet 8.4 to prioritize your outstanding debts, either from smallest to largest dollar amount or by interest rate (highest to lowest). Consider

financialfitness:
ACTION ITEM

Timelines

To calculate how long it will take to pay off your credit card debt, use an online calculator, like http://finance.yahoo.com/calculator/banking-budgeting/det01. Knowing how much debt you have and how long it will take to pay it off will help curb the temptation to add to the outstanding balance.

doing the MATH

8.1 Pay the Smallest Balance First

You have three credit cards: Card A, with a balance of $1,200 (minimum payment: $37); Card B, with a balance of $400 (minimum payment: $11); and Card C, with a balance of $57 (minimum payment: $9). You have $300 per month to put toward reducing debt. Lay out your payment plan following the pay-the-smallest-balance-first strategy.

Period 1 Payments	Period 2 Payments	Period 3 Payments
Credit Card A:	Credit Card A:	Credit Card A:
Credit Card B:	Credit Card B:	
Credit Card C:		
Total Payments:	Total Payments:	Total Payments:

What advantage does this strategy have over disbursing the payment funds proportionally over all three cards?

the extra cash you have saved from stopping little leaks, and set a goal of applying this extra money toward the debt you want to pay off first, making minimum payments on the rest of your debts. Once you pay off that first debt, apply the money to the next debt. Continue to apply your previous debt payments to the next debt until all your debts are paid off.

make payments on time Missing a payment, even by one day, can dramatically increase your interest rate and add penalties and fees to what you owe. If you have online banking, you can set up an automatic bill payment to pay your minimum amount. Always allow enough time so your payment arrives on time.

increase your income If your budget is so tight you are having a hard time making the minimum payments, sell unneeded items to pay off your debt. Look around the house for things you do not use. Can you sell the items online, take them to a consignment shop, or have a garage sale? If an auto payment is stressing your budget, could you sell the car and purchase a less expensive (but reliable) car? Is public transportation, bicycling, or a carpool an option to reduce expenses? The other option is to look at ways to increase your income: Take on a second job, work more hours, or sell things you make, using your talents and gifts to turn your passion into profit. You can then prioritize the use of your increased income to pay off debt.

Managing Past Credit Card Debt

The first step in managing past credit card debt is to contact the credit card companies and try to renegotiate the interest rate. One phone call can save hundreds of dollars in interest. The interest rate will not change unless you *ask* the lender to change it. If the lender says "no," ask what it would take to get a lower interest rate. If the credit card company gives a specific time frame—for example six months of regular payments—mark the calendar and call back in six months.

If you are struggling to make credit card payments, call the companies to explain your circumstances. Tell them your plan of action to pay off the debt. If the credit card company agrees to the plan, follow through. The credit card company will make notes on your file, so if you do not meet the commitment, you may not be able to negotiate a reduction with that company again.

Credit card companies are sometimes willing to lower your rate and waive fees if they are assured they will get paid. In a bankruptcy, the credit card company might end up with nothing. Let the credit card company know you will do whatever it takes to avoid bankruptcy if the creditor will work with you to set a realistic repayment plan. If the credit card company agrees to the repayment

plan, be sure to get it in writing. This will protect you and avoid any confusion or bad faith on the part of the creditor.

Beyond negotiating directly with credit card companies, there are other solutions to managing debt. Next we will consider the processes of *debt consolidation* and *credit counseling.*

debt consolidation Getting a debt consolidation loan is dangerous because it treats only the outcomes, not the source of the problem. Too many times, people will get a debt-consolidation loan and keep using their credit cards as they did in the past. Before long, their credit cards have a new balance

It can be easy to get trapped in debt, but planning and careful budget discipline will help you to avoid it.

and they are still paying off the consolidation loan. Going this route simply adds more debt instead of eliminating it.

A debt-consolidation loan often is structured as a second mortgage on your home. With a second mortgage, you put your home at risk if you cannot make the payments. If you do not have equity in your home, the lender might require you to collateralize the loan by securing it with your car. If you secure the consolidation loan, you are paying off unsecured debt with a lien on your car or home. If you declare bankruptcy, the new lender can take away your home or car, whereas unsecured lenders—such as credit card companies—do not have any claims to these assets.

credit counseling services If you feel you can't dig your way out of debt by yourself, you may want to turn to a credit counseling service for help. The National Federation for Credit Counseling (www.nfcc.org) is a network of nonprofit credit counselors who provide education and advice. Credit counseling services provide advice on how to manage money, offer solutions for your specific financial situation, and help you develop a financial spending plan to prevent future financial problems. Credit counseling agencies are designed for people who need help paying off credit card debt and who are struggling with long-term debt but don't know where to begin.

According to the National Federation for Credit Counseling (NFCC), one-third of its clients need just a single session to help them along, one-third are in too much debt for counseling to help, and one-third sign up for a debt-management plan. With a debt-management plan, you deposit money each month to be managed by the credit counseling agency and the agency pays your creditors. This may help to reduce fees, interest rates, and some of the outstanding principal. Of the one-third who sign up for a debt-management plan, only 55% successfully complete their debt-management program.[3]

debt-settlement companies Debt-settlement companies help settle debts by renegotiating rates, payments, and principal amounts. Be wary of promises that seem too good to be true. See Figure 8.4 for some screening tips to keep in mind when seeking either a debt-settlement company or a credit counseling agency.

Credit counseling and debt-settlement companies can assist in improving your credit. You can do a lot on your own, but if you feel you are sliding down the slope of financial trouble, reach out for help before it is too late. Be careful if credit counselors recommend bankruptcy right away. You should consider bankruptcy only as your last option.

consumer protection and debt collection Being behind on payments and receiving phone calls from debt collectors is not fun. The Fair Debt Collection Practices Act (FDCPA) is Title VIII of the Consumer Credit Protection Act and protects consumers from unfair debt-collection practices.

financialfitness:
JUST THE FACTS

Debt Settlement Resource

Fast and easy promises to get rid of your debt can often lead you into even deeper financial trouble. For some helpful information on debt-settlement companies, see the NFCC's Financial Fast Fact video on debt settlement at www.nfcc.org/ConsumerAlert/index.cfm.

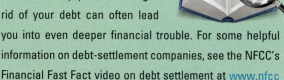

▼ **FIGURE 8.4**

Debt-settlement/credit counseling agency screening tips

Upfront Fees	• Examine what you are getting for the money you pay. If the agency asks for a large up-front fee, this is a red flag that it is not a legitimate business. As a point of reference, consumer credit counseling services typically charge a $10 set-up fee.
No Accreditation or Association Affiliation	• Make sure the credit counselor is associated with the NFCC or the Association of Independent Consumer Credit Counseling Agencies (AICCCA, www.aicca.org), which helps establish legitimacy and ethical standards.
Your Bills Are Not Being Paid	• Before you give a portion of your paycheck to an agency to manage, know how much is going to each creditor and when it will be paid. Some companies use your first month's payment as a fee, rather than paying your creditors. Missing payments hurt your credit rating, cause late payment fees, and increase the balance you owe.
Sounds Too Good to Be True	• Some companies promise that you can cut your debt in half or pay only cents on the dollar without hurting your credit rating. Repairing your credit takes time and effort. Legitimate credit counseling services help you be responsible by paying back what you owe.

[3]Marketplace Money Report, August 13, 2009, http://marketplace.publicradio.org/display/web/2009/08/13/mm-credit-counseling/ and http://marketplace.publicradio.org/display/web/2009/08/14/mm-cunningham/.

> "If I can control the person in the mirror, I can be skinny and rich."
>
> —DAVE RAMSEY, *American financial author, personality (1960–)*

Not all debt collectors are properly trained on the FDCPA, so it is good for you to know what collectors can and cannot do under the FDCPA. Under the FDCPA, a debt collector *cannot* do the following:

- Call you before 8:00 A.M. or after 9:00 P.M.
- Call you at work if you ask them not to call you at work
- Harass you, use obscene or profane language, or threaten the use of violence or other criminal means to harm you, your reputation, or your property
- Conceal his or her identity on the phone
- Lie or falsely imply you have committed a crime
- Disregard a written request from you to cease further contact
- Falsely represent the amount, character, or legal status of any debt

If you are being harassed by debt collectors, you can file complaints with the Federal Trade Commission, the local state attorney general's office, or the Better Business Bureau. If you feel your rights have been violated, you can sue a collector in a state or federal court within one year of the date on which the law was violated. If you win, the judge can require the collector to pay you for any damages suffered because of the illegal collection practices, like lost wages and medical bills. The judge also can require the debt collector to pay you up to $1,000, even if you can't prove that you suffered actual damages. You also can be reimbursed for attorney fees and court costs. Even if a debt collector violates the FDCPA in trying to collect a debt, it is important to remember the debt does not go away until you pay it off.[4]

Making $ense

8.6 What are the steps to digging out of debt?

8.7 What are some strategies for managing past credit card debt?

8.8 What risk does debt consolidation bring?

8.9 How do you identify legitimate credit counselors who can help you dig out of debt?

8.10 What types of activities are not permitted under the FDCPA?

financialfitness: JUST THE FACTS

Consumer Protection

The Federal Trade Commission provides a wealth of information for consumer protection at its website (www.ftc.gov) and has a home page for the Fair Debt Collection Practices Act (FDCPA) at www.ftc.gov/os/statutes/fdcpajump.shtm.

8.4 FORECLOSURE

LO 8-4 Describe options for protecting your credit if at risk of foreclosure.

Your home is one of your largest assets. Owning a home gives you the ability to live without making payments to anyone—except the government in the form of taxes. Therefore, it is important to protect your home and do everything you can to avoid foreclosure. When facing debt problems, you may be able to work out a temporary plan

[4]http://www.ftc.gov/bcp/edu/pubs/consumer/credit/cre18.shtm

Foreclosure is a last resort for many creditors; working to find a solution to financial problems with your lender can help you to avoid it entirely.

for making up missed payments, or it may be more beneficial to modify the loan terms. Sometimes the best option may be to sell the house. Keep the lender informed of your solution and how you are doing in your efforts to make the solution work. If these methods are not feasible, you need to understand the foreclosure process.

Avoiding Foreclosure

According to the Federal Trade Commission, the number of seriously delinquent residential mortgages jumped from 5% in 2005 to over 35% in 2009 (see Figure 8.5). *Seriously delinquent* loans are residential mortgages 90 days or more past due or already in foreclosure. During the financial crisis of 2008–2009, many mortgage holders found themselves at risk of losing their homes to foreclosure. If you find yourself in this position, you need to know what steps to take.

address mortgage problems If you are late or miss a mortgage payment, contact the lender before he or she contacts you, ideally before the payment is due. Mortgage lenders want to work with you to resolve the problem. Meet with the mortgage lender in person if possible. If the

mortgage lender is not in town, make a phone call and follow up every call with a written letter and/or e-mail. Explain your financial situation and ask to work with the

▼ **FIGURE** 8.5

Serious residential mortgage delinquency/ foreclosure rates 2000–2009

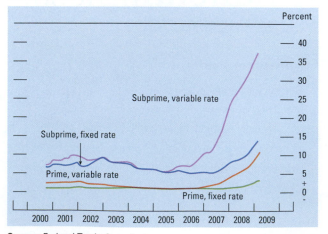

Source: Federal Trade Commission.

lender on a temporary payment plan or a manageable long-term solution. Take good notes during the meeting and summarize your understanding of the solution in a letter to the lender.

Before calling the lender, review the original mortgage loan papers. Re-evaluate your budget and personal cash flow statement completed in Chapter 3 (Worksheet 3.2). Make sure the documents are up-to-date. Can you stop some small leaks? Look at your debt-to-income ratio that you calculated in Chapter 5 (Worksheet 5.1). Be ready to explain to the lender where you currently stand and to recommend a payment to which you can commit. Keep in mind that it is much better to go to a lender with a proposed solution to the problem rather than just the problem itself.

In some cases, you may be able to negotiate a **cramdown** with the lender, an arrangement in which the lender will renegotiate the loan at a lower interest rate and/or a lower principal balance. The term "cramdown" comes from bankruptcy courts, which can modify the interest rate of principal payments on household debts (but not mortgages). Even without a bankruptcy court ordering a renegotiation of the interest and principal, a solution involving loan modification might interest the bank.

There are many benefits to the bank for choosing a mortgage loan modification. First, by doing so it will receive payments on a loan it would otherwise have to foreclose. The interest on these payments count as income to the bank, whereas possession of an asset (your house) does not generate income. Second, the process of foreclosure takes time and money. According to the Real Estate Bloggers (www .therealestatebloggers.com), the average foreclosure costs $60,000 for Freddie Mac and large banks. HSBC's average loss on a foreclosure is 20% to 25%. Knowing this, you can negotiate a win-win situation for both you and the bank. You win by staying in your house and having lower payments and a lower principal balance that is in line with what your property is currently worth. Although the bank suffers a loss in the reduced amount you owe (a direct loss for the bank) and your reduced interest rate (a reduction in interest income for the bank), the bank scores a semi-win: The bank is still getting paid on a loan, the value of the house stays up, and you are still maintaining the house.

temporary solutions If you are at risk for foreclosure due to a short-term financial problem, such as an illness or a recent job loss, you may need only a temporary solution if

you anticipate you will be back on your feet in a short time. In this case, your options include:

Reinstatement. Lenders will sometimes offer the option of **reinstatement**; that is, they will *reinstate* the loan if you make up the back payments in a lump sum by a specific date. A loan reinstatement will occur only after the loan has been *accelerated* (discussed later in the chapter).

Forbearance. Lenders can sometimes grant **forbearance,** or a temporary reduction or suspension of the mortgage payments for three or four months, followed by a new repayment plan for the loan. Banks will sometimes grant forbearance in situations in which you have had a reduction in income or an increase in living expenses.

Repayment plan. Lenders may agree to a plan that includes regular monthly payments plus a portion of the past-due payments each month until payments are current.

long-term solutions If your difficulty in making payments is due to a more long-term problem—for example, disability or divorce—you will need to look for a more permanent adjustment to the loan. In this case, your options include:

Loan modifications. Ask the lender to consider rewriting the terms of the original mortgage loan to make the monthly payments more affordable, either by extending the number of years or

---

cramdown
an arrangement in which the mortgage terms are altered in an attempt to keep the borrower from foreclosure

reinstatement
a temporary solution to the risk of foreclosure that involves re-establishing a loan if the terms of a new agreement are met

forbearance
a temporary reduction or suspension of mortgage payments for 3 or 4 months, followed by a new repayment plan for the loan

---

> ❝ One of the secrets of life is to make stepping stones out of stumbling blocks. ❞
>
> —JACK PENN, *Surgeon, sculptor, and author (1909–1996)*

---

financialfitness:
ACTION ITEM

Lending Counseling

If your lender won't meet with you, work through a housing counseling agency. Visit the Neighbor Works website at www.nw.org/network/home .asp for a list of counseling offices in your area or visit the U.S. Department of Housing and Urban Development's (HUD) website at www.hud.gov/offices/hsg/sfh/hcc/hccprof14.cfm.

Partial claim. Some insurers provide a one-time, interest-free loan to bring the account up to date. The interest-free loan is due when you refinance, pay off the mortgage, or sell the property.

changing the interest rate. This option might include changing an adjustable rate to a fixed rate. You may have to pay a processing fee to obtain a loan modification. If you have an FHA-approved loan, special loan-modification programs may be available to you.

Once you have the short-term or long-term solution in place, protect your home and your credit score by making timely payments. Prioritize bills and pay the most necessary ones, with the new mortgage payment at the top of the list. Unfortunately, in some cases, keeping your home may not be possible. In that situation, you still have some options that can help protect your credit score.

selling a home If keeping your home is not an option, consider these alternatives to safeguard your credit:

Sale. Lenders usually will provide a set amount of time for you to find a buyer and pay off the mortgage. Be sure to stay in good communication with the lender throughout this process. The sale of a home before foreclosure will normally bring a higher price than *after* the foreclosure process has begun. Once foreclosure is announced in public, as required by law, the buyer will know you need to sell the house and will try to get a bargain by offering less than market value.

Short sale. If you are unable to sell the property for the full amount of the loan, the lender may accept the selling price of the home as satisfying the mortgage. This is known as a preforeclosure sale or a **short sale**. A short sale occurs when the house is sold, with the lender's approval, for less than what is owed on the mortgage. When the house sells, the lender receives the money, and you walk away from the loan owing nothing more and with no damage to your credit.

Assumption of loan. In some cases the lender may allow a qualified buyer to assume (take over) the mortgage.

Deed-in-lieu of foreclosure. In a **deed-in-lieu of foreclosure** arrangement, the lender accepts the property and, in return, forgives the balance of the loan.

financialfitness:
JUST THE FACTS

Protection

Con artists prey on people who fall behind on their mortgage payments. If you are approached by a foreclosure counselor, make sure he or she is with a HUD-approved counseling agency before you do business together. For tips on spotting scam artists, visit the Federal Trade Commission's Foreclosure Rescue Scams website: www.ftc.gov/bcp/edu/pubs/consumer/credit/cre42.shtm.

▼ **FIGURE** 8.6

The preforeclosure process

Miss 1st payment	• The bank sends out a late notice once you are past-due five days on your loan. At the same time, the lender or collector will be notified and will try to contact you by phone to remind you to make your payments.
Miss 2nd payment	• The lender is becoming concerned if you have not made an alternate arrangement to pay. The bank and the banker will continue to try to contact you by phone and mail.
Miss 3rd payment	• If no arrangements have been made to come current on the loan, using its acceleration clause, the bank will send a demand letter for the balance of the loan. This is really the decision point for the bank to begin the foreclosure process. Once the demand letter has been sent, the bank will accept only full payment of the loan. If you are able to pay your past-due amount with interest, the lender might reinstate the original terms of the loan.
Unable to make payment	• The lender begins the foreclosure process.

The Foreclosure Process

A bank will not foreclose on your property the first time you are late on your payments. Most banks see foreclosure as the last option. They pursue foreclosure only when they suspect you will not make more payments on the loan. In that case, their only way to receive money on the loan is to take and sell the property to another buyer.

Although the process varies between states and individual banks, Figure 8.6 outlines the general steps involved in a preforeclosure. Missing payments with no attempt to negotiate a payment plan will force the lender to act on the loan's **acceleration clause**. This clause basically states that if you become past-due on your monthly payments, the bank can demand full repayment of the loan amount, thus "accelerating" the due date of the loan.

The foreclosure process is put in motion when the lender does not see a solution for getting the mortgage loan paid back. The lender can halt the foreclosure process at any time, assuming the borrower comes up with an acceptable plan for repayment. If you receive a demand letter or the foreclosure process has begun already, contact an attorney to discuss your specific rights. The steps involved in a foreclosure are illustrated in Figure 8.7.

Making $ense

8.11 If you are in a position in which you cannot make payments on your home, what should you do to prepare for a meeting with your mortgage lender?

8.12 What are your short-term and long-term options for maintaining your credit if you are at risk of foreclosure?

8.13 What can you do to protect your credit score in the event that you are no longer able to make your mortgage payments?

---

financialfitness:
JUST THE FACTS

Foreclosure Resources

If you are at risk for foreclosure, visit HUD's website (www.hud.gov/foreclosure/index.cfm) for an in-depth study regarding your options. Visit Foreclosure Resources for Consumers (www.federalreserve.gov/consumerinfo/foreclosure.htm) for links to local resources to assist you.

▼ **FIGURE** 8.7

The foreclosure process

• Bank sends 'Notice of Intent to Foreclose' by certified mail or sheriff

1. Bank files paper with courts to foreclose

You have 30 days to respond to the letter with full payment to avoid foreclosure

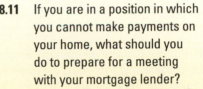

2. Required legal notices are published in local paper

• Court holds a hearing on the foreclosure and issues an order allowing the bank to foreclose

•Legal public notice of foreclosure sale and advertisements published in the local papers

3. Property sold to highest bidder at sheriff's auction

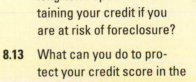

4. New owner evicts you from the property

•House sells; If the sale price does not cover the loan, you are still responsible for the balance of repayment

8.5 INS AND OUTS OF BANKRUPTCY

■ ■ **LO 8-5** Identify when bankruptcy is a viable option and know the consequences and how to restore your credit afterward.

If you have tried diligently, but unsuccessfully, to repay your debts, you may be considering bankruptcy. Before filing for bankruptcy, you should understand the different types of bankruptcy and their consequences. In addition, you need to know how to restore your credit after bankruptcy.

Types of Bankruptcy

Bankruptcy is the legal process by which a person declares the inability to pay debts owed to others. In the United States, there are two common forms of personal bankruptcy in the federal code: **Chapter 7**, which is the liquidation of the debtor's assets, and **Chapter 13**, which involves the reorganization, restructuring, and pay-out plan for bankrupt individuals.

Traditionally, people declare bankruptcy for three major reasons: bad luck, lack of preparation, and poor decision making. By being prepared with an emergency fund and exercising proper decision making and self-control, you can avoid bankruptcy when bad luck hits.

Chapter 7 bankruptcy Chapter 7 bankruptcy, the quickest and simplest form of bankruptcy, involves a **liquidation** of the debtor's assets, with the proceeds distributed to the creditors. This is commonly referred to as *straight bankruptcy*. Secured creditors are paid first, followed by those with a lien on the property. The remaining funds are divided among unsecured creditors under the supervision of a court-appointed trustee. Some property may be declared exempt (not subject to liquidation), but those items and amounts vary from state to state. Examples of exempt property include clothing, household goods, or an older car. Common obligations that do not get discharged in a Chapter 7 bankruptcy are student loans, child support, property tax, income tax less than three years old, fines and restitutions imposed by courts, and spousal support.

Chapter 13 bankruptcy In a Chapter 13 bankruptcy, you repay a portion of your debts and live within a strict budget monitored by the bankruptcy court–appointed trustee. Individuals file for Chapter 13 bankruptcy when they fall behind on secured debts (mortgage and auto loans) and plan to renegotiate the loan and make it current over time. Known as **wage earner bankruptcy**, Chapter 13 is for households with a regular source of income. You retain ownership of your current assets but must repay creditors over a specified period of time, usually three to five years. The bankruptcy court can issue a cramdown on your consumer loans, except your mortgage, ordering creditors to lower interest rates, principal amounts, or both. Filing a Chapter 13 bankruptcy allows you to stop foreclosure on your home; however, foreclosure is reinstated upon completion of the bankruptcy process.

means test To help a debtor determine which bankruptcy to file, the 2005 amendments to the Bankruptcy Code established a *means test* for Chapter 7 bankruptcy. This test attempts to prevent the abuse of bankruptcy by individuals with sufficient income to repay their debts. The means test uses a state's monthly median income as a benchmark against your median income to determine if you are eligible to file a Chapter 7 bankruptcy. If your income is below the state's median income, you are not subject to the means test. Bankruptcy fraud is a crime, and if you hide assets or documents when filing for bankruptcy, you are committing perjury.

Counseling and Education Requirements

In declaring personal bankruptcy, you are required to undergo mandatory prebankruptcy credit counseling and post-filing debtor education. A credit-counseling session includes an evaluation of your personal financial situation, a discussion of alternatives to bankruptcy, and a personal budget plan. A debtor education course includes information on developing a budget, managing money, and using credit wisely. You must present evidence (a certificate) of completing a debtor education course to have your debts discharged. Only credit counseling organizations and debtor education course providers approved by the U.S. Trustee Program may issue these certificates.

Consequences of Bankruptcy

Stemming from the Old Testament passages on forgiveness of debt, U.S. bankruptcy laws are intended to give those overburdened with debt a new start. However, there are consequences to this freedom from debt. As a result of declaring bankruptcy, you could lose your home and/or possessions, be bound to a strict budget to repay creditors, and lower your credit score—thus making it more expensive to get car insurance, buy phone service, rent an apartment, and get a loan. You will still be responsible for student loans and other court-ordered obligations. Bankruptcy shows up on your credit record for 7 to 10 years.

Declaring bankruptcy can keep you from getting a job in financial industries. More and more employers are pulling credit reports on prospective employees to measure their responsibility. You may have to explain the bankruptcy to a prospective employer to land a job. Bankruptcy also carries the social stigma of one who cannot manage credit or has little self-control. Bankruptcy is a public record, and your bankruptcy filing will be in the local newspaper and searchable on the Internet. It is very difficult to keep bankruptcy private. Filing for bankruptcy is a serious step; therefore, consider it cautiously and make certain you understand the benefits and the consequences before you make that choice.

moral and social consequences of bankruptcy

When you borrow from someone, you are expected to repay them. Even if you just are borrowing your roommate's car, the socially responsible thing to do is to replace the gas you have used. If you return the car on empty, your roommate will be less likely to let you borrow the car again.

Likewise, when you borrow money or buy something on credit, you are expected to pay back the amount as well as

any interest charged. When you receive a good or service on credit, to be repaid later, you create a contract and a moral obligation with that individual or business to pay for that service or good at a later date.

This much seems obvious, yet thousands of bankruptcy cases are filed on a daily basis and the rate continues to climb (see Figure 8.8). This means millions of creditors are not receiving any money for the goods or services they have provided. When bankruptcy occurs, someone does

▼ **FIGURE 8.8**

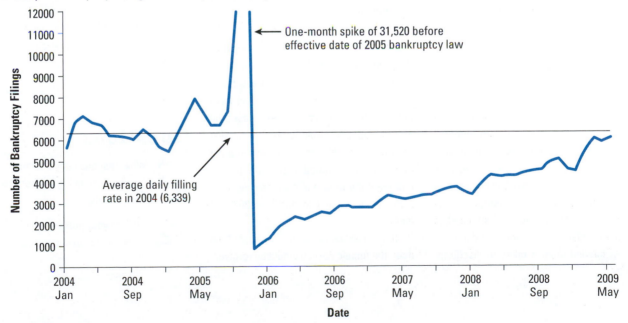

U.S. daily bankruptcy filings: January 2004–May 2009

One-month spike of 31,520 before effective date of 2005 bankruptcy law

Average daily filling rate in 2004 (6,339)

Source: www.law.gmu.edu/assets/files/publications/working_papers/01-18.pdf

Student must repay $350,000 court says

A Grand Marais lawyer tried to discharge his (student) loan debt through bankruptcy, but an appeals court says no way

If the bad economy has you thinking of taking on debt to go to grad school, consider the case of Mark Jesperson. The Eighth U.S. Circuit Court of Appeals has ruled that the 45-year-old Grand Marais man cannot escape more than $350,000 of student debt he piled up over more than a decade.

Jesperson had hoped to discharge the debt in bankruptcy and won the first couple rounds in court. But last week a three-judge panel reversed the lower courts' decision and said he must pay the money back. While the dollar amount involved is unusual, experts say the latest ruling is not. It's extremely difficult to get rid of student loan debt, even through bankruptcy. . . .

Jesperson has a law degree, but he's not putting it to much use these days—except for representing himself early in his case. He works as a painter, and lives in a camper. Struggles with alcohol brought him in and out of college; it took 11 years to complete his undergraduate degree. . . . Sober for several years, he passed the Minnesota bar on his first attempt in February 2002. Jesperson "borrowed heavily from government and private lenders" to finance his degrees, court documents state. Since passing the bar exam, he's never made more than $48,000 per year. In 2006, Jesperson went to bankruptcy court to rid himself of the debt. To succeed, a borrower must show "undue hardship"—a step beyond what it takes to discharge most other kinds of debt. The high standard is meant to encourage lenders to extend students credit and to prevent abuse. The bankruptcy court ruled in his favor, saying without discharging the "shockingly immense" debt, Jesperson "would, in effect, be sentenced to 25 years in a debtors' prison without walls." The lenders appealed, but the U.S. District Court upheld the bankruptcy court's decision.

The appeals court disagreed. It said that Jesperson's "young age, good health, number of degrees, marketable skills, and lack of substantial obligations to dependents or mental or physical impairments weigh in favor of not granting an undue hardship discharge." The lenders and courts pointed out that Jesperson hadn't made a single voluntary payment toward his student loans. That's true, Jesperson said. "I'm just like everyone else on the planet," he said. "I've been surviving. Housing and food and diapers." The ruling stated that Jesperson should have taken advantage of a program that would have allowed him to make payments based on his income and family's poverty level—regardless of his total unpaid student debt. Lenders argued that if Jesperson had used the program, his loan payments would have equaled no more than $629 per month.

If, after 25 years, he had not repaid the debt, the unpaid portion would be forgiven.

Courts are citing such programs more often as reasons to deny discharging student loan debt, said Deanne Loonin, director of the Student Loan Borrower Assistance Project at the National Consumer Law Center. "We've seen this reasoning for a while, but it has taken on new momentum," she said. A new student loan repayment plan went into effect just this month that applies to more people with more kinds of loans in bankruptcy court. For one, not everyone is eligible. The programs also don't provide relief from private loans. And they don't offer the "clean slate" bankruptcy does. Once a debtor makes it to 25 years, he or she pays taxes on the amount that's forgiven. For Jesperson, the repayment program "is basically a life sentence," he said. "It's like having the court say you and your family are relegated to poverty for the rest of your lives.". . .

JENNA ROSS, "Student Must Repay $350,000 Court Says," *Star Tribune*, July 15, 2009. Reprinted with permission.

Even for the purposes of education, it is important to be judicious in regard to the amount of debt you take on. Remember that someday it all has to be paid off, and the challenges of starting off so far in debt can be overwhelming.

Questions

1 What responsibility do you believe the lending institutions had in this situation?

2 What is your position on the federal court ruling and why?

not get paid. This someone could be a large financial institution, or it could be your neighbor's business.

For these businesses to stay afloat, they must pass along these losses due to bankruptcy to other customers who pay on time. This leads to higher credit card interest rates, larger fees, and stricter credit standards for those seeking credit in the future. A business recovers the cost of bankruptcy by raising the cost of its products for other customers. If a business is not prepared for the loss of unpaid obligations, it might have to close. Therefore, bankruptcy impacts all paying customers.

Bankruptcy is a personal choice and process. It is a program designed for those who truly need help, but its effects are wide-reaching throughout society.

Life after Bankruptcy

After a bankruptcy has been discharged (agreed-upon amounts have been repaid), the first priority is to re-establish good credit—either immediately, for a Chapter 7, or after reorganization, for a Chapter 13. Figure 8.9 lists a number of good habits to establish during this stage.

The good news is that time does indeed heal all wounds. It takes time to establish a good credit record, but if you have declared bankruptcy, hopefully you have learned from that experience and will avoid past mistakes. Bankruptcy provides a chance to start fresh, but it does come with a financial and emotional cost. ■

Making $ense

8.14 How does Chapter 7 bankruptcy compare to Chapter 13 bankruptcy?

8.15 Summarize the consequences of bankruptcy.

8.16 What steps can you take to restore your credit after bankruptcy?

▼ **FIGURE 8.9**

Beyond bankruptcy: good habits to follow

Change Your Lifestyle

• Eliminate the habits that got you into trouble. If you don't change your lifestyle, bankruptcy is only treating the symptoms and not the disease. Use self-control and self-discipline to stay within your budget and build up an emergency fund.

Pay Everything on Time

• Paying your rent, utilities, and phone bill on time will establish good habits and start rebuilding your credit.

Don't Use Credit

• Save for the things you want and need. You can use lay-away for items in a department store—for some money down, the store will hold your item until you pay for it in full.

Establish a Secured Credit Card

• To reestablish credit, apply for a secured credit card, where a lender issues you a credit card with a credit limit for the amount you deposit in an account. If you use this card, pay it off in full every time. You receive your deposit back when you close the account.

→ LEARN. In this chapter you learned about the warning signs of financial trouble. You also learned about the importance of stopping little leaks to keep your financial ship afloat and prioritizing needs over wants. Buying only what you need frees up cash flow and provides extra money to pay off past expenditures. When you purchase on credit, you are helping the banks and credit card companies make millions of dollars. You have the choice of who you want to make a millionaire: you or the credit card companies. You learned about the foreclosure process and your options if you are unable to make the mortgage payments on your home. Finally, you learned bankruptcy is a last resort that entails many consequences, both social and financial.

> ❝ It is easier to go down a hill than up, but the view is best from the top. ❞
>
> —ARNOLD BENNETT, *English novelist (1867–1931)*

SUMMARY

■■ **LO 8-1** Examine the early warning signs of financial trouble and learn how to avoid mistakes that can lead to financial crisis.

Getting a credit card and running up charges is easy. Paying off that debt after the fact is hard, and it requires discipline and restraint to not charge more than what you can pay off at the end of each month. Some signs that you may be heading toward financial trouble include living paycheck-to-paycheck, a decreasing net worth, and having no emergency fund. The best way to avoid a financial crisis is to take control one step at a time and arrive at a point where you are spending less than you make.

■■ **LO 8-2** Discover how little changes in your spending habits can make a big difference in your financial well-being.

To achieve financial success, begin by identifying essential versus nonessential spending. Follow the budgeting basics from Chapter 3 and keep a money journal in order to know where you stand financially and identify expenses you might want to trim. To get out of debt, eliminate nonessential spending for a time and assess your essential expenses to see if some of those can be trimmed. The key to staying the course is to keep it fun, so invite others to join you in taking on a more frugal lifestyle.

■■ **LO 8-3** Create a workable plan to become debt-free and in control of your finances.

Steps to digging out of debt include: (1) not using credit cards; (2) creating a realistic budget and using allocated cash for designated spending; (3) exercising the 10-second rule and month-end holds to combat impulsive buying; (4) not buying things you cannot afford; (5) paying off debt; (6) making payments on time; and (7) increasing your income. In managing past credit debt, be wary of the risk of backsliding if you choose to consolidate your debt. Credit counseling services and debt-settlement companies exist if you need to reach out for help. The Fair Debt Collection Practices Act protects consumers by specifying what a debt collector can and cannot do in attempting to collect on past-due debt.

■■ **LO 8-4** Describe options for protecting your credit if at risk of foreclosure.

To avoid foreclosure and maintain your credit score, address mortgage payment problems directly. The first step is to contact the mortgage lender to work out either a temporary or a long-term solution. Temporary options include reinstatement of the loan, forbearance, or creating a catch-up repayment plan. Long-term solutions include a loan modification or filing a partial insurance claim. If keeping the home is not an option, alternatives to safeguard your credit include executing a sale of the home, executing a short sale, having another qualified buyer assume the loan, or offering a deed-in-lieu of foreclosure to the bank.

■ ■ **LO 8-5** Identify when bankruptcy is a viable option and know the consequences and how to restore your credit afterward.

Before filing for bankruptcy, get professional help. Chapter 7 bankruptcy is a quick and simple form of bankruptcy in which your assets are liquidated and the funds are distributed to the creditors. In Chapter 13 bankruptcy, you retain your assets and propose a restructured debt-payment plan to your creditors. The 2005 amendments to the U.S. Bankruptcy Code established a means test to determine the type of bankruptcy for which an individual is eligible. Filing for bankruptcy includes mandatory credit counseling and debtor education. The first priority following bankruptcy is to reestablish your credit.

SCAN HERE for study quizzes for this chapter

➡ PLAN & ACT.

The online worksheets that accompany this chapter will help you determine whether you are headed for financial trouble and, if so, develop a debt priority pay-off plan to pay off your debts by starting with your smallest debt and building up momentum until you are debt-free. Other worksheets will help you identify savings opportunities and use those savings to build an emergency fund. By having an emergency fund, you will not be tempted to use credit cards as a safety net. Your Plan & Act to-do list is as follows:

- ☐ Check for early warning signs of financial trouble (Worksheet 8.1).
- ☐ Use the balance sheet you created in Chapter 3 (Worksheet 3.1) to derive a minimum amount for your emergency fund balance goal (Worksheet 8.2).
- ☐ Evaluate your spending journal from Chapter 3 to identify saving opportunities that could be reallocated to your emergency fund (Worksheet 8.3).
- ☐ Create a debt priority pay-off plan (Worksheet 8.4).

➡ EVALUATE.

By stopping little leaks and working within a budget, you can gain control of your financial health. As Dave Ramsey states, "If you can control the person in the mirror, you can be skinny and rich."[5] What you have learned in this chapter can improve your life, your fiscal health, and your well-being. You can live debt-free, be in control of your money and spending, and be confident that your money is working hard for you. Through disciplined savings and self-control, you will not only get out of debt, but you will also be able to achieve your financial goals.

❯❯ GoalTracker

Review your online **GoalTracker**. Record new-found savings opportunities from the worksheets that you can use to reach your goals. Identify the current balance of your emergency fund and the methods you plan to use to grow the fund to a healthy balance.

[5]Ramsey, D. *The Total Money Makeover: A Proven Plan for Financial Fitness*, Nelson Books, 2007.

key terms

Acceleration Clause

Bankruptcy

Chapter 7

Chapter 13

Cramdown

Deed-in-Lieu of Foreclosure

Forbearance

Liquidation

Reinstatement

Short Sale

Wage Earner Bankruptcy

self-test questions

1. The following is *not* a cautionary (yellow-flag) warning of financial trouble: (LO 8-1)

   a. Having a little bit left out of every paycheck
   b. Using credit cards without the cash to pay them off when the bill comes
   c. Paying the minimum amount due on the credit cards
   d. A decrease in net worth each month

2. The following is a red-flag warning of financial trouble: (LO 8-1)

   a. Losing your investment on a stock
   b. Tapping home equity to pay off credit cards
   c. Buying junk bonds
   d. Using your emergency fund to repair your car

3. What is the one simple rule to dig out of debt? (LO 8-1)

   a. Pay off the highest interest card first, to save on the amount of interest you pay
   b. Pay off the lowest balance credit card first, to more quickly reduce the number of your credit cards with a balance
   c. Consolidate all your credit cards to one home equity loan with a lower interest rate
   d. Spend less than you make, and save or invest the rest

4. In stopping little leaks, what are the first things you need to sort out? (LO 8-2)

   a. Needs from wants
   b. Bills from payments
   c. Ongoing bills vs. one-time payments
   d. Giving vs. spending

5. Which is *not* a recommended method to trim necessary spending? (LO 8-2)

   a. Refinance your mortgage
   b. Skip a meal one day weekly
   c. Opt for public transportation
   d. Drop your land line

6. Which is *not* an activity to help you dig out of debt? (LO 8-3)

   a. Stop using credit cards
   b. Exercise the 10-second and month-end holds
   c. Don't buy stuff you can't afford
   d. Postpone credit card payments to build an emergency fund

7. Which is *not* a risk of debt consolidation? (LO 8-3)

   a. Continued bad credit card habits
   b. Varying interest rates on the consolidation loan
   c. In an equity consolidation loan, the risk of losing your home if you fail to make payments
   d. The high fees of consolidation loans

8. Which of the following should you look out for in working with a debt-settlement company or a credit counseling agency? (LO 8-3)

   a. Up-front fees
   b. Whether or not your bills get paid
   c. If the offer sounds too good to be true
   d. All of the above

9. Which activity is a debt collector prohibited from doing under the Fair Debt Collection Practices Act? (LO 8-3)

   a. Calling between 8:00 A.M. and 9:00 P.M.
   b. Calling you at work
   c. Disregarding a written request from you to cease further contact
   d. Representing the amount, character, or legal status of your debt
   e. All of the above

10. Which is *not* true of cramdowns? (LO 8-4)

    a. The lender will renegotiate the loan at a lower interest rate
    b. The lender will renegotiate a lower principal balance
    c. The term comes from bankruptcy courts
    d. Bankruptcy courts have jurisdiction to cram down mortgage loans

11. Which is *not* true of the preforeclosure process? (LO 8-4)

    a. A bank will foreclose on a property following a first-time late payment
    b. The bank will send you a demand letter using the acceleration clause
    c. The bank will demand full repayment of the loan amount
    d. If you are able to pay the past-due amount with interest, the lender may reinstate the original terms of the loan

12. Which is *not* an option if the risk of foreclosure is due to short-term financial problems? (LO 8-4)

    a. Reinstatement
    b. Forbearance
    c. Repayment plan forbearance
    d. Reinstatement plan forbearance

13. Which of the following is a long-term solution to the risk of foreclosure? (LO 8-4)

    a. Short sale
    b. Assumption of the loan
    c. Deed-in-lieu of foreclosure
    d. All of the above

14. Which is a characteristic of Chapter 13 bankruptcy but not Chapter 7 bankruptcy? *(LO 8-5)*

 a. Quicker
 b. Simpler
 c. You repay a portion of your debts and live within a strict budget that is monitored
 d. You undergo a liquidation of assets with the proceeds distributed to the creditors

15. How does one know which type of bankruptcy to file or whether it is even an option? *(LO 8-5)*

 a. Means test
 b. Floating average test

 c. Good Samaritan test
 d. Debt-to-income ratio limit

16. Which is *not* a step you need to take to reestablish your credit following bankruptcy? *(LO 8-5)*

 a. Credit counseling and debtor education
 b. Make timely payments
 c. Stay away from credit cards
 d. Apply for a debit card

problems

1. Your first job pays $36,000 per year. How much should you have in your emergency fund? *(LO 8-1)*

2. You have $5,000 in your emergency fund. There has been a death in your family and you need to fly home to Alaska; the ticket price is $975. Your current budget allows for no more than $75/month to be moved from your savings to build back your emergency fund. How long will it take you to build your emergency fund back to a $5,000 balance? *(LO 8-1)*

3. You make $12/hour in a work-study program. You want to start training for a triathlon. You see a great pair of running shoes for $150 and running clothes for $90. How many hours will you need to work to buy the shoes and clothing? *(LO 8-2)*

4. You and your friends want to go to Napa Valley for a long weekend get-away in two months. You estimate the cost of the trip will be $400. If you start saving for the trip now, how much do you need to put into savings on a daily basis to be able to pay cash for the trip in two months? *(LO 8-2)*

5. You have a car payment of $300/month. You spent $675 on maintenance last year and you spend about $35/week on gasoline. Parking costs are $25/month. How much could you put toward debt reduction on an annual basis if you sold the car and instead used public transportation? The monthly transit pass is $45. *(LO 8-3)*

6. You have broken your arm and your major medical insurance does not cover $425 of the expenses. You can direct $75 from each paycheck (every other week) toward paying this bill. What payment period will you try to negotiate with the medical center in order to pay the bill in full? *(LO 8-3)*

7. You have the following debts:
 a. Student loan balance of $17,000 at 5.25% interest, with payments of $225/month
 b. Visa balance of $800 at 18% interest, with a minimum monthly payment of $32
 c. Car loan balance of $5,500, with monthly payments of $175
 d. Department store credit card balance of $300 at 24% interest, with minimum monthly payments of $25

By paying all of your expenses and living on a very tight budget, you stopped all the little leaks and now have an extra $300 each month and $1,000 in your emergency fund. You now are at war with your debts. Structure a repayment plan, listing the order in which you will pay off your debts and when they will be paid off. Use a worksheet like the one below to calculate the balances month-to-month for two years. *(LO 8-3)*

Debt	Beginning Balance	Current Balance	Minimum Payment	Current Payment Amount	Payments to Zero Balance	Date of Payoff
$	$	$	$	$	$	

1. Chang is a sophomore at college and currently has $1,500 in credit card debt. He has a work-study job and is making just the minimum payments on his credit card, using the rest of his money for entertainment and school supplies. He has no savings and wants to build a $1,000 emergency fund. Come up with an action plan whereby Chang can pay off his credit card debt and save $1,000 for an emergency fund. *(LO 8-1)*

2. Jimmy just graduated from college with $15,000 in student loans with a 10-year amortization, as well as credit card debt of $2,500. He just got his dream job in another city. His car is 10 years old; it doesn't look the best, but it runs well, is reliable, and is in good working order. He does not have any savings or an emergency fund. He wants to save at least $25,000 for a down payment on a house and would like to have six months' income saved in his emergency fund. His net pay is $2,500 a month. *(LO 8-3)*

   a. Create a realistic budget for Jimmy, including moving expenses, deposits, and so on.

   b. List and prioritize savings and debt-payoff goals for Jimmy.

   c. Describe spending and savings plans for the following goals, with specific dates for their achievement:
      (1) Have at least $1,000 in an emergency fund.
      (2) Pay off the credit card.
      (3) Pay off the student loan.
      (4) Save six months of income in an emergency fund.
      (5) Save for a down payment.

   d. What will it take to accomplish these goals, and what challenges do you forecast for Jimmy?

3. Unfortunately, two years after Callie bought her new home, the economy went into a recession, and she got laid off from her job. She has gone back to teaching, which she loves, but her household income has been drastically reduced—from $350,000 a year to $65,000 a year. What should Callie do to avoid foreclosure? *(LO 8-5)*

worksheets

Find the worksheets online at www.mhhe.com/walkerpf1e

8.1 EARLY WARNING SIGNS OF FINANCIAL TROUBLE CHECKLIST

Complete the checklist in Worksheet 8.1 to see if you exhibit any of the warning signs of financial trouble.

Check the following list for any early warning signs of financial trouble.

Early Warning Signs of Financial Trouble	Yes	No
I am living paycheck to paycheck.		
I am using my credit cards without the cash to pay the bill when it comes.		
I am paying only the minimum amount due on my credit cards.		
My credit card balances increase month to month (I'm gaining pounds).		
My net worth is decreasing each month.		
I am charging essentials like gas and groceries without a payoff plan.		
I do not have a budget and do not know my monthly income and expenses.		
When I get a raise, a new job, or win the lottery, I will live debt-free.		
My money runs out before the month does.		
I do not have at least six months' income in an emergency fund.		
Total Yes Count		

If you checked yes in any of the boxes, you may be heading toward financial trouble. Now is the time to make a plan for changing your bad financial habits. Stick to that plan to avoid a financial crisis.

8.2 BUILDING AN EMERGENCY FUND

Use Worksheet 8.2 to create a snapshot of where you have been and what you have to show for it. First review your balance sheet information from Chapter 3 and then create a plan for paying off your credit card debts and building an emergency fund.

Following a review of your balance sheet (worksheet 3.1):	
Current net worth:	
Current debt amount:	
Items purchased with the debt:	
Steps to Building an Emergency Fund	
1. Minimum Emergency Fund:	$,1000
2. Six Months Income:	
2. Twelve Months Income:	
Steps to take to pay off credt card debts and have a strong emergency fund:	
1)	
2)	
3)	
4)	
5)	

8.3 FINDING LITTLE LEAKS

Use Worksheet 8.3 to review your Every Penny Counts spending journal and determine which of your expenses are essential and which are nonessential. Then look for opportunities to eliminate or trim these expenses and increase your savings.

Referring to your Every Penny Counts spending journal entries from Chapter 3 over the past month, complete the following steps.
1) Review items from the previous month and mark them as 'E' essential or 'N' nonessential.
2) List nonessential items and their amount. Could you do without them? Is there a more frugal option? Could it be cut back by a portion? Consider what savings opportunities you could take on. Calculate what the new budgeted amount would be for each item.
3) Total the opportunity savings from the nonessential expenditures for the month.
4) List the essential items. Are there opportunities to trim on any of these expenses? Give thought to some of the options discussed in the chapter.
5) Calculate what the new budgeted amount would be for each item.
6) Total the opportunity savings from the essential expenditures for the month.

Nonessential		Opportunity?			
Item	Amount	Stop Little Leaks Plan	Amount	Savings	Done
Total Savings Opportunity			0		

Essential		Opportunity?			
Item	Amount	Stop Little Leaks Plan	Amount	Savings	Done
Total Savings Opportunity			0		

Total savings opportunity from nonessential spending	0	
Total savings opportunity from essential spending	0	
Total savings opportunity	0	

8.4 DEBT PRIORITY PAY-OFF PLAN

Use Worksheet 8.4 to list and create a prioritized plan for paying off your credit card debts and loans.

Worksheet 8.4 - Debt-Priority Pay-Off Plan

List all debts from smallest to largest.

Use a credit card calculator to figure out how long it will take to pay off your smallest debt by making only minimum payments on your other cards and loans and aggressively paying off that lowest credit debt.

As soon as you pay off that debt, use the same tactic to work on the next smallest balance.

Cross off the debt when you pay it off.

Yahoo! Finance has many different calculators to determine when you will reach your goals. Go to finance.yahoo.com/calculator/index.

Use finance.yahoo.com/calculator/banking-budgeting/det01 to calculate how long it will take to pay off your credit card debt.

Debt	Interest Rate	Beginning Balance	Current Balance	Minimum Payment	Current Payment Amount	Payments to Zero Balance	Date of Payoff

continuing case

906 E College Street

Karri is about to graduate, and she has landed a job paying $32,000 a year. However, her love of shoes and her latest trip to New York City left her with $10,000 in credit card debt. She is also graduating with $15,000 in student loans, and those payments will come to $180/month. She will not have to make any student loan payments until six months after graduation.

A summary of the housemates' goals can be found in the first Continuing Case problem on page 27.

1. What advice would you give Karri so she can build an appropriate emergency fund?

2. Think about typical living expenses, and then create a realistic budget for Karri.

> "The difference between death and taxes is death doesn't get worse every time Congress meets."
>
> —WILL ROGERS, *Humorist (1879–1935)*

section three

chapter nine

tax management

Taxes are an important part of planning your finances. In understanding the tax laws, you will be able to conserve more income, enhance your investments, and protect the transfer of wealth.

LEARNING OBJECTIVES

After reading this chapter, you should be able to:

LO 9-1 Describe the purposes of taxes, the different types of taxes, and the principles of progressive and regressive taxes.

LO 9-2 Examine the logic, terms, and process of filing taxes.

LO 9-3 Distinguish between different types of tax rates, and know when they apply and how to calculate them.

LO 9-4 Analyze strategies to legally minimize tax liabilities.

◀ Curtis, age 23, new graduate, project manager

Tax Reality

Curtis is in his first postgraduation job. He is single, has no children, and is renting. (Thus, he has no mortgage deductions.) His starting salary is $36,000. He was surprised at how much money was taken out of his first check for taxes, retirement, and health insurance. It was much more than he had anticipated or budgeted for when signing the lease to his new apartment: "The tax liability was a real shocker. I wish I would have realized how much money in taxes would be taken out of my check before I signed my lease. To compensate, I am thinking about getting a side job as a personal trainer on weekends. A warning should go on the back of your diploma: 'Don't buy anything until you get your first check.'"

9.1 TYPES OF TAXES

■ ■ **LO 9-1** Describe the purposes of taxes, the different types of taxes, and the principles of progressive and regressive taxes.

Taxes are fees charged by governments (federal, state, and local) on a product, income, or activity to finance government expenditures. If the tax is levied directly on personal income, it is a **direct tax**. If the tax is levied on the price of a good or service, it is an **indirect tax**.

financialfitness:
STOPPING LITTLE LEAKS

Retirement Tax-Friendly Picks

Some retired individuals will move to states such as Florida or Alaska that have little or no state and local taxes. In fact, Alaska pays all its citizens an annual rebate from its oil pipeline revenues each year. Other states without a state income tax are Nevada, South Dakota, Texas, Washington, and Wyoming. New Hampshire and Tennessee tax only dividend and interest income. It should be noted that some of these states do make up for this with higher property or sales taxes.

One of the most important uses of taxes is to finance government-provided services that protect the nation and support its citizens. These are known as **public goods and services**. Public goods and services include the military, fire departments, police departments, public schools, libraries, the Federal Emergency Management Agency (FEMA), and the Department of Homeland Security. Since public goods and services have to be available to all citizens, it is not possible to exclude nontaxpayers. For instance, the military cannot choose to protect some citizens but not others—it protects them all simultaneously. Because public goods and services cannot be offered equally to all citizens in a market, the government provides them and finances them largely through taxes.

U.S. federal taxes are the same regardless of where you live in the United States (although members of the military are excluded from paying taxes while serving combat duty.) State and local taxes vary greatly.

Principles of Progressive and Regressive Taxes

Taxes are categorized as being either progressive or regressive. A **regressive tax** is a fee that is applied uniformly. A regressive tax imposes a greater burden (relative to

["But in this world, nothing can be said to be certain, except death and taxes."

—BENJAMIN FRANKLIN *(1706–1790)*]

resources) on the poor than on the rich; it hits lower-income individuals harder. Regressive taxes include sales tax and taxes on tobacco, alcohol, and gasoline. If a person has an income of $100 and pays $10 in tobacco and gasoline taxes, he is taxed at a rate of 10% of his income. If the next person is making $200 and pays the same $10 in tobacco and gasoline taxes, she is paying an average tax rate of only 5% of her income. With regressive taxes, there is an inverse relationship between the tax rate and the taxpayer's ability to pay.

A regressive tax is often referred to as a fixed tax, meaning that every person has to pay the same amount of money. Some states do not have a state income tax, but instead finance their state governments through sales tax. This puts a larger tax burden (as a percentage of income) on the poor.

Examples of regressive taxes include:

Sales tax: Individuals pay sales taxes at the time of a purchase transaction. The magnitude of the sales tax varies across states and cities.

Excise taxes: These taxes are levied on consumer products like tobacco, alcohol, and gasoline.

Property taxes: Property owners pay a tax based on the value of their home and land.

Gift taxes: Gifts are taxable if they are for an amount greater than the annual exclusion dollar amount for the year. Itemized deductions to your income include tuition or medical expenses, gifts to your spouse, or gifts to a political organization.

Estate taxes: The federal government and some state governments tax estates depending on their size. Your estate is an accounting of everything you own or have interests in on the day you die. You must file an estate tax return nine months after a person dies. The value of an inherited estate can be tricky. Any inherited stocks, bonds, or other investments are valued at their prices on the day the person dies. When the individual inheriting the property disposes of the property, taxes are paid only on the difference between the sale price and the value on the day of death (not the price originally paid for the investment). Tax-protected investments like an IRA or 401(k) have complicated rules on how much you can withdraw and how much tax you are required to pay. You will want to get a professional (a lawyer, CPA, or tax professional) involved before touching any of the inherited funds; otherwise you may find yourself with an exceptionally large tax bill.

Social Security and Medicare taxes: Earned income (wages and salary) is subject to Federal Insurance Contributions Act (FICA) taxes, which are used to fund Social Security and Medicare. This tax payment is withheld from each paycheck. The Social Security tax is 6.2% of your salary up to a maximum salary level of $106,800 in 2011. The maximum salary level adjusts annually. Medicare taxes are 1.45% of your earned income. Your employer also pays 6.2% of your income toward Social Security and 1.45% of your income toward Medicare as part of your FICA tax obligation. If self-employed, you have to pay both the employer and employee

taxes
fees charged by the government on a product, income, or activity

direct tax
fee levied directly on personal income

indirect tax
fee levied on consumption or an expenditure, privilege, or right, but not on income or property

public goods and services government-provided services that protect and support citizens; examples are services provided by the police, fire, library, and military

regressive tax
fee that is applied uniformly, imposing a greater burden (relative to resources) on the poor than on the rich

doing the MATH

9.1 Burden of a Regressive Tax

You buy a car for $10,000 and the sales tax is 8%. Therefore, you pay $800 in taxes.
If you make $20,000/year, that $800 tax is

$800/$20,000 = 4.0%

of your income. If you make $100,000/year, that $800 tax is

$800/$100,00) = 0.8%

of your income. Based on this example, you can see that a regressive tax places a heavier tax burden on those making less money.

If you buy 400 gallons of gasoline a year, at $3/gallon, and one-third of the price is sales tax, what percentage of your income goes toward the gas sales tax?

1. Assume you are making $20,000/year.

2. Assume you are making $100,000/year.

financialfitness:
JUST THE FACTS

Saving on Sales Tax

In some states, consumers have avoided paying sales taxes by shipping purchases across state lines if the business does not operate in the state where the product is purchased. States increasingly are looking for ways to collect such sales taxes; Amazon.com has been in the news as they fight suits from several states that are trying to close this loophole.

parts of FICA. Therefore, the FICA tax for self-employed individuals is 15.3%.

A **progressive tax** system is designed to help create equity among citizens. The wealthy are taxed at a higher tax rate than the poor, and the tax rate increases as the taxable amount increases. The percentage of personal income tax is based on your adjusted gross income: the more you make, the higher the tax percentage you are levied. In 2010, the federal income tax percentage ranged from 0 to 35%. Progressive taxes attempt to reduce the tax burden on people with a lower ability to pay. Progressive taxes are sometimes referred to as a "Robin Hood" tax, meaning that the money is redistributed from the rich to help pay for government-led social programs for the poor.

fulfilling tax liabilities
The legislative branch of the government passes tax laws, which are then approved by the executive branch of government and afterward given to the Treasury Department. The Internal Revenue Service (IRS) is a bureau of the Treasury Department and is responsible for assessing and collecting taxes in the United States. This revenue consists of personal and corporate income taxes, excise taxes, estate taxes, and gift taxes, as well as employment taxes for the nation's Social Security system.

The goal of the government is to have a steady stream of income all year long. Therefore it collects a portion of your tax liability from each paycheck in the form of withholding taxes. The amount withheld is initially determined by completing the W-4 form.

the W-4 form
When you start a new job, you fill out a **W-4 form.** Officially known as the Form W-4 Employee's

Withholding Allowance Certificate, it is used to determine how much money should be withheld from each paycheck to pay your tax liability. That amount is called **withholdings.**

The amount can be changed at any time, and you should re-evaluate it every year when you do your taxes. Certain changes will result in the need to change your withholding, for example, if you add or lose a source of income, if you get married, if you have children, or if your children become independent and you no longer claim them on your taxes. The total number of personal allowances on line 5 of the W-4 form affects whether a little or a lot is taken from each paycheck for taxes. See Figure 9.1.

To figure out how much to withhold, the W-4 includes three different worksheets that may be completed if necessary. The Personal Allowances Worksheet (Figure 9.2) looks at how many people are in your household and how many jobs they have.

Next, the Deductions and Adjustments Worksheet (Figure 9.3 on page 226) tries to account for any tax deductions or adjustments you may have. Examples include interest on student loans, contributions to charities, and mortgage interest.

The final worksheet (Figure 9.4, page 226) is the Two-Earners/Multiple Jobs Worksheet. It estimates your withholdings: (1) if you are married, and you and your spouse are both earning income, and (2) if you have more than one job.

If you start employment mid-year, you can ask your employer to use the *part-year method* to adjust your withholdings downward. For example, if you are salaried for $30,000 but start your employment in July, you will earn close to $15,000 in the tax year. This puts you in a lower tax bracket and therefore lowers your withholdings each paycheck. (However, remember to change the withholding amount at the start of the next year, or you will under-withhold that year.)

If your taxable income is not money you receive in salary or if your employer withholds nothing, you may be required to make estimated payments four times a year to cover at least 100% of what you paid the previous year or at least 90% of what you will owe for the current year. Generally, no income tax is withheld on alimony, self-employment income, or investment income; however, all three are considered income by the IRS and are included in your income when you calculate your tax liability. If you have additional income from these sources, you usually will owe more in taxes than what is being withheld from your salary.

There is no penalty for not pre-paying if the tax that is due is less than $1,000 and you had no tax liability in the prior year. If you collected unemployment benefits, check to see if your state withheld taxes. If not, then you will need to pay taxes on your unemployment along with the rest of your income. In 2009, all or part of unemployment benefits received were tax-free for unemployed workers due to the American Recovery and Reinvestment Act. Tax laws change

W-4 tax form

Source: www.irs.gov/pub/irs-pdf/fw4.pdf

W-4 personal allowances worksheet

Source: www.irs.gov/pub/irs-pdf/fw4.pdf

every year, so you need to either research the changes in the tax laws every year or obtain advice from a tax professional.

You may consider using withholding as a form of forced savings. You will get a refund when you file your tax return if you choose to have more money withheld from your paychecks than necessary to cover your tax liability. Essentially, you will be making an interest-free loan to the government until the money is returned to you as a tax refund. A better financial decision would be to withhold only what is necessary for taxes and have money from each paycheck automatically placed in a savings account. With this method, you—not the government—will earn interest on the money in the savings account. And since you will not see it as part of your paycheck, you will not be tempted to spend it.

▼ FIGURE 9.3

W-4 deductions and adjustments worksheet

Deductions and Adjustments Worksheet

Note. Use this worksheet *only* if you plan to itemize deductions or claim certain credits or adjustments to income.

1	Enter an estimate of your 2011 itemized deductions. These include qualifying home mortgage interest, charitable contributions, state and local taxes, medical expenses in excess of 7.5% of your income, and miscellaneous deductions	1	$ _____
2	Enter: { $11,600 if married filing jointly or qualifying widow(er) $8,500 if head of household $5,800 if single or married filing separately }	2	$ _____
3	**Subtract** line 2 from line 1. If zero or less, enter "-0-"	3	$ _____
4	Enter an estimate of your 2011 adjustments to income and any additional standard deduction (see Pub. 919)	4	$ _____
5	**Add** lines 3 and 4 and enter the total. (Include any amount for credits from the *Converting Credits to Withholding Allowances for 2011 Form W-4 Worksheet* in Pub. 919.)	5	$ _____
6	Enter an estimate of your 2011 nonwage income (such as dividends or interest)	6	$ _____
7	**Subtract** line 6 from line 5. If zero or less, enter "-0-"	7	$ _____
8	**Divide** the amount on line 7 by $3,700 and enter the result here. Drop any fraction	8	_____
9	Enter the number from the **Personal Allowances Worksheet**, line H, page 1	9	_____
10	**Add** lines 8 and 9 and enter the total here. If you plan to use the **Two-Earners/Multiple Jobs Worksheet**, also enter this total on line 1 below. Otherwise, **stop here** and enter this total on Form W-4, line 5, page 1	10	_____

Source: www.irs.gov/pub/irs-pdf/fw4.pdf

▼ FIGURE 9.4

W-4 two-earners/multiple jobs worksheet

Two-Earners/Multiple Jobs Worksheet (See *Two earners or multiple jobs* on page 1.)

Note. Use this worksheet *only* if the instructions under line H on page 1 direct you here.

1	Enter the number from line H, page 1 (or from line 10 above if you used the **Deductions and Adjustments Worksheet**)	1	_____
2	Find the number in **Table 1** below that applies to the **LOWEST** paying job and enter it here. **However,** if you are married filing jointly and wages from the highest paying job are $65,000 or less, do not enter more than "3"	2	_____
3	If line 1 is **more than or equal to** line 2, subtract line 2 from line 1. Enter the result here (if zero, enter "-0-") and on Form W-4, line 5, page 1. **Do not** use the rest of this worksheet	3	_____

Note. If line 1 is **less than** line 2, enter "-0-" on Form W-4, line 5, page 1. Complete lines 4 through 9 below to figure the additional withholding amount necessary to avoid a year-end tax bill.

4	Enter the number from line 2 of this worksheet	4	_____
5	Enter the number from line 1 of this worksheet	5	_____
6	**Subtract** line 5 from line 4	6	_____
7	Find the amount in **Table 2** below that applies to the **HIGHEST** paying job and enter it here	7	$ _____
8	**Multiply** line 7 by line 6 and enter the result here. This is the additional annual withholding needed . .	8	$ _____
9	Divide line 8 by the number of pay periods remaining in 2011. For example, divide by 26 if you are paid every two weeks and you complete this form in December 2010. Enter the result here and on Form W-4, line 6, page 1. This is the additional amount to be withheld from each paycheck	9	$ _____

Table 1

Married Filing Jointly		All Others	
If wages from **LOWEST** paying job are—	Enter on line 2 above	If wages from **LOWEST** paying job are—	Enter on line 2 above
$0 - $5,000	0	$0 - $8,000	0
5,001 - 12,000	1	8,001 - 15,000	1
12,001 - 22,000	2	15,001 - 25,000	2
22,001 - 25,000	3	25,001 - 30,000	3
25,001 - 30,000	4	30,001 - 40,000	4
30,001 - 40,000	5	40,001 - 50,000	5
40,001 - 48,000	6	50,001 - 65,000	6
48,001 - 55,000	7	65,001 - 80,000	7
55,001 - 65,000	8	80,001 - 95,000	8
65,001 - 72,000	9	95,001 -120,000	9
72,001 - 85,000	10	120,001 and over	10
85,001 - 97,000	11		
97,001 -110,000	12		
110,001 -120,000	13		
120,001 -135,000	14		
135,001 and over	15		

Table 2

Married Filing Jointly		All Others	
If wages from **HIGHEST** paying job are—	Enter on line 7 above	If wages from **HIGHEST** paying job are—	Enter on line 7 above
$0 – $65,000	$560	$0 - $35,000	$560
65,001 – 125,000	930	35,001 - 90,000	930
125,001 – 185,000	1,040	90,001 - 165,000	1,040
185,001 – 335,000	1,220	165,001 - 370,000	1,220
335,001 and over	1,300	370,001 and over	1,300

Source: www.irs.gov/pub/irs-pdf/fw4.pdf

9.2 FILING TAXES

■ ■ **LO 9-2** Examine the logic, terms, and process of filing taxes.

Each April 15 (or the first business day after April 15 if it falls on a weekend or federal holiday), you have to file a federal income tax return, reporting what you earned from the previous year and what you owe or are requesting as an entitled refund. The amount of taxes you owe could depend on what you know, how you plan, and how you file.

Tax-Filing Basics

Before you file your taxes, you will need to know your filing status and your gross income, as well as any deductions and/or credits for which you may be eligible.

filing status The first thing to determine is your *filing status.* For federal income tax purposes, there are five filing statuses.

Single: Unmarried, widowed, divorced, or legally separated as of the last day of the year

Married filing jointly: Married couples, people with legally recognized common-law marriages, or anyone whose spouse has died over the past tax year

Married filing separately: Legally married couples, regardless of whether they live together, who choose to file separate returns

Qualified widow(er) with dependent child: Widowed in the past two years and with a qualifying dependent in the household

Head of household: Unmarried adult who maintains a home and supports a qualifying relative

The filing status is important because your tax bracket (and therefore the amount you must pay) is determined by your marital status, your number of dependent children, your occupation, and several other factors. You may fit more than one description and are free to choose the one providing the better tax advantage. Your filing status also determines your standard deductions, an amount of income that is not subject to tax. The regular standard deductions change each year.

gross income The next item you need to know is your **gross income**. Your gross income is your total income, including earned income and unearned income. *Earned income* is money you earn from work and includes wages, commissions, tips, farming profits, and other income.

$ense
Making

9.1 Why do we pay taxes?

9.2 What types of taxes are we subject to?

9.3 Explain the difference between progressive and regressive taxes.

9.4 What things should you consider when calculating how much personal income tax you should contribute on a monthly basis?

Unearned income includes money received from sources other than employment, such as interest and dividends from investments, or income derived from other sources such as rental property, royalties, pensions, alimony, and unemployment. Employers must report your annual wages and tips to both you and the government (the IRS) on a **W-2 form** by January 31 of the next year.

adjusted gross income   **Adjusted gross income (AGI)** is the U.S. tax term for the amount used in the calculation of an individual's tax liability. AGI is gross income minus the tax code's **deductions** for certain specific expenses. Among the adjustments you may be able to take are contributions to a traditional IRA (individual retirement account), interest paid on a student loan, alimony paid, moving expenses, and certain self-employment expenses.

deductions   Every taxpayer must decide whether to take the standard deduction or to itemize personal expenses, called **itemized deductions**. You automatically qualify for standard deductions; however, the amount depends upon your filing status and whether you are blind or older than 65. In some cases, by itemizing your deductions you may qualify for more than the standard-deduction amount. Common itemized deductions include:

- Mortgage interest
- State and local taxes
- Personal property taxes
- Charitable contributions
- Medical and dental expenses
- Casualty and theft losses
- Moving expenses
- Job-related and school expenses

Generally, taxpayers choose to deduct whichever is larger—their total itemized deductions or their standard deduction.

exemptions   An **exemption** is a dollar amount allowed by law that reduces your taxable adjusted gross income. Every taxpayer, unless you are a dependent on another taxpayer's return, may claim his or her own personal exemption. If filing a joint return, both you and your spouse can claim personal exemptions. If any individuals qualify as your dependents, you can claim their exemptions on your return.

There are five tests you must satisfy to qualify as a dependent. A *dependent* must be a U.S. citizen or resident, or a resident of Canada or Mexico who is either related to, or a member of, the taxpayer's household for the entire tax year. A dependent cannot file a joint return with a spouse, must have a gross income of less than $3,650 for 2010, and must have received over one-half of his or her total support from the taxpayer. The gross income requirement does not apply to a taxpayer's child who is either under the age of 19 or a full-time student under the age of 24. Finally, you must have provided more than half of the dependent's support, and he or she must live with you or be a relative.

taxable income   The result obtained by subtracting deductions and exemptions from adjusted gross income is called **taxable income**. Your tax liability is based on your taxable income.

In addition to deductions and exemptions, **tax credits** can reduce your tax liability dollar-for-dollar. These credits may even reduce your tax liability to zero or below. *Refundable credits* may reduce the liability below zero, with the difference refunded to the taxpayer. Refundable credits include child tax credits, adoption credits, earned income credits, and taxes on certain fuels. *Nonrefundable credits* mean the credits cannot reduce the taxpayer's liability below zero. Nonrefundable credits include taxes paid to a foreign country, child and dependent care expenses, qualified education expenses, and retirement savings contributions.

Isn't it appropriate that the month of the tax begins with April Fool's Day and ends with cries of 'May Day!'

— ROB KNAUERHASE, *Research Scientist and Adjunct Faculty at Portland State University School of Business Administration*

If you are listed as a dependent on another person's return and have unearned income of over $950 for 2010 or earned income over the standard deduction amount, you are required to file a federal tax return. If the total amount of your earned income is less than your personal exemptions plus the standard deduction, you do not owe income tax and do not have to file. If you had taxes withheld but you do not have to file, you should still file so you can get your withholdings refunded.

Using Tax Forms

If you are required to file a tax return, you may use one of the forms provided by the Internal Revenue Service (IRS) or file a return electronically using approved tax-preparation software.

U.S. citizens and resident aliens are required to file Form 1040EZ, Form 1040A, or Form 1040. Nonresident aliens who earn U.S. income are required to file Form 1040NR. The filing status, number of exemptions, taxable income, and signature sections appear on all three forms. Any taxpayer may use Form 1040. However, use of Form 1040EZ and 1040A is restricted. Your individual situation—as

defined by types and sources of income, deductions, adjustments to income, other taxes, and credits—determines which form you use.

Some forms are accompanied by schedules, worksheets, or statements. Schedules and forms are official IRS documents. You complete these documents and then enter the totals from them on Form 1040 or 1040A (and sometimes on another schedule as well). Statements are not official IRS forms, but they are attached to the return to explain the information reported directly on Forms 1040EZ, 1040A, or 1040. Worksheets are used in compiling information to be entered on the return but are not sent with the return. You simply keep them with your personal copy.

form 1040EZ *Form 1040EZ is the shortest form* and the easiest one to complete. It does not require additional schedules or forms. Form 1040EZ is designed for people who have only wages and a little bank interest income. You can use this form if you meet the following requirements:

- Your wages, salaries, tips, unemployment compensation, taxable scholarships, and fellowships add up to less than $100,000 and your taxable interest is under $1,500

- You have no dependents

- You are less than 65 and not blind

- Your filing status is single or married filing jointly

- You have no advance earned income tax credits (EITC), no adjustments to income, and no credits except EITC and you owe no household employment taxes

- You have no itemized deductions

form 1040A *Form 1040A is an intermediate form.* It consists of two pages and Schedules 1, 2, and 3. The 1040A can be used if you have paid student-loan interest, have dividend income, or have contributed to an IRA. You can use this form if you meet the following requirements:

- Your wages, salaries, tips, unemployment compensation, taxable scholarships and fellowships, investment income, capital gain distributions, and retirement plan income add up to less than $100,000

- You have no itemized deductions

- You claim only specific adjustments to income

- You owe only certain types of taxes

- You claim only specific credits

form 1040 *Form 1040 is the most comprehensive tax form* and generally requires additional schedules. Anyone may use

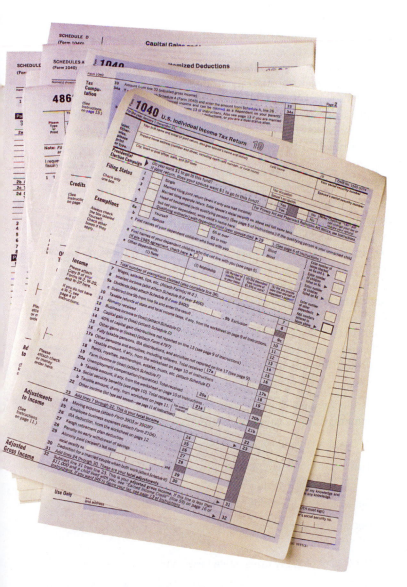

exemption
a dollar amount allowed by law that reduces your adjusted gross income that would otherwise be taxed

taxable income
adjusted gross income minus deductions and exemptions

tax credits
credits that reduce your tax liability, dollar-for-dollar

the Form 1040, and about 70% of all taxpayers do. If you do not meet the qualifications to file Form 1040EZ or Form 1040A, or if you have sold stock, want to claim moving expenses, plan to itemize deductions, have earned a taxable income of more than $100,000, or are self-employed, you must use Form 1040. In many cases, you will need to attach supplementary forms explaining certain kinds of income, expenses, or credits.

Each IRS form comes with detailed instructions that take you step-by-step through the process. Each line of the IRS form will indicate if an additional form (and which form) is needed to substantiate the value entered on the form. The IRS also provides worksheets to help with the calculations and to help you assess whether you are eligible for certain credits, deductions, or exemptions. As of January 2011, all schedules and forms are available electronically.

electronic and professional filing With so many requirements and exceptions, figuring out what you owe in taxes can be a challenge. Online or store-bought tax software programs can simplify tax preparation and filing. The software will help you determine which forms and schedules you need. You can also complete worksheets to determine the correct information to enter on the forms. If your adjusted gross income is low enough (less than $57,000 in 2010), you can file your return using the FreeFile service at www.IRS.gov. At the site, you can pay online if you owe money or sign up to have your refund directly deposited into your bank account. Because the IRS wants to equip taxpayers with the tools they need to get it right, it is investing in its web environment at www.IRS.gov and increasing support for the underserved—seniors, low-income families, and limited-English-speaking individuals.

If you find the whole process overwhelming, you may prefer to use a service to file your taxes. In hiring someone to prepare your tax returns, be mindful of considerations listed in Figure 9.5.

financialfitness:
JUST THE FACTS

Form Finder

You can find the standard IRS forms in post offices, banks, and libraries. You also can order copies by calling the IRS at 1-800-829-3676, or you can download and print the forms from the IRS website (www.irs.gov). If you wish, you may be able to complete the forms online, save them to your computer, and simply print and mail them or file them electronically.

financialfitness:
JUST THE FACTS

Preparation Ease

You may find that using one of the commercially available tax software programs simplifies the filing process. TurboTax (www.turbotax.intuit.com), Tax-Cut (www.taxcut.com), and TaxACT (www.taxact.com) are the current market leaders in tax software packages. Not only do programs such as these help virtually eliminate the issue of incomplete tax returns, but they also assist in simplifying the electronic filing process.

Tax Audits

Reputable preparers will ask to see receipts and will ask multiple questions to determine whether expenses, deductions, and other items qualify. By doing so, they are trying to help you avoid penalties, interest, or additional taxes that could result from an IRS examination. Tax evasion is a felony and is punishable by five years' imprisonment and a $250,000 fine. Figure 9.6 lists recent statistics on tax return–preparer fraud from the IRS Criminal Investigation Division.

The IRS may audit you for any reason within three years after a tax return is due or within two years after the tax is paid. The IRS may audit returns even older than three years if there is reason to believe you have underreported your income. During the 2008 filing year, the IRS examined 1.1 million returns through correspondence-examination programs with the taxpayer and assessed over $6.7 billion in unpaid taxes. Returns are selected for audit if they are deemed to have questionable deductions, expenses, or credits—including employee business expenses, charitable contributions, and self-employed business expenses. The IRS also conducts pre-refund examinations which aim to protect revenue by holding the refund during the audit process.

To protect yourself in case of an audit, keep the following documents for at least three years:

- W-2 statements showing your earnings for the year

- 1099 forms that show how much you received in dividends and gains on investments

- Bank account tax forms showing interest earned

- Documents pertaining to student loan and mortgage interest paid

- Records of property taxes, state taxes, and other taxes paid

Items to consider when selecting a tax preparer

Avoid preparers who charge a percentage fee based on your refund

Use a reputable tax professional who signs the tax return and provides a copy

Make sure the tax preparer is established and that he or she will be able to stand behind their work for the next 7 years in case you are audited

Look for credentials; attorneys, certified public accountants (CPAs), and enrolled agents can represent taxpayers before the IRS in all matters, including audits, collection, and appeals

Check for references—ask friends and family whether they know anyone who has used a tax professional and whether they were satisfied with the service they received

- Receipts for charitable contributions and medical expenses (if claimed)
- Receipts for work-related expenses if self-employed
- Receipts for purchases and sales of stocks, bonds, or mutual funds and any contributions to retirement accounts

- Credit-card statements showing business expenses or charitable contributions
- Records of scholarships and what the scholarship paid for
- Records related to sold property

▼ **FIGURE** 9.6

IRS criminal investigation statistics on tax return–preparer fraud

	Fiscal Year 2008	Fiscal Year 2007	Fiscal Year 2006
Investigations initiated	214	218	197
Prosecution recommendations	134	196	153
Indictments	142	131	135
Sentenced	124	123	109
Incarceration rate*	81.5%	81.3%	89.0%
Average months to serve	18	19	18

* Incarceration may include prison time, home confinement, electronic monitoring, or a combination.

Source: http://www.irs.gov/newsroom/article/0,,id=202123,00.html

financialfitness:
ACTION ITEM

Organization and Tax Prep

Keep one file for the year's tax documents and receipts. Keep another for home expenses, a third for insurance expenses, and a fourth for warranties. File documents as they come in (or at least once a month when you are reviewing how you did on your budget over the past month). Good record-keeping makes tax time *much easier*, and you are more likely to remember all the exemptions and deductions that you should take credit for.

Making $ense

9.5 Explain filing status.

9.6 How do you determine which tax form you should file?

9.7 What is gross income and how does it differ from adjusted gross income?

9.8 Explain the difference between earned and unearned income.

9.9 List the types of receipts you need to save if you plan to itemize your deductions.

9.10 What documents should you save as a precaution in case of audit?

9.3 TAX RATES

■ ■ **LO 9-3** Distinguish between different types of tax rates, and know when they apply and how to calculate them.

Understanding the concept of the marginal and average tax rate is beneficial for both single individuals and couples. Individuals can benefit from tax-year optimization. Making a sale of mutual fund investments or taking a lump sum from a pension plan can make a difference in how much you must pay in taxes. Wise planning can result in a reduction of the total tax paid.

Marginal Income Tax Rates

A **marginal income tax rate** is the tax rate levied on your last dollar of taxable income. This last dollar of income is often called the *marginal dollar of income.* For example, if you earn $33,951 in taxable income, the tax rate imposed on the last dollar earned (the dollar taking you from $33,950 to $33,951) is the marginal tax rate. The federal income tax employs a progressive tax rate schedule. This means that as your income increases, there is a jump in the marginal tax rate on the marginal dollar of income (at certain distinct income levels). Marginal income tax rates are set by the tax law. Your tax income bracket (income range) determines your marginal tax rate. There are six brackets; as shown in Figure 9.7, the lowest rate in 2009 was 10% and the highest was 35%. The more taxable income you have, the larger percentage you pay.

Doing the Math 9.2 walks you through the steps of determining your marginal income tax rate. As shown in the example, the 10% tax bracket is capped at $8,500, and each dollar made after that is taxed at 15% until you reach the ceiling of the next tax bracket.

Average Tax Rate

The **average tax rate** is calculated by dividing the total income taxes paid by the total income. The average tax rate incorporates taxes paid at all levels of income, so naturally it is less than the marginal rate, as demonstrated in *Doing the Math* 9.3 on page 234.

Alternative Minimum Tax (AMT)

The concept behind the **alternative minimum tax (AMT)** was to tax a few wealthy individuals who were trying to avoid paying taxes. It was designed to keep the rich from living tax-free. The alternative minimum tax was introduced in the Tax Reform Act in 1969 and set up as an extra tax to be paid in addition to regular income tax. The AMT now hits many more people than the few wealthy individuals who were the original target of the tax. Persons who have an income over $75,000 (or couples with a combined income of greater than $150,000) and who have

▼ **FIGURE 9.7**

Marginal federal tax rate on taxable income 2011

Filing Status	Single	Head of Household	Married Filing Jointly
10%	$0—$8,500	$0—$12,150	$0—$17,000
15%	Over $8,500—$34,500	Over $12,150—$46,250	Over $17,000—$69,000
25%	Over $34,500—$83,600	Over $46,250—$119,400	Over $69,000—$139,350
28%	Over $83,600— $174,400	Over $119,400—$193,350	Over $139,350—$212,300
33%	Over $174,400— $379,150	Over $193,350—$379,150	Over $212,300—$379,150
35%	Over $379,150	Over $379,150	Over $379,150

Source: www.IRS.gov

some large deductions are often affected by the alternative minimum tax. Taxpayers with capital gains, mortgage interest deductions, high state and local taxes, or incentive stock options are especially vulnerable to the AMT.

calculating and reporting the AMT The best way to figure out whether you owe any alternative minimum tax is to fill out the IRS Form 6251. The AMT rules and deductions are quite confusing and usually less generous than the regular income tax rules. The regular tax system allows itemized deductions for investment expenses, some medical and dental expenses, some employee business expenses, charitable contributions, and second mortgage interest. Under the alternative minimum tax rules, interest from some tax-exempt government bonds is treated as taxable income.

avoiding the AMT One way to avoid the alternative minimum tax is to have a simple tax return (fewer deductions or itemizations). Another way to avoid AMT liability is to stay out of the $75,000 to $415,000 income range. For example, if you are thinking about exercising your stock options, depending on the circumstances, it might be better to realize $1,000,000 in capital gains all in one year rather than dividing it into two or three years.

Comprehending Capital Gains

A **capital gain or loss** is the difference between the sale price and the purchase price of an investment asset, such as stock or real estate. You have a capital gain when the selling price of an asset (such as a house, a share of stock, or a mutual fund) exceeds the purchasing price. In other words, if you buy an asset for $1,000 and sell it sometime later for $1,500, your investment has generated a $500 capital gain.

A *short-term capital gain* is a gain on an asset held for 12 months or less. Inversely, a *long-term capital gain* is a gain on an asset held for longer than 12 months. The capital gains tax on short-term capital gains is based on your marginal tax rate (and treated like additional ordinary income). The capital gains tax on a long-term capital gain is currently restricted to a 15% maximum. For lower-income individuals, the rate may be 0% on some or all of the net capital gain. The government taxes capital gains on assets held for at least a year at a lower rate than regular income to encourage long-term investment and entrepreneurship. If you are in a year where you want to cash in an asset that will bring about a large capital gain, one way to even out your tax liability is to consider whether there is a stock or asset you can sell for a loss. That loss will help offset what you will owe the IRS.

Incentive stock options (ISOs) are a form of equity compensation that provides unique tax benefits and significant tax complexity. Consider the following example. Ronald Speltz of Ely, Iowa, earned $75,000/year. In 2000, he exercised (acquired) a McLeod Company ISO that increased his income to $700,000, resulting in $206,191 in federal taxes and $46,792 in state (Iowa) taxes, including the AMT. He did not sell the stock to pay his tax liability when he exercised his option because he was

doing the MATH

9.2 Computing the Marginal Income Tax Rate of a Dollar Earned

Assume you have taxable earnings of $8,550 and your filing status is single. Referring to Figure 9.7, the 10% tax bracket caps at $8,500, and each dollar made after that is taxed at 15% until you reach the ceiling of the next tax bracket.

Tax Bracket	Your Taxable Income within Given Bracket	Your Income
10%	$0–$8,500	$8,500
15%	Over $8,500–$8,550	50
Total		$8,550

You are earning $8,550, so you would pay 10% on the first $8,500 earned and then 15% on the next $50. The marginal income tax rate would be considered 15%.

What is your marginal income tax rate if you make $36,000 annually? (Refer to Figure 9.7.)

9.3 Comparison of Marginal and Average Tax Rate Calculations

Your earnings after deductions and exemptions are $100,000 and your filing status is single.

Step	Income	Marginal Tax Subsets	Bracket Total	*Tax rate %	Tax
1	$0 to $8,500	Earnings within 10% Bracket	$8,500	*0.10	$850
2	$8,500 to $34,500	Earnings within 15% Bracket	$26,000	*0.15	$3,900
3	$34,500 to $83,600	Earnings within 25% Bracket	$49,100	*0.25	$12,275
4	$83,600 to $100,000	Earnings within 28% Bracket	$16,400	*.28	$4,592
5		Total Marginal Tax			$21,617
6		Average Tax Rate ($21,617/$100,000)			0.2162

To determine your total marginal tax rate, complete the following steps:

1. $8,500 of the $100,000 is taxed at 10%
   $8,500 * .10 = $850 in taxes

2. $26,000 *($34,500 − $8,500 = $26,000)* of $100,000 is taxed at 15%
   $26,000 * .15 = $3,900 in taxes

3. $49,100 *($83,600 − $34,500 = $49,100)* of $100,000 is taxed at 25%
   $49,100 * .25 = $12,275 in taxes

4. $16,400 *($100,000 − $83,600 = $16,400)* of $100,000 is taxed at 28%
   $16,400 * .28 = $4,592 in taxes

5. Add all the taxes ($850 + $3,900 + $12,275 + $4,592 = $21,617) and the sum will be your total federal tax liability (marginal tax).

In contrast, your average tax rate is calculated as $21,617 (the amount you paid in taxes) divided by $100,000 (your income) = 21.6%.

The average tax rate (21.6%) is lower than the marginal tax rate (28%) because you are taxed less on the first dollar you make than on the last dollar you make.

What are the marginal and average tax rates for $30,000 in earnings after deductions and exemptions? Assume your filing status is single.

hoping the stock price would increase. The McLeod stock did not increase but instead collapsed, and Mr. Speltz found himself with a $253,000 tax bill on now-worthless McLeod ISO shares. Still owing his tax liability on the shares, he paid part of the tax with his 2000 return, borrowed $134,000 from a bank to pay some more, and then entered into an installment deal to pay the remaining $125,000.

Like Mr. Speltz, when the housing market bubble burst, many taxpayers who exercised ISOs found themselves AMT victims. In exercising ISOs, it is important to know exactly what you are doing; it is wise to get advice from a qualified financial planner or tax adviser. Consider selling enough shares immediately to cover your taxes. The ISO capital gain feature tempts some people to hold on—which is a huge gamble if you are riding a market bubble.

You have to save yourself

Okay, so what about YOUR Money? What should YOU be doing right now?

SUZE ORMAN, "You Have to Save Yourself," CBSNews.com, February 28, 2010. Reprinted with permission.

. . . We are now standing on land that in my opinion has financial faults going all the way through it. And if we have any financial tremors whatsoever, we will find ourselves, in my opinion, right back to where we were in 2008. So you have got to make sure that you are not dependent on anybody else's financial plan for you. The economy cannot save you. The administration cannot save you. You have got to save yourself. And you have got to make sure that your financial foundations don't have any cracks in them whatsoever. So, what do you need to know to make sure you are standing on solid ground?

Well, the first thing you need to understand is that most of you probably have debt on credit cards. Many of those credit cards are charging you 30% interest, charging fees, doing all these kinds of things, especially if they are with major banks. What I want all of you to do is go to www.creditcardconnection.org and find a good credit union near you. Anybody can join a credit union, where you get a credit union credit card.

Do you know by law federally chartered credit unions cannot charge you more than an 18% interest rate? Get yourself a credit card at a credit union. Next, a lot of you have 401(k) plans where you work. Now listen to me. You should be investing in your 401(k) plan, but only up to the point where your employer matches your contribution. After the point of your employer's match (or if your employer does not match), if you qualify for it, every single one of you should have a Roth IRA. A Roth IRA is simply a retirement account where you invest in it with money you have already paid taxes on. You want to do that because currently we are in the lowest income tax brackets of our lifetime. Later on you may be in the highest tax brackets of our lifetime to meet with the deficits that we have. So why not invest right now, pay the taxes, so that you can take out the money later, tax-free? If you don't qualify for the Roth, get a traditional IRA, make it nondeductible, and then convert to a Roth. Do those things and you will be on happy financial footing.

Questions

1 In switching from a traditional to a Roth IRA, you must pay the taxes at the time of the switch. For example, if you move $100,000 from a traditional to a Roth IRA and are in the 28% tax bracket, you will have to pay taxes of $28,000 following the switch. What is your opinion as to the wisdom of this move?

2 What if you anticipate that your income will continue to climb in the future?

3 In 1932, during the Great Depression, the top marginal tax rate was increased to 63% and steadily increased, reaching 94% (on all income over $200,000) in 1945. Given the size of our $1.75 trillion national debt, do you think it is possible that the marginal tax rate would ever climb this high again? If not, what other means does the United States have to bring down its national debt?

9.4 STRATEGIES TO MINIMIZE YOUR TAX LIABILITY

■ ■ **LO 9-4** Analyze strategies to legally minimize tax liabilities.

The tax laws can change each year, which is why it is important to stay current and take advantage of all of the tax credits and deductions for which you are eligible. For example, Congress passed the American Recovery and Reinvestment Bill in 2009, which led to an unprecedented number of tax credits to help stimulate the economy. The first step to using tax law to your advantage is to establish your exemptions, deductions, and adjusted gross income.

Exemptions and Deductions

You can determine your adjusted gross income (AGI) by adding your wages, salary, tips, taxable interest, and unemployment compensation, and then subtracting the

Making $ense

9.11 Differentiate between marginal and average tax rates.

9.12 Explain the purposes of the alternative minimum tax.

9.13 Distinguish between long-term and short-term capital gains and how they are taxed.

Track your spending now and you could save time—and money—at tax time.

exemptions and *deductions* to which you are entitled. AGI is your taxable income. Exemptions and deductions can save you money because they reduce the amount of income on which tax is due.

exemptions Exemptions are amounts you can subtract for yourself, your spouse (if your filing status is *married filing jointly*), and each of your dependents. The value of the exemption is fixed, but generally it increases each year to account for inflation. Also, the more dependents you have, the higher the amount of your exemptions.

The dependents for whom you claim an exemption must be either your children or another qualifying relative. Use the instructions that accompany the tax form to determine who you are entitled to claim. Remember that each qualifying dependent must have a Social Security number or an individual taxpayer identification number (ITIN).

deductions Deductions are amounts you can subtract from income to offset certain expenses during the past year. Most taxpayers use the standard deduction, which is a fixed amount that generally increases each year. The standard deduction depends on your filing status and is higher if you are age 65 or older or if you are legally blind.

Itemizing

If you spend more in specific areas than the amount allowed with the standard deduction, you may be able to itemize those expenses and take them as deductions. Expenses that can be itemized include home mortgage interest, state and local income taxes, real estate taxes, and charitable contributions. Two other deductions that may be itemized are business expenses exceeding 2% of your AGI and medical and dental expenses not covered by your insurance and exceeding 7.5% of your AGI.

If you plan to itemize, you will need to keep careful records of expenditures so you can verify your claims if the IRS questions your deductions. Letters from charities acknowledging your gifts are also important, especially if you give generously, and they must be dated.

retirement savings contributions credit Did you know that saving money for retirement may actually help

> "Intaxication: Euphoria at getting a refund from the IRS, which lasts until you realize it was your money to start with."
> —WASHINGTON POST *word contest*

```
```

Staying on top of your finances year-round will benefit you on April 15.

you save on taxes? If you contribute to a retirement savings plan, such as a traditional IRA or an employer plan such as a 401(k), you may qualify for the saver's credit. This credit will offset your contribution if your adjusted gross income (AGI) is less than the limit for your filing status.

mortgage interest credit Unless your house is very expensive, you will be able to take the mortgage-interest payments and property taxes as an income-tax deduction, assuming all your deductions total more than the standard deduction given to all taxpayers. The IRS designed the mortgage interest credit to help lower-income individuals own homes. If you took a mortgage loan to purchase a home and received a mortgage credit certificate (MCC) from your state or local government, you may qualify for a credit to offset the mortgage interest you pay. (However, if you take this credit, you must reduce any mortgage-interest deduction by the amount of the credit.)

Lowering Taxable Income

To calculate your total tax liability, add your state, local, and FICA tax liability. This is important to know when you first set up your budget. Like Curtis in the chapter opener, many new graduates are surprised to learn how much of their paycheck goes toward paying FICA and withholdings on personal income taxes. As a result, they may overcommit on their rental agreement or their new car payment, not realizing until after the first paycheck how much of each check goes toward their tax liability.

One way to reduce your tax liability is to lower the amount of your taxable income through deductions and credits. You can lower your tax liability by taking advantage of a

401(k) plan or traditional IRA and by using your **cafeteria plan** at work. Cafeteria plans include:

- Accident and health benefits
- Health savings accounts
- Group-term life insurance coverage
- Adoption assistance
- Dependent-care assistance

Since these qualified benefits are paid by the employee on a pretax basis, the amount paid reduces the taxable salary for the individual. Figure 9.8 shows an example of how to use a cafeteria plan to lower your taxable monthly income.

Some money market funds focus on tax-free investments, shielding your return from federal income taxes. Tax-free funds pay a lower interest rate than taxable investments, but because they offer a tax break, they are beneficial if your income level puts you in the highest tax brackets. Some investments are **tax-deferred**, meaning you do not pay taxes until you withdraw funds. Ideally, you withdraw the funds when you are retired and in a lower tax bracket so you pay a lower marginal tax rate. Another way to lower taxes is to lower your income. Examples of ways to lower your income include the following.

Municipal bonds: If you buy a corporate bond and hold on to it, you will pay tax on the interest you receive. If you sell the bond at a profit, you will also pay tax on the gain. By

▼ FIGURE 9.8

Reducing taxable income using cafeteria-plan options

Assume your taxable monthly income is $3,000 and your paid qualified benefits total $1,615 monthly.

Monthly salary before deductions	$3,000
Employee 401(k) contribution	300
Dependent care (day care)	700
Health savings account (unreimbursed medical expenses)	100
Health insurance	500
Group life insurance	15
Total	$1,615
Taxable salary per month	$1,385

Your taxable monthly income is reduced by the amount of your paid qualified benefits, so your taxable income reduces to $1,385 per month ($16,620 per year), as opposed to $3,000 per month ($36,000 per year).

contrast, interest paid on municipal bonds (bonds issued by the state and local governments) are exempt from federal taxes and state taxes in the state in which they are issued.

Health savings accounts: Health savings accounts help people who have health care plans with high deductibles. You can contribute pretax dollars to these accounts and the money will grow tax-free. The funds can be used to pay for medical expenses and, unlike a flexible spending account, they carry over from year to year.

Dependent care account: Offered through employers, these accounts allow working parents to save up to $5,000 of pretax dollars toward child care for children under the age of 13. These funds can then be used to pay expenses related to day care, nannies, or day camps.

Timing income from investments: The income you earn from investments is added to your income from all other sources. As a result, each additional dollar of investment income is taxed at the highest rate applicable to your total income. Therefore, you should plan the most advantageous time to sell your investments. For example, if you know that your income will be high this year but not next year, you will want to defer the sale of your investments to the year when your marginal tax rate will be lower.

Pension plans: You also can time withdrawals from your pension plan— 401(k), IRA, and so on—to your advantage. Taking a lump sum out of your pension plan can easily move you to a higher tax bracket. Therefore, if you have the option of taking a lump sum in a later year when your total annual income will be lower, doing so may have a significant positive impact on your tax liability.

Reinvestments: If a couple, filing separately, has investments in the name of the higher-income-earning spouse, the investment income is likely to be taxed at a higher rate than necessary. There may be advantages to transferring the assets to the lower-income earner.

Income split between spouses: If one of the spouses makes little money and the other one is a high earner, it makes sense to distribute the two incomes more evenly between the

spouses. For example, the higher income earner should receive the couple's tax deductions.

Salary payments to your spouse or children: If you own your own business, you can pay your spouse or children a salary for work performed. This work must be documented and reasonable. The wage or salary you pay to your spouse must correspond with prevailing market rates.

Tax Credits

Whereas tax deductions reduce your taxable income, tax credits reduce tax liability for the *full amount* of the credit. That makes them an even more valuable way to reduce what is owed. Since various tax credits have different eligibility limits, you will want to check to make sure you qualify. Tax credits are given for various considerations, such as families, children, elders, and education.

Figure 9.9 compares a tax credit with a tax deduction. Assuming a federal tax liability of $12,000 and a 25% marginal tax bracket, a $1,500 tax credit reduces taxes by $1,500. In comparison, a $1,500 tax deduction reduces tax liability by only $375 (25% of $1,500).

family values credits Many of the most popular tax credits are designed to help families in one way or another. While most of these credits have been around for years, some were expanded in 2006. If you have not claimed these credits before, or if your family or financial situation has changed, you may now qualify.

education deductions and credits You may also qualify for tax breaks on certain higher education expenses that you pay either for yourself or for someone else. Higher education generally includes undergraduate and graduate degree programs, as well as vocational or technical certificate programs at an eligible institution. Remember that you subtract education deductions as adjustments to income, thus reducing your adjusted gross income (AGI); in contrast, you subtract education credits directly from the amount of tax you owe.

education deductions As an example, you may be able to deduct up to $2,500 for student loan interest you pay for yourself or your spouse if your modified adjusted gross income (MAGI) is less than $65,000 (if you are single) or $135,000 (if you are married and file a joint return). You are eligible to take the deduction each year of the loan term, provided you continue to meet the MAGI requirement. If you cosign a loan for a dependent and make payments on the loan, you can deduct up to $2,500 of that loan's interest.

You may also qualify to reduce your AGI by deducting up to $4,000 in tuition and tuition-related fees paid for

> "There's nothing wrong with the younger generation that becoming taxpayers won't cure."
>
> —DAN BENNETT, *Performer (1962–)*

▼ FIGURE 9.9

Comparison of a tax credit and a tax deduction

Credit of $1,500 of Tax Liability	Deductions to Income of $1,500
	$1,500 deducted from income
$12,000 owed	× .25 marginal tax rate
− 1,500 credit	= $375 less tax liability
= $10,500 total taxes	$12,000 − $375 = $11,625 total taxes

financialfitness:
ACTION ITEM

Keeping Up on Tax Credits

Tax credits change frequently. Make sure you visit www.irs.gov each year to see if there are new credits that may apply to your situation. Visit a tax adviser if you are uncertain what credits you may qualify for.

Making $ense

9.14 Compare exemptions to deductions.

9.15 How do tax credits work?

9.16 What are some strategies you can use to lower your tax liability?

yourself, your spouse, or a dependent you claim on your tax return. You can deduct money you borrow to pay those bills, but not money you withdraw from a tax-free education savings account or money you receive in tax-free interest from U.S. savings bonds.

If you work as an elementary or secondary school teacher, teacher's aide, counselor, or principal, you can deduct up to $250 of supplies purchased for your classroom—provided you are not reimbursed for those expenses. If both you and your spouse qualify for this deduction, you can deduct up to $500.

education credits   There are two kinds of education credits: Hope and Lifetime Learning. The Hope credit

financialfitness:
STOPPING LITTLE LEAKS

Taxes and Retirement Savings

In a 401(k) plan, the employee elects to have a portion of wages deposited directly into a special retirement savings account. The contributions are pretax, therefore reducing taxable income. In some cases, the employer will match contributions from your salary before taxes. The funds grow tax-free until withdrawn, at which point they can be converted into an IRA. Funds can be transferred if you change employers, or you can manage the investments yourself via an IRA.

is for students enrolled at least half-time in the first two years of higher education toward a degree, certificate, or diploma at a qualified institution. The Lifetime Learning credit is for all qualifying higher education expenses for an eligible student at any point in his or her life. The student—you, your spouse, or a dependent for whom you claim an exemption—can take any type of course, whether or not the study leads to a degree or certificate. You may qualify for only one or for both of the education credits; however, you can take only one credit per student. In addition, your MAGI must be less than the annual limit in order for you to be eligible.

Remember, credits are potentially bigger tax savers than deductions because they directly reduce the amount of tax you owe. That becomes an issue, for example, if you have to choose between taking a deduction for tuition and fees or a Hope or Lifetime Learning credit for the same expenditure; you cannot take both the deduction and the credit for the same expense. You may want to calculate your taxes both ways and choose the one that saves you the most money or ask your tax adviser to help you compare the potential savings. Be sure to keep detailed records of what you spend on school expenses during the year in order to get the most from either credit.

the earned income tax credit Congress originally approved the earned income tax credit in 1975 to offset the burden of Social Security taxes and to provide an incentive to work. The earned income tax credit (EITC) is a refundable federal income tax credit for low- to moderate-income individuals and families. When the EITC exceeds the amount of taxes owed, it results in a tax refund to those who claim and qualify for the credit. To qualify, taxpayers must meet certain requirements and file a tax return, even if they did not earn enough money to be obligated to file a tax

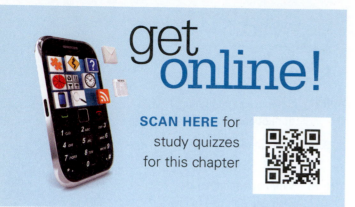

return. Requirements include having a child or being at least age 25, but less than 65, and not being claimed as anyone's dependent.

other credits In addition to the many tax credits mentioned in this chapter, many other credits are available that you may want to investigate. Examples include credits for energy-efficient cars and homes. There is no limit on the number of credits you can take, provided you qualify for each of them. And while some have income limits, others are available no matter how much you earn. ■

Learn. ⟩ Plan & Act. ⟩ Evaluate.

➡ **LEARN.** Taxes are the means by which the government finances public goods and services. Taxes are an important responsibility of citizenship and your contribution to your community. However, it is also important to not be wasteful with your resources or pay more in taxes than necessary.

In this chapter, you learned about both direct and indirect taxes and the difference between a regressive and a progressive tax. You learned how to reduce your overall tax liability through deductions and credits, by taking advantage of a 401(k) plan or traditional IRA, by using your cafeteria plan at work, and by investing in municipal money market funds that are either tax-free or tax-deferred. You also learned about the alternative minimum tax (AMT) and the importance of how and when you exercise stock options and take on capital gains or losses.

SUMMARY

■ ■ **LO 9-1** Describe the purposes of taxes, the different types of taxes, and the principles of progressive and regressive taxes.

Taxes are a fee charged by the government on a product, income, or activity to finance government expenditures. There are both direct and indirect taxes. Taxes are necessary to finance public goods and services. A regressive tax is applied uniformly, thereby imposing a greater burden (relative to resources) on the poor than on the rich. A progressive tax increases as the amount subject to taxation increases. Examples of a regressive tax include sales tax, excise tax, property tax, gift tax, estate tax, Social Security tax, and Medicare tax. An example of a progressive tax is personal income tax. The Internal Revenue Service (IRS), a bureau of the Treasury Department, is responsible for assessing and collecting taxes in the United States. In order for the government to have a steady stream of income all year long, employees pay a portion of their tax liability with each paycheck. The W-4 Employee's Withholding Allowance Certificate helps you compute your withholdings each pay period.

■ ■ **LO 9-2** Examine the logic, terms, and process of filing taxes.

In filing taxes, it is important to have a good handle on your filing status, gross income, and any deductions or credits you may be eligible for. U.S. citizens and resident aliens are required to file Form 1040EZ, Form 1040A, or Form 1040. Nonresident aliens who earn U.S. income are required to file Form 1040NR. Form 1040EZ is designed for people who have only wages and a little bank interest income. The 1040A is an intermediate form and can be used if you have paid student-loan interest, had dividend income, or contributed to an IRA. Form 1040 is the most detailed form, eligible to all citizens and required if you are self-employed, have sold stock, want to claim moving expenses, plan to itemize deductions, or if your taxable income is more than $100,000.

■ ■ **LO 9-3** Distinguish between different types of tax rates, and know when they apply and how to calculate them.

Knowing your marginal tax rate can drive decisions about how and when to sell investments or take a lump sum from a pension. Wise planning will help narrow the percentage difference between a couple's marginal and average tax rates, resulting in a reduction of the total tax paid. Your average tax rate is an important factor when establishing a budget. One way to reduce your tax liability is to lower the amount of your taxable income through deductions and credits, by taking advantage of a 401(k) plan or traditional IRA, and by using your cafeteria plan at work. Some municipal money market funds focus on tax-free investments, shielding your return from federal income taxes. Tax-free funds are beneficial if your income level puts you in the highest tax brackets. Tax-deferred investments are attractive if you plan to postpone using the investment until after retirement, when you are in a lower tax bracket and therefore paying a lower tax rate. The alternative minimum tax (AMT) was designed to tax wealthy individuals who were trying to avoid paying taxes, but it now applies to a wider swath of taxpayers. When exercising your stock options and taking on capital gains or losses, use care to avoid the AMT. Being judicious as to when and how you execute these options can help offset what you owe the IRS.

■ ■ **LO 9-4** Analyze strategies to legally minimize tax liabilities.

Tax laws change each year so it is important to stay current to be sure you are taking advantage of all of the tax credits and deductions for which you are eligible. Exemptions and deductions reduce your taxable income, and so can itemizing certain items such as retirement savings contribution credits and mortgage interest credits. Methods for lowering taxable income include investments in a 401(k), a traditional IRA, municipal bonds, health savings accounts, dependent care accounts, income from investments, pension plans, reinvestments, splitting income between spouses, spousal loans, or paying a salary to your spouse or children. Tax credits directly reduce, dollar-for-dollar, the amount of tax owed. Among the tax credits available are credits for children and the elderly, education deductions and credits, and earned income tax credits.

➲ PLAN & ACT. Your Plan & Act to do list is as follows:

☐ Calculate your withholdings using the W-4 Employee's Withholding Allowance Certificate. Use the Personal Allowances and the Deductions and Adjustments worksheets as necessary.

☐ Validate your withholdings via the IRS online calculator (go to www.irs.gov and follow the prompts). If you are not on target, follow the calculator's recommendations to adjust your withholdings so you do not under- or overpay your tax liability.

☐ Review the tax credits and deductions and look for those that may apply to your situation last year and this year. If you qualify, plan to take advantage of them (Worksheet 9.1).

☐ Calculate your marginal and average tax rates. Remember to adjust your budget whenever life events impact your income tax liability (and remember, a raise is taxed at your marginal tax rate versus your average tax rate).

☐ Maintain a tax folder system, filing receipts that qualify for deductions and credits. When it is time to complete the appropriate tax forms, you will be prepared to take advantage of all the deductions and credits for which you are eligible, including those for education expenses.

→ EVALUATE. Are you withholding the appropriate amount to cover your tax liability? Are you taking advantage of all the credits and deductions for which you are eligible? It is important to keep yourself current on the tax laws and maintain good records of expenditures in these areas to prove your eligibility. When thinking about that next raise, be sensitive to whether this will put you in a new tax bracket and how this will impact your average tax rate.

» GoalTracker

Does any of this information impact your savings and investment goals on your Goal-Tracker? Look at your long-term savings and types of IRA accounts and make sure you are making the right investment choices given your income plans, your current income bracket, and your anticipated income bracket. Are you making wise choices in managing your tax liability?

key terms

Adjusted Gross Income (AGI)	Gross Income	Tax-Deferred
Alternative Minimum Tax (AMT)	Indirect Tax	Taxable Income
Average Tax Rate	Itemized Deductions	Taxes
Cafeteria Plan	Marginal Income Tax Rate	W-2 Form
Capital Gain/Loss	Progressive Tax	W-4 Form
Deductions	Public Goods and Services	Withholdings
Direct Tax	Regressive Tax	
Exemption	Tax Credits	

self-test questions

1. Which tax places a disproportionate burden on the poor? *(LO 9-1)*
   a. Direct
   b. Indirect
   c. Progressive
   d. Regressive

2. Which tax provides funds for public goods and services? *(LO 9-1)*
   a. Direct
   b. Indirect
   c. Progressive
   d. Regressive

3. Which tax is designed to create equity among citizens? *(LO 9-1)*
   a. Direct
   b. Indirect
   c. Progressive
   d. Regressive

4. Which is an example of a progressive tax? *(LO 9-1)*
   a. Property tax
   b. Excise tax

   c. Personal income tax
   d. Social Security tax

5. Which form do you use to determine how much money should be withheld from your paycheck to pay your tax liability? *(LO 9-1)*
   a. W-2
   b. W-4
   c. 1040EZ
   d. 1040A

6. You may be eligible for more than one tax-filing status, so you should experiment with the different filing-status options to determine which one provides you the best tax advantage. *(LO 9-2)*
   a. True
   b. False

7. Which of the following is *not* considered earned income? *(LO 9-2)*
   a. Interest
   b. Wages
   c. Commissions
   d. Tips

8. Your adjusted gross income (AGI) is your gross income minus tax code deductions for certain specific expenses. Which of the following is *not* a qualifying expense? *(LO 9-2)*

   a. Contributions to a traditional IRA
   b. Interest paid on a student loan
   c. Alimony you paid
   d. Mortgage interest

9. Which is *not* one of the three tax-form options U.S. citizens must file? *(LO 9-2)*

   a. 1040EZ
   b. 1040E
   c. 1040A
   d. 1040

10. Your marginal tax rate is always greater than your average tax rate. *(LO 9-3)*

    a. True
    b. False

11. What is the alternative minimum tax (AMT)? *(LO 9-3)*

    a. A minimum tax all citizens must pay
    b. A tax for wealthy individuals who are trying to avoid paying taxes
    c. An alternative to filing as a single or filing jointly
    d. All of the above

12. Which is *not* true of taxes on long-term capital gains? *(LO 9-3)*

    a. They apply to assets held for 12 months or more
    b. They are based on your marginal tax rate
    c. They are restricted to a 15% maximum
    d. They are restricted to only 5% for lower-income taxpayers

13. Which would *not* be considered a tax deduction? *(LO 9-4)*

    a. Real estate taxes
    b. Charitable contributions
    c. Student loan interest
    d. Car loan interest

14. Which is *not* an option for lowering your tax liability by lowering your income? *(9-4)*

    a. Municipal bonds
    b. A health savings account
    c. A Roth IRA
    d. A dependent care account

15. Which directly reduces the amount of tax you owe, dollar-for-dollar? *(LO 9-3)*

    a. A tax credit
    b. An exemption
    c. A deduction
    d. All of the above

problems

1. You make $17,500/year. You pay $100 in gasoline tax, which is the same amount your parents pay. *(LO 9-1)*
   a. What percentage of your income goes toward this "gasoline" tax?
   b. Is this a regressive or progressive tax?
   c. How might you reduce the rate of this tax?

2. You make $100,500/year. You budget $5,000 for gasoline annually, half of which is tax. What percentage sales tax do you pay? *(LO 9-1)*

3. If you earned a salary of $30,000, what would be your total FICA taxes? *(LO 9-1)*
   a. How much would you pay in taxes for Social Security for the year? For Medicare?
   b. How much did your employer pay in Social Security tax and Medicare tax on your behalf?

4. You are in the 28% marginal tax rate. Stock you purchased at the beginning of the year has increased in value by $20,000. *(LO 9-2)*
   a. If you sell the stock today, your capital gain will be classified as short-term. At what rate would you be taxed, and what would be your tax liability?
   b. If you waited a month, your capital gain would be classified as long-term. At what rate would you be taxed, and what would be your tax liability given this scenario?

   c. You earned a salary of $35,000, had interest income of $500 and dividend income of $101, and you experienced the short-term capital gain described in 4(a). What is your gross income?
   d. You made a traditional IRA contribution of $2,000 and paid $900 in student loan interest. What is your adjusted gross income (AGI) based on the gross income described in 4(c)?

5. Assuming an income of $34,000/year, apply the marginal tax rate in Figure 9.7: *(LO 9-3)*
   a. What is your marginal tax rate?
   b. What is your average tax rate?

6. Assuming an income of $12,000/year, apply the marginal tax rate in Figure 9.7: *(LO 9-3)*
   a. What is your marginal tax rate?
   b. What is your average tax rate?

7. You own a home and are thinking of doing some home repairs. This year there is a tax credit of one-third the cost of materials for adding insulation and for replacing windows and external doors, up to a $3,000 tax-credit maximum. *(LO 9-4)*
   a. You decide to add insulation to your attic, which costs $1,000 in materials, and you install it yourself. What is the dollar amount of the tax credit?

b. You are in a 28% tax bracket. How much does the home-repair tax credit reduce your tax liability?

c. How much would you have to spend on qualified improvement materials to maximize your $3,000 tax credit?

you're the expert

1. It's December and Elizabeth is doing an assessment of the past year's tax liabilities. It has been a tough year for her company. There will be no raise next year as well as one furlough day each month, which will lower her income. To minimize taxes owed, what should Elizabeth do in the following cases? In each case, explain why. *(LO 9-1–LO 9-4)*

   a. Should Elizabeth accelerate deductions in the current year or hold off until January of next year?

   b. Should she delay the receipt of income from a contract until next year or request it in the current year?

   c. Should she purchase a hybrid car in December or January?

   d. Should she get married on December 31 or on January 1?

   e. Should she deliver twins by c-section on December 31 or on January 1?

2. Johnna is 63 years old, retired, and considering what to do with her $200,000 traditional IRA. She must start taking distributions from her traditional IRA at age 70½. At that point, the combination of her pension's income and her Social Security benefit will move her into the 25% federal tax bracket. She has no pressing financial needs. *(LO 9-1–LO 9-4)*

   a. What are the advantages and disadvantages of starting to make withdrawals from her IRA now?

   b. What are the advantages of waiting until she is 70½ and taking the minimum mandatory withdrawals? Consider the tax implications in both (a) and (b).

3. George ended up having to pay $5,000 in taxes last April. He doesn't want to go through that pain again. *(LO 9-1–LO 9-4)*

   a. What changes can he make to his payroll deduction now to avoid this scenario next April?

   b. What options can he explore to reduce his overall tax liability?

4. You are a single parent with one child. You work as a full-time educator, making $40,000/year plus $6,000 in the summer tutoring students. You spend $700/month on child care. What is the total number of allowances you should claim on your W-4 form?

worksheet

Find the worksheets online at www.mhhe.com/walkerpf1e

9.1 REDUCING YOUR TAX LIABILITY

Review the many tax credits and deductions available and use Worksheet 9.1 to create a list of those for which you may be eligible.

1. Go to http://www.irs.gov/individuals/index.html to review tax credits and deductions that are applicable for this past year and upcoming for next year.	
2. Upon review, create a list of deductions and credits for which you may be eligible (below).	
3. Invest in a file folder and label each deduction and credit.	
4. Each time you have a receipt, drop it into the folder so you are prepared when it comes time to complete your tax forms.	

Credits	Deductions

Blake works during the semester breaks for the family business and has earned $14,000 this past year. Any investment income above $800 is taxed at the same rate as his parents, who are in the top bracket. His parents have advised him to invest in a Roth IRA for retirement savings and a 529 for educational expenses next year.

A summary of the housemates' goals can be found in the first Continuing Case problem on page 27.

1. What are the benefits to following this strategy?

2. Next year, Blake has the opportunity to work during the summer for his parents; this job will be out of the country. What tax advantage does this job have for Blake?

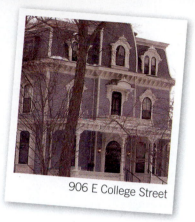

906 E College Street

> "Needing insurance is like needing a parachute. If it isn't there the first time, chances are you won't need it again."
>
> —*Unknown*

insurance: covering your assets

According to the *Commonwealth Fund Biennial Health Insurance Survey*, 26 million Americans are underinsured, meaning their insurance does not adequately protect them against catastrophic health care expenses.[1] Nearly 3 out of every 10 (28 percent) working-age adults, an estimated 52 million people, were uninsured for at least some time during 2010. Health Affairs reports approximately 50 percent of personal bankruptcies are due to medical expenses.[2] Of the bankruptcies that included medical bills, 75 percent of the people had health insurance. As Annie in the chapter opener on the next page learned too late, insurance is an important tool for protecting your assets and net worth in the event of a catastrophe, accident, or health problem. It is important not only to have insurance, but also to have the appropriate amount of insurance. ■

LEARNING OBJECTIVES

After reading this chapter, you should be able to:

LO 10-1 Understand the basics of insurance.

LO 10-2 Examine your state's minimum requirements for auto liability insurance, and identify the proper coverage for your vehicle.

LO 10-3 Explain the importance of homeowner's/renter's insurance, and determine the proper coverage for your home or apartment.

LO 10-4 Distinguish between the different types of health insurance, and identify the proper coverage for your situation.

LO 10-5 Understand the importance of disability and long-term care insurance, and determine the proper coverage for your situation.

LO 10-6 List different types of life insurance, and recognize the appropriate amount of coverage given your responsibilities.

[1] http://www.commonwealthfund.org/~/media/Files/Publications/Fund%20Report/2011/Mar/1486_Collins_help_on_the_horizon_2010_biennial_survey_report_FINAL_v2.pdf

[2] http://content.healthaffairs.org/content/suppl/2005/01/28/hlthaff.w5.63.DC1

◄ Annie, age 23, recent graduate of a large eastern university, liberal arts major

Health Insurance: Expensive but Worth Every Penny

Annie is a recent graduate in liberal arts. She decided to take a year off and head to the Rockies. While there, she got a job as a waitress, which was good for tips and left her free time for the slopes, but included no health insurance benefits. Because she had always been in good health and was a great skier, she figured she would run the risk of no health insurance. However, she took a bad spill and broke her elbow. She now recalls, "Not only was I not able to work for three months, but I tallied up over $27,000 in medical expenses. I have no health insurance. Since I wasn't able to work, I could no longer cover my rent, car, and phone payments. Unfortunately, I had to move back home with my parents. Since then, I have worked out a payment plan with the medical facility, but I will be making payments to them for the next 10 years. Avoiding the expense of health insurance is not worth the risk."

10.1 THE IMPORTANCE OF INSURANCE

■ ■ **LO 10-1**   Understand the basics of insurance.

You don't know when an accident will happen, whether your home will flood or catch fire, or whether you will be a victim of robbery, poor health, or an untimely death. Without insurance, any of these events could jeopardize the financial well-being of you or your family, forcing you or your loved ones to liquidate assets or file for bankruptcy. Not only is it crucial to have insurance to cover your assets

and protect your personal wealth, but it also is important to have the proper coverage for your circumstances. You need to carefully research and understand the offerings of different insurance companies before making your choice. (In the online worksheet supplement, refer to Worksheet 10.1 for an insurance checklist you can use to determine the appropriate amount of coverage you need to protect your assets.)

Insurance Basics

Insurance protects your assets. With insurance, you pay a **premium** (a periodic payment) to the insurance company based on your risk of filing a claim. Insurance companies estimate how many of their customers will file claims and how many dollars they will have to pay out. Then they calculate the estimated claims and include their risk in your premium. Insurance companies diversify their risk by insuring many people. Not every car covered by an insurance company will be in an auto accident this year, so the risk and premiums are distributed among all policyholders.

You can purchase insurance online or through an insurance agent. Any agent has to be licensed and regulated by your state's insurance commissioner. He or she may be a single-company provider who sells insurance from only one company, such as State Farm, Allstate, or Geico, or an independent insurance agent. Independent agents represent more than one insurance company and can sell insurance from a wide range of insurance companies.

The state insurance commissioner's primary responsibility is to protect the interests of insurance consumers through the regulation and licensing of insurance agents. Through the National Association of Insurance Commissioners (NAIC), the insurance commissioner can provide consistency of regulation between states and regulate multistate agencies.

Selecting an Insurance Company

When selecting an insurance company, it is important to look for one with fair rates and a history of financial strength and good service. According to the Insurance Information Institute, you should consider rates, financial security, service ratings, and licensing when selecting an insurance company. See Figure 10.1.

Knowing the Terms of the Policy

When purchasing insurance, it is important to understand the terms. You will receive an insurance policy and a **declaration page**. The declaration page is the first page of the policy and summarizes the coverage. It lists the names of the insured, the property insured (with vehicles this includes the make, model, year, and vehicle identification number or VIN), the effective dates, the coverage type and limits, the deductible, and the policy premium amount. It is very important to review the declaration page

Making $ense

10.1 Why do you need to purchase insurance?

10.2 Where can you go to purchase insurance?

10.3 How do independent agents differ from single-company insurance agents?

10.4 Who regulates insurance companies?

for accuracy and coverage limits and to read through the insurance policy for coverage and exclusions.

10.2 AUTO INSURANCE

■ ■ **LO 10-2** Examine your state's minimum requirements for auto liability insurance, and identify the proper coverage for your vehicle.

The privilege of driving a car comes with a great deal of responsibility and liability. Even if you are an extremely safe and cautious driver, someone else can hit your vehicle and cause hundreds of thousands of dollars in personal and material damage. Because of this, auto insurance is a safe investment at relatively little cost.

Auto insurance premiums are determined by your credit history, age, driving record, home location, and marital status, as well as by the make and model of your vehicle and the safety equipment in the vehicle (such as air bags, anti-lock brakes, and stability control). Insurance companies fold this information into complex statistical equations to rate your individual risk of filing a claim.

Males have higher insurance rates because they usually drive more miles and file more claims. Young people have a higher risk because they lack experience in driving. The type of vehicle also determines the insurance rate: The highest rates are levied on sports cars, muscle cars, and sport utility vehicles (SUVs). Insurance premiums usually decrease when you turn 25, get married, or if you drive a car that has a good safety record.

It is always wise to check the insurance rates and consider the insurance premiums before you buy a vehicle. For instance, a higher sports car or SUV insurance premium could have a dramatic impact on your budget and your cash flow. It is also important to have a clear understanding of the difference between full and liability auto insurance, the varying amounts of coverage they offer, and their corresponding rates.

premium
the periodic payment made on an insurance policy

declaration page
the policy page that lists the insurance company's name and address, the policyholder, the coverage dates, and the contracted coverage amounts

▼ **FIGURE 10.1**

Factors to consider when selecting an insurance company

Rates	• Get quotes from at least three insurers, either through their websites, by phone, or in person.
	• Ask about discounts, savings, and overall price. A company that offers few discounts still may have lower rates.
	• Ask if an insurer reduces premiums if you buy more than one type of insurance.
Financial Security	• Choose a company that is likely to be there when you need it.
	• Consult consumer publications, A.M. Best Insurance Company reports, and your state's department of insurance.
Service Ratings	• Select a company that treats you courteously and fairly.
	• Ask family, friends, and neighbors what they like or dislike about their insurers.
	• Visit your state's insurance department website to find out whether complaints have been filed against a particular company.
Licensing	• Visit your state's insurance department website to learn if a company is licensed in your state. Buying from a company licensed in your state means your state's insurance department can help if there is a problem.

Source: http://www.iii.org/articles/how-do-i-choose-an-insurance-company.html

liability insurance
insurance that only covers the driver's legal responsibilities if they are at fault for an accident

loss payee
in an insurance contract , the third party lien holder who gets paid if there is a claim on the insurance

full coverage
insurance that includes comprehensive and collision insurance

comprehensive insurance insurance that covers an insured vehicle for damage other than collision such as fire, theft, weather, impacts with animals, or vandalism

deductible
the amount of money one must pay before the insurer will begin to pay on a claim

Liability Auto Insurance

Because of the legal responsibility of driving a vehicle, most states have implemented a minimum liability insurance requirement. You can view your state's minimum automobile insurance coverage at www.insure .com. **Liability insurance** covers only your legal responsibility if you are at fault in an accident. It often breaks down into three categories as follows:

C1: Bodily injury liability dollar amount for one person injured in an accident.

C2: Bodily injury liability dollar amount for all people injured in an accident.

C3: Personal property liability dollar amount for one accident.

Each category pays a different dollar amount. The amounts for each category (C1/C2/C3) are shown with the numbers (in thousands) separated by a forward slash. Figure 10.2 provides an example of a minimum auto liability insurance requirement of 20/40/15.

▼ **FIGURE 10.2**

Minimum coverage example

The amounts for each category (C1/C2/C3) are shown with the numbers (in thousands) separated by a forward slash.

Example: A minimum auto liability insurance requirement of 20/40/15 means:

C1: $20,000 for bodily injury liability for one person injured in an accident

C2: $40,000 bodily injury liability for all people injured in an accident

C3: $15,000 coverage for personal property liability for one accident

The amount of liability insurance you purchase on your auto depends on your financial situation. According to *Consumer Reports* recommendations, your liability coverage should be at least 100/300/100 (in thousands of dollars) and you should consider increasing your liability coverage to 250/500/100 if you have sizable assets. If you cause an accident in which you damage another vehicle as well as your own, your liability insurance covers only the repairs on the other vehicle, not your vehicle. If you want insurance to cover repairs on your own car, you will need comprehensive and collision insurance.

Full Coverage Auto Insurance

A vehicle is usually the second largest purchase you make, and you need to protect that asset from damage due to accidents, weather, or vandalism. If you buy your car using money borrowed from a financial institution, it will normally require you to have full coverage auto insurance, naming the financial institution as lien holder and **loss payee**. If the vehicle is damaged, the loss payee is notified and the insurance payment goes to the loss payee.

Insurance companies provide **full coverage** insurance consisting of comprehensive and collision coverage. **Comprehensive insurance** covers vehicles for the repair of any damage to the vehicle not sustained as a result of an accident. Comprehensive insurance normally pays for repairs, less your deductible, for any of the following events:

- Hail
- Flood
- Fire
- Theft
- Vandalism
- Breakage of glass
- Earthquake
- Impacts with animals

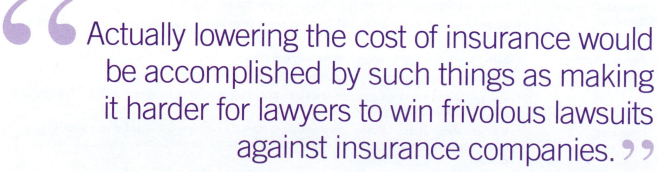

" Actually lowering the cost of insurance would be accomplished by such things as making it harder for lawyers to win frivolous lawsuits against insurance companies. "

—THOMAS SOWELL, *American economist (1930–)*

Check your individual policy for specific inclusions and exclusions.

The **deductible** is the amount of money you must pay before the insurance company will begin to pay on an insurance claim. If you accept a higher deductible, the insurance company will assume less of the risk; as a result, your premium will be lower. Many lenders may limit you to a $500 deductible. If you could increase your deductible to $1,000, you could save as much as 40 percent of your insurance cost; however, you would have to pay the first $1,000 out of your own pocket. If you increase your deductible, be sure to set aside money in an emergency fund to cover the full amount.

Collision insurance provides coverage for your vehicle for damages sustained in an accident. It pays for the repairs as long as the cost is less than the value of the vehicle minus the salvage value of the vehicle. The **salvage value** of the vehicle is how much money the insurance company would get if it were to sell the damaged car in its current damaged condition. If the cost of repairs minus the salvage value is greater than the cash value of the vehicle, the insurance company will likely *total* the vehicle and write you a check for the cash value. If there is a lien on the vehicle, the check will be made payable to you and the lien holder, so the loan can be paid off. In the scenario in which the car is totaled, the insurance company receives the title of the vehicle.

To illustrate, suppose you have a Honda Civic worth $8,000 but then you have a car accident that pushes the car's value (or salvage value) to $3,000. The repairs would need to cost $5,000 or less in order to avoid totaling the car. If you have an older vehicle, it may not be worth the insurance premium to have comprehensive and collision coverage.

financialfitness:
STOPPING LITTLE LEAKS

Comprehensive Savings

Drop comprehensive and collision insurances on old, near-end-of-life vehicles. The cost of a few years of this insurance payment is usually more than the car is worth. Instead, put this money into a savings account to go toward the purchase of your next car. If you are involved in an accident, you have the savings ready to purchase your next vehicle.

³ http://www.ircweb.org/News/IRC_UM_012109.pdf

Uninsured/underinsured motorist insurance covers you, your passengers, and your vehicle in an accident that is not your fault in the event that the at-fault driver does not have insurance (or enough insurance) to cover all the damages. This is very important insurance to have, given the low amounts of liability insurance many states require. Even though states require insurance, the Insurance Research Council estimates that the number of uninsured drivers is as high as 29 percent in some states and approximately one in six drivers in the United States may be driving uninsured in 2010.³ You need to review your individual policy and your state's uninsured/underinsured motorist coverage endorsement for the specifics of your coverage.

You can also purchase roadside assistance and rental reimbursement to protect your vehicle. **Roadside assistance** insurance pays for vehicle towing, but you may not need this coverage if you are a member of an auto club that includes towing in its coverage. **Rental reimbursement** covers the expense of a rental vehicle if your vehicle is being repaired due to an accident or if it has been stolen.

It is important to shop for the best rate, the best coverage, and the easiest claim-filing process. Insurance policies usually are written for six months or one year and generally renew automatically as long as you avoid any accidents or driving violations. The insurance company may bill you monthly or at the beginning of the policy. Be careful, though, because some companies will charge a service fee for each payment if you choose to pay monthly.

If you have multiple serious driving violations, your state may classify you as a high-risk driver and require you to have **SR-22 liability insurance**. You can be classified as a high-risk driver if you are cited for: driving under the influence, reckless driving, serious moving violations, causing an accident without having insurance, having too many tickets in a short period of time, or having a suspended or revoked license. The state's department of motor vehicles will notify you if you are required to get SR-22 insurance, and if you do not own a vehicle, you will be required to purchase "non-owners" SR-22 insurance.

collision insurance
insurance that covers the payment of repairs to a vehicle damaged in a collision

salvage value
the value of a damaged vehicle if it were sold for scrap metal or to an individual or company for repair

roadside assistance
insurance coverage to pay for towing if your vehicle is disabled

rental reimbursement
insurance to cover the cost of a rental vehicle if your vehicle is stolen or being repaired; usually involves a per-day limit as well as a limit on the number of days

SR-22 liability insurance liability insurance required by states for high-risk drivers

Making $ense

10.5 What is the difference between liability and full coverage auto insurance?

10.6 When do you need to purchase comprehensive and collision insurance?

10.7 What factors contribute to the calculation of your insurance premiums?

10.8 Why is it important to have uninsured/underinsured motorist insurance?

Lowering Your Costs

You can do a number of things to help lower the cost of auto insurance. When comparing insurers, ask which discounts they offer and take advantage of any of those listed in Figure 10.3.

10.3 HOMEOWNER'S AND RENTER'S INSURANCE

■■ **LO 10-3** Explain the importance of homeowner's/renter's insurance, and determine the proper coverage for your home or apartment.

A home is normally a family's largest purchase, an asset that grows in value, and a place of rest and relaxation. If anything were to happen to your home, you would want it and your personal belongings insured so you could rebuild your home and replace your belongings without financial hardship. Therefore, it is important to understand the basics of home and property insurance and make the right choices to protect these assets.

Home Insurance Basics

As with vehicle insurance, home insurance includes a premium, a deductible, and a renewal cycle of typically six months or one year. However, a home usually appreciates in value, so you will want to increase your insurance coverage over time as well. Home insurance should not cover the price of the land, only the building on the land. For example, if you are selling a house and asking $200,000 for it, that price includes the structure ($150,000) and the lot ($50,000); however, your homeowner's insurance needs to cover only the $150,000 value of the house.

Typical homeowner's insurance covers the dwelling, other structures, personal property, and loss of use. Most homeowner's insurance goes into effect if the dwelling is damaged because of:

- Fire
- Hail
- Windstorms
- Lightning
- Explosions
- Falling objects
- Vehicles
- Vandalism
- Ice
- Accidental discharges or overflows of water
- Volcanic eruptions

Homeowner's insurance generally does not cover earthquakes or floods. You may be able to purchase **flood insurance** as a separate rider or policy; however, many insurers do not

▼ **FIGURE 10.3**

Discounts: Ways to lower auto insurance costs

Good Student: For students who are under 25 years of age and attend a high school, college, or university and have a B average or better from the previous semester

Student Away at School: For students who are away at school, attending a college or university, and do not have a vehicle with them at school

Driver Training and Defensive Driving Courses: For drivers who have taken an approved driver education course

Good Driver (California only): For drivers who meet the statutory definition of a good driver

Mature driver: For drivers between the ages of 50 to 65 years

Multi-Vehicle: For drivers insuring more than one vehicle on the same policy and garaged within the same area

Restricted Mileage: For drivers who drive only a limited number of miles in a single year

provide flood insurance. In response, the federal government has established the National Flood Insurance Program through which individuals may purchase flood insurance if their home is at risk of being flooded.

After Hurricane Katrina, many homeowners were denied their insurance claims on the basis that the flood, not wind or rain, damaged their property. Homeowners had to prove their home was first damaged by the storm, wind, rain, or hail before the insurance companies would pay on the claims. In 2008, the Cedar River in Iowa rose above the 500-year floodplain. Very few of the hundreds of thousands of people who suffered damage from the flooded river owned flood insurance. FEMA (Federal Emergency Management Agency) provided some relief, but not nearly enough to cover their financial losses.

Earthquakes are also normally excluded as part of a homeowner's policy. **Earthquake insurance** covers your property from damage due to an earthquake. California requires insurance companies selling homeowner's insurance to offer earthquake insurance also. It is important to review your homeowner's policy. If your home is at risk of being flooded or in an earthquake, you may want to contact your insurance agent, the National Flood Insurance Program, or the insurance commissioner in your state to explore your insurance options.

Insuring Your Personal Property

With homeowner's insurance, you normally insure your personal property (the contents of your home) as well. If you are renting, you can purchase **renter's insurance**, which will cover only your personal property. Renter's insurance is most commonly purchased from the same insurance company insuring your vehicle. Insurance companies can insure personal property at replacement cost or current value, with replacement cost being preferable in most cases. For example, the current value of your clothes would not come close to the cost of replacing your wardrobe. Some insurers offer similar insurance for students living on campus at residential colleges and universities.

If you have valuable items, you will want to insure them separately with an insurance rider on your homeowner's or renter's insurance. An **insurance rider** covers something specific that is not covered on your primary policy. Common riders are for jewelry, antiques, coins, or other collectibles. For these items to be insured, you have to provide your insurance agent with a certified appraisal on the

flood insurance
special insurance coverage to protect your home and property from damage sustained from a flood

earthquake insurance special insurance coverage to protect your home and property from damage sustained in an earthquake

renter's insurance insurance that covers your personal property in a structure you do not own; generally there is liability insurance associated with this coverage, to cover the liability of accidents occurring within the rented property

insurance rider an addendum to your primary coverage to cover something specific that is not covered on your primary policy

Protect yourself from additional financial headaches if thieves break in to your home.

umbrella liability insurance
a supplemental policy that provides high limits of additional liability coverage above the limits of a homeowner's or auto policy

specific property. The rider is then attached to your primary coverage as an addendum.

home inventory If your home burns down, a natural disaster strikes, or you are robbed, you will need to provide your insurance company with a list of your lost or damaged personal property and its value. A home inventory can be a priceless document to help you remember all that may have been lost. One of the easiest ways to take a home inventory is to walk room to room making a video recording, filming everything you own and describing it as you film. It is important to mention the brand of each item and its details, including the serial number, the time frame of the purchase, the purchase price, and the estimated value. Many software packages such as Quicken include a household inventory

Video recording is an easy way to take a home inventory.

function. You can use Worksheet 10.4 in the online supplement to document your personal property.

After you have completed your home inventory, keep this document up to date and store it in a safe, off-site place. A bank safety deposit box is an ideal place in which to keep your inventory video, pictures, and written documentation. If you choose to use a spreadsheet, you can store the document online. If you e-mail the document to yourself or store it with a free service like Google Docs, you will be able to access it anywhere and anytime you have access to the Internet.

In the case of widespread disaster such as a hurricane or flood, insurance adjusters are under strict deadlines from state officials to see everyone who has filed a claim within a certain time period. In this case, adjusters may provide a rough estimate of damages and give you an initial check. If more damage is discovered later, you can submit an amended claim. See Figure 10.4 on how to file a claim.

liability insurance A homeowner's or renter's insurance policy usually contains liability insurance for accidents that occur in the home or on the property. Homeowners and renters are responsible for maintaining safe conditions for people on or about the property. If someone trips, slips, or falls as a result of an unsafe environment, you could be held fully responsible and the person injured could sue for damages and lost income. A homeowner's or renter's insurance policy could save you from costly medical bills and other expenses for accidents in your home or on your property. As with auto insurance coverage, the declaration page of the policy lists the limits and coverage of personal liability insurance.

umbrella liability insurance An **umbrella liability insurance** policy is an additional supplemental policy that covers your liability usually up to $1 million or higher,

▼ FIGURE 10.4

How to file an insurance claim

If you need to file a claim, the following steps can help smooth the process:

- ☐ Immediately report a burglary or theft to the police.
- ☐ Photograph the damage to your home or property.
- ☐ From a copy of your home inventory list, highlight any stolen or damaged property.
- ☐ Review your insurance coverage before reporting a claim and notify the insurer as soon as possible.
- ☐ Meet the insurance adjuster to survey the damage, providing any documentation to support the claim.
- ☐ Make only temporary repairs that help prevent further damage to property. Do not allow contractors to make permanent repairs until the claims adjuster has inspected the damage.
- ☐ Keep receipts of materials purchased and repairs made for reimbursement. If you have to move out of the home due to a disaster, keep receipts of your expenses.
- ☐ Complete the paperwork your insurer sends quickly and completely, and make copies.
- ☐ Keep a journal of the details of your conversations with insurers, contractors, estimators, or anyone else associated with the claim.

Making $ense

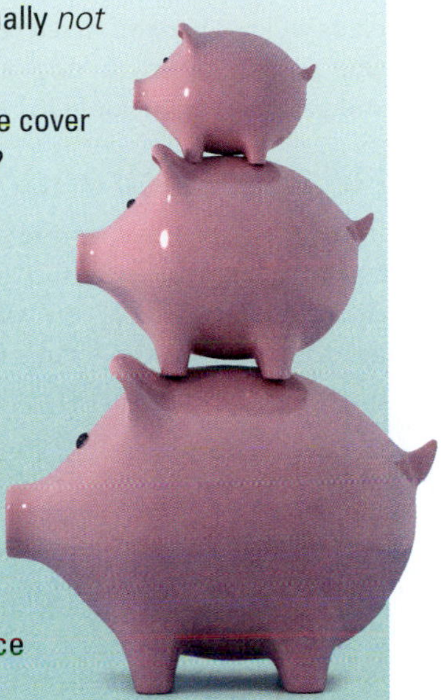

10.9 What two risks does your home-owner's insurance usually *not* cover?

10.10 What types of insurance cover your personal property?

10.11 What is the difference between replacement value and actual value for personal property insurance?

10.12 Why should you compile a home inventory?

10.13 What is the purpose of an umbrella insurance policy?

financialfitness:
NUMBERS GAME

Insurance Pricing Advantage

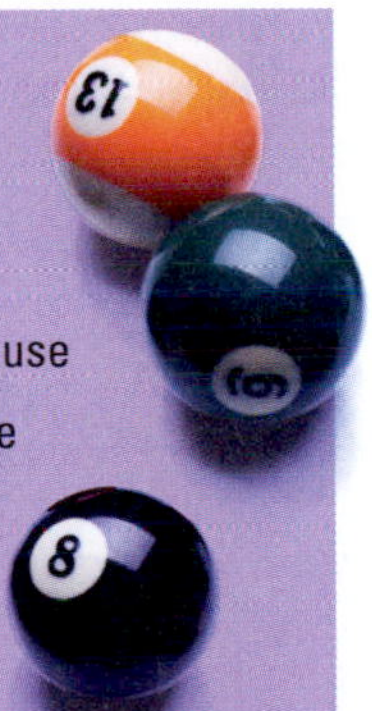

In most cases, patients who do not have insurance are charged higher prices for their care than those covered by insurance because the insurance companies often negotiate lower rates with the care provider. As a result, those who elect to "self-pay," or use health savings accounts in place of insurance, are at a cost disadvantage.

If you self-pay for care, try to negotiate the charges in exchange for paying cash. Some offices offer a sliding scale discount, based on income, for self-pay patients.

depending on the policy limits. This policy is in addition to the liability coverage from auto and homeowner's insurance. An umbrella policy goes into effect after you reach your liability limits on other policies. People with a large number of assets that would be put at risk in a lawsuit should consider an umbrella policy of at least a million dollars.

Lowering Your Costs

Figure 10.5 lists some steps you can take to lower the cost of your overall homeowner's or renter's insurance.

10.4 **HEALTH INSURANCE**

■ ■ **LO 10-4** Distinguish between the different types of health insurance, and identify the proper coverage for your situation.

Health insurance is the most important insurance to have in protecting both your personal health and your assets. As Annie in the chapter opener learned, minor medical procedures can cost thousands, if not tens of thousands, of dollars. Moreover, major medical procedures can cost hundreds of thousands of dollars. Medical insurance protects your wealth if you should have any illness or injury requiring medical attention. Many different types of health insurance plans are available to help cover the cost of doctors, hospitals, medical tests, and prescription drugs. You should understand the various terms and costs of coverage before selecting the best plan for you.

Health Insurance Basics

Health insurance is very complicated and sometimes difficult to understand. Even with coverage from what seems like extensive health insurance, it is easy to find yourself paying for a lot of medical expenses. In March 2010, President Obama signed into law the health care bill which will go into effect in 2014. The impact of the bill is that most Americans will be required to either have health insurance or pay a fine. Larger employers will be required to provide coverage or risk financial penalties. Lifetime coverage limits will be banned, and insurers will be barred from denying coverage based on gender or pre-existing conditions. The goal of the bill is to make health care more accessible and affordable to all.

▼ **FIGURE 10.5**

Lowering your homeowner's or renter's insurance cost

Inspect your home regularly and make necessary repairs to keep claims to a minimum.

Do not smoke—smoke-free homes are cheaper to insure.

Install smoke detectors, fire extinguishers, deadbolt locks, and a security system.

Maintain a good credit rating.

terms and costs There are two sets of costs in health insurance: the *premium* (the amount paid for health insurance coverage) and the *deductible* (the amount of money you must pay before the insurer will begin to pay on a claim). For health insurance, your deductible amount is commonly referred to as your *out-of-pocket* expense. The higher the deductible is, the lower your premium insurance cost will be. Health insurance deductibles range from $500 to over $10,000. Some policies have a maximum out-of-pocket limit, which states the insured person's maximum payment obligation for a specific benefit year.

A **copayment** is the amount you must pay before the insurer will pay for a particular visit, service, or drug. For example, if you have a $25 copayment for a clinic visit and you go to your physician for a check-up or a strep-test, the charge may be $125 but you will pay only $25 and your insurance will cover the rest. **Coinsurance** is a percentage you must pay until you reach your maximum out-of-pocket expense, which could be in addition to the copay amount. For an example illustrating coinsurance, see *Doing the Math* 10.1.

Some policies have **exclusions** stating what is *not* covered in the insurance coverage. Common exclusions are elective surgeries, which would include plastic surgery for face-lifts, tummy tucks, and so on. Many health insurance plans have a **network** of doctors, labs, clinics, and hospitals with whom they have negotiated set prices. Under these plans, you will pay less at the locations within the network. Some plans will require you to select a **primary care physician** who will be your main doctor. You must go to this doctor and get a referral if you need to see a specialist.

Health Insurance Options

In general, the cheaper the insurance is, the less choice and flexibility the health care plan will have. If you want choice and flexibility, you will either need to pay a larger up-front cost (in the form of the premium) and pay less when seeking medical care, or pay less up front and then a larger amount when in need of medical care (in the form of a higher deductible). Health insurance plans are usually classified as: (1) fee-for-service, (2) high deductible, or (3) managed care. Figure 10.6 lays out the three types of health care plans and how they differ.

managed care plans The purpose of managed care is to control the employer's health care costs and improve the methods used to select health care providers. This goal is accomplished through the introduction of practice guidelines for health care providers. Based on the method of payment, there are three types of managed care arrangements: health maintenance organizations (HMOs), preferred provider organizations (PPOs), and point-of-service plans (POSs).

A **health maintenance organization (HMO)** is a group of doctors and other medical professionals who offer care

doing the MATH

10.1 Coinsurance Example

You have a $20 copayment plus a 20% coinsurance policy. Consider the following scenario:

   a. You have a prescription for a generic drug costing $100.
   b. You pay a $25 copayment; the remaining amount is ($100 – $25) = $75.
   c. Your 20% coinsurance portion of the balance is ($75 × 0.20) = $15.
   d. With your copayment and coinsurance, your $100 prescription actually costs you: $25 (copayment) + $15 (coinsurance) + $40 (total cost). Your insurance company pays the remaining $60.

  1. What would be your total cost to fill the prescription if your doctor had selected to go with the brand-named drug at a cost of $250 instead of the generic option?

  2. What amount of the cost would the insurance company have covered?

for a flat monthly rate with no deductibles. The policy covers only visits to professionals within the HMO network. The HMO also must approve all visits, prescriptions, and other care. A primary physician within the HMO handles referrals.

A **preferred provider organization (PPO)** provides health care services at a reduced fee. A PPO is similar to an HMO, but care is paid for as it is received instead of in advance (in the form of a scheduled fee). PPOs offer more flexibility by allowing visits to out-of-network professionals. Visits within the network require only the payment of a small fee, and there is often a deductible for out-of-network expenses and a higher copayment. A policyholder has a primary physician within the network who also handles referrals to specialists covered by the PPO. After any visit, the policyholder must submit a claim to be reimbursed for the visit, minus the copayment.

Point-of-service (POS) plans give the patient a single primary care provider, but that primary provider can make referrals to other providers both in and out of the network. The plan covers in-network providers at a more favorable rate. The patient is responsible for higher out-of-pocket costs if he or she uses an out-of-network physician. This type of plan is more flexible than an HMO because the enrollee does have the option of going outside of the network; however, out-of-network care is billed at a higher rate.

government health care plans Medicare is a federal program that pays for certain health care expenses for people age 65 or older. Enrolled individuals must pay deductibles and copayments, but many of their medical costs are covered by the program. Medicare is less comprehensive than some other health care programs, but it is an important source of postretirement health care.

Medicare is divided into multiple parts. Part A covers hospital bills; Part B covers doctor bills; Part C provides the option to choose from a package of health care plans; and Part D provides prescription drug coverage. **Medigap policies** are supplemental insurance policies designed to cover the "gap" between total out-of-pocket costs and expenses reimbursed by Medicare.

Medicaid is a public-assistance program funded by the federal and state governments. It pays for medical care for those with limited income who cannot afford other coverage. The Medicaid rules vary widely from state to state.

point-of-service (POS) plan the patient has a single primary care provider, but that provider can make referrals to providers both in and out of the network

Medigap policies supplemental insurance policies sold by private insurance companies to fill "gaps" in the original Medicare plan coverage

▼ **FIGURE** 10.6

Types of health insurance plans

Plan Type	Characteristics
Fee-for-Service	• You can see any physician or receive medical services without a primary care physician's referral.
	• You and/or the employer pay a monthly premium.
	• Providers bill separately for each medical visit.
	• The insurance company pays all or a set percentage of the fee after you have paid the annual deductible.
	• If applicable, you pay a coinsurance amount, a portion of covered health care expenses for which you are responsible, usually a fixed percentage.
High Deductible	• The plan can work in conjunction with a health savings account or a health reimbursement account.
	• These plans generally have higher annual out-of-pocket maximums than traditional health care plans.
	• Preventive care services may be paid after a copayment. A maximum preventive care amount may apply.
Managed Care	• Insurance companies contract with physicians and medical service providers, forming a service network in an effort to control costs.
	• You receive financial incentives for using network physicians and health care providers.
	• You may be required to choose or be assigned a primary care provider (PCP).
	• You, or you and your employer, pay a monthly premium.
	• You generally pay a copayment for each office visit, prescription, and service.
	• You can choose the managed care arrangement right for you:
	○ Health maintenance organizations (HMOs) provide comprehensive medical services for a fixed, prepaid premium.
	○ Preferred provider organizations (PPOs) combine managed care with traditional fee-for-service plans.
	○ Point-of-service plans (POSs) allow patients to choose providers at the time service.

Source: The USAA Education Foundation at www.usaaedfoundation.org/insurance/bi06.asp.

The State Children's Health Insurance Program (SCHIP) provides health insurance for children under the age of 19 whose family income is too high to qualify for Medicaid but who cannot afford private health insurance. The program pays for clinic appointments, immunizations, hospitalizations, and emergency room visits.

Consolidation Omnibus Budget Reconciliation Act (COBRA)

The Consolidation Omnibus Budget Reconciliation Act (**COBRA**) is a law that allows you to extend health insurance for a period of time after a job loss, death, divorce, or other transitional life event. If you lose your job, you can continue the health insurance coverage from your employer. COBRA also allows you to continue coverage under your parents' insurance if you are a student or recently graduated but not yet fully employed (for up to three years after graduation or up to the age of 26). Many colleges also will offer their recent grads a health care plan they can purchase at a reasonable rate.

Lowering Your Costs

In choosing a type of health care plan, take into consideration such items as your current state of health, your health risks, and your saving discipline. Figure 10.7 provides some items to consider in selecting a health care plan and shows how these considerations align with the different plans.

You can use online Worksheet 10.5 to compare the different types of health care insurance based on their key criteria. For a list of things you can do to help lower the overall cost of your health care insurance, see Figure 10.8.

▼ **FIGURE 10.7**

Considerations in selecting a health care plan

Questions to Consider in Selecting a Health Care Plan	No	Yes
Do I have the discipline to keep enough in my savings to cover a large deductible?	Select a plan with a lower deductible and pay more as you go	Choose a cheaper monthly premium and opt for a higher deductible
Am I particular about which doctors I see?	Opt for plans with a cheaper premium, in which you see a primary care physician first and accept referrals from inside the network	Choose to pay more and have total freedom to choose your doctors and specialists
Do I make regular visits to the doctor?		Select a plan with a lower copay
Do I take prescription medicine?		Prioritize good prescription drug benefits

▼ **FIGURE 10.8**

Cutting health care insurance costs

Opt for a higher deductible if you and your dependents are generally in good health.

Save enough money to cover the deductible when you need it.

Participate in your employer's group medical plan if available.

Request a three-month prescription for medications that treat chronic conditions, like diabetes and arthritis; this can reduce costs up to 33 percent (compared with paying monthly).

Select cheaper generic drugs over the brand names whenever possible.

Enroll in your company's flexible-spending account, paying out-of-pocket expenses with pretax dollars.

See a dental student for checkups; many dental schools have free clinics that treat patients, where care is supervised by a dentist and supply fees are discounted 50 percent.

Take advantage of preventive care benefits such as annual physical exams or flu shots.

Get silver fillings in your back teeth; they are half the cost of white composite fillings and last four times longer.

Avoid a no-show penalty; if not able to keep your appointment, cancel it in advance.

Stay healthy. Some employers/insurers offer wellness incentives that save dollars for employees if they visit the gym regularly, eat healthily, or enroll in smoking-cessation classes. Excess pounds are associated with high blood pressure, diabetes, heart disease, and other chronic illnesses that require expensive daily medication and frequent check-ups.

financialfitness:
STOPPING LITTLE LEAKS

Making $ense

10.14 What two cost terms are key to understanding health insurance policies?

10.15 What characteristics differentiate the three different types of health insurance options?

10.16 How can COBRA help you during transition phases?

10.5 DISABILITY AND LONG-TERM CARE INSURANCE

■ ■ **LO 10-5** Understand the importance of disability and long-term care insurance, and determine the proper coverage for your situation.

If you become disabled and are unable to work (temporarily or permanently), how will you pay your bills and provide for your family? You can purchase disability and long-term care insurance to protect you in such unfortunate circumstances. But what if you are so impaired that you cannot make decisions about your care? Once you are an adult, federal privacy laws limit what information the provider and facility can share without your permission. Therefore, it is important to designate someone who can speak with your care team on your behalf.

Advance Directives

Advance directives are specific instructions you prepare in advance with the intent to direct your medical care in the event you are unable to do so. Two important advance directives include the *power of attorney* and a *living will*.

power of attorney   You will want to designate a **power of attorney**, a document that identifies who you want to make business and legal decisions on your behalf in the event you are not able to make them for yourself. Your power of attorney (*attorney-in-fact*) can pay your bills, file your tax return, and buy or sell property and assets for you.

living will   You should also have a **living will**, which will document your position on prolonging your life if you are on life support or severely brain impaired. The infamous case of Terri Schiavo illustrates the value of having a living will: Schiavo became severely brain impaired in her 20s, and her families went through much grief and financial pain while her husband and parents disagreed on what Terri would have wanted. To protect your family's assets and avoid this emotional drain, designate your wishes now by completing a living will form.

Disability Insurance

Disability insurance provides you a portion of your income if you are unable to work for a stated period of time. Some employers offer disability insurance as an option, but you can also purchase it as an individual. With disability insurance, the premium is dependent on: (1) how much of your income you would like to replace, (2) how long you want those payments to continue, and (3) when the payments would start. Disability insurance cannot replace more than what you make; common disability policies replace 60 to 70% of your income. Some disability insurance policies have caps on the amount they will pay over a lifetime, and most disability policies have a waiting period. The waiting period is the time between your becoming disabled and the date the payments start (commonly 90 days). This means you have to be disabled 90 consecutive days before you start to receive 70 percent of your income. During this waiting time, you might be able to use accrued sick leave and vacation to cover your missing income.

Scan here for more information on the latest events "In the News"

Major ways the overhaul will affect those who currently have health insurance and those who do not.

If you are insured and pay on your own, you can keep your current plan or you can buy coverage through new state-run insurance marketplaces starting in 2014. Existing plans don't have to meet higher benefit standards of new policies, but will face tighter regulations. . . .

If you are insured by an employer, you can keep your plan or you can buy coverage through new state-run insurance marketplaces starting in 2014. Families making more than $250,000 will pay higher taxes. Some tax breaks for medical costs will also be reduced . . .

If you are insured by Medicare, you will pay less for preventive care and prescription drugs. If you receive benefits through a private Medicare Advantage plan, you could pay more or receive reduced benefits.

If you are insured by Medicaid, you and your children can stay on the program. States will be required to maintain current eligibility levels for adults until 2014 and for children until 2019 . . .

If you are uninsured . . . If you are currently unable to get private insurance due to a pre-existing medical condition, you will be eligible for subsidized coverage through a new high-risk insurance program . . . If your household income is below 133 percent of the poverty level—or about $29,327 in 2009 for a family of four, you qualify today for Medicaid insurance . . . The uninsured can buy private insurance—federally subsidized for lower-income people—through new state-run insurance marketplaces starting in 2014. All plans in the exchanges will offer a minimum set of benefits . . . .

Starting in 2014, you will pay penalties if you are required to buy coverage but do not. Most Americans will be required to buy insurance. American Indians, those with religious objections, and low-income people may be exempt . . . .

FARHANA HOSSAIN and Kevin Quealy, "Major Ways the Overhaul Will Affect Those Who Currently Have Health Insurance and Those Who Do Not," *The New York Times*, March 21, 2010. Reprinted with permission.

Retrieve the article online and use the interactive grid to select the category into which you fall. Read the details of the law's impact as it pertains to you.

Questions

1 How does the law affect you directly?

2 What type of safety net does the new law present?

3 What challenges do you forecast for the law?

How the Health Care Overhaul Could Affect You

Major ways the overhaul will affect those who currently have health insurance and those who do not.

Choose a category

Insured	On your own
Uninsured	By employer
	By Medicare
	By Medicaid

You can keep your current plan or you can buy coverage through new state-run insurance marketplaces starting in 2014. Existing plans don't have to meet higher benefit standards of new policies, but will face tighter regulations.

If you are self-employed, you will have to buy disability insurance from a private insurance provider. The premiums charged through a group plan are typically low but vary according to the length of the coverage, renewability/cancellation options, scheduled adjustments, and your occupation.

social security Through the Social Security program, the federal government supplements your income if you are disabled. There is no age limit to this disability insurance. Even a two-pound premature newborn is eligible for Social Security disability payments until the point that the child is determined to be no longer disabled.

financialfitness:
ACTION ITEM

Setting up Advance Directives

The U.S. Living Will registry at http://www.uslwr.com/formslist.shtm provides living will and power of attorney forms. Once you have downloaded the forms and completed the documents, keep a copy in your home file and take another copy of the forms to your doctor the next time you have an appointment. It will be scanned into your medical record and be on file if you ever need it. Social workers at your local hospital also can assist you in completing the forms.

Long-term care insurance can help you—or those you love—live a long life with fewer financial concerns.

Little Jordan in Figure 10.9 was born 2½ months early, weighing 2 pounds, 6 ounces. Babies born this premature need a lot of help and care and it is not uncommon for them to take two years to grow enough to catch up to other children their same age. During this time, they are classified as disabled and can receive a Social Security check. The social service representative at the hospital helped Jordan's parents complete the paperwork to apply for Social Security. Even though Jordan's parents had great insurance, he was in the Neonatal Intensive Care Unit for seven weeks, and the hospital bill totaled over $350,000. Jordan's parents

negotiated an interest-free payment plan with the hospital; over the next two years they were able to pay off the copay of $4,000. The Social Security check helped offset their copay expenses as well as pay for the cost of the in-home nurse visits Jordan required until he had developed further.

workers' compensation If you become disabled in your workplace, you may receive income through your state workers' compensation program. The laws regarding workers' compensation vary between states, and the amount you receive is based on your salary.

Long-Term Care Insurance

Long-term recovery patients and the elderly sometimes need assisted care for their living arrangements. Both at-home care and nursing-home care can be very expensive and extend for a long period of time. Medicare does not cover the cost of long-term care. You can purchase long-term care insurance policies through private insurance companies, an insurance agent, or sometimes your employer. Premiums are based on your age, your health, and the type of coverage you select. Nursing homes and assisted-living facilities have rates that vary widely from state to state. Most long-term care policies are guaranteed renewable as long as you pay the premiums. However, premiums may increase if the insurer raises them for an entire class of policyholders.

Nursing-home costs can be well over $5,000 a month and can deplete all of your assets over time—to the point that you have nothing left to leave to your loved ones. Long-term care policies usually have a waiting period, like disability insurance, before they actively start covering your day-to-day expenses. They usually pay if you

▼ **FIGURE 10.9**

Newborn at 28½ weeks

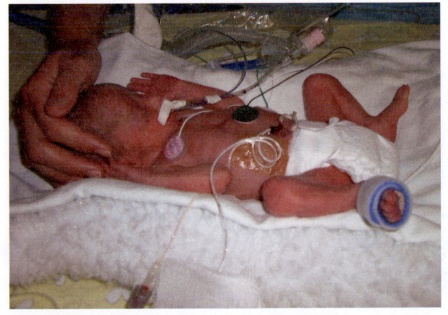

Even a 2-pound, 6-ounce newborn baby can qualify for Social Security.

are unable to perform two or more activities of daily living, such as bathing, dressing, eating, walking, and moving from a bed to a chair.

Lowering Your Costs

Figure 10.10 offers some tips for lowering your overall disability and long-term care insurance costs.

10.6 LIFE INSURANCE

■ ■ **LO 10-6**   List different types of life insurance, and recognize the appropriate amount of coverage given your responsibilities.

Life insurance protects your family and loved ones at the time of your death by providing a one-time, lump sum of money to help make up for the loss of your income. Life

insurance is cheapest and most accessible when you are young and healthy. It can be harder to acquire life insurance as you get older and develop health problems. Generally, the larger the dollar amount of the policy, the higher the premium.

There are many reasons why you might want to purchase life insurance, including paying for your final medical expenses and funeral costs, paying off your debts, replacing income for your family, and planning your estate. If you do not have dependents, you need only minimal life

▼ **FIGURE 10.10**

Tips for lowering disability and long-term care insurance costs

Disability Insurance
Opt for a longer waiting period before benefits begin.
Save enough money to pay for expenses while you are waiting for benefits to begin.
Select a shorter benefit period, but bear in mind you must be able to provide for yourself if your disability continues beyond the stated benefit period.

Long-Term Care Insurance
Consider purchasing long-term care insurance while you are younger and in good health, which will help you qualify for better rates.
Buy a policy with a longer waiting period before benefits begin.
Save enough money to pay for care during the time when you are not receiving benefits.
Consider buying a joint policy for yourself and your spouse.

insurance. If you are a stay-at-home parent with dependent children, you may want to buy insurance to cover the cost of maintaining your home and providing child care if something should happen to you.

When you are buying life insurance, the insurer will ask you about your weight and preventive health habits, such as the use of tobacco, alcohol, and illegal drugs. The insurer may ask you to have a physical in order to assess the company's risk in covering you and to determine how much to charge you for insurance.

Types of Life Insurance

There are two general types of life insurance: term life and permanent insurance. **Term life insurance** covers you for a fixed amount for a certain period of time at a relatively low cost. When the term is over, you make no more insurance payments and the insurance goes away. **Permanent life insurance**, which is much more expensive, is an account that builds up over time.

term life insurance Term life insurance is the cheapest form of life insurance. It insures your life for a specific amount for a specific length of time. If you were to die while your term life insurance policy was in effect, your beneficiary would receive the face value of the life insurance. Many insurance companies sell term life insurance for 1-, 5-, 10-, 15-, 20-, and even 30-year periods.

On the other hand, if you were to die one day after your term life insurance policy expired, your beneficiary would receive no money. At the end of the term, you may have the option of renewing the term policy for another specific time period or converting the policy to a permanent life insurance policy. If you do nothing, the term insurance will expire and you will outlive the insurance. The good news is that you are alive; the bad news is that you spent money on something you didn't use.

permanent life insurance Permanent life insurance policies are meant to last your whole life. They usually build in value in the form of a cash amount or mutual funds and investments. You have the insurance as long as you make your premium payments on

> ## "There are worse things in life than death. Have you ever spent an evening with an insurance salesman?"
> —WOODY ALLEN, *American film director and screenwriter (1935–)*

financialfitness:
STOPPING LITTLE LEAKS

Long- vs. Short-Term Policy

Short-term policies may have a lower payment now, but over the long run, a longer term policy is the better deal. It is more expensive to buy another term policy in 10 years when you are 10 years older than to buy the long-term policy now while you are young. In the long run, opting for the long-term policy will save you money.

time. The three major types of permanent life insurance policies are whole life, universal life, and variable life. The two most popular are whole life and universal life. (We will not cover variable life in detail in this chapter, but Figure 10.12 on page 265 provides a basic outline if you are curious.)

whole life insurance **Whole life insurance** provides a fixed amount of life insurance and also a cash value as long as you pay the premiums. The premiums are for a fixed amount of money and part of each premium goes to fund the life insurance. The remainder goes into a savings vehicle that builds value. The value it builds usually has a minimum guaranteed rate of interest and therefore a minimum guaranteed cash value.

universal life insurance **Universal life insurance** is similar to whole life insurance, except it does not have a guaranteed minimum return. With universal life insurance, part of the premium goes for life insurance and the remainder goes toward your choice of investments. Universal life insurance was very popular during the 1990s when the stock market was outperforming savings. You can usually change the investment in universal life insurance to minimize the risk as you get older.

Recommended Amount of Life Insurance

The amount of life insurance you buy is up to you, and no one is going to look out for your future better than you. Many financial planners provide a free assessment of your

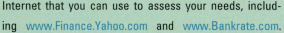

financialfitness:
JUST THE FACTS

Online Insurance Calculators

There are many insurance calculators available on the Internet that you can use to assess your needs, including www.Finance.Yahoo.com and www.Bankrate.com. If you visit an insurer's website, remember the organization is trying to sell life insurance, so be sure to validate its recommendation.

▼ **FIGURE 10.11**

Example of life-event impact on the amount of life insurance needed

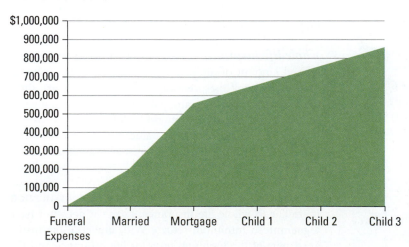

financial condition and will recommend that you increase your life insurance protection. They may be right in recommending that you buy more insurance, but bear in mind they make a high commission on any life insurance they sell.

The rule of thumb on how much life insurance to have is between 5 and 20 times your annual salary. In the event of your death, your life insurance proceeds will go to the beneficiaries you have designated on the policy. Any time you have a major life event, such as getting married or divorced or having children, you should review and revise your life insurance policy (see Figure 10.11).

If you do need life insurance, decide which form of insurance is best for *you* and the amount of coverage *you* need. It is usually less expensive if you buy life insurance with face values of $100,000, $250,000, $500,000, or $1,000,000. If your goal is the cash value (the investment value of permanent life insurance), it is better to buy term and invest the rest in another investment vehicle. Permanent insurance does not build respectable cash value until the 12th year, and you will be paying the insurance agents a commission for the first 2 to 10 years.[4] Figure 10.12 compares the life insurance options discussed in this section.

Personal Finance Life Stages

Your life insurance needs will change across your life stages. Therefore, it is important to understand what insurance products are best suited for each life stage.

dependent life stage (age < 16) Since the risk of dying during this stage is so low, many insurance companies offer dependent life insurance, which covers $8,000 to $10,000 for pennies a day. For that small amount, you could cover unexpected funeral expenses.

independent life stage (age 16–24) As an independent person, aged 16–24, you probably do not need much life insurance. However, even if you have few assets and no family members who depend on your income, life insurance can cover your final medical expenses and funeral costs, freeing your extended family from carrying that financial burden. Funeral expenses range from $5,000 on up, depending on how elaborate a funeral you want. Usually a $10,000 life insurance policy is sufficient to cover funeral expenses. If you are a dependent of someone else who has life insurance, you might be able to buy $10,000 worth of coverage for a small fee on their plan. Many employers offer this as a benefit to their employees. If you have student loans or have other high debts, you may want to increase the amount of your life insurance to cover those liabilities.

[4] http://www.investopedia.com/articles/pf/05/012405.asp?partner=yahoofin&viewed=1

Life insurance options: a comparison

	Term	Whole Life	Universal Life	Variable Life
Protection	No coverage after age 85	Provides permanent protection		
Premium	Premium increases dramatically upon renewal after the coverage period	No renewal or conversion required; premium guaranteed same throughout lifetime	No renewal or conversion required	No renewal or conversion required
Cash Value	Policy has no cash value	Value accumulates and can be taken out or borrowed against		
Tax Advantages	None	Enjoy tax-free compound growth on the investment		
Cost/Payment Flexibility	Least expensive type of insurance during coverage period	Most expensive due to the high overfunding amount required; payment amount is decided, and the schedule is inflexible	Flexible on payment amount and payment schedule	
Investment Type	None	Insurance company controls investment choices and returns	Options to choose and change investment vehicle; certain level of investment knowledge is required to make investment decision	Similar to universal life insurance, but includes a broader selection of investment products, including stocks
Suitability	Best choice if you need a large amount of coverage with low cost for a specific period of time, such as personal debt which will be paid off in a certain period of time (mortgage), or financial support for children up to a specific age	Good choice if you have substantial and stable monthly income, want to take advantage of tax-shelter benefits, and don't have time to manage the investment; the cash value can be used for retirement funding	Best choice for anyone who has permanent insurance needs and certain knowledge of investing; it is most popular among business owners and can be used for businesses as funding for a partnership agreement	

early family life stage (age 25–40) During the early-family years, your life insurance needs will probably be the highest. The need for life insurance increases dramatically when you become a parent. At the beginning of this life stage, one of the most valuable assets you have is the ability to continue to earn an income for your dependents in the future. If you are 25 years old, earn $40,000 per year, and plan to work until age 65, your earnings in today's terms will be $1.6 million, without consideration of any increases in pay over that time. Life insurance can be an inexpensive way to make sure there is ready cash to cover any financial obligations you leave behind.

Both parents will want to consider coverage, even if one does not work outside the home. Term insurance is a popular type of coverage during these years because it provides the most coverage at the lowest cost. Some young couples start with a permanent policy or a combination of term and permanent insurance. A benefit of buying a whole life policy when you are young is that you can lock in a fixed lower premium.

At this stage, you typically are paying on a home mortgage, saving for your children's college expenses, and saving for

retirement. Were you to die at this point, you most likely would not have had a chance to build up your liquid assets to meet cash flow demands. Therefore, one goal at this life

Your life insurance needs may never be higher than when you are in the Early Family life stage.

stage might be to have a policy that would provide over $100,000 for an educational fund for each child and cash to pay off the mortgage, in addition to two or three years' salary to provide your family an adjustment period and hopefully allow them to stay in the same home.

empty nest life stage (age 41–65) These are the years when your children leave home and your income usually continues to increase. You may want to consider dropping some of your term insurance and converting the remaining coverage to permanent insurance as you look toward retirement. The cash value of permanent insurance can be used to purchase long-term care insurance to protect your family from any financial burdens.

retirement life stage (age 66+) If your assets are modest, you will need the life insurance proceeds to provide income for a surviving spouse, if need be. If you have developed income-producing assets and have a good pension, you will not need as much life insurance during this stage. If you need additional retirement income, you can use the cash value of permanent insurance. Most retirees maintain some coverage to pay funeral and burial expenses, to cover the cost of a final illness or estate taxes, to make a final bequest, or to provide money for children and grandchildren. You can use life insurance as an estate-planning strategy to potentially reduce estate taxes and to pass more money on to your heirs.

Lowering Your Costs

There are a number of things you can do to reduce your overall insurance costs. Key activities for lowering your life insurance costs are listed in Figure 10.13. ▪

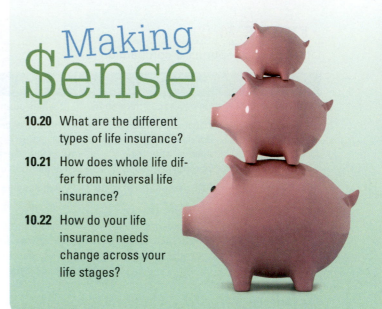

Making $ense

10.20 What are the different types of life insurance?

10.21 How does whole life differ from universal life insurance?

10.22 How do your life insurance needs change across your life stages?

▼ **FIGURE 10.13**

Tips for lowering your life insurance costs

Exercise, eat well, and do not smoke.

Maintain a healthy weight.

Purchase life insurance at a young age to get a lower rate.

Purchase the appropriate amount of life insurance using a combination of term and permanent insurance to meet short-term and long-term financial needs.

> "In a hospital they throw you out into the street before you are half cured, but in a nursing home they don't let you out until you're dead."
>
> —George Bernard Shaw, *Irish dramatist and critic (1856–1950)*

Learn. ▶ Plan & Act. ▶ Evaluate.

➲ LEARN. In this chapter you learned about protecting your assets against natural disasters, accidents, medical emergencies, and disabilities. You health is one of your most important assets, and the cost of health care continues to increase. It is imperative to have health insurance coverage. You also learned about auto insurance, homeowner's/renter's insurance, disability and long-term care insurance, and life insurance. For each of these types of insurance, this chapter provided tips for lowering costs while maintaining adequate coverage.

SUMMARY

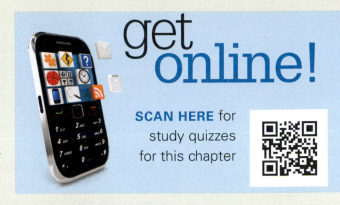

■■ **LO 10-1** Understand the basics of insurance.

Insurance provides a way to protect assets from loss in the event of a catastrophe, accident, or health problem. To secure assets and avoid the risk of bankruptcy, you need the appropriate amount of insurance. Insurance premiums are based on your risk of filing a claim against the insurance company. Insurance can be purchased online or through an insurance agent. The declaration page of the policy includes the names of the insured, the property insured (with vehicles this includes the make, model, year, and vehicle identification number), the effective dates, the coverage type and limits, the deductible, and the policy premium amount. Review the declaration page for accuracy and coverage limits, and review the policy for a full understanding of the coverage and exclusions.

■■ **LO 10-2** Examine your state's minimum requirements for auto liability insurance, and identify the proper coverage for your vehicle.

Auto insurance premiums are determined by credit history, age, driving record, location, marital status, the make and model of the vehicle, and the safety equipment in the vehicle (air bags, anti-lock brakes, stability control). Consider the cost of insurance premiums and their impact on your budget when buying a car.

Liability insurance on a vehicle is broken down into three different categories: (1) the bodily injury liability dollar amount for one person injured in an accident, (2) the bodily injury liability dollar amount for all people injured in an accident, and (3) the personal property liability dollar amount for one accident. If you are in an accident for which you are at fault, liability insurance covers only the repairs on the other vehicle. Comprehensive and collision insurance cover repairs on your own car. If you have a car loan, the lender will require you to have full coverage insurance, naming the financial institution as lien holder and loss payee. If the vehicle is damaged, the loss payee is notified and payment is made to the loss payee. Full coverage consists of comprehensive and collision insurance, and it protects you and the vehicle regardless of fault or if the other driver has no insurance. If you have many serious driving violations, your state may require you to have SR-22 liability insurance in order to drive.

■■ **LO 10-3** Explain the importance of homeowner's/renter's insurance, and determine the proper coverage for your home or apartment.

Home insurance protects you from financial hardship in repairing or replacing your home and belongings in the event of damage or loss. Homeowner's insurance generally does not cover earthquakes or floods. If you are at risk for those events, contact your insurance agent, the National Flood Insurance Program, or the insurance commissioner to explore your options.

Renter's insurance safeguards your personal property if you are not a homeowner. A guaranteed replacement cost or an extended replacement cost policy insures that your personal property will be replaced even if its cost exceeds policy limits. Consider an insurance rider for jewelry, antiques, coins, or other collectibles and maintain an inventory of your personal property to ease replacement.

A homeowner's or renter's insurance policy usually contains liability insurance for accidents that occur in the home or on the property to safeguard you if someone else should be hurt on your property. People can sue for many reasons, and an umbrella policy covers your assets in the event of a liability lawsuit or if you have reached the liability limits on other insurance policies.

■■ **LO 10-4** Distinguish between the different types of health insurance, and identify the proper coverage for your situation.

Health insurance requires a basic understanding of monthly premiums, deductibles, copayments, coinsurance, and exclusions. Types of health insurance plans fall into three categories: fee-for-service, high deductible, and managed care. The driving force behind managed care

(PPO, HMO, and POS) plans is to control the employer's health care costs through the introduction of practice guidelines and to improve the methods used to select health care providers. The Consolidation Omnibus Budget Reconciliation Act (COBRA) allows a student to extend coverage under his or her parents' policy for up to three years. It also allows you to extend health insurance for a period of time after a job loss, death, divorce, or other transitional life event.

■■ **LO 10-5** Understand the importance of disability and long-term care insurance, and determine the proper coverage for your situation.

Federal privacy laws limit what the care provider/care facility can share without your permission. Therefore, it is important to designate a power of attorney so that, in the event that you are not able to make decisions on your own, this attorney-in-fact can tend to your financial matters on your behalf. You should also have a living will in place to protect your family's assets and ease their emotional challenge. It is common for employer disability insurance policies to have a waiting period of 90 consecutive days; after this period of time, you receive 75 percent of your income while you are disabled. Factors affecting the premium costs of disability insurance include length of coverage, renewability, cancellation, automatic adjustments, and occupation. Other forms of disability pay include Social Security and the state workers' compensation program. Long-term care insurance protects your assets if you should require at-home or nursing-home care for an extended period of time.

■■ **LO 10-6** List different types of life insurance, and recognize the appropriate amount of coverage given your responsibilities.

Life insurance protects your family and loved ones at the time of your death by providing a sum of money to cover their financial needs and to help make up for the loss of your income. Term life insurance covers you for a fixed amount over a certain time period at a relatively low cost. Permanent life insurance is an account that builds up value over time and is much more expensive than term life. The two most popular types of permanent life insurance policies are whole life and universal life.

➔ **PLAN & ACT.** To assess your current insurance needs, create a plan with the appropriate coverage to protect your current assets. In addition, create a plan that takes into account how your future insurance needs will change as you progress through the personal finance life stages. Your Plan & Act to do list is as follows:

☐ Use an online calculator to derive the appropriate amount of insurance for you at this time (Worksheet 10.1).

☐ Compile a listing of your current insurance coverage (Worksheet 10.2).

☐ Assess the appropriateness of your current auto insurance (Worksheet 10.3).

☐ Prepare a record of your home inventory (Worksheet 10.4).

☐ Assess the appropriateness of your current health insurance (Worksheet 10.5).

➔ **EVALUATE.** Based on the worksheets, what is the overall balance of your insurance coverage? Walking through your inventory review, does your insurance provide the appropriate level of coverage? Use this new information to determine whether you should increase or decrease your insurance coverage, given your risk tolerance, your life stage, and your net worth. Online insurance calculators (www.finance.yahoo.com, www.bankrate.com) can help you to determine your insurance needs. Are you getting a good price on your insurance? Comparison insurance shopping can be done on the Internet or by contacting your local insurance agent.

After you complete the worksheets, open your online GoalTracker to make notes on how your insurance supports your SMART goals. Assess how you are tracking in achieving your stated goals. Note in your GoalTracker any changes you need to make to your insurance to ensure your assets are covered against accidents, natural disasters, and liability issues.

key terms

Advance Directives

COBRA

Coinsurance

Collision Insurance

Comprehensive Insurance

Copayment

Declaration Page

Deductible

Earthquake Insurance

Exclusions

Flood Insurance

Full Coverage

Health Maintenance Organization (HMO)

Insurance Rider

Liability Insurance

Living Will

Loss Payee

Medigap Policies

Network

Permanent Life Insurance

Point-of-Service (POS) Plan

Power of Attorney

Preferred Provider Organization (PPO)

Premium

Primary Care Physician

Rental Reimbursement

Renter's Insurance

Roadside Assistance

Salvage Value

SR-22 Liability Insurance

Term Life Insurance

Umbrella Liability Insurance

Universal Life Insurance

Whole Life Insurance

self-test questions

1. Why do you need insurance? *(LO 10-1)*

    a. To protect your assets in case of accident, fire, or other disaster
    b. To repair your assets when need be
    c. To protect your family's financial well-being
    d. All of the above

2. The insurance declaration page states: *(LO 10-1)*

    a. The type of insurance you have
    b. The maximum amount an insurance company will pay
    c. Who is covered under the insurance policy
    d. All of the above

3. What type of auto insurance will you need to get your car repaired if you are in a hail storm? *(LO 10-2)*

    a. Liability
    b. Collision
    c. Comprehensive
    d. Uninsured motorist

4. If you are at fault in an auto accident, what insurance coverage will you need to get the funds to have your car repaired? *(LO 10-2)*

    a. Liability
    b. Collision
    c. Comprehensive
    d. Uninsured motorist

5. If you are at fault in an auto accident and your passenger sustains injuries and is required to go to a hospital for treatment, what type of insurance will cover those expenses? *(LO 10-2)*

    a. Liability
    b. Collision
    c. Comprehensive
    d. Health

6. You can purchase insurance only through an insurance agent who is licensed in your state. *(LO 10-1)*

    a. True
    b. False

7. An independent insurance agent can sell you insurance: *(LO 10-1)*

    a. From only one company
    b. From any company she represents
    c. Only for your automobile
    d. Cheaper than purchasing insurance online

8. Your insurance deductible is: *(LO 10-1)*

   a. The amount you have to pay if you make an insurance claim
   b. The cost of insurance that is deducted from your paycheck
   c. The maximum the insurance company will pay
   d. A fee insurance companies charge

9. Minimum automobile liability insurance is: *(LO 10-2)*

   a. Not something you need, but is a suggested amount of coverage
   b. The same in every state
   c. Different in every state
   d. Sufficient to cover your legal responsibilities if you cause an accident

10. Insurance companies are regulated by: *(LO 10-1)*

    a. The National Insurance Regulation Commission (NIRC)
    b. The Federal Insurance Assurance Commission (FIAC)
    c. The Independent Association of Insurance Regulators (IAIR)
    d. The state in which they do business

11. Auto insurance rates are determined by: *(LO 10-2)*

    a. The likelihood that you will make a claim against the insurance company
    b. Your age
    c. Your driving record
    d. All of the above

12. SR-22 liability insurance is: *(LO 10-2)*

    a. Required by the state if you are classified as a high-risk driver
    b. Issued by the state
    c. Required only if you are cited for driving under the influence
    d. Required only if you own a car

13. The insured value of your home is usually less than the market price because: *(LO 10-3)*

    a. Homeowner's insurance covers just the value of the buildings and structures and not the value of the land
    b. Your home depreciates over time and is not worth the market price
    c. Insurance companies cannot afford to cover the replacement value of your home
    d. All of the above

14. Flood insurance is: *(LO 10-3)*

    a. Automatically included in your homeowner's insurance policy
    b. Required only if you live near a river
    c. Not important if you live in a 500-year flood plain
    d. Purchased from the National Flood Insurance Program

15. When purchasing homeowner's or renter's insurance, replacement value: *(LO 10-3)*

    a. Reimburses you for only the amount originally spent to acquire personal property
    b. Costs less than purchase price insurance
    c. Reimburses you for the amount required to replace your personal property at today's values
    d. Is a way for insurance companies to charge you more money

16. Insurance riders: *(LO 10-3)*

    a. Cover passengers in your automobile
    b. Are additional insurance to protect specific items of value not covered on your primary policy
    c. Are extremely expensive and not worth getting
    d. Are a way for insurance agents to make more money

17. A home inventory: *(LO 10-3)*

    a. Helps you recall your personal possessions in case of fire, theft, or destroyed property
    b. Should be documented with video or photographs
    c. Should be kept in a secure, off-site location
    d. All of the above

18. Umbrella liability insurance coverage: *(LO 10-3)*

    a. Provides additional liability coverage above your homeowner's and auto policies
    b. Is unaffordable for many people
    c. Covers you on a rainy day
    d. Is just for the rich

19. With health insurance, the copayment is: *(LO 10-4)*

    a. The amount you must pay before insurance pays
    b. Not counted against your out-of-pocket maximum
    c. Included in your premium
    d. Covered under Medicaid

20. A health maintenance organization (HMO): *(LO 10-4)*

    a. Has a greater selection of doctors than a preferred provider organization (PPO)
    b. Is more expensive than a PPO
    c. Provides less flexibility in selecting doctors than a PPO
    d. Has a deductible for out-of-network expenses

21. Medicare: *(LO 10-4)*

    a. Is for those with limited income
    b. Is for the health care expenses of people age 65 and older
    c. Is a government program that covers all medical expenses
    d. Has two parts to it

22. COBRA: *(LO 10-4)*

    a. Allows you to keep health insurance for a limited time under your employer's health insurance plan even if you no longer work there
    b. Is paid by the employer

c. Is not available to students after they graduate from college
  d. Is covered under Medicaid

23. Disability insurance: *(LO 10-5)*
  a. Pays 100 percent of your salary if you are hurt and have to miss work
  b. Starts immediately when you are injured
  c. Usually has a waiting period before you can make a claim
  d. Is offered only by your employer or the government

24. Life insurance: *(LO 10-6)*
  a. Benefits you after you die
  b. Is to help support those who depend on your income in the event of your death
  c. Costs the same for everyone
  d. Needs do not change over time

25. In what life stage are you likely to need the most life insurance coverage? *(LO 10-6)*

  a. Dependent
  b. Independent
  c. Early family
  d. Empty nest
  e. Retirement

26. Term life insurance: *(LO 10-6)*
  a. Covers you only for the term of the policy
  b. Is the cheapest form of life insurance you can purchase
  c. May have the option to renew
  d. Can be outlived
  e. All of the above

27. Permanent life insurance: *(LO 10-6)*
  a. Builds a cash value
  b. Is known as whole life, universal life, and variable life
  c. Provides you with a fixed amount of insurance
  d. All of the above

problems

1. If you are at fault in an auto accident and carry an auto liability insurance requirement of 20/40/15, what is the total dollar amount of your coverage? *(LO 10-2)*

2. If you carry an auto liability insurance requirement of 20/40/10 and are in a car accident where there are three persons in the other car whose medical bills are $7,250, $10,500, and $30,000, how short are you on coverage? *(LO 10-2)*

3. If you carry an auto liability insurance requirement of 10/20/10 and are at fault for an accident that totals the other driver's car, will your insurance cover the replacement value? The other driver's car is worth $12,000. *(LO 10-2)*

4. You moved into an apartment and brought your parents' second-hand furniture and dishes from home. You purchased a new TV, computer, and microwave for $2,000. You have all your clothes with you, which fill up a 6-foot long closet. What type and how much renter's insurance should you purchase? *(LO 10-3)*

5. You have a copay of $25 per clinic visit and a maximum out-of-pocket expense of $500. How many times can you visit the doctor this year before you no longer have to pay the copayment? *(LO 10-4)*

6. If your prescription drugs cost $150 and your plan calls for a $25 copayment plus 20 percent coinsurance, how much will the prescription end up costing you, and how much will the insurance company end up paying? *(LO 10-4)*

7. You make $45,000 a year and have disability insurance that will kick in at 70 percent of your salary after a 90-day disability period. Collectively, how many vacation and sick days do you need to build up to carry you until your disability pay begins, and what will be the value of your monthly disability paycheck? *(LO 10-5)*

you're the expert

1. Richard is having a party at his home when someone trips on his skateboard and breaks her leg falling against Richard's car in the driveway. What type of insurance provides Richard's liability coverage for this type of accident? *(LO 10-1–LO 10-3)*

2. Jane has done very well after taking this class, and her net worth is approaching $2 million at age 58. What type of liability insurance should she have, and what type of insurance should she use to cover her assets? *(LO 10-1–LO 10-5)*

3. Sally just started her own business and is talking to an insurance agent about covering her assets. What type of insurance should she buy and why? *(LO 10-1–LO 10-5)*

4. Ward and June have three children and a mortgage with an outstanding balance of $250,000. Ward works

outside the home, and June is a stay-at-home mom. How much life insurance should they have in order to make sure they have enough set aside for the children's college—as well as enough to cover the loss of income or to help pay for child care if one or both of them should die? What factors should they use in deciding how much life insurance they need? Go to www.bankrate.com and use the life insurance calculator to help determine how much life insurance they will need. Print out the details and give your reasoning for agreeing or disagreeing with the recommendations. (LO 10-1–LO 10-5)

worksheets

Find the worksheets online at www.mhhe.com/walkerpf1e

10.1 INSURANCE CHECKLIST

Use the insurance checklist in Worksheet 10.1 to assess the appropriate amount of coverage you need to protect your assets.

Worksheet 10.1 - Insurance Checklist

1) Go to www.Bankrate.com. Use the online calculator to derive the appropriate amount of insurance for you at this time.
2) Fill out the table to identify the appropriate coverage and annual premium payment to be budgeted.
3) Make note of the deductible and plan for savings in the emergency fund to cover the amount.

Insurance Type	Coverage Needed	Premium	Deductible
Auto			
Homeowner's/Renter's			
Riders			
Health			
Long-Term Care			
Disability			
Life			

10.2 INSURANCE INVENTORY LIST

It is important to have a handy list of all your insurance policy numbers. Complete Worksheet 10.2 online and print copies. Be sure to file one copy in a safety deposit box or other secure, off-site location.

Insurance Inventory List

It is important to have a handy list of all your insurance policy numbers. Complete the table and make multiple copies with one to be filed in your Safety Deposit Box.

Insurance Name	Type	Policy Number	Agent Name	Contact Number	Premium	Deductible

10.3   AUTO INSURANCE ASSESSMENT

Complete Worksheet 10.3 to determine the minimum auto insurance required by your state and to see if your existing insurance is sufficient. Go online to compare other auto insurers' rates and to find the correct coverage and insurance policy for your needs.

COVERAGE	LIMIT	PREMIUM	LIMIT	PREMIUM	LIMIT	PREMIUM
A1 Bodily Injury						
Each Person						
Each Accident						
Property Damage Liability						
Each Accident						
B1 Medical Payments						
Uninsured/Underinsured Motorist						
Each Person						
Each Accident						
D Damage to Auto						
Other than Collision						
Actual Cash Value Less Deductible						
Collision						
Actual Cash Value Less Deductible						
ADDITIONAL COVERAGES	LIMIT	PREMIUM	LIMIT	PREMIUM	LIMIT	PREMIUM
Transportion Expenses						
Per Day / Maximum						
Towing and Labor Cost						
Each Disablement						
OTHER						
TOTAL						

10.4   HOME INVENTORY

Use Worksheet 10.4 to conduct a home inventory and make a record of your personal property in every room in your home. Keep this document in a safety deposit box or other secure, off-site location.

Worksheet 10.4 - Home Inventory

Use the following worksheet to conduct a home inventory for every room in your home.

Room:				Date:		
Item	Description	Model/Manufacturer	Serial #	Purchase Date	Purchase Price	

10.5 HEALTH INSURANCE COMPARISON

Use Worksheet 10.5 to compare health insurance options and evaluate which plan best suits your needs.

Worksheet 10.5 – Health Insurance Comparison

The goal of this worksheet is to summarize your options on one sheet to more easily evaluate which plan best suits your needs.

1. Read the list of items in the table below and rank them.
2. Complete the table for three of your healthcare options.
3. Highlight in yellow the lines that are your top 5 criteria.
4. Review the data, then rank the plans on the last line in order of preference.

	Priority	Plan A	Plan B	Plan C
Plan name				
Type of plan (HMO, OAP, POS, PPO)				
Annual premium amount				
Annual deductible amount				
Clinic visit copayment amount in network				
Urgent care visit copayment amount in network				
Emergency room visit copayment amount in network				
Hospitalization copayment amount in network				
Prescription copayment				
Emergency room				
Preventive health screenings covered? (Yes/No)				
Maximum out-of-pocket amount annually				
Out-of-pocket maximum				
Does the policy have lifetime limits? (Yes/No)				
If so, what are the lifetime $ limits?				
My physicians in network?				
Primary care provider required before seeing specialist (Yes/No)				
Can refer to specialist outside the plan if needed? (Yes/No)				
What will it cost?				
Dental care (Yes/No)				
Vision care (Yes/No)				
Mental health (Yes/No)				
Chemical dependency (Yes/No)				
Covered if become ill away from home (Yes/No)				
Covered if traveling abroad? (Yes/No)				
	Rank			

continuing case

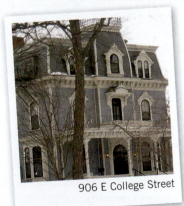

906 E College Street

Peter is considering his insurance needs once he opens his own business. He currently has no debt, is not married, and has no children. His current employer provides health insurance, the equivalent of one year's salary for life insurance, and 70 percent of his salary for disability insurance after 90 days. Peter will need to borrow $400,000 to open his restaurant. His parents purchased a $40,000 whole life insurance policy for him when he was born.

What type of insurance does Peter need and how much would you recommend he purchase? Use the Internet to get cost estimates for Peter. Give the supporting reasons for your recommendation.

A summary of the housemates' goals can be found in the first Continuing Case problem on page 27.

> "I've never been poor, only broke. Being poor is a frame of mind. Being broke is only a temporary situation."
>
> —MIKE TODD, *Actor (1907–1958)*

chapter eleven

investment basics

You work hard for your money, and you want the money you save and invest to work hard for you. There are thousands of options for you to consider, including savings accounts, certificates of deposit, Treasury bills, mutual funds, stocks, bonds, pork bellies, derivatives, precious metals and gems, artwork, and collectibles like old cars. This chapter will help you decide which investments are right for you. ◼

LEARNING OBJECTIVES

After reading this chapter, you should be able to:

LO 11-1 Distinguish between savings and investments.

LO 11-2 Analyze the risk and return on varying investment products.

LO 11-3 Interpret the hierarchies of the investment pyramid.

LO 11-4 Examine the importance of varying your investments.

LO 11-5 Compare portfolio asset allocations for the different personal finance life stages.

◀ Ozlem, age 22, business major from Turkey, senior at a small, private midwestern U.S. university

Investment Strategies

Ozlem comes from a privileged background and is taking the opportunity to study abroad in the United States. She believes that great resources come with great responsibility. She wants her family to be proud of her decisions and how she is taking what has been given to her and making it grow. She selected a quality university that provides a good value education and then invested a large portion of her allocated funds in a number of different account types to help minimize her market risk. Ozlem shares, "It has been a tough four years for investments, but I'm in it for the long run, and I have my investments spread between secure and more risk-taking options. I'm hoping that buying into the market when prices are low will pay off down the road."

11.1 SAVINGS VERSUS INVESTMENTS

■ ■ **LO 11-1** Distinguish between savings and investments.

Most of us are convinced that having more assets would make us feel more secure. As Benjamin Franklin noted, it is difficult to say you are content with the funds at hand. When deciding

Reading financial publications regularly will make you a more well-informed investor.

whether to save or invest and which vehicle to use, the first question to ask yourself is *when* you will need the money. If the time horizon is under 10 years, you should save your money in risk-free savings or low-risk investment instruments. For example, you might choose a savings account or a certificate of deposit with FDIC (Federal Deposit Insurance Corporation) or NCUA (National Credit Union Association) insurance. Or you might choose to invest in U.S. Treasury bills, notes, or bonds. With these **savings** vehicles, you are guaranteed to receive back your principal (the amount you deposited) plus interest, as long as you hold them to maturity.

Savings should be used for accumulating money for things such as an emergency fund, a down payment for a car or a house, or for college (if you will be using it within the next 10 years). Savings is your foundation of financial planning. In Jane Bryant Quinn's words, "Savings is not to make you rich, but it is to keep you from being poor."[1] You should have six to nine months of income in savings as an emergency fund. This fund is your safety net to cover necessities in the event you lose your job, become seriously ill, or have other unplanned expenses. Once you have this amount in savings, you can feel more confident in taking on some risks with your investments to help them grow faster.

Impact of Inflation on Savings

Inflation is the overall increase in the price of goods and services over time. As inflation rises, your dollar buys a

---

[**"Who is rich? He that is content. Who is that? Nobody."**
—BENJAMIN FRANKLIN (1706–1790)]

---

[1] Quinn, J.B. *Making the Most of Your Money Now*, p. 213, Simon & Schuster, 2009.

smaller amount of goods and services. For example, if inflation is at 3%, then the energy bar that cost $1 a year ago now costs $1.03. Inflation whittles away your dollar's purchasing power. Cash in a cookie jar will not maintain its value, but saving money in a low-risk account will hopefully keep your purchasing power in line with inflation so your money does not lose its value.

You need to monitor your savings to make sure its value keeps pace with inflation. If you put all your money into low-risk savings options, it will be difficult to make your money increase in purchasing power. For example, if you put your money in a savings account earning 2% annually and inflation is 4%, the purchasing power of your savings will decrease 2% in that year. The advantage of **investment** over savings is that it gives you a chance to beat inflation. Figure 11.1 outlines the decision process of putting money into savings versus investing it.

Risk of Investing

When you invest, you run the risk of losing some or all of your investment, but you also have higher expected returns. The higher the risk of an investment, the higher the potential return should be. In selling an investment, the seller rewards the buyer for taking on the associated risk; therefore, the seller pays a **risk premium** to the buyer. This risk–return relationship makes sense: If you were paid to change a light bulb in your room, you would do it for very little money because there is a low risk that you would get hurt. On the other hand, if you were being paid to change the light bulb on top of the half-mile tall KVLY-TV tower in Blanchard, North Dakota, you would demand more money. This additional pay would be your compensation for the additional risk. The risk associated with different investments is like changing a light bulb at different heights.

Accounts insured by the Federal Deposit Insurance Corporation (FDIC) and the National Credit Union Association (NCUA), as well as U.S. Treasury bills, notes, and bonds, have zero default risk and therefore do not require a risk premium. In contrast, investing in a small business is a risky investment. According to the Small Business Administration, start-up companies have about a 50% chance of not being in business five years after they open their doors. To entice investors, small business investments therefore pay a higher rate of return to make up for the risk involved.

In summary, the risk premium is the difference between the risk-free rate of return and the expected yield of an investment that involves risk. It is a form of compensation for the investor who takes on the risk of the investment and it also provides an incentive for the investor to buy nonguaranteed investments.

savings
money set aside for future use in a secure, no-risk instrument

inflation
the overall increase in the price of goods and services over time

investment
an outlay of money for a profit, where the risk exists that either some or the entire original amount may be lost

risk premium
compensation for taking a risk

▼ **FIGURE 11.1**

Investment vs. savings decision process

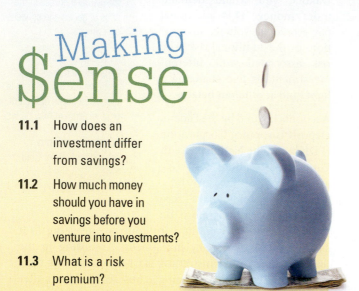

Making $ense

11.1 How does an investment differ from savings?

11.2 How much money should you have in savings before you venture into investments?

11.3 What is a risk premium?

2013, this insurance coverage will revert to $100,000. The FDIC and NCUA are funded through premiums charged to banks and credit unions. These premiums are used to fund a reserve in the event of a bank or credit union failure. If a bank or credit union were to declare bankruptcy, the FDIC or NCUA would take over that institution and pay depositors up to the maximum insured level using funds from the reserve.

Interest Rate Risk

Interest rate risk is the risk you take on when you lock into a fixed-rate investment for a specific length of time. A United States Treasury bond is backed by the full faith and credit of the U.S. government and therefore is considered to have no default risk, however, it does have interest rate risk.

The current value of a bond is dependent on its fixed interest rate as it compares with other investment options at the current interest rate. When interest rates go up on new bonds being offered, the selling price of your bond (with the lower fixed interest rate) goes down. When interest rates go down on new bonds being offered, the value of

> ❝ You can only get poor quickly; getting rich is slow. ❞
>
> —JANE BRYANT QUINN, *American financial journalist (1939–)*

11.2 RISK AND RETURN

■■ **LO 11-2** Analyze the risk and return on varying investment products.

To determine the risk premium on an investment, it is important to know the different types of risk associated with investment options. The major types of risk are: default risk or credit risk, interest rate risk, market risk, and liquidity risk.

Default or Credit Risk

Default or **credit risk** is the risk that the company you have invested in may declare bankruptcy; as a result, you might lose part or all of your investment in the company. In the 2009 Chrysler bankruptcy, secured bondholders received only $0.26 on every dollar they invested. In most bankruptcies, the stockholders lose all of their investment.

For deposits at banks and credit unions, the federal government takes on the credit risk through the FDIC and NCUA. These federal agencies currently insure bank and credit union accounts up to $250,000, but on December 31,

your bond (which is paying a higher fixed interest rate) increases. Figure 11.2 reflects the inverse relationship between bond prices and the interest rate. Bonds are discussed in more detail in Chapter 14.

There is great risk investing in companies that may not make it through an economic rough spell—but also possible reward.

Interest rate risk example

Assume you purchase a $10,000, 10-year bond at 5% with interest payments of $500/year. If you hold the bond until maturity (10 years), you will receive $500 every year plus the original $10,000 investment after 10 years. On the other hand, consider how the interest rate impacts your investment if you sell the bond after five years (before maturity):

If the current interest rate for similar investments is 10%, the value of your bond will be $8,104.

Since competing bonds are earning 10%, you will need to *discount* your bond (lower your price to make up for the difference in earnings for the remaining five years).

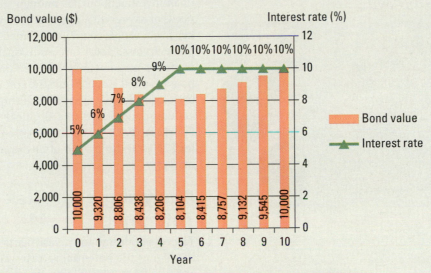

If the current interest rate for similar investments is 2%, the value of your bond will be $11,414.

Since competing bonds are earning only 2%, you will be able to sell your bond at a *premium* (to accommodate for the difference in earnings for the remaining five years).

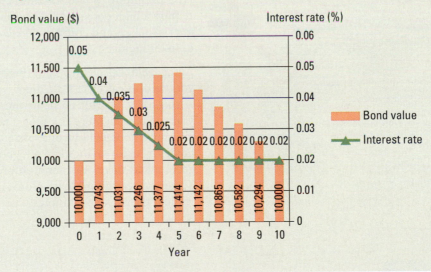

Market Risk

Market risk is the risk that an investment's value will decrease due to changes in the market. In 2008, market risk spiked and investment values plummeted in the housing market, mainly due to subprime mortgages. *Subprime mortgages,* mortgages made to home buyers with low credit ratings, have a higher default risk, so the lender charges a higher interest rate. Before the housing market collapsed, people with low credit ratings were able to receive financing for new homes and bigger homes easily. Through substandard lending practices (such as offering low "teaser" interest rates, failing to verify applicants' income, and committing loan application fraud) many people received loans they could not afford, and many of them eventually lost their homes.

liquidity risk

risk of not being able to cash out an investment quickly enough to meet cash flow needs or to prevent a loss

An overbuilt housing market, along with the flood of home foreclosures, caused the supply of houses on the market to spike. Following these events, banks tightened their lending, and those with lower credit ratings were unable to get loans. Supply was greater than demand, and houses in many different areas of the country lost up to 40% of their value. At this point, many people owed more on their houses than they were worth.

Liquidity Risk

Liquidity risk is the risk of not being able to get cash out of an investment quickly enough either to meet cash flow needs or to prevent a loss. Again, in the 2008 housing market crash, people could not sell their houses fast enough to prevent a loss. Houses are traditionally very illiquid investments. It can sometimes take six months to a year to sell a house. To sell a house quickly, you may have to lower the price considerably. Those caught up in the housing market crash and forced to sell quickly suffered huge losses. For example, a $500,000 home (pre-crash) might have sold for $250,000 during and after the collapse of the housing market.

Analyzing Your Risk Tolerance

The rule of thumb for investments is the higher the risk, the higher the potential return—and the less likely you are to achieve this higher return. As an investor, you must differentiate between different types of investment risks and determine your willingness to pay the risk premium. Some investors are risk-averse and require a high potential return to offset the risk. Others are risk takers and enjoy the thrill of the ups and downs of investments.

Along with calculating your investment-risk tolerance, you need to calculate how much you can afford to lose. A single doctor with no debt who is making $250,000 a year can take on more risk than a family of four living on an annual household income of $60,000. The family has a higher need for savings and a higher risk of family emergencies and therefore cannot afford to lose any money. The doctor can afford to lose some money on investments without the risk of bankruptcy.

financialfitness:
NUMBERS GAME

T-Bill Security

Treasury bills (also known as T-bills) are one of the most marketable securities. T-bills are issued with 4-, 13-, 26-, or 52-week maturities. They minimize interest rate risk because they tie up your money for only a short period. When the Treasury bill matures, you receive your principal plus interest.

financialfitness:
ACTION ITEM

Measuring Your Risk Tolerance

To find out your investment risk tolerance, there are numerous online risk tolerance quizzes you can take. Two quiz options are provided by MSNmoney (http://www.moneycentral.msn.com/investor/calcs/n_riskq/main.asp) and Rutgers University (http://www.njaes.rutgers.edu/money/riskquiz/).

doing the MATH

11.1 Interest Rate Risk

Based on the example illustrated in Figure 11.2 on the previous page,

1. If you sold your bond after three years, what would its value have been if the current interest rate was 3%?

2. Would you be selling the bond at a discount or a premium?

11.3 THE INVESTMENT PYRAMID

■ ■ **LO 11-3** Interpret the hierarchies of the investment pyramid.

Your investment options should form a pyramid, with three distinct tiers layered on top of a foundation of savings (see Figure 11.3). To maintain a secure amount but still allow your money to grow, it is important to diversify your investments across the different risk tiers.

The theory of the investment pyramid is to diversify investments in proportion to their risk. Depending on your risk tolerance, time horizon, and investment goals, the percentage of investments found in each tier will vary.

Base: No-Risk, Known-Return Investments

The base of the pyramid is your savings. It is easily accessible cash you can use to smooth out unplanned events and expenditures. This savings base keeps you financially secure overall and keeps your budget stream on an even keel. It is important to maintain a strong foundation on which to build your investment pyramid.

Making $ense

11.4 Describe the four major types of investment risks.

11.5 Explain the relationship between investment risk and potential return on investment.

▼ **FIGURE 11.3**

Investment pyramid

Tier III: High-Risk, High-Potential Returns: options, futures, commodities, precious metals

Tier II: Riskier Intermediate Investments: junk bonds, real estate, aggressive growth funds

Tier II: Intermediate Risk: quality growth stocks and mutual funds, blue-chip stocks

Tier I: Relatively Low-Risk Investments: balanced mutual funds which include stocks and bonds, convertible bonds, preferred stock

Tier I: Low-Risk, Low-Return Investments: money market accounts, fixed-income mutual funds, high-grade corporate bonds, municipal bonds

Savings: U.S. Treasury securities, insured checking, savings and certificates of deposit, U.S. savings bonds

diversification
spreading assets among different investment options to reduce risk

portfolio
all the investments you hold

asset allocation
the diversification of the portfolio

Tier I: Low-Risk, Low-Return Investments

Tier I is your investment base and represents the strongest portion of your investment pool. Your low-risk investment options include money market accounts, fixed-income mutual funds, high-grade corporate bonds, and municipal bonds with foreseeable short-term returns. This tier is typically the largest percentage of your investment assets. These investments do have default risk, market risk, and interest rate risk associated with them, but the risk can be minimized by investing carefully.

Tier II: Intermediate-Risk, Intermediate-Return Investments

The middle investment tier is composed of intermediate-risk investments offering a stable return while still allowing for capital appreciation. Although more risky than the assets in your Tier I investment layer, these investments should still be relatively safe. This layer typically includes quality growth stocks, mutual funds, blue-chip stocks, bonds, real estate, and aggressive growth funds. Compared to Tier I investments, these investments have greater default risk, market risk, and interest rate risk associated with them. Upper Tier II investments, especially real estate, are associated with default risk and liquidity risk.

> " **Money is better than poverty, if only for financial reasons.** "
> —WOODY ALLEN, *American film director and screenwriter (1935–)*

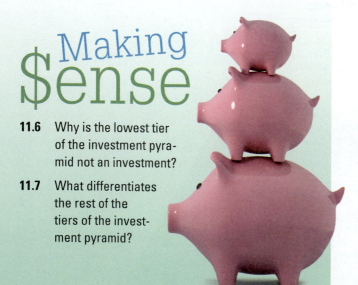

Making $ense

11.6 Why is the lowest tier of the investment pyramid not an investment?

11.7 What differentiates the rest of the tiers of the investment pyramid?

Tier III: High-Risk, High-Potential Return Investments

At the peak of the investment pyramid are high-risk investments. These investments may include foreign stocks or currencies, commodities, options, futures, and other complicated derivative investments that are beyond the scope of this introductory text. This should be the smallest percentage of your invested assets and should be made up of money you can lose without fear of bankruptcy. The money you invest here should not be indisposable, since taking a bad risk can lead to a loss in capital.

11.4 DIVERSIFICATION OF ASSETS

■ ■ **LO 11-4** Examine the importance of varying your investments.

You have heard the old saying "Don't put all your eggs in one basket." This is especially true when it comes to making wise investments.

Why Diversify?

Distributing your savings and investments among different bases lessens the risk of losing all of your "eggs" if the basket is dropped. You want to put your assets in several different investment baskets so that if one doesn't do so well, the assets in the other baskets are still intact. Spreading your assets among different investment options to reduce risk is known as **diversification**.

When you put money into more than one investment, you are building a **portfolio**. Diversification reduces your default risk, your interest rate risk, and your market risk. Diversification of your portfolio is also known as **asset allocation**. Using the investment pyramid to allocate your investments in proportion to their risk gives you a strong, secure base with appropriately proportioned building blocks to help maintain growth. When you allocate your money to each risk tier proportionally, you help offset your overall risks while continuing to grow your wealth.

Targeted and Automatic Asset-Allocation Mutual Funds

Many investment companies have established funds with targeted retirement dates that are diversified based on the

Making $ense

11.8 Why do you need to diversify your asset investments?

11.9 Why do investment companies have established funds with targeted retirement dates?

> ❝ **"The safest way to double your money is to fold it over and put it in your pocket."**
> —Kin Hubbard, *American journalist (1868–1930)* ❞

date on which you want to retire. These accounts automatically adjust your asset allocation to reduce your market risk as you approach retirement. These funds invest in U.S. stocks, international stocks, corporate bonds, and Treasury bonds. The investment companies typically allocate 80 to 90% of the retirement funds in domestic and international stocks and the remaining 10 to 20% in corporate bonds until you are about 25 years from retirement. As you get closer to retirement, the account shifts your asset allocation from stocks to bonds. At retirement, the portfolio has an asset allocation of 50% stocks and 50% bonds. During your retirement years, the asset allocation amount of stocks in the portfolio continues to decrease and bonds and cash increase so there is less exposure to risk from market swings as you come closer to withdrawing funds.

Investing in targeted retirement funds or asset-allocated mutual funds may not be right for you. Every investor has different goals, levels of risk tolerance, and time horizons for his or her investment strategies. The benefits of these target retirement funds or asset-allocated funds is that the fund manager takes on the task of deciding which stocks and bonds to buy or sell and how to structure the portfolio. This can save you time, and you may benefit from the professional expertise. A financial adviser can help you evaluate your options and manage your entire portfolio, if you would rather have a more hands-on role.

11.5 PORTFOLIO EVALUATION

■ ■ **LO 11-5** Compare portfolio asset allocations for the different personal finance life stages.

If you choose to manage your own portfolio, you must re-evaluate your investment goals, risk tolerance, portfolio returns, and asset allocation annually, if not more often, to make sure you have the right mix of investments. Be aware that your investment goals and risk tolerance will vary as you move through different life stages.

Maintaining Balance

It requires regular analysis and reallocation to maintain the proper balance in your portfolio. For example, say you have chosen a portfolio with 70% domestic stocks, 10% international stocks, and 20% corporate bonds. At the end of the first year, the international stocks have outperformed the others. As a result, your portfolio has shifted to

15% international stocks, 68% domestic stocks, and 17% corporate bonds. To maintain your original goals and risk tolerance and rebalance your portfolio, you may want to sell some of your international stocks and buy more corporate bonds and domestic stocks.

Life Stages and Investments

Your investment plans will change across your life stages. Therefore, it is important to know which investments are most appropriate at which stages.

independent life stage (age 16–24) Many young independent-stage adults have a lot of savings goals, yet they still want to enjoy a variety of life experiences. The key to achieving financial success is to have balance and discipline. At this stage, your most important savings goals include your education and retirement.

Checking your asset allocation regularly will help you to meet your investment goals.

For your education expenses, consider investing in a 529 college savings account. Established by the federal government, these accounts do not require you to pay taxes on their earnings and anyone (mom, dad, grandparents, uncles, aunts, etc.) can contribute to the account. In some state-sponsored plans, the contribution is deductible from state taxes as well.

Keep in mind that if you use birthday or other gift money to pay for certain qualified educational expenses, those earnings are tax-free. If relatives and parents wonder what to give as gifts, be creative and ask them to make a contribution to your future by making a deposit into a 529 college savings plan. Even if you are already in college, you can contribute to a 529 plan and the earnings will not be taxed. Since you will soon be in college, are in college, or are saving for graduate school in this life stage, your time horizon is short. Therefore you want to minimize your risks, maximize your liquidity, and invest in savings vehicles (savings account, inflation-proof bond mutual funds, or any guaranteed savings vehicles) on the base tier of the investment pyramid.

The other important investment goal in this life stage is your retirement. With a Roth IRA, you can become a millionaire by starting early, like Smart Sam and Dedicated Dave in Chapter 3. As of 2009, individuals can contribute up to $5,000 a year into a Roth IRA. Although there is no tax advantage on the contribution, a Roth IRA grows tax-free and all withdrawals are tax-free.

Since you are not going to retire for 40 to 50 years, you can take on more risk in the stock market. If the market declines, you have a long time for the market to recover. Therefore, your investment pyramid at this stage could be balanced across Tiers I, II, and III. See Figure 11.4 for a sample savings/investment strategy for the Independent Life Stage.

early family life stage (age 25–44) As you transition from the Independent to the Early Family Stage, you may or may not get married or have children. Most people will start their full-time working career in the Early Family Stage. If you contributed the maximum to your Roth IRA during your Independent Stage, you have made a great start toward financial independence during retirement. You need to keep contributing to your Roth IRA. Your time horizon for retirement is still 20 to 40 years away, so you can still tolerate market swings.

Independent life stage: sample savings/investment strategy

Savings/Investment Goals	Vehicle for Saving
Auto	Direct deposit into savings account
College savings for self	529 college savings plan
House down payment	Conservative mutual fund/money market account
Retirement	Roth IRA in stocks and bonds

Your place of employment may offer a 401(k) retirement savings plan. In some cases, employers also will match your contribution; this doubles your investment, so be sure to take full advantage of this opportunity. For example, your employer may match your contributions dollar for dollar up to 6% of your income. In such plans, if you contribute 6% of your income through a payroll deduction, your employer will match that amount so your total contribution is 12% of your salary. You may think that it is difficult to contribute 6% (or whatever the maximum) in order to take full advantage of your company's match but, in reality, you cannot afford to *not* take advantage of

this opportunity. If you contribute less, you are throwing away freely available money. By meeting the match, you are immediately doubling your money.

All 401(k) contributions are on a pretax basis, and the earnings are tax-deferred. This means your taxable earnings are decreased by your contribution amount. Being pretax and tax-deferred, you pay tax when you withdraw the money. With pretax contributions, you are reducing your take-home pay by only a little more than half of your contributed amount. For example, if you are in the 28% federal tax bracket and pay a 7% state tax and a 7.6% Social Security tax (for a total tax of 42.6%), then for every extra $1 you make, $0.42 goes toward taxes and $0.57 is take-home pay. When you contribute $100 to your 401(k) and your employer matches that $100, you are adding $200 to your retirement and reducing your take-home pay by only $57.00.

college savings and 529 plans In the Early Family Stage, you will probably want to establish savings accounts for the education of your children. In many states, one can contribute over $320,000 in 529 plans, and generally there are no income limitations or age restrictions.

Coverdell Education Savings Accounts (ESAs) The education IRA, renamed the Coverdell Education Savings

doing the MATH

11.2 Triple-Digit Earnings through 401(k) Contributions

Your tax liability is 40% of your salary of $100,000. For every $1,000 earned, $400 ($1,000 × 0.40) goes toward taxes and $600 ($1,000 − $400) is take-home pay.

All 401(k) contributions are on a pretax basis. Therefore, if you contribute $1,000 to a 401(k) and your employer matches $1,000, then $2,000 is added to your retirement fund, for what would have been only $600 in take-home pay. This is an immediate return on investment (ROI) of 333%.

If your tax liability is 30% of your salary of $50,000:

1. For every $1,000 earned, how much goes toward taxes?

2. How much of the $1,000 is take-home pay?

3. If you contribute $2,000 to your 401(k) and your employer matches $2,000, how much is added to your retirement that year?

4. How much will your $2,000 contribution to your 401(k) affect your take-home pay for the year?

5. What is your immediate ROI given your decision to contribute $2,000 to your 401(k)?

Making $ense

11.10 How do you maintain a balanced portfolio?

11.11 List some of the advantages of 529 college savings plans.

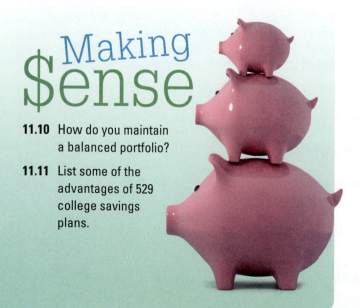

Savings/Investment Goals	Vehicle for Saving
Auto	Direct deposit into savings account
College savings for children	529 college savings plan, ESAs
House down payment	Move funds from conservative mutual fund/money market account to savings to purchase a house
Retirement	Roth IRA, 401(k)

Account (ESA) in 2002, is attractive for families saving for college and for elementary and secondary school expenses. However, there are more restrictions on ESAs than on 529 plans. An ESA is similar to a Roth IRA: Contributions are made after-tax and grow free of federal income tax. If you follow all the restrictions and use the money for qualified education expenses, withdrawals are tax-free. Before opening an ESA, consult with a tax adviser as to your eligibility, the maximum amount you can contribute, and the specific rules and regulations. As of 2010, you can contribute $2,000 annually to an ESA. See Figure 11.5 for a sample savings/investment strategy for the early family life stage.

empty nest life stage (age 41–65) The Empty Nest Life Stage is the time when you are making withdrawals from your 529 or educational savings account for your children. In this life stage, it may seem like all of your money is going to pay for college expenses, and you might have to put off buying a new car until the college tuition bills are paid. While this is going on, it is very important to continue contributing to your retirement plans—your 401(k) and Roth IRA. Your children may also be able to help contribute to their college education.

In this life stage, you are in your prime earning years. After the kids have graduated from college and the house and car have been paid off, you will have more disposable income than ever before. This is the time to contribute the maximum amount to your retirement accounts. This will help you both lower your taxable income and reach financial independence sooner. If you have been a regular contributor to your retirement plans since you started working, these final years will be icing on the cake. Your early-retirement dollars have been growing for over 40 years. If you started to contribute to your retirement funds late in life, you may have to work a little longer and contribute more to reach your financial independence point.

At this life stage, you may be looking for a second home to use for vacations, provide rental income while you are working, and then serve as a retirement home when you finish your career. Be wary of a long financing period for your second home. Your goal should be to have your home paid for by the time you retire.

retirement life stage (age 66+) Now is the time to enjoy your retirement savings and work only for the fun of it. You may choose to volunteer or work for a favorite charity, but you will no longer need to work for money. If your retirement nest egg is not large enough, you may choose to work part-time to supplement your retirement income. An income of $20,000 a year is equal to a $400,000 retirement savings earning 5% interest. You may have the opportunity to travel more often and do what you have always wanted to do. Your investments should be conservative, yet you should still own stocks to outpace inflation. ■

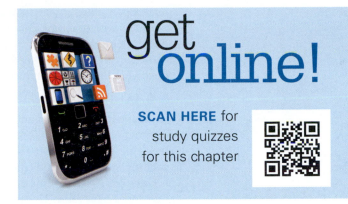

get online!

SCAN HERE for study quizzes for this chapter

Learn. ❯ Plan & Act. ❯ Evaluate.

➡ **LEARN.** This chapter defined the difference between savings and investments and described the various financial tools that fall into these two categories. It is important to maintain a secure amount of savings as well as to invest in order to grow your purchasing power. Building your portfolio according to the investment pyramid will help to diversify your investments across the risk tiers; the proportion of your investment in each tier will vary depending on your risk tolerance, time horizon, and investment goals. Typically, the higher the risk level of the investment, the greater the potential for substantial gains—and for substantial losses. No money should ever be placed in a high-risk, Tier III investment option that you could not afford to lose. The nature of the market dictates that there will be periodic upturns and downturns. Not everyone is cut out for the investment roller coaster ride, particularly not for the extreme volatility that can accompany the highest-risk investments. Investing is a long-term process and, if your assets are well-diversified, your money should grow as time passes.

SUMMARY

■■ **LO 11-1** Distinguish between savings and investments.

Deciding whether to save or invest and knowing which savings or investment vehicle to use depend on when you will need the money. Money needed within the next 10 years should be saved in a risk-free savings instrument—for example, a savings account, a certificate of deposit, or U.S. Treasury bills, notes, and bonds.

Inflation is the overall increase in the price of goods and services over time. The value of a dollar is its purchasing power. As inflation rises, your dollar buys a smaller amount of goods and services. Saving your money in a low-risk account keeps your purchasing power in line with inflation and maintains its value, but that money will not grow in terms of purchasing power. The advantage of investing over saving is that it gives you a chance to beat inflation.

With investing, you risk losing some or all of your investment. The risk premium is a form of compensation for the investor who takes on the risk of the investment.

■■ **LO 11-2** Analyze the risk and return on varying investment products.

The major types of risk are: default (credit) risk, interest rate risk, market risk, and liquidity risk. *Default (credit) risk* is the risk that a company in which you have invested may declare

 Money frees you from doing things you dislike. Since I dislike doing nearly everything, money is handy. ❞

—GROUCHO MARX, *American actor (1890–1977)*

bankruptcy. *Interest rate risk* is the risk you take when you lock into a fixed-rate investment for a specific length of time. *Market risk* is the risk that the value of your investment will decrease due to changes in the market. *Liquidity risk* is the risk of not being able to cash out an investment quickly enough either to meet cash flow needs or to prevent a loss. The higher the risk, the higher the potential return, and the less likely you are to achieve the higher return.

■ ■ ■ LO 11-3 Interpret the hierarchies of the investment pyramid.

To maintain a secure amount but still grow your money, diversify your investments across the different risk options. The investment pyramid suggests diversifying investments in proportion to their risk. Your base is a *no-risk, known-return* savings zone. Tier I, the *low-risk, low-return* zone, is your investment base and represents the strongest portion of your investment pool (money market accounts, fixed-income mutual funds, high-grade corporate bonds, and municipal bonds that have foreseeable returns). Tier II, the *intermediate-risk, intermediate-return* zone, is composed of intermediate-risk investments offering a stable return while still allowing for capital appreciation (quality growth stocks and mutual funds, blue-chip stocks, junk bonds, real estate, and aggressive growth funds). Tier III, the *high-risk, high-return* zone, is at the peak of the investment pyramid and includes the riskiest investments. These should be the smallest percentage of your invested assets and should be made up of money you can lose without fear of bankruptcy. Not every investor will feel comfortable selecting an investment from Tier III.

■ ■ ■ LO 11-4 Examine the importance of varying your investments.

When you put money into more than one investment, you are building a portfolio. Diversification (asset allocation) reduces your risks by allocating your investments proportionally to the investment pyramid; as a result, you have a strong secure base with appropriately proportioned building blocks to help maintain growth. When you allocate your investments to each tier in proportion to their risk, you mitigate your overall risk while continuing to grow your wealth. Many investment companies have established targeted funds that are diversified based upon how many years you have to reach a given goal. These accounts automatically adjust your assets to reduce market risk as you approach your stated goal.

■ ■ ■ LO 11-5 Compare portfolio asset allocations for the different personal finance life stages.

If you choose to manage your own portfolio, you must re-evaluate your investment goals, risk tolerance, portfolio returns, and asset allocation on at least an annual basis and more often during times of economic volatility. Depending on your financial life stage, your investment allocations will vary.

⮕ PLAN & ACT. As you assess your current financial needs, start to think about which savings and investment options best fit. Your *Plan & Act* to do list is as follows:

☐ To assess your risk tolerance, take the MarketPsych Questionnaire, online at http://www.marketpsych.com, and complete Worksheet 1.1.

☐ Given your risk tolerance and current goals, customize your own investment pyramid (Worksheet 11.2).

⮕ EVALUATE. Following the completion of the worksheets, assess your investment strategy. If you need access to your money in the next 10 years, make sure you are investing in the lower two rungs of the investment pyramid (i.e., in money market accounts, fixed-income mutual funds, bonds, savings accounts, and certificates of deposit). Before starting any investment plan, make sure you understand the balance between risk and return and know your own comfort level with assuming investment risk.

›› GoalTracker

Open your online GoalTracker and consider how you have allocated your investments in the investment pyramid (Worksheet 11.2). Are you making the appropriate allocations in building your emergency fund? Does your investment strategy support your overall SMART goals?

Asset Allocation

Credit Risk

Default Risk

Diversification

Inflation

Interest Rate Risk

Investment

Liquidity Risk

Market Risk

Portfolio

Risk Premium

Savings

self-test questions

1. The first question to ask yourself when deciding whether to save or invest is: *(LO 11-1)*

   a. How much money do I have in an emergency fund?

   b. When will I need the money?

   c. Is the money insured?

   d. Can I get at least a 10% return on this money?

2. You just received a $5,000 gift from your rich uncle and you don't know whether to invest or save the money. You want to use the money to help purchase a new car in four years. Where should you invest the money? *(LO 11-1)*

   a. In a safe, insured, guaranteed investment

   b. In an index mutual fund

   c. In gold or other precious metals

   d. Under your mattress

3. Which of the following would *not* be considered an appropriate savings vehicle for an emergency fund? *(LO 11-1)*

   a. Savings account

   b. Certificate of deposit

   c. High-quality stocks

   d. Antique cars

4. Savings: *(LO 11-1)*

   a. Should be used for accumulating enough money to cover day-to-day expenses

   b. Will not necessarily make you rich, but will keep you from being poor

   c. Should consist of six to nine months of income

   d. All of the above

5. Which instrument does *not* have a zero default risk? *(LO 11-1)*

   a. A Federal Deposit Insurance Corporation (FDIC) account

   b. A National Credit Union Association (NCUA) account

   c. A mutual fund account

   d. U.S. Treasury bills

6. Inflation: *(LO 11-1)*

   a. Has no impact on your savings and investments

   b. Causes prices to decrease over time

   c. Makes your money grow faster

   d. Is the overall increase in the price of goods and services over time

7. What proportion of your income should you have in savings? *(LO 11-2)*

   a. 2–3 months of income

   b. 6–9 months of income

   c. 12 months of income

   d. 2 years of income

8. The general rule of thumb is the _____ the risk, the _____ the return will be. *(LO 11-2)*

   a. higher; higher

   b. lower; higher

   c. higher; lower

   d. lower; lower

   e. (a) and (d)

   f. (b) and (c)

9. For people to invest in riskier investments, the investment must pay a/an _____ to offset the risk. *(LO 11-2)*

   a. investment premium

   b. investment incentive

   c. personal guarantee

   d. risk premium

10. Default risk: *(LO 11-2)*

    a. Is the risk that a firm in which you have invested will declare bankruptcy and your investment will become worthless

    b. Should be calculated as part of your risk premium

    c. Is zero for FDIC- and NCUA-insured accounts, up to $250,000.

    d. All of the above

11. Interest rate risk: *(LO 11-2)*

    a. Is the risk associated with an increase or decrease in interest rates

    b. Applies only to bonds

    c. Is not considered in the risk premium

    d. All of the above

12. Market risk: *(LO 11-2)*

    a. Is the risk that the value of your investment will decrease due to changes in the market

    b. Spiked during the housing crisis of 2007–2009

    c. Should be calculated as part of your risk premium

    d. All of the above

13. Liquidity risk: *(LO 11-2)*

    a. Is the risk that you will not be able to cash out your investment quickly enough to either meet your cash flow needs or prevent a loss

    b. Only applies to the housing market

    c. Increases as the liquidity of an investment increases

    d. All of the above

14. Risk tolerance for savings and investments: *(LO 11-2)*

    a. Is the same for every individual

    b. Is dependent on the individual

    c. Is not important when deciding on an investment strategy

    d. Should be increased to meet your financial goals

15. If you have a high risk tolerance and you want to invest money for the long-term, you might invest in: *(LO 11-3)*

    a. Certificates of deposit

    b. Fixed-income mutual funds and high-grade corporate bonds

    c. Balanced mutual funds

    d. Precious metals

16. The base of the investment pyramid consists of: *(LO 11-3)*

    a. U.S. Treasury securities, insured savings, checking accounts, certificates of deposit, and U.S. savings bonds

    b. Money market accounts, fixed-income mutual funds, high-grade corporate bonds, and municipal bonds

    c. Blue-chip stocks

    d. Junk bonds, real estate, and aggressive growth funds

17. The investment pyramid: *(LO 11-3)*

    a. Was created in Egypt

    b. Is not reflective of the risk of investments

    c. Is only for people with incomes over $100,000 annually

    d. Is a guideline for investing and saving

18. You should evaluate your investments: *(LO 11-5)*

    a. Only when you make the initial investment

    b. At least once a year or any time there is a major life change

    c. Only when you sell an investment

    d. Only when the market decreases 10% or more

19. Which instrument is *not* typical for persons in the independent personal finance life stage? *(LO 11-5)*

    a. Direct deposit into savings account

    b. 529 college savings plan

    c. Conservative mutual fund

    d. Quality stocks

    e. Roth IRA

20. Which life stage is the best time to start putting money into a Roth IRA to start building your retirement fund? *(LO 11-5)*

    a. Independent

    b. Early Family

    c. Empty Nest

    d. Retirement

problems

1. What is the impact of a savings account's purchasing power if it is earning 3% APY and inflation has been 4% for the past year? *(LO 11-1)*

2. A family with an annual take-home pay of $120,000 a year needs how much in its emergency fund? *(LO 11-1)*

3. A decade ago, your parents purchased a 20-year, $1,000 Treasury bond. The interest rate at the time of purchase was 5%. Today, comparable bonds are paying 7%. Approximately how much could they sell this bond for? *(LO 11-1)*

4. You and a friend want to go on a bike trek through France. Your friend wants to invest $200 a month for four years in a money market account that is earning 4%. You would prefer to go now, taking out a loan for $10,000 at 11% and paying it off over the next four years. If inflation runs at 2% for the next four years, what is the true difference in cost between the two options? *(LO 11-1)*

5. It is deemed that your niece, Jenny (who is two), will be going to a four-year college that will cost her no more than $30,000/year. If Grandpa is going to buy U.S. Treasury bonds at 4% interest for Jenny, what dollar amount will he need to buy so that she has $120,000 at the start of college? *(LO 11-2)*

6. You like to keep your investment risks at a 70–20–10 proportion (stocks-bonds-cash). After the first year, your $10,000 investment doubled in value to $20,000, with $16,000 in stock, $2,750 in bonds, and $1,250 in cash. How should you allocate your assets to maintain your original goals and rebalance your portfolio to retain the 70–20–10 proportion in investments? *(LO 11-5)*

7. When you first started working, your target retirement account allocated 90% of the funds to domestic and international stocks and 10% to corporate bonds, with plans to shift to an allocation of 50% stock and 50% bonds upon retirement. You are now ready for retirement with $5,750,000 in your fund. How much money should be in stocks, and how much should be in bonds? *(LO 11-5)*

8. If your tax liability is 25% of your salary of $40,000, *(LO 11-5)*
   a. For every $1 earned, how much goes toward taxes?
   b. How much of each $1 is take-home pay?
   c. If you contribute $1,000 to your 401(k) and your employer matches $1,000, how much is added to your retirement that year?
   d. How much did the $1,000 contribution to your 401(k) affect your take-home pay for the year?
   e. What was your immediate ROI when you decided to contribute $1,000 to your 401(k)?

you're the expert

1. A decade ago, Monty purchased a 30-year, $1,000 Treasury bond. The interest rate at the time of purchase was 7%. Today, comparable bonds are paying 5%. Approximately how much could Monty sell his bond for? Explain why the bond has increased in value. *(LO 11-1)*

2. Elaine is young, healthy, and single. Fresh out of college, she has just started a new job with a $32,000 annual salary. She has approximately $500 left at the end of each month after covering budgetary needs.

   a. How many months will it take to build her emergency fund? *(LO 11-1)*
   b. What are some appropriate emergency fund investment options? *(LO 11-1)*
   c. After her emergency fund is established, how should Elaine begin allocating her $500/month? *(LO 11-3)*
      (1) If she has a low risk tolerance?
      (2) If she has a medium risk tolerance?
      (3) If she has a high risk tolerance?

3. Casey has $1,000 that she will not need for three months. Her bank is offering three-month CDs at 3%. Disney stock has been doing well lately, averaging about an 8% return. Calculate the risk-return trade-off amount. Which investment option should Casey exercise? Why? *(LO 11-4)*

4. Pat would like to invest in a targeted retirement fund diversified across U.S. stocks, international stocks, corporate bonds, and Treasury bonds. *(LO 11-4)*

   a. What asset allocation would you recommend to Pat if he is 30 years from retirement?
   b. How should Pat adjust those allocations when he is 10 years from retirement?
   c. What adjustments would you suggest Pat make at the time of retirement?

5. Annie and Frank are married, with one toddler and another baby on the way. They have their emergency fund built up. Of their monthly budget, $1,200/month can be allocated toward their savings for their next car, a down payment for a house, and a college savings account for their two children. Additionally, it would be nice if they could start putting aside a little for retirement. *(LO 11-5)*

   a. Which instruments would you recommend for them to explore for each goal?
   b. What amount would you suggest they allocate to each instrument over the next 24 months (which is when they hope to be moving into a new home as well as buying a car)? Why?

11.1 FINANCIAL PSYCHOLOGY QUESTIONNAIRE

Complete the MarketPsych Questionnaire at http://www.marketpsych.com/test_question.php?id=8. The questionnaire takes you through thought-provoking questions in the areas of financial anxiety, interest in learning about and tracking investments, your discipline in staying organized and preparing for contingencies, and your "thrill-seeking" investment desires. The quiz also helps you evaluate your risk-tolerance level. After completing the questionnaire, you will receive a detailed wealth-psychology profile. Your customized profile will help you in selecting the right tools for your wealth-accumulation journey. Open Worksheet 11.1 to answer the following questions:

1. What did you learn about your wealth-management personality traits?

2. Knowing this, what types of investment tools will you be most likely to invest in?

11.2 ASSESS YOUR RISK TOLERANCE

Using your current age, personal finance life stage, and financial risk tolerance, create a balanced investment portfolio according to the appropriate descriptions on Worksheet 11.2.

continuing case

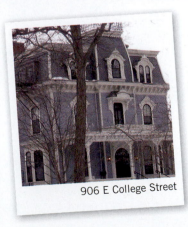

906 E College Street

Blake bought into a stock mutual fund as a retirement investment six months ago. Since then, he has watched the prices slowly drop each month. He realizes that there are periodic downturns in the market, and this retirement investment is not something he will tap for close to 40 years, but he is afraid that his investment will soon be worthless. He is tempted to cash in the stock and move what funds are left to another instrument. What advice would you give him?

A summary of the housemates' goals can be found in the first Continuing Case problem on page 27.

> "Little to little added, if oft done, in small time makes a good possession."
>
> —HESIOD, *Greek poet (~700 BC), Works and Days*

chapter twelve

mutual funds

n this chapter, you will learn about different types of mutual funds and how to determine which type best matches your savings objectives and risk tolerance. ■

LEARNING OBJECTIVES

After reading this chapter, you should be able to:

LO 12-1 Appreciate the history of mutual funds and understand mutual fund basics.

LO 12-2 Examine the types of mutual funds.

LO 12-3 Assess the benefits and risks of mutual funds.

LO 12-4 Evaluate mutual funds in terms of their class, commission, and fee structure.

LO 12-5 Plan how and where to invest in mutual funds.

◄ Max, age 27, political science undergrad, graduate student in history and education

Investment Seed Money

Max received $10,000 as a gift from his grandmother upon finishing college, and he did not want to spend the money frivolously. Since he had some savings, he saw this as an opportunity to start investing: "Being out of college, I had a lot of expenses and a lot of wants. I ended up investing my savings in the S&P (Standard and Poor's) 500 mutual funds to start my emergency fund and a nest egg. I wasn't making very much money at the time, but I set it up to add a continuous, automatic investment of $50 per month to help grow the fund." Max later went back to graduate school and used some of the money for tuition. "It was hard to take money out of the mutual fund, so I wanted to be sure I spent it on something that would make my grandmother proud. I continue to invest money into the fund and think of my grandmother every 15th of the month when I make my investment."

12.1 MUTUAL FUND BASICS

■ ■ **LO 12-1** Appreciate the history of mutual funds and understand mutual fund basics.

Mutual funds are investment instruments in which individuals pool their funds for investing in stocks, bonds, money markets instruments, and other assets. Mutual funds are managed by a professional money manager known as the **fund manager**, who buys and sells individual assets to best maximize the return on the fund given its specific investment objectives. Mutual funds are popular because they: (1) diversify investment risk by buying many different types of investments, (2) are managed by professional fund managers, and (3) allow people to invest with small amounts. Before investing in mutual funds, you should understand how they developed as financial instruments and how they operate today.

History of Mutual Funds

Mutual funds have been around since the 1800s, but they did not gain popularity until the 1980s when the stock market took off on a long **bull run** (a period during which stock prices in general are consistently rising). The **stock market** is a public market for trading ownership **shares** (known as *stock*) of a company among investors. At the time of this bull run, many companies were in the process of eliminating their defined-benefit pension retirement plans for employees and encouraging them to open 401(k) retirement plans instead. Mutual funds became popular vehicles for this purpose.

Disclosure of a fund for sale to the public is done in the form of a **prospectus**. The prospectus contains the facts an investor needs to know in order to make an informed investment decision and includes the fund's strategy, risk, and fees.

The first mutual fund in the United States was a closed-end fund started in 1893 as the Boston Property and Trust. **Closed-end mutual funds** raise a fixed amount of money for a company, and investors receive a fixed number of shares through the company's **initial public offering**, or IPO (first sale of stock to the public). The value of the shares is based on the total value of the fund. No new money is added to the fund, thus the name *closed-end*. In contrast, an **open-end mutual fund** allows continued investment into the fund and issues shares based on the value of the fund. The fund company will also buy back shares when investors want

Mutual funds can help you to capitalize on a bull run without as much exposure to risk as you may have if you invest in individual stocks.

to sell. In the stock market crash of 1929, most closed-end funds were wiped out; most mutual funds today are open-end funds.

By the end of 2009, mutual funds represented a significant component of many U.S. households' financial holdings. Among households owning mutual funds, the median amount invested in mutual funds was $80,000. Today, mutual funds also play a key role in achieving both the long- and short-term savings goals of U.S. households. In 2009, 76% of mutual fund–owning households indicated that their primary financial goal for their fund investments was saving for retirement; 96% of households that owned mutual funds held shares inside workplace retirement plans, individual retirement accounts (IRAs), and other tax-deferred accounts (see Figure 12.1 on the next page).

Mutual Fund Regulation

With the Securities Act of 1933 and the Securities Exchange Act of 1934, Congress enacted regulations requiring mutual funds to register with the **Securities and Exchange Commission (SEC)**. As the primary federal regulatory agency for the securities industry, the SEC promotes full disclosure and protects investors against fraudulent and manipulative practices in the securities markets.

Costs and Fees of Mutual Funds

No-load mutual funds became increasingly popular in the 1970s. A **no-load mutual fund** is a fund offered to the public that carries no purchase fee (front-end load) or redemption fee (back-end load). When you invest your money in a mutual fund, your asset ownership is not direct. Instead, you own a part of a fund which is invested in multiple assets. The price you pay for a share of a mutual fund is based on the net asset value of the fund. The **net asset value (NAV)** is the total value of all the assets in the mutual fund minus the cost and divided by the number of outstanding shares. The NAV is commonly referred to as the *share price* of the mutual fund.

All mutual funds have operating expenses that are passed along to shareholders. These expenses include payments to the fund's investment manager, recordkeeping expenses, custodial service expenses, taxes, legal expenses, and accounting and auditing fees. Total operating expenses divided by the average dollar value of the fund's assets under management is known as the fund's **expense ratio**. Expense ratios can also include a **12b-1 fee** to cover the marketing of the fund to potential investors as well as expenses involved in printing and mailing statements. Not all funds charge a 12b-1 fee, but if they do, they are required to disclose it in the prospectus. Most funds have an expense ratio between 0.2 and 2.5%, which lowers the return on the fund.

12.2 TYPES OF MUTUAL FUNDS

■ ■ **LO 12-2** Examine the types of mutual funds.

There are many types of mutual funds. The funds vary in terms of asset allocation (percentages of stocks, bonds, and short-term reserves), risk tolerance, and investment preferences and objectives. It is important to understand the different types of funds in order to select the type that best fits your goals.

Mutual funds are classified as being either open-end or closed-end funds. Within the open- and closed-end

Making $ense

12.1 What differentiates a closed-end fund from an open-end fund?

12.2 What does net asset value (NAV) measure?

12.3 What factors are considered in calculating a mutual fund's expense ratio?

▼ **FIGURE** 12.1

Characteristics of mutual fund investors, May 2009

How Many People Own Mutual Funds?

87 million individuals

50.4 million U.S. households

Who Are They?

50 years of age (median head of household)

76% are married or living with a partner

47% are college graduates

74% are employed (full- or part-time)

18% are Silent or GI Generation

44% are Baby Boomers

25% are Generation X

13% are Generation Y

$80,000 (median household income)

What Do They Own?

$150,000 (median household financial assets)

66% hold more than half of their financial assets in mutual funds

67% own IRAs

78% own defined-contribution retirement plan accounts

4 mutual funds (median number owned)

$80,000 (median mutual fund assets)

77% own equity funds

How and When Did They Make Their First Fund Purchase?

54% bought their first fund before 1995

62% purchased their first mutual fund through an employer-sponsored retirement plan

Why Do They Invest?

94% are saving for retirement

49% hold mutual funds to reduce taxable income

46% are saving for emergencies

26% are saving for education

Source: Investment Company Institute, http://www.icifactbook.org/fb_ch6.html#6.2.

financialfitness:
NUMBERS GAME

Expense Ratio Comparisons

Typical index funds have expense ratios from 0.15% to 1.00%, depending on the index. By comparison, an actively managed fund runs on an average expense ratio of about 1.5%.

fund categories, mutual funds can be categorized by the types of assets purchased (bond funds, equity/stock funds, balanced funds, global/international funds, or sector funds) and whether the fund is actively managed or is an index fund.

Actively Managed Mutual Funds

Actively managed mutual funds have a professional fund manager who looks for assets that will meet the investment objectives of the fund and maximize returns given those investment objectives. To meet the investment objectives of the fund, the fund manager researches different companies to decide if investing in them is a wise choice. At the same time, the fund manager looks at the current holdings in the portfolio to see which assets should be sold. Actively managed mutual funds usually have higher expense ratios to cover the compensation of the fund manager and staff and to pay administrative fees. These funds also buy and sell assets more frequently than index funds, which can result in higher short-term capital gains and higher transaction costs.

Index Market Funds

Index funds imitate well-known stock indexes such as the **Standard & Poor's 500** or the **Russell 2000** (two commonly used benchmarks for the overall U.S. stock market) or the entire stock market. These funds are not actively managed by a fund manager looking for the best asset to buy; these funds try to hold all of the securities in the same proportion. As a result, index funds usually have lower expense ratios and do not buy and sell assets as often. The lower turnover in buying and selling assets as compared to actively managed funds results in lower capital gains tax (because the assets are usually held longer). Many index funds use computer modeling to make investment decisions about which securities to buy and sell.

Exchange-Traded Funds (ETFs)

A relatively recent innovation (see Figure 12.2 on p. 303), *exchange-traded funds (ETFs)* are a little like closed-end mutual funds and a little like stocks. They are often structured as open-end investments but they are traded throughout the day on a stock exchange, just like closed-end mutual funds, at prices generally approximating the ETF's net asset value.

Most ETFs are index funds and track stock market indexes. Institutional investors issue or redeem the shares in large blocks (typically of 50,000 shares), making ETFs more efficient than traditional mutual funds and thereby resulting in lower expenses.

Individuals may purchase ETFs through full-service brokers, discount brokers, online brokers, and many mutual fund companies. ETFs can be purchased to meet practically any investment strategy or style. ETFs are also valuable for foreign investors who are often able to buy and sell securities traded on a stock market, but who, for regulatory reasons, are limited in their ability to participate in traditional U.S. mutual funds.

Equity Mutual Funds

Equity funds (also known as stock funds) consist mainly of stock investments and are the most common type of mutual fund. Often, equity funds focus on specific types of investments according to a particular strategy or type of issuer. The objective of an equity fund is long-term growth through capital gains, although dividends also have been an important source of total return historically. Specific equity funds may focus on a certain sector of the market or may be geared toward a certain level of risk. Equity funds can be distinguished by several properties. These properties are discussed further in Chapter 13 but, in general, equity funds typically focus on:

1. A specific style according to Morningstar Style Box (i.e., value, blend, growth)

2. Securities solely from one country or from many countries, such as the European Stock Index and emerging markets stock indexes

no-load mutual fund a fund offered to the public that carries no purchase fee (front-end load) or redemption fee (back-end load)

net asset value (NAV) the dollar value of a single mutual fund share based on the value of the underlying assets of the fund, minus its liabilities, divided by the number of shares outstanding; calculated at the end of each business day

expense ratio (of a mutual fund) the operating costs expressed as a percentage of the fund's average net assets for a given time period

12b-1 fee an extra fee charged by some mutual funds to cover promotion, distributions, marketing expenses, and sometimes commissions to brokers

Scan here for more information on the latest events "In the News"

Why investment choices in your 401(k) might change

Have the investment offerings in your 401(k) plan changed recently? If not, they might soon. That's because as plan sponsors scrutinize the cost of 401(k) plan investment options more closely, there is a growing trend away from higher-cost retail mutual funds to lower-cost "institutional" versions of these funds and to low-cost index funds. According to a recent survey by Hewitt Associates, a human resources consulting company, 74% of employers are making efforts to reduce 401(k) plan expenses, up from 57% in 2007. Moreover, according to the Hewitt study, 51% of employers are moving to lower-cost investment options.

To understand what's going on, a history lesson is helpful. When 401(k) plans were first introduced in the 1980s, plan design was largely a function of Department of Labor regulations, which required that a plan have at least three diversified investment alternatives. Typical plans in those days featured only about five or six investment options. But in the 1990s, as companies began scaling back traditional pensions and 401(k)s became central to workers' retirement security, plans started providing many more investment options. The thinking was this would enhance plan participants' ability to meet their retirement savings goals and better diversify their portfolio to mitigate risk. In this stage of 401(k) plan design, sponsors turned to the mutual fund industry to supply the investment vehicles to augment existing plans. A typical design would retain a core of investment options, supplemented by an expanded lineup of retail mutual funds. Many plans grew to include dozens, and in some cases, hundreds of investment choices. This new structure was largely praised by participants, as 401(k) plans were taking on an ever-increasing role in funding their retirement income needs.

There is, however, a problem with using retail mutual fund shares—they typically have the same cost structure, known as the expense ratio, within a 401(k) plan as they do when offered to retail investors. Why is the expense ratio of a mutual fund an issue? Some costs are related to the management of the fund to pay for investment research, professional management, and trading costs for the underlying securities. When a fund exhibits superior performance relative to its peers and its benchmarks, those costs are justified. But other costs can include marketing the fund to the public to help a fund company stand out from the competition. In other words, retail fund shareholders are paying not just for the management of their money, but also for all of those TV commercials. With retail mutual fund shares in a 401(k) plan, the plan participant may still pay for these marketing costs (known as a 12b-1 fee) in addition to the management fees.

To critics, marketing and advertising costs for retail funds offered to the general investing public make sense within reasonable limits but do not make much sense when they are being tacked on to investment options within a 401(k) plan. After all, plan participants are not shopping among thousands of retail funds, they are merely choosing between a few dozen options within their 401(k) plan. These marketing and advertising costs associated with retail funds within 401(k) plans essentially drain money away from retirement savers. So now, we've moved into a new stage, where 401(k) plans are evolving yet again as sponsors assume a fiduciary duty to participants to keep costs modest.

. . . While expense ratio and other mutual fund internal costs are important, the investment recommendations we make for clients are primarily driven by expected total return, portfolio diversification attributes, and risk reduction potential. When a plan sponsor adds a lower-cost investment option that demonstrates superior performance compared to the fund it replaced, we view it as a "win-win" for plan participants.

DAVID KUDLA, "Why Investment Choices in Your 401(k) Might Change," *Forbes*, July 8, 2010. Reprinted with permission.

Questions

1 What is your position on 401(k) plans that spend earnings on marketing costs?

2 How can you educate yourself on your 401(k) options?

> ❝ When I think I have found the solution I must prove I am right. I know of only one way to prove it; and that is, with my own money. ❞
> —JESSE LIVERMORE, *Famous early 20th century stock trader (1877–1940)*

3. Specific sectors of the economy, such as energy, health care, and technology

4. The size of the companies in which the fund invests. Companies are classified by their capitalized size (or *cap*) and are generally labeled small (<$1 billion), medium ($1 − $5 billion), or large (>$5 billion) cap.

Bond Mutual Funds

Bond funds specify the term or the fixed set of time (short-, medium-, or long-term) before they mature. Government bond funds (municipal, state, and federal) generally have lower returns, but they offer tax advantages and lower risk. Corporate bonds have a default risk and do not have the special tax advantages that government bonds offer, but pay a higher rate of return. Corporate bond funds are generally categorized into investment-grade bonds and high-yield or junk bonds. We will cover bonds in more detail in Chapter 14.

Bond funds can be made up of federal, state, municipality, or corporate bonds and are generally classified by the type of bonds held in the fund. An entity issues bonds when it needs to raise money. For example, if your local city needs to build a new parking garage, it may issue revenue bonds. In effect, investors who buy the revenue bonds are lending the bond issuer (the city) money to build the parking garage. This bond is classified as a revenue bond because the money being lent to the city will be repaid by the revenue generated by the new parking garage. Corporations also issue bonds to finance plant expansions or large capital improvements.

Money Market Mutual Funds

Money market funds hold the least risk, pay the lowest rates of return, and offer high quality with high liquidity.

You can redeem money market shares at any time, unlike certificates of deposit (CDs). However, the FDIC (Federal Deposit Insurance Corporation) does not insure money market mutual funds, as it does savings accounts or CDs. Money market funds are open-end mutual funds that invest in short-term debt securities. Under the Securities and Exchange Commission's Investment Company Act, money market funds must focus on buying the highest rated debt (or bonds) maturing in less than 13 months. This act also regulates the money market mutual fund's weighted-average maturity limit.

A mutual fund's **weighted-average maturity (WAM)** is the length of time until the average security in a fund will mature or be redeemed by its issuer. The WAM is an indication of the money market fund's sensitivity to interest rate changes: A longer weighted-average maturity implies greater volatility in response to interest rate changes. A money market portfolio must maintain a WAM of 90 days or less and not invest more than 5% in any one issuer, except for government securities and repurchase agreements. Eligible money market securities include **commercial paper** (unsecured

Standard & Poor's 500 (S&P 500)
a market-performance measurement index, derived from the stock of 500 large companies on the U.S. market; designed to be a leading indicator of U.S. equities; it is meant to reflect the risk/return characteristics of the large-cap companies

Russell 2000
a market-performance measurement index, derived from the stock of the 200 smallest companies on the U.S. market

weighted-average maturity (WAM)
the length of time until the average security in a fund will mature or be redeemed by its issuer

commercial paper
an unsecured obligation issued by a corporation to finance its short-term credit needs

▼ **FIGURE** 12.2

Total net assets and number of ETFs, 1998–2009

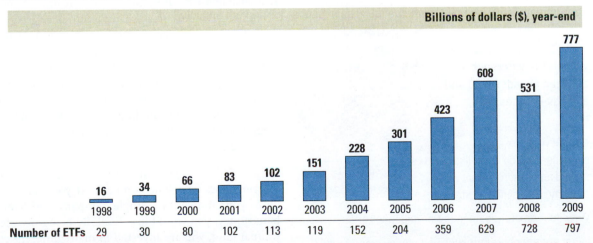

Note: Data prior to 2001 provided by Strategic Insight Simfund; data include ETFs not registered under the Investment Company Act of 1940; data exclude ETFs that invest primarily in other ETFs.

Sources: Investment Company Institute and Strategic Insight Simfund.

obligations issued by a corporation to finance its short-term credit needs), **repurchase agreements** (contracts whereby an entity sells some securities, agreeing to buy back the securities at a specified future time and price), short-term bonds, or other money funds.

Other Specialized Funds

Balanced mutual funds have a combination of stocks, bonds, and cash. Targeted retirement funds are balanced funds that hold all three investments in different proportions. The closer the date is to the targeted retirement date, the fewer number of stocks the fund will hold, and the more bonds and cash it will hold. You can also buy balanced funds set to a specific ratio, such as 65% stocks, 30% bonds, and 5% cash.

Global and **international funds** invest in companies from foreign countries. International funds generally invest only in foreign companies, while global funds will invest in international and domestic companies.

Sector funds invest in one identifiable sector of the economy. Common sector funds invest in technology, steel, energy, health care, finance, agribusiness, or other identifiable sectors. These funds can be more volatile

than others due to their lack of diversity across various industries.

12.3 BENEFITS AND RISKS OF MUTUAL FUNDS

■ ■ **LO 12-3** Assess the benefits and risks of mutual funds.

Mutual funds offer several advantages over investing in individual stocks, such as professional fund management and diversification. Whether actively managed or passively indexed, mutual funds are not immune to risks, though. They share the same risks associated with the underlying investments. If a fund invests primarily in stocks, it is subject to the same ups and downs as the stock market. If the mutual fund also invests in bonds, however, you still have interest rate risk but you have diversified your holdings.

Benefits

There are many benefits to investing in mutual funds, including convenience, efficiency, and transparency. These and other benefits are summarized in Figure 12.3.

professional fund manager A professional fund manager or investment adviser of a mutual fund is responsible for the investments in that fund. Fund managers are seasoned professionals with access to the best available research. Their sole responsibility is to make money for the fund, which is your reason for investing in the fund. Since in most cases fund managers' compensation is tied to the performance of the fund, they are motivated to make the fund grow. You do not have to analyze stocks, evaluate and rate bonds, or look for other assets when you find a mutual fund that meets your investment objectives.

diversification Diversification reduces the risk of a serious loss from one company. If you were to invest all of your money in a single company and it declared bankruptcy, you would lose it all. By being invested in a mutual fund, you are invested in many different companies. If one goes bankrupt or has serious problems, you do not lose your entire investment. Many experts say that

Making $ense

12.4 How are mutual funds classified?

12.5 What is the difference between an index fund and an actively managed fund?

12.6 In what way are exchange-traded funds like mutual funds, and in what way are they more similar to stock?

12.7 Why do index funds have lower expense ratios?

12.8 What are the characteristics of a money market fund?

Benefits of investing in mutual funds

Professionally Managed	• The fund manager's job is to make money for the fund, investing in assets that match the investment/risk strategy of the fund
Diversification	• In a mutual fund, your investment is as diversified as the entire fund
Variety	• 8,000+ funds; varying degrees of risk/investment objectives; helps align investment objectives with risk tolerance
Easy to Understand	• Mutual fund prospectuses are written in common English; fees, major holdings, risks, and investment strategy are readily explained
Easy to Research	• Online websites allow you to examine the past performance, expense ratio, and what others have to say
Low Initial Investment	• Many allow investors to establish an account for as little as $50 if automatic monthly transfers into the account are set up
Automatic Investment	• Can take advantage of continuous automatic investing by setting up an automatic transfer from checking account
Dividends and Capital Gains Reinvested	• Dividend checks and capital gains are automatically reinvested into mutual fund account
Recordkeeping Ease	• Mutual fund companies carry out all the recordkeeping and each January, automatically send tax information for previous year
Liquidity	• Many funds allow transfer of funds from the sale of mutual fund shares directly into a checking or savings account (1–2 days after the sale)

it would take 100 or more stocks and over $250,000 to reduce the risk of owning individual stocks and achieve the diversification of mutual funds.

variety Mutual funds offer many different investment strategies to meet your investment needs. Mutual funds may be entirely invested in federal bonds, municipal bonds, corporate bonds, gold, silver, or stocks, or they may invest in a variety of stocks, bonds, and other investments. Within each asset classification, you can pick a fund that matches your risk tolerance and investment objectives. For example, in the bond asset classification, you can choose from federal short-term bonds, state bonds, tax-exempt bonds, investment-grade corporate bonds, and high-yield corporate bonds.

easy to understand Mutual funds were designed to be easy to understand. You do not have to have a master's degree in finance to pick a mutual fund that meets your investment criteria. Each fund has a prospectus

that clearly states its investment strategy and risks. A professional fund manager does the investing and trading of assets. However, you do have to actively monitor your fund and its holdings to be sure that the fund is meeting your investment objectives. You should also be aware of the history of your fund manager and pay particular attention if or when your fund manager changes. He or she is making decisions for the mutual fund in which you are investing. While a change of fund manager does not automatically mean you should sell your fund, you do need to monitor the new fund manager's performance to make certain it aligns with your expectations.

easy to research Many publications post "best of" lists that rate funds and investments on their performance, fees, customer service, and satisfaction. The lists are fun to look at, but you need to look beyond the list before you make any investment decisions. There are numerous websites and publications where you can research mutual funds. Popular websites for research include the following:

- Morningstar (www.morningstar.com)
- Yahoo Finance (http://finace.yahoo.com)
- Google Finance (www.google.com/finance)
- Value Line (www.valueline.com)
- *The Wall Street Journal* (www.wsj.com)
- MSN Money (www.money.msn.com)
- CNN Money (http://money.cnn.com)

low initial investment Many mutual funds make it easy to invest on a regular basis by allowing you to open the account with an automatic deposit into the mutual fund for as little as $50 per month. This allows you to invest in the stock market, bonds, balanced funds, or money market funds with a relatively small investment. You can challenge yourself to find $50 a month by stopping little leaks and then invest it in a mutual fund. All you have to do is stop a $1.65 little leak per day and you can invest over $600

a year. Then you will be on your way to saving your first $1 million, like Dedicated Dave in Chapter 3.

automatic investment By investing monthly or at regular intervals, not only are you able to invest small dollar amounts, but you also are able to take advantage of *continuous automatic investing*. Like Max in our chapter opener, you could have a strategy to invest $50 into a mutual fund on the 15th of every month. When the price of the mutual fund is high, your $50 will buy fewer shares. When the price of the mutual fund is low, your $50 will buy more shares. With this strategy, you will not have to worry about timing the market to buy low.

Continuous automatic investing is often confused with dollar-cost averaging, but they are different. Continuous automatic investing does not have any stated lump sum or end date. In contrast, **dollar-cost averaging** involves investing specific portions of a lump sum at specific times until the entire sum is invested, instead of investing the entire sum all at once.

For example, say your aunt gives you $10,000 because she is so proud of you for taking a personal finance class. You could invest the $10,000 all at once, or you could decide to invest $1,000 a month for 10 months. Like continuous automatic investing, you could buy some mutual fund shares at high prices and others at low prices, without trying to time the market. This method allows you to spread out your market risk. In contrast, if you invest all of your money at once and the market declines, you will have overpaid. Or, if the market is going up, you could lose out on the upswing. Figure 12.4 provides an illustration of $10,000 invested over 10 months using dollar-cost averaging.

There are pros and cons to dollar-cost averaging. If you are more risk-averse, you might feel more comfortable with investing that $10,000 over 10 months. If you are willing to take on more risk, you might invest it as a lump sum, knowing that the market could go up or down the next day. The disadvantage of incurring multiple transaction costs may outweigh the advantages of dollar-cost averaging if you spread the investment over just a short window of time.

financialfitness:
STOPPING LITTLE LEAKS

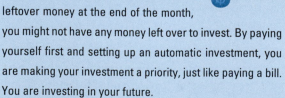

Automatic Investing

The other advantage of continuous automatic investing is that it encourages self-discipline. You will be paying yourself first, but you won't miss the money. If you wait to invest your leftover money at the end of the month, you might not have any money left over to invest. By paying yourself first and setting up an automatic investment, you are making your investment a priority, just like paying a bill. You are investing in your future.

dividends and capital gains reinvested With mutual funds, you do not receive dividend checks when the companies in your mutual fund pay dividends. The dividends from the individual stocks in the mutual fund are automatically reinvested into the mutual fund. You are issued more shares of the mutual fund based on the amount of the dividends, the net asset value, and how much you own. When a mutual fund sells an asset for a profit, it receives capital gains. These capital gains automatically reinvest into the mutual fund.

The federal government requires mutual funds to distribute their dividends and capital gains to shareholders at least once a year. Many mutual fund companies distribute dividends and capital gains once a quarter to the person of record on a specific date. The **person of record** is the person holding shares in the mutual fund on the day the fund distributes dividends and capital gains. This transaction is reflected on your monthly statement, and at the end of the year, you are also issued a Form 1099-DIV as a tax record for your dividend distribution and capital gains. With capital gains and dividend distributions, instead of receiving a check, you receive more shares of your mutual fund. This income is taxable in the year you receive the income. The downside to being issued more shares of the mutual fund is that you either have to sell some shares of your mutual fund or save cash from another resource to pay the taxes due.

ease of recordkeeping Mutual fund companies will send you a 1099-DIV form at the end of the

dollar-cost averaging
an investment strategy designed to reduce volatility in which securities, typically mutual funds, are purchased in fixed dollar amounts at regular intervals, regardless of what direction the market is moving

person of record
the individual holding shares in the mutual fund on the day the fund distributes dividends and capital gains

▼ **FIGURE** 12.4

Dollar-cost averaging example

Example: Investment of $1,000/month for 10 months			
Period	Invested	Share Price	Shares Bought
1/31/2011	$ 1,000	$100.01	10.00
2/28/2011	1,000	$ 98.54	10.15
3/31/2011	1,000	$101.20	9.88
4/30/2011	1,000	$103.43	9.67
5/31/2011	1,000	$102.23	9.78
6/30/2011	1,000	$103.78	9.64
7/31/2011	1,000	$104.23	9.59
8/31/2011	1,000	$106.02	9.43
9/30/2011	1,000	$105.99	9.43
10/31/2011	1,000	$108.87	9.19
Period End	$10,000		96.76

Average share price: $103.43 ($1,034.3 Sum of share prices / 10 prices)

doing the MATH

12.1 Cost Averaging

You plan to invest $100/month for six months. Given the share prices listed below, complete the table with the amount invested and the number of shares bought for the six months.

Period	Invested	Share Price	Shares Bought
1/31		$50.01	
2/28		$48.54	
3/31		$51.20	
4/30		$53.43	
5/31		$51.23	
6/30		$49.78	
Period end investment		Total shares bought	

What was the average share price over the last six months?

calendar year, reporting the dividends and capital gains you have received. If you sell your shares of the mutual fund, the fund company will determine the cost basis of your investment. The **cost basis** is the original value of a purchased asset, usually the purchase price. When you redeem your mutual fund shares, your capital gains are determined by subtracting the cost basis from your redemption value.

If you continuously automatically invest, your purchase prices could vary, making it difficult to keep track of the purchase price every month. The mutual fund company calculates this for you to determine whether you have a capital gain or loss when you redeem your shares. Many mutual fund companies now provide online access so you can review your portfolio and statement, as well as place buy and sell orders.

liquidity Mutual funds are traded only after the markets close, when they are able to calculate the net asset value (NAV) of the fund. This could be frustrating or beneficial depending on what the market does. When you place a buy or sell order, the order will not be executed until the end of the business day. From the time you decide to sell, the market could go up or down, therefore increasing or decreasing the amount of money you receive. For a buy order, this could increase or decrease the number of shares purchased, based on the same amount of money invested. On the other hand, buy or sell orders for *stocks*

are executed when the orders are received and at the price known when the orders are received. You know within minutes how much money your shares cost you or how much money you will receive from your sale.

The liquidity of mutual funds is not like walking in to a bank and making an immediate cash withdrawal. Once the sale is executed, money can be wired to a bank and either issued to you in a check or directly deposited into your account. For example, if you place a sale order today, it will be executed after the close of business and wired or directly deposited the next day. If you have a check issued, it will take longer, depending on the speed of the post office or service delivering the check.

Risks

An actively managed mutual fund is influenced by the people managing the fund. You want managers with proven track records of generating strong returns. Information about fund managers and their experience can be found online on www.Morningstar.com or in *The Wall Street Journal*. A fund's trading activity is measured by the **turnover rate** (the percentage of stocks bought and sold every year). The higher the turnover rate, the more likely it is that managers are buying and selling stocks quickly rather than holding them for a longer time. More trading is costly, as it results in more transaction fees and potentially higher short-term capital gains.

If you start with a small investment, you may have to choose a fund with somewhat higher expenses. As your account builds, you should be able to switch to a lower cost fund. If it is a retirement account, making this change should be tax-free. If not, you will want to consider the tax consequences of switching funds.

As with any investment, there is the possibility that your mutual fund may lose value. Case in point: In September 2008, the credit crisis took a dangerous downturn when New York's Reserve Primary Fund (the nation's oldest money fund) dropped its share prices below the standard $1 a share to 97 cents after marking down the value of $785 million in Lehman debt securities, following Lehman's filing for bankruptcy court protection. As stated in Chapter 11, mutual funds are low risk, but they are not a *no*-risk investment vehicle.

Making $ense

12.9 When are mutual fund buy and sell orders executed?

12.10 What is the difference between dollar-cost averaging and continuous automatic investing?

12.11 How are dividends and capital gains distributed in a mutual fund?

12.12 In a mutual fund, what does a high turnover rate indicate?

12.4 COSTS AND CLASSES OF MUTUAL FUNDS

■ ■ **LO 12-4** Evaluate mutual funds in terms of their class, commission, and fee structure.

Section 12.3 reviewed the benefits and reasons you would want to select mutual funds as an investment instrument.

In this section we will look at some of the costs involved. As we will see, the various classes of funds entail different costs.

Finding the Mutual Fund Price

The first and foremost cost of a mutual fund is its price. Information about mutual funds is readily available online. Figure 12.5 provides an example of the Vanguard 500 Index Fund Investor Shares (VFINX) online report. It lays out both current and comparable trending information across multiple tabs in an easy-to-read, easy-to-access format.

Mutual Fund Costs

The costs of investing in mutual funds include management fees, loads and commissions, and losses caused by delay in the sale or purchase of shares. Fees are charged for managing the mutual fund and for expenses associated with the fund. These fees are passed directly on to the shareholders of the fund, reducing the yield of the fund. A fee may also be charged whenever you buy or sell the mutual fund. All purchases and sales are performed at the close of business when the net asset value can be cal-

▼ **FIGURE 12.5**

Finding mutual fund prices sample

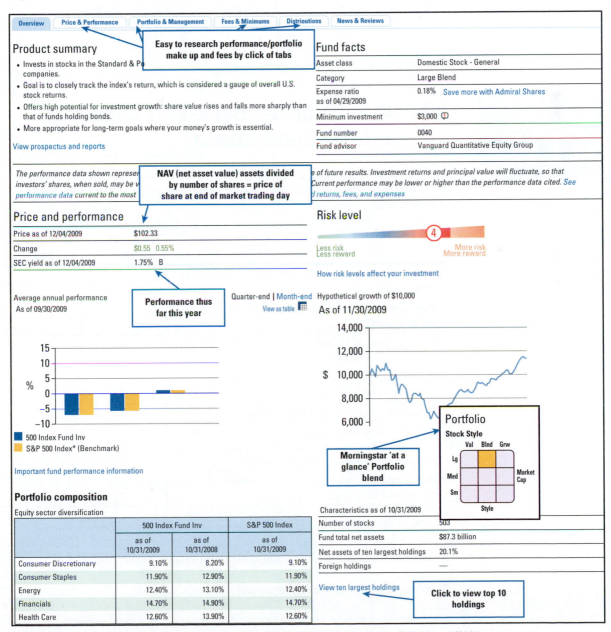

Source: https://www.personal.vanguard.com/us/FundsSnapshot?FundId=0040&FundIntExt=INT#hist=tab%3A0

culated; this end-of-day delay could also cost you in lost profits.

fees Like most things in life, mutual funds come with additional costs attached. When you buy mutual fund shares, you may have a front-end or back-end load, and you will have maintenance fees known as the expense ratio.

A **front-end load** is the fee charged when you buy a mutual fund, which could include the commission of the financial planner or selling agent who sold you the fund. For example, if you have a 5% front-end load and you invest $100, only $95 will be invested in the mutual fund, with a $5 load taken out to pay commissions.

A **back-end load**—sometimes called a redemption fee or deferred sales charge—works in the same way, except you are charged the load when you take money out of the fund. For example, if you invest $100, the whole $100 is put into the mutual fund. Say your $100 investment then grows to $1,000. When you withdraw the $1,000, if the back-load fee is 5%, then $50 (5% of $1,000) is subtracted from what you withdraw. Some mutual fund companies have back-load fees only if you sell the fund within a specific time frame. For example, there may be a 2% back-load fee if you sell your mutual fund within one year. Your prospectus will explain all of your fees and charges.

doing the MATH

12.2 Front-End vs. Back-End Loads: A Cost Comparison

You have $100 to invest in a mutual fund for the next 10 months. One fund has a 5% front-end load; another has a 5% back-end load. Use the table below to compare the two funds.

	Front-End Load	Back-End Load
For each time you invest $100, what amount is invested in the mutual fund?		
What amount is taken out to pay commissions at the time of deposit?		
Over the course of 10 months, at $100/month, what is the total amount invested in the mutual fund?		
What has been the total amount taken out to pay commissions at the time of deposit?		
The value of your fund after 10 months at 5% return is:	$1,005.26	$1,058.17
If you were to withdraw the balance from the mutual fund after 10 months, what amount would be subtracted from your withdrawal to pay commissions?		
What is your ending balance from the investment, after all fees have been paid?		

1. Which fee option proved to be the better alternative in the above scenario?

2. In what situations is a front-end load more advantageous?

3. When is a back-end load preferable?

Taking time to meet with and understand your financial planner can help you achieve great results.

commissions Many financial planners and financial advisers receive a large part of their compensation from commissions. Even though they are obligated to sell you the most appropriate fund for your situation, advisers may receive a higher commission from a particular fund. Some financial planners and advisers are fee-based and do not receive commissions. It is not uncommon for fee-based financial planners to charge $150 an hour or more. They are providing a service for you and deserve to be compensated. It is important that you trust your financial planner and that your financial planner discloses all fees and charges to you.

Vanguard and Fidelity funds are two major mutual fund companies that market their funds online (no sales force or financial planners) and do not charge a load on most of their funds. These funds often outperform loaded funds when you consider that 100% of your investment is working for you. If you feel comfortable in researching and picking your own investments, no-load funds may be right for you.

> **It's far better to buy a wonderful company at a fair price than a fair company at a wonderful price.**
> —WARREN BUFFETT, *Venture capitalist (1930–)*

Share Classes

Many mutual funds offer more than one class of shares. Each class will invest in the same pool (or investment portfolio) of securities and will have the same investment objectives and policies. However, each class will have different shareholder services and/or distribution arrangements with different fees and expenses. These differences reflect the unequal costs involved in servicing investors in the various classes.

For example, one class may be sold through brokers with a front-load fee. Another class may be sold directly to the public with no load but with a 12b-1 fee included (sometimes referred to as *Class C* shares). Still a third class might have a minimum investment of $10,000,000 and be available only to financial institutions (a so-called *institutional* share class). In some cases, by aggregating regular investments made by many individuals, a retirement plan—such as a 401(k) plan—may qualify to purchase institutional shares (and gain the benefit of their typically lower expense ratios) even though no members of the plan would qualify individually.

contingent deferred sales load (CDSL) a fee triggered if fund shares are redeemed before a given number of years of ownership

Because of their divergent fees and expenses, each class will likely have different performance results. A multiclass structure offers investors the ability to select a fee and expense structure most appropriate for their investment goals (including the length of time that they expect to remain invested in the fund).

load share classes Load share classes usually include a sales load and/or a 12b-1 fee to compensate financial advisers and other investment professionals for their services. They also may include a **contingent deferred sales load (CDSL)**, which is a fee triggered if fund shares are redeemed before a given number of years of ownership. The load share class of funds is divided into three classes (A, B, and C), which differ in how and when they charge their fees (see Figure 12.6).

no-load share classes No-load share classes do not have front-load or CDSL fees, but they do have a 12b-1 fee of 0.25% or less. Originally, no-load share classes were offered by mutual fund sponsors that sold directly to investors. Now, investors can purchase no-load funds through employer-sponsored retirement plans, mutual fund clearinghouses, discount brokerage firms, and bank trust departments as well as directly from mutual fund sponsors. Some financial advisers who charge investors separately for their services rather than through a load or 12b-1 fee also use no-load share classes.

12.5 CHOOSING AND BUYING A MUTUAL FUND

■ ■ **LO 12-5** Plan how and where to invest in mutual funds.

The first things you need to do before choosing a mutual fund are to determine your investment objectives and your risk level. If you are looking to use your invested money in the next few months or even the next few years, you might want to buy low-risk mutual funds—for example, money market funds, government bonds, or investment-grade bond funds. However, if you are investing in mutual funds for retirement and you are not going to retire for the next 30 years, you can assume more risk and invest in stock mutual funds. The risk of the fund is explained in the prospectus, and many mutual fund companies will rate their fund on risk, from low risk to high risk.

Investment Strategies

Matching your investment objectives with a mutual fund's objectives will take a little time and research. You can

financialfitness:
STOPPING LITTLE LEAKS

Low-Fee Shopping

Fees, loads, and expense ratios are clearly stated in a fund's prospectus. It is important you research expense ratios and loads before you buy because they will reduce your total returns. Vanguard has a reputation for low fees and expense ratios. You can compare the fees of mutual funds at www.morningstar.com.

▼ **FIGURE 12.6**

Load share class fee comparison

	Load Share Classes		
	Class A	**Class B**	**Class C**
Load	Front-load	Back-load	Back-back
Fees/Timing	12b-1 fee of about 0.25% (at the time of purchase)	12b-1 fee and CDSL (typically decreases each year for 6–7 years until it reaches zero, then back-load shares convert to Class A)	Annual 12b-1 fee (typically 1%) and a CDSL (also often 1%) that shareholders pay if they sell their shares within the first year after purchase
Benefits	Fund sponsors typically waive the sales load for purchases made through employer-sponsored retirement plans		

Making $ense

12.13 What is the difference between a front-load and a back-load fee?

12.14 What is a no-load mutual fund?

research a fund's objectives and risk by reading its prospectus online. There are two kinds of prospectuses: (1) the statutory prospectus, and (2) the summary prospectus.

The *statutory prospectus* is the traditional, long-form prospectus. The *summary prospectus* is only a few pages long and contains key information about a fund. Both versions include information on the fund's investment objectives, its strategies for achieving the objectives, the principal risks of investing in the fund, the fund's fees and expenses, and its past performance. The statutory prospectus

includes information about the fund's investment advisers and portfolio managers and how to purchase and redeem shares. It also shows the holdings (individual stocks and/ or bonds). You will have to decide if those holdings match what you want in a mutual fund. If the first company you look at does not have a mutual fund that matches your investment objectives, keep looking; there are over 8,000 different mutual funds to choose from.

Morningstar has developed a Style Box that shows you at a glance how the fund is invested (see Figure 12.7). On the vertical axis, the Morningstar Style Box shows whether the mutual fund holds stocks of large, medium, or small capitalized companies. The horizontal axis reports the company valuation, whether the stocks are from value-based companies (based on the price/earnings ratio), growth companies, or a blend of value-based and growth companies. A Standard and Poor's 500 (S&P 500) index fund would appear as a large blend in the Morningstar Style Box. You can see the box in actual use in the Vanguard example seen earlier in Figure 12.5 (page 309).

If you feel uncomfortable managing your own investments, you might want to talk to a financial planner, financial adviser, stock broker, or your local banker. Many banks now offer investment centers to help their customers choose investments. All of these people are paid for their services, either in the form of a direct fee (as in a fee-only investment adviser) or through commissions and service charges on your account. If you are not confident making these financial decisions, the fee or commission could be worth the price.

▼ **FIGURE** 12.7

Morningstar style box

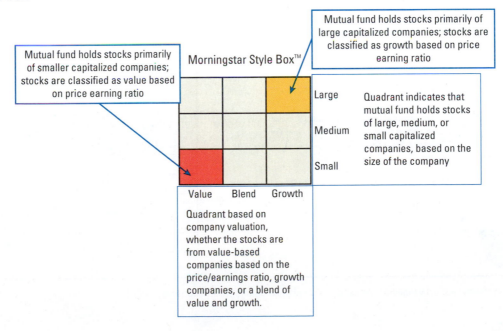

Once you determine your investment objectives and find mutual funds that meet those objectives, you will need to decide which one you want to purchase. To compare different funds, you want to look at loads, expense ratios, the historical performance of the fund, the fund's manager, and the turnover rate. Ideally, you want to find a no-load mutual fund with a low expense ratio. This will allow more of your money to work for you instead of being spent on commissions, loads, and larger operating expenses.

Although the past does not predict the future, you can get an idea of how well a fund and its fund manager have performed in the past. The performances of many mutual funds are judged against the S&P 500. On different mutual funds' financial websites, you can see a graph of the mutual fund compared with the S&P 500. The S&P 500 is used as a measuring stick, just as par is

used as a measuring stick on a golf course. Not many golfers shoot under par, and not many mutual funds beat the S&P 500. Only about 25% of fund managers beat the S&P 500 consistently, and they usually have higher expense ratios than index funds. Measuring against the S&P 500 will also show you the consistency of the fund's returns.

Turnover shows how long a fund typically holds an asset it buys. A mutual fund that has a turnover of 50% sells half of all its holdings in a year. The higher the turnover, the more you will pay in transaction fees (incorporated in the expense ratio), and the more you will pay in capital gains. Low turnover funds will have lower transaction costs and lower capital gains.

Balanced funds and targeted retirement funds can help you target your goals. For example, see Figure 12.8 for

▼ **FIGURE 12.8**

Target fund sample

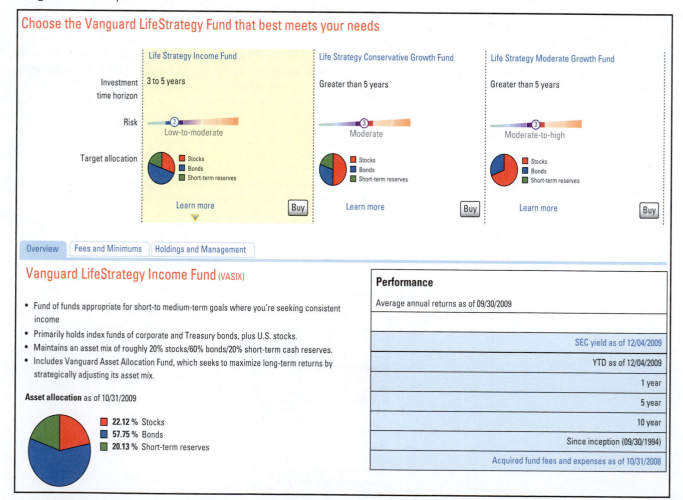

Source: https://www.personal.vanguard.com/us/funds/vanguard/LifeStrategyList#lifeStrategyAnchor

> " A public-opinion poll is no substitute for thought. "
>
> —WARREN BUFFETT, *Venture capitalist (1930–)*

several different Life Strategy funds offered by Vanguard, each designed to help you match particular savings objectives with a mutual fund. Each fund option provides a targeted allocation of stocks, bonds, and short-term reserves based upon your savings objectives.

Where to Buy Mutual Funds

You can buy many mutual funds directly from the mutual fund company. Some of the big mutual fund companies are Vanguard, Fidelity, and Oppenheimer. These companies usually do not charge a transaction fee, and many of their funds are no-load funds. However, these companies have minimum opening balances that could be $3,000 or higher. These companies could also have minimum additional contributions of $100 or higher.

Discount brokerage houses are another place to buy mutual funds. Some of these companies are available online, such as e-Trade, Scottrade, and TD Ameritrade. These brokerage houses sometimes charge commissions or fees to make purchases or sales.

You might also seek the assistance of financial planners, advisers, and full-service brokerage houses, all of which provide investment advice and can help you buy mutual funds. They also will sell you the financial products they recommend, but remember: They make their money from commissions, fees, and loads.

Banks and insurance companies have financial service advisers who can recommend and advise you on the products and services that are the best fit for your financial situation. However, they also will sell you the products they recommend. Like financial planners and full-service brokers, they make their money on commissions, fees, and loads. ◼

⊃ **LEARN.** This chapter explored the history of mutual funds and offered an overview of how mutual funds work, their benefits and risks, the commissions and fees involved, the various types of mutual funds available, and where to buy mutual funds.

SUMMARY

■ ■ **LO 12-1** Appreciate the history of mutual funds and understand mutual fund basics.

Mutual funds can be traced back to the 1800s, but they did not grow in popularity until the 1980s when many companies eliminated their defined-benefit pension plans and encouraged employees to invest in their own retirement through 401(k) plans. Modern mutual funds in the United States can be traced back to 1924 with MFS Investment Management.

The first mutual funds were closed-end mutual funds; today, the majority of mutual funds are open-end. Mutual funds are now regulated by the Securities and Exchange Commission (SEC) through the Securities Act of 1933 and the Securities Exchange Act of 1934. Mutual fund fees range from front-load to back-load to no-load, depending on where you buy. All mutual funds have an expense ratio, which represents the operating expenses of the fund, assessed to the owners of the fund. Mutual funds are valued at their net asset value (NAV), which is the total value of all the assets minus costs divided by the number of shares outstanding.

■ ■ **LO 12-2** Examine the types of mutual funds.

Mutual funds are first categorized as being either open-end or closed-end funds. From there, they are classified as being either no-load or load funds. Next, they are classified according to the types of assets held in the fund, generally stocks, bonds, and balanced funds. Within each classification, the fund can be further identified by the investment objective of the fund, such as international growth stock or a municipal bond fund. With over 8,000 mutual funds, there are funds to meet almost every investment objective and risk tolerance.

■ ■ **LO 12-3** Assess the benefits and risks of mutual funds.

The major benefits of owning mutual funds are the diversification they offer, professional fund management, the variety of funds available to investors, the ease in understanding their processes, the ease of researching, the low entrance costs, the ability to automatically invest, the automatic reinvestment of dividend and capital gains, the ease of recordkeeping, generally good liquidity, and relatively low expense ratios and fees. However, as with any investment, mutual funds do carry some risk, potentially unforeseen tax effects, and it is wise to be aware of the specific risks linked to your fund before you buy.

■ ■ **LO 12-4** Evaluate mutual funds in terms of their class, commission, and fee structure.

There are two main fees associated with mutual funds: expense ratios and loads. An expense ratio refers to the operating expenses of the fund divided by the total assets of the fund, expressed as a percentage. All mutual funds have an expense ratio, but there are no-load funds as well as funds with loads. A load is a sales charge that is assessed either when you make investments into the fund (front-load) or when you withdraw money from the fund (back-load). When purchasing mutual funds, you need to evaluate the fees and loads as well as the performance of the fund.

■ ■ **LO 12-5** Plan how and where to invest in mutual funds.

Mutual funds can be purchased directly from mutual fund companies, financial planners, financial advisers, full-service brokerage houses, discount brokerage houses, insurance companies, and banks. If you feel confident in your investment knowledge, you can buy directly. If you would like assistance in making your investment decisions, you can consult with full-service brokerage houses, financial planners, financial advisers, insurance agents, or your local banker. These advisers will charge a fee or commission for using their services, which will reduce your investment return.

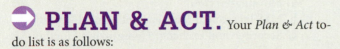

➡ PLAN & ACT. Your *Plan & Act* to-do list is as follows:

☐ Research mutual funds as options to support your short-term, intermediate, and long-term savings objectives (Worksheet 12.1).

☐ Look into three similar funds at different mutual fund companies that have similar holdings according to the Morningstar Style Box (Worksheet 12.2).

☐ Construct an investment plan that includes the appropriate use of mutual funds as an investment (Worksheet 12.3).

➡ EVALUATE. Review the goals you established at the beginning of this course. Is there a mutual fund option that will put you on the path to achieve your goals?

›› GoalTracker

Use the worksheets that accompany this chapter and your online GoalTracker to assess your investments and your savings goals. Every year, reevaluate your investment portfolio to decide if it is indeed meeting your investment objectives. Near the beginning of each year you will receive all of your tax forms and final investment statements from the previous year. You can refer to this information when you make your annual evaluation.

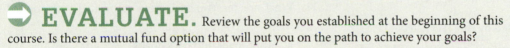

key terms

Back-End Load

Balanced Mutual Funds

Bull Run

Closed-End Mutual Funds

Commercial Paper

Contingent Deferred Sales Load (CDSL)

Cost Basis

Dollar-Cost Averaging

Expense Ratio

Front-End Load

Fund Manager

Global Funds

Initial Public Offering (IPO)

International Funds

Mutual Fund

Net Asset Value (NAV)

No-Load Mutual Fund

Open-End Mutual Funds

Person of Record

Prospectus

Repurchase Agreements

Russell 2000

Sector Funds

Securities and Exchange Commission (SEC)

Shares

Standard & Poor's 500 (S&P 500)

Stock Market

Turnover Rate

Weighted-Average Maturity (WAM)

12b-1 Fee

1. What is the purpose of a mutual fund manager? *(LO 12-1)*

   a. Buy and sell assets
   b. Maximize the growth of the fund given the specific investment objective
   c. Minimize the losses of the fund
   d. All the above

2. Closed-end mutual funds: *(LO 12-1)*

   a. Allow investors to add new money at any time
   b. Have a fixed number of shares
   c. Are priced based on the return of a one-year Treasury bill
   d. Have no commission

3. Open-end mutual funds: *(LO 12-1)*

   a. Open up for investors to add new money at the end of each quarter
   b. Are priced based on the net asset value (NAV) of the fund
   c. Became popular in the 1920s
   d. Have no commission

4. Mutual funds are regulated by the: *(LO 12-1)*

   a. Federal Deposit Insurance Corporation (FDIC)
   b. National Stock and Mutual Fund Association (NSMFA)
   c. Stock Insurance Protection Agency (SIPA)
   d. Securities and Exchange Commission (SEC)

5. When you buy a mutual fund, you own: *(LO 12-1)*

   a. The individual stock directly
   b. Part of a fund that owns the assets
   c. Stock in the mutual fund company
   d. Stocks and bonds

6. Net asset value is calculated by the total value of all the assets the: *(LO 12-1)*

   a. Fund holds
   b. Fund holds for the historical average for one year, divided by the number of mutual fund shares outstanding
   c. Fund holds, divided by the number of mutual fund shareholders
   d. Fund holds, divided by the number of mutual fund shares outstanding

7. Categorizations of mutual funds include: *(LO 12-2)*

   a. No-load and load
   b. Types of assets held
   c. Investment objective
   d. All the above

8. How do index funds keep their expense ratios low? *(LO 12-2)*

   a. By trading stocks often for maximum gains for the funds
   b. By maintaining their holdings similar to well-known indexes

   c. By having a team of professional money managers look for the best options for the fund's performance
   d. By holding fewer than 10 companies in the fund

9. Information about fund managers and their experience can be found at: *(LO 12-3)*

   a. Morningstar.com
   b. MFS Investment Management Annual Report
   c. Securities and Exchange Commission Monthly Publication
   d. DOW Monthly Journal

10. What is/are the major benefit(s) in mutual funds? *(LO 12-3)*

    a. Professional money managers
    b. Low initial investments
    c. Diversification
    d. Dividend and capital gains reinvestment
    e. All of the above

11. What are the two main fees associated with mutual funds? *(LO 12-4)*

    a. Front-loads and back-loads
    b. Purchase and commission fees
    c. Expense ratios and loads
    d. Commissions and sales charges

12. _____ are share classes that are level-load shares and generally do not have a front load. *(LO 12-4)*

    a. Class A
    b. Class B
    c. Class C
    d. Class D

13. The Morningstar Style Box evaluates mutual funds based on: *(LO 12-5)*

    a. The capital asset size of the companies a fund holds and whether the companies in the fund are value, blend, or growth
    b. The performance of the mutual fund since the inception of the fund
    c. The performance of the mutual fund, excluding the expense ratio since the inception of the fund
    d. The individual performance of each stock in the fund

14. What is the advantage of buying mutual funds from a full-service broker or financial planner? *(LO 12-5)*

    a. No fees or commissions
    b. Professional advice for making your investment decisions
    c. Knowing that all full-service brokers and financial planners do everything in the best interests of their customers
    d. Knowing that your returns are guaranteed

1. Net asset value (NAV) is the total value of all the assets in the mutual fund minus cost, divided by the number of shares outstanding. What is the NAV of a mutual fund with assets totaling $150 million and 3,750,000 shares outstanding? *(LO 12-1)*

2. Your mutual fund has varying asset allocations of stocks, bonds, and short-term reserves; if it allocates 25% to stocks and 40% to bonds, what percentage of the mutual fund is comprised of short-term reserves? *(LO 12-2)*

3. If you wanted to venture into investing but felt you could start at a rate of only $5/day, what is the total amount you would be able to invest over the course of a year? *(LO 12-3)*

4. If you have a 5% front-load charge and you invest $1,000, how much of this money will be invested in the mutual fund? *(LO 12-4)*

5. If you have a 5% back-load charge and you invest $1,000, how much of this money will be invested in the mutual fund? *(LO 12-4)*

6. If you have a 5% front-load mutual fund and you withdraw $10,000 of your investment, how much will be subtracted from your withdrawal to pay commission fees? *(LO 12-4)*

7. If you have a 5% back-load mutual fund and you withdraw $10,000 of your investment, how much will be subtracted from your withdrawal to pay commission fees? *(LO 12-4)*

1. Margot just received a gift of $10,000 from her uncle for her newborn son, Will. She would like to invest this money for Will's college in 18 years. What type of mutual fund would you recommend Margot invest in and why? *(LO 12-2)*

2. Geoff has two mutual fund options with the same investment objective and the same risks. One is a no-load mutual fund with an expense ratio of 0.50%; it has historically returned 7.5%. The other fund has a 5% front-load fee and an expense ratio of 1.20%; it has historically returned 8.2%. In which fund would you suggest Geoff invest and why? *(LO 12-4)*

3. Jack just started a new job that offers a 401(k) retirement plan. His company will match his investment dollar for dollar up to 6% of his salary. Jack decides to invest 6%, so the total investment to his 401(k) will be 12% of his salary after the company matches his contribution. He is allowed to invest in Vanguard funds, so go to www.vanguard.com and recommend the fund or funds in which you think Jack should invest. Explain your reasoning for picking the particular funds. *(LO 12-4)*

4. Sherri is automatically investing $100 a month in a mutual fund. She has no plans for this money other than wealth accumulation. Suggest three funds in which Sherri should invest and explain your reasoning, along with the pros and cons of each mutual fund. *(LO 12-5)*

12.1 MUTUAL FUNDS FOR DIFFERENT TIME HORIZONS AND OBJECTIVES

Use Worksheet 12.1 to compare different mutual funds that support your short-term, intermediate, and long-term objectives.

Worksheet 12.1 - Mutual Funds for Different Time Horizons and Objectives

and long-term objectives. Compare funds based on their past performance, expense ratios, loads, risks, and holdings.

Short-Term Investment (< 1 Year)			
Mutual Fund	Initial Investment	Load/Expense Ratio	Holdings

Intermediate Investment (1 - 5 Years)			
Mutual Fund	Initial Investment	Load/Expense Ratio	Holdings

Long-Term Investment (> 5 Years)			
Mutual Fund	Initial Investment	Load/Expense Ratio	Holdings

12.2 COMPARISON OF MUTUAL FUND COMPANIES

Research three different mutual fund companies that offer similar funds with similar holdings. Use Worksheet 12.2 to compare the three funds based on past performance, expense ratios, loads, risks, and holdings. Where do they fit in the Morningstar Style Box?

Research different mutual fund companies and choose three similar funds with similar holdings. Compare the three funds based on past performance, expense ratios, loads, risks, and holdings. Where do they fit in the Morningstar Style Box?

	Fund 1	Fund 2	Fund 3
Fund name			
Fund symbol			
Benchmark index			
Benchmark return over:			
1 year			
3 years			
5 years			
10 years			
Fund return over:			
1 year			
3 years			
5 years			
10 years			
Fund manager			
Minimum initial investment			
Minimum continuous automatic			
Annual expense			
Load?			
How much?			
12b-1 fee?			
Turnover rate			

12.3 MUTUAL FUND PLANNING WORKSHEET

Based on your research in Worksheets 12.1 and 12.2, use Worksheet 12.3 to construct an investment plan that includes an appropriate use of mutual funds as an investment. Be sure to log this information in your online GoalTracker.

Worksheet 12.3 - Mutual Fund Planning Worksheet

Construct an investment plan that includes appropriate use of mutual funds to meet your short-term, intermediate, and long-term savings objectives. Then log this information in your online GoalTracker.

	Short-Term	Intermediate	Long-Term
Goal/Purpose			
Fund Name			
Symbol			
Holdings/Style Box			
Risk Level			
Fund return over:			
1 year			
3 years			
5 years			
10 years			
Fund manager tenure			
Minimum initial investment			
Minimum continuous, automatic investment			
Annual expense ratio			
Load/How much?			
12b-1 fee?			
Turnover rate			

Jen is earning her degree at the local community college and just got promoted to full-time status at her work. She is now eligible to participate in the company's 401(k) plan. Her company will match her 401(k) contribution up to 6% of her pretax income but Jen is not sure she can do without 6% of her income since she is paying her way through college.

Jen knows you are taking this personal finance class and she asks for your help and advice. Her company uses Fidelity funds for its 401(k) plan. Research the funds at www.fidelity.com and make a recommendation for Jen. Support your answer. Be sure to look at historical performance, the expense ratio, the fund manager, and the Morningstar Style Box in considering which fund, if any, she should invest.

A summary of the housemates' goals can be found in the first Continuing Case problem on page 27.

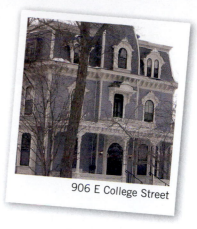

906 E College Street

> Lampis, the ship owner, on being asked how he acquired his great wealth, replied, 'My great wealth was acquired with no difficulty, but my small wealth, my first gains, with much labor.'
>
> —EPICTETUS, *Greek Stoic philosopher (55–135 AD)*

stocks

The stock market is a complex investment engine that is part business sense and part social science. The goal of this chapter is to give you basic information on stocks as an investment option. ■

LEARNING OBJECTIVES

After reading this chapter, you should be able to:

LO 13-1 Understand the basic principles of stocks and the stock market.

LO 13-2 Explain how stocks are valued.

LO 13-3 Contrast how companies on the stock market are valued.

LO 13-4 Summarize the basics of buying and selling stocks.

◄ Glen, age 33, economics graduate from a large public university

Starting in Stocks

Glen graduated with a degree in economics. At the time there were no local job opportunities in his field of study. He settled for a software-testing position, helping the company prepare for the new millennium. As a social outlet, he joined an investment club made up of recent graduates. "No one had a great deal of money, but we all had a great interest in investing in stocks and getting rich, fast. We were all young so we could ride out the ups and downs of the market. Each month, we took turns volunteering to research new stock options, pooling our funds to buy the stock. Doing it as a club allowed me to gain experience in the stock market despite my limited resources, make money, and learn from others who had already been investing in the stock market. It was both socially and financially rewarding."

13.1 STOCK BASICS

■ ■ **LO 13-1** Understand the basic principles of stocks and the stock market.

A **stock** is a certificate representing partial ownership of a company. As a stockholder, you are a part-owner of the company and benefit from the profits of the company.

The more profitable the company, the more your stock is worth. When the company loses money, the stock price declines. Stock can be either privately held or publicly traded on a stock exchange. Let's look more closely at the different types of stocks and exchanges.

Private and Public Companies

Privately held companies have a relatively small number of stockholders, and the stock is not traded publicly on a stock exchange. Many companies are privately held. According to Forbes.com, Cargill—a firm that provides services ranging from selling grains and commodities to offering financial services—is the largest privately held company, with an estimated $106 billion in revenue and over 131,000 employees. Other familiar examples of privately held companies include Levi Strauss & Co., Hallmark Cards, Hyatt Hotels Corporation, and PETCO Animal Supplies.

When companies want to raise money for growth and new projects, or when a firm's owners want to cash-out and sell their company, they can go public. An **initial public offering (IPO)** (also known simply as an *offering*) takes place when a company first sells its stock to the public on a stock exchange. In an IPO, the company usually obtains

Lego is an example of a large, internationally known, privately held company.

> "Look at market fluctuations as your friend rather than your enemy; profit from folly rather than participate in it."
>
> —WARREN BUFFETT, *Venture capitalist (1930–)*

the assistance of an investment bank, which helps it determine what type of security to issue (*common stock* or *preferred stock*) and the best offering price and time to bring it to market.

An IPO can cost a company hundreds of thousands of dollars in filing, legal, and administrative fees, in addition to the fees paid to the underwriting firm. The decision to go public costs the company additional money in terms of reporting expenses and closer scrutiny of the company by the Securities and Exchange Commission (SEC) and the company's new stockholders. On the other hand, going public with an IPO can be very profitable.

In its initial public offering on August 19, 2004, Google raised $1.67 billion, selling over 19 million of its 271 million shares. The majority of the remaining shares remain under Google's control. The money raised by the IPO was used to hire more staff and build more offices. This investment in the company helped it launch Google Earth and other projects, as well as acquire different companies and incorporate them into Google. One of the most famous buys for Google was the purchase of YouTube in late 2006 for $1.65 billion in stock.

An IPO can be a risky investment. For an individual investor, it is impossible to predict exactly what the stock or shares will do since there is often little historical data available to analyze the company. The fact that most IPOs are issued by companies going through a transitory growth period also makes it difficult to predict the future value of the shares.

Types of Stock

There are two types of stock: common and preferred.

Most companies issue only **common stock**. It is termed *common* to distinguish it from preferred stock. Common stockholders receive a return on their investment through the payout of dividends and the potential increase in the company's stock price. *Dividends* are a percentage of profits (determined by the board of directors) paid to the stockholders. After paying dividends, the company retains the remaining profit, which increases the value of the company and its stock price.

Start-up companies and high-growth companies do not usually pay dividends; instead, they use the money to build the company. The stockholders hope the stock price increases as the company grows, which increases the value of their investment. Established companies in stable environments usually pay higher dividends. In this case, the investor receives a return in the form of dividend payments and does not expect the stock price to increase rapidly. The potential return on investment through an increase in stock price provides investors in all kinds of companies the best opportunity to increase wealth in the long run.

Common stock usually carries voting rights. These rights allow the stockholder some influence in the direction of the company. Voting stockholders elect the company board of directors, attend annual shareholder meetings, and vote on establishing corporate objectives, policy, and stock splits. The largest shareholders of many companies are usually institutional investors, such as mutual funds and insurance companies. As holders of large amounts of stock, they typically have more influence over the company than an individual shareholder.

If a company declares bankruptcy, common stockholders are the last to receive any money, assuming any money remains. In a bankruptcy, those who receive their money first are the secured lenders, followed by unsecured lenders (bondholders), then preferred stockholders, and finally common stockholders.

Preferred stock (also known as *preferred shares* or *preference shares*) typically carries no voting rights, but it is a higher-ranking stock than common stock. Preferred stockholders are paid their dividends before common stockholders, and if the company experiences financial difficulties or declares bankruptcy, preferred stockholders are paid before common stockholders. The terms of preferred stock are negotiated between the corporation and the investor and are specific to each corporation. Most preferred stock issues pay dividends as a percentage of the par value of the stock and have characteristics similar to debt (by paying a fixed amount to the debtholder) and equity (by offering appreciation in growth potential). Some preferred stock (called *convertible preferred*) includes a provision by which it can be converted into common stock.

There is no guarantee of dividends or capital appreciation with *any* stock, so keep in mind that money invested in stocks is at risk and does not have a guaranteed return.

Stock Exchanges

Publicly traded stocks are bought and sold on **stock exchanges**. A stock has to be listed on a stock exchange in order to be traded there. To list a stock, the company must meet the criteria for minimum size and number of stock shares outstanding. There are several different stock exchanges to keep in mind when investing.

stock
equal parts or shares of a company's capital; a method of sharing ownership of a company with other investors

initial public offering (IPO)
a company's first sale of stock to the public

common stock
stock that carries voting rights, but in the event of bankruptcy, owners receive their funds after preferred stockholders

preferred stock
stock that carries no voting rights but takes priority over common stock in the payment of dividends to stockholders and upon liquidation

stock exchange
a market in which shares of stock and common stock equivalents are bought and sold

New York Stock Exchange (NYSE)

Known as *The Big Board*, the New York Stock Exchange (NYSE) is the largest stock exchange in the United States. The NYSE was established in 1792 when a group of brokers met under a tree in Manhattan and signed an agreement to trade securities. **Securities** are tradable documents issued by a corporation, government, or other organization which show evidence of ownership. Unlike the newer exchanges, the NYSE still conducts its transactions on a trading floor. On Wall Street in New York City, **brokers** (representatives of buyers and sellers) shout out prices in order to strike a deal (in what is called an **open outcry**). To facilitate the exchange of stocks, the NYSE employs **specialists** (or **market makers**), who manage the buying and selling of stocks. The NYSE also has electronic trading. Of the exchanges, the NYSE is the most rigorous in terms of its listing requirements.

National Association of Securities Dealers Automated Quotation Stock Market (NASDAQ)

NASDAQ is the largest electronic equities trading market in the United States. It trades more in volume per hour than any other stock exchange in the world. All NASDAQ trading is done over a computer network. The process is similar to the NYSE, except buyers and sellers are electronically matched, and a market maker manages the buying and selling of stocks.

American Stock Exchange (Amex)

Known as *The Curb*, the Amex is the second-largest stock exchange in the United States. Its listing rules are more lenient than those of the NYSE, resulting in a larger representation of stocks and bonds issued by small companies. The Amex started as an alternative to the NYSE, originating with brokers meeting on the curb outside the NYSE in order to trade stocks that failed to meet the Big Board's listing requirements. Amex now has its own trading floor on Wall Street, adjacent to the NYSE. NASDAQ purchased the Amex in 1998 and combined their markets, although the two continued to operate separately. In 2008, the exchange was purchased by NYSE Euronext and eventually renamed NYSE Amex Equities.

over-the-counter (OTC) market

When a security is traded in some context *other than* on a formal exchange (e.g., the NYSE or Amex), it is said to trade **over-the- counter (OTC)**. Typically, a stock is traded over-the- counter because the company is too small to meet the requirements of an exchange. Known as *unlisted stock,* these securities are traded by broker-dealers who negotiate directly with one another over computer networks or by phone.

OTC stocks trade on the Over-the-Counter Bulletin Board (OTCBB) or on *pink sheets* (so named because they were originally printed on pink paper). Companies trading on pink sheets do not need to meet the minimum requirements or file with the SEC. Take caution with the OTCBB stocks because they could be **penny stocks**. These shares often trade for less than $5.00 and are offered by companies with poor credit records. As such, they are considered very high risk investments.

foreign stock exchanges

Most developed countries have at least one stock exchange where local stocks are traded. Popular exchanges are the Nikkei Stock Average in Japan and the FTSE (Financial Times Stock Exchange or "Footsie") in the United Kingdom.

The increasing globalization of financial markets means that these markets often indicate how U.S. markets will react to world events. Just as the S&P 500, the Dow Jones Industrial Average, and the NASDAQ Composite indexes are seen as indicators for U.S. markets, the Nikkei Stock Average and the FTSE 100 are followed in Japan and the United Kingdom, respectively, as indicators for the health and stability of their markets.

Making $ense

13.1 What is involved in going public?

13.2 Why are IPOs a risky investment?

13.3 How does common stock differ from preferred stock?

13.4 Why are some stocks exchanged over-the-counter?

IN THE **NEWS**

How Tiger Woods destroyed $12 billion of stock-market value

How much can one car crash cost?

If you are Tiger Woods, as much as $12 billion. That is the amount Tiger's corporate sponsors lost in stock value since he crashed his sport utility vehicle the day before Thanksgiving, according to a study from two economics professors.

Much has been written and said about the impact the scandal would have on Tiger's personal wealth. The world's best golfer derives 90% of his income from endorsements, appearance fees, licensing agreements, and a host of other off-the-course activities. It is unclear how much of that income will be affected by the crash.

More difficult to determine, though, is how the scandal would hit his corporate sponsors. So Victor Stango and Christopher Knittel, two economics professors at the University of California—Davis, decided to take a stab at quantifying the effect—performing what is called an "event study." To do this, the professors looked at the nine sponsors for which stock price data were available and compared stock returns for those companies for the 13 days after the accident, both to the entire stock market and a group of competitors. The market value of the sponsors fell 2.3%.

The ones hit the hardest? The three sports-related companies—Gatorade (owned by PepsiCo), Nike, and Electronic Arts. Those companies experienced a 4.3% decline in stock value. Meanwhile, consulting firm Accenture "experienced no ill effects."

Overall, the pace of the losses slowed by Dec. 11, the day Woods announced he would take a leave from golf, but as of Dec. 17, shareholders had not recovered their losses, according to the study.

Of course, caveats abound. Woods's sponsors are mostly subsidiaries of larger parent companies and the statistical margin of error is particularly large. Still, "the overall pattern of losses at the parent companies is unlikely to stem from ordinary day-to-day variation in their stock prices," the professors say.

STEPHEN GROCER, "How Tiger Woods Destroyed $12 Billion of Stock-Market Value," *The Wall Street Journal*, December 28, 2009. Reprinted with permission.

Questions

1 Do you think the drop in the market value of the affected stocks will be short- or long-term? Why?

2 What does this example (the impact of the Tiger Woods's incident on stock prices) tell you about the volatility of the stock market?

3 List seven types of events and what type of impact each event has on the stock market.

4 Can you think of a past news-worthy event that did *not* affect stock market prices? How can you show any proof?

13.2 STOCK EVALUATION

■ ■ **LO 13-2** Explain how stocks are valued.

Stocks are valued according to what you and other investors are willing to pay for them. Investors make decisions based on expectations. In making their evaluations, investors can look at the market indexes and stock quotations.

Expectations

Expectations of future earnings and data from past performances largely determine stock market prices. For example, if a drug company were to find a cure for obesity, we would expect the profits of that company to increase. Stock analysts would estimate increased future sales and earnings for the company, so investors would be willing to pay a higher price for the drug company's stock, thus increasing demand for the stock. If everyone had equal access to this information, the markets would be *efficient* in determining a new price for the drug company. In this case, the stock market is said to be "forward-looking" because a large part of the stock's price is based on future expectations.

Because the stock market is based on expectations and can change quickly, government officials and investors watch it for information on how businesses are doing and for a reading of consumer confidence. A **bull market** is one in which overall stock prices are rising. A **bear market** is one in which prices on multiple broad market indexes have decreased 20% or more over at least a two-month period. Factors that affect stock prices include changing interest rates, traumatic world events, consumer confidence, and market expectations. In the 10-year picture of the market shown in Figure 13.1, you can see periods in which the market moved between a bull market (upward-trending) and a bear market (downward-trending).

The Market and Indexes

In the stock markets, the term *market* is often used as slang for the performance of key stock market indexes. For instance, the Dow Jones Industrial Average (also known as the *Dow*) is made up of 30 large, well-known stocks, but is often used as a representation of the *whole* stock market. The S&P 500 Stock Index represents large-company stocks, the NASDAQ 100 is technology heavy, and the Russell 2000 index represents small company stocks—yet the performance of each of these acts as a stand-in for the expectations of the entire financial world. Figure 13.2 is a snapshot of the major market indexes on a given day. On the day illustrated, all indicators across the board reflect a downward trend.

the Dow The Dow Jones Industrial Average (DJIA), or Dow, is the most widely used indicator of the overall condition of the stock market. It is a price-weighted average of 30 actively traded blue-chip stocks, primarily industrial. The 30 stocks, listed in Figure 13.3, are chosen by the editors of *The Wall Street Journal* and published by Dow Jones & Company. The Dow was officially started by Charles Dow in 1896, and originally consisted of only 11 stocks. The Dow is computed by adding up the prices of all the stocks and then dividing by the number of stocks in the index.

the S&P 500 The Standard & Poor's 500 (S&P 500), created in 1957, is a collection of 500 large- and mid-sized capitalized company stocks that are considered to be widely held and representative of the

▼ **FIGURE** 13.1

Stock price index trends 2001–2009

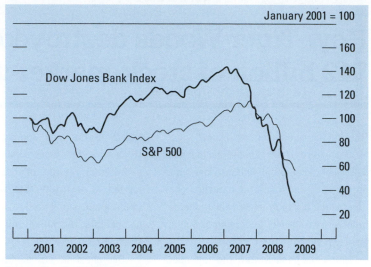

Source: Standard & Poor's and Dow Jones.

▼ **FIGURE** 13.2

Sample online market check report

U.S. STOCKS | See all U.S. Stocks Data

Major Indexes

1:24 p.m EST 11/27/09

	Last	Change	% Chg
DJIA*	10309.92	−154.48	−1.48
DJ Transportation Average*	3922.84	−49.48	−1.25
DJ Utility Average*	375.71	−6.28	−1.64
DJ Total Stock Market*	11153.11	−203.80	−1.79
Nasdaq*	2138.44	−37.61	−1.73
Nasdaq 100*	1765.46	−28.21	−1.57
S&P 500*	1091.49	−19.14	−1.72
S&P 100*	508.98	−8.16	−1.58
S&P 400 Mid-Cap*	683.79	−13.99	−2.00
S&P 600 Small-Cap*	305.38	−7.39	−2.36
NYSE Composite*	7070.09	−162.03	−2.24
Russell 2000*	577.21	−14.98	−2.53
Amex Composite*	1760.78	−56.47	−3.11
KBM Bank*	43.04	−1.18	−2.67
PHLX Gold/Silver*	183.52	−7.28	−3.82
PHLX Housing Sector*	96.80	−2.47	−2.49
PHLX Oil Service*	189.25	−5.29	−2.72
PHLX Semiconductor*	309.82	−5.27	−1.67

* at close

See All Major U.S. Indexes

Markets Diary

5:11 p.m EST 11/27/09

Issues	NYSE	Nasdaq	Amex
Advancing	450	446	122
Declining	2,547	2,122	329
Unchanged	89	165	76
Total	3,086	2,733	527
Issues at			
New 52 Week High	36	35	4
New 52 Week Low	12	30	2

Source: http://online.wsj.com/mdc/public/page/marketsdata.html

financialfitness:

JUST THE FACTS

The Bull and The Bear

Using the bull and the bear to represent market movements comes from the way the animals attack their prey. The bear swipes down with its paws, and the bull thrusts its horns up in an attack. If the market is down, it's a bear. If it's up, it's a bull.

stock market These stocks are selected based upon their size, liquidity, and sector, and provide a broad snapshot of the overall U.S. equity market. Most experts consider the S&P 500 to be one of the best benchmarks to judge overall U.S. market performance because it tracks over 70% of U.S. equities. Vanguard's S&P 500 mutual fund was established August 31, 1976, and as of November 30, 2009, had an overall average annual return of 10.45%.

Comparison of Indexes

To evaluate a stock, you will want to compare how the company's stock is doing on different indexes. Online tools are readily available to help you with this analysis at sites such as Yahoo! Finance or *The Wall Street Journal Online* (see www.online.wsj.com). Figure 13.4 on the next page provides a screenshot example to show how these interactive online tools can be used to compare how a stock is performing on the different indexes. In this example, Walt Disney Company (DIS) stock is tracked over the course of one day as it compares to the S&P 500, the Dow Jones Industrial Average (DJIA), and the NASDAQ. These tools help you compare your potential purchase against multiple key market indexes.

Stock Quotes

Online financial stock quote web pages provide information about the stock, including share prices, dividends, yields, and price-to-earnings ratios. Each stock is labeled with an acronym (no more than five letters) that is shorthand for the company's name. Figure 13.5 (also on the next page) is an example of Walt Disney Company's stock quote showing the previous day's performance.

price The following prices will be reflected in the quote:

Open: The price of the stock when the market opened that day

Low: The lowest price of the stock for the day

High: The highest price of the stock for the day

Close: The price of the stock when the market closed

▼ **FIGURE 13.3**

Listing of companies in the Dow Jones Industrial Average (DJIA)

Company	Symbol	Industry
3M Co.	MMM	Conglomerate
Alcoa Inc.	AA	Aluminum
American Express Co.	AXP	Consumer finance
AT&T Inc.	T	Telecommunications
Bank of America Corp.	BAC	Banking
Boeing Co.	BA	Aerospace and defense
Caterpillar Inc.	CAT	Construction
Chevron Corp.	CVX	Oil and gas
Cisco Systems Inc.	CSCO	Computer networking
Coca-Cola Co.	KO	Beverages
E. I. du Pont de Nemours and Co.	DD	Chemical industry
ExxonMobil Corp.	XOM	Oil and gas
General Electric Co.	GE	Conglomerate
Hewlett-Packard Co.	HPQ	Technology
Home Depot Inc.	HD	Home improvement retailer
Intel Corp.	INTC	Semiconductors
International Business Machines Corp.	IBM	Computers and technology
Johnson & Johnson	JNJ	Pharmaceuticals
JPMorgan Chase & Co.	JPM	Banking
Kraft Foods Inc.	KFT	Food processing
McDonald's Corp.	MCD	Fast food
Merck & Co., Inc.	MRK	Pharmaceuticals
Microsoft Corp.	MSFT	Software
Pfizer Inc.	PFE	Pharmaceuticals
Procter & Gamble Co.	PG	Consumer goods
Travelers Companies Inc.	TRV	Insurance
United Technologies Corp.	UTX	Conglomerate
Verizon Communications Inc.	VZ	Telecommunications
Wal-Mart Stores Inc.	WMT	Retail
Walt Disney Co.	DIS	Broadcasting and entertainment

Source: Derived from info on www.money.cnn.com/data/markets/dow.

Stocks with a wide range in prices over a period of time are sometimes thought to be risky; their stock price is considered *volatile*. Most quotes provide the past day's high, low, open, and close, as well as the 52-week high and low.

dividends Dividends, or payouts, are taxable payments declared by a company's board of directors and distributed to shareholders out of the company's current or retained earnings. Dividends can be paid quarterly, twice a year, or annually; most companies pay dividends quarterly. Dividends are usually given as cash (known as a *cash dividend*), but they can also take the form of stock (a *stock dividend*) or other property. The steady return dividends provide is an incentive to own stock in stable companies, even if they are not experiencing much growth.

▼ **FIGURE** 13.4

Stock quote market index comparison example

Source: http://www.finance.aol.com/quotes/the-walt-disney-company/dis/nys

▼ **FIGURE** 13.5

Online stock quote example: Walt Disney Co. (DIS)

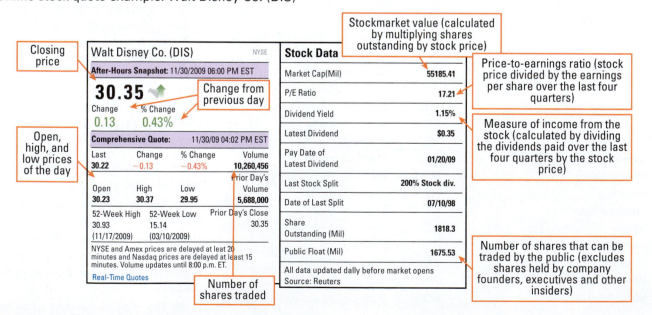

Source: http://www.online.wsj.com/quotes/main.html?symbol=dis&type=djn

Companies are not required to pay dividends and may decide to keep their profits to fund future growth or to pay down debt. Companies that offer dividends are most often companies that have progressed beyond the growth phase and no longer reap large benefits from reinvesting their profits; therefore, they choose to distribute their profits to their shareholders in the form of a dividend.

dividend yield   The **dividend yield** is the annual return received from dividends if you purchase the stock and the dividend payments remain unchanged. The dividend yield is computed as follows:

Dividend yield = Annual dividends per share/Price per share

The dividend yield will tell you how much cash flow you will receive from an investment. If you want a high cash return on an investment, you should look for a high dividend yield. If you want a capital gain in an investment, look for a stock with a low dividend yield or a company that does not pay dividends.

Start-up and growth companies are cash sponges. They reinvest their money in the company so it can grow. These companies usually do not pay dividends. The stockholders receive a return on their investment when they sell the stock. Hopefully, the price is higher when sold than when purchased, and the capital appreciation in the value of the company is reflected in the stock price. In the Disney stock quote example in Figure 13.5, the annual dividend yield of 1.15% means investors purchasing the stock at the time of this quote would earn an annual dividend equal to 1.15% of their investment based on the last dividend payout.

price-to-earnings(P/E)ratio
The **price-to-earnings (P/E) ratio** is a formula that helps you assess the value of a stock by comparing the company's current share price to its per share earnings. The P/E ratio is calculated as:

P/E ratio = Market value per share/Earnings per share (EPS)

dividends
taxable payments declared by a company's board of directors and distributed to its shareholders out of the company's current or retained earnings

dividend yield
annual return received from dividends if you purchase the stock and the dividend payments remain unchanged

price-to-earnings (P/E) ratio   an assessment tool for valuing a stock in which market value per share is divided by earnings per share

> ❝ October: This is one of the peculiarly dangerous months to speculate in stocks. The others are July, January, September, April, November, May, March, June, December, August and February. ❞
>
> —MARK TWAIN, *American author and humorist (1835–1910)*

doing the MATH

13.1 Purchasing Decisions Based on Dividend Yield

Suppose you want a high cash return on an investment and you can choose between Company Alpha and Company Omega stock.

Company Alpha: stock price $40 per share; dividend $3.60 per share
Company Omega: stock price $80 per share; dividend $7.00 per share

Which stock would you buy? Explain your reasoning.

For example, if a company is currently trading at $50 per share and earnings over the last 12 months were $2 per share, the P/E ratio for the stock would be 25 ($50/$2). In the Disney example in Figure 13.5, the price-to-earnings ratio is 17.21, which means that the prevailing stock price of Disney is 17.21 times its annual earnings per share.

Generally, a high P/E ratio suggests higher earnings growth in the future compared to companies with a low P/E ratio. The higher the earnings, the more likely it is that funds will be available to pay dividends to shareholders or to reinvest in the company to keep it growing. It is important to compare the P/E ratios of companies within the same industry. For example, the P/E ratio of a technology company is typically high compared with that of a utility company, as the two industries have different growth prospects.

Most years, stocks have an average P/E ratio between 15 and 20. This means investors are willing to pay $15 to $20 for each $1 of profit as reflected in the stock price. **Growth stocks** (stocks of companies that are growing at a faster than average rate) tend to have a P/E ratio of 30 or higher, reflecting the investor's belief of a higher potential future return. Investors will pay far more for each $1 of earnings if they believe the company's outlook is strong and that returns at a later date will be reflected in a much higher stock price.

price-to-earnings valuation process As an investor, after you look at how a company handles its profits—paying a quarterly dividend, paying cash to the shareholders, or reinvesting its earnings—you should next focus on earnings per share (how much profit the company earns for each share that has been issued). **Value stocks**, which may have single-digit P/E ratios, are the underappreciated underdogs in the market. They may be in out-of-favor industries or from a company that has gone through a rough spot.

Investors buy value stocks because they believe the market has undervalued them. Warren Buffett, one of the world's best-known and most successful investors, made his billons by seeking out and investing in value stocks.

Many online sites make it easy to compare a company's stock against its peers. See Figure 13.6 for a comparison of Disney stock with the stock of three of its media peers: CBS, NWS (News Corporation), and TWX (Time Warner).

Figure 13.7 shows an example of one of the many online research tools provided by *The Wall Street Journal Online;* the page featured in this figure includes a list of popular stock indexes and the changes for the day. In referencing these online tools, you can pull together the necessary information to determine if the stock is a good fit for your financial goals. For a sample quote comparison matrix, see Figure 13.8 on page 334.

Based on Figure 13.8, if you are looking for a higher cash return on an investment, TWX—with the high dividend yield

financialfitness:
STOPPING LITTLE LEAKS

Cheaper Trading

Using online brokers such as E*TRADE for trading securities can save you a significant amount in terms of trading costs. The online tools offered by such brokers also provide references, help guide you with a target strategy, and assist you in executing your trading strategy with ease.

doing the MATH

13.2 Purchasing Decisions Based on the Price-to-Earnings (P/E) Ratio

You are thinking of investing in one of the following three companies:

Alpha Co.: stock price of $35 per share; annual earnings of $2.85 per share
Beta Co.: stock price of $35 per share; annual earnings of $5.35 per share
Kappa Co.: stock price of $35 per share; annual earnings of $0.85 per share

Based on their P/E ratios, which company will most likely have the funds available to either pay dividends to shareholders or reinvest in the company to keep it growing?

▼ FIGURE 13.6

Online stock quote example: Walt Disney Co. (DIS) vs. media peers

Source: http://www.finance.aol.com/quotes/the-walt-disney-company/dis/nys

▼ FIGURE 13.7

Example of online research tools

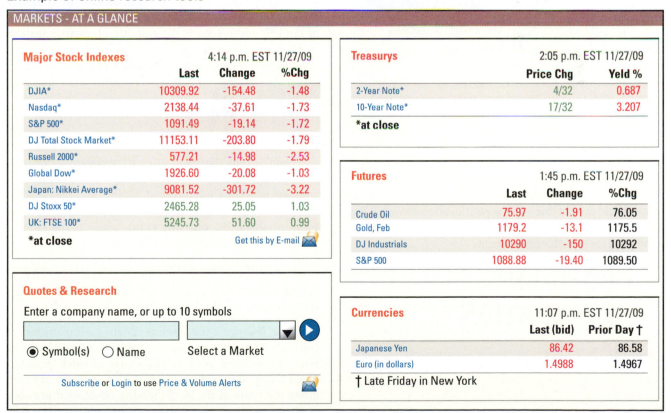

MARKETS - AT A GLANCE

Major Stock Indexes	4:14 p.m. EST 11/27/09		
	Last	Change	%Chg
DJIA*	10309.92	-154.48	-1.48
Nasdaq*	2138.44	-37.61	-1.73
S&P 500*	1091.49	-19.14	-1.72
DJ Total Stock Market*	11153.11	-203.80	-1.79
Russell 2000*	577.21	-14.98	-2.53
Global Dow*	1926.60	-20.08	-1.03
Japan: Nikkei Average*	9081.52	-301.72	-3.22
DJ Stoxx 50*	2465.28	25.05	1.03
UK: FTSE 100*	5245.73	51.60	0.99
*at close			Get this by E-mail ✉

Treasurys	2:05 p.m. EST 11/27/09	
	Price Chg	Yield %
2-Year Note*	4/32	0.687
10-Year Note*	17/32	3.207
*at close		

Futures	1:45 p.m. EST 11/27/09		
	Last	Change	%Chg
Crude Oil	75.97	-1.91	76.05
Gold, Feb	1179.2	-13.1	1175.5
DJ Industrials	10290	-150	10292
S&P 500	1088.88	-19.40	1089.50

Quotes & Research

Enter a company name, or up to 10 symbols

⦿ Symbol(s) ◯ Name   Select a Market

Subscribe or Login to use Price & Volume Alerts ✉

Currencies	11:07 p.m. EST 11/27/09	
	Last (bid)	Prior Day †
Japanese Yen	86.42	86.58
Euro (in dollars)	1.4988	1.4967
† Late Friday in New York		

Source: http://www.online.wsj.com/mdc/public/page/marketsdata.html

Decision indicators quote comparison matrix

QUOTE COMPARISON MATRIX			
	DIS	CBS	TWX
52-wk Price Range; Close Price/Trend	15.14-30.93 30.35 ⬆	3.06-14.25 13.13 ⬆	29.64-30.74 30.85 ⬆
Dividend	$0.35	$0.20	$0.75
Dividend Yield	1.1%	1.4%	2.4%
EPS	1.764	.448	−11.91
P/E Ratio	17.75	30.99	N/A

Making $ense

13.5 What differentiates a bull from a bear market?

13.6 What are key market-performance indexes, and how are they used?

13.7 How do dividends work?

of 2.4%—may be most attractive to you. However, if you want a capital gain in your investment, such as when you hold stocks inside a retirement account, DIS—with a low dividend yield of 1.1%—might be more attractive. If you want a track record of higher earnings, where the company has demonstrated it has enough funds to either pay dividends or reinvest in the company to keep it growing, then CBS may look more attractive, with its P/E ratio of 30.99%. If you have done your research and predict that TWX is positioned to do well in the future, you may consider it an underdog in the market and a good value for growth in investment.

13.3 COMPANY EVALUATION

■ ■ **LO 13-3** Contrast how companies on the stock market are valued.

Before buying stock in a company, you will want to review the company's financial statements, look at industry trends, and consider future demand and profit for the company. A study of the company's current state will help provide a feel for its future performance and profitability and will help you decide if you want to be a part-owner of the company.

Research

The government requires publicly held companies to file certain reports and financial statements. When researching a company as a possible stock investment, you will want to look at these documents. They provide information on everything an investor would want to know before buying or selling a company's stock.

financial reports and statements When investors review a company, they typically turn to the 10K, 10Q, and the annual reports. The *10K* is an annual report filed with the Securities and Exchange Commission (SEC). Required parts of a 10K include: (1) an explanation of a company's operations (how it makes its money) and the markets in which it operates; (2) disclosures of risks the company faces, including current lawsuits; (3) the financial statements (such as the income statement and balance sheet), which show how much money the company made; and (4) its debt levels. The *10Q* is a smaller version of the 10K and is filed at the end of each quarter instead of each year. The *annual report* includes reports from the company's chairman, CEO, and CFO. It provides an explanation of the previous year's performance and what the officers forecast for the coming year. It also includes the company's balance sheet and income statement.

evaluation criteria Information on the firm's balance sheet and income statement helps you evaluate the company's liquidity (its ability to cover its expenses) and financial leverage, which are indicators of stability and the possibility for future growth. To assess the firm's liquidity, you will want to look at the **current ratio**, which is the ratio of short-term assets to short-term liabilities:

Current ratio = Short-term assets/Short-term liabilities

A high current ratio relative to the industry norm represents a relatively high degree of liquidity.

Financial leverage is the amount of debt a company has. A company can raise funds either by borrowing from suppliers or creditors or by selling shares of stock to investors. Issuing additional shares of stock to raise money may dilute the value of the stock, placing downward pressure on the stock price. If a company borrows too much money, it may have difficulty making loan payments. Financial leverage indicates a reliance on debt to support operations and can be measured by the **debt ratio**, which calculates the proportion of total assets financed with debt:

Debt ratio = Total debt/Total assets

A high debt ratio relative to the industry norm signifies a high degree of financial leverage and therefore indicates a relatively high risk of default on future debt payments, depending on the company's cash flow. To measure whether the company's cash flow can cover its current debt, compare the **times interest earned ratio** (which is earnings before interest and taxes, or EBIT) to its total interest payments:

Times interest earned ratio = EBIT/Interest payments

current ratio
an indicator of liquidity; calculated as short-term assets/short-term liabilities

debt ratio
a measurement of the proportion of total assets financed with debt; calculated as total debt/total assets

times interest earned ratio
an indicator of financial leverage; calculated as earnings before interest and taxes (EBIT)/total interest payments

A high times interest earned ratio (relative to the industry norm) is an indication that the company should be able to cover its debt payments.

Ratios are used as performance indicators to compare different companies within the same industry. Deviations within the industry are often in line with good and proper management, but they can also indicate that the company is struggling.

---

doing the MATH

13.3 Deriving Evaluation Criteria from the Balance Sheet and Income Statement

You are thinking of investing in a company with the following balance sheet and income statement data:

Short-term assets: $1,500,000
Short-term liabilities: $500,000
Total debt: $750,000
Total assets: $2,500,000
EBIT: $300,000
Interest payments: $100,000

The industry standard times interest earned ratio is 2.

1. Calculate the current ratio to assess the company's liquidity (the company's ability to cover its expenses).

2. Calculate the debt ratio to assess the company's financial leverage (the extent of the company's reliance on debt to support operations).

3. Calculate the times interest earned ratio to assess the company's ability to cover debt payments compared to its peers.

4. Is this a company whose stock you want to buy? Why or why not?

Making $ense

13.8 What reports should you study before buying stock?

13.9 Why is a review of the 10K important in stock selection?

13.10 What information do the balance sheet and income statement provide?

13.11 What is the purpose of analyzing ratios based on financial data?

13.4 BUYING AND SELLING STOCKS

■ ■ **LO 13-4** Summarize the basics of buying and selling stocks.

The process of buying, selling, and evaluating stocks takes a considerable amount of research and time. For this reason, some people are better served investing in mutual funds, as discussed in Chapter 12. Developing a basic understanding of how the stock market works and how stocks are valued will help you select a mutual fund.

Common stock represents ownership in a business and gives you the right to vote in the election of company directors and on issues raised at the annual shareholders' meetings. Companies can buy back their stock by making an offer directly to shareholders or by buying the shares on the stock market. Stocks are traded on most working days on the stock exchanges.

Types of Brokers

You can purchase stock from an SEC-licensed agent or brokerage house recognized by the exchange on which

> " In Wall Street, the only thing that's hard to explain is next week. "
> —LOUIS RUKEYSER, *Financial journalist and broadcaster (1933–2006)*

the stock is listed. You can also purchase stock from an online brokerage house, a discount brokerage house, or a full-service brokerage house. Fees, services, and the advice you receive will vary, depending on which type of broker you select.

full-service brokerage houses Full-service brokerage houses, such as Merrill Lynch, Wells Fargo Securities, and Edward Jones, provide the most personal advice, and also have the highest fees. A good stockbroker will get to know you, your risk tolerance, and your investment objectives. She or he will then give advice regarding when and what type of stocks, bonds, or commodities to buy or sell. Brokers also may offer financial and tax planning. Full-service brokers normally charge a commission for stock transactions or a fee for their advice.

discount brokers Discount brokers, such as Fidelity, E*TRADE, TD Ameritrade, Charles Schwab, and Scottrade, execute stock trades on your behalf but do not provide advice. Discount brokers generally charge a set fee for trades; this fee is typically lower than that charged by full-service brokers. Many online brokerage houses are discount brokers who provide stock information and research online. Likewise, many full-service brokerage houses now offer discount and online brokerage services, with fees and commissions adjusted for the amount of service you receive.

Types of Trades

After choosing a broker, you can begin buying investments such as stocks, bonds, mutual funds, or exchange-traded funds. Before that, however, it is important to learn the 12 types of trades that can be placed and how they work. These trades are summarized in Figure 13.9.

market orders A **market order** is the simplest type of stock trade. If you want to buy or sell shares of a stock, the market order gets transmitted to the exchange and will be filled at the current price when the order is executed (which is not necessarily the same price as when you placed the order). These orders typically charge the lowest commission. Shares of stock are normally purchased 100 shares at a time, which is referred to as a **round lot**. Any purchase less than 100 shares is considered an **odd lot**.

limit orders A **limit order** lets you set a minimum or maximum price before your stock trade gets converted to a market order and sent to the stock exchange. Until you are very experienced

The trading floor of a stock exchange can be an overwhelming place, but many people love to be close to the action.

▼ **FIGURE** 13.9

Mechanics of trading stocks

Market order	• Guarantees execution but not price
Limit order	• Guarantees price but not execution
All-or-none order	• Executed if enough shares as a block are offered to fill your order
Stop order	• Automatically converts to market order at predetermined stop price
Stop-limit order	• Automatically converts to a limit order when stop price reached
Short-sell order	• Sale of stock you do not own with assumption that stock prices will fall
Buy-to-close order	• Closes the transaction of the short-sell order
Day order	• Expires at the end of a trading day
Good-til-canceled order	• An order that stays on the books until complete, canceled, or 60 days expires
Extended-hours order	• Executed after the close of market as an electronic trade request
Trailing-stop order	• An order to sell if the price falls a said amount from its highest price
Bracketed order	• A trailing-stop order with an upper limit trigger price that places a sell order

in stock trading, you should place almost all orders as limit orders, to protect yourself. The primary difference between a market order and a limit order is that there is no guarantee the order will take place because the limit must be reached before the trade can be executed.

all-or-none orders An **all-or-none order** is a request to execute an order only if it can be done in a single transaction. The minimum size of an all-or-none order is 300 shares. Normally, when purchasing a substantial amount of a company's common stock, the broker will fill your order over the course of several hours or even days, which keeps you from "moving the market"—that is, drastically affecting the price of the stock by flooding the market with a single, large order. An all-or-none order is an efficient way to place your order with a minimum amount of bookkeeping.

stop and stop-limit orders A **stop order** is an order to buy or sell a stock once the price reaches the *stop price*. Stop and stop-limit orders are known as *stop-loss* orders because investors use them to lock in the profits of their trades. A *stop-limit order* combines the features of a stop order and a limit order. Once a stop price is reached, the stop-limit order becomes a limit order to buy or sell at a specified price. The benefit of a stop-limit order is that you control the price at which the trade will be executed. But, as with all limit orders, a stop-limit order may never get filled if the stock's price never reaches the specified limit price. This happens especially in fast-moving markets where prices fluctuate wildly.

short-sell and buy-to-close orders A *short sale* is the sale of a stock you do not own. Thus, a **short-sell order** is an order for a trade that involves selling borrowed stocks. Investors who sell short believe the price of the stock will fall. It is an extremely speculative practice that can lead to unlimited losses or to high profits from a decline in a stock price. If the stock price falls, you can close the transaction

with a *buy-to-close order,* replacing the borrowed stock and pocketing the difference minus the commission and expenses for borrowing the stock. However, if the price of the stock climbs, your losses could be extreme. It is a very risky technique, and sales of this type are closely monitored by the SEC.

day and good-til-canceled (GTC) orders A **day order** expires at the end of the trading day if it is not filled. A **good-til-canceled (GTC) order** will not expire for up to 60 days. Placed orders must have an expiration date. All market orders are placed as day orders. The risk in using GTC orders is that you may forget you placed the order, and a lot can change in 60 days. If you place a large trade with a GTC status, you will pay a commission each day your order is partially filled.

extended-hours orders An **extended-hours order** allows you to place orders through electronic trading networks after the market is closed. This enables investors to react to late-day corporate announcements and evening news prior to the opening of the market the next day. Risks associated with extended-hours orders include a lack of liquidity and larger quote spreads (with less trading activity, you have wider spreads between the bid and ask prices, making it more difficult to get your order executed or to get as favorable a price).

trailing-stop orders A **trailing-stop order** can be helpful in protecting your profits. As the stock price goes up, you can request to sell only if it falls a specific amount from its highest price. At that point, the order gets converted to a market order.

bracketed orders A **bracketed order** is a buy order that is accompanied by a *sell-limit order* above the buy order's price and a *sell-stop order* below the buy order's price. You set the price at the time you place the bracketed order. This type of order allows you to lock in profits with an upside movement and limit your losses in the event of a downside movement. Bracketed orders and trailing-stop orders are not good options for you if you plan to hold a particular investment for its long-term potential; stocks are notorious for their volatility. Under the bracketed order, trailing-stop orders might be triggered as a result of ordinary volatility—and if an upper limit is reached, the stock would be sold automatically.

Investment Clubs

In the stock market, diversification is the key to financial security. As stated in Chapter 12, mutual funds provide diversification. You should not think about investing in individual stocks until you are diversified in mutual funds, unless you can afford to lose the money you invest in stocks. One way to invest in stocks without risking a lot of money is to join an investment club, where members contribute a set amount of money in their individual accounts each month and take turns studying companies (as Glen did in our chapter opener). This is a good way to gain experience researching, buying, and selling stocks. Your college or university might have an investment club that you can join. If not, there are many websites that will walk you through the steps of starting an investment club (see the nearby Financial Fitness box).

Diversification in individual stocks takes a lot of money. Every time you buy or sell stock, you encounter transaction and sales commission fees. If there is a transaction fee of $20, your investment will need to gain at least $20 for you to break even. Frequent trading will run up the costs of your investment and reduce your returns. To diversify, you will need to own a variety of stocks—from large caps to small caps and from growth stocks to undervalued stocks. An investment club can help ensure your stock purchases are of different types and sizes and from different industries.

Buying individual stocks also requires research. An investment club is a great place to learn how to research a stock. Avoid taking tips at face value from television, the Internet, magazines, or mailings. Study the company's current financial statements, future financial prospects, and the quality of its business and management; these subjects are covered in respected business publications. In the words of Warren Buffett: "It's far better to buy a wonderful company at a fair price than a fair company at a wonderful price."

Buying Stock Directly

While opening a brokerage account is the most popular way to buy and sell investments, it is not absolutely

Participating in an investment club is a great way to gain experience.

financialfitness:
STOPPING LITTLE LEAKS

Cheap Learning

Like traditional clubs, *self-directed* investment clubs meet regularly to share analysis, insight, and information in pursuit of investment opportunities. After investment decisions are made, club members invest through their own accounts, rather than using pooled funds. Visit www .betterinvesting.org/Public/StartLearning/clubs/default.htm to learn more on the benefits of investment clubs.

necessary. Although working with a qualified broker definitely has advantages, it may be better, in some cases, to purchase stock directly from a company. As always, it is important to read the prospectus before investing. Let's look at several ways to make direct investments.

direct stock-purchase plans A number of companies offer direct stock-purchase plans. These plans allow investors to buy shares of stock directly from the company. Most companies have a minimum initial deposit but may be willing to waive it if you agree to automatic monthly withdrawals from a checking or savings account. This way, the company automatically purchases stock for you by debiting your bank account every month. This can be an easy and relatively painless way to invest.

dividend reinvestment plans (DRIPs) If the company you want to invest in does not offer a direct stock-purchase plan, find out if it has a dividend reinvestment plan (DRIP). DRIPs are a great tool for growing your portfolio. In this type of plan, the company reinvests your dividends in company stock by issuing you partial shares for the dividend. Most of these plans also have a lesser-known feature: the cash investments option. This feature allows you to send a check in any amount over $10 (or sometimes $25) to the program administrator, who will then purchase additional shares for you. The big benefit of DRIPs is that you are allowed to purchase fractional shares, allowing your money to begin building wealth. The catch is you may have to own one share of the company before you can enroll.

buying single shares Companies such as One Share allow you to buy a single share of stock in many leading corporations and send you a stock certificate in a frame.

financialfitness:
ACTION ITEM

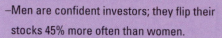

The Gift That Keeps Giving

The perfect gift for holiday giving can be found at www.OneShare.com. It is a framed decorative stock certificate complete with a quick reference guide to the stock market. This starter kit teaches kids how the market works and lets them take pride in being an owner of a company whose product they enjoy. Whether it is Disney for the toddler, DreamWorks Animation for the grade schooler, or Domino's Pizza for a teenager, it is a gift that more than retains its value long after the holidays have passed.

While this may seem like a novelty gift, it provides the needed requisite to enroll in a DRIP. Once the share is in your possession, the enrollment paperwork takes only a few minutes. After you are enrolled, you can start building positions in your favorite stocks while avoiding brokerage commissions. Some companies do charge a slight service fee for DRIP plans.

Personal Finance Life Stages and Stock Ownership

The number and types of stocks you own should vary according to your personal finance life stage. Stocks are an

Making $ense

13.12 How do investment clubs work?

13.13 What option do you have for buying stock if you can't afford a full share?

financialfitness:
NUMBERS GAME

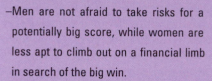

Mars and Venus

According to a study in 2008 by the University of Oregon:[1]

- Men are confident investors; they flip their stocks 45% more often than women.
- Men are not afraid to take risks for a potentially big score, while women are less apt to climb out on a financial limb in search of the big win.
- Female investors tend to incur fewer dramatic losses in their portfolios than men, as well as fewer dramatic wins.
- Female risk-adjusted returns beat male returns by an average of about 1 percentage point annually.

investment to take on when you have more capital to work with and can afford to lose money.

dependent life stage (age <16) to independent life stage (age 16–24) For young people, stocks make a great gift, both to learn from and to build on. Once you have one share of stock, you can buy additional shares through a direct stock-purchase plan using additional gift money.

early family life stage (age 25–40) After you have an emergency fund in place and are ready to take on more risk, you can start to allocate funds toward a DRIP in order to build your wealth. A University of Oregon study found men tend to better anticipate and take advantage of the soaring highs of a bull market. In contrast, women tend to approach the stock market with more patience, deliberation, and caution and, over time, they achieve a more dependable, risk-adjusted return on investments.[1] These traits are generalized and do not apply to everyone. As an example, Warren Buffett's style of investment more characteristically resembles traits attributed to the female investors in the study. Couples should take advantage of any complementary styles they each bring to the table. Just as couples should work together in defining and managing a budget, so too should they be partnered in their stock investment decisions during this stage.

empty nest life stage (age 41-65) Revisit and investigate all the investment options offered in your 401(k)

[1] Barber, B.,M., & Odean, T. (2001). Boys will be boys: Gender, overconfidence, and common stock investment. *The Quarterly Journal of Economics*, 116(1).

plan. You should rebalance your current investment allocations and expand into investments that will preserve asset value, especially in a recession period. Make sure no single industry, business sector, geographical area, company size, or type of investment amounts to more than 20% of your portfolio.

retirement life stage (age 66+) At this stage it is important to review your potential combined retirement income. If necessary, reallocate your current investments so that you have the income you need while still providing for some growth in capital to help beat inflation and fund your later years. ◼

Learn. ❯ Plan & Act. ❯ Evaluate.

⮕ **LEARN.** This chapter covered the basics of stocks. To develop confidence when working directly with stocks as an investment option, spend time researching the companies in which you want to invest. Because stocks require capital, they are an investment to take on when you have capital to work with. Investing in stocks can also involve risk, and no guarantee of returns, so you should only invest in stocks if you can afford to lose money.

SUMMARY

◼◼ **LO 13-1** Understand the basic principles of stocks and the stock market.

Stock is equity that represents ownership in a company. Selling stock (going public) is a way for companies to raise money; the first time a company sells stock is referred to as an IPO (initial public offering). Stocks are common or preferred. Preferred stock pays dividends as a percentage of the par value of the stock. Common stock has voting rights, allowing stockholders to elect the board of directors, attend annual shareholder meetings, and vote on establishing corporate objectives, policies, and stock splits—and thus influence the direction of the company. If a company were to declare bankruptcy, secured lenders would receive their money first, followed by unsecured lenders (bondholders), and then preferred stockholders before common stockholders. There is no guarantee of dividends or capital appreciation with any stock, so money invested in stocks is at risk and does not have a guaranteed return. Stock is bought and sold on stock exchanges. Over-the-counter (OTC) refers to stocks traded in some context other than on a formal exchange.

◼◼ **LO 13-2** Explain how stocks are valued.

The value of stock is determined by the amount investors are willing to pay in order to buy it. Online sites make it easy to see how a company's stock is doing in comparison with that of its peers. Government officials and investors watch the stock market for indications of how businesses are doing and for a reading of consumer confidence. A bull market is one in which stock prices overall are rising. A bear market is one in which prices on multiple broad market indexes have decreased 20% or more over at least a two-month period.

The term *market* is commonly used to represent the performance of key stock market indexes. The Dow Jones Industrial Average (Dow) is made up of 30 large, well-known stocks used to represent the whole stock market. The S&P 500 Stock Index represents large-company stocks,

> ["It isn't as important to buy as cheap as possible as it is to buy at the right time."]
>
> —JESSE LIVERMORE, *Famous early 20th century stock trader (1877–1940)*

SCAN HERE for
study quizzes
for this chapter

the NASDAQ 100 is technology heavy, and the Russell 2000 index represents small company stocks.

Stock quotes give information with which to assess how the stock is doing and make market comparisons. Included in the quote is information on the price, dividend, dividend yield, and price-to-earnings (P/E) ratio. A high P/E ratio suggests investors are expecting higher earnings growth in the future. Investors focus on how a company shares its profits (paying a quarterly dividend, making a cash payment to the shareholders, or investing profits in retained earnings), and earnings per share (how much profit the company earns for each share that has been issued). Value stocks are "underdogs" and typically have single-digit P/E ratios.

■■ LO 13-3 Contrast how companies on the stock market are valued.

Three documents useful for researching a company are the 10K, the 10Q, and the annual report. The financial statements to examine within these reports are the income statement and the balance sheet. Refer to the balance sheet and income statement to evaluate the firm's liquidity and financial leverage, as measured by various financial ratios. Additionally, the annual report includes management's assessment of the previous year and the company's prospects for the year to come. It also discloses significant financial risks, including pending lawsuits.

■■ LO 13-4 Summarize the basics of buying and selling stocks.

You can purchase stock from an SEC-licensed agent or brokerage house recognized by the exchange on which the stock is listed. You also can purchase it from an online brokerage house, a discount brokerage house, or a full-service brokerage house. To protect yourself from significant losses, be mindful of the mechanics of buying stocks. There are several types of trades that range from simple (market and limit orders) to complex (trailing-stop and bracketed orders). Investment clubs provide a good way to gain experience researching, buying, and selling stocks. Direct stock-purchase plans allow investors to buy shares of stock directly from the company, with automatic monthly withdrawals from a checking or savings account. DRIPs support purchasing fractional shares, allowing your money to begin building wealth, but you may have to own one share of the company before you can enroll. Through companies such as One Share, you can buy a single share of stock, which positions you to enroll in a DRIP.

⟶ PLAN & ACT. Engage in activities that will help you gain experience with stock investments. Your Plan & Act to-do list is as follows:

- ☐ Log on to the WSJ Market Watch and request that the daily market report be e-mailed to you (www.marketwatch.com).

- ☐ Review the current trends over the past few weeks and consider the impact those trends have had on the market (Worksheet 13.1).

- ☐ Pretend that you have $10,000 to invest. Select your stock choices and monitor them for the rest of the semester to get acquainted with the reports and the movement of the market (Worksheet 13.2).

- ☐ Research three companies that you would consider investing in that have DRIPs (Worksheet 13.3).

- ☐ Research accessible investment clubs in your community (Activity 13.4).

→ EVALUATE. Are stocks the right tool to help grow your savings? To keep pace—or better yet, outpace—inflation, it is important to diversify your portfolio and take some risk. Can you do that with just mutual funds, or do you want to venture into stock investments by investing in a DRIP or joining an investment club? Even if you do not plan to get into the complexity of buying stocks directly, understanding the basics of the stock market will help you be more knowledgeable and have greater confidence in selecting mutual funds.

» GoalTracker

Open up your online **GoalTracker**. From your worksheet assessments, note how the investment ideas from this chapter may help support your SMART goals.

key terms

All-or-None Order	Good-til-Canceled Order	Round Lot
Bear Market	Growth Stocks	Securities
Bracketed Order	Initial Public Offering (IPO)	Short-Sell Order
Brokers	Limit Order	Specialist
Bull Market	Market Maker	Stock Exchange
Common Stock	Market Order	Stocks
Current Ratio	Odd Lot	Stop Order
Day Order	Open Outcry	Times Interest Earned Ratio
Debt Ratio	Over-the-Counter	Trailing-Stop Order
Dividend Yield	Penny Stock	Value Stocks
Dividends	Preferred Stock	
Extended-Hours Order	Price-to-Earnings (P/E) Ratio	

self-test questions

1. Stock represents _____. *(LO 13-1)*

    a. Ownership in a company
    b. Profits from a company
    c. Debt from a company
    d. Mutual fund holdings

2. Companies receive money from the sale of stock_____. *(LO 13-1)*

    a. Any time it is traded on a stock exchange
    b. Only at an IPO or secondary offering
    c. When the company sells bonds
    d. When the company sells its product or service

3. Preferred stock_____. *(LO 13-1)*

    a. Provides voting rights
    b. Pays out dividends as a percentage of par value
    c. Is converted to common stock
    d. Has a lower priority than common stock

4. Common stock_____. *(LO 13-1)*

    a. Has guaranteed dividends
    b. Is the first to be paid in the event the company declares bankruptcy
    c. Has guaranteed returns
    d. Provides voting rights

5. The rights of common stock allow you to ____. *(LO 13-1)*

    a. Veto decisions made by the board of directors
    b. Attend the annual shareholders meeting
    c. Trump the vote of bondholders
    d. Receive an SEC annual report

6. If a company declares bankruptcy, common stockholders are _____. *(LO 13-1)*

    a. Paid before preferred stockholders
    b. Paid before bondholders
    c. Usually the last to get paid
    d. Not at risk of losing any money

7. Market capitalization of a company represents the value of the company by _____. *(LO 13-1)*

    a. Multiplying the current stock price by the number of shares outstanding

    b. Subtracting the liabilities from the assets

    c. Subtracting the liabilities from the adjusted market value of the assets

    d. Comparing it to the value of similar companies

8. Stock values are determined by _____. *(LO 13-2)*

    a. The net worth of a business divided by shares outstanding

    b. Calculating the price/earnings ratio

    c. The past performance of the company

    d. What investors are willing to pay for the stock

9. What defines a bear market? *(LO 13-2)*

    a. The market prices are increasing.

    b. The market is going up and down with no determined trend.

    c. The market indexes decrease 20% for at least two months.

    d. Your stock portfolio is losing money.

10. Which of the following is a characteristic of the Dow Jones Industrial Average? *(LO 13-2)*

    a. It contains 30 well-known stocks that represent the whole stock market.

    b. It has had the same stocks since its inception.

    c. It is another name for the S&P 500.

    d. It is stronger than the S&P 250.

11. Which of the following is *not* a stock index? *(LO 13-2)*

    a. DJIA

    b. Russell 2000

    c. S&P 500

    d. Buffett 10,000

12. Which is *not* a recommended consideration when reviewing and researching companies in order to buy stock? *(LO 13-2)*

    a. P/E ratio

    b. Television and radio marketing

    c. Future outlook for the company and the industry

    d. Dividend yield

13. The dividend yield _____. *(LO 13-2)*

    a. Represents annual dividend payments per share divided by the price per share

    b. Is not reflected in the stock price

    c. Should never be zero

    d. All of the above

14. What indications should you derive from a firm's balance sheet and income statement when conducting research prior to buying the firm's stock? *(LO 13-3)*

    a. Liquidity and financial leverage

    b. Income over liabilities ratios

    c. Bankruptcy risk

    d. P/E yield

15. What type of order tells the broker to buy or sell stock at the current price? *(LO 13-4)*

    a. Market order

    b. Limit order

    c. Stop order

    d. Day order

16. What type of order tells the broker to buy or sell stock at a specific price? *(LO 13-4)*

    a. Market order

    b. Limit order

    c. Stop order

    d. Day order

17. What plan allows outside investors to buy shares of stock directly from the company? *(LO 13-4)*

    a. The S&P 500

    b. An SEC plan

    c. An investment club

    d. A dividend reinvestment plan

18. Which is an option through which you can continuously invest small amounts of money in a specific company's stock? *(LO 13-4)*

    a. Extended-hours order

    b. Bracket order

    c. Trailing-bracket order

    d. Dividend reinvestment plan (DRIP)

19. When you buy or sell stock, _____. *(LO 13-4)*

    a. It is free through a discount broker

    b. There is almost always a transaction cost that should be calculated in your total return

    c. Using a full-service broker is your least expensive alternative

    d. It is too expensive to make money on small orders

problems

1. Overall stock prices on multiple broad market indexes have decreased 17% over the last two months. How much more must the market indexes drop before it is determined to be a bear market? *(LO 13-2)*

2. You invested in stock for which you paid $4,000. What is the rate of return if the stock increases in value by $200 and pays an annual dividend of $50? *(LO 13-2)*

3. You bought 100 shares for $40/share plus a commission of $25 for the lot. You ended up selling the shares at $43.27/share plus a commission of $35 for the lot. What is the overall profit from the stock sale? *(LO 13-2)*

4. What is the earnings per share if a company's after-tax income is $1,500,000 and the number of shares outstanding is 750,000? *(LO 13-2)*

5. What is the price/earnings (P/E) ratio if the price per share is $75 and the earnings per share is $2.50? *(LO 13-2)*

6. What is the dividend yield if the dividend amount is $0.75 and the stock price per share is $30? *(LO 13-2)*

7. What is the dividend yield if the annual dividend per share is $5 and the market price of a share of stock is $75? *(LO 13-2)*

8. You have two stocks from which to pick. The first stock has a current stock price of $40 and earnings per share of $3.33. The second stock has a current stock price of $33.50 and earnings per share of $4.01. Both firms are in the media industry, and the average P/E ratio for the industry is 12. Use the P/E ratio to determine which stock you expect to have higher earnings. *(LO 13-2)*

9. What is the current ratio if a company's short-term asset balance is $135,000,000 and its short-term liabilities balance is $60,000? *(LO 13-3)*

10. Which company has a higher degree of liquidity: Company A with a current ratio of 2, or Company B with a current ratio of 1.7? *(LO 13-3)*

11. What is the debt ratio if the total assets financed with debt total $1,700,000 and assets total $2,500,000? *(LO 13-3)*

12. Which company has a higher reliance on debt to support operations: Company A with a debt ratio of 0.2, or Company B with a current ratio of 0.7? *(LO 13-3)*

13. What is the times interest earned ratio if a company's EBIT is $2,700,000 and the total interest payments are $750,000? Should the company be able to cover its debt? *(LO 13-3)*

1. Jim's emergency fund is in place, and he just received a nice bonus of $10,000. He decides he is going to invest in stock and wants your opinion on how to invest it. Jim is single, has no immediate plans for the bonus money, loves adventure sports, and tends to be a risk taker, but he is very careful with his money. *(LO 13-4)*

   a. In what type of industry would you suggest he invest?
   b. On what stock exchange is the industry traded?

   c. How would you value the stock offerings of the companies in the market?
   d. Based on the findings above, would you support Jim's decision to invest $10,000 in the stock of that company?
   e. How would Jim go about purchasing the stock?
   f. What type of order would Jim use and why?

2. Walter is considering investing in the Bikes Ahoy Company. He goes online and looks up the company's 10K, 10Q, and annual report, where he finds the latest balance sheet and income statement, shown below. *(LO 13-3)*

BIKES AHOY
Balance sheet
(*numbers in the thousands*)

Assets	
Cash and marketable securities	$ 150
Accounts receivable	250
Inventories	250
Net fixed assets	900
Total assets	$ 1,550
Liabilities and Stockholders' Equity	
Accounts payable	$ 200
Short-term debt	100
Long-term debt	350
Stockholders' equity	900
Total liability/stockholders' equity	$ 1,550

BIKES AHOY
Income Statement
(*numbers in the thousands*)

Revenue	$ 2,900
Cost of goods sold	1,500
Gross profit	1,400
Operating expenses	800
EBIT	600
Interest paid	275
EBT	325
Taxes	132
Earnings after taxes	$ 193

a. What is the company's current ratio?
b. If the average current ratio for the bike-travel industry is 3.0, is Bikes Ahoy liquid?
c. What is the financial leverage for Bikes Ahoy?
d. Other companies in this industry collect their receivables in 25 days on average. How does this compare to Bikes Ahoy?
e. What is Bikes Ahoy's profitability ratio?

3. Darla decides to start buying stock in Walt Disney Company and Kellogg Company on a regular basis. She is trying to decide between using a dividend reinvestment plan (DRIP) offered by the companies or purchasing the stocks through a discount broker. She asks for your help in researching the two companies' DRIP plans online and comparing their costs in terms of fees, minimum investments, and monthly deposits. Relevant information on these companies can be found at http://www.dailyfinance.com/market-news/. *(LO 13-4)*

a. If she plans to invest $500/month, should Darla go with a DRIP or a direct stock-purchase plan via a discount broker? Why?

b. If she plans to invest $100/month, should she go with a DRIP or a direct stock-purchase plan via a discount broker? Why?

c. If Darla chooses only one company's DRIP plan, is one company a better option than the other if she plans to deposit $500/month vs. $100/month? Which one, and why?

worksheets

Find the worksheets online at www.mhhe.com/walkerpf1e

13.1   THE SOCIAL SCIENCE OF THE STOCK MARKET

Use Worksheet 13.1 to assess how current events impact the market.

Worksheet 13.1 - The Social Science of the Stock Market
(1) Review the top news stories over the past few weeks and consider the impact they have had on the market (Dow).
(2) After completing Worksheet 13.1, what characteristics or patterns do you see?
(3) How does this observation impact your decisions as to what type of stock to buy or sell and when?

Date	Event	Impact on the Dow

13.2   PLAYING THE MARKET

Use Worksheet 13.2 to select a number of stocks and use the worksheet to track the progress and performance of your selections, assessing how current events impact your stock choices.

Worksheet 13.2 - Playing the Market

Pretend that you have $10,000 to invest. Select your stock choice and monitor it for the rest of the semester to become familiar with the reports and the movement of the market.

Company		Date/Price	Date/Price	Date/Price	Date/Price	Date/Price
Symbol						
Stock price						
52 week high/low						
Annual earnings per share						
P/E ratio						
Annual dividend						
Dividend pay date						
Dividend yield						

Date/News about the Company/Industry/World (What happens to the stock price?)

13.3 DRIPS

Use Worksheet 13.3 to evaluate DRIPs offered by three different companies and to determine which one you would most like to invest in.

CRITERIA	Company 1:	Company 2:	Company 3:
Symbol			
Stock price			
52-week high/low			
Annual earnings per share			
P/E ratio			
Annual dividend			
Dividend pay date			
Dividend yield			
Enrollment fee			
Minimum investment			
Minimum automatic investment			
Investment fees			

13.4 INVESTMENT CLUBS (Web Activity)

To learn more about investment clubs, go to www.betterinvesting.org/Public/StartLearning/clubs/default.htm.
Search your community to see what options exist. List three investment clubs in your community. Is an investment club something that would interest you? Why or why not?

continuing case

Blake's college does not currently have an investment club on campus. Blake would like to establish an investment club to get experience buying and selling stocks; he also would like to help his housemates learn more about stocks so they can start aggressively moving toward some of their long-term goals (provided, of course, that they're in a good position to do so).

A summary of the housemates' goals can be found in the first Continuing Case problem in Chapter 1 (page 27).

1. What are the benefits to establishing an investment club?

2. How might Blake go about convincing his housemates to start an investment club?

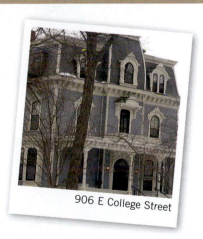

906 E College Street

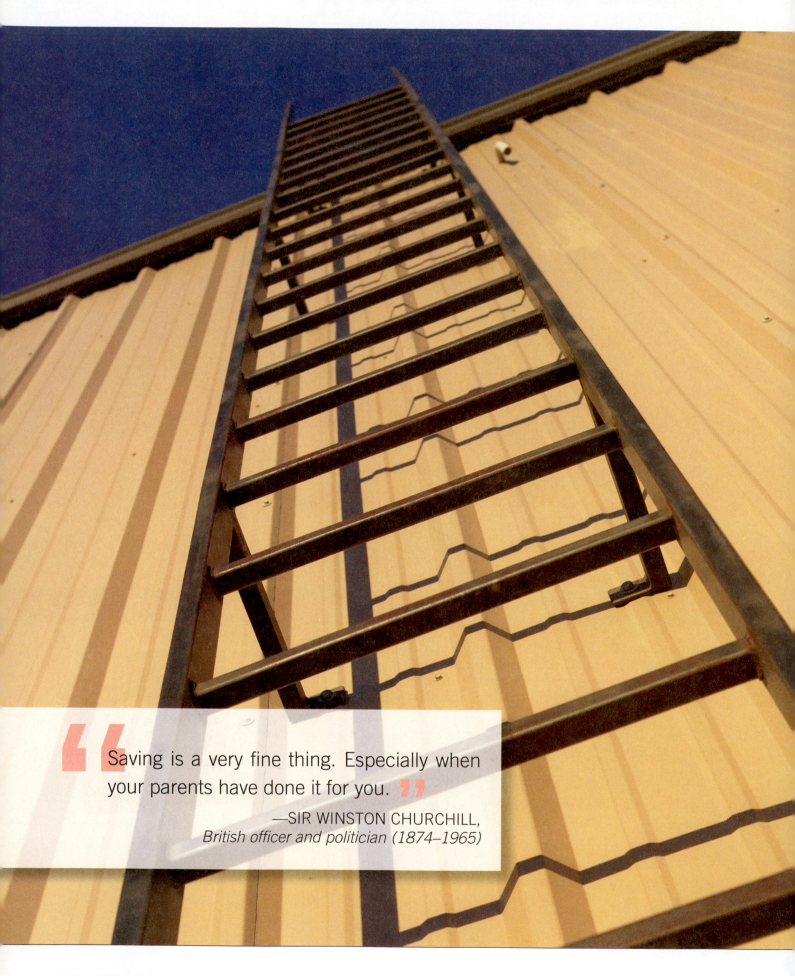

"Saving is a very fine thing. Especially when your parents have done it for you. "

—SIR WINSTON CHURCHILL,
British officer and politician (1874–1965)

bonds

Bonds are a core investment tool in growing wealth, and make up the largest component of the securities market. Bonds are not only a way to invest and earn a return on your money; they are also a way to invest in the security and infrastructure of your community. Regardless of who issues them, bonds play a critical role in the daily economic life of your world. The next time you drive on a smoothly paved highway, visit a local library, see a new hospital tower being built, or hear of a business expansion that is creating new jobs, know that it is likely being financed through the bond market.

There are different types of bonds and several ways to invest in bonds. You can buy bonds individually or diversify your investments through a mutual fund that invests solely in bonds. In this chapter, you will learn the fundamentals of bonds, why companies and governments issue bonds, how bonds are evaluated, and why bonds help you maintain balance in your investment portfolio. You will also be introduced to the mechanics of how and when to invest in bonds.

LEARNING OBJECTIVES

After reading this chapter, you should be able to:

LO 14-1 Define the basics of bonds.

LO 14-2 Contrast the different types of bonds.

LO 14-3 Explain how bonds are valued.

LO 14-4 Evaluate bond risks and returns.

LO 14-5 Plan where and how to buy bonds.

◄ Sam, age 25, teacher, graduate from a large public university

Buried Treasure

Every Christmas and birthday, Sam received a U.S. savings bond from her grandparents. Her parents put each bond in a safety deposit box, so Sam did not put much thought into their value. After she landed her first teaching job out of college, her parents gave her a stack of bonds. Given that she didn't remember having these, it felt like she had unearthed a treasure. She said, "I didn't know that bonds were worth so much. I've heard that government bonds have some tax advantages. I think I might cash in the savings bonds and look to buy Treasury bonds."

14.1 BOND BASICS

■■ ■■ **LO 14-1** Define the basics of bonds.

The United States government needs to borrow money when tax revenues are down. During recessionary periods, the government spends more money on unemployment benefits, student financial aid, job re-training programs, and other social programs that help put people back to work. When more people are working, tax revenues increase, and the government can reduce its debt. When you buy a government bond, you are lending money, unsecured, so that the government can maintain or expand operations.

The same is true with corporate bonds. If a company needs to borrow money for expansion, growth, or retooling, it can go to a bank and get a loan, or it can go directly to investors and issue bonds. For example, if Boeing wanted to build a new aircraft assembly plant for its 787 Dreamliner, it could issue corporate bonds and borrow the money directly from investors. In 2009, Boeing did just that, issuing $1.85 billion in three debt issues to finance its new assembly plant in South Carolina (see Figure 14.1).

Bonds are not as exciting as stocks or other complex investments, but they do provide a steady source of fixed income that can help balance and diversify your portfolio. Because of this, bonds can be an important source of income during retirement. Before purchasing a bond, however, you should fully understand what this instrument is and how it works.

What Are Bonds?

A **bond** is a debt instrument issued by a government or a company for the purpose of raising money to fund construction, take on new projects, or grow the business. A bond is a promise to repay the principal along with interest (**coupons**) by a specified date (**maturity**).

Historically, bonds (such as the example pictured in Figure 14.2) were all "bearer bonds," meaning whoever possessed the bond had the rights to the interest and principal. Bearer bonds were popular ways to exchange money in the illegal-drug trade because a briefcase could hold more money in bearer bonds than in $100 bills, and the bonds were just as hard to trace as currency. Today, nearly all interest payments are sent electronically to the registered bondholder.

When you buy a bond, you become a *creditor* of the issuer. Unlike stock, you do not gain any kind of ownership rights to the issuer. However, bondholders can force a company into bankruptcy if the company does not pay the interest as promised, and if the company does declare bankruptcy, bondholders have a greater priority claim on the issuer's assets than do the shareholders of company stock.

How Do Bonds Work?

If you buy a school bond for $10,000 with an interest rate of 5%, and you hold onto it until its maturity date in 10 years, you will receive interest payments of $250 every six

financialfitness:
JUST THE FACTS

Clipping Coupons

Early bonds were issued with interest coupons attached to the bottom of the bond. To redeem the interest due, every six months the bondholder would cut a coupon from the bond and take it to a bank. The bank would then send the coupon to the company that issued the bond, so the bondholder could receive the interest payment. As a bondholder, you would not receive the interest payment until you had sent in the clipped coupon.

months. On the maturity date, you will get your original $10,000 back. Most bonds are bought and sold on a secondary market. If you need your $10,000 before the end of the 10 years, you can sell the bond to someone else. The price someone is willing to pay for your bond could be less or more than $10,000, depending on the current interest rate payments being offered for other available bonds.

Bond prices and interest rates move in inverse directions. When interest rates go up, bond prices fall. When interest rates go down, bond prices rise. As seen in Figure 14.3, if interest rates were to fall to 2% for a similarly issued bond, your

$10,000 bond would be worth more than $10,000. In this case, you would charge a **premium** for the bond, because there are no similar investments with the same risk paying 5% interest.

Likewise, as shown in Figure 14.4 on the next page, if interest rates for a similar investment were to rise to 10%, you would have to sell your bond for less than

▼ FIGURE 14.1

Excerpt of Reuters report on Boeing

```
BORROWER: BOEING CO
AMT $700 MLN          COUPON 5.00 PCT      MATURITY 3/15/2014
TYPE SR NOTES         ISS PRICE 99.558     FIRST PAY 9/15/2009
MOODY'S A2            YIELD 5.101 PCT      SETTLEMENT 3/13/2009
S&P A-PLUS            SPREAD 310 BPS/      PAY FREQ SEMI-ANNUAL
FITCH A-PLUS            MORE THAN TREAS    MAKE-WHOLE CALL 50 BPS

AMT $650 MLN          COUPON 6.00 PCT      MATURITY 3/15/2019
TYPE SR NOTES         ISS PRICE 98.466     FIRST PAY 9/15/2009
MOODY'S A2            YIELD 6.208 PCT      SETTLEMENT 3/13/2009
S&P A-PLUS            SPREAD 320 BPS/      PAY FREQ SEMI-ANNUAL
FITCH A-PLUS            MORE THAN TREAS    MAKE-WHOLE CALL 50 BPS

AMT $500 MLN          COUPON 6.875 PCT     MATURITY 3/15/2039
TYPE SR NOTES         ISS PRICE 97.913     FIRST PAY 9/15/2009
MOODY'S A2            YIELD 7.043 PCT      SETTLEMENT 3/13/2009
S&P A-PLUS            SPREAD 330 BPS/      PAY FREQ SEMI-ANNUAL
FITCH A-PLUS            MORE THAN TREAS    MAKE-WHOLE CALL 50 BPS
```

Source: www.reuters.com

▼ FIGURE 14.2

A bond coupon

Source: Unknown auction site.

▼ FIGURE 14.3

Premium bond (Example: after 5 years, the current interest rate is 2%; a $10,000 bond paying 5% interest, valued at a premium, would equal $11,414)

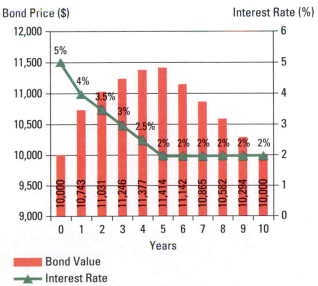

Discount bond (Example: after 5 years, the current interest rate is 10%; a $10,000 bond paying 5% interest would be discounted to $8,104)

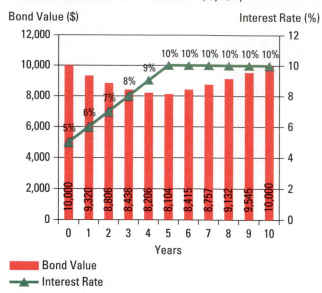

Bond Value ($)   Interest Rate (%)

Bond values: 10,000, 9,320, 8,806, 8,438, 8,206, 8,104, 8,415, 8,757, 9,132, 9,545, 10,000

Interest Rate: 5%, 6%, 7%, 8%, 9%, 10%, 10%, 10%, 10%, 10%, 10%

Years (0–10)

■ Bond Value
▲ Interest Rate

$10,000. This is known as selling at a **discount**. Why would someone pay full face value ($10,000) for your bond at 5% when they could buy a similar bond at 10%? To sell the bond, you would have to reduce the price so the return on the bond would equal 10%.

Bond prices can rise or fall from day to day. For example, the closer your school bond gets to its maturity date, the more likely it is to be close to the original (**par**) value of $10,000, as there is less time to maturity and less time to accrue interest.

Making $ense

14.1 What does a coupon represent when associated with a bond?

14.2 Why do bond prices and interest rates move in inverse directions?

14.3 Describe how a call provision works with bonds.

A **call feature** on a bond allows the issuer to buy back the bond before its maturity date. This feature allows the issuer to retire existing bonds that have coupon rates higher than current interest rates. As an investor, you will want to purchase bonds with a call feature only if the bonds offer a slightly higher return than similar bonds without a call feature. This premium compensates you for the possibility of the bond being called before maturity, and you miss out on the promised interest.

Returning to our example, suppose the school bond includes a call feature stating that the issuer (the school) will pay you an extra six months of interest if it calls the bond. (The call provision states the particulars of the repayment penalty.) Our school bond was issued at 10% for 10 years. If interest rates drop to 5%, the school will

doing the MATH

14.1 **Mechanics of Bonds**

You purchase a $10,000, 10-year bond at 5%.

1. How often will you receive an interest payment?

2. How much will each interest payment be?

3. How much interest will you earn over the 10-year period?

4. How much will you get back on the bond maturity date?

5. If you were to sell your bond after holding it for only three years and interest rates for other similar bonds were at 3%, would you be able to sell your bond at a premium or would you need to sell it at a discount?

want to call the bond (pay off the bond early) by paying the current bondholders an extra six months of interest premium. The school will save money by issuing another bond at 5% to pay off the bond at 10%. This is similar to refinancing a car or house at a lower interest rate.

14.2 TYPES OF BONDS

■ ■ **LO 14-2**   Contrast the different types of bonds.

Both governments and corporations issue bonds. Before purchasing a bond, it is important to fully understand how these bonds differ, so you select the option that best meets your specific investment goal.

United States Savings Bonds

United States savings bonds were introduced in 1935 when President Franklin D. Roosevelt signed the first "baby bonds" legislation. These bonds were issued in four successive series, from 1935 to 1941, and were sold in denominations from $25 to $1,000 at 75% of their face value. For example, a $100 bond cost $75 to purchase and paid 2.9% interest when held until maturity in 10 years.

These federal bonds were sold through post offices and offered in small denominations to encourage wide public participation in government financing. The government offered these bonds as a savings type of security—with a schedule of interest payments and redemption values, redeemable at any time after a short holding period for the purchase price plus accrued interest. Savings bonds differ from other bonds in that the interest is accrued and paid out at maturity rather than twice a year as income.

In 1941, the federal government introduced the Series E bond, known as the "All American Investment," to help fund defense programs during WWII. Sales outlets for U.S. savings bonds moved from only post offices to multiple venues, including banks and payroll deductions through employers.

discount
a price below the face value of a bond

par
the face value of a bond

call feature
an option for the issuer of a bond to buy back the bond prior to its maturity date

municipal bond
a debt security issued by a state, municipality, or county to finance its capital expenditures

Treasury Bonds, Bills, Notes, and TIPS

Along with savings bonds, the government now issues Treasury bonds, Treasury bills, Treasury notes, and Treasury Inflation-Protected Securities (TIPS). *Treasury bonds* are issued with a 30-year maturity date, and they pay interest every six months. *Treasury bills* are short-term government securities with maturities ranging from a few days to 52 weeks. Treasury bills are sold at a discount and mature at face value. *Treasury notes* (sometimes called T-notes) have longer maturity periods than Treasury bills (up to 10 years) and pay interest every six months.

TIPS are marketable securities whose principal is adjusted by changes in the consumer price index to protect them against inflation. The principal increases with inflation or decreases with deflation. When TIPS mature, you are paid the adjusted principal or original principal, whichever is greater. There are slight variations to when and how TIPS pay interest as well as tax implications.

Figure 14.5 on the next page lays out the differences and details of federal bonds.

Municipal Bonds

A **municipal bond** is a debt security issued by a state, municipality, or county to finance its capital expenditures. For example, municipal bonds may be used to fund the construction of highways, bridges, or schools. Municipal bonds (also known as *munis*) are generally exempt from federal taxes and from most state and local taxes. Taxation depends upon the state in which you live and the location of the bond issuer. Munis are bought for their favorable tax implications and are popular with people in high-income tax brackets.

financialfitness:
STOPPING LITTLE LEAKS

Treasury Hunt

Each year, 25,000 bond interest payments revert to the Treasury Department because the bondholders do not cash them. At www.treasurydirect.gov, you can check if you or a family member has savings bonds no longer earning interest. If so, the bonds should be either cashed in or reinvested to begin accruing money again.

Government bonds: a comparison

	U.S. Savings Bonds (I)	U.S. Savings Bonds (EE)	Treasury Bills	Treasury Notes	Treasury Bonds	Treasury TIPS
Investment Type	Nonmarketable (registered in names of holders)	Nonmarketable (registered in names of holders)	Marketable short-term government securities	Marketable intermediate-term government securities	Marketable long-term government securities	Marketable—can be bought and sold in the secondary securities market
Denominations	Electronic: purchased in amounts $25 or more, to the penny Paper: $50, $75, $100, $200, $500, $1,000, and $5,000	Electronic: purchased in amounts $25 or more, to the penny Paper: $50, $75, $100, $200, $500, $1,000, and $5,000	Min $100; increments of $100	Min $100; increments of $100	Min $100; increments of $100	Min $100; increments of $100
Purchase Price	Face value	Electronic: Face value; Paper 1/2 face value	Sold at a discount from face value	Price and yields are determined at auction and can be priced higher, lower, or at face value of the bond	Price and yields are determined at auction and can be priced higher, lower, or at face value of the bond	Price and yields are determined at auction and can be priced higher, lower, or at face value of the bond
Purchase Limit	$5,000/person	$5,000/person	None	None	None	Auction: Noncompetitive bidding:* up to $5 million; Competitive bidding: up to 35% of offering amount
Span	30 years	30 years	Days to 52 weeks	2, 3, 5, 7, 10 years	30 years	5, 10, 30 years
Interest Earnings	Combined fixed rate & variable semiannual inflation rate (based on CPI-U for Mar & Sept); interest compounds semiannually for 30 years	Fixed or variable rates, depending on date of purchase; interest compounds semiannually for 30 years	Fixed rate	Fixed rate	Fixed rate	Principal increases/decreases with inflation/deflation; interest calculations are based upon adjusted principal; fixed interest rate
Interest Payment	Accrues; paid upon redemption	Accrues; paid upon redemption	Accrues; paid upon redemption	Paid every six months	Paid every six months	Paid every six months
Redemption	Can be redeemed after 12 months; 3-month interest penalty if redeemed during the first 5 years	Can be redeemed after 12 months; 3-month interest penalty if redeemed during the first 5 years	Can be sold prior to maturity in the secondary market or held until it matures	Can be sold prior to maturity in the secondary market or held until it matures	Can be sold prior to maturity in the secondary market or held until it matures	Can be sold prior to maturity in the secondary market or held until it matures
Taxes	Exempt from state & local income tax; exempt from federal tax if used for education	Exempt from state & local income tax; exempt from federal tax if used for education	Exempt from state & local income tax	Exempt from state & local income tax	Exempt from state & local income tax	Exempt from state & local income tax
Risk	Low	Low	Low	Low	Low	Low
How to Buy	Electronic: A Treasury Direct Paper: most banks, credit unions, or savings institutions	Electronic: A Treasury Direct Paper: most banks, credit unions, or savings institutions	Auctioned on a regular schedule; issued electronically	Electronically: Treasury Direct; or banks, brokers, or dealers	Electronically: Treasury Direct; Or banks, brokers, dealers-place a non-/competitive bid	Auction through Treasury Direct, Legacy Treasury Direct, or banks, brokers, or dealers

*Noncompetitive Bid: Agreement to accept yield determined at auction.

Source: Information gathered from www.treasurydirect.gov.

Municipal bonds are generally classified into two categories: *general obligation* bonds and *revenue* bonds. If a municipality issues a bond to build a new water plant, it can designate it as a revenue bond. The revenue the new water plant generates can then be used to pay back the bond. For road repairs and improvements, a municipality would issue general obligation bonds backed by the taxing authority of the municipality. Unlike federal bonds, there is some default risk associated with municipal bonds.

Corporate Bonds

Corporate bonds (also known as *corporate* or *commercial paper*) are debt obligations issued by private and public corporations. Companies use the funds they raise from selling bonds for a variety of purposes, from building facilities or purchasing equipment to expanding their businesses. Unlike stocks, bonds do not give you an ownership interest in the issuing corporation, but they do have to be paid back. The downside for a company issuing bonds is that it must pay interest to bondholders as agreed, or face bankruptcy.

Corporate bonds are evaluated and rated by the credit-rating agencies—Moody's, Fitch, and Standard & Poor's. The ratings provide investors with information about a company's health and stability when buying a bond. Corporate bonds are often listed on major stock exchanges, along with their symbol, coupon rate, maturity, price, percent change, and yield. Corporate bonds can be sold above face value (at

a *premium*), below face value (at a *discount*), or at face value (*par*), depending on the prevailing interest rate in the market. Corporate bonds include convertible bonds and high-yield (junk) bonds.

convertible bonds A *convertible bond* allows the holder to convert the bond into shares of common stock in the issuing company at an agreed-upon price. It is a hybrid security with features of both debt and equity. Convertible bonds typically have low coupon rates but they have additional value in that they can be converted into stock and provide further growth in the company's equity value. When you invest in convertible bonds, you have the benefit of potential conversion into equity as well as cash flow from the coupon payments. When the bond is converted, the company does not pay back the bondholder in dollars, but in company shares.

The benefit to the corporation issuing convertible bonds is that it is borrowing money at a low interest (or coupon payment) rate. The downside to the issuer is that the value of shareholders' equity is reduced due to the stock dilution expected when bondholders convert their bonds into new shares. For the bondholder, the benefit is that a convertible bond may have a large payoff if the company's share price increases, yet the security still retains the properties of a bond (e.g., stability, regular payments) if it is not converted.

corporate bonds
debt obligations issued by private and public corporations

Bonds provide a source of funding for government and business.

high-yield (junk) bonds *High-yield bonds* are corporate bonds issued by organizations that do not qualify for investment-grade ratings. Bonds rated BB+, Ba1, or lower are considered speculative. Based on their rating, these organizations are deemed at greater risk of default on paying interest or principal in a timely manner. To compensate investors for the risk associated with investing in organizations of lower credit quality, the issuers must pay a higher interest rate to attract investors to buy their bonds. Junk bonds, as they are often called, are a high-risk, fixed-income investment.

Figure 14.6 summarizes the different municipal and corporate bond options.

14.3 BOND EVALUATION

■ ■ **LO 14-3** Explain how bonds are valued.

Investing in corporate or municipal bonds is not risk-free. There is a risk that the company or municipality will declare bankruptcy and you will lose your money. New York City barely avoided bankruptcy in 1975 by obtaining a large federal loan. In 1978, Cleveland, Ohio, was the first major U.S. city to default on a financial obligation when the Cleveland Trust Company did not renew the city's credit on a $14 million loan. Many companies declare bankruptcy and default

> " Someone's sitting in the shade today because someone planted a tree a long time ago. "
> —WARREN BUFFETT, *Venture capitalist (1930–)*

▼ **FIGURE 14.6**

Municipal and corporate bonds: a comparison

	Municipal Bonds	**Corporate Bonds**	**Convertible Bonds**	**Junk Bonds**
Investment Type	Marketable debt security issued by a state, municipality, or county	Marketable debt security issued by private and public corporations	Marketable hybrid security (debt & equity); can be converted into common stock	Marketable high-risk debt obligations issued by private and public corporations
Denominations	Typically issued in multiples of $1,000 and $5,000 or higher	Typically issued in multiples of $1,000 and $5,000 or higher	Typically issued in multiples of $1,000 and $5,000 or higher	Typically issued in multiples of $1,000 and $5,000 or higher
Purchase Price	Sold above (premium), below (discount), or at face value (par) depending on the interest rate	Sold above (premium), below (discount), or at face value (par) depending on the interest rate	Sold above (premium), below (discount), or at face value (par) depending on the interest rate	Sold above (premium), below (discount), or at face value (par) depending on the interest rate
Purchase Limit	None	None	None	None
Span	Varying	Varying	Varying	Varying
Interest Earnings	Fixed rate	Fixed rate	Fixed rate	Fixed rate
Interest Payment	Varying	Varying	Varying	Varying
Redemption	Can be sold prior to maturity in the secondary market or held until it matures	Can be sold prior to maturity in the secondary market or held until it matures	Can be sold prior to maturity in the secondary market or held until it matures	Can be sold prior to maturity in the secondary market or held until it matures
Taxes	Exempt from federal taxes and most state and local taxes	No exemptions	No exemptions	No exemptions
Risk	Varying	Varying	Varying	High
How to Buy	From financial institutions, financial advisors, or brokers	From financial institutions, financial advisors, or brokers	From financial institutions, financial advisors, or brokers	From financial institutions, financial advisors, or brokers

on financial obligations. When investing in bonds, it is important to understand the guidance provided by bond ratings.

Bond Ratings

Just as a credit score indicates the likelihood that you will be able to repay your debt, a bond credit rating assesses the creditworthiness of the government or corporation issuing the bonds. The creditworthiness of the borrower (or issuer) affects a bond's risk factor and therefore the interest rate that the issuer has to pay. Standard & Poor's, Moody's, and Fitch are the three largest bond credit-rating companies. Figure 14.7 compares the scoring ranges used by these companies, from *prime* to *in default*.

The higher the bond rating, the less the risk of nonrepayment on debt, and the safer the investment in the bond. The higher the rating on the bond, the lower the interest rate the issuer has to pay to compensate for the default risk. Just like your credit score, a higher bond rating indicates a lower probability of default, which translates into lower interest rates. Conversely, a lower bond rating indicates a higher probability of default, which makes the bond riskier; therefore, the issuer has to pay a higher interest rate.

Companies are very protective of their bond ratings, just as you should be protective of your credit score. A decrease in

Making $ense

14.4 What are the different debt obligations issued by the U.S. Treasury?

14.5 How is interest taxed on Treasury-issued bonds? How could it be taxed on municipal bonds?

14.6 What are the advantages of a convertible corporate bond?

14.7 Why would someone invest in junk bonds?

a company's bond rating can cost the company thousands or even millions of dollars in increased interest payments to bondholders on new bond issues. If a company's bond rating increases, the company can call in old issues of bonds that have higher rates and refinance at lower rates.

Bonds can be classified as senior or subordinate debt by the company's hierarchy of borrowing and priority of repayment. *Senior* debt obligations often have lower interest rates because of the reduction of risk compared with *subordinate* debt obligations. If the government or company runs into financial trouble and ends up in bankruptcy court, the liens are repaid in the following sequence: (1) IRS, (2) banks, (3) senior bondholders, (4) subordinate bondholders, and (5) stockholders. If there is not enough money in the end, the stockholders are not paid. This is a key reason why bonds are generally less risky than stocks.

Researching Bonds

In researching bonds, first look at Treasury bonds, bills, and notes and compare the coupon rate or interest rate to the bond you are thinking

▼ **FIGURE 14.7**

Bond ratings

Moody's		S&P		Fitch		Ratings
Long-Term	Short-Term	Long-Term	Short-Term	Long-Term	Short-Term	
Aaa		AAA		AAA		Prime
Aa1		AA+	A-1+	AA+	A1+	High-grade
Aa2	P-1	AA		AA		High-grade
Aa3		AA–		AA–		High-grade
A1		A+	A-1	A+	A1	Upper medium-grade
A2		A		A		Upper medium-grade
A3	P-2	A–	A-2	A–	A2	Upper medium-grade
Baa1		BBB+		BBB+		Lower medium-grade
Baa2	P-3	BBB	A-3	BBB	A3	Lower medium-grade
Baa3		BBB–		BBB–		Lower medium-grade
Ba1		BB+		BB+		Noninvestment grade; speculative
Ba2		BB		BB		Noninvestment grade; speculative
Ba3		BB–	B	BB–	B	Noninvestment grade; speculative
B1		B+		B+		Highly speculative
B2		B		B		Highly speculative
B3		B–		B–		Highly speculative
Caa1	Not Prime	CCC+		CCC		Substantial risks
Caa2		CCC	C	CCC	C	Extemely speculative
Caa3		CCC–				In default with little prospect for recovery
Ca		CC				In default with little prospect for recovery
/				DDD		In default
/		D	/	DD	/	In default
/				D		In default

Source: www.municipalbond.org/wp-content/uploads/2009/02/bond-table1-857x1024.jpg

Yahoo! Finance bond screener

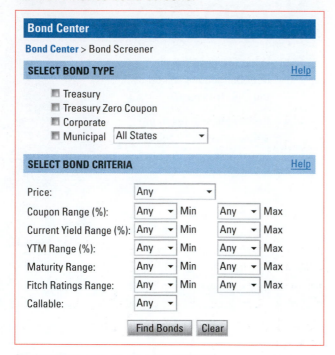

Source: http:///screen.yahoo.com/bonds.html

about buying. U.S. Treasury bonds have virtually no default risk, and the interest is not taxable by state and local governments. Even though the interest rate may be lower, you benefit by not paying state and local taxes, and you are not taking on default risk. The more risk you take on, the higher the interest rate you should receive.

Once you decide on your investment objective and time horizon, find the yield on government bonds with a similar time span; then start to look at corporate bonds within the same time period. In order to do this, you may need to use a bond screener, which searches for bonds according to criteria you set. Figure 14.8 shows a bond screener from Yahoo! Finance. The bond screener first asks you to select the type of bond you want. You then can specify the range for your coupon rate, current yield, yield-to-maturity, maturity, and bond rating, as well as whether or not you would like the bond to be callable. If the screener finds any bonds that meet your requirements, it will provide a list of bonds with the issuer's name, price, and information.

From the list provided by the stock screener, select some issuers, perhaps ones you know and a few others of interest. The next step is to go to the company websites, where you can download and read the companies' annual reports, 10ks, and press releases. Also search the Internet for articles on the company by using your library's databases, *The Wall Street Journal,* Morningstar, and other financial publications. Watch for how each company compares to overall bonds offered in its class (see the online bond report in Figure 14.9).

Look at each company's rating by Standard & Poor's, Moody's, and Fitch, being careful to see if the different agencies rate the company differently. Read reports about the company written by the rating agencies. Be a visionary and try to predict the future for each company you are researching. What circumstances might cause the company to go bankrupt? How likely is business growth and under what circumstances might it occur during your investment period? If you are investing for the long term with bonds, you want to be as certain as possible the company will still be around when the bond matures.

You can use Worksheet 14.2 (online) to evaluate different bonds and find one that meets your specific demands. Always compare the corporate bonds in which you are interested with Treasuries. Do not forget about the transaction costs of buying corporate bonds. Transaction costs and state, local, and federal taxes on the interest

► **FIGURE** 14.9

Sample online bond report

Source: Yahoo! Finance.

yield
the interest rate of a bond

yield to maturity
the interest rate you receive between the date you buy the bond and the date it is repaid, including all payouts, coupons, and capital gains/losses

yield to call
the interest rate you receive between now and the early repayment date

current yield
the interest rate paid on the bond as a percentage of the bond's current market price

income can decrease your yield by as much as 1% compared with the yield on Treasuries. Now all you have to decide is which bond you want to add to your investment portfolio.

Bond Value

There are a number of features you should look at when comparing bond options and assessing value (see Figures 14.10 and 14.11 for market data on corporate bonds and tax-exempt bonds, respectively). First, evaluate the bond for the interest rate (or **yield**) you will receive relative to the risk you would take. You want a bond with a high bond rating that pays a reasonable return relative to similar bonds. The yield varies depending on the bond's par value at the time you buy or sell it.

The **yield to maturity** is the interest rate you receive if you buy the bond today and hold it to maturity, including all payouts, coupons, and capital gains or losses. The yield to maturity calculation assumes all interest payments can be reinvested at the same interest rate as the coupon rate. Some bonds can be called, or repaid earlier than the maturity date. The **yield to call** is the interest rate you receive between now and the call or early repayment date. The **current yield** is the interest rate paid on the bond as a percentage of the bond's current market price.

▼ **FIGURE** 14.10

Researching bond value: online review of corporate bonds

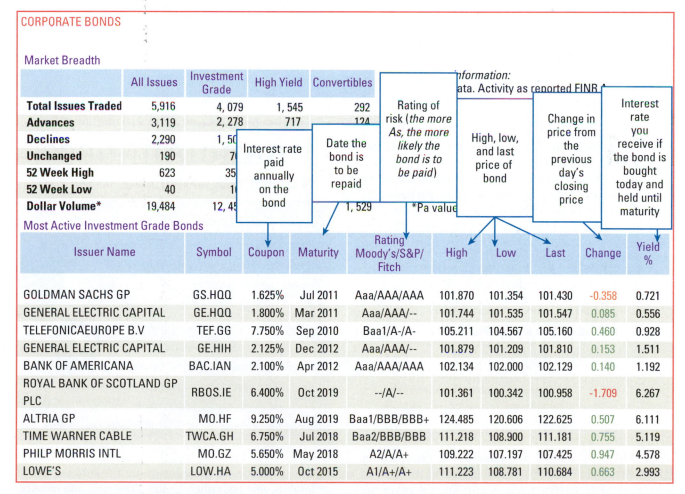

CORPORATE BONDS

Market Breadth

	All Issues	Investment Grade	High Yield	Convertibles
Total Issues Traded	5,916	4,079	1,545	292
Advances	3,119	2,278	717	124
Declines	2,290	1,50		
Unchanged	190	7		
52 Week High	623	35		
52 Week Low	40	1		
Dollar Volume*	19,484	12,45		1,529

Most Active Investment Grade Bonds

Issuer Name	Symbol	Coupon	Maturity	Rating Moody's/S&P/Fitch	High	Low	Last	Change	Yield %
GOLDMAN SACHS GP	GS.HQQ	1.625%	Jul 2011	Aaa/AAA/AAA	101.870	101.354	101.430	-0.358	0.721
GENERAL ELECTRIC CAPITAL	GE.HQQ	1.800%	Mar 2011	Aaa/AAA/--	101.744	101.535	101.547	0.085	0.556
TELEFONICAEUROPE B.V	TEF.GG	7.750%	Sep 2010	Baa1/A-/A-	105.211	104.567	105.160	0.460	0.928
GENERAL ELECTRIC CAPITAL	GE.HIH	2.125%	Dec 2012	Aaa/AAA/--	101.879	101.209	101.810	0.153	1.511
BANK OF AMERICANA	BAC.IAN	2.100%	Apr 2012	Aaa/AAA/AAA	102.134	102.000	102.129	0.140	1.192
ROYAL BANK OF SCOTLAND GP PLC	RBOS.IE	6.400%	Oct 2019	--/A/--	101.361	100.342	100.958	-1.709	6.267
ALTRIA GP	MO.HF	9.250%	Aug 2019	Baa1/BBB/BBB+	124.485	120.606	122.625	0.507	6.111
TIME WARNER CABLE	TWCA.GH	6.750%	Jul 2018	Baa2/BBB/BBB	111.218	108.900	111.181	0.755	5.119
PHILP MORRIS INTL	MO.GZ	5.650%	May 2018	A2/A/A+	109.222	107.197	107.425	0.947	4.578
LOWE'S	LOW.HA	5.000%	Oct 2015	A1/A+/A+	111.223	108.781	110.684	0.663	2.993

Callout boxes: Interest rate paid annually on the bond · Date the bond is to be repaid · Rating of risk (*the more As, the more likely the bond is to be paid*) · High, low, and last price of bond · Change in price from the previous day's closing price · Interest rate you receive if the bond is bought today and held until maturity · *Pa value

▼ FIGURE 14.11

Researching bond value: online review of tax-exempt bonds

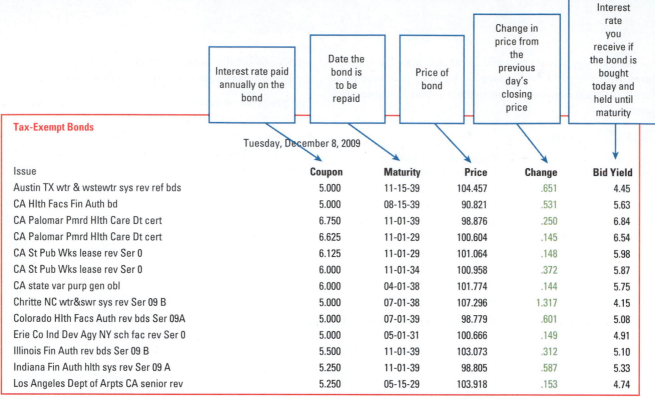

Tax-Exempt Bonds

Tuesday, December 8, 2009

Issue	Coupon	Maturity	Price	Change	Bid Yield
Austin TX wtr & wstewtr sys rev ref bds	5.000	11-15-39	104.457	.651	4.45
CA Hlth Facs Fin Auth bd	5.000	08-15-39	90.821	.531	5.63
CA Palomar Pmrd Hlth Care Dt cert	6.750	11-01-39	98.876	.250	6.84
CA Palomar Pmrd Hlth Care Dt cert	6.625	11-01-29	100.604	.145	6.54
CA St Pub Wks lease rev Ser 0	6.125	11-01-29	101.064	.148	5.98
CA St Pub Wks lease rev Ser 0	6.000	11-01-34	100.958	.372	5.87
CA state var purp gen obl	6.000	04-01-38	101.774	.144	5.75
Chritte NC wtr&swr sys rev Ser 09 B	5.000	07-01-38	107.296	1.317	4.15
Colorado Hlth Facs Auth rev bds Ser 09A	5.000	07-01-39	98.779	.601	5.08
Erie Co Ind Dev Agy NY sch fac rev Ser 0	5.000	05-01-31	100.666	.149	4.91
Illinois Fin Auth rev bds Ser 09 B	5.500	11-01-39	103.073	.312	5.10
Indiana Fin Auth hlth sys rev Ser 09 A	5.250	11-01-39	98.805	.587	5.33
Los Angeles Dept of Arpts CA senior rev	5.250	05-15-29	103.918	.153	4.74

The boxes above the table point to columns and read:
- Interest rate paid annually on the bond → Coupon
- Date the bond is to be repaid → Maturity
- Price of bond → Price
- Change in price from the previous day's closing price → Change
- Interest rate you receive if the bond is bought today and held until maturity → Bid Yield

Source: http://online.wsj.com/mdc/public/page/2_3024-bondbuyer.html?mod5topnav_2_3021

calculating the value of a bond If you want to buy a bond at a market price different from the bond's par value, how do you determine its actual value? The present value of a bond is calculated by discounting the future cash flows (the coupon payments and principal payment) you will receive from the bond. The cash flow discount rate should reflect your required rate of return. The formula is:

$$\text{Value of a bond} = c/(1+i)^1 + c/(1+i)^2 + \ldots + c/(1+i)^Y + B/(1+i)^Y = P$$

where

c = Annual coupon payment in dollars

i = Interest rate (yield to maturity)

Y = Number of years to maturity

B = Par value

P = Purchase price

accounting for taxes Some bonds are exempt from taxes. These bonds are typically issued by municipal, county, or state governments, whose interest payments are not subject to federal income tax. Sometimes, the

interest payments on these bonds are not subject to state or local income tax, either. Unlike Treasuries and munici-pal bonds, corporate bonds do not have favorable tax

14.2 Calculating Bond Value

Your bond is selling for $950 and has a coupon rate of 7%; it matures in five years, and its par value is $1,000.

What is the bond's yield to maturity (YTM)?

The coupon payment is $70 (i.e., 7% of $1,000), so the equation is:

$$70/(1 + i)^1 + 70/(1 + i)^2 + 70/(1 + i)^3 + 70/(1 + i)^4 + 70/(1 + i)^5 + 1,000/(1 + i)^5 = \$950$$

i = 8.261% (Using the formula or a bond yield calculator such as www.money-zine.com/Calculators/Investment-Calculators/Bond-Yield-Calculator/0), the interest rate or yield to maturity (*i*) is 8.261%.

1. What is the YTM if your bond is selling for $950 but has a coupon rate of 6%?

2. What is the value of your $1,000 bond if the YTM is 5% and the bond has a coupon rate of 5% and matures in five years?

financialfitness:
STOPPING LITTLE LEAKS

Minimizing Tax Liability

When you invest in U.S. savings bonds, you can claim your interest as income each year on your federal income taxes. This is extremely advantageous for students as it allows them to make claims when they are in a much lower tax bracket as opposed to waiting to redeem the bond and taking the interest as income at the point of maturity. Additionally, all Treasury interest is exempt from state and local income tax.

Making $ense

14.8 What is the difference between the coupon yield and the yield to maturity?

14.9 How do you calculate the value of a bond and what does it take into consideration?

14.10 Why do investments in corporate bonds lack the favorable tax advantages of Treasuries and municipal bonds?

advantages. With corporate bonds, you pay taxes only on the interest you receive, and the interest is treated as ordinary income. If you sell the bond at a profit, you also pay taxes on the gain.

Municipal bonds generally pay a lower interest rate than corporate bonds, to account for the difference in how they are taxed. Since municipal and Treasury bonds are exempt from state and local tax, they are a good choice if you are in a high tax bracket. Corporate bonds make more sense if you are in a lower tax bracket.

14.4 BENEFITS AND RISKS OF BONDS

■■ **LO 14-4**   Evaluate bond risks and returns.

As an investor, you buy a bond for the interest income, which is often higher than what you would earn from a savings account or a money market mutual fund. However, you

bond ladder
a method of managing investments by buying bonds that mature in intervals

should also be aware of the risks involved in buying bonds.

Benefits

In general, bonds are low-risk investments that help to mitigate the overall risk of your investment portfolio; bonds have relatively low volatility compared with stocks. Bonds are known as *fixed-income* securities because they pay a fixed amount of cash interest, usually twice a year. As you move through your personal finance life stages, increasing the percentage of bonds in your investment portfolio is a good way to gradually reduce your overall portfolio risk.

If you want to receive a regular income from your investment, you can buy individual bonds that pay interest regularly. As an investment strategy, you can build a **bond ladder**, buying bills, notes, and bonds that mature in different years (see Figure 14.12). When one bond matures, you can replace it with another that matures in a future year. Using this strategy, you benefit from the higher interest rates on longer-term bonds, but without the risk you would incur if you were to invest only in long-term bonds.

Laddering helps reduce interest-rate risk by having bonds come due at different times. If you have $10,000 to invest in bonds, you might ladder your bonds by purchasing a 10-year bond for $1,000 every year for 10 years. You will then have a 10-year, $1,000 bond coming due every year. The interest you receive will be the average interest rate for 10-year bonds over the 10-year period. Some of your bonds will have

> " **Dollars do better if they are accompanied by sense.** "
>
> —EARL RINEY, *American clergyman (1885–1955)*

an interest rate higher than others because of the changes in interest rates.

Risks

Bonds are repaid or redeemed on their maturity date. This makes them safer than stock as a stock purchase is never "repaid." However, as with all debt instruments, you are never *guaranteed* that the bond issuer will not default on its debt. The risks of investing in bonds include interest rate risk, default risk, liquidity risk, inflation risk, and call risk.

- *Interest rate risk.* Bonds have a fixed coupon rate for a specific period of time. If you buy your bond and then interest rates go up, your bond will lose value if you have to sell it.

- *Default risk.* The value of the bond may increase or decrease because of problems or opportunities the company faces. If the company is having financial trouble, the value of the bond will decrease because the probability that the firm will default on the financial obligation and declare bankruptcy has increased.

- *Liquidity risk.* Some bonds do not trade daily and have fewer buyers and sellers. If you are unable to find a buyer for the bond, you may have to hold it to maturity.

- *Inflation risk.* An increase in inflation will decrease the purchasing power of the dollar and result in a less-valuable bond. Deflation will increase the purchasing power of the dollar and therefore increase the value of the bond.

- *Call risk.* Bonds with a call feature may have to be sold back to the issuer prior to maturity. You may be unable to replace the bond with an investment of equal risk that pays as much interest.

balancing bond risk One method of balancing your bond risk is to invest in a bond mutual fund that owns many different corporate bonds. With this method there is less risk of default than if you were to own only one bond. Through the fund, your investment is spread among government, corporate, and mortgage-backed bonds, giving you further protection through diversification.

In a bond mutual fund, you can have a mix of bonds of varying terms. Short-term bonds are considered the least risky as they reach maturity within one year, which is when you would be repaid at par. In a year's time frame, the bond price will not have much time to drop or rise. Long-term bonds generally have a higher interest rate, but they are riskier because their prices can be fairly volatile over the 10-year (or longer) period. Intermediate-term bond funds (notes) are likely to pay a

▼ **FIGURE 14.12**

Sample bond ladder investment strategies

Example 3-rung, 3-year bond ladder (over a 6-year period)

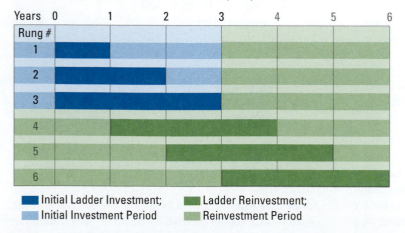

Legend:
- ■ Initial Ladder Investment;
- ■ Ladder Reinvestment;
- ■ Initial Investment Period
- ■ Reinvestment Period

Source: www.tdameritrade.com/offer/global/img/cnt-retire-fixed.gif

Junk bonds: Savvy investment or fool's gold?

The 8 percent solution? Investing in junk (bonds) is risky but could pay off in weak market

CHICAGO (AP)—A sideways stock market has investors searching for other places to make a decent return on their money. And junk bonds, for better or worse, are starting to look like gems to many. The appeal is easy to understand. Junk bonds, known more politely as high-yield bonds, are bonds with very low credit ratings that corporations pay more interest on so they can attract investors. As of last week, they were yielding 8.34 percent, down from 9 percent earlier in July. That number is mighty enticing at a time when the Standard & Poor's 500 index is up just 1 percent for 2010 and down 22 percent from a decade ago. And a murky economic outlook hampers prospects of a strong rebound any time soon. Virtually nowhere else can you get 8 percent back on your money these days. . . . But investors beware: They're called junk for a reason. Bonds below investment grade, or those with S&P ratings below BBB and Moody's ratings below Baa, are much likelier to default. Not only that, junk bonds act more like stocks than other bonds. That's because their prices are closely tied to the corporations that issue them and their ability to service debts. So if you are considering adding them to your portfolio to diversify, think again.

"Don't expect a junk bond to hold its value if equities are doing poorly," says John Donaldson, director of fixed income at Haverford Trust Co. in Radnor, Pa. "It will have good years when equities have good years and bad years when equities have bad years." High-yield bonds as a group lost about 35 percent in price in 2008 during the credit crisis, when stocks also tanked. A casual investor may want to think more about the return OF capital than the return ON capital. That doesn't necessarily mean to steer clear of junk bonds entirely. There could be a place for them in your portfolio if you have a strong appetite for risk and a grasp of the pitfalls as well as the rewards. "Junk bonds may provide an attractive income stream, as long as they are part of a diversified portfolio and the downside risks are clearly understood," says Joseph Jennings, director of investments for PNC Wealth Management in Baltimore. Here's a look at some other points for investors to consider if they decide to chase those 8 percent yields:

- **Stick with funds.** The average investor should not invest in individual junk bonds. There's too big a risk of a default that can cost you a big chunk of money. A casual investor doesn't have sufficient knowledge to assess them anyway. A good mutual fund with a broad portfolio of junk bonds can generate enough extra income to offset any defaults.

- **Investing in junk is speculating.** There's nothing wrong with speculating. But if you do that, choose only an investment that you can afford to lose money on. "There's a reason why investors are offered such a 'bounty' relative to what they are earning on their CDs or savings accounts," says Michael Kay, a certified financial planner based in Livingston, N.J. "An investor should always ask himself or herself, if a total loss is sustained, how will that affect one's portfolio, wealth, and life?" Risk of total loss, of course, should be minimal if you own bonds through a fund rather than individually.

- **Experience and diversification really matter.** In researching a fund, pay extra attention to how long the portfolio manager has been there. Given the volatility of high-yield funds, you want a management team that has been tested by a variety of market conditions over the last 5 to 10 years and come through it with solid results. Spreading your money among different types of corporate junk also is extra important because of the risk that defaults in one weak sector could cost you heavily.

- **Junk bond funds vary dramatically in credit quality.** Check the credit quality before you decide on your preferred level of risk. "High-yield portfolios can vary in quality from 'a little junky' to 'stinky,'" says Dina Lee, a personal financial specialist with the American Institute of Certified Public Accountants. A good way to invest in junk bonds is through a low-cost exchange-traded fund. . . .

Just don't load up your portfolio with junk. Indulge with moderation, as with emerging-market stocks or with wine.

DAVE CARPENTER, "Junk Bonds: Savvy Investment or Fool's Gold?" Associated Press, August 1, 2010. Reprinted with permission.

Questions

1. Given the past-period performance of investment options across the board, what role do junk bonds play in balancing a portfolio in today's market?

2. At what point might junk bonds be a good option for you, and at what percentage of your portfolio?

Making $ense

14.11 What are the benefits of buying bonds?

14.12 What are the risks associated with bonds?

14.13 How does laddering protect you from interest rate risk?

14.14 What are the advantages and disadvantages of bond mutual funds?

Strategy

If the start-up cost makes it difficult for you to invest in a diversified portfolio of bonds, a bond mutual fund is a good alternative. Mutual funds often allow you to enter with as little as $1,000. If you expect interest rates

higher interest rate than short-term bond funds, and their prices should be somewhat more stable than longer-term bond funds.

The advantage of bond mutual funds is that you have immediate diversification of your bond portfolio—and you have a professional fund manager evaluating what bonds to buy and sell. The disadvantage of bond mutual funds is that you have to pay for the professional fund manager and other expenses, which lowers your yield. If you feel you have the expertise to pick and buy bonds, many professionals advise investing directly in bonds rather than in bond mutual funds to avoid these additional expenses. The website www.TreasuryDirect.gov makes it easy for individuals to buy Treasury bonds.

14.5 BUYING BONDS

■■ **LO 14-5** Plan where and how to buy bonds.

The most important strategy in investments is diversification. One way to accomplish this is to include in your investment portfolio a mixture of Treasuries, corporate bonds, and municipal bonds. In addition, you will want to have bonds of varying maturities and yields. In this section we will discuss where and how to buy and sell these different kinds of bonds.

Bonds make up an important part of your investment portfolio, and the stability they provide will help you climb toward your goals.

[**"Like the cosmetics industry, the securities business is engaged in selling illusions."**

—PAUL SAMUELSON, *American economist (1915–2009)*]

Buying bonds online is easy!

to decline, you should invest more heavily in long-term bonds whose prices will increase the most with the fall of interest rates. Conversely, if you expect interest rates to go up, you should put your money into bonds with short terms to maturity, thus minimizing the adverse impact of higher interest rates.

A more passive strategy is to invest in a diversified portfolio of bonds and then hold it for a long period of time, generating interest income in the form of coupon payments. You might consider using a *target strategy,* a practice in which you align the maturity date with the savings goal (such as a child's high-school graduation) so that the principal can be made available to fund the goal, all the while receiving income from the investment. Laddering bonds, as mentioned above, is another way to reduce the interest rate risk associated with bonds. Of course, you will want to diversify your bond portfolio to reduce its default risk.

Where to Buy Bonds

You can buy U.S. Treasury bonds at www.TreasuryDirect .gov, at most local financial institutions, or through payroll deduction plans with a minimum purchase of $100. You can purchase corporate bonds through a full-service broker, discount broker, or online broker. Corporate bonds are primarily for institutional investors; Treasury bonds are available for both institutional and individual investors.

Buying and selling corporate bonds is harder than buying and selling stocks. Bonds tend to trade only every few days and have fewer buyers and sellers. You can find a listing of the most actively traded bonds in the market section of *The Wall Street Journal* (http://online.wsj.com/mdc/public/page/mdc_bonds.html) and other popular financial websites. Many brokers now list their inventories of corporate bonds online.

You can buy and sell bonds in the secondary market before the bonds reach maturity. To sell on the secondary market, you will have to use a broker. Whenever you buy or sell a bond, you will have a transaction fee, which reduces your yield. Some bonds are traded on stock exchanges. Others are traded in the over-the-counter market. ■

financialfitness:
JUST THE FACTS

Smart Exchanges

SmartExchange allows TreasuryDirect account owners to convert their Series E, EE, and I paper savings bonds to electronic securities in a special Conversion Linked Account online. Paper EE Bonds are still available for purchase through most local financial institutions or participating employers' payroll deduction plans.

Making $ense

14.15 Why is diversification important in portfolio bond management?

14.16 Where can you buy bonds?

14.17 Where can you trade bonds?

→ **LEARN.** In this chapter you learned the fundamentals of bonds and why companies and governments issue bonds. You also became familiar with the bond rating system and learned why bonds make good investment options for your portfolio.

SUMMARY

■■ **LO 14-1** Define the basics of bonds.

A bond is a debt instrument issued by governments and companies for the purpose of raising money to fund construction, take on new projects, or grow the business. Bondholders can force a company into bankruptcy if the company does not pay the interest as promised, and in the case of bankruptcy, bondholders have a higher priority claim on an issuer's income than shareholders. Bond prices can rise or fall on any given day.

A call feature on a bond allows the issuer to buy back the bond before the maturity date and retire existing bonds with coupon rates that are higher than current interest rates. As an investor, you should purchase bonds with a call feature only if the bonds offer a slightly higher return than similar bonds without a call feature; this higher return compensates you for the call risk.

■■ **LO 14-2** Contrast the different types of bonds.

U.S. savings bonds differ from other bonds in that the interest is accrued and paid out at maturity rather than twice a year as income. Treasury bills are short-term government securities with maturities of 52 weeks or less. TIPS are marketable securities whose principal is adjusted against the consumer price index to protect them from inflation. The principal increases with inflation or decreases with deflation. When TIPS mature, you are paid the adjusted principal or original principal, whichever is greater.

A municipal bond is a debt security issued by a state, municipality, or county to finance its capital expenditures. Corporate bonds are debt obligations issued by private and public corporations. A convertible bond can be converted into shares of common stock in the issuing company at an agreed-upon price. It is a hybrid security with features of both debt and equity. Convertible bonds typically have low coupon rates, but they provide additional value in that they can be converted into stock and provide further growth. High-yield bonds (also known as junk bonds) are corporate bonds issued by organizations that do not qualify for investment-grade ratings.

■■ **LO 14-3** Explain how bonds are valued.

The bond credit rating assesses the creditworthiness of the government or corporation issuing the debt. The creditworthiness of the issuer affects a bond's risk and the interest rate that the issuer has to pay. Standard & Poor's, Moody's, and Fitch are the three largest credit-rating agencies. Bond values can be derived by evaluating their yield, yield to maturity, call risk, yield to call, and coupon yield.

The present value of a bond is calculated by discounting the future cash flows (the coupon payments and principal payment) to be received from the bond. Price and yield have an inverse relationship. A bond might be sold at above or below par, but the market price will approach par value as the bond approaches maturity. A riskier bond has to provide a higher payout to compensate for that additional risk. Some bonds are tax-exempt, and these are typically issued by municipal, county, or state governments whose interest payments are not subject to federal income tax; sometimes these interest payments are exempt from state or local income tax as well.

■■ **LO 14-4** Evaluate bond risks and returns.

Bonds are known as fixed-income securities because they pay a fixed amount of cash interest. Building a bond ladder involves buying bills, notes, and bonds that mature in different years. An investor using a bond ladder strategy benefits from the higher interest rates on longer-term bonds while incurring less risk than a strategy of investing only in long-term bonds. Because bonds are repaid or redeemed on their maturity date, they are safer than stock as a stock purchase is never "repaid."

Bond risks include interest rate, default, liquidity, inflation, and call risk. Bond mutual funds spread the investor's risk among government, corporate, and mortgage-backed bonds. Short-term bonds are considered the least risky. Long-term bonds generally have a higher interest rate but are considered riskier because their prices can be fairly volatile over the 10-year or longer period to maturity.

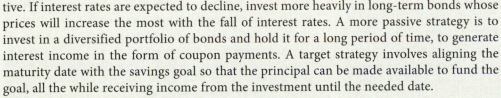

get online!

SCAN HERE for study quizzes for this chapter

■■ **LO 14-5** Plan where and how to buy bonds.

If start-up costs make it difficult to invest in a diversified portfolio of bonds, a bond mutual fund is a good alternative. If interest rates are expected to decline, invest more heavily in long-term bonds whose prices will increase the most with the fall of interest rates. A more passive strategy is to invest in a diversified portfolio of bonds and hold it for a long period of time, to generate interest income in the form of coupon payments. A target strategy involves aligning the maturity date with the savings goal so that the principal can be made available to fund the goal, all the while receiving income from the investment until the needed date.

U.S. Treasury bonds can be bought online. Buying and selling corporate bonds is harder than buying and selling stocks as bonds tend to trade only every few days and have fewer buyers and sellers. You can buy and sell bonds in the secondary market before the bonds reach maturity. To sell on the secondary market, however, you must use a broker and pay a transaction fee, which reduces your yield. Some bonds are traded on stock exchanges. Others are traded in the over-the-counter market.

⮕ PLAN & ACT. After reading this chapter, you should be able to determine whether bonds are an appropriate instrument to include in your portfolio. Your Plan & Act to-do list is as follows:

- ☐ Confirm that you or family members do not have any buried treasure (i.e., unclaimed U.S. savings or Treasury bonds) (www.treasurydirect.gov).

- ☐ Investigate options for a ladder strategy for bond investments (Worksheet 14.1).

- ☐ See if your city has a bond offering and assess its appeal as an investment option for you (Worksheet 14.2).

⮕ EVALUATE. As you move through your personal finance life stages, a good way to help your portfolio gradually reduce risk is to increase your percentage of bonds. Every year you should re-evaluate your asset allocation.

›› GoalTracker

Review your online **GoalTracker**. How can bonds play a role in helping you achieve your goals? From your worksheet assessments, note how the investment ideas in this chapter may support your SMART goals.

It is easier to make money than to save it; one is exertion, the other self-denial. 〞

—THOMAS HALLIBURTON, *Canadian author (1796–1865)*

Bond

Bond Ladder

Call Feature

Corporate Bonds

Coupon

Current Yield

Discount

Maturity

Municipal Bond

Par

Premium

Yield

Yield to Call

Yield to Maturity

self-test questions

1. As a bondholder you _____. *(LO 14-1)*

   a. Are lending money to a corporation or government entity

   b. Are a part owner of the corporation

   c. Have no risk of losing your money

   d. Will receive only your principal investment when the bond matures

2. If you need to sell your bond on the secondary market before the maturity date, _____. *(LO 14-1)*

   a. You will receive only the exact amount you invested

   b. If current interest rates are higher than your bond, you will receive less than face value

   c. If current interest rates are lower than your bond, you will receive more than face value

   d. If current interest rates are higher than your bond, you will receive more than face value

   e. If current interest rates are lower than your bond, you will receive less than face value

   f. Both (b) and (c)

   g. Both (d) and (e)

3. Selling a bond at a discount is _____. *(LO 14-1)*

   a. Selling the bond for more than face value

   b. Selling the bond for less than face value

   c. Selling the bond for face value

   d. Lowering the interest rate on the bond

4. Selling a bond at a premium is _____. *(LO 14-1)*

   a. Selling the bond for more than face value

   b. Selling the bond for less than face value

   c. Selling the bond for face value

   d. Increasing the interest rate on the bond

5. The closer the bond comes to reaching its maturity date, _____. *(LO 14-1)*

   a. The more impact changes in the interest rate will have on its value

   b. The more interest rates will align with its value

   c. The closer it comes to its par value

   d. (a), (b), and (c)

6. Bonds with a call feature _____. *(LO 14-1)*

   a. Have a phone number on them where you can check the value of the bond

   b. Can be bought back by the issuer before the maturity date

   c. Stay at the current interest rate

   d. Can be stored electronically on a cell phone

7. Series EE U.S. savings bonds differ from most other bonds in that _____. *(LO 14-2)*

   a. Interest is paid out quarterly

   b. Interest is paid out semiannually

   c. Interest is paid out monthly

   d. Interest accrues and is paid out at maturity

8. Treasury bills _____. *(LO 14-2)*

   a. Pay interest semiannually

   b. Pay interest monthly

   c. Are typically issued at a discount from the face amount

   d. Are issued for greater than 10 years

9. Treasury notes _____. *(LO 14-2)*

   a. Can be purchased only through a broker

   b. Can be purchased only through a national bank

   c. Can be purchased only through TreasuryDirect

   d. Pay interest that is exempt from state and local income taxes

10. TIPS _____. *(LO 14-2)*

    a. Have an interest rate adjusted by changes in the consumer price index

    b. Have a principal adjusted by changes in the consumer price index

    c. Have to be held to maturity

    d. Pay interest monthly

11. Municipal bonds _____. *(LO 14-2)*

    a. Have no default risk

    b. Have tax advantages

    c. Are issued by the federal government

    d. Are repaid by the revenue generated by the project funded

12. Corporate bonds _____. *(LO 14-2)*

    a. Have default risk

    b. Have tax advantages

    c. Are issued by the federal government

    d. Give you ownership in the corporation

13. Convertible bonds are corporate bonds _____. (LO 14-2)

    a. That can be converted to common stock
    b. That can be called early by the issuer
    c. That can be converted to the present interest rate
    d. That do not pay interest but issue common stock

14. Junk bonds or high-yield bonds _____. (LO 14-2)

    a. Are investment-grade bonds
    b. Are bad investments that should always be avoided
    c. Are classified BB, BA, or lower by the bond rating agencies
    d. Have a guaranteed return

15. Bond rating agencies classify bonds based on the _____. (LO 14-3)

    a. Creditworthiness of the issuer
    b. Potential for growth and success of the issuer
    c. Personal guarantee of the corporate officers and board of directors
    d. Stock value of the corporation

16. In corporate bankruptcy, _____. (LO 14-3)

    a. Subordinate bondholders get paid before senior bondholders
    b. Senior bondholders get paid before subordinate bondholders
    c. Bondholders are the last to get paid
    d. Bondholders are the first to get paid

17. The three biggest credit rating companies for bonds are _____. (LO 14-3)

    a. Bloomberg, Moody's, and Standard & Poor's
    b. Bloomberg, Fitch, and Moody's
    c. Bloomberg, Fitch, and Standard & Poor's
    d. Fitch, Moody's, and Standard & Poor's

18. The higher the rating on the bond, the_____. (LO 14-3)

    a. Higher the interest rate the issuer has to pay
    b. Higher the risk of default of the bond
    c. Lower the risk of default on the bond
    d. The rating has no effect on the interest rate and does not rate the risk of a bond.

19. When researching a bond to add to your portfolio, you should first _____. (LO 14-3)

    a. Know your investment objective
    b. Look at the return on U.S. Treasuries to determine the risk-free rate
    c. Ask a broker/dealer/financial planner what to buy
    d. Look at a bond screener to find a bond you would like to buy

20. The value of a bond is determined by _____. (LO 14-3)

    a. Calculating the present value of the future cash flows
    b. Calculating the future value of future cash flows
    c. Calculating the return for a similar-risk investment
    d. Discounting its present cash value to determine its future value

21. The tax advantage of corporate bonds is _____. (LO 14-3)

    a. You do not have to pay federal income tax on the interest and capital gains you earn
    b. You do not have to pay state income tax on the interest and capital gains you earn
    c. You do not have to pay federal or state income tax on the interest and capital gains you earn
    d. There is no tax advantage for corporate bonds.

22. A bond ladder _____. (LO 14-4)

    a. Helps reduce the risk of changes in interest rates by spacing out the maturities
    b. Is a monthly contribution into a bond mutual fund
    c. Guarantees to always get the best interest rates on the bonds
    d. Is a strategy that helps achieve financial goals by "climbing the ladder."

23. Bond mutual funds _____. (LO 14-4)

    a. Provide immediate bond diversification
    b. Have a professional fund manager evaluating what bonds to buy and sell
    c. Have management fees associated with them
    d. All of the above

24. If you expect interest rates to go up, you should buy _____. (LO 14-5)

    a. Long-term bonds
    b. Short-term bonds
    c. Intermediate-term bonds
    d. A bond mutual fund

25. The website www.TreasuryDirect.gov is _____. (LO 14-5)

    a. Only for major investors who can buy U.S. government bonds
    b. The only place to buy Treasury bills, notes, and bonds
    c. Too complicated for the common person to understand
    d. Where anyone can go to purchase EE-Bonds, I-Bonds, Treasury bills, notes, and bonds

26. Which statement is true? (LO 14-5)

    a. It is easier for individuals to buy and sell corporate bonds.
    b. It is easier for individuals to buy and sell government bonds.
    c. All bond transactions should be handled through an investment adviser.
    d. Bonds are too complicated for individuals to buy on their own.

problems

Use the data below to answer problems (1) and (2).

BORROWER: APPLE CO		
AMT $500 MLN	COUPON 5.00 PCT	MATURITY 3/15/2015
TYPE SR NOTES	ISS PRICE 99.558	FIRST PAY 9/15/2010
MOODY'S A2	YIELD 5.101 PCT	SETTLEMENT 3/13/2010
S&P A-PLUS	SPREAD 310 BPS/	PAY FREQ SEMI-ANNUAL
FITCH A-PLUS	MORE THAN TREAS	MAKE-WHOLE CALL 50 BPS
AMT $700 MLN	COUPON 6.00 PCT	MATURITY 3/15/2020
TYPE SR NOTES	ISS PRICE 98.466	FIRST PAY 9/15/2010
MOODY'S A2	YIELD 6.208 PCT	SETTLEMENT 3/13/2010
S&P A-PLUS	SPREAD 320 BPS/	PAY FREQ SEMI-ANNUAL
FITCH A-PLUS	MORE THAN TREAS	MAKE-WHOLE CALL 50 BPS
AMT $600 MLN	COUPON 6.875 PCT	MATURITY 3/15/2040
TYPE SR NOTES	ISS PRICE 97.913	FIRST PAY 9/15/2010
MOODY'S A2	YIELD 7.043 PCT	SETTLEMENT 3/13/2010
S&P A-PLUS	SPREAD 330 BPS/	PAY FREQ SEMI-ANNUAL
FITCH A-PLUS	MORE THAN TREAS	MAKE-WHOLE CALL 50 BPS

1. Apple issued three debt issues of corporate bonds to borrow money to finance the building and operating of its new research lab. How much money did Apple raise collectively from its issues of corporate bonds? *(LO 14-1)*

2. If you bought a $99.558 Apple bond, how many years would pass between the first payment and maturity? *(LO 14-1)*

3. You buy a municipal bond for $20,000 with an interest rate of 5%, and you hold it until its maturity date in 10 years. *(LO 14-1)*
   a. What is the amount of the interest payment you will receive every six months?
   b. What amount will you receive back in 10 years?

4. A $100 U.S. savings bond that originally cost $75 to purchase pays 2.9% interest if held to maturity in 10 years. How much will it pay at maturity? *(LO 14-2)*

5. You have a $1,000 bond at 4% that matures in five years and pays interest annually. You want to sell it, but the current interest rate on a similar investment that matures in five years is now paying 8% interest. What is the current value of your bond? *(LO 14-3)*

6. You have a $1,000, 8% bond that matures in five years and pays interest annually. You want to sell it, but the current interest rate on a similar investment that matures in five years is now paying 4% interest. What is the current value of your bond? *(LO 14-3)*

7. You buy a $10,000 Treasury note that matures in seven years at 5% interest. What will the interest payments be, and how often will you receive interest? *(LO 14-3)*

8. If you had $5,000 to invest in bonds and your intent was to ladder the bond investments at segments of $1,000 every year, for what period of time would each bond be set? *(LO 14-4)*

you're the expert

1. Jenn invested in a corporate bond for $10,000 at 7% interest three years ago. She is now planning a wedding and would like to cash in her bond to help finance the event. The current interest rate is 5%. *(LO 14-1–LO 14-4)*
   a. What should she be able to sell her bond for in relation to its par value?
   b. How should she go about selling her bond?
   c. How will the bond be taxed?

2. At the birth of twin grandchildren, the grandparents gave the parents $10,000 to buy bonds for the newborns as a start to their college savings. *(LO 14-1–LO 14-4)*
   a. Which type of bonds should be bought and why?
   b. What options are there to diversify this bond investment?
   c. In this example, if $5,000 had been invested in a corporate convertible bond at year 5 and the company's stock price has been trending well,

what would be the motivators (if any) for converting the bond to stock?

3. Clay really likes Nike and has purchased stock in the company. Nike has just announced that it is issuing $10 million in bonds at 5% for 10 years. *(LO 14-1– LO 14-4)*

a. Should Clay buy Nike bonds? What are the advantages?
b. If Clay buys Nike bonds, what are the drawbacks?
c. What should Clay consider before purchasing Nike bonds?

14.1 BOND COMPARISON

Use Worksheet 14.1 to compare a U.S. Treasury bond, a corporate bond, and a municipal bond. Use your comparison to create a ladder strategy for bond investing.

Worksheet 14.2 - Bond Comparison

Investigate bond options and consider using a ladder strategy approach to bond investing. Select a U.S. Treasury bond, a corporate bond, and a municipal bond and complete the comparison worksheet.

Issuer	U.S. Treasury Bond	Corporate Bond	Municipal Bond
Name:			
Price			
Min. amount ($)			
Transaction cost			
Coupon %			
Coupon pay date			
Maturity			
Yield to maturity			
Current yield			
Fitch rating			
S&P rating			
Moody's rating			
Callable (Y/N)			
Comments			

14.2 LOCAL MUNICIPAL OFFERINGS

Use Worksheet 14.2 to assess local municipal bond offerings and consider their appeal as investment options.

See if your city (nearby city or state) has a bond offering and assess its appeal as an investment option. Would you consider this as an investment option? Why or why not?	
Municipal offering	
Price	
Min. amount ($)	
Transaction cost	
Coupon %	
Coupon pay date	
Maturity	
Yield to maturity	
Current yield	
Fitch rating	
S&P rating	
Moody's rating	
Callable (Y/N)	

continuing case

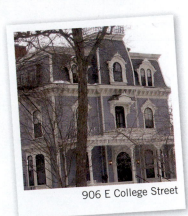

906 E College Street

Blake and his housemates started an investment club, and it has been going well. So far, Brett has presented a pharmaceutical company with the potential of hitting it big with a drug that is about ready to go to market after clinical trials. Peter has presented a new sushi fast-food chain that is going public in order to expand throughout the United States.

Leigh is ready to present her recommendation to the group but is hesitant. Leigh's concern is that she wants the investment club to diversify and buy bonds. She knows they are not as exciting as the stock options Peter and Brett have presented, but she wants something less risky. Leigh knows you are taking this class, so she comes to you to talk about bonds. What advice would you give her to convince her fellow investment club members to buy bonds?

A summary of the housemates' goals can be found in the first Continuing Case problem on page 27.

> **"** There is no fortress so strong that money cannot take it. **"**
>
> —CICERO, *Roman philosopher and statesman* (B.C. 106–43)

real estate investments

A good investment strategy maintains a diversification of assets. Real estate can help you diversify your investment portfolio. Real estate can be purchased to provide a home, an option to grow your wealth, or both. ■

LEARNING OBJECTIVES

After reading this chapter, you should be able to:

LO 15-1 Understand the different types of real estate investments.

LO 15-2 Contrast the benefits and drawbacks of owning rental property.

LO 15-3 Understand how to grow a real estate portfolio through real estate investment trusts.

LO 15-4 Evaluate the risks and returns involved in short-term real estate investments.

Long-Term Gains

In search of long-term investment options, Mackenzie came across six one-bedroom apartment units. She computed the cash flow of the investment, taking into consideration the rental rate, the location, the necessary appeal to renters, and the costs of membership in a condo association, which reduces the time required for manual landlord labor. After calculating the depreciation, rental income, mortgage interest, operating expenses, and mortgage payments, she determined the apartments would have a positive cash flow. The bank hesitated to give her the loan based on her financial statement, but instead of giving up, Mackenzie partnered with three other people to purchase the units, sharing both the management tasks and the financial burden. Over the next four years the partnership was able to acquire five more units. In 2008, the partnership dissolved, leaving Mackenzie with three units that had doubled in value, rents that were twice their original amounts, and a loan worth only 33% of the appraised value of the apartments. Mackenzie shares, "The investment is great supplementary income for now and retirement, and continues to provide tax advantages. The size of the investment provides me with income without being too large and complicated to manage. I'm happy I pushed for it."

15.1 REAL ESTATE BASICS

■ ■ **LO 15-1** Understand the different types of real estate investments.

Some people think a house should be viewed as a home, a place you find rest, peace, family, and joy. In their view, a house or apartment is not something purchased only to make money. Others treat real estate as a part of an asset allocation strategy and see it as an investment. In either case, getting into the real estate market can be an important part of your financial planning. The term **real estate** refers to homes or holdings in rental property and land. Before buying real estate, you should investigate all types of real estate and know how to measure the return on investment.

Types of Real Estate Investments

The goal of investing in real estate is for the property to provide income and appreciate in value. This can be done through rental properties, real estate investment trusts, or reselling properties for profit. We will briefly introduce these different types of real estate investments here and then cover them in more depth later in the chapter.

rental property One strategy in real estate investment is to buy property and **rent** it to other individuals. **Rental property** is housing, farm land, or commercial property that is leased out to others in return for a stated amount of money. A **lease** is a contract that stipulates the use and possession of the property for a specified time and for fixed payments. As the landlord, or lessor, your return on investment (ROI) is based on the income you receive in the form of rent payments, minus maintenance and operating expenses (including property taxes, depreciation, and interest payments), plus the capital gains from the appreciation of the property when you sell it. In other words:

$$\text{Rental ROI} = \text{Rent} - \text{Expenses} + \text{Capital gains}$$

If you think you would like to invest in rental property and you are ready to purchase a home, one strategy is to buy a duplex and live in one side and rent out the other half. The rent from the other side of the duplex can be used to offset some of the cost of the mortgage payment. Eventually

> ## "The best investment on earth is earth."
> — LOUIS J. GLICKMAN, *Manhattan real estate investor and philanthropist (1905–1999)*

you may move into a single-family home and either sell the duplex or rent out both sides.

To increase your profits as a landlord, you can personally assume some or all of the repair work and business management of the rental property. Doing so requires an investment of your time and skills. This means conducting credit checks on prospective renters, following building codes, and maintaining the property in good condition. If the task of buying and maintaining rental property seems overwhelming, consider creating a partnership, limited liability company (LLC), or S corporation. In this way, the business management and maintenance tasks can be shared among the members of the partnership or corporation.

real estate investment trusts (REITs) If you do not have the time or skills necessary to be a landlord, an alternative is a **real estate investment trust (REIT)**. A REIT pools funds from a group of individuals and invests in real estate. Many REITs invest in commercial property such as office buildings and shopping malls.

flipping properties Another strategy for making money in real estate is referred to as **flipping**—buying property under market value, upgrading it, and reselling it. With real estate flipping, your returns are based on "sweat equity." In other words, you are investing your time and effort to build equity and value in the property. Before the housing crisis of 2008–2011 (see Figure 15.1), housing prices were on the rise and credit was easy to obtain. In this booming market, many people saw flipping houses as a sure way to make money.

Money can be made in flipping, even in a slumping market, if you take the proper precautions as outlined later in this chapter (see Section 15.4).

Measuring Return on Investment

There is no guarantee you will make money from a real estate investment. You may spend more money than you

▼ **FIGURE** 15.1

Housing price index (HPI) (measurement of movement of single-family house prices) during the first two years of the housing crisis

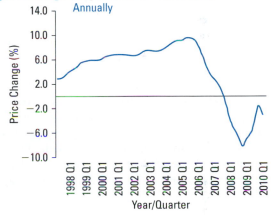

Source: U.S. Federal Housing Finance Agency (www.fhfa.gov/Default.aspx?Page=14).

doing the MATH

15.1 Calculating the ROI of Rental Property

If you buy an empty lot for $10,000, pay a total of $500 in taxes for five years, and then sell the lot for $25,000, your return on investment (ROI) is:

Purchase price (P_o) .... = $10,000

Cost of ownership/upgrades (C) ... = $500

Today's price (P_t) .... = $25,000

$ROI = [P_t - (P_o + C)]/P_o$

$ROI = [\$25,000 - (\$10,000 + \$500)]/\$10,000$

$\qquad = \$14,500/\$10,000 = 1.45$, or 145% ROI; -> 145%/5 years = **29% ROI per year**

Now suppose you have built a house on the property for $180,000 and you are able to sell the lot with the newly built home for $220,000. What is the ROI now?

collect in rent, or the property may lose value from the time you buy it to the time you sell it. For investments that do not provide set payments (such as rent checks), the **return on investment (ROI)** is measured by the percentage change in the price of the property between the original purchase price (P_o) plus the cost of ownership/upgrades (C) and the price for which it sells today (P_t). The formula for ROI is as follows:

$$ROI = [P_t - (P_o + C)]/P_o$$

You can use this ROI formula to determine returns on capital gains or appreciation on the property you own. For example, if you purchase a duplex for $150,000 in cash and sell it five years later for $200,000, your return on investment in capital gains will be $50,000 in five years (assuming you did not have any other costs, such as real estate taxes or home repairs). If you did have additional costs, you would subtract them from the upgrades part of the equation (C), which reduces your ROI.

There are many ROI calculators on the Internet that can help you calculate the potential profit and return on a rental property investment. For example, see the real estate investment calculator illustrated in Figure 15.2. These calculators lead you through the purchase, debt, income, and expense assumptions that need to be considered, as well as evaluating your marginal tax rate, duration for keeping the

property, real estate sales commission fees, and long-term capital gains tax percentages.

15.2 RENTAL PROPERTY

■ ■ **LO 15-2** Contrast the benefits and drawbacks of owning rental property.

Rental properties provide both advantages and disadvantages for the owner. You should weigh all the pluses and minuses of being a landlord before deciding whether owning a rental property is right for you. In this section we will discuss both the advantages and the disadvantages of owning rental property (see Figure 15.3).

Advantages of Rental Property

Owning rental property provides some overall advantages to growing your wealth. Among the advantages are tax savings, passive income, and asset appreciation.

▼ **FIGURE 15.2**

Return on real estate investment calculator

Purchase		
Purchase price ($)	0	
Market value (if different from purchase price) ($)	0	
Cash invested ($)	0	
Depreciable value (%)	80%	
Debt		
"Interest-only" loan? (Y/N)	No ▼	
Loan amount (may include estimated rehad) ($)	0	
Interest rate (%)	0%	
Term (years)	5	
Closing costs ($)	0	
Income		
Gross rental income ($)	0	
Income frequency ($)	Monthly ▼	
Annual rent increases: (%)	0%	
Occupancy rate	100%	
Expenses		
Annual property tax ($)	0	
Annual insurance ($)	0	
Annual maintenance ($)	0	
Annual HDA ($)	0	
Annual Increase in expenses (%)	0%	
Other Information		
Duration of analysis (years)	20	
Realtor fees upon future sale (%)	0%	
Annual appreciation rate (%)	0%	
Marginal tax bracket (%)	25%	?
Long-term capital gains bracket (%)	15%	

Submit

Source: www.calcxml.com/do/inv04

Making $ense

15.1 What are some options for investing in real estate?

15.2 Which type of real estate investment focuses on short-term gains?

15.3 When you invest in real estate rental property, what do you need to consider in calculating the true return on investment?

The advantages and disadvantages of owning rental property

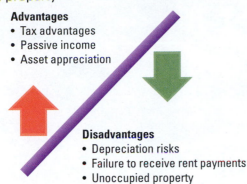

Advantages
- Tax advantages
- Passive income
- Asset appreciation

Disadvantages
- Depreciation risks
- Failure to receive rent payments
- Unoccupied property

the rental properties and her rental income will allow her to retire more comfortably.

asset appreciation   When buying rental property, you hope to make money from the rent, but you also hope to make money through increasing property values. When selling rental property, the difference between the selling price and the purchase price is considered capital appreciation and is taxed at a capital gains tax rate if you have held the property for more than two years. However, if you sell the property and buy a like-property, the IRS will allow you to reinvest 100% of the equity from the sale of the property to the like-property, thus deferring the gain. This is a great way to build a real estate portfolio without paying taxes on the gains until you liquidate all of your investment real estate.

> ❝❝More money has been made in real estate than in all industrial investments combined. ❞❞
>
> —ANDREW CARNEGIE, *Industrialist and philanthropist (1835–1919)*

tax advantages   Owning real estate for income purposes provides the benefits of any ownership in a small business. For example, you can deduct legitimate expenses associated with the rental property. In addition, you can deduct mileage when you go to the rental property or buy things for the rental property. Before deducting any expenses, however, you should consult with a tax adviser, as tax laws can change.

passive income   When you buy real estate that will be used as rental property, you are developing a stream of passive income. Passive income is income that comes to you without requiring you to work actively for it. The Internal Revenue Service (IRS) defines passive income as income from "trade or business activities in which you do not materially participate." Even if you spend significant time managing and repairing the property, the IRS generally considers the rent payment you receive as passive income. Being classified as passive income limits the amount of losses you can take on your income tax annually.

The income stream you receive from your rental property can be used to supplement your income now or help you in retirement. As illustrated in the chapter opener, Mackenzie uses her rental income to supplement her working income. When she retires, she will have paid off the mortgage on

Disadvantages of Rental Property

Owning rental property involves risks as well, including risks related to asset depreciation, failure to receive rent payments, and unoccupied property.

depreciation risks   Not all property is going to appreciate in value. During the housing crisis of 2008–2011, real estate property values fell by as much as 50% in some areas. The idea with any investment is to buy low and sell high, but many real estate investors experienced the reverse scenario when the real estate bubble burst; they purchased high and sold low.

Real estate values can also change due to changing demographics and demand. If you live in a college town and are renting a house, your landlord charges rent based on supply and demand. If enrollment in the college increases, places to live may be harder to find and your rent might go up. However, if a new 250-unit student housing complex is being built nearby, your landlord might make concessions and lower the rent to keep you as a tenant.

failure to receive rent payments   If your tenant loses her or his job, you may not receive rent payments and thus you may have to evict the tenant. You should not become

As a landlord, you need to be ready to protect the value of your property. If you found your yard looking like this, would you let the tenants stay?

a landlord if you cannot evict a tenant from your property, regardless of their situation.

For instance, Todd got into real estate, buying small houses to rent out. During the 2009 recession, his tenant was laid off at Christmas and did not have the funds to make either his car or his rent payments. Todd had to evict the tenant for failure to make rent payments. The tenant also had his car repossessed for failure to make loan payments. This experience was tough for Todd, but when he got into real estate rentals he understood that he would need to be able to evict people, even during the holidays. Not only did Todd not get two months' rent, but his property sat vacant for another two months before he could rent it out again. During this time, he had to pay the utilities for four months, and it cost him time and money to file all the necessary paperwork. If you aren't comfortable taking action to protect your investments, rental property may not be right for you.

unoccupied property When tenants move out, there is a chance the property will sit vacant until other tenants move in. When your property is vacant, there is no rental income, yet you still need to make mortgage payments. The advantage of buying a four-plex instead of a duplex is that if one unit is vacant in a four-plex, your income is

reduced by only 25%, rather than 50%. Either way, you need to have enough money in reserve to make payments for any time the unit is vacant.

Landlordship

When done correctly, being a landlord can be a great way to increase your net worth and also develop a stream of passive income. To be a successful landlord, however, you need to manage a number of areas, including tenant screening, advertising, maintenance, and repairs (see Figure 15.4).

tenant screening Not all tenants will be good tenants. Do not be so eager to fill a rental property that you neglect to fully screen the prospective tenant. This includes asking for a reference, talking to their previous landlord, and conducting a credit check. You need to follow a consistent policy so as not to discriminate against certain tenants and risk a lawsuit. You can check to see if your town has a landlord-tenant association to help with the tenant-screening process.

budgeting expenses Most people do not realize that rental property expenses add up to more than just taxes, insurance, and mortgage payments. Make sure you have savings set aside for repairs, vacancies, and unpaid rents.

▼ FIGURE 15.4

Areas to manage as a landlord

advertising One of the most common ways for landlords to find renters is through advertising. Advertising in traditional newspapers and magazines can be expensive; the Internet has reduced the cost of advertising and allows you to post pictures of your rental property. CraigsList (www.craigslist.com) is a popular advertising site. Another online apartment rental service, Rent King (http://www.rentking.com/list_property.php), helps tenants find their way to you. Potential residents are able to see a picture of your property, so you will spend your time showing the property to people who are genuinely interested.

communication As the landlord, you need to be in contact with your tenants. The best way to make sure your tenants pay the rent and treat your property well is to maintain a one-on-one relationship with them. If they feel you are looking after their interests, then they will look after yours. Most tenants have an idea of how long they plan to stay. Knowing their intentions lets you plan ahead and can help reduce your vacancy rate.

resolve disputes informally Try to resolve any tenant problems with an informal meeting first. This will help save money on lawyers' fees and will serve both parties better in the long run. If an informal meeting does not work, then consider using a neutral third party to mediate between you and the resident. In some communities, there is a landlord/tenant association that will help you avoid or resolve problems when they do happen, or your college or university might have a tenant/landlord service that helps students understand their rights. Only after exhausting all possible avenues should you get lawyers involved.

home checklist It is crucial to do a check of the premises before a tenant moves in or out. This process helps tenants know exactly what condition the apartment is in. Obviously, there will be wear and tear, but if damage is done or you need to make extensive repairs, the checklist serves as a point of reference. The checklist should be signed by both parties. This document provides proof of any changes in condition the property has undergone, should the condition of the apartment be disputed by the tenant when he or she moves out.

rules for your tenants Having a clearly defined set of rules for residents can save time and money. When drawing up a list of rules, make sure the same rules apply to all residents, so as not to discriminate. If a resident does break a rule, keep written records of the time and date when the incident took place. Keeping records will make it far easier to evict the resident and win lawsuits if there are any problems in the future. By providing clearly laid out rules and guidelines for residents, they will know what is expected of them before they agree to rent. The rules must follow state laws and city and local ordinances, as well as adhere to

Be realistic about the condition of the property. If something looks like it is not going to last or will require repairs in the near future, address those issues before tenants move in. This approach will save you money, because you will have the opportunity to either fix the problem yourself or find a good quote from someone else who can fix it. Once tenants have moved in, your priority will be to solve problems as quickly as possible, which may mean increased costs. Be sure you can afford to maintain the upkeep and loan payments if the rental property is not occupied for a period of time.

maintenance and repairs Plan to make timely repairs as needed. A small problem can soon escalate into a big one if not acted upon quickly. Acting quickly to repair problems will mean the rental and sales price of your property will not decline. If you do not act quickly, good residents may want to leave (sometimes without giving notice). They can also sue if they suffer any injuries due to improper maintenance. Your responsibilities as a landlord are covered under the Fair Housing Act and state landlord/tenant laws.

insurance Make sure you have enough insurance to cover your property. Talk to an insurance agent to get the right coverage. A well-designed insurance package can protect your property from losses caused by everything from fire and storms to vandalism, personal injuries, and discrimination lawsuits. For a small amount of money, you can protect yourself from the risk of losing a large amount of your wealth.

rules under the U.S. Department of Housing and Urban Development (HUD) and the Fair Housing Act.

get it in writing Even if you plan to rent to friends, you need a written contract or lease. Without a written contract, any disputes will become a case of "your word against their word" and you will have less standing in the eyes of the court. The contract needs to include: (1) the names of all the people renting the property; (2) rules regarding when and who is responsible for repairs or maintenance; (3) how much notice the landlord must provide prior to visiting renters; (4) the deposits and fees payable; (5) the price of monthly rent; and (6) the length of the contract.

Shared Ownerships

If the thought of being a landlord scares you and you feel you may not have the necessary skills to take it on alone, you could get others to help and become part-owners in the property. Options include a partnership, a limited liability company (LLC), or an S corporation, with someone whose skill-set complements yours. For example, one of you may be handy at maintenance while the other is skilled at bookkeeping and tenant relationships. Partnerships allow you to share the benefits and the responsibilities of the investment and also provide additional start-up capital. Figure 15.5 outlines how partnerships compare to LLCs and S corporations.

▼ **FIGURE** 15.5

Partnerships, S corporations, and LLCs: a comparison

	Partnership vs. S Corporation vs. Limited Liability Company (LLC)		
	Partnership	**S Corporation**	**Limited Liability Company (LLC)**
Formation, Requirements, Costs	None	Must file with state, state specific filing fee required	Must file with state, state specific filing fee required
Personal Liability	Unlimited liability	Shareholders not typically held liable	Members not typically held liable
Administrative Requirements	Relatively few	Election of board of directors/officers, annual meetings, and annual report filing	Relatively few requirements
Management	Full control	Shareholders elect directors who manage business activities	Members can set up structure as they choose
Term	Terminated when proprietor ceases doing business or upon death	Perpetual: can extend past death or withdrawal of shareholders	Perpetual, unless state requires fixed amount of time
Taxation	Entity not taxable; Partners pay taxes	No tax at the entity level; income passed through to the shareholders	No tax at the entity level; income passed level through to members
Self-Employment Tax	Subject to self-employment tax	Salary subject to self-employment tax, but shareholder distributions are not subject to employment tax	Salary subject to self-employment tax
Transferability of Interest	No	Yes, but must observe IRS regulations on who can own stock	Possibly, depending on restrictions outlined in the operating agreement
Capital Raising	Individual provides capital	Shares of stock are sold to raise capital; Limitations prevent S corp stock ownership by corporations	May sell interests, but subject to operating agreement
Ease of Operation	Easiest	Must have annual meetings, board of directors, corporate minutes, and stockholder meetings	Easy; some states may require more than others

A **partnership** is voluntary contract between two or more persons to place their capital, labor, and skills in a business corporation with the understanding there will be a sharing of the profits and losses among the partners. It is best to have a written partnership agreement to define responsibilities and clarify any misconceptions. Going into a partnership is like getting married, and the partnership agreement is like a prenuptial agreement. Partnerships involve unlimited liability exposure for all partners and their personal assets. In other words, if you get sued while in a partnership, all your personal assets are at risk. You can limit your risk exposure by increasing your insurance. Also, in a partnership your income is taxed at your individual tax rate.

An S corporation and a limited liability company (LLC) protect personal assets by setting up a separate entity. You may consider establishing an S corporation or an LLC to protect personal assets even if you own 100% of the property. Both the S corporation and the LLC pass the income of the business to the individual's personal income tax rate. An **S corporation** is a corporation that has between 1 and 100 shareholders and that passes net income or losses on to shareholders in accordance with Internal Revenue Code, Chapter 1, Subchapter S. These corporations must meet specific eligibility criteria, and they must notify the IRS of their choice to be taxed as an S corporation within a certain period of time. An S corporation is not subject to corporate tax rates.

A **limited liability company (LLC)** limits personal liability and allows you to pass the rental income to your personal taxes or be taxed as a corporation. An LLC has members, which are the owners of the LLC, much like shareholders in corporations. LLCs must file articles of organization with the secretary of state in the company's home state. It is common for LLCs also to have an operating agreement, which defines the rights of the members and manager, but it is not filed with the state in which it was organized.

Don and Harriet provide an excellent example of how to use a company formation for real estate investment. They inherited their father's farm and, to share in the management, they created H&D, an S corporation, in which each acre reflected a share in the company. When Harriet wanted to sell her ownership, the S corporation made the transfer of ownership easier to manage. The expenses and income from the farm were much simpler to distribute, as well. It is best to work through a lawyer to establish any type of partnership or corporation. Within the articles of the corporation, all the rules of responsibility and methods of terminating the business can be detailed to avoid any misunderstandings or difficult discussions in the future.

Temporary Rentals

If you are buying a new home but are not able to sell your existing home, you might consider renting the first home to offset the mortgage. You can treat this property as *temporary rental property*. Doing this provides a small tax break in that all rental expenses can be deducted against your rental income. Once you sell your home, you should be able to tax-defer the profit. If you decide to make your home a permanent rental, you will owe a capital gains tax on the property when you sell it. In order to maintain the temporary status, keep offering the house for sale while renting it.

financialfitness:
STOPPING LITTLE LEAKS

Rental Contract

Going through a lawyer to establish the leasing agreement can be expensive. You can create your own rental agreements online, saving both money and time. Two website options include: www.LawDepot.com and www.legalzoom.com.

$Making $ense

15.4 What should you consider before getting into the rental business?

15.5 What are some of the advantages provided by rental property ownership?

15.6 How does a partnership differ from an S corporation or an LLC?

15.3 REAL ESTATE INVESTMENT TRUSTS

■■ **LO 15-3**   Understand how to grow a real estate portfolio through real estate investment trusts.

Real estate investment trusts (REITs) are similar to closed-end mutual funds. They are companies that buy and usually manage apartment complexes, office buildings, shopping centers, and warehouses. REITs sell shares to the public on stock exchanges. The shares can be purchased with a small amount of money, making REITs an easy way to start investing in real estate. REITs are managed by skilled real estate professionals who decide what properties to purchase and manage the maintenance of the properties. Unlike mutual funds, REITs focus only on the real estate sector. They were created as a tax protection for some corporations, as well as a way for small investors to invest in commercial real estate (see Figure 15.6).

There are two types of REITs. **Equity REITS** invest money directly in property. **Mortgage REITs** invest in mortgage loans that finance the development of properties. The performance of an equity REIT is based on the changes in the value of property over time, therefore returns are determined by general real estate conditions. The performance of a mortgage REIT is based on the interest payments received from the loans it has provided.

How to Invest in REITs

As with any investment, do your homework before investing in a REIT fund. One resource is the National Association of Real Estate Investment Trusts (see the Financial Fitness box on the facing page). Another option is to consult a professional, as REITs are a fairly specific type of investment. Working with a broker or financial adviser with experience investing in REIT mutual funds is a good idea.

To select a REIT, order the **prospectus** for each REIT in which you have an interest. The prospectus is a legal document that explains the offer, including the terms, the issuer, the objectives (if it is a mutual fund) or the planned use of the money (if it deals in securities), and historical financial statements. Read each prospectus thoroughly to decide which one best fits your financial goals and investment capabilities. The prospectus contains the specifics of each mutual fund, as well as information about the risks of investing.

▼ **FIGURE** 15.6

How real estate investment trusts (REITs) work

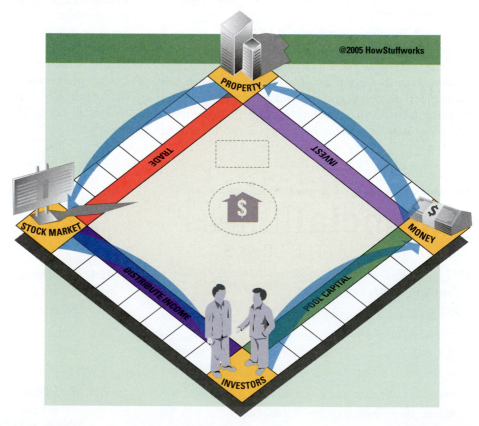

Source: www.static.howstuffworks.com/gif/reit-4.gif

Making $ense

15.7 How do real estate investment trusts (REITs) compare to closed-end mutual funds?

15.8 Explain the difference between an equity REIT and a mortgage REIT.

15.9 What things should you look for to avoid becoming the victim of a REIT scam?

About 200 REITs are traded on major stock exchanges, and you can learn about them by reading annual reports and other public documents. Focus on REITs that are at least three years old. In studying their annual reports, look for financial strength: A healthy REIT's debt is usually less than 50% of its market capitalization (the number of all outstanding shares multiplied by the price per share). The REIT's revenue should come largely from operations and not from the sale of properties or from borrowed funds. Look for REITs that have shown steady growth in dividends over several years. Make sure executives and managers of the REIT own a substantial amount of stock in the REIT. After making your decision, contact your investment adviser to make your initial investment.

By law, U.S. REITs are required to pay out at least 90% of their taxable income to their shareholders in the form of dividends. Consequently, REITs can generate a stable and consistent income stream for their investors. Remember: The key to the success of an investment portfolio is diversification. Different REITs focus on different aspects of the real estate industry. Do not put all your eggs in one basket. In general, REITs should not make up more than 5 to 10% of your portfolio.

How to Avoid Scams

A REIT can be a nice investment, adding value to a diversified portfolio. Both commercial and residential real estate have been increasing in value for decades and should perform well in the future. However, be wary of REITs offering quick profits over the short term. REITs have been used to scam investors who are not proficient in the real estate market. To protect yourself from REIT scams, you should:

- *Research the history of the REIT.* Evaluate the REIT's performance on the stock market over a period of time. If the REIT is privately held, ask for statements from the past three years.

- *Consult a tax accountant.* Ask an accountant what tax advantages or disadvantages an investment in a REIT presents for you.

- *Have an attorney review the paperwork.* Make sure to consult an attorney who is experienced with the real estate market and knowledgeable as to the kinds of language and issues involved in past REIT scams.

- *Beware of offers that seem too good to be true.* Even though REITs can provide solid profits, the structure has attracted dishonest types who are able to make an offer sound irresistible. Investigate the company's leadership to see what type of past associations turn up.

> " Put not your trust in money, but put your money in trust. "
> —OLIVER WENDELL HOLMES, *Author and physician (1809–1894)*

15.4 FLIPPING REAL ESTATE

■ ■ **LO 15-4** Evaluate the risks and returns involved in short-term real estate investments.

As noted earlier in this chapter, *flipping* is the practice of acquiring real estate at substantially less than the market value and reselling it quickly at full market value. The key to making money in flipping is to buy property that is at least 20% below the market value. Successful flipping involves buying a house with a problem that is overwhelming to the seller (foundation issues, flood damage, lead paint, and so on) but that you have the resources to solve inexpensively.

Measuring Your ROI on Flipping

The return on investment (ROI) for flipping houses is driven by leverage. **Leverage** is the amount of debt carried relative to the investment. For example, if you purchase a house for $200,000 cash (no leverage) and, by making improvements, raise its value by $20,000, you have made 10% on the invested money. Because you purchased the house with cash, you have 100% of your money at risk (and therefore no leverage). However, if you buy the house with a $40,000 down payment, you have invested 20% and the bank has financed 80% (which results in higher

leverage). You have less money at risk, and the bank is risking more money by giving you a loan. Your ROI on your $40,000 investment is now 50% based on a $20,000 profit from the sale of the house.

If you carry a mortgage while flipping the property, you will need another source of income to cover the mortgage payments. This is part of the cost of investment and will decrease your ROI. In rental investment properties, the income from rent covers the expense of the mortgage. If you decide to flip houses, make sure you have enough capital, income, and skills to make the necessary improvements and cover the cost of repairs and mortgage payments until the house sells.

Steps to Successful Flipping

In order to succeed in flipping, you need the vision of what a property could be. Without foresight, it is difficult to make money in real estate. You also need a substantial cash reserve or a good credit score to get a loan and make necessary repairs before selling the property. The three steps to successful flipping involve: (1) finding property to buy; (2) fixing up and adding value; and (3) reselling the property (see Figure 15.7).

finding property to buy Finding property well under market value is a task unto itself. To understand the phenomenon of flipping, it is important to understand that in an appreciating marketplace, the principles of a *shortage* are at work. The demand for property is so great that prices increase because people want to purchase the property and are willing to pay higher prices for it because of its location, area, or status.

doing the MATH

15.2 Leveraging

You are buying a house and considering the following financing arrangements:

No Leverage: Buy a house for $100,000 cash (no leverage), raise value by $10,000. You made a 10% ROI ($10,000/$100,000) on your $100,000 investment.

Higher Leverage: Buy a house with a $20,000 down payment. You invested 20%, and the bank financed 80% (higher leverage). You made a 50% ROI ($10,000/$20,000) on your $20,000 investment.

1. Suppose you buy a house with a 20% down payment of $20,000 and then sell for $150,000. What would be your ROI?

2. What would be your ROI on that same investment if you used no leverage?

▼ FIGURE 15.7

Steps to successful flipping

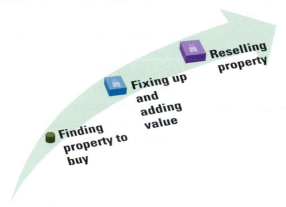

In looking for houses to flip, look for areas with generally strong employment, a growing population, and a good school system. These characteristics will create competition for houses if a shortage develops. Values are driven by supply and demand, the local economy, and people's wants and desires to own a home. It may be quite possible to buy real estate for less than the value of comparable properties in parts of the nation experiencing job loss, but it will be virtually impossible to sell that property quickly for substantial profits. That leaves new construction, distress sales, fixer-uppers, and foreclosures as possible sources of undervalued real estate. Bear in mind, though, real estate markets are local, and every property is unique.

Look for houses that are a good buy and have the best potential for resale. For example:

- *One-bedroom homes:* These sell cheaply but rent well as they appeal to single renters.

financialfitness:
STOPPING LITTLE LEAKS

Home Maintenance

Save costs on home repairs. Go to your local Lowe's or Home Depot and take advantage of their free Saturday morning do-it-yourself classes. You will learn tons and become acquainted with the staff, so there will be a familiar face when you have questions about the best tool for a project or when you need suggestions on how to attack a home maintenance problem.

- *Two houses on one lot:* Renters may not care about their proximity to the street or their neighbor.

- *Absentee owner:* If the owner has been gone for some time, he or she may welcome someone coming in to help make an easy sale of the asset.

- *Probate sales:* Sales of a deceased person's real property to close their estate can be a good opportunity.

- *Foreclosure sales:* Homes and real property sold in a foreclosure can usually be bought below market value.

fixing up and adding value Homeowners living in fixer-uppers, in distressed situations, or under the threat of foreclosure offer opportunities for investors interested in buying real estate below market value and reselling it quickly at a substantial profit. If you have the expertise, ample spare time, access to inexpensive labor and materials, and enough cash to carry the property for at least several months, you may be able to add sufficient value to a fixer-upper to reap a healthy return, but be aware that the odds are against you.

reselling property People often overlook or underestimate the costs associated with selling real estate. **Multiple Listing Service (MLS)** listing is vital to assure maximum exposure and obtain the highest possible price. The MLS allows real estate agents to share their properties for sale with other real estate agents, thus expanding the exposure of your property. Real estate agents charge a commission of 6 to 7% to sell your property, which usually includes the fee to list your property in the MLS database. In addition, there are a host of regulatory requirements placed upon the seller that are often best handled by a paid professional.

Sometimes flippers buy a house or condo before it is constructed, hoping to sell it at a higher price when it is completed. This can take patience and time. Once a project is approved by area planning, zoning, and city councils, it may still be two to three years before the first units are available for occupancy. Pre-selling offers an increased sense of security to the builder and its finance partners. In a traditional suburban "horizontal" subdivision, the builder has the option of building in phases that reflect the rate of demand; this allows the builder to realize an immediate return, minimize the risk of a market shift, and retain the ability to adjust prices in each phase. In a "vertical" subdivision like a high-rise, of course, it is more difficult to build in phases.

Investors who are able to tie up a healthy deposit and wait years for their return can realize a substantial profit in a hot market. However, they can just as easily get stuck with a property they never intended to own, do not want, and cannot

---

Multiple Listing Service (MLS)

an arrangement among brokers who are real estate board members, through which brokers share information regarding their listings with one another and may negotiate the transaction

Scan here for more information on the latest events "In the News"

10 mistakes that made flipping a flop

SACRAMENTO—If there's a poster child for everything that went wrong in the real estate boom, it just might be Casey Serin. In one year, the 24-year-old website-designer-turned-real estate-flipper bought eight homes in four states—and in every case but one, he put no money down. At his peak, in April, Serin had $93,000 he'd taken out of the homes as he bought them. By July, he was broke, desperate for one last deal. Now? Serin has $140,000 in credit card and credit-line debt and five houses in foreclosure. Last month, he started iamfacingforeclosure.com, a blog that's drawn both notes of condolence and expletive-laced condemnation. "I did some stuff shady, but I'm not going to hide from it," he says. "Somebody can learn from it. I've already had people contact me and say, 'Hey, I'm in the same place.'"

The rise and fall of Casey Serin is a tale with moral and financial lessons for real estate buyers, lenders, and regulators. Having consumed real estate guides and seminars, Serin made just about every mistake a newbie could make—most of them, he admits, were no one's fault but his own—from fudging loan applications

to buying homes sight-unseen. That he began with bold dreams of class mobility makes his fall a peculiarly American saga. Serin didn't know much about real estate at 19, when he bought his first condo. As a website designer, Serin was earning $35,000 a year at S.M.A.R.T. Association, a maker of marketing systems for health care providers. He quit to start his own web-design company but couldn't earn enough to cover his mortgage. So he moved in with his parents and sold the condo a few months later. His profit: $30,000.

"My goal was to reinvest that money," Serin says. "But I also needed a car. My car was falling apart. I used some of it to keep me going, and for living expenses and things. And I used some of it to go on dates." He also stopped working for three months. By the time he married in 2004, the money was gone. He and his wife used credit cards to cover living costs because Serin's business wasn't bringing in enough money. When he found a job that summer as a web designer, the couple had piled up nearly $20,000 in card debt, half of which they'd spent on real estate courses. He

bought Carleton Sheets' No Down Payment real estate program and attended seminars by Russ Whitney, author of *The Millionaire Real Estate Mindset,* and others. "Sure, they used pressure sales tactics to get you into it, but looking back on it, I don't regret it," he says. "They told me how to start safe, but I really didn't start safe. I went all out. So it was my own fault." . . .

Along the way, Casey made multiple mistakes, including: (1) he lied on his loan applications, (2) he overpaid on his purchases, (3) he lacked cash, (4) he quit his day job, (5) he hired an unlicensed contractor, (6) he bought property sight-unseen, (7) he bought out-of-state property, (8) he bought too many properties too fast, (9) he underestimated the remodeling costs, and (10) he had a poor exit strategy.

NOELLE KNOX, "10 Mistakes That Made Flipping a Flop," *USA Today*, October 22, 2006. Reprinted with permission.

Question

1 What precautions should you heed if you are considering flipping as an option to build wealth?

rent for anywhere near the amount of the mortgage payment. This occurred in Florida during the housing bubble. In 2006, investors were buying condos before they were constructed, with the intention of selling the completed condos for a hefty profit. However, when the real estate market collapsed, these investors were left with unfinished condos and were forced to battle companies through the courts to either have the projects completed or receive their deposits back.

In strong markets, few properties make their way through the foreclosure process. Generally, sales occur quickly

enough to prevent foreclosure, and lenders tend to be cooperative with defaulting borrowers who have a viable plan for curing the default. In those cases where a property does wind up in a foreclosure auction, you will be bidding against professional buyers armed with cash. They are disciplined, patient, and prepared to walk away. Ironically, the word "foreclosure" has enough draw that it can bring prices to or above market value.

Very few people get rich quickly in real estate. To get rich, it takes time, money, a willingness to take risks, good luck, hard work, and the ability to deal with renters. Real estate wealth, like almost anything of value, is built over time, not overnight.

Flipping Land

Raw land can be a good investment if you believe that, within a reasonable time period, something will be happening in the community to make the land more valuable. The changes could include a new company coming in, growth of the town and subdivisions, a new access road, or a re-zoning from residential single-family to multi-family or commercial. Short of having some insider knowledge, you typically will have to hang on to land for quite a few years to get a decent return on investment. If you can rent it as farm land in the interim, you will have a greater chance of getting ongoing value from the land.

As with any real property, land, or buildings, the key to success is location, location, location. Unfortunately, you cannot always predict what will happen with the location. Even if you check with city hall and the planning office, the zoning can change. At some point in the future, there may be multiple-family homes in an area once zoned for single-family homes. Once you buy, you cannot change the location.

Making $ense

15.10 What are some of the characteristics you should look for if you want to be successful in flipping?

15.11 How do you compute leverage when flipping houses?

15.12 How might land be a good investment option?

Scams are everywhere, promising riches with little work and little time. This is especially true in real estate. Do not believe everything you read or hear about getting rich quick in real estate. It takes time, effort, good planning, and know-how to make money on real estate investments. ■

Learn. ▸ Plan & Act. ▸ Evaluate.

➡ **LEARN.** This chapter covered ways to diversify your portfolio with investments in real estate. It covered simple steps from home ownership to acquiring passive income via owning rental property or investments in REITs.

SUMMARY

■■ **LO 15-1** Understand the different types of real estate investments.

One way to enter the real estate market is to purchase a duplex, where the rent from one side covers (or offsets the cost of) the mortgage payment. Eventually you may move into a single-family home, retain the duplex, and rent out both sides. If you do not have the time or skill to be a landlord, an alternative investment for you may be real estate investment trusts (REITs).

There are two strategies for investing in real estate. One is to hold on to the property and rent it in return for period payments, according to the terms of a lease, a contract that stipulates the use and possession of the property for a specified time and fixed payments. The other strategy is through flipping the property, buying it at a price under market value, upgrading it, and then reselling it for profit. Here your returns come from sweat equity and the value you bring to the property through upgrades.

For investments that do not provide set payments (such as rent checks), the return on investment (ROI) is measured by the percentage change between the original purchase price (P_o) plus the cost of ownership and upgrades (C) and the price for which you can sell it today (P_t).

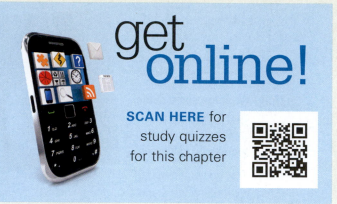

get
online!

SCAN HERE for
study quizzes
for this chapter

■ ■ **LO 15-2** Contrast the benefits and draw-backs of owning rental property.

Owning rental property provides a way to grow your wealth and offers some overall advantages, including tax advantages, passive income, and appreciation; however, there are also risks. Being a landlord can provide passive income, as well as ownership of assets that may continue to appreciate in value. If the responsibilities involved in being a landlord seem overwhelming, you might consider taking on rental investments in a partnership, S corporation, or LLC.

■ ■ **LO 15-3** Understand how to grow a real estate portfolio through real estate investment trusts.

Real estate investment trusts (REITs) are like closed-end mutual funds, but unlike mutual funds, REITs focus only on the real estate sector. REITs were created as a tax protection for some corporations and offer a way for small investors to invest in commercial real estate. There are two types of REITs: equity REITs and mortgage REITs. To begin investing in REITs, order the prospectus for each REIT mutual fund in which you have an interest and decide which one best fits your financial goals and investment capabilities.

■ ■ **LO 15-4** Evaluate the risks and returns involved in short-term real estate investments.

Flipping is the practice of acquiring real estate at substantially less than the market value and reselling it quickly at full market value. The key to making money in flipping is buying property that is at least 20% below the market value. Profits are driven by leverage, or the amount of debt you carry relative to your investment.

⮕ **PLAN & ACT.** After reading this chapter, you should be able to determine whether investments in real estate are an appropriate instrument to include in your portfolio. Your Plan & Act to-do list is as follows:

☐ Evaluate rental property options in your community and estimate your potential return on investment (http://www.calcxml.com/do/inv04).

☐ Research REIT investment options (Worksheet 15.1).

⮕ **EVALUATE.** Over the centuries, people of great wealth have done well investing in real estate. Is real estate a viable investment option for you? If you do not already own a home, is homeownership via purchasing rental property an option you would consider? In researching REITs, does this look like an affordable, safe investment option for you?

》GoalTracker

Review your online GoalTracker. How can investment in real estate play a role in helping you achieve your goals?

[*"The major fortunes in America have been made in land."*]

—JOHN D. ROCKEFELLER, *American industrialist (1839–1937)*

Equity REIT

Flipping

Lease

Leverage

Limited Liability Company (LLC)

Mortgage REIT

Multiple Listing Service (MLS)

Partnership

Prospectus

Real Estate

Real Estate Investment Trust (REIT)

Rent

Rental Property

Return on Investment (ROI)

S Corporation

self-test questions

1. Home ownership is_____. (*LO 15-1*)

   a. For everyone
   b. The only way to be secure in retirement
   c. An asset and could be seen as an investment
   d. A guaranteed way to make money

2. To be profitable in personal real estate investment, _____. (*LO 15-1*)

   a. You must be able to make your own repairs and improvements
   b. You can make money only by flipping property after you fix it up
   c. You can make money only by leasing the property
   d. There is no guarantee you will make money in real estate

3. To calculate your return on investment (ROI) on real estate, you _____. (*LO 15-1*)

   a. Use only the purchase price and the selling price
   b. Use the purchase price, the cost of ownership/ upgrades, and the selling price
   c. Should not worry about real estate commissions on the sale of the property
   d. Should not use a ROI real estate calculator

4. Which is *not* an advantage of owning rental property? (*LO 15-2*)

   a. Tax deductions
   b. Passive income
   c. Property appreciation
   d. Depreciation risks

5. When renting a property, you need to set aside money for all of these expenses *except* _____. (*LO 15-2*)

   a. Repairs
   b. Vacancies
   c. Unpaid rents
   d. Snow removal

6. Having rules for your tenants helps you by _____. (*LO 15-2*)

   a. Establishing expectations for the tenants
   b. Avoiding discrimination
   c. Making it easier to evict a tenant
   d. All of the above

7. Partnerships, LLCs, and S corporations differ in _____. (*LO 15-2*)

   a. The way income is passed to its owners
   b. The liability exposure to the owner
   c. The paperwork that must be completed
   d. All of the above

8. Real estate investment trusts (REITs) _____. (*LO 15-3*)

   a. Are like closed-end mutual funds
   b. Are investments in commercial real estate properties like office buildings and shopping centers
   c. Offer shares traded on stock exchanges
   d. All of the above

9. Real estate investment trusts _____. (*LO 15-3*)

   a. Are guaranteed to make a profit
   b. Provide an option to diversify your investment portfolio
   c. Have never been used in scams to defraud investors
   d. Are not required to produce a prospectus

10. All of the following *except* _____ are good places to look for houses to buy if you want to flip them. (*LO 15-4*)

    a. Foreclosure sales
    b. Probate sales
    c. Homes with absentee owners
    d. Homes for sale by owner

11. When flipping houses you should _____. (*LO 15-4*)

    a. Have enough capital income and skills to make the necessary improvements and cover the cost of repairs and mortgage payments
    b. Quit your day job so you have time to make the repairs and flip the house sooner, to get a better return on your investment
    c. Hire unlicensed contractors because they are cheaper and will save you a lot of money
    d. Borrow as much money as the bank will lend so you have a financial cushion; then you can use that money to pay off other debts and credit cards

problems

1. If you purchased a lot for $10,000, paid $500 in taxes over a five-year period, and then sold the lot for $15,000, what is your ROI? What would your annual ROI be? *(LO 15-1)*

2. You purchased a house for $100,000 cash and you sold it in one year for $125,000. You had to pay $5,000 in taxes and repairs before you sold it. What is your ROI? If you financed $80,000 with a bank, used only $20,000 for a down payment, and paid $4,000 for taxes, repairs, and interest expense, what would be your ROI? *(LO 15-1)*

3. You purchased two condos for $100,000 cash down, with loan/insurance payments of $1,500/month for the next 10 years. Your association fees are $150/month. You plan to rent out one of the condos to cover 80% of your housing expenses. What rent amount do you need to charge your tenant? *(LO 15-2)*

4. REITs are required by the IRS to pay out annual dividends of 90% of their taxable income. If a REIT's taxable income is $1.5 million, what will be the total payout of its annual dividends? *(LO 15-3)*

5. If you follow the recommendation that investments in a REIT should not make up more than 10% of your investment portfolio, what is the maximum dollar amount you should have tied up in a REIT if the total assets of your portfolio equal $730,000? *(LO 15-3)*

6. You are considering buying the house next to your home, in order to fix it up and sell it to make a profit. You estimate that you will need to invest about $5,000 to make necessary repairs and upgrades; after these improvements, you should be able to sell it for $185,000. If the general guideline for flipping is to buy at least 20% below the market value, what is the most you should be willing to pay for the home? *(LO 15-4)*

7. You bought a lot for $20,000 and have paid $75/year in taxes for the past five years. A new golf course is going in across the street, and you have been approached by a buyer to sell your lot for $95,000. What will be your ROI? *(LO 15-4)*

you're the expert

1. Two years ago Sam purchased a duplex for $180,000 cash. She has rented out one side for $1,000/month. Taxes have been $1,800 every six months. Sam put in new carpeting throughout the duplex and gave it fresh paint when she purchased it; these improvements cost about $5,000. She now is considering selling the duplex and moving into a single-family home. *(LO 15-1)*

   a. At what price should Sam sell the duplex to earn a 10% ROI?

   b. If she goes through a realtor to sell the property, Sam will have to pay a commission of 6% of the selling price. To maintain a 10% ROI and accommodate the expense of the realtor's fee, what should her asking price be?

   c. Sam is offered $225,000 for the duplex. After paying the 6% realtor's commission, what is her actual ROI?

2. To diversify Jack's investment portfolio, he and his neighbor have decided to go into business together to purchase and manage rental property. They need to decide on the legal status of their partnership. *(LO 15-2)*

   a. What advantages would they have under a limited liability company (LLC)?

   b. Under an S corporation?

   c. What responsibilities do they need to articulate before entering into business together?

3. Doug has decided to purchase the run-down one-bedroom home next door in order to clean up the neighborhood and, he hopes, make a profit. He guesses that with $10,000 in improvements and repairs over the next 12 months, including the selling time, he can sell the property for $180,000. Realtor fees will be 6%. He has the cash necessary to make the purchase. In order for this to be worth his time, Doug wants to make 20% on his investment. *(LO 15-1)*

   a. What price should he offer to pay for the house?

   b. As he starts into repairs, Doug discovers rotting floorboards throughout the first floor, running up his repair cost an additional $2,000. What will be his new asking price for the house?

   c. Doug made the repairs in the floorboard, so his total investment in improvements and repairs was $12,000. When he put the house on the market, he received an offer for $175,000. He purchased the house for $130,000 cash and did not have any other expenses. If he accepts the offer, what will be his ROI?

15.1 REIT COMPARISON GRID

Use Worksheet 15.1 to compare two REIT investment options. Based on the consideration factors, in which REIT would you prefer to invest?

Consideration	Name of REIT 1:	Name of REIT 2:
REIT debt % in relation to market capitalization (# outstanding shares * price per share; less is good with goal <50%)		
Revenue source (operations vs. sale of properties or from borrowed funds)		
Steady growth in dividends over last 3 years		
REIT executives/managers own a substantial amount of REIT stock		
>=12% annual return to shareholders for the past few years (total returns are dividends plus appreciation in the stock price)		

continuing case

Peter finds the perfect location for his sushi restaurant and wants to buy or rent the space. Although it is three years earlier then he wanted to open his restaurant, he does not want to miss this opportunity. However, he does not have the money to buy it.

During an investment club meeting with all of his housemates, Peter brings up the idea of the investment club buying the building and renting it to him so he could open up his business. The housemates decide this is an idea worth considering, but they want to do it separately from the investment club.

A summary of the housemates' goals can be found in the first Continuing Case problem on page 27.

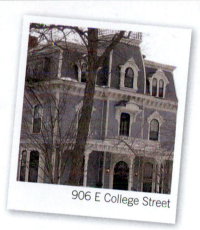

906 E College Street

1. What form of ownership would you recommend using for the new business, and why?

2. You meet with Leigh and she tells you about the housemates' interest in buying the building and renting it to Peter for his restaurant. What advice would you give her about the dangers of real estate investing before they buy the property?

3. Leigh also wants to know about the benefits of investing in real estate. What would you tell her?

4. What would you do if you were one of the housemates? Why?

> "True, you can't take it with you, but then that's not the place where it comes in so handy."
>
> —BRENDON FRANCIS, *Irish poet (1923–1964)*

sixteen

retirement and estate planning

In this chapter, you will learn why it is so important to start a retirement savings account early and how to track progress toward your retirement goals. You will also learn the importance of end-of-life legal documents and the value of charitable giving. ■

LEARNING OBJECTIVES

After reading this chapter, you should be able to:

LO 16-1 Recognize the benefits of retirement planning and the importance of starting early, and determine the appropriate retirement savings strategy for your current life stage.

LO 16-2 Understand the importance of a will and advance directives and recognize estate planning methods you can use to transfer wealth.

LO 16-3 Evaluate different means of charitable giving and their impact on your tax liability.

◀ Colette, age 29, research assistant

Trade-Offs

Colette works for a university as a research assistant. As a benefit for all full-time employees, the university contributes 6% of each worker's annual salary to his or her employee retirement plan. Colette began contributing another 10% of her salary in the retirement savings plan from the day she was hired. In her fifth year of employment, she learned she could make a one-time withdrawal. She comments, "At the time, we had one toddler and a baby on the way. I was desperate to move out of our apartment and into a single-family home with a yard. Cashing out my retirement savings seemed like an easy way to come up with the down payment for our home. The tax penalty was 10% on top of having to pay taxes on the balance and it emptied out our retirement savings, but I traded it for my sanity. I know that once we get the kids through college, we'll have to work hard to bolster our retirement fund. At this point, I don't imagine we will be able to retire until we are in our 70s."

16.1 RETIREMENT PLANNING

■ ■ **LO16-1** Recognize the benefits of retirement planning and the importance of starting early, and determine the appropriate retirement savings strategy for your current life stage.

Poor economic times can be nerve-racking when the market declines and negatively impacts your retirement savings. You cannot control the stock market's ups and downs or the interest rates paid on bonds, savings accounts, or certificates of deposit. The key is to focus on things you *can* control, such as your career plans, how much you put toward your savings and investments, how you allocate your retirement savings assets, and how you handle debt.

You can save for retirement through company plans (40l[k]s), individual savings (IRAs, annuities), and government-sponsored plans (Social Security). The general rule is that you will need at least 70% of your pre-retirement annual salary to live comfortably at retirement if you have paid off your mortgage and are in good health. To be safe, you should target 80% or higher.

As a college student or a fresh graduate, it may be difficult to think about retirement. You may feel like you will never want to retire or that you cannot afford to put money into retirement savings given all of your current expenses. You may have a hard time putting money needed today toward a retirement plan that may be 40 to 50 years in the future. Even if you think you may never retire, Figure 16.1 lists a few reasons why you should start saving for retirement when you begin your first career job.

Company Savings Plans

By taking advantage of savings plans at your place of employment, you can grow a comfortable retirement nest egg. Most companies offer a retirement savings plan such as a 40l(k), which requires you to make regular contributions if you choose to participate. Your contributions may be deducted from each paycheck on a before-tax basis, thus lowering your taxable income, or on an after-tax basis. It is up to the company to decide what amount of your contribution, if any, it will match. Many companies offer to match a percentage of every dollar you contribute, up to a given percentage of your salary. A matching

fund of this type is *free money* from the employer, and you should take full advantage of the offer. Since the 401(k) account is tax-deferred, it compounds faster than regular savings. Any matching funds contributed by your company usually require you to be **vested** in the company (i.e., to have been employed by the company for a minimum number of years) before the company contribution is yours.

When starting a new job, you will make choices as to how you want your 401(k) to be invested and how much of your salary you want to contribute. Try to contribute enough to maximize the employer match and, if at all possible, contribute the maximum amount allowed. In addition to building your retirement fund more quickly, you will benefit from the tax savings.

401(k) plans A 401(k) plan is a qualified plan established by employers to which eligible employees may make salary-deferral (salary-reduction) contributions on a pretax and/or a post-tax basis. Employers offering a 401(k) plan may make matching or nonelective contributions to the plan on behalf of eligible employees and may also add a profit-sharing feature to the plan. Earnings accrue on a tax-deferred basis. The post-tax 401(k) is commonly referred to as a *Roth 401(k)*. Plans that allow participants to direct their own investments provide a core group of investment products from which participants may choose. Otherwise, professionals hired by the employer direct and manage the employees' investments.

Roth 401(k) plans As noted above, contributions to a Roth 401(k) are made on a post-tax basis; that is, you are contributing money that you have earned and that has already been taxed. Your contributions into a Roth 401(k) account grow and compound tax-free. There are no taxes owed on any funds withdrawn from a Roth 401(k) account after retirement. The Roth 401(k) makes sense for people who think their tax rate in retirement may be higher than their current tax rate. If you are currently in a 15% tax bracket, you might consider a Roth 401(k) over a traditional 401(k).

Once you have settled on your contributions (how much and which type), you must next decide how to invest them. Many 401(k) plans offer target-date or life-cycle funds which remove the guesswork by allowing you to invest in one diversified fund and then forget about it. Target-date funds adjust asset allocations based on a planned retirement date, proportionally adjusting the asset allocation (as discussed in Chapter 11) as you draw closer to retirement.

vested
when one has satisfied the terms of employment and thereby has access to pension benefits contributed by the employer

simplified employee pension (SEP) plan a low-overhead retirement savings account in which employers make contributions to traditional IRAs set up for employees (including self-employed individuals)

▼ **FIGURE 16.1**

Reasons to start saving for retirement (even if you don't think you will ever retire)

Change of Heart
• As a new graduate, you may feel like you could work forever, but there are no guarantees that you will feel the same way when you are in your 60s. Better to save now and have the option to retire than to be 65 years old, burn out, and have no savings.

Lack of Choice
• Many older workers are forced into retirement due to health reasons. Your company may downsize or merge with another company and your position may be eliminated.

Family
• Retirement savings can be passed on to your children if you end up not needing them.

Sabbatical Options
• While you plan to work forever, there may be some value in taking time off to rejuvenate. Retirement savings can help you finance a sabbatical.

Second Lifetime Career Option
• Down the road, you may find yourself wanting to explore a new career path. Having sizable savings allows you the financial independence to select a career that provides you joy regardless of pay. Having enough money saved frees you to pursue other passions or devote time to a cause without taking a prohibitive drop in your standard of living.

16.1 Matched Contributions

Your company will match $2 for every $1 you contribute, up to 7% of your $50,000 salary.

1. If you invest $2,000, what amount does your company contribute to your retirement savings?

2. To maximize this benefit, what is the top dollar amount you should strive to contribute?

3. Without consideration of the tax advantages, what is the ROI of the first dollar upon deposit?

Simplified Employee Pension Plans

Those who are self-employed can invest in a **simplified employee pension (SEP) plan**. A SEP is a retirement plan that employers or self-employed individuals—including sole proprietors, partnerships, and S corporations—can establish. Some of the advantages of a SEP are that administrative costs are low, contributions are tax-deductible, the business pays no taxes on the earnings on the investments, and the employer-contribution limit is higher. Additionally, you are not locked into making contributions every year, and you may be eligible for a tax credit for each of the first three years for the cost of starting the plan.

Individual Retirement Accounts

Chapter 4 introduced individual retirement accounts (IRAs), which are special savings instruments in which a portion of an individual's income is set aside for retirement. There are two types of IRAs: traditional and Roth.

traditional IRAs A traditional IRA allows you to invest pretax income (up to specific annual limits) in accounts that can grow tax-deferred (no capital gains or dividend income is taxed). Individual taxpayers are allowed to contribute 100% of their earned income up to a specified maximum dollar amount. Contributions to the traditional IRA may be tax-deductible, depending on the taxpayer's income, tax-filing status, and other factors.

Traditional IRAs are held by commercial banks, retail brokers, and discount brokers. Investors can place IRA funds into stocks, bonds, mutual funds, and other financial assets and are limited only by what the custodian offers. Some assets, such as real estate, come with heavy restrictions from the IRS and may be taxed differently. Interest and earnings grow tax-deferred: You pay the taxes when you withdraw the money. When you begin to receive distributions from a traditional IRA, the income is treated as

The sooner you understand terms like these, the better off you'll be in retirement.

ordinary income and may be subject to income tax. This differs from the Roth IRA, which uses taxable contributions to provide tax-free distributions.

Roth IRAs A Roth IRA is similar to a traditional IRA, but contributions are *not* tax-deductible. You pay tax on the amounts that you put into the Roth IRA, and the interest and earnings in the Roth IRA grow tax-free. The advantage of a Roth IRA is that qualified distributions are tax-free. There is no income tax to be paid on qualified withdrawals. A qualified distribution is one taken at least five years after the taxpayer has established his or her first Roth IRA and when he or she is age 59½, disabled, using the withdrawal to purchase a first home (limit $10,000), or deceased (in which case the beneficiary collects). Since qualified distributions from a Roth IRA are tax-free, a Roth IRA may be more advantageous than a traditional IRA if you anticipate that the tax rate during the years of your IRA withdrawals will be higher.

By using a tax-advantaged individual retirement account, your earnings are either not taxed or are tax-deferred until you withdraw the money. Not paying taxes on your earnings allows your investments to grow faster. Figure 16.2 compares two investments in the same mutual fund: A Roth IRA (in which returns grow tax-free) and a taxable account. The example assumes annual contributions of $2,000, an 8% annual return after expenses, and a total tax rate of 30% (for the taxable account) imposed on the total return each year. Despite identical investment returns, the Roth IRA grows almost a quarter of a million dollars more than the taxable account.

spousal IRAs A **spousal IRA** is a traditional or Roth IRA established and funded by an individual for his or her spouse. These plans are typically set up when the spouse has little or no income. The contribution limits and eligibility requirements for a spousal IRA are the same as those for a regular IRA.

annuities An **annuity** is a product sold by financial institutions, designed to accept and grow funds from an individual and then pay out a stream of payments at a later point in time. Annuities are primarily used as a means of securing a steady cash flow during your retirement years. Annuities are typically sold by insurance companies and regulated by state insurance commissions. Annuities can be created so that payments will continue so long as either the annuitant or his or her spouse is alive.

Figure 16.3 on the next page is a matrix of the different retirement fund options, comparing a 401(k), Roth 401(k), traditional IRA, and Roth IRA. Studying each and reviewing how you plan to use the accounts will help you select the options that best fit your needs.

Social Security

For many people, Social Security is the foundation of their retirement savings. The Social Security Act was signed into law August 14, 1935, by President Franklin D. Roosevelt and was meant to provide a safety net against poverty brought on by unemployment, illness, disability, death, and old age. It is a source of income that has been guaranteed to last for life and keep pace with inflation.

The amount of your monthly Social Security check depends on when you retire, how much you and/or your spouse have earned, and whether you work during retirement. Social Security benefits are based on the average lifetime earnings of your 35 highest years of wages. The longer you wait to draw Social Security, the higher the monthly amount will be (see Figure 16.4, page 401). If your spouse dies, you receive a survivor's benefit of up to 100% of what your spouse was collecting (if that amount is higher than your own payment). If you are divorced, you may still be eligible for spouse and survivor benefits.

Usually your Social Security check is automatically adjusted for inflation each January based on the consumer

spousal IRA
traditional or Roth IRA established and funded by an individual for his or her spouse

annuity
financial product designed to accept and grow funds then pay out a stream of payments at a later point in time

▼ **FIGURE** 16.2

Tax-free vs. taxable accounts (with a $2,000 annual contribution, 8% return, and a 30% tax rate)

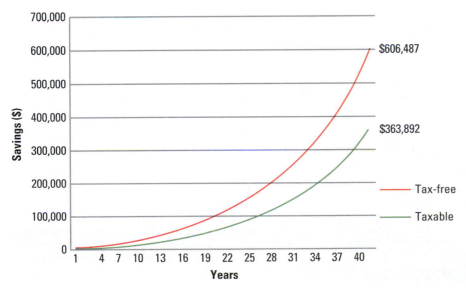

Retirement fund comparison

	Company-Sponsored		Independently Established	
	401(k)	**Roth 401(k)**	**IRA**	**Roth IRA**
Tax Implications	Contributions are deposited as "tax-deferred" and then taxed at the normal income bracket for distributions.	Contributions are from post-tax money, and no taxes have to be paid under normal distributions.	Contributions are tax-deductible and reduce one's tax basis for the tax year. Distributions are taxed as normal income.	Contributions are from post-tax money, and no taxes have to be paid under normal distributions.
Income Limits	Generally none, but somewhat complicated due to HCE (highly compensated employees) rules.		Based on your adjusted gross income (AGI): for 2010, phases out between $105,000 and $120,000 for single filers and $167,000 to $177,000 for those who are married and file jointly .	
Contribution Limits	$16.5k/yr for under 50, $22k/yr for 50 + in 2011; limits are a total of traditional 401(k) & Roth 401(k) contributions. Employee/employer combined contributions must be < 100% of employee's salary or $46k.		$5k/yr for age 49 or below; $6k/yr for age 50 or above in 2011; limits are total for traditional IRA and Roth IRA contributions combined.	
Set Up	Employer sets up this plan.		Individual sets up this plan.	
Matching Contributions	Matching contributions may be available from employers.	Matching contributions may be available through employers, but must sit in a pretax account.	No matching contributions available.	
Distributions	Distributions can begin at age 59½ or if the owner becomes disabled.	Distributions can begin at age 59½ and if the account has been open for at least 5 years, or if the owner becomes disabled. (There are exceptions.)	Distributions can begin at age 59½ or if the owner becomes disabled.	Distributions can begin at age 59½ as long as contributions are "seasoned" (have been in the account for at least 5 years) or the owner becomes disabled.
Forced Distributions	Must start withdrawing funds at age 70½ unless employee is still employed. Penalty is 50% of minimum distribution.	Must start withdrawing at age 70½ unless employee is still employed or still working and not a 5% owner. Penalty is 50% of minimum distribution.	Must start withdrawing funds at age 70½. Penalty is 50% of minimum distribution.	None
Early Withdrawal	10% penalty plus taxes (taxed at normal income tax rate)	Proportion of withdrawal = proportion of profits to contributions in the account subject to 10% penalty + taxes.	10% penalty plus taxes for distributions before age 59½, with exceptions.	Early withdrawal greater than contributions plus seasoned conversions are subject to normal income taxes + 10% penalty if not qualified distributions.
Home Down Payment	Purchase of primary residence and avoidance of foreclosure or eviction of primary residence is subject to 10% penalty.		Can withdraw up to $10k for a first-time home purchase down payment, with stipulations.	Up to $10k can be used for primary home down payment. Must not have owned a home in last 24 months. House must be owned by IRA owner or direct lineal ancestors/descendants.
Education Expenses	Can pay educational expenses in last 12 months for employee, spouse, or dependents, subject to 10% penalty.	None	Can withdraw for qualified higher education expenses of owner, children, and grandchildren.	
Medical Expenses	Uncovered medical expenses for employee, spouse, or dependents subject to 10% penalty.		Can withdraw for qualified unreimbursed medical expenses that are more than 7.5% of AGI; medical insurance during period of unemployment; during disability.	
Conversions	Employment termination — can be rolled to IRA/Roth IRA. If Roth IRA, taxes must be paid during the year of the conversion.	Cannot be converted to traditional 401(k), but upon termination of employment, can be rolled into Roth IRA.	Can be converted to a Roth IRA. Taxes must be paid during year of the conversion. Other limitations.	None
Changing Institutions	Can roll over to another employer's 401(k) plan or to a traditional IRA at an independent institution.	Can roll over to another employer's Roth 401(k) plan or to a Roth IRA at an independent institution.	Can be transferred to another institution or sent to owner who has 60 days to put in another institution in rollover to another traditional IRA.	Can be transferred to another institution or sent to owner who has 60 days to put the money in another institution in a rollover contribution to another Roth IRA.

Source: Extracted from www.retirementplans.irs.gov and www.schwab.com.

financialfitness:
JUST THE FACTS

price index for urban wage earners and clerical workers (CPI-W). If you have an average life expectancy or better, you will come out ahead if you wait for larger monthly payments. Additionally, you will have a bigger check later in your life when your retirement savings are diminished and you are perhaps no longer able to work to supplement your income. As a strategy for married couples, the higher-earning spouse should delay taking Social Security

for as long as possible because survivor benefits are based on the larger of the two. The other spouse should claim benefits earlier. This strategy typically provides the greatest amount of income for a married couple over their retirement years.

Life Stages of Retirement Planning

Putting money aside now for a long-term goal such as retirement may feel like a sacrifice. However, remember Smart Sam in Chapter 2; the sooner you start saving, the faster your savings will grow. If the long-term goal is hard to appreciate, focus on the silver lining—the tax breaks you will get this year for contributing to an IRA or a 401(k). With retirement savings, strike a balance where you can both enjoy today and plan for tomorrow. Bear in mind your retirement savings allocation will change as you pass through the different personal finance life stages.

late dependent/independent life stages (age 14–24) The only requirement to open a traditional or Roth IRA is that you have earned income. Some states allow you to start working at age 14; most people have their first summer jobs at around age 16. If you were to deposit $1,000 in a Roth IRA at age 16 and were able to get a 10% annual return, 50 years later that $1,000 would be worth $117,390. Depositing $5,000 in a Roth IRA would amount to $586,954.26 in 50 years. If you waited until you were 70 years old to make withdrawals from the fund, the $1,000 would be worth $171,871.95, and the $5,000 would be worth $859,359.74 (see Figure 16.5 on the next page). As these examples illustrate, it is never too early to start saving for retirement. A little discipline now pays off big later.

Early Family Life Stage (Age 25–40) Stashing away the maximum amount for retirement in the Early Family Life Stage will give you the biggest boost from tax-deferred compounding. However, retirement saving at this time of your life can be a challenge. Your retirement goal should be to have twice your annual salary in a retirement account by age 44. According to the Federal Reserve Board, most Americans by the age of 40 have an average retirement savings of only 0.8 times their annual income and an average home equity of 43% of their annual salary.

empty nest life stage (age 41–65) The biggest wealth hazard in the Empty Nest Stage of your life is overspending on housing. Aim to put no more than 30% of your pretax income toward any debt, including a mortgage. Earnings are at a peak during this period and your savings and investing should be as

▼ **FIGURE 16.4**

Social Security benefits and age of enrollment

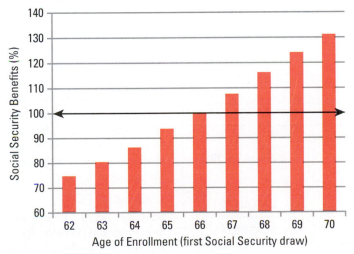

Source: www.SSA.com

financialfitness:
NUMBERS GAME

Retirement Savings Estimator

To estimate what your Social Security monthly check will be, go to http://www .socialsecurity.gov/planners/calculators .htm. The Retirement Estimator can give you an idea of what your monthly payments will be, based on current law, real-time access to your earnings, and the age you elect to start drawing on your benefits.

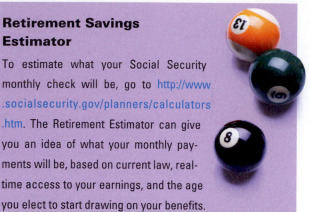

financialfitness:
ACTION ITEM

Retirement Savings Calculators

Use the following calculator to see how much you need to save each year for retirement savings: http://cgi.money.cnn.com/tools/saveyoung/index.html. Are you on target? This same site also offers a calculator to see if you can retire early: http://cgi.money.cnn.com/ tools/retireyoung/index.html.

well. Aim to have more than four times your income saved in your retirement account by age 54. According to the Federal Reserve Board, the reality is that Americans at this stage have an average retirement savings of 1.1 times their annual income, and their average home equity is 55%.

If you are not on track with your retirement savings, there are a few things you can do to catch up. For example, workers age 50 and older can contribute $5,000 more to a 401(k) and $1,000 more to traditional and Roth IRAs than younger workers. If you are older, a traditional IRA may be a better choice than a Roth because it lowers your current

earnings now and does not become a taxable income until you withdraw from it.

Colette, from the chapter opener, is putting off her retirement to get back on track. Working past the traditional retirement age will allow you to postpone withdrawals from a retirement account. Your savings will have more time to grow, and you will reduce the number of years needed to draw on those funds. Working longer also may let you delay taking Social Security, potentially increasing the size of your monthly benefit by as much as 30%. Another option is to take a part-time job after you retire. For example, if you work part-time in a job you enjoy after you have retired and are able to earn $20,000 per year, that income is equivalent to having a $400,000 investment that pays 5% interest.

▼ FIGURE 16.5

Impact of compound interest on early savings

One small investment at age 16 pays big 50/54 years later

	Initial Investment at Age 16	Value at Age 66	Value at Age 70
Series 1	$ 1,000	$ 117,390.00	$ 171,871.95
Series 2	$ 5,000	$ 586,954.26	$ 859,359.74

retirement life stage (age 66+) It is wonderful if you are able to retire by age 66, but if you delay tapping your accounts by a few years, you will be even more secure down the road. If by the Retirement Stage you have paid off your home, you can live on 10 to 15% less than those who have not. Moving to a lower-cost region can also stretch your retirement savings significantly.

Short of a change in our national health care plan, a 65-year-old person retiring today needs $120,000

> ## "I have enough money to last me the rest of my life, unless I buy something."
>
> —J. PAUL GETTY, *American industrialist (1892–1976)*

for future health costs (even with Medicare). A long-term care policy is not necessary as long as you have prepared for the cost of assisted living (a semi-private room in a nursing home costs $70,000 per year or more). According to the Federal Reserve Board, Americans at age 64 have an average retirement savings of 2.0 times their annual income, and their average home equity is 57%.

See Figure 16.6 for a breakdown of actual compared to recommended financial goals for different life stages. Saving to get what you need will take work and planning. Do yourself a favor and start now!

financialfitness:
ACTION ITEM

Cost-of-Living Comparisons

The cost of living can vary greatly from one region to the next. When making a decision on where to live in your retirement years, visit cgi.money.cnn.com/tools/costofliving/costofliving.html. If you plan on moving after retirement, selecting an area with a low cost of living can help stretch your savings further.

Making $ense

16.1   What are the pros and cons of starting to draw Social Security benefits?

16.2   What are some of the reasons you should start a retirement fund when you get your first job?

16.3   How do traditional IRAs and 401(k)s differ from Roth IRAs and Roth 401(k)s?

▼ **FIGURE 16.6**

Actual retirement savings compared to recommended goals

Comparison at Different Life Stages Actual Averages 2009 vs. Recommended Goals *(an example in dollars using a person with an annual income of $100,000 who owns a $200,000 home)*			
Actual Averages from Federal Reserve Board 2009			**What You Should Have in Retirement Savings**
Age	Average 401(k) Contribution of Annual Salary	Average Retirement Savings as % of Annual Income	Average Home Equity	
40	6.40% ($6,400)	80% ($80,000)	43% ($86,000)	2x salary ($200,000)
54	7.60% ($7,600)	110% ($110,000)	55% ($110,000)	4x salary ($400,000)
66	9% ($9,000)	200% ($200,000)	57% ($124,000)	8x salary ($800,000)

Source: Table information derived from the Federal Reserve Board.

will
a legal declaration of your decision as to the dispersion of your assets and the caring for your dependents following your death

testate
having made a legally valid will

intestate
without a valid will

executor
the person who will tend to your estate according to the wishes outlined in your will

letter of intent
a letter to the heirs and executor outlining your wishes for your funeral arrangements, who to notify of your death, and other wishes

estate tax
a tax imposed on a property owner's right to transfer the property to others after his or her death

16.2 ESTATE PLANNING

■ ■ **LO 16-2** Understand the importance of a will and advance directives and recognize estate planning methods you can use to transfer wealth.

It is inevitable that someday you will die. As a gift to those you leave behind, keep your will, advance directives, and other legal documents in good order. It will help your family carry out your wishes and deal with your assets as you would have wanted.

Wills

A **will** (formally known as your *last will and testament*) is a legal document that specifies how you want your assets distributed and your dependents cared for after your death. If you die with a will, you die **testate** (having a will). If you die **intestate** (without a will), a court determines who gets what. Everything you own is part of your estate. Typically, if you are single, all your assets will go to your parents and/or siblings. If you have children and are without a will, a judge will decide who will raise your children. The state will appoint a guardian to take custody of your children and manage any funds for their health, education, maintenance, and support. A will ensures you have a say in how your estate is handled after you are gone.

An **executor** is a person who will tend to your estate according to your wishes as outlined in your will. Tasks performed by the executor include preparing an inventory of your assets, collecting any money due to the estate, paying off your debts, and preparing and filing all income and estate tax returns. This person also may need to make decisions about selling or reinvesting assets to pay off debt or provide income for your family while the estate is being settled. This person will distribute the assets of the estate and make a final accounting to your beneficiaries and to the probate court (the court that will oversee and settle your will).

Banks, trust companies, or attorneys can be named as an executor of your will, a

service for which your estate will pay a fee. The advantage of this over naming a family member is that there would be no fighting or hard feelings between siblings. Executor fees vary from state to state, but they often range from 2 to 4% of the value of the assets subject to probate.

legal documents of the estate Along with the will, the executor of your estate will need access to a number of your legal documents to handle your affairs appropriately and in a timely fashion. These documents must be reviewed and verified before your assets can be dispersed. Figure 16.7 lists important papers to keep organized and accessible by the executor of your will.

In addition to a will, you should prepare a **letter of intent** or last instructions to your executor and heirs. The letter is not legally binding, but it provides your heirs and executor with important information such as wishes for your funeral arrangements and who should be informed of your death. If by chance the will is deemed invalid for some reason, a letter of intent will help the probate judge determine your intentions in the distribution of your assets.

estate and inheritance taxes Over 200 years ago, Benjamin Franklin observed that "in this world nothing can be said to be certain, except death and taxes." Although not much can be done about the certainty

▼ **FIGURE 16.7**

Important papers checklist

Certificates and Registrations
• Birth certificates (yours, spouse's, dependents')
• Marriage certificates
• Divorce papers
• Legal name changes
• Social Security documents
• Automobile registrations

Armed Service Records
• Military service records
• Veterans' documents

Policies and Banking Records
• Insurance policies
• Transfer records of joint bank accounts
• Safety-deposit box records/keys
• Titles to stocks and bond certificates

▼ **FIGURE** 16.8

Estate tax rates by state for 2010

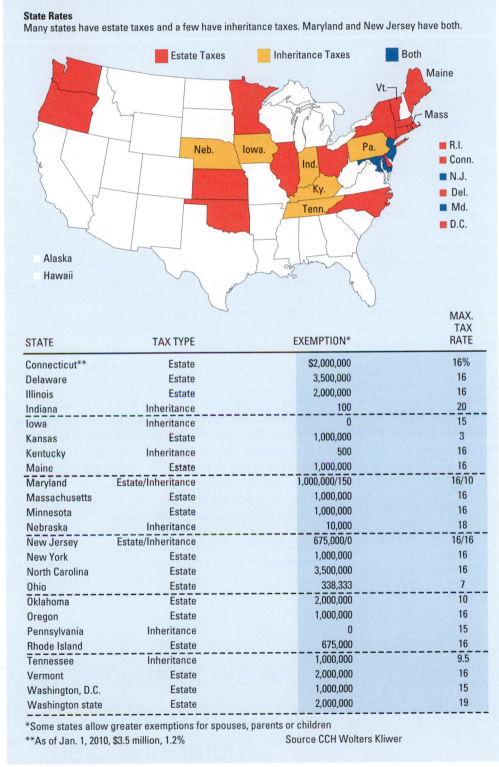

State Rates
Many states have estate taxes and a few have inheritance taxes. Maryland and New Jersey have both.

■ Estate Taxes ■ Inheritance Taxes ■ Both

Maine
Vt.
Mass

■ R.I.
■ Conn.
■ N.J.
■ Del.
■ Md.
■ D.C.

Alaska
Hawaii

STATE	TAX TYPE	EXEMPTION*	MAX. TAX RATE
Connecticut**	Estate	$2,000,000	16%
Delaware	Estate	3,500,000	16
Illinois	Estate	2,000,000	16
Indiana	Inheritance	100	20
Iowa	Inheritance	0	15
Kansas	Estate	1,000,000	3
Kentucky	Inheritance	500	16
Maine	Estate	1,000,000	16
Maryland	Estate/Inheritance	1,000,000/150	16/10
Massachusetts	Estate	1,000,000	16
Minnesota	Estate	1,000,000	16
Nebraska	Inheritance	10,000	18
New Jersey	Estate/Inheritance	675,000/0	16/16
New York	Estate	1,000,000	16
North Carolina	Estate	3,500,000	16
Ohio	Estate	338,333	7
Oklahoma	Estate	2,000,000	10
Oregon	Estate	1,000,000	16
Pennsylvania	Inheritance	0	15
Rhode Island	Estate	675,000	16
Tennessee	Inheritance	1,000,000	9.5
Vermont	Estate	2,000,000	16
Washington, D.C.	Estate	1,000,000	15
Washington state	Estate	2,000,000	19

*Some states allow greater exemptions for spouses, parents or children
**As of Jan. 1, 2010, $3.5 million, 1.2%

Source CCH Wolters Kliwer

Source: *The Wall Street Journal* , October 31, 2009.

of death, you can take a number of actions to reduce, if not avoid, the estate tax, while ensuring your assets are transferred exactly as you wish. The **estate tax** is the tax on your estate at the time of your death. Federal laws have been changing in recent years and state laws vary, so keep an eye on estate tax legislation. For example, in 2009 the federal estate-tax exemption was $3.5 million per individual or $7 million per married couple. The federal estate tax disappeared in 2010 but was reinstated in 2011 with an exemption amount set at $5 million per individual or $10 million per married couple and the maximum tax rate set at 35%. After 2011, the exemption amounts are indexed for inflation.

You must file estate taxes within nine months after the owner's death. An **inheritance tax** is the tax your heirs pay on property they inherit. A few states exercise both an estate and an inheritance tax (see Figure 16.8). Some people select their retirement residence in tax-free states to avoid estate taxes at the state level.

domicile
a place where an individual has a fixed and permanent home for legal purposes

trustor
a person who puts money into a trust

trustee
a person who manages the money in a trust

beneficiary
the person or persons who are entitled to the benefit of any trust arrangement

revocable living trust a trust over which the settler has retained the power of revocation

In calculating the estate value, any stocks, bonds, or other investments inherited are valued at their prices on the day the person dies. You pay taxes only on the difference between the sale price and the value on the day of the donor's death (not the price originally paid for the stock). Tax-protected investments like IRAs and 401(k)s have tricky rules on how much can be withdrawn and how much tax you must pay. You will want to get a professional involved before you touch any of the funds; otherwise, you may find yourself with an exceptionally large tax bill.

One way to avoid these taxes is to establish a **bypass trust** in your will. A bypass trust allows married couples to maximize exemptions from state taxes. At the death of the first spouse, assets go into a trust the survivor can draw from if necessary. When the second spouse dies, the remaining assets pass tax-free to heirs, preserving the value of both individual exemptions. For example, if a married couple lives in a state with a $1 million individual exemption, a bypass trust lets them pass as much as $2 million tax-free to heirs.

Even if taxpayers live in states without estate taxes, they may be liable for estate taxes if they own property in a state that does have such a tax. More so than residency, the **domicile** of a taxpayer determines where that person pays income tax. The determinants of a person's domicile include:

- The amount of time spent in a state
- The state where a taxpayer votes
- The location of any church or club memberships
- The location of the individual's car registration
- The location of a burial plot, if owned

Even though a taxpayer may live and spend most of his or her time in a state that does not have an estate tax, if s/he keeps a second home and memberships in another state, s/he may be considered to be domiciled there.

In the worst case scenario, a taxpayer could be domiciled in more than one state and owe taxes to each. Following the 1930 death of Campbell Soup magnate John Dorrance, both New Jersey and Pennsylvania claimed they were due $15 million in estate taxes. Twice, the U.S. Supreme Court refused to break the deadlock. After a six-year battle, the John Dorrance estate paid estate taxes of $15 million to each state.

Trusts

Another way to leave money to your heirs is by creating a trust, whereby you (the **trustor**) set aside money controlled by a **trustee** who invests money in the trust and delivers it to the **beneficiaries** according to your directions. You can establish and fund a trust while you are still alive, or you can instruct that a trust be created in your will.

There are two main types of trusts. **Revocable living trusts** can be changed at any time, but any assets in them will be included as part of your estate when you die. **Irrevocable trusts** cannot be changed, meaning that once you create an irrevocable trust, it is permanent. The advantage of an irrevocable trust is that the assets in this trust (including the proceeds from life insurance policies) are not included as part of your estate.

charitable remainder trusts A **charitable remainder trust** is an irrevocable trust whose beneficiary is a charitable organization. When you establish

I made my money the old fashioned way.
I was very nice to a wealthy relative right
before he died.

— MALCOLM FORBES, *Publisher of* Forbes *magazine (1919–1990)*

this trust, the trust owns the assets. Naming a charity as the beneficiary allows you to receive a tax deduction for the contribution to the charity when the assets are turned over to the trust. As the trustor, you can stipulate that the earnings of the assets go to you as long as you are living. After your death, the beneficiary receives the assets.

revocable living trusts   The main advantage of setting up a revocable living trust is to avoid **probate** (a costly, time-consuming, and public court proceeding in which your property is transferred to your heirs). Since probate affects only the assets you own at the time of your death, assets placed in a revocable trust are treated as owned by the trust and are not subject to probate.

Another practical reason for having a revocable living trust is to provide for the possibility of your becoming disabled. If all of your property is held in a revocable trust and you become disabled, the successor trustee you named in the trust document can step in and manage your property for your benefit in accordance with the terms of your trust. This avoids, in most cases, the need for the courts to appoint someone to manage your affairs in the event of your incapacitation.

Power of Attorney

When you complete a **power of attorney** document, you designate a representative, known as an **attorney in fact**, to perform certain actions for you should you become ill, incapacitated, or otherwise unable to manage your affairs. This person can pay your bills, file your tax returns, and sell securities or make major financial decisions on your behalf, depending on how broad or narrow you limit his or her powers. Without a power of attorney, your spouse or other loved ones must endure the delay and expense of seeking court approval to carry out needed financial transactions.

Advance Directives

Competent adults have the right to refuse or accept medical treatment after being informed of the procedures and risks involved. An **advance directive** is a legal document that states your health care choices and designates who will make choices for you if you become unable to do so.

financialfitness:
ACTION ITEM

Advance Directives

State laws vary on the requirements of advance directives. Go to http://www .caringinfo.org/stateaddownload to get copies of the forms that are appropriate for your state. Generally, you must have two witnesses over age 18 or use a notary. At least one of the witnesses must not be related to you by blood, marriage, or adoption.

Making $ense

16.4   In what situations do advance directives come into play?

16.5   What advantage is there to setting up a bypass trust for a spouse or children?

16.6   What are some of the ways you can reduce your tax liability on the assets and property you pass on to your heirs?

advance directive a legal document that expresses your wishes regarding medical treatment in the event of incapacitation

living will a document that outlines your preferences or directions for the administration and the withdrawal or withholding of life-sustaining medical treatment in the event of terminal illness or permanent unconsciousness

durable power of attorney for health care a power of attorney that becomes effective in the event that you become incompetent or unable to manage your affairs; often identified within an advance directive

financialfitness:
ACTION ITEM

Making a Will

Some software, such as Family Lawyer and Quicken Willmaker, can help you create your own will. Other online references include www.legalzoom.com and www.nolo.com. Once drawn up, the will must be signed by two witnesses who will not inherit anything and, in some states, it must be notarized.

Having advance directive documents saves the people you love from the additional grief of making difficult health care decisions during an already emotional time.

Advance directives are more commonly known as living wills and durable powers of attorney for health care. A **living will** is a written declaration of what life-sustaining medical treatment you will or will not allow in the event you become incapacitated. For example, you may request that artificial nourishment be, or not be, withheld if you are terminally ill. The **durable power of attorney for health care** authorizes a person to make medical decisions on your behalf, generally to carry out what you have specified in your living will. Share these documents and your decisions with your family early, so they will be more comfortable executing your wishes if the situation presents itself.

Make sure you have multiple copies of your will and advance directives. Be sure to give copies to key players

(your executor and your attorney of fact). Take a copy of your advance directives to your doctor or hospital to be scanned into your medical record. Because your personal and family circumstances will change over the years, it is important to review your documents every four to five years. A simple guide is to review the documents every presidential election year and update them to reflect any changes in state or federal laws or to accommodate changes in your personal circumstances.

16.3 CHARITABLE GIVING

■■ **LO 16-3** Evaluate different means of charitable giving and their impact on your tax liability.

Giving your money to charities is one way to reflect your personal values. If you have enough tax deductions to itemize, you can also take advantage of the tax break the government offers for charitable contributions. Keeping track of your donations will help you keep your spending priorities in line with your values.

Selections

Once you decide on the amount you want to budget toward charitable giving, you have options to give a little money to many organizations or a lot to one; you can donate to a local community initiative (such as a neighborhood crisis center) or a national organization (such as the American Red Cross, Goodwill, or your college or university). To be assured your gift is being used for its intended purpose, research how much of the gift goes to the group's work and how much goes to raising more money. Sites such as www.give.org and www.charitynavigator.org identify what charitable groups do with their funds and evaluate their financial strengths and weaknesses.

Impact on Taxes

To qualify for tax deductions, a charitable group must be not-for-profit and meet certain other criteria. Items you can deduct include donations of cash, clothing, household items, used vehicles, art, and stock. Used items are valued at garage-sale prices. Works of art require an appraisal.

> " One must be poor to know the luxury of giving.
> —GEORGE BERNARD SHAW, *Irish playwright (1856–1950)* "

Scan here for more
information on the
latest events
"In the News"

Timing of George Steinbrenner's death saves family $500 million in taxes

TOM WEIR, "Timing of George Steinbrenner's Death Saves Family $500 Million in Taxes," *USA Today*, July 14, 2010. Reprinted with permission.

We don't mean to in any way make light of George Steinbrenner's passing yesterday, but it's ironic that a man obsessed with winning appears to have beaten the adage that the two inevitable things in life are death and taxes. The timing of Steinbrenner's death, according to the *New York Post,* will save his family about $500 million in estate taxes. The paper says Steinbrenner's death occurred six months after the federal estate tax of 45% expired in January. It is scheduled to be renewed in 2011, at 55%. *Forbes* last year estimated Steinbrenner's net worth at $1.15 billion, so it's conceivable that a $500 million tax bill could have compelled the family to sell the Yankees. Steinbrenner owned 55% of the Yankees's parent company, which includes the team, the YES Network, and the new Yankee Stadium. Value of the Yankees has been estimated at $1.6 billion.

Questions

1 Why do you think the government eliminated estate taxes for one year?

2 Why does the government have estate taxes?

3 What are some things your family can do to minimize your estate tax liability?

You cannot deduct donations to an individual, contributions to a political campaign or group, or raffle tickets—nor can you deduct your donated time. If you buy a ticket to a dinner that is in support of a cause, you may deduct only the amount over and above the cost of the meal. The IRS requires a receipt for every donation (no matter how small the amount). Put these receipts in a tax folder throughout the year so that, come tax time, your donations are easy to tally.

financialfitness:
NUMBERS GAME

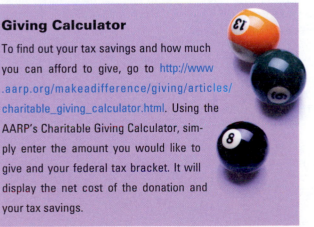

Giving Calculator

To find out your tax savings and how much you can afford to give, go to http://www.aarp.org/makeadifference/giving/articles/charitable_giving_calculator.html. Using the AARP's Charitable Giving Calculator, simply enter the amount you would like to give and your federal tax bracket. It will display the net cost of the donation and your tax savings.

opportunities for lifetime gifting The Internal Revenue Code provides two basic mechanisms for transferring property to individuals free of the gift tax: (1) the lifetime gift-tax exemption, and (2) the annual exclusion amount. The lifetime-gifting opportunities are some of the simplest and most effective ways to reduce your taxable estate without incurring any wealth transfer taxes, and they should be considered as part of any estate plan.

As of 2010, you can give away up to $13,000 per individual without paying the gift tax. The gift tax is paid by the giver, not the receiver, and was established to prevent people from avoiding federal estate tax by giving away their assets before they die. Unlike giving the money to a not-for-profit charitable organization, which is a tax deduction, these gift-tax opportunities represent a tax exemption. Both forms of giving provide tax advantages. ■

Making $ense

16.7 What types of giving can be deducted on your income taxes?

16.8 On an annual basis, how much can a married couple give as a gift to an individual without having to pay a gift tax?

["A billion here, a billion there, pretty soon it adds up to real money."]

—EVERETT DIRKSEN, *U.S. senator (1896–1969)*

Learn. ⟩ Plan & Act. ⟩ Evaluate.

➡ **LEARN.** This chapter covered ways to save for retirement, how to pass your assets on to your heirs, and the paperwork you should have in place to make sure your end-of-life decisions are carried out as you wish. It also identified ways to demonstrate your values and decrease your tax liability through charitable giving.

SUMMARY

■■ **LO 16-1** Recognize the benefits of retirement planning and the importance of starting early, and determine the appropriate retirement savings strategy for your current life stage.

In planning for retirement, the general rule is you will need 70% of your pre-retirement annual salary to live comfortably, assuming your mortgage is paid off and you are in good health. To be safe, target 80%.

Most companies offer a retirement plan that requires monthly contributions. Take advantage of any matching funds offered. Contributions to a 401(k) are made with pretax dollars. Contributions to a Roth 401(k) are made with money you have earned that has already been taxed.

Social Security benefits are based on the average lifetime earnings of your 35 highest wage-earning years. The longer you wait to draw Social Security, the higher the monthly amount will be. Social Security is not likely to cover all of your cost-of-living expenses, so it is important to have a retirement savings plan in place.

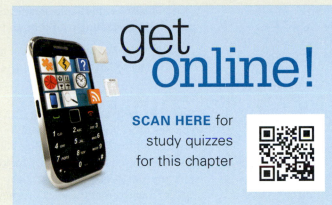

get online!

SCAN HERE for study quizzes for this chapter

■■ **LO 16-2** Understand the importance of a will and advance directives and recognize estate planning methods you can use to transfer wealth.

A will ensures that your estate will be handled according to your wishes and specifies who will care for children under the age of 18. Estate and inheritance taxes are levied at the passing of property at the time of your death. The applicability of the tax and the amount is dependent on domicile, the estate value, and your relationship with those receiving your property. One way to avoid these taxes is to establish a bypass trust in your will. Setting up a revocable living trust avoids probate.

Other important documents to have in place are a power of attorney and advance directives (including a living will and a durable power of attorney for health care) should you become ill, incapacitated, or otherwise unable to manage your affairs.

■■ **LO 16-3** Evaluate different means of charitable giving and their impact on your tax liability.

Charitable giving reflects your personal values. Financially, it can provide tax advantages. Charitable remainder trusts have estate-planning benefits. Keeping track of your donations will help you keep your spending priorities in line. Research charities before you give to ensure that they will be good stewards of your time and money.

⟹ **PLAN & ACT.** Some of the Financial Fitness boxes in this chapter reference online calculators that can be used to assess your retirement savings. Check your Social Security benefits and determine how much savings you need to budget monthly in order to obtain your financial goals for retirement. Another link provided in one of the Financial Fitness boxes can help you draft advance directives. Communicating your end-of-life wishes to loved ones, appointing a health care power of attorney, and addressing the transfer of your assets are just a few of the issues you can address today to plan ahead. Your Plan & Act to-do list is as follows:

☐ Research your future Social Security monthly benefits (Worksheet 16.1).

☐ Identify how much to allocate annually toward retirement savings (Activity 16.3; http://cgi.money.cnn.com/tools/saveyoung/index.html).

☐ If you have earned income, look into opening a traditional IRA or a Roth IRA.

☐ Create/review your need for a will. Identify steps to have it in place.

☐ Create your advance directives and discuss your wishes with your family (Activity 16.4; http://www.caringinfo.org/stateaddownload).

☐ Identify a charitable organization you want to help either through financial support or by volunteering your time and talents (Worksheet 16.2).

☐ Identify how much you want to give on an annual basis to charitable organizations, and create a plan to act upon it (Activity 16.5; http://www.charitynavigator.org).

⊃ EVALUATE.

At what age do you want to retire? How much should you set aside for retirement savings? Compare this amount to your current retirement savings allocations. Determine your personal finance life stage and evaluate when and how much to budget monthly for retirement. Are you where you need to be? If not, what can you do to get on track? Keep these savings allocations in mind as you make your 401(k) decisions at the start of a new job. If your employer does not offer a 401(k) benefit, take it upon yourself to allocate the appropriate amount in your budget to cover yourself in the long run.

Have you set up a will and your advance directives? How much of your budget or time do you allocate to charitable giving today? The returns are twofold, a small one being the tax deductions. Do you track charitable giving today? If not, does completing Worksheet 16.2 motivate you to start?

›› GoalTracker

Give some thought to the decisions you make in your advance directives. It is important to reassess these documents every few years to confirm that they reflect your current needs and family situation. Document your reflections in your online GoalTracker.

key terms

Advance Directive	Estate Tax	Revocable Living Trust
Annuity	Executor	Simplified Employee Pension (SEP) Plan
Attorney in Fact	Inheritance Tax	
Beneficiary	Intestate	Spousal IRA
Bypass Trust	Irrevocable Trust	Testate
Charitable Remainder Trust	Letter of Intent	Trustee
Domicile	Living Will	Trustor
Durable Power of Attorney for Health Care	Power of Attorney	Vested
	Probate	Will

self-test questions

1. With savings, investing, and retirement savings, you can control _____. *(LO 16-1)*

   a. Interest rates
   b. Inflation
   c. The ups and downs of the stock market
   d. How much money you allocate

2. Your Social Security benefits are based on _____. *(LO 16-1)*

   a. Where you live
   b. How much you have in retirement savings
   c. The average lifetime earnings of your 35 highest wage-earning years
   d. What your company contributes toward your retirement savings

3. Factors that affect how much you will receive monthly from Social Security include _____. *(LO 16-1)*

   a. Your age when you decide to start drawing your Social Security checks
   b. How much money you earned
   c. Whether you are working during retirement
   d. All of the above

4. When calculating retirement income and Social Security, _____. *(LO 16-1)*

   a. Do not worry about Social Security because it probably will be around when you are ready to retire
   b. File for Social Security at the same time as your spouse
   c. Have the spouse with the higher income draw his or her Social Security last
   d. File for Social Security with your spouse as soon as possible while there is still money in the fund

5. The total amount you receive in Social Security retirement income depends on _____. *(LO 16-1)*

   a. Your previous earnings and the amount you paid into Social Security
   b. The age at which you retire
   c. How long you live
   d. All of the above

6. Once you start receiving Social Security payments, _____. *(LO 16-1)*

   a. Your amount is set for life
   b. You receive an adjustment for inflation on your birthday
   c. The amount you receive is recalculated based on your life expectancy and your physician's report of your health
   d. You receive an annual adjustment each January for inflation

7. At retirement, what is the minimum suggested percentage of pre-retirement income you should have if your mortgage is paid off and you are in good health? *(LO 16-1)*

   a. 60%
   b. 70%
   c. 80%
   d. 90%

8. What can be done to catch up on retirement savings if you are not reaching the targeted amount? *(LO 16-1)*

   a. Work longer
   b. Add more money to Roth and traditional IRAs

   c. Work a part-time job after retirement
   d. All of the above

9. The best way to have enough saved for retirement is to _____. *(LO 16-1)*

   a. Start saving for retirement as soon as you have earned income
   b. Work for a company with a good retirement plan
   c. Rely on Social Security
   d. Don't worry, be happy

10. Traditional IRA accounts _____. *(LO 16-1)*

    a. Allow you to save for retirement using pretax dollars
    b. Defer taxes on all their earnings
    c. Pay taxes on withdrawals
    d. All of the above

11. Roth IRA accounts _____. *(LO 16-1)*

    a. Allow saving for retirement using after-tax dollars
    b. Have tax-free earnings
    c. Do not tax withdrawals
    d. All of the above

12. Both Roth and traditional IRA accounts _____. *(LO 16-1)*

    a. Allow you to deposit 100% of your earned income for retirement
    b. Allow you to deposit $5,000 annually if you are under the age of 50 or $6,000 annually if you are age 50 and over
    c. Are employee-sponsored retirement plans
    d. Can be invested only in mutual funds

13. Characteristics of a 401(k) plan include _____. *(LO 16-1)*

    a. Employers are required to match a minimum of 3% of salary for all full-time employees
    b. You can deposit a maximum of $22,000 if you are under age 50
    c. You can invest only in mutual funds
    d. You can have either a traditional 401(k) or a Roth 401(k)

14. When you change jobs, your 401(k) account _____. *(LO 16-1)*

    a. Has to stay with your past employer
    b. Is considered a withdrawal and you have to pay taxes on the entire amount
    c. Can be transferred to another plan administrator, such as a mutual fund company or your new employer's plan
    d. Cannot be rolled over into an IRA

15. The importance of a last will and testament is _____. *(LO 16-2)*

    a. You decide how assets will be distributed following your death
    b. The court decides how assets will be distributed following your death
    c. You can provide an advance directive in your will
    d. Heirs do not have to pay inheritance tax if you have a will

16. Estate taxes _____. *(LO 16-2)*

    a. Are taxes you pay before you die
    b. Are taxes based on the value of your estate at the time of your death
    c. Are of concern only if you are very wealthy
    d. Cannot be avoided

17. An irrevocable trust _____. *(LO 16-2)*

    a. Can be changed at any time
    b. Is a good way to give to charities

    c. Is a way to increase your estate tax
    d. All of the above

18. A general power of attorney allows the attorney in fact to _____. *(LO 16-2)*

    a. Conduct business on your behalf
    b. Sign loans in your name
    c. Sell your property
    d. All of the above

19. Which item is *not* noteworthy for tax purposes? *(LO 16-3)*

    a. The market value of clothing given to Goodwill
    b. The appraised value of art given to your university
    c. Cash given to the American Red Cross
    d. The blue book price of a car donated to a local crisis center

problems

1. You are 25 years old and need to have $1,000,000 in savings before you retire at age 75. You estimate you will receive an annual return of 8% on investments. *(LO 16-1)*

    a. How much do you need to put into retirement savings on an annual basis?
    b. How much do you need to put into retirement savings on an annual basis if you get an annual return of 10%?

2. You are just starting your first job out of college. You and your best friend are competing to see who will have more in their savings when you retire; you both plan to retire at age 52, just 30 years out. You will need $5 million to retire. If you average an annual return of 7% on your investment, how much do you need to put into retirement savings on an annual basis? *(LO 16-1)*

3. You have made an appointment with a lawyer to begin estate planning. Your current balance sheet shows a net worth of $2.7 million. If executor fees range from 2 to 4% of the value of the assets, what should you plan on paying? *(LO 16-2)*

4. Your parents gave you $30,000 worth of Apple stock in 2008. In 2010, the shares are worth $55,000. *(LO 16-3)*

    a. What is the taxable amount for the gift tax in 2008?
    b. By what amount was your parents' estate value reduced after giving you this gift?
    c. What would the taxable amount of the gift tax be if your parents waited until 2010 to give you the Apple stock?

5. You have four children, and you and your spouse want to maximize the amount you can give to each child each year before you have to pay the gift tax. *(LO 16-3)*

    a. How much would you give each child?
    b. What would the total gifts be in a single year?

6. You give $1 million to your college in an irrevocable trust with the stipulation that you receive the earnings from the gift. You are guaranteed an 8% return on your investment. *(LO 16-3)*

    a. What would be the income from your gift?
    b. How much of your gift would be a tax deduction?

7. Your 75-year-old grandparents have over $10,000,000 in assets. They have three children and nine grandchildren. How much money can they gift to each of the children and grandchildren in 2010 without any gift-tax liability? *(LO 16-3)*

1. Sara is 30 years old and makes $40,000 per year. She has $10,000 in a traditional IRA, which is growing at 5%. She plans not to touch it until she retires at age 70. Sara believes she will make $3,000 per month from Social Security. *(LO 16-1)*

   a. With cost of living and merit salary increases, she estimates that she will be making $200,000 annually prior to retiring. How much should she budget for living expenses on a monthly basis after retirement?

   b. How much will her IRA be worth by age 70?

   c. Assuming that her IRA is growing at 5%, how much will Sara need to put in her company 401(k) plan over the next 40 years in order to reach her retirement income goals?

2. Sam has just been informed that he will be laid off in a month but may be hired back as an independent contractor. He has been with the ABC Corporation for five years with a full-employee benefit package. He has two children, ages 8 and 10. One is diabetic and the other has asthma attacks. Sam's last physical exam raised alarms about his own health. List the questions Sam should ask the employer before being laid off. What actions should he consider? *(LO 16-1)*

3. Joel's new love wants to take a leave of absence for two months and backpack through Europe for the summer. Joel's emergency fund savings would cover only the first month. *(LO 16-1)*

   a. Is withdrawing from his IRA an option? Why or why not?

   b. Is transferring his traditional IRA to a Roth IRA an option?

   c. Would this transfer of funds make the original deposit a more accessible option?

   d. What could Joel suggest to his new love as a more affordable compromise?

4. Noah's grandparents recently died, and his parents now find themselves with a large inheritance as well as the wake-up call that they themselves should venture into estate planning. Noah's older, established brother suggests they set up a bypass trust so all the grandparents' money goes to their grandchildren. He himself has three children. Although Noah someday hopes to have a family, he is currently back in college pursuing a master's degree and very much unattached. Noah is a bit of a free spirit, and his mother is putting more pressure on Noah to settle down and give her more grandchildren. *(LO 16-3)*

   a. What argument can you provide your parents to convince them that Noah's brother's proposal is not ideal?

   b. What counter-proposal could Noah make?

Find the worksheets online at www.mhhe.com/walkerpf1e

worksheets

16.1   SOCIAL SECURITY CALCULATOR

Use Worksheet 16.1 to calculate your Social Security benefit based on your actual earnings history and the age at which you plan to retire.

The Social Security web site maintains a Retirement Estimator that calculates your benefit based on:	
1) Your actual earnings history as maintained by the Social Security Administration;	
2) Additional information you provide about future earnings; and	
3) The age at which you expect to stop working.	
Go to http://www.socialsecurity.gov/planners/calculators.htm and complete the following:	
At your current earnings rate, if you stop working and start receiving Social Security benefits; At age 62, your monthly benefit will be about:	
At full retirement *(age 67 if born on/after 1960)* your monthly benefit will be about:	
At age 70, your monthly benefit will be about:	
How much more a month are Social Security benefits if wait to age 67 vs. starting at age 62?	#VALUE!
Percentage difference?	#VALUE!
How much more a month do you earn if wait and retire at age 70 vs. age 62?	#VALUE!
Percentage difference?	#VALUE!
Is the wait worth it to you?	
If you are in good health and know that the average American lives to age 85, does it impact your decision differently?	
On the table below, record the dollar amount and reasons that one might opt for one age over another option.	
	Motivators for selecting one retirement age over another
Retire at Age 62: $ /month	
Retire at Age 67: $ /month	
Retire at Age 70: $ /month	
How does reviewing this information impact your current retirement savings goals?	

16.2 EVALUATING CHARITIES

Use Worksheet 16.2 to identify and research charitable organizations that you would like to support, either financially or by volunteering your time and talents.

Name of charity			
Website			
Vision			
Mission			
Program expenses			
Administrative expenses			
Fund-raising expenses			
Fund-raising efficiency			
Efficiency ratings			
Comments on this charity			

16.3 RETIREMENT SAVINGS CALCULATOR (Web Activity)

CNN.Money.com hosts an online calculator that estimates how much money you need to put away each year if you want to retire at age 65 with 80% of your pre-retirement income. Go to http://cgi.money.cnn.com/tools/saveyoung/index.html to see your results.

If you are currently a full-time student, plug in your age at graduation and the annual salary you guess you will be making. Annual amount: $_____

To calculate how much you need to save each year to retire early at age 60, go the site and plug in your numbers. Annual amount: $ _____

What are your current thoughts about retirement and your target age for retirement? How does knowing this information influence your retirement savings goals?

16.4 ADVANCE DIRECTIVES (Web Activity)

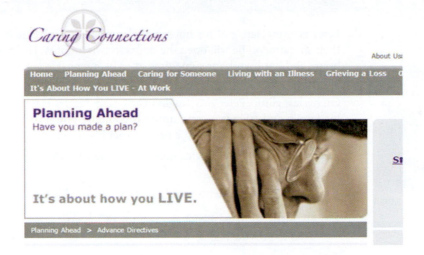

Go to the website http://www.caringinfo.org/stateaddownload and download a copy of the forms that are appropriate for your state. Discuss the forms with your family members and give serious thought to how to complete the documents. First ask permission to have this conversation, as people cope with this discussion differently. Make a decision on how you would want to be treated if you were faced with a life-limiting illness. Let your family know your choices and tell them who you have named as your health care decision maker.

Your medical power of attorney should be someone you trust, such as a close family member or good friend who understands your wishes. Make sure this person is comfortable and confident about the type of medical care you want to receive. You can also select a second agent as an alternate in case your first person is unavailable.

It is very important you use advance directive forms specifically created for your state so that they are legal. Read the forms carefully and make sure you follow the legal requirements determined by your state. You may need to have a witness signature and get the forms notarized (signed by a notary public).

Keep your completed advance directives in an easily accessible place and give photocopies to your primary medical power of attorney and your secondary, alternate agent. Contact your local hospital and doctor and ask that they file a copy of your advance directives in your medical record. This document stays in effect unless you cancel it or decide to complete a new one with changes.

16.5 CHARITABLE GIVING TAX SAVINGS CALCULATOR (Web Activity)

To find out your tax savings on charitable giving, go to Charity Navigator and enter the amount you'd like to give and your federal tax bracket (using the displayed chart at the site). The calculator will display the net cost of the donation and your tax savings. What benefits does knowing this information provide? Do you keep receipts of your charitable giving today? If not, make a plan to start.

Charitable Giving Tax Savings Calculator

Donation:		Tax Rate %:		Net Cost of Donation	Tax Savings
$	x	10% ▼ =		$	$
		Calculate			

2009 Federal Income Tax Brackets

Marginal Tax Rate	Single	Married Filing Jointly or Qualified Widow(er)	Married Filing Separately	Head of Household
		Taxable Income		
10%	$0 - $8,350	$0 - $16,700	$0 - $8,350	$0 - $11,950
15%	$8,350 - $33,950	$16,700 - $67,900	$8,350 - $33,950	$11,950 - $45,500
25%	$33,950 - $82,250	$67,900 - $137,050	$33,950 - $68,525	$45,500 - $117,450
28%	$82,250 - $171,550	$137,050 - $208,850	$68,525 - $104,425	$117,450 - $190,200
33%	$171,500 - $372,950	$208,850 - $372,950	$104,425 - $186,475	$190,200 - $372,950
35%	Over $372,950	Over $372,950	Over $186,475	Over $372,950

Source: http://www.charitynavigator.org/index.cfm?bay=content.view&cpid=40

906 E College Street

Peter is appreciative of his housemates' confidence in his new restaurant. Thanks to their investment, he will open the doors in two months. He knows that it will be long hours and hard work for some time after he opens. He is tempted to take on one last adventure before the opening day and decides to go climbing.

On his last climb, Peter gets caught in an avalanche. He is not seriously hurt, but it gives his family and friends a scare until his climbing group is found. Before he leaves for another climb, Peter realizes he needs to get his affairs in order.

A summary of the housemates' goals can be found in the first Continuing Case problem on page 27.

1. What legal documents should he create before his next departure?

2. He plans to name Blake as executor of his estate. What information does Peter need to provide Blake?

3. What should he give to his primary care provider before his departure?

" Money won't buy happiness, but it will pay the salaries of a large research staff to study the problem. "

—BILL VAUGHAN, *American columnist (1915–1977)*

financial planning for life

Personal finance management is not just a course, it is a life skill. The key to achieving financial independence, goals, and financial success is to plan and act according to your personal values, vision, and mission. ∎

LEARNING OBJECTIVES

After reading this chapter, you should be able to:

LO 17-1 Assess your financial plan against your values, vision, and life goals.

LO 17-2 Evaluate the sustainability of your financial plan, as it is the key to your plan's success.

LO 17-3 Recognize the importance of reevaluating your life goals and your progress on an annual basis.

◀ **Erin and Seth**, happy ever after

Foundation-Setting

The big day was coming. Erin had been dating Seth since her freshman year in high school. Seven years later, they were making the commitment to a life-long partnership, for richer, for poorer, until death do they part. Like any good partnership, they evaluated where they had been and where they were going: "We grew up together; we are in sync with our priorities and our plans. We know managing a budget is more than a household responsibility; it is an important cornerstone of our commitment to one another. Our short-term and long-term goals include going back to school to get our master's degrees, buying our first home, having children, and being able to provide for them. Setting up our spending and savings budget will keep us on track to achieving our goals and will keep our marriage strong and healthy. We have committed not only to the plan but also to how we will continue, ever after, to stay on course through open dialogue and continual assessment."

17.1 BALANCE

■ ■ **LO 17-1** Assess your financial plan against your values, vision, and life goals.

Money in itself does not create peace of mind. When you are in step with your values, vision, and life goals and are adhering to a financial plan that supports them, you are then in financial balance. More money is nice, but it will not create financial serenity; balance will. Balance can be reached through simplicity.

Simplicity is taking the clutter of material things out of your life—things that can be physically and mentally exhausting. To simplify, you need to prioritize, minimize, organize, and economize. Doing this will bring you clarity, balance, and energy.

prioritize Think back to your values, vision, and mission statement. Focus on what matters most. Choose the objects, obligations, and activities that bring meaning to your life and focus on them. Learn to say no to the things that do not matter and are not high on your list of priorities. Think about your opportunity cost when you say yes. Saying yes to things that are *not* a priority can cause a lot of little leaks in time, energy, and money.

minimize Eliminate the nonessential. Pursue activities that you enjoy or that allow you to be productive. Take a more minimalist approach to the number of material things that make you comfortable. This does not have to be painful; in fact, it can be liberating. If you have the things that mean the most to you and are aligned with your values, vision, and mission, you might be surprised how little you need and how much joy a minimalist approach brings. You also will be freed from tending to things not important to you. You will find that you do not need a lot of possessions to have a lot of fun.

organize As you reduce your obligations and the things you own, make sure everything has its place. Create a routine and cultivate the discipline to stick to that routine. If you take care of the essentials, you will have time and room for fun without feeling stressed. Being disorganized can waste time as you look for things and lose things. Being disorganized can put you in a bad mood and contribute to a feeling of being out of control. By being organized, you gain control over your space and time.

Balance can be tough to maintain.

economize If you prioritize, minimize, and organize, you will naturally reduce your overall spending. To make sure you are living within your means, develop a budget. Pay yourself first. Save for retirement. Buy quality instead of quantity. Be an intelligent consumer. This habit will give you the feeling of maximizing your dollars.

energize Be industrious; do not procrastinate. Pursue your passions with passion. Eat well, exercise, and get enough rest so that you can work hard. Play hard and learn to have fun while getting things done.

A final statement about balance is best summed up in the words of Steve and Annette Economides in their book, *America's Cheapest Family*:

> Life is more than the money you have in the bank, the cars you drive and houses you own. When you come to your last days, your investment portfolio won't matter nearly as much as the relationships into which you have invested your time. Make your emergency plans, set aside your savings, put some of your money into investments but all the while be sure that you are putting as much time and energy into those precious relationships that surround you. If your investments ever fail or emergencies deplete your savings, having strong bonds with friends and family will pull you through. These are the investments that really matter.[1]

Making $ense

17.1 What steps can you take to reduce clutter in your life?

17.2 How do your current actions reflect your values, vision, and mission?

17.2 SUSTAINABILITY

■ ■ **LO 17-2** Evaluate the sustainability of your financial plan, as it is the key to your plan's success.

A large part of building your financial future is learning the methods and tools necessary to manage your personal finances successfully and knowing which tools come into play during the different personal finance life stages. Learning how to adopt a frugal and fun lifestyle is a small part of building that future. The overall goal of personal finance is to incorporate financial health and sustainability into your life. Sustainability is the capacity to endure. In ecology, the word *sustainability* describes how biological systems remain diverse, adaptive, and productive over time. For humans, *sustainability* is the potential for long-term well-being, which in turn is dependent on the

---

[1] Steve and Annette Economides, *America's Cheapest Family—Gets You Right on the Money* (New York: Three Rivers Press, 2007), pp. 250–251. Reprinted with permission.

well-being of your physical and fiscal well-being. By practicing frugality and staying focused on your goals, you will achieve sustainability.

Frugality

Frugality is *not* deprivation. Being frugal is not about being cheap; it is about not being wasteful. Quality does not have to be expensive. Quality is about doing things well. Frugality does not necessarily mean washing sandwich bags or reusing gift wrapping and bows. Your time and money are too important to let slip away. When you are more frugal with your resources, you are able to spend your money according to your priorities and vision for the future. Being frugal also is being creative; it is finding savings and more efficient ways to achieve your objectives. Being frugal is having your money work for you, thus freeing you from working for the money. It is being in control of your income and expenses.

Do not associate frugality with drudgery. It should be approached as a fun challenge, a bit of a game. For example, some find pleasure in shopping thrift stores with family or friends and finding real bargains. For a great low-carbon date or a healthy family outing, ride your bike to a farmers' market to buy locally grown produce. Be creative, have fun, and enjoy life, living it to the fullest. The key to sustainability is enjoying and taking pride in what you are doing.

Focus on Goals

Goals give you something to strive for; they stretch you and help you to grow. How badly do you want to reach your goal? It takes hard work, dedication, and discipline now to get what you want later.

Keeping it simple and focusing on what matters help you to live a more meaningful and fulfilling life.

Making $ense

17.3 What are some ways you can have fun being frugal?

17.4 What should you do with your goals when life does not go as you expected?

17.5 What methods can you use to remember your goals as you balance buying decisions against the opportunity costs?

financialfitness:
STOPPING LITTLE LEAKS

Repurposing

Do not toss leftovers. Last night's vegetables mix well into tomorrow's rice or the next morning's scrambled eggs. A chicken or turkey carcass makes exceptional broth. Watch expiration dates and challenge yourself to create a culinary delight with items you have on hand. A smart way to save on groceries is to efficiently use what you buy.

A visual reminder of your savings goal can remind you to evaluate the opportunity cost involved before you make other purchases. For example, put a picture of the home you are saving for in your wallet, and you will see it every time you want to buy something. This is not to deprive you of things you need, but to help you focus on whether the purchase is a need or a want.

Along the way, life will throw you some curveballs and get you off track. Think of these occasions as a test to see how badly you want to achieve your goal. Some of these hurdles may be empowering, or they may be wake-up calls indicating that your goals are changing. Each hurdle encountered is an opportunity to reevaluate your goals, to make sure they are in line with your values, vision, and mission. You can and will change your goals as your circumstances change and as you change.

17.3 REASSESSMENTS

■ ■ **LO 17-3** Recognize the importance of reevaluating your life goals and your progress on an annual basis.

By completing the online worksheets that accompany this textbook, you have created an overall financial plan to get you through college and beyond. You have planned the work; now you have to *work the plan*. To be successful in executing your plan, you need to set aside specific times to reassess where you are and where you want to go. Look at your long-term, intermediate, and short-term goals on a regular basis.

When you are first getting started, it is good to review your budget weekly. Assess your lifestyle decisions: Are they in line with your budget, savings, and spending goals? Weekly checks of the family budget encourage good communication and keep everyone on the same page. For example, children are more sensitive to leaving all the lights on in the house if they know how much electricity costs, and they get excited about saving money for the family trip.

Monthly Budget Review

To keep a budget, you have to know where you are spending your money. Make tracking your expenses a lifelong habit. Have a formal budget assessment at least once a month to review last month's income and expenses and to plan for the next month. Keep the budget the focus of the review. Refer back to Chapter 3 for the rules of a budget. Start by reviewing your values, vision, mission, and goals to keep focused on what is important to you. Think about your upcoming expenses and your priorities. If you are

sharing your budget with another person, talk about your financial goals and budget often to help you stay on track and be accountable.

Annual Budget Review

You need to review and revise your budget at least once a year. At the end of the year or after major events (such as a new home, a new job, a baby, or a raise), sit down and reassess your overall annual budget. This will help you establish your priorities for the next period, given your new circumstances or the new year. Look at your previous year's budget. Where did you spend more than your estimates? Where did

Major life events often require a budget review and taking the time to update your goals.

> ## All wealth is the product of labor.
> —JOHN LOCKE, *Political theorist (1632–1704)*

you spend less? What do you want to do differently next year? This is a good time to set New Year's resolutions.

Other Financial Reassessments

In addition to tracking your budget, you should also assess your other financial plans and needs, such as investments and insurance coverage, at least once a year or when major life changes occur. Making necessary adjustments in a timely fashion will keep you on track to meet your goals.

reassessment of investments An ideal time to reassess your financial goals and investments is when you complete your tax returns. When you do your taxes, you have a record of all your income from investments, work, and other sources of income. You also have records of the interest you paid on debts. This is a great time to complete a balance sheet to see if you are making progress toward your financial goals. You may find it encouraging to look back and see how far you have come in just a short period.

insurance reviews Are your car, life, and health insurance appropriate for your needs? Your birthday is a great time to reassess your life, auto, and health

> " Money may be the husk of many things but not the kernel. It brings you food, but not appetite; medicine, but not health; acquaintances, but not friends; servants, but not loyalty; days of joy, but not peace or happiness. "
>
> —HENRIK IBSEN, *Norwegian playwright (1828–1906)*

insurance. Do you have enough coverage, or is it too much or too little? Your life insurance needs will change when you buy a house, have children, and gain assets—and they will change again when your children become independent.

Major life events should be a good reminder to check all of your insurance coverage. When you change jobs, you will need to check your new health and life insurance coverage. You may want to add money to your health care spending account or reduce the amount you contribute. Your new employer may also provide more or less life insurance than your previous employer. If you need more life insurance, you will want to talk to an insurance agent or buy insurance online.

continual reassessment Your life will keep changing. You may marry, have children, divorce, remarry, have more children, or retire. You may never marry. You may change jobs and careers every three years, or you may work for the same company your entire life. You may go back to graduate school; you may stay in school for as long as possible; you may enter the work world without completing college. Each person takes a separate path in life, and each person has different financial goals.

As you proceed down life's path, make sure you are assessing your goals and evaluating the progress you are making toward them. Remember: It is *your* life and *you* are in control of your destination. ◼

Making $ense

17.6 How often should you reassess your budget? Why?

17.7 When is a good time to reassess your investment plans? Why?

17.8 Why is it important to reassess your goals?

get online!

SCAN HERE for study quizzes for this chapter

➡ **LEARN.** Throughout this book, you have learned that money is a resource for accomplishing your goals; however, it is only *one* resource you have to help you reach your goals. Your goals should be based on your values, vision, and mission. By following your values, vision, and mission, you can put your money to work for you.

You learned money does not bring happiness, but *using* your money to accomplish your goals does bring you happiness. Values-based spending, investing, and giving are different ways to use the resource of money.

In this book, you also learned about the 90/10 and the 80/10/10 rules. Strive to live on 90% of your income and to save 10%. As you progress through the personal finance life stages, you may find you can live on 80% of your income, save 10%, and contribute 10% to charitable causes that matter most to you. During your college years, you may not have 10% of your income to give away, so volunteer your time in the community. Your time is also a precious resource that you do not want to waste.

You learned about goal setting, budgets, savings, investing, insurance, and buying cars and houses. You learned about opportunity costs. Every dollar you spend cannot be spent again; you cannot save it or invest it. It is gone. You learned that the definition of financial success is what you want it to be. Personal finance is personal; it is all about you. You are in control to achieve your goals.

➡ **PLAN & ACT.** Planning for financial success is the easy part. The hard part is acting on your plan. You have the tools now to reach your financial goals and be successful. As you plan and act, do not be afraid to ask for help along the way or refer back to this book for specific strategies. Share your successes with others, and encourage others to achieve their financial goals. As the old saying goes, "If you really want to learn something, teach it to others." Use your life experiences to help others succeed. This will reinforce the principles you have learned throughout this class.

➡ **EVALUATE.** Learning throughout life requires constant reevaluation of the environment around you, your values, vision, goals, and mission, as well as the resources you have to achieve your goals. Constantly reevaluate, learn, and act on new information you have gained.

》 GoalTracker

Look over your online GoalTracker. Are you set for success? You now have a great foundation for your future. Live your life to the fullest and use your resources to accomplish your goals and mission so that you may achieve your personal vision.

"He that is known to pay punctually and exactly to the time he promises, may at any time, and on any occasion, raise all the money his friends can spare.... The way to wealth, if you desire it, is as plain as the way to market. It depends chiefly on two words, INDUSTRY and FRUGALITY; Waste neither Time nor Money, but make the best use of both."

—BEN FRANKLIN, *American statesman (1706–1790)*

It is graduation day for Jen. The past four years have flown by. She is excited to move to Madison and start her career. She has come such a long way from when she first moved to 906 East College Street. Never would she have imagined she could start a Roth IRA while she was in college, join an investment club, or be a small-time investor in a sushi restaurant. Jen is entering this next life stage debt-free, and she wants to follow that path as closely as she can.

A summary of the housemates' goals can be found in the first Continuing Case problem on page 27.

1. Without the support group of her housemates, what advice do you have for Jen to keep her financial plan foundation strong?

2. With the close of this course, what activities will you put into place to assure your personal financial plan foundation remains strong?

Peace of mind comes from knowing your goals and striving to achieve them. You're on your way, and best of luck!

A appendix

Financial Tables

Tables begin on the next page.

Future Value Interest Factors (FVIF)

Period	1%	2%	3%	4%	5%	6%	7%	8%	9%	10%
1	1.0100	1.0200	1.0300	1.0400	1.0500	1.0600	1.0700	1.0800	1.0900	1.1000
2	1.0201	1.0404	1.0609	1.0816	1.1025	1.1236	1.1449	1.1664	1.1881	1.2100
3	1.0303	1.0612	1.0927	1.1249	1.1576	1.1910	1.2250	1.2597	1.2950	1.3310
4	1.0406	1.0824	1.1255	1.1699	1.2155	1.2625	1.3108	1.3605	1.4116	1.4641
5	1.0510	1.1041	1.1593	1.2167	1.2763	1.3382	1.4026	1.4693	1.5386	1.6105
6	1.0615	1.1262	1.1941	1.2653	1.3401	1.4185	1.5007	1.5869	1.6771	1.7716
7	1.0721	1.1487	1.2299	1.3159	1.4071	1.5036	1.6058	1.7138	1.8280	1.9487
8	1.0829	1.1717	1.2668	1.3686	1.4775	1.5938	1.7182	1.8509	1.9926	2.1436
9	1.0937	1.1951	1.3048	1.4233	1.5513	1.6895	1.8385	1.9990	2.1719	2.3579
10	1.1046	1.2190	1.3439	1.4802	1.6289	1.7908	1.9672	2.1589	2.3674	2.5937
11	1.1157	1.2434	1.3842	1.5395	1.7103	1.8983	2.1049	2.3316	2.5804	2.8531
12	1.1268	1.2682	1.4258	1.6010	1.7959	2.0122	2.2522	2.5182	2.8127	3.1384
13	1.1381	1.2936	1.4685	1.6651	1.8856	2.1329	2.4098	2.7196	3.0658	3.4523
14	1.1495	1.3195	1.5126	1.7317	1.9799	2.2609	2.5785	2.9372	3.3417	3.7975
15	1.1610	1.3459	1.5580	1.8009	2.0789	2.3966	2.7590	3.1722	3.6425	4.1772
16	1.1726	1.3728	1.6047	1.8730	2.1829	2.5404	2.9522	3.4259	3.9703	4.5950
17	1.1843	1.4002	1.6528	1.9479	2.2920	2.6928	3.1588	3.7000	4.3276	5.0545
18	1.1961	1.4282	1.7024	2.0258	2.4066	2.8543	3.3799	3.9960	4.7171	5.5599
19	1.2081	1.4568	1.7535	2.1068	2.5270	3.0256	3.6165	4.3157	5.1417	6.1159
20	1.2202	1.4859	1.8061	2.1911	2.6533	3.2071	3.8697	4.6610	5.6044	6.7275
21	1.2324	1.5157	1.8603	2.2788	2.7860	3.3996	4.1406	5.0338	6.1088	7.4002
22	1.2447	1.5460	1.9161	2.3699	2.9253	3.6035	4.4304	5.4365	6.6586	8.1403
23	1.2572	1.5769	1.9736	2.4647	3.0715	3.8197	4.7405	5.8715	7.2579	8.9543
24	1.2697	1.6084	2.0328	2.5633	3.2251	4.0489	5.0724	6.3412	7.9111	9.8497
25	1.2824	1.6406	2.0938	2.6658	3.3864	4.2919	5.4274	6.8485	8.6231	10.8347
26	1.2953	1.6734	2.1566	2.7725	3 5557	4.5494	5.8074	7.3964	9.3992	11.9182
27	1.3082	1.7069	2.2213	2.8834	3.7335	4.8223	6.2139	7.9881	10.2451	13.1100
28	1.3213	1.7410	2.2879	2.9987	3.9201	5.1117	6.6488	8.6271	11.1671	14.4210
29	1.3345	1.7758	2.3566	3.1187	4.1161	5.4184	7.1143	9.3173	12.1722	15.8631
30	1.3478	1.8114	2.4273	3.2434	4.3219	5.7435	7.6123	10.0627	13.2677	17.4494
31	1.3613	1.8476	2.5001	3.3731	4.5380	6.0881	8.1451	10.8677	14.4618	19.1943
32	1.3749	1.8845	2.5751	3.5081	4.7649	6.4534	8.7153	11.7371	15.7633	21.1138
33	1.3887	1.9222	2.6523	3.6484	5.0032	6.8406	9.3253	12.6760	17.1820	23.2252
34	1.4026	1.9607	2.7319	3.7943	5.2533	7.2510	9.9781	13.6901	18.7284	25.5477
35	1.4166	1.9999	2.8139	3.9461	5.5160	7.6861	10.6766	14.7853	20.4140	28.1024
36	1.4308	2.0399	2.8983	4.1039	5.7918	8.1473	11.4239	15.9682	22.2512	30.9127
37	1.4451	2.0807	2.9852	4.2681	6.0814	8.6361	12.2236	17.2456	24.2538	34.0039
38	1.4595	2.1223	3.0748	4.4388	6.3855	9.1543	13.0793	18.6253	26.4367	37.4043
39	1.4741	2.1647	3.1670	4.6164	6.7048	9.7035	13.9948	20.1153	28.8160	41.1448
40	1.4889	2.2080	3.2620	4.8010	7.0400	10.2857	14.9745	21.7245	31.4094	45.2593
41	1.5038	2.2522	3.3599	4.9931	7.3920	10.9029	16.0227	23.4625	34.2363	49.7852
42	1.5188	2.2972	3.4607	5.1928	7.7616	11.5570	17.1443	25.3395	37.3175	54.7637
43	1.5340	2.3432	3.5645	5.4005	8.1497	12.2505	18.3444	27.3666	40.6761	60.2401
44	1.5493	2.3901	3.6715	5.6165	8.5572	12.9855	19.6285	29.5560	44.3370	66.2641
45	1.5648	2.4379	3.7816	5.8412	8.9850	13.7646	21.0025	31.9204	48.3273	72.8905
46	1.5805	2.4866	3.8950	6.0748	9.4343	14.5905	22.4726	34.4741	52.6767	80.1795
47	1.5963	2.5363	4.0119	6.3178	9.9060	15.4659	24.0457	37.2320	57.4176	88.1975
48	1.6122	2.5871	4.1323	6.5705	10.4013	16.3939	25.7289	40.2106	62.5852	97.0172
49	1.6283	2.6388	4.2562	6.8333	10.9213	17.3775	27.5299	43.4274	68.2179	106.7190
50	1.6446	2.6916	4.3839	7.1067	11.4674	18.4202	29.4570	46.9016	74.3575	117.3909

FVIF for $1 compounded at i percent for n periods ($FV = PV \times FVIF_{i,n}$)

11%	12%	13%	14%	15%	16%	17%	18%	19%	20%
1.1100	1.1200	1.1300	1.1400	1.1500	1.1600	1.1700	1.1800	1.1900	1.2000
1.2321	1.2544	1.2769	1.2996	1.3225	1.3456	1.3689	1.3924	1.4161	1.4400
1.3676	1.4049	1.4429	1.4815	1.5209	1.5609	1.6016	1.6430	1.6852	1.7280
1.5181	1.5735	1.6305	1.6890	1.7490	1.8106	1.8739	1.9388	2.0053	2.0736
1.6851	1.7623	1.8424	1.9254	2.0114	2.1003	2.1924	2.2878	2.3864	2.4883
1.8704	1.9738	2.0820	2.1950	2.3131	2.4364	2.5652	2.6996	2.8398	2.9860
2.0762	2.2107	2.3526	2.5023	2.6600	2.8262	3.0012	3.1855	3.3793	3.5832
2.3045	2.4760	2.6584	2.8526	3.0590	3.2784	3.5115	3.7589	4.0214	4.2998
2.5580	2.7731	3.0040	3.2519	3.5179	3.8030	4.1084	4.4355	4.7854	5.1598
2.8394	3.1058	3.3946	3.7072	4.0456	4.4114	4.8068	5.2338	5.6947	6.1917
3.1518	3.4785	3.8359	4.2262	4.6524	5.1173	5.6240	6.1759	6.7767	7.4301
3.4985	3.8960	4.3345	4.8179	5.3503	5.9360	6.5801	7.2876	8.0642	8.9161
3.8833	4.3635	4.8980	5.4924	6.1528	6.8858	7.6987	8.5994	9.5964	10.6993
4.3104	4.8871	5.5348	6.2613	7.0757	7.9875	9.0075	10.1472	11.4198	12.8392
4.7846	5.4736	6.2543	7.1379	8.1371	9.2655	10.5387	11.9737	13.5895	15.4070
5.3109	6.1304	7.0673	8.1372	9.3576	10.7480	12.3303	14.1290	16.1715	18.4884
5.8951	6.8660	7.9861	9.2765	10.7613	12.4677	14.4265	16.6722	19.2441	22.1861
6.5436	7.6900	9.0243	10.5752	12.3755	14.4625	16.8790	19.6733	22.9005	26.6233
7.2633	8.6128	10.1974	12.0557	14.2318	16.7765	19.7484	23.2144	27.2516	31.9480
8.0623	9.6463	11.5231	13.7435	16.3665	19.4608	23.1056	27.3930	32.4294	38.3376
8.9492	10.8038	13.0211	15.6676	18.8215	22.5745	27.0336	32.3238	38.5910	46.0051
9.9336	12.1003	14.7138	17.8610	21.6447	26.1864	31.6293	38.1421	45.9233	55.2061
11.0263	13.5523	16.6266	20.3616	24.8915	30.3762	37.0062	45.0076	54.6487	66.2474
12.2392	15.1786	18.7881	23.2122	28.6252	35.2364	43.2973	53.1090	65.0320	79.4968
13.5855	17.0001	21.2305	26.4619	32.9190	40.8742	50.6578	62.6686	77.3881	95.3962
15.0799	19.0401	23.9905	30.1666	37.8568	47.4141	59.2697	73.9490	92.0918	114.4755
16.7386	21.3249	27.1093	34.3899	43.5353	55.0004	69.3455	87.2598	109.5893	137.3706
18.5799	23.8839	30.6335	39.2045	50.0656	63.8004	81.1342	102.9666	130.4112	164.8447
20.6237	26.7499	34.6158	44.6931	57.5755	74.0085	94.9271	121.5005	155.1893	197.8136
22.8923	29.9599	39.1159	50.9502	66.2118	85.8499	111.0647	143.3706	184.6753	237.3763
25.4104	33.5551	44.2010	58.0832	76.1435	99.5859	129.9456	169.1774	219.7636	284.8516
28.2056	37.5817	49.9471	66.2148	87.5651	115.5196	152.0364	199.6293	261.5187	341.8219
31.3082	42.0915	56.4402	75.4849	100.6998	134.0027	177.8826	235.5625	311.2073	410.1863
34.7521	47.1425	63.7774	86.0528	115.8048	155.4432	208.1226	277.9638	370.3366	492.2235
38.5749	52.7996	72.0685	98.1002	133.1755	180.3141	243.5035	327.9973	440.7006	590.6682
42.8181	59.1356	81.4374	111.8342	153.1519	209.1643	284.8991	387.0368	524.4337	708.8019
47.5281	66.2318	92.0243	127.4910	176.1246	242.6306	333.3319	456.7034	624.0761	850.5622
52.7562	74.1797	103.9874	145.3397	202.5433	281.4515	389.9983	538.9100	742.6506	1020.6747
58.5593	83.0812	117.5058	165.6873	232.9248	326.4838	456.2980	635.9139	883.7542	1224.8096
65.0009	93.0510	132.7816	188.8835	267.8635	378.7212	533.8687	750.3783	1051.6675	1469.7716
72.1510	104.2171	150.0432	215.3272	308.0431	439.3165	624.6264	885.4464	1251.4843	1763.7259
80.0876	116.7231	169.5488	245.4730	354.2495	509.6072	730.8129	1044.8268	1489.2664	2116.4711
88.8972	130.7299	191.5901	279.8392	407.3870	591.1443	855.0511	1232.8956	1772.2270	2539.7653
98.6759	146.4175	216.4968	319.0167	468.4950	685.7274	1000.4098	1454.8168	2108.9501	3047.7183
109.5302	163.9876	244.6414	363.6791	538.7693	795.4438	1170.4794	1716.6839	2509.6506	3657.2620
121.5786	183.6661	276.4448	414.5941	619.5847	922.7148	1369.4609	2025.6870	2986.4842	4388.7144
134.9522	205.7061	312.3826	472.6373	712.5224	1070.3492	1602.2693	2390.3106	3553.9162	5266.4573
149.7970	230.3908	352.9923	538.8065	819.4007	1241.6051	1874.6550	2820.5665	4229.1603	6319.7487
166.2746	258.0377	398.8813	614.2395	942.3108	1440.2619	2193.3464	3328.2685	5032.7008	7583.6985
184.5648	289.0022	450.7359	700.2330	1083.6574	1670.7038	2566.2153	3927.3569	5988.9139	9100.4382

Present Value Interest Factors (PVIF)

Period	1%	2%	3%	4%	5%	6%	7%	8%	9%	10%
1	0.9901	0.9804	0.9709	0.9615	0.9524	0.9434	0.9346	0.9259	0.9174	0.9091
2	0.9803	0.9612	0.9426	0.9246	0.9070	0.8900	0.8734	0.8573	0.8417	0.8264
3	0.9706	0.9423	0.9151	0.8890	0.8638	0.8396	0.8163	0.7938	0.7722	0.7513
4	0.9610	0.9238	0.8885	0.8548	0.8227	0.7921	0.7629	0.7350	0.7084	0.6830
5	0.9515	0.9057	0.8626	0.8219	0.7835	0.7473	0.7130	0.6806	0.6499	0.6209
6	0.9420	0.8880	0.8375	0.7903	0.7462	0.7050	0.6663	0.6302	0.5963	0.5645
7	0.9327	0.8706	0.8131	0.7599	0.7107	0.6651	0.6227	0.5835	0.5470	0.5132
8	0.9235	0.8535	0.7894	0.7307	0.6768	0.6274	0.5820	0.5403	0.5019	0.4665
9	0.9143	0.8368	0.7664	0.7026	0.6446	0.5919	0.5439	0.5002	0.4604	0.4241
10	0.9053	0.8203	0.7441	0.6756	0.6139	0.5584	0.5083	0.4632	0.4224	0.3855
11	0.8963	0.8043	0.7224	0.6496	0.5847	0.5268	0.4751	0.4289	0.3875	0.3505
12	0.8874	0.7885	0.7014	0.6246	0.5568	0.4970	0.4440	0.3971	0.3555	0.3186
13	0.8787	0.7730	0.6810	0.6006	0.5303	0.4688	0.4150	0.3677	0.3262	0.2897
14	0.8700	0.7579	0.6611	0.5775	0.5051	0.4423	0.3878	0.3405	0.2992	0.2633
15	0.8613	0.7430	0.6419	0.5553	0.4810	0.4173	0.3624	0.3152	0.2745	0.2394
16	0.8528	0.7284	0.6232	0.5339	0.4581	0.3936	0.3387	0.2919	0.2519	0.2176
17	0.8444	0.7142	0.6050	0.5134	0.4363	0.3714	0.3166	0.2703	0.2311	0.1978
18	0.8360	0.7002	0.5874	0.4936	0.4155	0.3503	0.2959	0.2502	0.2120	0.1799
19	0.8277	0.6864	0.5703	0.4746	0.3957	0.3305	0.2765	0.2317	0.1945	0.1635
20	0.8195	0.6730	0.5537	0.4564	0.3769	0.3118	0.2584	0.2145	0.1784	0.1486
21	0.8114	0.6598	0.5375	0.4388	0.3589	0.2942	0.2415	0.1987	0.1637	0.1351
22	0.8034	0.6468	0.5219	0.4220	0.3418	0.2775	0.2257	0.1839	0.1502	0.1228
23	0.7954	0.6342	0.5067	0.4057	0.3256	0.2618	0.2109	0.1703	0.1378	0.1117
24	0.7876	0.6217	0.4919	0.3901	0.3101	0.2470	0.1971	0.1577	0.1264	0.1015
25	0.7798	0.6095	0.4776	0.3751	0.2953	0.2330	0.1842	0.1460	0.1160	0.0923
26	0.7720	0.5976	0.4637	0.3607	0.2812	0.2198	0.1722	0.1352	0.1064	0.0839
27	0.7644	0.5859	0.4502	0.3468	0.2678	0.2074	0.1609	0.1252	0.0976	0.0763
28	0.7568	0.5744	0.4371	0.3335	0.2551	0.1956	0.1504	0.1159	0.0895	0.0693
29	0.7493	0.5631	0.4243	0.3207	0.2429	0.1846	0.1406	0.1073	0.0822	0.0630
30	0.7419	0.5521	0.4120	0.3083	0.2314	0.1741	0.1314	0.0994	0.0754	0.0573
31	0.7346	0.5412	0.4000	0.2965	0.2204	0.1643	0.1228	0.0920	0.0691	0.0521
32	0.7273	0.5306	0.3883	0.2851	0.2099	0.1550	0.1147	0.0852	0.0634	0.0474
33	0.7201	0.5202	0.3770	0.2741	0.1999	0.1462	0.1072	0.0789	0.0582	0.0431
34	0.7130	0.5100	0.3660	0.2636	0.1904	0.1379	0.1002	0.0730	0.0534	0.0391
35	0.7059	0.5000	0.3554	0.2534	0.1813	0.1301	0.0937	0.0676	0.0490	0.0356
36	0.6989	0.4902	0.3450	0.2437	0.1727	0.1227	0.0875	0.0626	0.0449	0.0323
37	0.6920	0.4806	0.3350	0.2343	0.1644	0.1158	0.0818	0.0580	0.0412	0.0294
38	0.6852	0.4712	0.3252	0.2253	0.1566	0.1092	0.0765	0.0537	0.0378	0.0267
39	0.6784	0.4619	0.3158	0.2166	0.1491	0.1031	0.0715	0.0497	0.0347	0.0243
40	0.6717	0.4529	0.3066	0.2083	0.1420	0.0972	0.0668	0.0460	0.0318	0.0221
41	0.6650	0.4440	0.2976	0.2003	0.1353	0.0917	0.0624	0.0426	0.0292	0.0201
42	0.6584	0.4353	0.2890	0.1926	0.1288	0.0865	0.0583	0.0395	0.0268	0.0183
43	0.6519	0.4268	0.2805	0.1852	0.1227	0.0816	0.0545	0.0365	0.0246	0.0166
44	0.6454	0.4184	0.2724	0.1780	0.1169	0.0770	0.0509	0.0338	0.0226	0.0151
45	0.6391	0.4102	0.2644	0.1712	0.1113	0.0727	0.0476	0.0313	0.0207	0.0137
46	0.6327	0.4022	0.2567	0.1646	0.1060	0.0685	0.0445	0.0290	0.0190	0.0125
47	0.6265	0.3943	0.2493	0.1583	0.1009	0.0647	0.0416	0.0269	0.0174	0.0113
48	0.6203	0.3865	0.2420	0.1522	0.0961	0.0610	0.0389	0.0249	0.0160	0.0103
49	0.6141	0.3790	0.2350	0.1463	0.0916	0.0575	0.0363	0.0230	0.0147	0.0094
50	0.6080	0.3715	0.2281	0.1407	0.0872	0.0543	0.0339	0.0213	0.0134	0.0085

Table header: PVIF for \$1 discounted at i percent for n periods (PV = FV × $PVIF_{i,n}$)

11%	12%	13%	14%	15%	16%	17%	18%	19%	20%
0.9009	0.8929	0.8850	0.8772	0.8696	0.8621	0.8547	0.8475	0.8403	0.8333
0.8116	0.7972	0.7831	0.7695	0.7561	0.7432	0.7305	0.7182	0.7062	0.6944
0.7312	0.7118	0.6931	0.6750	0.6575	0.6407	0.6244	0.6086	0.5934	0.5787
0.6587	0.6355	0.6133	0.5921	0.5718	0.5523	0.5337	0.5158	0.4987	0.4823
0.5935	0.5674	0.5428	0.5194	0.4972	0.4761	0.4561	0.4371	0.4190	0.4019
0.5346	0.5066	0.4803	0.4556	0.4323	0.4104	0.3898	0.3704	0.3521	0.3349
0.4817	0.4523	0.4251	0.3996	0.3759	0.3538	0.3332	0.3139	0.2959	0.2791
0.4339	0.4039	0.3762	0.3506	0.3269	0.3050	0.2848	0.2660	0.2487	0.2326
0.3909	0.3606	0.3329	0.3075	0.2843	0.2630	0.2434	0.2255	0.2090	0.1938
0.3522	0.3220	0.2946	0.2697	0.2472	0.2267	0.2080	0.1911	0.1756	0.1615
0.3173	0.2875	0.2607	0.2366	0.2149	0.1954	0.1778	0.1619	0.1476	0.1346
0.2858	0.2567	0.2307	0.2076	0.1869	0.1685	0.1520	0.1372	0.1240	0.1122
0.2575	0.2292	0.2042	0.1821	0.1625	0.1452	0.1299	0.1163	0.1042	0.0935
0.2320	0.2046	0.1807	0.1597	0.1413	0.1252	0.1110	0.0985	0.0876	0.0779
0.2090	0.1827	0.1599	0.1401	0.1229	0.1079	0.0949	0.0835	0.0736	0.0649
0.1883	0.1631	0.1415	0.1229	0.1069	0.0930	0.0811	0.0708	0.0618	0.0541
0.1696	0.1456	0.1252	0.1078	0.0929	0.0802	0.0693	0.0600	0.0520	0.0451
0.1528	0.1300	0.1108	0.0946	0.0808	0.0691	0.0592	0.0508	0.0437	0.0376
0.1377	0.1161	0.0981	0.0829	0.0703	0.0596	0.0506	0.0431	0.0367	0.0313
0.1240	0.1037	0.0868	0.0728	0.0611	0.0514	0.0433	0.0365	0.0308	0.0261
0.1117	0.0926	0.0768	0.0638	0.0531	0.0443	0.0370	0.0309	0.0259	0.0217
0.1007	0.0826	0.0680	0.0560	0.0462	0.0382	0.0316	0.0262	0.0218	0.0181
0.0907	0.0738	0.0601	0.0491	0.0402	0.0329	0.0270	0.0222	0.0183	0.0151
0.0817	0.0659	0.0532	0.0431	0.0349	0.0284	0.0231	0.0188	0.0154	0.0126
0.0736	0.0588	0.0471	0.0378	0.0304	0.0245	0.0197	0.0160	0.0129	0.0105
0.0663	0.0525	0.0417	0.0331	0.0264	0.0211	0.0169	0.0135	0.0109	0.0087
0.0597	0.0469	0.0369	0.0291	0.0230	0.0182	0.0144	0.0115	0.0091	0.0073
0.0538	0.0419	0.0326	0.0255	0.0200	0.0157	0.0123	0.0097	0.0077	0.0061
0.0485	0.0374	0.0289	0.0224	0.0174	0.0135	0.0105	0.0082	0.0064	0.0051
0.0437	0.0334	0.0256	0.0196	0.0151	0.0116	0.0090	0.0070	0.0054	0.0042
0.0394	0.0298	0.0226	0.0172	0.0131	0.0100	0.0077	0.0059	0.0046	0.0035
0.0355	0.0266	0.0200	0.0151	0.0114	0.0087	0.0066	0.0050	0.0038	0.0029
0.0319	0.0238	0.0177	0.0132	0.0099	0.0075	0.0056	0.0042	0.0032	0.0024
0.0288	0.0212	0.0157	0.0116	0.0086	0.0064	0.0048	0.0036	0.0027	0.0020
0.0259	0.0189	0.0139	0.0102	0.0075	0.0055	0.0041	0.0030	0.0023	0.0017
0.0234	0.0169	0.0123	0.0089	0.0065	0.0048	0.0035	0.0026	0.0019	0.0014
0.0210	0.0151	0.0109	0.0078	0.0057	0.0041	0.0030	0.0022	0.0016	0.0012
0.0190	0.0135	0.0096	0.0069	0.0049	0.0036	0.0026	0.0019	0.0013	0.0010
0.0171	0.0120	0.0085	0.0060	0.0043	0.0031	0.0022	0.0016	0.0011	0.0008
0.0154	0.0107	0.0075	0.0053	0.0037	0.0026	0.0019	0.0013	0.0010	0.0007
0.0139	0.0096	0.0067	0.0046	0.0032	0.0023	0.0016	0.0011	0.0008	0.0006
0.0125	0.0086	0.0059	0.0041	0.0028	0.0020	0.0014	0.0010	0.0007	0.0005
0.0112	0.0076	0.0052	0.0036	0.0025	0.0017	0.0012	0.0008	0.0006	0.0004
0.0101	0.0068	0.0046	0.0031	0.0021	0.0015	0.0010	0.0007	0.0005	0.0003
0.0091	0.0061	0.0041	0.0027	0.0019	0.0013	0.0009	0.0006	0.0004	0.0003
0.0082	0.0054	0.0036	0.0024	0.0016	0.0011	0.0007	0.0005	0.0003	0.0002
0.0074	0.0049	0.0032	0.0021	0.0014	0.0009	0.0006	0.0004	0.0003	0.0002
0.0067	0.0043	0.0028	0.0019	0.0012	0.0008	0.0005	0.0004	0.0002	0.0002
0.0060	0.0039	0.0025	0.0016	0.0011	0.0007	0.0005	0.0003	0.0002	0.0001
0.0054	0.0035	0.0022	0.0014	0.0009	0.0006	0.0004	0.0003	0.0002	0.0001

Future Value Interest Factors for Annuity (FVIFA)

Period	1%	2%	3%	4%	5%	6%	7%	8%	9%	10%
	FVIFA for $1 annuity compounded at i percent for n periods (FVA = PMT × FVIFA$_{i,n}$)									
1	1.000	1.000	1.000	1.000	1.000	1.000	1.000	1.000	1.000	1.000
2	2.010	2.020	2.030	2.040	2.050	2.060	2.070	2.080	2.090	2.100
3	3.030	3.060	3.091	3.122	3.153	3.184	3.215	3.246	3.278	3.310
4	4.060	4.122	4.184	4.246	4.310	4.375	4.440	4.506	4.573	4.641
5	5.101	5.204	5.309	5.416	5.526	5.637	5.751	5.867	5.985	6.105
6	6.152	6.308	6.468	6.633	6.802	6.975	7.153	7.336	7.523	7.716
7	7.214	7.434	7.662	7.898	8.142	8.394	8.654	8.923	9.200	9.487
8	8.286	8.583	8.892	9.214	9.549	9.897	10.260	10.637	11.028	11.436
9	9.369	9.755	10.159	10.583	11.027	11.491	11.978	12.488	13.021	13.579
10	10.462	10.950	11.464	12.006	12.578	13.181	13.816	14.487	15.193	15.937
11	11.567	12.169	12.808	13.486	14.207	14.972	15.784	16.645	17.560	18.531
12	12.683	13.412	14.192	15.026	15.917	16.870	17.888	18.977	20.141	21.384
13	13.809	14.680	15.618	16.627	17.713	18.882	20.141	21.495	22.953	24.523
14	14.947	15.974	17.086	18.292	19.599	21.015	22.550	24.215	26.019	27.975
15	16.097	17.293	18.599	20.024	21.579	23.276	25.129	27.152	29.361	31.772
16	17.258	18.639	20.157	21.825	23.657	25.673	27.888	30.324	33.003	35.950
17	18.430	20.012	21.762	23.698	25.840	28.213	30.840	33.750	36.974	40.545
18	19.615	21.412	23.414	25.645	28.132	30.906	33.999	37.450	41.301	45.599
19	20.811	22.841	25.117	27.671	30.539	33.760	37.379	41.446	46.018	51.159
20	22.019	24.297	26.870	29.778	33.066	36.786	40.995	45.762	51.160	57.275
21	23.239	25.783	28.676	31.969	35.719	39.993	44.865	50.423	56.765	64.002
22	24.472	27.299	30.537	34.248	38.505	43.392	49.006	55.457	62.873	71.403
23	25.716	28.845	32.453	36.618	41.430	46.996	53.436	60.893	69.532	79.543
24	26.973	30.422	34.426	39.083	44.502	50.816	58.177	66.765	76.790	88.497
25	28.243	32.030	36.459	41.646	47.727	54.865	63.249	73.106	84.701	98.347
26	29.526	33.671	38.553	44.312	51.113	59.156	68.676	79.954	93.324	109.182
27	30.821	35.344	40.710	47.084	54.669	63.706	74.484	87.351	102.723	121.100
28	32.129	37.051	42.931	49.968	58.403	68.528	80.698	95.339	112.968	134.210
29	33.450	38.792	45.219	52.966	62.323	73.640	87.347	103.966	124.135	148.631
30	34.785	40.568	47.575	56.085	66.439	79.058	94.461	113.283	136.308	164.494
31	36.133	42.379	50.003	59.328	70.761	84.802	102.073	123.346	149.575	181.943
32	37.494	44.227	52.503	62.701	75.299	90.890	110.218	134.214	164.037	201.138
33	38.869	46.112	55.078	66.210	80.064	97.343	118.933	145.951	179.800	222.252
34	40.258	48.034	57.730	69.858	85.067	104.184	128.259	158.627	196.982	245.477
35	41.660	49.994	60.462	73.652	90.320	111.435	138.237	172.317	215.711	271.024
36	43.077	51.994	63.276	77.598	95.836	119.121	148.913	187.102	236.125	299.127
37	44.508	54.034	66.174	81.702	101.628	127.268	160.337	203.070	258.376	330.039
38	45.953	56.115	69.159	85.970	107.710	135.904	172.561	220.316	282.630	364.043
39	47.412	58.237	72.234	90.409	114.095	145.058	185.640	238.941	309.066	401.448
40	48.886	60.402	75.401	95.026	120.800	154.762	199.635	259.057	337.882	442.593
41	50.375	62.610	78.663	99.827	127.840	165.048	214.610	280.781	369.292	487.852
42	51.879	64.862	82.023	104.820	135.232	175.951	230.632	304.244	403.528	537.637
43	53.398	67.159	85.484	110.012	142.993	187.508	247.776	329.583	440.846	592.401
44	54.932	69.503	89.048	115.413	151.143	199.758	266.121	356.950	481.522	652.641
45	56.481	71.893	92.720	121.029	159.700	212.744	285.749	386.506	525.859	718.905
46	58.046	74.331	96.501	126.871	168.685	226.508	306.752	418.426	574.186	791.795
47	59.626	76.817	100.397	132.945	178.119	241.099	329.224	452.900	626.863	871.975
48	61.223	79.354	104.408	139.263	188.025	256.565	353.270	490.132	684.280	960.172
49	62.835	81.941	108.541	145.834	198.427	272.958	378.999	530.343	746.866	1057.190
50	64.463	84.579	112.797	152.667	209.348	290.336	406.529	573.770	815.084	1163.909

11%	12%	13%	14%	15%	16%	17%	18%	19%	20%
1.000	1.000	1.000	1.000	1.000	1.000	1.000	1.000	1.000	1.000
2.110	2.120	2.130	2.140	2.150	2.160	2.170	2.180	2.190	2.200
3.342	3.374	3.407	3.440	3.473	3.506	3.539	3.572	3.606	3.640
4.710	4.779	4.850	4.921	4.993	5.066	5.141	5.215	5.291	5.368
6.228	6.353	6.480	6.610	6.742	6.877	7.014	7.154	7.297	7.442
7.913	8.115	8.323	8.536	8.754	8.977	9.207	9.442	9.683	9.930
9.783	10.089	10.405	10.730	11.067	11.414	11.772	12.142	12.523	12.916
11.859	12.300	12.757	13.233	13.727	14.240	14.773	15.327	15.902	16.499
14.164	14.776	15.416	16.085	16.786	17.519	18.285	19.086	19.923	20.799
16.722	17.549	18.420	19.337	20.304	21.321	22.393	23.521	24.709	25.959
19.561	20.655	21.814	23.045	24.349	25.733	27.200	28.755	30.404	32.150
22.713	24.133	25.650	27.271	29.002	30.850	32.824	34.931	37.180	39.581
26.212	28.029	29.985	32.089	34.352	36.786	39.404	42.219	45.244	48.497
30.095	32.393	34.883	37.581	40.505	43.672	47.103	50.818	54.841	59.196
34.405	37.280	40.417	43.842	47.580	51.660	56.110	60.965	66.261	72.035
39.190	42.753	46.672	50.980	55.717	60.925	66.649	72.939	79.850	87.442
44.501	48.884	53.739	59.118	65.075	71.673	78.979	87.068	96.022	105.931
50.396	55.750	61.725	68.394	75.836	84.141	93.406	103.740	115.266	128.117
56.939	63.440	70.749	78.969	88.212	98.603	110.285	123.414	138.166	154.740
64.203	72.052	80.947	91.025	102.444	115.380	130.033	146.628	165.418	186.688
72.265	81.699	92.470	104.768	118.810	134.841	153.139	174.021	197.847	225.026
81.214	92.503	105.491	120.436	137.632	157.415	180.172	206.345	236.438	271.031
91.148	104.603	120.205	138.297	159.276	183.601	211.801	244.487	282.362	326.237
102.174	118.155	136.831	158.659	184.168	213.978	248.808	289.494	337.010	392.484
114.413	133.334	155.620	181.871	212.793	249.214	292.105	342.603	402.042	471.981
127.999	150.334	176.850	208.333	245.712	290.088	342.763	405.272	479.431	567.377
143.079	169.374	200.841	238.499	283.569	337.502	402.032	479.221	571.522	681.853
159.817	190.699	227.950	272.889	327.104	392.503	471.378	566.481	681.112	819.223
178.397	214.583	258.583	312.094	377.170	456.303	552.512	669.447	811.523	984.068
199.021	241.333	293.199	356.787	434.745	530.312	647.439	790.948	966.712	1181.882
221.913	271.293	332.315	407.737	500.957	616.162	758.504	934.319	1151.387	1419.258
247.324	304.848	376.516	465.820	577.100	715.747	888.449	1103.496	1371.151	1704.109
275.529	342.429	426.463	532.035	664.666	831.267	1040.486	1303.125	1632.670	2045.931
306.837	384.521	482.903	607.520	765.365	965.270	1218.368	1538.688	1943.877	2456.118
341.590	431.663	546.681	693.573	881.170	1120.713	1426.491	1816.652	2314.214	2948.341
380.164	484.463	618.749	791.673	1014.346	1301.027	1669.994	2144.649	2754.914	3539.009
422.982	543.599	700.187	903.507	1167.498	1510.191	1954.894	2531.686	3279.348	4247.811
470.511	609.831	792.211	1030.998	1343.622	1752.822	2288.225	2988.389	3903.424	5098.373
523.267	684.010	896.198	1176.338	1546.165	2034.273	2678.224	3527.299	4646.075	6119.048
581.826	767.091	1013.704	1342.025	1779.090	2360.757	3134.522	4163.213	5529.829	7343.858
646.827	860.142	1146.486	1530.909	2046.954	2739.478	3668.391	4913.591	6581.496	8813.629
718.978	964.359	1296.529	1746.236	2354.997	3178.795	4293.017	5799.038	7832.981	10577.355
799.065	1081.083	1466.078	1991.709	2709.246	3688.402	5023.830	6843.865	9322.247	12693.826
887.963	1211.813	1657.668	2271.548	3116.633	4279.546	5878.881	8076.760	11094.474	15233.592
986.639	1358.230	1874.165	2590.565	3585.128	4965.274	6879.291	9531.577	13203.424	18281.310
1096.169	1522.218	2118.806	2954.244	4123.898	5760.718	8049.770	11248.261	15713.075	21938.572
1217.747	1705.884	2395.251	3368.838	4743.482	6683.433	9419.231	13273.948	18699.559	26327.286
1352.700	1911.590	2707.633	3841.475	5456.005	7753.782	11021.500	15664.259	22253.475	31593.744
1502.497	2141.981	3060.626	4380.282	6275.405	8995.387	12896.155	18484.825	26482.636	37913.492
1668.771	2400.018	3459.507	4994.521	7217.716	10435.649	15089.502	21813.094	31515.336	45497.191

Present Value Interest Factors for Annuity (PVIFA)

Period	1%	2%	3%	4%	5%	6%	7%	8%	9%	10%
	PVIFA for $1 annuity discounted at *i* percent for *n* periods (PVA = PMT × PVIFA$_{i,n}$)									
1	0.990	0.980	0.971	0.962	0.952	0.943	0.935	0.926	0.917	0.909
2	1.970	1.942	1.913	1.886	1.859	1.833	1.808	1.783	1.759	1.736
3	2.941	2.884	2.829	2.775	2.723	2.673	2.624	2.577	2.531	2.487
4	3.902	3.808	3.717	3.630	3.546	3.465	3.387	3.312	3.240	3.170
5	4.853	4.713	4.580	4.452	4.329	4.212	4.100	3.993	3.890	3.791
6	5.795	5.601	5.417	5.242	5.076	4.917	4.767	4.623	4.486	4.355
7	6.728	6.472	6.230	6.002	5.786	5.582	5.389	5.206	5.033	4.868
8	7.652	7.325	7.020	6.733	6.463	6.210	5.971	5.747	5.535	5.335
9	8.566	8.162	7.786	7.435	7.108	6.802	6.515	6.247	5.995	5.759
10	9.471	8.983	8.530	8.111	7.722	7.360	7.024	6.710	6.418	6.145
11	10.368	9.787	9.253	8.760	8.306	7.887	7.499	7.139	6.805	6.495
12	11.255	10.575	9.954	9.385	8.863	8.384	7.943	7.536	7.161	6.814
13	12.134	11.348	10.635	9.986	9.394	8.853	8.358	7.904	7.487	7.103
14	13.004	12.106	11.296	10.563	9.899	9.295	8.745	8.244	7.786	7.367
15	13.865	12.849	11.938	11.118	10.380	9.712	9.108	8.559	8.061	7.606
16	14.718	13.578	12.561	11.652	10.838	10.106	9.447	8.851	8.313	7.824
17	15.562	14.292	13.166	12.166	11.274	10.477	9.763	9.122	8.544	8.022
18	16.398	14.992	13.754	12.659	11.690	10.828	10.059	9.372	8.756	8.201
19	17.226	15.678	14.324	13.134	12.085	11.158	10.336	9.604	8.950	8.365
20	18.046	16.351	14.877	13.590	12.462	11.470	10.594	9.818	9.129	8.514
21	18.857	17.011	15.415	14.029	12.821	11.764	10.836	10.017	9.292	8.649
22	19.660	17.658	15.937	14.451	13.163	12.042	11.061	10.201	9.442	8.772
23	20.456	18.292	16.444	14.857	13.489	12.303	11.272	10.371	9.580	8.883
24	21.243	18.914	16.936	15.247	13.799	12.550	11.469	10.529	9.707	8.985
25	22.023	19.523	17.413	15.622	14.094	12.783	11.654	10.675	9.823	9.077
26	22.795	20.121	17.877	15.983	14.375	13.003	11.826	10.810	9.929	9.161
27	23.560	20.707	18.327	16.330	14.643	13.211	11.987	10.935	10.027	9.237
28	24.316	21.281	18.764	16.663	14.898	13.406	12.137	11.051	10.116	9.307
29	25.066	21.844	19.188	16.984	15.141	13.591	12.278	11.158	10.198	9.370
30	25.808	22.396	19.600	17.292	15.372	13.765	12.409	11.258	10.274	9.427
31	26.542	22.938	20.000	17.588	15.593	13.929	12.532	11.350	10.343	9.479
32	27.270	23.468	20.389	17.874	15.803	14.084	12.647	11.435	10.406	9.526
33	27.990	23.989	20.766	18.148	16.003	14.230	12.754	11.514	10.464	9.569
34	28.703	24.499	21.132	18.411	16.193	14.368	12.854	11.587	10.518	9.609
35	29.409	24.999	21.487	18.665	16.374	14.498	12.948	11.655	10.567	9.644
36	30.108	25.489	21.832	18.908	16.547	14.621	13.035	11.717	10.612	9.677
37	30.800	25.969	22.167	19.143	16.711	14.737	13.117	11.775	10.653	9.706
38	31.485	26.441	22.492	19.368	16.868	14.846	13.193	11.829	10.691	9.733
39	32.163	26.903	22.808	19.584	17.017	14.949	13.265	11.879	10.726	9.757
40	32.835	27.355	23.115	19.793	17.159	15.046	13.332	11.925	10.757	9.779
41	33.500	27.799	23.412	19.993	17.294	15.138	13.394	11.967	10.787	9.799
42	34.158	28.235	23.701	20.186	17.423	15.225	13.452	12.007	10.813	9.817
43	34.810	28.662	23.982	20.371	17.546	15.306	13.507	12.043	10.838	9.834
44	35.455	29.080	24.254	20.549	17.663	15.383	13.558	12.077	10.861	9.849
45	36.095	29.490	24.519	20.720	17.774	15.456	13.606	12.108	10.881	9.863
46	36.727	29.892	24.775	20.885	17.880	15.524	13.650	12.137	10.900	9.875
47	37.354	30.287	25.025	21.043	17.981	15.589	13.692	12.164	10.918	9.887
48	37.974	30.673	25.267	21.195	18.077	15.650	13.730	12.189	10.934	9.897
49	38.588	31.052	25.502	21.341	18.169	15.708	13.767	12.212	10.948	9.906
50	39.196	31.424	25.730	21.482	18.256	15.762	13.801	12.233	10.962	9.915

11%	12%	13%	14%	15%	16%	17%	18%	19%	20%
0.901	0.893	0.885	0.877	0.870	0.862	0.855	0.847	0.840	0.833
1.713	1.690	1.668	1.647	1.626	1.605	1.585	1.566	1.547	1.528
2.444	2.402	2.361	2.322	2.283	2.246	2.210	2.174	2.140	2.106
3.102	3.037	2.974	2.914	2.855	2.798	2.743	2.690	2.639	2.589
3.696	3.605	3.517	3.433	3.352	3.274	3.199	3.127	3.058	2.991
4.231	4.111	3.998	3.889	3.784	3.685	3.589	3.498	3.410	3.326
4.712	4.564	4.423	4.288	4.160	4.039	3.922	3.812	3.706	3.605
5.146	4.968	4.799	4.639	4.487	4.344	4.207	4.078	3.954	3.837
5.537	5.328	5.132	4.946	4.772	4.607	4.451	4.303	4.163	4.031
5.889	5.650	5.426	5.216	5.019	4.833	4.659	4.494	4.339	4.192
6.207	5.938	5.687	5.453	5.234	5.029	4.836	4.656	4.486	4.327
6.492	6.194	5.918	5.660	5.421	5.197	4.988	4.793	4.611	4.439
6.750	6.424	6.122	5.842	5.583	5.342	5.118	4.910	4.715	4.533
6.982	6.628	6.302	6.002	5.724	5.468	5.229	5.008	4.802	4.611
7.191	6.811	6.462	6.142	5.847	5.575	5.324	5.092	4.876	4.675
7.379	6.974	6.604	6.265	5.954	5.668	5.405	5.162	4.938	4.730
7.549	7.120	6.729	6.373	6.047	5.749	5.475	5.222	4.990	4.775
7.702	7.250	6.840	6.467	6.128	5.818	5.534	5.273	5.033	4.812
7.839	7.366	6.938	6.550	6.198	5.877	5.584	5.316	5.070	4.843
7.963	7.469	7.025	6.623	6.259	5.929	5.628	5.353	5.101	4.870
8.075	7.562	7.102	6.687	6.312	5.973	5.665	5.384	5.127	4.891
8.176	7.645	7.170	6.743	6.359	6.011	5.696	5.410	5.149	4.909
8.266	7.718	7.230	6.792	6.399	6.044	5.723	5.432	5.167	4.925
8.348	7.784	7.283	6.835	6.434	6.073	5.746	5.451	5.182	4.937
8.422	7.843	7.330	6.873	6.464	6.097	5.766	5.467	5.195	4.948
8.488	7.896	7.372	6.906	6.491	6.118	5.783	5.480	5.206	4.956
8.548	7.943	7.409	6.935	6.514	6.136	5.798	5.492	5.215	4.964
8.602	7.984	7.441	6.961	6.534	6.152	5.810	5.502	5.223	4.970
8.650	8.022	7.470	6.983	6.551	6.166	5.820	5.510	5.229	4.975
8.694	8.055	7.496	7.003	6.566	6.177	5.829	5.517	5.235	4.979
8.733	8.085	7.518	7.020	6.579	6.187	5.837	5.523	5.239	4.982
8.769	8.112	7.538	7.035	6.591	6.196	5.844	5.528	5.243	4.985
8.801	8.135	7.556	7.048	6.600	6.203	5.849	5.532	5.246	4.988
8.829	8.157	7.572	7.060	6.609	6.210	5.854	5.536	5.249	4.990
8.855	8.176	7.586	7.070	6.617	6.215	5.858	5.539	5.251	4.992
8.879	8.192	7.598	7.079	6.623	6.220	5.862	5.541	5.253	4.993
8.900	8.208	7.609	7.087	6.629	6.224	5.865	5.543	5.255	4.994
8.919	8.221	7.618	7.094	6.634	6.228	5.867	5.545	5.256	4.995
8.936	8.233	7.627	7.100	6.638	6.231	5.869	5.547	5.257	4.996
8.951	8.244	7.634	7.105	6.642	6.233	5.871	5.548	5.258	4.997
8.965	8.253	7.641	7.110	6.645	6.236	5.873	5.549	5.259	4.997
8.977	8.262	7.647	7.114	6.648	6.238	5.874	5.550	5.260	4.998
8.989	8.270	7.652	7.117	6.650	6.239	5.875	5.551	5.260	4.998
8.999	8.276	7.657	7.120	6.652	6.241	5.876	5.552	5.261	4.998
9.008	8.283	7.661	7.123	6.654	6.242	5.877	5.552	5.261	4.999
9.016	8.288	7.664	7.126	6.656	6.243	5.878	5.553	5.261	4.999
9.024	8.293	7.668	7.128	6.657	6.244	5.879	5.553	5.262	4.999
9.030	8.297	7.671	7.130	6.659	6.245	5.879	5.554	5.262	4.999
9.036	8.301	7.673	7.131	6.660	6.246	5.880	5.554	5.262	4.999
9.042	8.304	7.675	7.133	6.661	6.246	5.880	5.554	5.262	4.999

B appendix

Limited Solutions

1 MONEY MATTERS: VALUES, VISION, MISSION AND YOU

Making $ense

1.1 Money personality is part nurture and part nature. It is a combination of your values, how you were raised, and your parents' traits.

1.2 Take control of spending by creating a **financial plan**—a goal-based activity that incorporates your future income plan *(career goals)*, budget plan *(spending goals)*, investment plan *(gaining assets goals)*, insurance plan *(protection goals)*, and estate plan *(giving goals)*.

1.3 In the relationship between consumer purchasing and consumer fulfillment, "Enough" is the point where if you were to purchase an additional luxury item, your overall satisfaction would actually decrease.

1.4 Passive income is money received from investments and savings.

1.5 Strategies to reaching financial independence sooner: (1) lower the expense line by reducing expenses and living more frugally; (2) increase savings and/or invest more money sooner; or do both (1) and (2), lower expenses and increase income.

1.6 In dollar cost averaging, by depositing a set amount on a regular basis into an investment account, there is no worry about timing the market and buying low. You will end up investing some money at low prices and some at high prices, but in consistently paying yourself first, your savings will grow and the overall price will average out in the long run.

1.7 A financial plan helps you control finances by being proactive in making decisions and by anticipating expected increases and/or decreases in income and expenses.

1.8 Primary principles of a mission statement: to reflect your strengths *(the things you do best)*, your passions *(the things that you really enjoy doing)*, your gifts *(what you do naturally well without effort)*, and your stakeholders *(those who have helped you and those who you have helped)*.

1.9 A SMART goal is: S – Specific, M – Measurable, A – Attainable, R – Realistic, T – Time-bound, having a specific end date and timeline

1.10 Happiness is determined by genes (50%), circumstances (10%), and intentional activity (40%).

1.11 To be happy, choose a career that allows you to pursue your passions, that is in line with your values, and that provides enough money to cover your needs, and learn to live within your means.

1.12 Find information on career options in the *Occupational Outlook Handbook* and at college career centers as well as via internships and job shadowing.

Doing the Math

1.1 (1) To retire now, you need to downsize $4,000/month. ($10,000 Current Budget − $6,000 Passive Income) = $4,000 (the amount to reduce monthly budget).
(2) According to the graph, in five years, you could afford an annual budget of $8,000/month − 12 = $96,000/year.
(3) According to the graph, to maintain your current lifestyle, you must keep working for 10 more years (the point at which your monthly budget = your monthly passive income).

Self-Test Questions

2 TIME VALUE OF MONEY

Making $ense

2.1 U.S. dollar currency gets its value from limited supply and a relatively high demand.

2.2 The role of the Bureau of Engraving and Printing is to print Federal Reserve Notes (paper money) and the role of the United States Mint is to produce coins. Both supply the Federal Reserve Banks with currency.

2.3 Annual Percentage Yield (APY) = $(1 + r/n)n - 1$

   r = the stated annual interest rate and

   n = the number of times the interest payment is compounded per year

2.4 The sooner you start to save, the more time the interest payments will have to add to the balance, making each additional payment that much larger.

2.5 The present value of a lump sum is the **current value** of a given dollar amount. The future value of a lump sum is the **projected value** of a given dollar amount based on the interest rate and time in the account.

2.6 The present value of an annuity is the **current value** of a series of equal payments that are made at equal intervals over time *(day, month, year)*. The future value of an annuity is the **projected value** of a series of equal payments that are made at equal intervals over time.

2.7 An annuity due is identical to an ordinary annuity, except that the payments occur at the beginning of a period instead of at the end of a period. Each payment of an annuity due occurs one period earlier.

2.8 Three methods that can be used to work the present value and future value formulas are: (1) the long-hand method, (2) the reference factor table method, and (3) a financial calculator.

Doing the Math

2.1 (1) The value difference on earned interest for $10,000 @ 12% simple interest is $10,000.00 \times .12$ = \$120.00 vs. 12%/12 months = 1% a month.

$1,000.00	*0.01	=$10.00
$1,010.00	0.01	$10.10
$1,020.10	0.01	$10.20
$1,030.30	0.01	$10.30
$1,040.60	0.01	$10.41
$1,051.01	0.01	$10.51
$1,061.52	0.01	$10.62
$1,072.14	0.01	$10.72
$1,082.86	0.01	$10.83
$1,093.69	0.01	$10.94
$1,104.62	0.01	$11.05
$1,115.67	0.01	$11.16
$1,126.83		$126.83

Interest compounded monthly over the course of 1 year = 126.83.

Difference = $126.83 - 120.00 = $6.83

(2) The APY earned on $10,000 @ 12% interest compounded monthly over the course of 1 year = $126.83

2.2 (1) $PV(1 + i)^n = 20,000(1 + .04)^5 = 20,000 (2.32665) = $24,330.00$ by long hand

   (2) $24,334.00 using the reference table method

   (3) $24,333.06 using a financial calculator

2.3 (1) $FV/(i + 1)^n = 100,000/(1 + .04)^6 = 100,000/ 1.2653 = $79,032.64$

   (2)$79,030 using the reference table method

   (3)$79,031.45 using a financial calculator

2.4 (1) $PMT[(1 + i)^n - 1/i)] = 15,000[(1 + .04)^6 - 1/.04)] = 15,000 \times 6.633 = $99,495$

   (2) $99,495 using the reference table method

   (3) $99,494.63 using a financial calculator

Self-Test Questions

3 PLANNING AND BUDGETING

Making $ense

3.1 The value of a spending journal is that you are better able to track all expenditures (little leaks)—to help identify ways to better control spending. By making minor changes in your spending, you can stop the "small leaks" and your ship can stay afloat without major adjustments to your lifestyle.

3.2 Elements of a personal financial statement are a listing of all the items of value you own (assets), the claims against those assets (liabilities), and the balance (net worth).

3.3 Net worth is the difference between what is owned and what is owed.

3.4 A balance sheet should be done annually (beginning of each new year).

3.5 A small leak, as it relates to budgets, is when a little money is spent often on items that are not a priority. Then when the time comes to purchase a bigger ticket item of higher priority, the funds do not exist.

3.6 The opportunity cost of completing college in 5 years vs. 4 years is the cost of a year of schooling plus the cost of lost wages for one year.

3.7 Prioritizing putting money into savings at the beginning of each month safeguards against accidental spending of it.

3.8 Automatic transfer to savings; increase income; reduce expenditures.

3.9 Methods for staying on a budget include cash allocations to budgeted buckets and sustainable consumption.

3.10 Sustainable consumption is not spending more than you make and not being wasteful with resources.

3.11 Components of a budget are (1) how much is going to be spent and (2) how much is going to be saved.

3.12 A budget is a plan for spending and sets aside savings to cover variable expenses. Creating a plan helps to reserve funds for priorities and to ensure you always have a positive cash flow.

3.13 Weekly budget meetings keep priorities and methods to fund the priorities at the forefront. They provide an opportunity to assess if adjustments are necessary to stay on track with overall priorities and goals.

Doing the Math

3.1 *Students should use their own expenses to do this problem.* Example: Purchase soda pop from vending machine twice a day, seven days a week, each costs $1.50.

To calculate the daily, weekly, yearly, and decade costs of something bought almost every day:
Item: 2 cans of soda pop @ cost of $3.00.
$3.00 daily cost $\times$ 7 = $21.00 weekly cost
$21.00 weekly cost $\times$ 52 = $1,092.00 yearly cost
$1,092.00 yearly cost $\times$ 10 = $10,920.00 decade cost

3.2 *Students should use their own expenses to do this problem.* Example: To calculate opportunity cost of one extra year of college:

Tuition, room, board, books, fees, spending money:	$40,000
Plus your estimated salary upon graduation	+$35,000
Equals opportunity cost of 1 extra year of college	=$75,000

3.3 *Students should use their own expenses to do this problem.* Example:

Estimate yearly variable expenses: ($10,000) / 12 months = ($833.33) is the amount to set aside each month to cover future anticipated expenses.
$166.67 should be put toward cover variable expenses on a weekly basis.

Self-Test Questions

(1) d; (2) c; (3) c; (4) d; (5) b; (6) b; (7) d; (8) d; (9) c; (10) b

4 FINANCIAL INSTRUMENTS AND INSTITUTIONS

Making $ense

4.1 Start a savings plan for college during the dependent life stage (0–15).

4.2 529 plans are designed to encourage savings for future college expenses.

4.3 Certificates of deposit (CDs) are time deposits that usually pay a higher rate of interest the longer time period the money is deposited.

4.4 A home equity line of credit (HELOC) is a line of credit secured by a mortgage on a home and is similar to a credit card. If you needed money, you could advance yourself money by writing a check on the HELOC account. You are normally only charged interest on the amount you borrow. You do have to make minimum payments but the amount that you pay back is available for you to borrow again.

4.5 ATM cards do not carry a credit card logo and must be used with a personal identification number (PIN). Debit cards carry a credit card logo, are tied to checking or share draft accounts with your authorization (with a PIN number), can be used like ATM cards to take money out of an ATM, and without using a PIN number. You can also use the debit card like a check, transferring money from your account to the retailer's account for the amount purchased.

4.6 It is important to maintain a check register so as not to overdraw the account.

4.7 Reconcile the check register with the bank statement each month so you know the account balance and whether there has been any unauthorized activity and to make sure that all transactions are accurate.

4.8 Advantages of overdraft protection are a savings of money in overdraft fees and merchant fees. It can also save your reputation and your time.

4.9 Credit unions are "member owned," not-for-profit, financial cooperatives where the depositors are the members; there are no stockholders. Instead of interest on their deposit accounts, members receive dividends based on the amount of money in an account.

4.10 The financial competitive edge of a credit union over a commercial bank or savings and loan is that credit unions do not pay federal or state income tax; this allows them to offer higher interest rates and lower loan rates and to take greater risks on loans than commercial banks.

4.11 A reason to select a small community bank over a national commercial bank is that they usually make their loan decisions locally.

4.12 The advantages of a large national bank over a small community bank or credit union include more products and services and more ATMs if traveling.

4.13 Select a financial institution that offers overall higher-valued products and services as defined by your personal needs.

Doing the Math

4.1 Current Balance = **$333.00**

Number or Code	Date	Transaction Description	Payment Amount	√	Fee	Deposit Amount	Balance
	1/1	Opening of account				$500.00	$500.00
101	1/25	Text Books	$117.00				$383.00
	1/25	ATM	$50.00				$333.00

4.2 Reconciled account balance: $333

Date	Amount	Checks	Amount
		1/25	$117
		1/25	$50
Total A	$0	Total B	$167
This statement's ending balance	$500		
Add deposits/other credit not yet on this statement (Total A)	$0		
Subtotal	$500		
Subtract checks/other debits not listed on this statement (Total B)	$167		
Your current checking account balance	$333		

Self-Test Questions

(1a) 1; (1b) 3; (1c) 5; (1d) 2; (1e) 2; (1f) 3; (1g) 3; (1h) 1; (1i) 1; (1j) 2; (2) b; (3) c; (4) d; (5) d; (6) a; (7) d; (8) d; (9) c (238,095 × 1.05 = 249,999.75 at 12 months)

5 CONSUMER CREDIT: CREDIT CARDS AND STUDENT LOANS

Making $ense

5.1 Character, capacity, collateral, capital, and conditions

5.2 The debt-to-income ratio is used to calculate your capacity or ability to repay the loan based on your income and other debt obligations.

5.3 A cosigner may be necessary if you do not have a credit history and the lender does not know you or if you do not have enough capacity.

5.4 Credit risk

5.5 30%

5.6 Select wisely, pay on time, maintain a balance that is less than 30% of your credit line, pay off the balance each month (ideally), look out for new fees, be judicial about all your activity, and complain if rates or fees increase.

5.7 Be sure to pay the balance on time so as not to incur interest.

5.8 Contact the credit card company in writing within 60 days after the statement date on the bill with the error. Send the letter to the "billing inquiries" address on the statement. Include your name and account number and state the error and the date of the error. Include copies of any documents that would support your argument. Keep a copy.

5.9 The main difference is that the interest of subsidized student loans is paid by the government while you are in school and maintaining a half-time student status or greater; for unsubsidized student loans, interest is not paid by the government while you are in school.

5.10 Options for managing the repayment of student loans are loan consolidation and refinance, deferment, forbearance, and alternate payment options.

5.11 Payday or title loans are considered predatory lending because they charge triple digit annual percentage rates (APRs).

5.12 The disadvantage of utilizing a rent-to-own contract is that the effective interest rate in some of these transactions averages over 1,800%.

5.13 Some alternatives to a payday or title loan include: A personal loan from a credit union or small loan company, a cash advance on a credit card, an account with overdraft protection, and a paycheck advance.

Doing the Math

5.1 Credit Limit: $1,000

Charge: $300

Available Credit: $700

How much more can I borrow: $700 what I owe: $300

Payment: $200

Available Credit: $900

How much more can I borrow: $900 what I owe: $100

Payment: $100

Available Credit: $1,000

How much more can I borrow: $1,000 what I owe: $0

5.2 (1) $500 − $105 = $395 × .02 = $7.90

(2) [$395 × 14 + $895 × 15]/29 = $653.62 × .02 = $13.07

(3) $13.07

5.3 (1)

Amortization Table			
Loan Amount	$ 10,000.00		
Annual Interest Rate	6	(whole number)	
Payments per Year	12		
Number of Payments	120		
Payment Amount	$ 111.02		

(2) 10,000 = PV, 120 = N, 6 = I/YR, PMT is $111.02

5.4 (1) The loan for $200 would cost $20 × 6 rollovers = $120

(2) 20/200 = .01, or 10% interest

10% interest / 14 days = .1/14 = .00714285 = 0.714284% per day

0.714284% per day × 365 days = 260.7% APY

Self-Test Questions

(1) c; (2a) 3; (2b) 2; (3) c; (4) b; (5) d; (6) b; (7) a; (8) f; (9) c; (10) d

6 CREDIT BUREAU REPORTS AND IDENTITY THEFT

Making $ense

6.1 Perma-debt is when an outstanding balance on credit cards is barely reduced over decades, based on making only the minimum payments and being charged a high annual percentage rate.

6.2 It is important to establish a credit record so as to demonstrate responsibility with credit. When it comes time to purchase a first car or home and you plan to pay for it by taking out a loan, creditors will want to know how you have handled credit in the past.

6.3 To establish a credit record, apply for a credit card. Use it wisely and pay it off on time and in full each month.

6.4 Items that can be found on the credit report include account info; type, terms and monthly payments; date opened; date last reported; credit limit or original amount and high balance; recent balance and required payment; and comments.

6.5 A low credit score number is an indication of challenges with past obligations and reflects poorly on a person's trustworthiness in terms of paying future credit.

6.6 All credit purchases are data mined and certain types of purchases are associated with higher risk.

6.7 A FICO score predicts how well you will manage credit in the future.

6.8 A good FICO score is $>= 700$.

6.9 The five most important measures are payment history, how much is owed, how long you have had credit, your last application for credit, and the types of credit used.

6.10 You can check your credit report and credit score at www.annualcreditreport.com.

6.11 It is important to check your credit report for errors.

6.12 To improve your credit score, never miss a payment and pay your bills on time; if carrying a balance, keep all credit card balances under one-third of their credit limit, pay off outstanding balances, and never transfer a balance between cards. Limit the number of new credit accounts opened.

6.13 If you find an error on your credit report, contact the credit bureau in writing, stating the information you believe is incorrect. Include copies of all documents that support your position.

6.14 Negative information stays on your credit report for seven years and bankruptcy information stays on for 10 years. Unpaid judgments can be reported for seven years or until the statute of limitations runs out, whichever is longer. There is no time limitation on reporting information about criminal convictions.

6.15 Identity theft is a crime of obtaining the personal or financial information of another person so as to assume that person's name or identity in order to make transactions or purchases.

6.16 Strategies you can exercise to reduce your risk include checking your financial statements; monitoring your credit report on a regular basis; not giving out personal information over the phone if you did not initiate the call or ever on a wireless or cell phone; shredding papers with financial information before throwing them out; not carrying unnecessary credit cards or personal information with you and always keeping these items locked up when not with you; exercising good computer security habits: keeping incoming and outgoing mail protected, being on the watch for skimming, and covering the keyboard when using your PIN number in public.

6.17 **Step 1:** Contact one of the three major credit bureaus and then follow up in writing. Additionally, place a fraud alert on your credit report. The credit bureau is required to contact the other two agencies to place a fraud alert on your credit file. The fraud alert is good for 90 days and can be extended to seven years if you provide the credit bureau with an "identity theft report."
Step 2: Get a copy of your credit report from all three companies. Examine them closely for errors and/or fraud.
Step 3: Contact local police and file a report. Get a copy of the report and the report number. Creditors will want a copy of the police report to clear your credit.
Step 4: Contact all of your creditors to alert them of the fraud and close the accounts where the fraud took place. Follow up all phone calls with letters to the creditors and retain a copy of the letters for your own records.
Step 5: File a complaint with the Federal Trade Commission at www.ftc.gov/idtheft or by phone at 1-877-IDTHEFT (438-4338).
Step 6: Place a freeze on your credit reports at all three credit bureaus.
Step 7: Continue to monitor your credit bureau reports for future identity theft.

6.18 Side effects of irresponsible use of debt can lead to defaulting on payments and a decreasing credit score, resulting in higher interest rates and the possibility of not qualifying for a future loan.

6.19 In the independent life stage, in order to begin to build a credit rating, apply for and receive a credit card; always make payments on time and do not use more than 30% of your credit line. Review every financial statement you receive carefully, looking for errors and any irregularities. As your credit report builds, be very careful with your personal information. Never give out your Social Security number or any log-ins or passwords, and be careful with what financial information you carry. Begin monitoring your credit bureau reports from www.annualcreditreport.com and look for errors. Contact the credit bureaus if you notice any problems or inaccuracies on your credit report.

Self-Test Questions

(1) d; (2) d; (3) b; (4) b; (5) a; (6) c; (7) b; (8) c; (9) b; (10) c; (11) b; (12) a; (13) b; (14) b; (15) a; (16) b; (17) b

7 AUTO AND HOME LOANS

Making $ense

7.1 To determine how much you can afford, multiply your monthly gross income by 36% to determine the limit of how much could be put to service debt each month. Subtract from this value all your monthly debt obligations. If the result is a positive balance, then this is the amount that you can afford for a new car.

7.2 There are advantages to leasing (versus buying) an automobile if you want to drive a new car every two to three years, you drive a low number of miles, and you take good care of your car.

7.3 Many of these deals also offer a cash discount if you do not take advantage of the 0% financing. To calculate the advantage of the 0% offer, compare the opportunity cost of the 0% to the cash discount.

7.4 Advantages of renting include:

- Can move easily at the end of the lease without a termination fee, or with a termination fee if it is during the lease
- Someone else is responsible for all the repairs
- No unexpected repair bills
- No property tax
- No homeowners association fees
- No homeowners insurance, just renters insurance on contents of the apartment
- No risk of losing money on your investment if the housing market goes down
- Low initial cost
- May not have to pay utilities

7.5 Advantages to buying include:

- Gain equity as you pay down the mortgage
- Value of the house may increase
- Can personalize your living space
- Eventually live payment-free
- Can provide tax advantages on the interest and property taxes you pay
- Capital gains exclusion if you have lived in your house for at least two of the past five years before selling
- Can get second mortgage home equity loans

7.6 It makes more financial sense to buy rather than rent if you will be staying there long enough to break even on the purchase for the intended time you will be there.

7.7 Selection criteria to include are: price, location, maintenance, school systems, insurance, taxes, homeowners associations, and resale value.

7.8 The role of a realtor in brokering the sale of a home includes linking the buyers with the sellers, listing the house on the multiple listing service (MLS) where other real estate agents can see that it is for sale, placing a for-sale sign in your yard and having "open houses," and informing you of when prospective buyers will be shown the house.

7.9 Mortgage loans can be fixed-rate and fixed-term loans, adjustable rate mortgages, and balloon mortgages. A fixed-rate/fixed-term loan has a specified payment amount and a specified repayment schedule. An adjustable rate mortgage (ARM) loan has an interest rate that varies based on a benchmark plus an additional spread, called an ARM margin; this is also known as a "variable-rate mortgage" or a "floating-rate

mortgage." In a balloon payment mortgage, payments are amortized over a longer period than the actual loan period. At the end of the loan period, the remaining balance ("balloon payment") is due.

7.10 Up-front costs to expect at the time of closing include fees for loan application, origination, points, appraisal, home inspection, and title search.

7.11 It makes sense to refinance your home if you plan to own the home past the cost of refinancing the loan's break-even point.

7.12 Home equity line of credit (HELOC); fixed-rate/fixed-term loan; and balloon payment.

7.13 Typical uses of a home equity loan are for home improvement, large purchases such as a car or boat, a second home, and education or debt consolidation.

7.14 Comparatively shop for a home equity loan the same as you would for a mortgage.

7.15 Do not incur any more unsecured debt until the home equity loan is paid in full.

Doing the Math

7.1 *Example monthly income of $2,000, no other debt*

Your Total Monthly Income: ($2,000) × 0.36 = ($720)

Subtract Other Debt   −(0)

Affordable Auto Payment: = ($720)

7.2 $1,199 − $955 = $244 × .72 = $511.40 = 4.8 months

Self-Test Questions

(1) b; (2) c; (3) c; (4) a; (5) d; (6) e; (7) c; (8) b; (9) a; (10) d; (11) False; (12) d; (13) c; (14) e; (15) b; (16) d; (17) d; (18) d; (19) d; (20) b; (21) c; (22) b; (23) b; (24) d; (25) b

8 DEBT, FORECLOSURE, AND BANKRUPTCY

Making $ense

8.1 Early warning signs of financial trouble include: living paycheck to paycheck; using credit cards without the cash to pay them off when the bill comes; paying only the minimum amount due on credit cards; credit card balances increase month to month; net worth decreases each month; charging essentials without a payoff plan; not having a budget and not knowing your monthly income and expenses; and no emergency fund.

8.2 Signs of out-of-control credit card spending include: unable to make minimum payments; tapping home equity to pay off credit cards; taking money from retirement savings to pay off credit cards; borrowing money from family members or friends to cover payments; getting cash advances on credit cards; and using a bail out lender.

8.3 Fiscal fitness compares to physical fitness in the following way: If you want to lose weight, you need to eat fewer calories and exercise more; to achieve personal financial success, you need to spend less and make more.

8.4 To be frugal is to avoid waste and be resourceful when looking into options on how to fulfill your needs for goods and services.

8.5 By paying yourself first, you are making a commitment to your future financial fitness. Regular saving from paying yourself first is a life-long habit to develop financial security.

8.6 Steps to digging out of debt: (1) stop using credit cards; (2) create a realistic budget; (3) exercise the "ten seconds" and "month-end" spending holds; (4) don't buy stuff you cannot afford; (5) pay off debt; (6) make payments on time; and (7) increase income.

8.7 Some strategies for managing past credit card debt include contacting the credit card companies and trying to renegotiate the interest rate. If you are struggling to make credit card payments, call the companies to explain your circumstances; create a plan of action to pay off the debt and follow through on the plan.

8.8 The risk of debt consolidation is that it only treats the outcome, not the source of the problem. If you keep using credit cards as you did in the past, you soon will be carrying a new balance on the credit cards as well as paying off the consolidation loan. Doing so just adds more debt to the pile instead of eliminating it. If you secure the consolidation loan, you are paying off unsecured debt with a lien on the car or home. If you declare bankruptcy, the new lender can take away the home or car that was used as collateral, whereas unsecured lenders do not have any claims to these assets.

8.9 Make sure the credit counselor is associated with the NFCC or the AICCCA.

8.10 Under the FDCPA, collectors cannot do the following:
- Call you before 8:00 a.m. or after 9:00 p.m.
- Call you at work if you ask them not to call you at work
- Harass you, use obscene or profane language, or threaten the use of violence or other criminal means to harm you, your reputation, or your property
- Conceal his or her identity on the phone
- Lie or falsely imply that you have committed a crime
- Disregard a written request from you to cease further contact
- Falsely represent the amount, character, or legal status of any debt

8.11 Before calling the lender, review the original mortgage loan papers and re-evaluate your budget and personal cash flow statement. Look at your debt-to-income ratio. Make sure documents are up-to-date. Be ready to explain to the lender where you currently stand and be ready to recommend a payment plan.

8.12 Temporary options include reinstatement of the loan, forbearance, or creating a catch-up repayment plan. Long-term solutions are a loan modification or filing a partial insurance claim.

8.13 Alternatives to safeguard your credit include: sale of the home, through a direct sale; a short sale; and assumption of the loan by the lender.

8.14 Chapter 7 bankruptcy is a quick and simple form of bankruptcy where liquidation of assets is distributed to the creditors. Chapter 13 bankruptcy is where you retain your assets and propose a reorganized debt payment plan to the creditors.

8.15 Consequences of bankruptcy include possible loss of your home and/or possessions, being bound to a strict budget to repay creditors, and having a low credit score, thus making it more expensive to get car insurance, buy phone service, rent an apartment, and get a loan. You will continue to be responsible for student loans and other court-ordered obligations. Bankruptcy shows up on your credit record for 7 to 10 years.

8.16 Steps to restoring your credit after bankruptcy include: (a) change your lifestyle, (b) pay everything on time, (c) plan to buy with saved cash instead of using credit, and (d) establish a secured credit card.

Doing the Math

8.1 The advantage of paying the smallest balance first is that it is the quickest way to reduce your number of outstanding credit card balances. It also helps build momentum in getting debt under control.

Period 1 Payments	Period 2 Payments	Period 3 Payments
Of $1,200 on A, Pay $37	Of $1,163 on A, Pay $106	Of $1,057 on A, Pay $300
Of $400 on B, Pay $206	Of $194 on B, Pay $194	
Of $57 on C, Pay $57		
Total Payments: $300	Total Payments: $300	Total Payments: $300

Self-Test Questions

(1) a; (2) b; (3) d; (4) a; (5) b; (6) d; (7) b; (8) d; (9) c; (10) d; (11) a; (12) d; (13) d; (14) c; (15) a; (16) a

9 TAX MANAGEMENT

Making $ense

9.1 Taxes are paid to finance government expenditures.

9.2 Direct and indirect taxes

9.3 The term "regressive tax" is often referred to as a fixed tax, where every person has to pay the same amount of money. A progressive tax is designed to help create equity among the citizens; the wealthy are taxed at a higher tax rate than the poor and the tax rate increases as the taxable amount increases.

9.4 To determine how much personal income tax you should contribute on a monthly basis, complete the W-4 Tax Form Allowance Worksheet, the W-4 Deductions and Adjustment Worksheet, and the W-4 Form Two-Earner/ Multiple Jobs Worksheet.

9.5 Filing status is important because your tax bracket (and therefore the amount paid) is determined by marital status, number of children, occupation, and several other factors. You may fit more than one description and, if so, you can choose the one that provides the better tax advantage. The filing status also determines standard deductions.

9.6 Your individual situation (types and sources of income, deductions, adjustments to income, other taxes, and credits) determines which tax form you use.

9.7 Your gross income is your total income, including money you earn from work and unearned income. Your adjusted gross income is your gross income minus the tax code's deductions for certain specific expenses.

9.8 Earned income includes wages, commissions, tips, farming, and other income. Unearned income includes money received from the investment of money or other property, such as interest, dividends, royalties, pensions, alimony, and unemployment income.

9.9 Types of receipts you need to save if you are planning to itemize deductions include: mortgage interest, state and local taxes, personal property taxes, charitable contributions, medical and dental expenses, casualty and theft losses, moving expenses, and job-related and school expenses.

9.10 Records that need to be kept for at least three years:

- W-2 statements showing your earnings for the year
- 1099 form showing amount received in dividends/ gains on investments
- Bank account tax forms showing interest earned
- Student loan and mortgage interest paid
- Records of property taxes, state taxes, and other taxes paid
- Receipts for charitable contributions and medical expenses (if claimed)
- Receipts for work-related expenses if self-employed

- Receipts for purchases and sales of stocks, bonds, or mutual funds and any contributions to retirement accounts.
- Credit card statements that show business expenses or charitable contributions
- Record of scholarships and what the scholarship paid for

9.11 A **marginal income tax rate** is the tax rate levied on your last dollar of taxable income. This last dollar of income is often called the marginal dollar of income. The **average tax rate** is calculated by dividing the total income taxes paid by the total income. The average tax rate incorporates taxes paid at all levels of income, so naturally it is less than the marginal rate.

9.12 The concept for the **alternative minimum tax (AMT)** was to tax wealthy individuals who were trying to avoid paying taxes. It was designed to keep the rich from living tax-free.

9.13 A short-term capital gain is a gain on assets that were held for 12 months or less. A long-term capital gain is a gain on assets that were held for longer than 12 months. The capital gains tax on short-term capital gains is based on your marginal tax rate (treated like additional ordinary income). The capital gains tax on a long-term capital gain is currently restricted to a 15% maximum.

9.14 Deductions are items that help reduce the income tax owed by reducing taxable income. An exemption is a dollar amount reduction from adjusted gross income that would otherwise be taxed.

9.15 Whereas tax deductions reduce taxable income, tax credits reduce tax liability for the full amount of the credit.

9.16 Strategies that can be used to lower your tax liability include making sure you are taking full advantage of all deductions, exemptions, and credits for which you are eligible. Also, look at possibly lowering your tax liability by taking advantage of a 401(k) plan or traditional IRA, and by using your cafeteria plan at work. Some money market funds focus on tax-free investments, shielding your return from federal income taxes. Some investments are tax-deferred, meaning you don't pay taxes until you withdraw funds, with the idea of withdrawing the funds when you are retired and in a lower tax bracket and can pay a lower rate. Other examples of ways to lower income include: municipal bonds; health savings accounts; dependent care accounts; income from investments; pension plans: reinvestments; income split between spouses; and salary payments to your spouse or children.

Doing the Math

9.1 $3 price of gas × 1/3 sales tax = $1/gal is tax; 400 gallons × $1 = $400/year in sales tax.

(1) $400/$20,000 = 2% of income goes to gas sales tax

(2) $400/$100,000 = 0.4\%$ of income goes to gas sales tax

9.2 On earnings of $36,000, you pay 10% on the first $8,500 earned, 15% on the next $26,000 earned, and 25% on the last $500 earned. Your marginal income tax rate would be considered 25%.

Tax Bracket	Income	Income
10%	$0 — $8,500	$8,500
15%	$8,351— $34,500	$26,000
25%	$34,501—$36,000	$500
Total		$36,000

9.3 On earnings of $30,000, your marginal tax rate is 15% and your average tax rate is 13.61%.

Step	Income	Marginal Tax Subsets	Bracket Total	×Tax rate %	Tax
1	$0 — $8,500	Subset in 10% Bracket	$8,500	× 0.1 =	$850
2	$8,501 — $34,500	Remainder falls to 15% Bracket	$21,500	× 0.15 =	$3,225
5		Total Marginal Tax =			$4075
6		Average Tax Rate ($4,075/$30,000) =			0.1358

Self-Test Questions

(1) d; (2) b; (3) c; (4) c; (5) b; (6) a; (7) a; (8) d; (9) b; (10) a; (11) b; (12) b; (13) d; (14) c; (15) a

10 INSURANCE: COVERING YOUR ASSETS

Making $ense

10.1 You need to purchase insurance to cover your assets and protect your personal wealth.

10.2 You can purchase insurance online or through an insurance agent.

10.3 The insurance agent may be a single company provider who only sells insurance from one company, such as State Farm, Allstate, or Geico. Independent insurance agents represent more than one insurance company and can sell insurance from a wide range of insurance companies.

10.4 The state's insurance commissioner's primary responsibility is to protect the interests of insurance consumers through regulation and licensing of insurance agents. Through the National Association of Insurance Commissioners (NAIC), the insurance commissioner can provide consistency of regulation between states and regulate multistate agencies.

10.5 The difference between liability and full coverage auto insurance is that liability insurance only covers the driver's legal responsibilities if at fault in an accident. Full coverage is insurance that includes comprehensive and collision insurance.

10.6 If borrowing money from a financial institution, it will normally require that you have full coverage insurance, naming the financial institution as lien holder and loss payee.

10.7 Auto insurance premiums are determined by credit history, age, driving record, where you live and marital status, the make and model of the vehicle, and safety equipment in the vehicle (air bags, anti-lock brakes, stability control, etc).

10.8 Uninsured/underinsured motorist insurance covers you, your passengers, and your vehicle if you are in an accident that is not your fault, and the at-fault driver does not have insurance, or not enough insurance, to cover all the damages. This is very important insurance to have, given the low amounts of liability insurance many states require.

10.9 Two risks that your homeowner's insurance usually does *not* cover are flood and earthquake.

10.10 Types of insurance that cover personal property are homeowner's and renter's insurance.

10.11 Replacement value is the cost to replace an item; actual value is the amount you could get for selling the item at a garage sale.

10.12 You should compile a home inventory to ease the process of filing a report or claim in the event of stolen or damaged property.

10.13 The purpose of an umbrella insurance policy is to protect your assets in the event of a liability lawsuit. An umbrella policy goes into effect after you reach your liability limits on your other policies.

10.14 Two cost terms basic to understanding health insurance policies are the *premium* (the amount paid for health insurance coverage) and the *deductible* (the portion of your health expenses that you pay as you use medical services).

10.15 Health insurance plans are usually classified as (1) fee-for-service, (2) high deductible, and (3) managed care.

10.16 COBRA helps you during transitional phases by allowing you to extend health insurance for a period of time after a job loss, death, divorce, or other transitional life event.

10.17 A power of attorney and living will are advance directives of specific instructions you prepare in advance with the intent to direct your medical care in the event that you are unable to do so in the future.

10.18 During this waiting time, you could use accrued sick leave and vacation to cover your missing income.

10.19 The best time for you to start shopping for long-term care insurance is when you are in your 50s to early 60s. Some things you can do to contain the cost of long-term care insurance are: (1) consider purchasing long-term care insurance while you are younger and in good health, which will help you qualify for better rates; (2) buy a policy with a longer waiting period before benefits begin; (3) save enough money to pay for care during the time when you will not be receiving benefits; and (4) consider buying a joint policy for you and your spouse.

10.20 There are three main types of life insurance: term life insurance, whole life insurance, and universal life insurance.

10.21 Whole life is insurance that provides a fixed amount of life insurance and also a cash value as long as you pay the premiums. Universal life is insurance that is similar to whole life insurance, except it does not have a minimum guaranteed return.

10.22 During the Dependent and Independent Life Stages, your risk of dying is low and you have no dependents and few assets, so you need just enough to cover funeral expenses and any outstanding debt. Once you are responsible for dependents, you will want to carry enough insurance to provide for them as well as outstanding debt, at least to keep them comfortable for the first few years following your death—giving them time to adjust financially. At the Empty Nest and Retirement Life Stages, you may consider dropping some term insurance and converting the remaining coverage to permanent as you look toward retirement. Life insurance can be used as an estate planning strategy to pass wealth on to beneficiaries.

Doing the Math

10.1 (1) $250 − $25 = $125 × .20 = $25; $25 + $25 = $50 would be the total cost paid by you

(2) $250 − $50 = $200 would be the cost covered by the insurance company

Self-Test Questions

(1) d; (2) d; (3) c; (4) b; (5) a; (6) b; (7) b; (8) a; (9) c; (10) d; (11) d; (12) a; (13) a; (14) d; (15) c; (16) b; (17) d; (18) a; (19) a; (20) c; (21) b; (22) a; (23) c; (24) b; (25) c; (26) e; (27) d

11 INVESTMENT BASICS

Making $ense

11.1 Saving your money in a low-risk account keeps your purchasing power in check with inflation and maintains its value; however, your money will not grow its purchasing power. The advantage of investing over saving is that it gives you a chance to beat inflation. Investing is putting money at risk.

11.2 You should have 6–9 months of income in savings as an emergency fund. This fund is your safety net to cover necessities in the event that you lose your job, become seriously ill, or have other unplanned expenses. Once you have enough in savings, you can feel more confident in taking on some risks with your money to help it grow faster.

11.3 A risk premium is the difference between the risk-free rate of return and the expected yield of an investment associated with risk. It is a form of compensation for the investor who takes on the risk of the investment and it entices the investor to buy nonguaranteed investments.

11.4 The four major types of risk are: (1) default (credit) risk, the risk that the company invested in will declare bankruptcy; (2) interest rate risk, the risk you take when you lock into a fixed-rate investment for a specific length of time; (3) market risk, the risk that the value of your investment will decrease due to changes in the market; and (4) liquidity risk, the risk that you will not be able to cash out an investment quickly enough to either meet cash flow needs or prevent a loss.

11.5 The higher the risk, the higher the potential return and the less likely you will achieve the higher return.

11.6 The base of an investment pyramid is savings. It is easy accessible cash that can be called upon to smooth out unplanned events and expenditures. This keeps you financially secure overall and your budget stream on an even keel. It is important to maintain a strong foundation on which to build your investment pyramid.

11.7 The level of risk differentiates the rest of the tiers of the investment pyramid.

11.8 You need to diversify your asset investments so as to maintain a secure amount but still have money grow. Diversification (asset allocation) reduces your risks by allocating investments proportionally to the investment pyramid; a strong secure base with appropriately proportioned building blocks to help maintain growth. When allocations are made to each tier proportionally, you mitigate overall risks while continuing to grow wealth.

11.9 Based on how far out you are planning to start drawing from the fund, you should balance your portfolio in order to both protect against market swings and take advantage of market growth; as you get closer to drawing funds, the fund is rebalanced to reduce the risks.

11.10 To maintain a balanced portfolio, re-evaluate your investment goals, risk tolerance, portfolio returns, and asset allocation on at least an annual basis to make sure you have the right mix of investments. Be aware that your investment goals and risk tolerance will vary as you move through different life stages.

11.11 Advantages of 529 college savings plans include: you pay no taxes on the account's earnings; anyone (mom, dad, grandparents, uncles, aunts, etc.) can contribute to the account; and, in some state-sponsored plans, the contribution is deductible from state taxes. Even if you are currently in college, you can contribute to a 529 plan and the earnings won't be taxed if they are used for qualified educational expenses.

Doing the Math

11.1 (1) If you sold your bond after three years and the current interest rate was 3%, its value would be $11,246.

(2) You would be selling the bond at a premium.

11.2 (1) For every $1,000 earned ($1,000 × .30), $300 goes to taxes.

(2) $1,000 − $300 = $700 is take-home pay.

(3) If you contribute $2,000 to your 401(k) and your employer matches $2,000, then $4,000 is added to your retirement that year.

(4) The $2,000 contribution to your 401(k) only impacts $1,400 take-home pay for the year because your marginal tax rate is 30%.

(5) Your immediate ROI given your decision to contribute $2,000 to your 401(k) is $4,000/1,400 = 286% immediate ROI.

Self-Test Questions

(1) b; (2) a; (3) c; (4) d; (5) c; (6) d; (7) b; (8) e; (9) d; (10) d; (11) a; (12) d; (13) a; (14) d; (15) d; (16) a; (17) d; (18) b; (19) d; (20) a

12 MUTUAL FUNDS

Making $ense

12.1 **Closed-end mutual funds** raise a fixed amount of money for the company and investors receive a fixed number of shares through the company's **initial public offering** (first sale of stock to the public). The value of the shares is based on the total value of the fund. No new money is added to the fund, thus the name, closed-end. An **open-end mutual fund** allows continued investment into the fund and will issue shares based on the value of the fund. With an open-end mutual fund, you can invest at any time.

12.2 The net asset value (NAV) is the total value of all the assets in the mutual fund minus cost, divided by the number of shares outstanding. The NAV is commonly referred to as the share price of the mutual fund.

12.3 These expenses include the fee paid to the fund's investment manager, as well as recordkeeping, custodial services, taxes, legal expenses, and accounting and auditing fees. The total of operating expenses is divided by the average dollar value of the fund's assets under management and is known as the fund's expense ratio. Expense ratios can also include a 12b-1 fee, to cover the marketing of the fund to potential investors, and expenses such as printing and mailing statements.

12.4 Mutual funds are classified as either open-end or close-end funds. Within the open- or closed-end funds, mutual funds can be categorized by the types of assets purchased (bond funds, equity (stock) funds, balanced funds, global/international funds, sector funds) and whether the mutual fund is actively managed or is an index fund.

12.5 Actively managed funds have a professional funds manager looking for assets that will meet the investment objective of the fund. Actively managed mutual funds usually have higher expense ratios to cover the compensation of the fund manager and staff and administrative fees. These funds also buy and sell assets more frequently than index funds. Index funds are not actively managed by a fund manager who is looking for the best asset to buy; instead they try to hold all of the securities of an index in the same proportions as the index. As a result, index funds usually have lower expense ratios.

12.6 Exchange-traded funds are often structured as an open-end investment company, but they are traded throughout the day on a stock exchange, just like closed-end mutual funds, at prices generally approximating the ETF's net asset value.

12.7 Index funds have lower expense ratios because these funds are not actively managed by a fund manager who is looking for the best asset to buy; instead they try to hold all of the securities of an index in the same proportions as the index. Index funds usually have lower turnover in buying and selling assets in the fund compared to actively managed funds. This can result in lower capital gains tax, because the assets are usually held longer before being sold.

12.8 Characteristics of a money market fund include: they hold the least risk, as well as the lowest rates of return; they are of high quality with high liquidity; they can be redeemed at any time; they are not FDIC (Federal Deposit Insurance Corporation) insured; they are open-end mutual funds that invest in short-term debt securities; and they are regulated by the Securities and Exchange Commission's (SEC) Investment

Company Act. Money market funds must focus on buying the highest rated debt (bonds), which matures in less than 13 months.

12.9 Mutual fund buy and sell orders are not executed until the end of the business day.

12.10 Continuous automatic investing doesn't have any stated lump sum or end date. Dollar cost averaging is when you have a large amount of money to invest and, instead of investing the entire sum all at once, you invest specific portions of the lump sum at specific times until the entire sum is invested.

12.11 The dividends from the individual stocks in the mutual fund are automatically reinvested into the mutual fund. You are issued more shares of the mutual fund based on the amount of the dividends, the net asset value, and how much you own. When a mutual fund sells an asset for a profit, it receives capital gains. These capital gains are distributed in this same way.

12.12 The higher the turnover rate, the more likely it is that managers are buying and selling stocks quickly rather than holding them for a longer time. More trading is costly as it results in more transaction fees and potentially more in short-term capital gains.

12.13 A front-load fee is charged when you buy a mutual fund, and includes the commission of the financial planner or selling agent who sold you the fund. A back-load fee works the same way, except you are charged the load when you take money out of the fund.

12.14 A no-load mutual fund is a fund in which the companies market their funds online (no sales force or financial planners) and do not charge a load on most of their funds. These funds can often outperform load funds when considering that 100% of the investment is working for you. If you are comfortable researching and picking your own investments, no-load funds may be right for you.

12.15 You can find a mutual fund's holdings, expense ratio, and loads in its prospectus.

12.16 The Morningstar Style Box shows on the vertical axis if the mutual fund holds stocks of large, medium, or small capitalized companies. The horizontal axis is based on company valuation, whether the stocks are from value-based companies (based on the price/earnings ratio), growth companies, or a blend of value and growth.

12.17 You can buy many mutual funds directly from the mutual fund company. These companies usually do not charge a transaction fee and many of the funds are no-load funds. However, these companies have minimum opening balances that could be $3,000 or higher. These companies could also have minimum additional contributions of $100 or higher.

Discount brokerage houses are another place where you can buy mutual funds. In placing orders to buy or sell, there may be commissions and fees. Financial planners, advisers, and full-service brokerage houses provide investment advice for your situation. They will also sell you the financial products they recommend. They make their money from commissions, fees, and loads.

Banks and insurance companies have financial service advisers that can recommend and advise you on the financial products and services appropriate for your financial situation. They will also sell you the products they recommend. Like financial planners and full-service brokers, they make their money on commissions, fees, and loads.

Doing the Math

12.1 The average share price over the last 6 months was $50.70.

Period	Invested	Share Price	Shares Bought
1/31	$100	$50.01	1.9992
2/28	$100	$48.54	2.0602
3/31	$100	$51.20	1.9531.
4/30	$100	$53.43	1.8716
5/31	$100	$51.23	1.9520
6/30	$100	$49.78	1.0088
Period End Investment	$100	Total Shares Bought	11.8449

	Front-End Load	Back-End Load
For each time you invest $100, what amount is invested in to the mutual fund?	$95.00	$100.00
What amount is taken out to pay commissions at the time of deposit?	$5.00	$0.00
Over the course of 10 months, at $100/month, what is the total amount invested in the mutual fund?	$950.00	$1,000.00
What has been the total amount taken out to pay commissions at the time of deposits?	$50.00	$0.00
The value of your fund after 10 months at 15% return is	$1,005.26	$1,058.17
If you were to withdraw the balance from the mutual fund after 10 months, what amount would be subtracted from your withdrawal to pay commissions?	$0.00	$52.91
What is your ending balance from the investment, after all fees have been paid?	$1,005.26	$1,005.26

(1) Both fee options worked in the given time period. The back-end load fund would have to make at least 15% to match the front-end load in overall earnings.

(2) A front-load fee is more advantageous if return rates are lower.

(3) A back-end load fee is preferred if return rates are higher.

Self-Test Questions

(1) d; (2) b; (3) b; (4) d; (5) b; (6) d; (7) d; (8) b; (9) a; (10) e; (11) c; (12) c; (13) a; (14) b

13 STOCKS

Making $ense

13.1 When a company first "goes public" (sells its stock to the public on a stock exchange), it is called an **initial public offering (IPO)** (also known as an "offering"). In an IPO, the company usually obtains the assistance of an underwriting firm, which helps it determine what type of security to issue (*common* or *preferred stock*), the best offering price, and the best time to bring it to market.

13.2 An IPO can be a risky investment. For the individual investor, it is tough to predict what the stock or shares will do on its initial day of trading or in the near future since there is often little historical data with which to analyze the company. Most IPOs are of companies going through a transitory growth period, which also makes it difficult to predict future value.

13.3 Preferred stock carries no voting rights but it takes priority over common stock in the payment of dividends to stockholders and upon liquidation. Common stock carries voting rights but, in the event of bankruptcy, investors receive their funds after preferred stockholders.

13.4 Typically the reason a stock is traded over-the-counter is usually because the company is too small to meet the requirements of the exchange.

13.5 A bull market is upward trending and a bear market is downward trending.

13.6 The Standard & Poor's 500 (S&P 500) is a collection of 500 large- and mid-sized capitalized company stocks that are considered to be widely held and representative of the stock market. This index provides a broad snapshot of the overall U.S. equity market, and companies are selected based upon their market size, liquidity, and sector.

13.7 Dividends can be paid quarterly, twice a year, or annually; however, most companies pay dividends quarterly. They are usually given as cash (cash dividend), but they can also take the form of stock (stock dividend) or other property. Dividends provide an incentive to own stock in stable companies even if they are not experiencing much growth.

13.8 Review a company's 10K, 10Q, and annual report before buying its stock.

13.9 A review of the 10K is important as it provides an explanation of a company's operations (how it makes its money) and the markets in which it currently operates; discloses any risks the company faces, including current lawsuits; includes the company's financial statements (such as the income statement and balance sheet, which show you how much money the company made); and provides information on the company's debt levels.

13.10 From the balance sheet and the income statement you can extract criteria to evaluate the company's liquidity and financial leverage, which are indicators of stability and the possibility for future growth.

13.11 Calculate the current ratio to assess liquidity (*indicator of the company's ability to cover any expenses*). Calculate the debt ratio to assess financial leverage (*indicator of the company's reliance on debt* to support operations). Calculate the times interest earned ratio to assess the company's ability to cover debt payments as it compares to its peers.

13.12 Investment clubs meet regularly to share analysis, insight, and information in pursuit of investment opportunities. After investment decisions are made, club members invest through their own accounts, rather than using pooled funds.

13.13 A dividend reinvestment plan (DRIP) is an option for buying stock if you cannot afford to purchase a full share.

Doing the Math

13.1 Dividend yield of Company Alpha: stock price $40.00 per share; dividend $3.60 per share; yield is 3.6/40 = .09. Dividend yield of Company Omega: stock price $80.00 per share; dividend $7.00 per share; yield is 7/80 = .0875. If you were looking for a high cash return, you would invest in Company Alpha as it has the higher dividend yield of .09.

13.2 The higher the earnings, the more likely funds will be available to pay dividends to shareholders or to reinvest in the company to keep it growing. Beta Co., with a stock price of $35/share and annual earnings of $5.35/share, has the highest earnings of the three, so it is most likely to have the funds available to pay dividends to shareholders or to reinvest in the company to keep it growing.

13.3 (1) **Current Ratio** = $1,500,000 Short-Term Assets/ $500,000 Short-Term Liabilities = **3.** A high ratio relative to the industry norm represents a relatively high degree of liquidity.

(2) **Debt Ratio** = $750,000 Total Debt/$2,500,000 Total Assets = .3. A high debt ratio relative to the industry norm means a high degree of financial leverage and therefore a relatively high risk of default on future debt payments, depending on their cash flow. A debt ratio of .3 is nice and low.

(3) **Times Interest Earned Ratio** = $300,000 EBIT/ $100,000 Interest Payments = **3.** A high times interest earned ratio (relative to the industry norm) is an indication that the company should be able to cover its debt payments. A times interest earned ratio of 3 is higher than the industry standard of 2.

(4) Criteria support moving forward with a purchase of stock from this company.

Self-Test Questions

(1) a; (2) b; (3) b; (4) d; (5) b; (6) c; (7) a; (8) d; (9) c; (10) a; (11) d; (12) b; (13) a; (14) a; (15) a; (16) b; (17) d; (18) d; (19) b

14 BONDS

Making $ense

14.1 The coupon is the interest payment of a bond.

14.2 When interest rates go up, bond prices fall. When interest rates go down, bond prices increase.

14.3 A call provision allows the bond issuer to buy back the bond before the maturity date, if the coupon rates are higher than the current interest rates.

14.4 Different debt obligations issued by the U.S. Treasury include: U.S. Savings Bonds I, U.S. Savings Bonds EE, Treasury bills, Treasury notes, Treasury bonds, and Treasury TIPS.

14.5 Interest on United States Treasury bonds is not taxable by state and local governments. Municipal bonds are generally exempt from federal taxes and from most state and local taxes.

14.6 Advantages of a convertible corporate bond include its potential conversion into equity as well as cash flow from the coupon payments. The company does not pay the bondholder in dollars but in company shares when the bond is converted.

14.7 A person would want to invest in junk bonds to diversify their portfolio and to achieve a higher return on their investment (for the percentage they can afford to risk).

14.8 The **coupon yield** (**coupon rate**) is the interest rate paid on the bond as a percentage of the bond's current market price The **yield to maturity** is the interest rate received if buying the bond today and holding it to maturity, including all payouts, coupons, and capital gains or losses.

14.9 The present value of a bond is calculated by discounting the future cash flows (coupon payments and principal payment) to be received from the bond. The formula is:

Value of a bond = $c(1 + r) - 1 + c(1 + r) - 2 + \ldots + c(1 + r)^{-Y} + B(1 + r)^{-Y}$

where c = annual coupon payment in dollars, r = interest rate (yield to maturity), Y = number of years to maturity, and B = par value.

14.10 With corporate bonds, you pay taxes only on the interest received and it is considered like ordinary income. If you sell the bond at a profit, you pay taxes on the gain. Interest paid on municipal bonds (issued by state and local governments) is exempt from federal taxes and usually state taxes in the state where they are issued. Municipal bonds generally pay a lower interest rate than corporate bonds to account for the difference in taxes. Since municipal and Treasury bonds are exempt from state and local tax, they are a good choice if you are in a high tax bracket. Corporate bonds make more sense if you are in a lower tax bracket.

14.11 Benefits of buying bonds are that they are low risk investments that help to spread the overall risk of your investment portfolio as bonds have relatively low volatility compared to stocks. Bonds are known as fixed-income securities because they pay a fixed amount of cash interest, usually twice a year. Increasing the percentage of bonds in an investment portfolio serves as a good way to gradually reduce overall portfolio risk.

14.12 Risks associated with bonds include interest-rate risk, default risk, liquidity risk, inflation risk, and call risk.

14.13 Laddering protects you from interest rate risk by buying bills, notes, and bonds that mature in different years. When one matures, you replace it with another that matures in a future year. Doing so will bring you the benefit of higher interest rates on longer-term bonds while taking less risk than investing only in long-term bonds. Also it helps reduce the interest rate risk by having bonds coming due at different times.

14.14 The advantages of bond mutual funds are immediate diversification of your bond portfolio and having a professional funds manager evaluating what bonds to buy and sell. The disadvantages of bond mutual funds are paying for the professional funds manager and other expenses in the expense ratio, which lower the yield.

14.15 Diversification is important to reduce the effect of default risk on your portfolio.

14.16 You can buy U.S. Treasury bonds at www.TreasuryDirect.gov, at most local financial institutions, or through payroll deductions. Corporate bonds can be purchased through a full-service broker, discount broker, or online broker.

14.17 Some bonds are traded on stock exchanges. Others are traded in the over-the-counter market.

Doing the Math

14.1 (1) You will receive an interest payment every 6 months.

(2) Each interest payment is $10,000 × .05 = $500/ year, or $250 each payment.

(3) 10 × $500 = $5,000

(4) You will get $10,000 back on the bond maturity date.

(5) Sell it at a premium because your bond is earning 5% and similar ones are earning only 3%.

14.2 (1) If your bond is selling for $950 but instead has a coupon rate of 6%, YTM = 7.227%.

Bond Yield Calculator	
Current Bond Price ($)	950.00
Bond Par Value ($)	1,000.00
Bond Coupon Rate (%)	6.000%
Years Until Maturity (Years)	5.0

Calculator Results:	
Current Bond Yield (%)	6.316%
Bond Yield to Maturity (%)	7.227%

(2) If the value of your bond was $1,000, the YTM was 5%, and it had a coupon rate of 5%, then the current value of the bond would be $1,000.

Bond Yield Calculator	
Current Bond Price ($)	1,000.00
Bond Par Value ($)	1,000.00
Bond Coupon Rate (%)	5.000%
Years Until Maturity (Years)	5.0

Calculator Results:	
Current Bond Yield (%)	5.000%
Bond Yield to Maturity (%)	5.000%

Self-Test Questions

(1) a; (2) f; (3) b; (4) a; (5) c; (6) b; (7) d; (8) c; (9) d; (10) b; (11) b; (12) a; (13) a; (14) c; (15) a; (16) b; (17) d; (18) c; (19) a; (20) a; (21) d; (22) d; (23) d; (24) b; (25) d; (26) b

15 REAL ESTATE INVESTMENTS

Making $ense

15.1 Options of real estate investment include rental property, real estate investment trusts, or reselling properties for profit.

15.2 "Flipping" is a real estate investment that focuses on short-term gains.

15.3 Return on investment (ROI) is measured by the percentage change in the price of the purchase between the original purchase price (P_0) plus the cost of ownership/upgrades (C) and the price for which it sells today (P^t). The formula: ROI = $[P^t - (P_0 + C)]/P_0$.

15.4 Things to take into consideration before getting into the rental business include the responsibilities of being a landlord as well as the risks of asset depreciation, failure to receive rent payments, and the possibility of having unoccupied property.

15.5 Advantages provided by rental property ownership include tax savings, passive income, and asset appreciation.

15.6 A partnership differs from an S Corporation or an LLC as shown in the table:

15.8 Equity REITS invest money directly in property. Mortgage REITs invest in mortgage loans that finance the development of properties.

15.9 Things you should do to protect yourself from REIT scams include:

- Research the history of the REIT. Evaluate its performance on the stock market over a period of time. If privately held, ask for statements from the past three years.
- Consult a tax accountant. Ask an accountant what tax advantages or disadvantages an investment in a REIT holds for you.
- Have an attorney review the paperwork. Consult an attorney who is experienced with the real estate

Partnership vs. S Corporation vs. Limited Liability Company (LLC)		
	Partnership	**S Corporation**	**Limited Liability Company (LLC)**
Formation, Requirements, Costs	None	Must file with state; state specific filing fee required	Must file with state; state specific filing fee required
Personal Liability	Unlimited liability	Shareholders not typically held liable	Members are not typically held liable
Administrative Requirements	Relatively few	Election of board of directors/officers, annual meetings, and annual report filing	Relatively few requirements
Management	Full control	Shareholders elect directors who manage business activities	Members can set up structure as they choose
Term	Terminated when proprietor ceases doing business or upon death	Perpetual: can extend past death or withdrawal of shareholders	Perpetual, unless state requires fixed amount of time
Taxation	Entity not taxable; partners pay taxes	No tax at the entity level; income passed through to the shareholders	No tax at the entity level; income passed level through to members
Self-Employment Tax	Subject to self-employment tax	Salary subject to self-employment tax, but shareholder distributions are not subject to employment tax	Salary subject to self-employment tax
Transferability of Interest	No	Yes, but must observe IRS regulations on who can own stock	Possibly, depending on restrictions outlined in the operating agreement
Capital Raising	Individual provides capital	Shares of stock are sold to raise capital; limitations prevent S corp stock ownership by corporations	May sell interests, but subject to operating agreement
Ease of Operation	Easiest	Must have annual meetings; board of directors, corporate minutes, and stockholder meetings	Easy; some states may require more than others

15.7 Real estate investment trusts (REITs) are like closed-end mutual funds except REITs focus on the real estate sector only and were created as a tax protection for some corporations, as well as a way for small investors to invest in commercial real estate.

market and knowledgeable on the kinds of language and issues that have cropped up in past scams.
- Beware of "Too good to be true." Even though REITs can provide solid profits, the structure has attracted dishonest types who can make an offer sound

irresistible. Google the principals of the company to see what types of past associations turn up.

15.10 To be successful in flipping, look for areas that generally have strong employment and a growing population (shortage in houses). Also, look for new construction, distress sales, fixer uppers, and foreclosures as possible sources of undervalued real estate.

15.11 Leverage is the amount of debt you carry relative to your investment.

15.12 Raw land can be a good investment if, within a reasonable time period, something will be happening in the community that will make the land more valuable (i.e., a new company coming in, growth of the town and subdivisions, a new access road, rezoning from residential single-family to multifamily or commercial). Short of having "insider knowledge," you typically have to hang on to land for quite a few years to get a good ROI on its sale. If you can rent it as farm land in the interim, you will have a greater chance of getting ongoing value from the land.

Doing the Math

15.1 If you build a house on the property for $180,000 and are able to sell the lot with the newly built home for $220,000, your ROI is:

$ROI = [P^t - (P_0 + C)]/P_0$
$ROI = [220,000 - (190,000 + 500)]/190,000$
$= 25,000/190,000 = 0.13$, or 13% ROI; 13%/5 years = 2.60% ROI per year

15.2 (1) If you buy a house with a 20% down payment of $20,000 and then sell it for $150,000, the ROI is:

$ROI = [P^t - (P_0 + C)]/P_0$
$ROI = [150,000 - (20,000 + 80,000)]/110,000$
$= 50,000/20,000 = 2.50$, or 250% ROI (given no interest was charged on the loan)

(2) Your ROI on your investment if you used no leverage would be:

$ROI = [P^t - (P_0 + C)]/P_0$
$ROI = (150,000 - 100,000)/100,000$
$= 50,000/100,000 = 0.50$, or 50% ROI

Self-Test Questions

(1) c; (2) d; (3) b; (4) b; (5) d; (6) d; (7) d; (8) d; (9) b; (10) d; (11) a

16 RETIREMENT AND ESTATE PLANNING

Making $ense

16.1 The longer you wait to draw Social Security, the higher the monthly amount will be. If you have an average life expectancy or better, you come out ahead by waiting for larger monthly payments. As a strategy for married couples, the higher earning spouse should delay taking Social Security for as long as possible because survivor benefits are based on the larger of the two. The other spouse should claim benefits earlier. This strategy typically provides the greatest amount of income for a married couple over their retirement years.

16.2 You should start a retirement fund when you get your first job to take advantage of the larger impact that compounding will have on the balance.

16.3 Traditional 401(k) contributions are deposited as "tax deferred" and then taxed at the normal income bracket for distributions; Roth 401(k) contributions are post-tax money and no taxes have to be paid under normal distributions.

16.4 Advance directives express your wishes regarding medical treatment in the event of your incapacitation.

16.5 By setting up a bypass trust to be the beneficiary of a life insurance policy, the trust can pass the benefits of the insurance policy on to the spouse and/or children, avoiding paying estate taxes on life insurance proceeds.

16.6 Some of the ways to reduce tax liability on the assets and property passed on to heirs include (a) retire in a tax-free state to avoid estate taxes or (b) establish a bypass trust in your will, which allows married couples to maximize exemptions from state taxes (at the death of the first spouse, assets go into a trust that the survivor can draw on if necessary; when the second spouse dies, the remaining assets pass tax-free to heirs, preserving the value of both individual exemptions).

16.7 Types of giving that can be deducted on income taxes include: (1) the lifetime gift tax exemption, and (2) the annual exclusion amount.

16.8 On an annual basis, a married couple can give a gift to an individual in the amount of $13,000 each without having to pay a gift tax, thus $26,000.

Doing the Math

16.1 (1) $2,000 × 2 = $4,000 company contribution to your retirement savings (but the ceiling is hit at $3,500).

(2) You should strive to contribute $3,500/2 = $1,750.

(3) The ROI of the first dollar upon deposit is 200%.

Self-Test Questions

(1) d; (2) c; (3) a; (4) c; (5) d; (6) d; (7) b; (8) d; (9) a; (10) d; (11) d; (12) a; (13) d; (14) c; (15) a; (16) d; (17) b; (18) b; (19) d; (20) a

17 FINANCIAL PLANNING FOR LIFE

Making $ense

17.1 Steps to reduce clutter in your life include: (a) Prioritize what matters most, (b) minimize, eliminating the nonessential, (c) organize with everything having its place, (d) economize overall spending as an offset from prioritizing, minimizing, and organizing, and (e) be industrious; don't procrastinate.

17.2 *Student self-assessment.*

17.3 Ways to have fun being frugal include: potluck get-togethers, outdoor exercising with friends, and neighborhood cleanups and swap meets.

17.4 Reassess your goals to make sure they are in line with your values, vision, and mission. Adjust your goals as appropriate and create a new plan accordingly.

17.5 To stay focused on your goals and weigh the opportunity costs of other buying decisions, you can: create visual reminders; put goals on your calendar and set mini-milestones in place; celebrate your achievements; and strategize in the event of setbacks.

17.6 Budgets should be reassessed monthly to review the last month's expenses and income and to plan for the next month. They should be reviewed annually to assess whether you are still on target given your current life stage and long-term goals.

17.7 A good time to reassess investment plans is at tax time because you will have a record of all income from investments, work, and other sources of income, as well as interest paid on debts. This is also a great time to complete a balance sheet to see if you are making progress toward your financial goals.

17.8 It is important to reassess your goals because major life events can impact them.

glossary

A

acceleration clause clause that allows the lender to demand full repayment of the loan amount if payments are past due (p. 207)

adjustable-rate mortgage (ARM) loan in which the interest rate varies based on a benchmark plus an additional spread, called an ARM margin; also known as a *variable-rate mortgage* or a *floating-rate mortgage* (p. 176)

adjusted gross income (AGI) gross income from taxable sources minus allowable deductions (p. 228)

advance directive a legal document that expresses your wishes regarding medical treatment in the event of incapacitation (pp. 259, 407)

all-or-none order a trade request executed only if the broker has enough shares, as a block, to fill the order in a single transaction (p. 338)

alternative minimum tax (AMT) extra tax you have to pay on top of your regular income tax (p. 232)

amortization the process of reducing debt through regular installment payments of principal and interest that will result in the payoff of a loan at its maturity (p. 125)

annual percentage rate (APR) the annual rate charged for borrowing or earned by investing (pp. 31, 119)

annual percentage yield (APY) effective yearly rate of return taking into account compounding interest (p. 31)

annuity a series of equal payments made at equal intervals over time (day, month, year); financial product designed to accept and grow funds then pay out a stream of payments at a later point in time (pp. 35, 399)

annuity due stream of equal payments that occurs at the beginning of a period (p. 39)

asset money and other items of value that you own (p. 56)

asset allocation the diversification of the portfolio (p. 284)

attorney in fact a person who is given written authority to act on your behalf should you become incapacitated (p. 407)

automated teller machines (ATMs) machines that allow bank customers to perform banking transactions without the aid of a teller (p. 93)

average tax rate tax rate calculated by dividing the total income taxes paid by the total income (p. 232)

B

back-end load a redemption fee or deferred sales charge that deducts a percentage when you take money out of the fund (p. 310)

balance sheet a snapshot of your equity at a given point in time, derived from a summation of your assets and liabilities (p. 56)

balanced mutual funds funds with a combination of stocks, bonds, and cash (p. 304)

balloon-payment mortgage payments are amortized over a longer period than the actual loan period; at the end of the loan period, the remaining balance (the balloon payment) is due (p. 176)

bankruptcy a legal procedure for dealing with debt problems; specifically, a case filed under one of the chapters of Title 11 of the United States Bankruptcy Code (p. 208)

bear market a period in which stock prices in general are consistently falling (p. 328)

beneficiary the person or persons who are entitled to the benefit of any trust arrangement (p. 406)

bond debt issued by the government or a company with a promise to repay the original amount plus interest by a given date (p. 350)

bond ladder a method of managing investments by buying bonds that mature in intervals (p. 362)

bracketed order a trailing-stop order with an upper price-limit trigger (p. 338)

brokers individuals or firms that act as an intermediary between a buyer and seller (p. 326)

budget an itemized summary of estimated income and expected expenditures in a given period (p. 66)

budget variance difference between a planned expenditure and the actual amount spent (p. 67)

bull market a period in which stock prices in general are consistently rising (p. 328)

bull run a period during which stock prices in general are consistently rising (p. 298)

bypass trust a trust that allows you to possibly bypass estate and inheritance taxes (p. 406)

C

cafeteria plan a benefits plan that allows employees to select from a pool of choices, some or all of which may be tax-advantaged (p. 237)

call feature an option for the issuer of a bond to buy back the bond prior to its maturity date (p. 352)

capacity ability to repay debt based on income and other obligations (p. 113)

capital net worth (assets minus liabilities) (p. 115)

capital gain/loss a gain or loss on the sale of an investment asset like stock or real estate (p. 233)

cash inflow cash coming in (i.e., salary, gifts, and interest income) (p. 59)

cash outflow cash going out (i.e., rent, utilities, and groceries) (p. 59)

cash value (of life insurance) amount of funds received if the policy is canceled (p. 56)

certificate of deposit (CD) an instrument issued by a bank that guarantees the payment of a fixed interest rate for holding a sum of money until a designated time in the future (p. 81)

Chapter 7 the quickest and simplest form of bankruptcy; the liquidation of assets with the proceeds distributed to the creditors (p. 208)

Chapter 13 a reorganization bankruptcy, where the debtor proposes a plan of reorganization to keep his or her assets and pay creditors over an extended time period, usually three to five years (p. 208)

charitable remainder trust an irrevocable trust that provides for a specific distribution, at least annually, to one or more charitable beneficiaries for a term of not more than 20 years (p. 406)

checking account an account that allows the holder to write checks against deposited funds (p. 82)

closed-end mutual funds publicly traded mutual funds that raise capital through an initial public offering (IPO); a limited number of shares are issued and no investment funds can be added (p. 298)

closing final steps in a home sale where documents are signed and recorded and ownership of the property is transferred (p. 177)

COBRA the Consolidation Omnibus Budget Reconciliation Act, which extends health insurance for a period of time after a job loss, death, divorce, or other transitional life event (p. 258)

coinsurance the percentage you must pay until you reach your maximum out-of-pocket expense amount (p. 256)

collateral asset of value that secures a loan; this item is given to the lender if the borrower defaults on the loan (pp. 83, 114)

collision insurance insurance that covers the payment of repairs to a vehicle damaged in a collision (p. 251)

commercial bank a financial institution that accepts deposits and uses the funds to provide private business loans and personal loans (p. 88)

commercial paper an unsecured obligation issued by a corporation to finance its short-term credit needs (p. 303)

common stock stock that carries voting rights, but in the event of bankruptcy, owners receive their funds after preferred stockholders (p. 325)

compounding process whereby the value of an investment increases exponentially over time due to earning interest on interest previously earned (p. 31)

comprehensive insurance insurance that covers an insured vehicle for damage other than collision such as fire, theft, weather, impacts with animals, or vandalism (p. 250)

contingent deferred sales load (CDSL) a fee triggered if fund shares are redeemed before a given number of years of ownership (p. 312)

copayment the amount you pay before the insurer will pay for a particular visit, service, or drug (p. 256)

corporate bonds debt obligations issued by private and public corporations (p. 355)

cosigner another person who signs your loan and assumes equal responsibility for repayment (p. 113)

cost basis the original value of a purchased asset, usually the purchase price (p. 308)

coupon the interest payment of a bond (p. 350)

coupon rate the interest rate paid on the bond as a percentage of the bond's current market price; also called *coupon yield* (p. 359)

cramdown an arrangement in which the mortgage terms are altered in an attempt to keep the borrower from foreclosure (p. 205)

credit a contractual agreement in which a borrower receives something of value now and agrees to repay the lender at some date in the future, generally with interest (p. 110)

credit risk risk that the company invested in may declare bankruptcy; also called *default risk* (p. 280)

credit union a nonprofit depository institution that serves members who have a common affiliation (p. 86)

current ratio an indicator of liquidity; calculated as short-term assets/short-term liabilities (p. 334)

current yield the interest rate paid on the bond as a percentage of the bond's current market price (p. 359)

D

day order a stock trade request that expires at the end of a trading day (p. 338)

debit card transfers money from a checking account to the account of the retailer, usually through the Visa/MasterCard network (p. 93)

debt ratio a measurement of the proportion of total assets financed with debt; calculated as total debt/total assets (p. 335)

debt-to-income ratio monthly recurring debt payments divided by monthly gross income (p. 113)

declaration page the policy page that lists the insurance company's name and address, the policyholder, the coverage dates, and the contracted coverage amounts (p. 248)

deductible the amount of money one must pay before the insurer will begin to pay on a claim (p. 251)

deductions items that help reduce the income tax owed by reducing taxable income (p. 228)

deed-in-lieu of foreclosure an arrangement whereby property is given to the lender in return for forgiveness of the mortgage balance (p. 206)

default risk risk that the company invested in may declare bankruptcy; also called *credit risk* (p. 280)

demand deposit account a transaction account that is payable on demand (p. 88)

direct tax fee levied directly on personal income (p. 222)

discount a price below the face value of a bond (p. 352)

discounting finding the present value of a future payment (p. 37)

diversification spreading assets among different investment options to reduce risk (p. 284)

dividend yield annual return received from dividends if you purchase the stock and the dividend payments remain unchanged (p. 331)

dividends taxable payments declared by a company's board of directors and distributed to its shareholders out of the company's current or retained earnings (p. 330)

dollar-cost averaging an investment strategy designed to reduce volatility in which securities, typically mutual funds, are purchased in fixed dollar amounts at regular intervals, regardless of what direction the market is moving (pp. 12, 306)

domicile a place where an individual has a fixed and permanent home for legal purposes (p. 406)

downshifting giving up all or part of one's work commitment and income in exchange for an improved quality of life (p. 11)

durable power of attorney for health care a power of attorney that becomes effective in the event that you become incompetent or unable to manage your affairs; often identified within an advance directive (p. 408)

E

earthquake insurance special insurance coverage to protect your home and property from damage sustained in an earthquake (p. 253)

80-10-10 rule living on 80% of income, saving 10%, and giving away 10% (p. 7)

enough point at which increased spending has a diminishing rate of fulfillment (p. 6)

equity the difference between what is owned and what is owed (p. 171)

equity REIT a real estate investment trust that invests money directly in property (p. 384)

estate tax a tax imposed on a property owner's right to transfer the property to others after his or her death (p. 405)

exclusions stated items that are not covered by an insurance policy (p. 256)

executor the person who will tend to your estate according to the wishes outlined in your will (p. 404)

exemption a dollar amount allowed by law that reduces your adjusted gross income that would otherwise be taxed (p. 228)

expense ratio (of a mutual fund) the operating costs expressed as a percentage of the fund's average net assets for a given time period (p. 299)

extended-hours order a stock trade request placed after the close of market (p. 338)

F

face value (of life insurance) amount of money the beneficiary receives when you die (p. 56)

FICO credit score a credit score method that reflects your credit risk based on a snapshot of your credit report at a particular point in time (p. 142)

financial independence sufficient means to support oneself (p. 8)

financial intermediaries financial institutions that accept money for deposits and then lend the money to others (p. 94)

financial life stages general financial situations that people experience throughout their lifetime (p. 12)

financial literacy ability to understand finances (p. 9)

financial plan goal-based activity related to future income, spending, investment, protection, and giving (p. 4)

529 plan funds set aside for post-secondary education expenses (p. 80)

fixed-rate/fixed-term mortgage a loan with a specified payment amount and a specified repayment schedule (p. 176)

floating-rate mortgage loan in which the interest rate varies based on a benchmark plus an additional spread, called an ARM margin; also known as an *adjustable-rate mortgage* or a *variable-rate mortgage* (p. 176)

flipping the process of buying, upgrading, and selling property over a short time period for a profit (p. 377)

flood insurance special insurance coverage to protect your home and property from damage sustained from a flood (p. 252)

forbearance a temporary reduction or suspension of mortgage payments for 3 or 4 months, followed by a new repayment plan for the loan (p. 205)

foreclosure if the borrower fails to pay on a mortgage loan, the lender can seek a court order sale of the property; money from the sale of the property goes to paying off the debt of the mortgage (p. 85)

401(k) retirement plan money set aside to be used after the worker retires; employees can make tax-deferred contributions to a trust and direct their funds to be invested among a variety of choices, taking payment when they retire or leave employment (pp. 11, 84)

front-end load a fee charged as a percent of what you invest in a mutual fund (p. 310)

frugal avoiding waste; to be resourceful when fulfilling one's need for goods and services (p. 6)

full coverage insurance that includes comprehensive and collision insurance (p. 250)

fund manager the person or people responsible for an investment fund, its investing strategy, and the management of its portfolio trading activities (p. 298)

future value projected value of an asset based on the interest rate and time in the account (p. 35)

future value interest factor (FVIF) factor multiplied by today's amount so as to determine the value of said amount at a future date (p. 36)

future value interest factor of an annuity (FVIFA) factor multiplied by the annuity (payment) to determine the amount in the account at a future date (p. 40)

G

global funds funds that invest in international and domestic companies (p. 304)

good-til-canceled (GTC) order a stock trade request that stays on the books until completely filled, canceled, or 60 calendar days have passed (p. 338)

gross income wages, bonuses, tips, interest earnings, dividends, and gains from selling investments (p. 227)

growth stocks stocks of companies that are growing at a fast rate (p. 332)

H

health maintenance organization (HMO) a group of doctors and other medical professionals who offer care for a flat monthly rate with no deductibles (p. 256)

home equity value of the house minus any loans secured by the house (p. 85)

home equity line of credit (HELOC) line of credit secured by a mortgage on a home; similar to a credit card (p. 85)

I

identity theft the crime of obtaining the personal or financial information of another person and assuming that person's name or identity in order to make transactions or purchases (p. 149)

indirect tax fee levied on consumption or an expenditure, privilege, or right, but not on income or property (p. 222)

individual retirement account (IRA) funds set aside to be withdrawn after age 59½ without penalty (p. 83)

inflation the overall increase in the price of goods and services over time (p. 278)

inheritance tax a tax levied upon the privilege of receiving property as heir or next

of kin under the law of intestacy; the tax is measured by the value of the property received (p. 405)

initial public offering (IPO) a company's first sale of stock to the public (pp. 298, 324)

insurance rider an addendum to your primary coverage to cover something specific that is not covered on your primary policy (p. 253)

interest rate risk risk undertaken on when you lock into a fixed-rate investment for a specific length of time (p. 280)

interest rate spread the difference between the interest rate of deposits and the interest rate of loans (p. 112)

intermediate goal objective to be attained in one to five years (p. 15)

international funds funds that invest in companies from foreign countries (p. 304)

intestate without a valid will (p. 404)

investment an outlay of money for a profit, where the risk exists that either some or the entire original amount may be lost (p. 279)

investment account outlay of money into a bank or stock with the objective of making a profit (p. 12)

irrevocable trust a trust for the benefit of the spouse and/or children that allows the trustor to avoid paying estate taxes on life insurance proceeds (p. 406)

itemized deductions if total tax deductions are greater than the standard deduction allowed by the IRS, you can list (itemize) them on Form 1040, thus reducing your overall income tax bill (p. 228)

L

lease a contract by which the landlord (lessor) gives to the tenant (lessee) the use and possession of lands, buildings, or property for a specified time and for fixed payments (p. 376)

letter of intent a letter to the heirs and executor outlining your wishes for your funeral arrangements, who to notify of your death, and other wishes (p. 404)

leverage the amount of debt you carry relative to your investment (p. 386)

liability debt or obligation that you owe (p. 58)

liability insurance insurance that only covers the driver's legal responsibilities if they are at fault for an accident (p. 250)

limit order a trade with a guaranteed price but not a guaranteed execution (p. 336)

limited liability company (LLC) a company with limited personal liability that allows you to pass the income to your personal taxes or be taxed as a corporation (p. 383)

liquidation a sale of a debtor's nonexempt property and the distribution of the proceeds to creditors (p. 208)

liquidity how quickly an asset can be turned into cash without substantial loss of value (p. 56)

liquidity risk risk of not being able to cash out an investment quickly enough to meet cash flow needs or to prevent a loss (p. 282)

living will a document that outlines your preferences or directions for the administration and the withdrawal or withholding of life-sustaining medical treatment in the event of terminal illness or permanent unconsciousness (pp. 259, 408)

loan to value (LTV) ratio ratio expressing the amount of a first mortgage lien as a percentage of the total appraised value of real property (p. 175)

long-term goal objective to be reached sometime after five years (p. 15)

loss payee in an insurance contract, the third party lien holder who gets paid if there is a claim on the insurance (p. 250)

lump sum single, one-time payment (p. 35)

M

margin loan when money is borrowed to buy stocks or bonds and those stocks or bonds serve as the collateral (p. 114)

marginal income tax rate tax rate levied on your last dollar of taxable income (p. 232)

market maker a person who manages the buying and selling of stocks; also called a *specialist* (p. 326)

market order a trade with a guaranteed execution but not a guaranteed price (p. 336)

market risk risk that the value of your investment will decrease due to changes in the market (p. 281)

maturity the repayment date of bond debt (p. 350)

Medigap policies supplemental insurance policies sold by private insurance companies to fill "gaps" in the original Medicare plan coverage (p. 257)

money personality style and habits of money management (p. 5)

mortgage a legal document used to allow a lender to use real property as collateral; a loan secured to buy property by putting a lien (legal claim) on the property that is not released until the loan is paid (pp. 85, 170)

mortgage REIT a real estate investment trust that invests in mortgage loans that finance the development of properties (p. 384)

Multiple Listing Service (MLS) an arrangement among brokers who are real estate board members, through which brokers share information regarding their listings with one another and may negotiate the transaction (p. 387)

municipal bond a debt security issued by a state, municipality, or county to finance its capital expenditures (p. 353)

mutual fund an investment vehicle in which many people pool their funds for investing in stocks, bonds, money market instruments, and other assets; each fund is operated by a fund manager with a specific investment objective (p. 298)

N

negotiable instrument an agreement that is dated, payable for a specific amount of money, signed by the person who owns the account, and payable to another party (p. 88)

net asset value (NAV) the dollar value of a single mutual fund share based on the value of the underlying assets of the fund, minus its liabilities, divided by the number of shares outstanding; calculated at the end of each business day (p. 299)

net cash flow cash inflows minus cash outflows for a specific time period (p. 59)

net worth amount left over if you sold all your assets and repaid all your liabilities (assets minus liabilities) (p. 58)

network doctors, labs, clinics, and hospitals with whom an insurance plan has negotiated set prices (p. 256)

90-10 rule saving 10% of income and living on 90% (p. 7)

no-load mutual fund a fund offered to the public that carries no purchase fee (front-end load) or redemption fee (back-end load) (p. 299)

non-earned income defined by the IRS as income from investments (p. 8)

O

odd lot any purchase of less than 100 shares (p. 336)

open-end mutual funds mutual funds in which investors can buy shares at the net asset value of the fund (p. 298)

open outcry a method of public auction in which verbal bids and offers are made in the trading rings or pits (p. 326)

opportunity cost cost of an alternative that must be forgone in order to pursue a certain action (p. 60)

ordinary annuity stream of equal payments that occurs at the end of a period (p. 39)

over-the-counter (OTC) stocks that trade via a dealer network rather than on a formal exchange (p. 326)

P

par the face value of a bond (p. 352)

partnership a voluntary contract between two or more persons to place their capital, labor, and skills in a business corporation with the understanding there will be a sharing of the profits and losses (p. 383)

passive income income received from investments and savings (p. 8)

penny stock a share in a company that trades for less than $5.00 (p. 326)

perma-debt the condition of having an outstanding balance on credit cards that is barely reducible over time because one is able to make only the minimum payments and is being charged a high annual rate (p. 138)

permanent life insurance an insurance account that builds up over time and is much more expensive than term life insurance (p. 263)

person of record the individual holding shares in the mutual fund on the day the fund distributes dividends and capital gains (p. 307)

personal cash flow statement measures your cash inflows and outflows in order to show your net cash flow for a specific time period (p. 59)

personal financial plan strategy to improve current financial situation based on an analysis of your liabilities, cash flow, savings, investments, and long-term accumulation plans (p. 12)

personal financial statement (or balance sheet) a snapshot of your equity at a given point in time, derived from a summation of your assets and liabilities (p. 56)

personal financial success achieving financial goals and living life in accordance with your values, vision, and mission (p. 7)

personal mission statement formal statement that reflects one's strengths, passions, gifts, and stakeholders (p. 14)

personal values those things that are most important to you and to which you must be true to lead a happy and fulfilled life (p. 5)

phishing bogus marketing schemes by phone, mail, or e-mail designed to gain personal information for the purpose of stealing your identity and committing fraudulent actions for financial gain (p. 150)

point-of-service (POS) plan the patient has a single primary care provider, but that provider can make referrals to providers both in and out of the network (p. 257)

points the initial fee charged by the lender; each point is equal to 1% of the amount of the loan (p. 177)

portfolio all the investments you hold (p. 284)

power of attorney a legal document that designates another person to act on your behalf should you become incapacitated (pp. 256, 407)

predatory lending the act of lending money at an unreasonably high interest rate, making repayment excessively difficult or impossible for the borrower (p. 125)

preferred provider organization (PPO) provides health care services at a reduced fee (p. 257)

preferred stock a stock that carries no voting rights but takes priority over common stock in the payment of dividends to stockholders and upon liquidation (p. 325)

premium (bond) a price above the face value of a bond (p. 351)

premium (insurance) the periodic payment made on an insurance policy (p. 248)

present value current value of an asset to be received in the future (p. 35)

present value interest factor (PVIF) factor multiplied by a future amount so as to determine value of said amount today (p. 38)

present value interest factor of an annuity (PVIFA) factor multiplied by the annuity (payment) to determine the value of the annuity today (p. 43)

price-to-earnings (P/E) ratio an assessment tool for valuing a stock in which market value per share is divided by earnings per share (p. 331)

primary care physician your main doctor (p. 256)

private banker customer service representative and/or loan officer trained to provide special services and help meet the financial needs of high net worth customers (p. 96)

private mortgage insurance (PMI) insurance for the lender if it needs to foreclose on the home and the sale of the home does not cover the mortgage and the cost of the foreclosure (p. 175)

probate a process of proving in a court that a document is the last valid will and testament of a deceased person (p. 407)

progressive tax fee designed to help create equity among citizens; the wealthy are taxed at a higher rate than the poor (p. 224)

prospectus a legal document detailing the fund's investment objectives, fees, risks, and major holdings; it is required to be sent to investors prior to investing so they can make an informed decision (pp. 298, 384)

public goods and services government-provided services that protect and support citizens; examples are services provided by the police, fire, library, and military (p. 222)

R

real estate rental or owned property and land (p. 376)

real estate investment trust (REIT) an organization that pools funds from a group of individuals and invests in real estate (p. 377)

regressive tax fee that is applied uniformly, imposing a greater burden (relative to resources) on the poor than on the rich (p. 222)

reinstatement a temporary solution to the risk of foreclosure that involves re-establishing a loan if the terms of a new agreement are met (p. 205)

rent a stated payment for the temporary possession of a house, land, or other property, made usually at fixed intervals by the tenant to the owner (p. 376)

rental property housing, farm land, or commercial property that is rented or leased to others (p. 376)

rental reimbursement insurance to cover the cost of a rental vehicle if your vehicle is stolen or being repaired; usually involves a per-day limit as well as a limit on the number of days (p. 251)

renter's insurance insurance that covers your personal property in a structure you do not own; generally there is liability insurance associated with this coverage, to cover the liability of accidents occurring within the rented property (p. 253)

repossess to take possession of an item that was used as collateral to secure a loan (p. 114)

repurchase agreements contracts whereby a seller of securities agrees to buy back the securities at a specified time and price (p. 304)

return on investment (ROI) the ratio of money gained or lost on an investment relative to the amount of money invested (p. 378)

reverse mortgage a loan secured by the value of one's home whereby the homeowner receives either a monthly or a lump sum from the lender; the loan is paid in full from the proceeds of the sale of the house when the homeowner dies or moves out of the house (p. 86)

revocable living trust a trust over which the settler has retained the power of revocation (p. 406)

revolving lines of credit you pay a fee and can take and repay funds at will (p. 111)

risk premium compensation for taking a risk (p. 279)

roadside assistance insurance coverage to pay for towing if your vehicle is disabled (p. 251)

roll over extension of a loan (p. 127)

round lot a purchase of 100 shares at a time (p. 336)

Russell 2000 a market-performance measurement index, derived from the stock of the 200 smallest companies on the U.S. market (p. 301)

S

S corporation a regular corporation that has between 1 and 100 shareholders and that passes net income or losses on to shareholders (p. 383)

salvage value the value of a damaged vehicle if it were sold for scrap metal or to an individual or company for repair (p. 251)

savings money set aside for future use in a secure, no-risk instrument (p. 278)

sector funds funds that invest in one identifiable sector of the economy (p. 304)

secured credit card a credit card linked to a savings account where the lender may claim the funds in the account in the event that payments are not made (p. 111)

securities tradable documents issued by a corporation, government, or other organization that show evidence of ownership (p. 326)

Securities and Exchange Commission (SEC) the primary federal regulatory agency for the securities industry, it promotes full disclosure and protects investors against fraudulent and manipulative practices in the securities markets (p. 299)

share draft account an account held in a credit union that operates like a checking account in a regular bank (p. 88)

shares equal parts of a company's capital stock; they provide a method for sharing ownership of a company among investors (p. 298)

short sale when a residential property cannot be sold for the full amount of the loan and the lender accepts the selling price as satisfying the mortgage (p. 206)

short-sell order a stock trade request that involves selling borrowed stocks (p. 338)

short-term goal objective to be reached in less than one year (p. 15)

signature loans unsecured loans, where guarantee of payment is based on your word (your signature on the written agreement) (p. 111)

simplified employee pension (SEP) plan a low-overhead retirement savings account in which employers make contributions to traditional IRAs set up for employees (including self-employed individuals) (p. 398)

skimming stealing information from a credit card by swiping it through a processing machine that gathers the information (p. 151)

SMART goal objective that is Specific, Measurable, Achievable, Realistic, and Timely (p. 16)

specialist a person who manages the buying and selling of stocks; also called a *market maker* (p. 326)

spousal IRA traditional or Roth IRA established and funded by an individual for his or her spouse (p. 399)

SR-22 liability insurance liability insurance required by states for high-risk drivers (p. 251)

Standard & Poor's 500 (S&P 500) a market-performance measurement index, derived from the stock of 500 large companies on the U.S. market; designed to be a leading indicator of U.S. equities; it is meant to reflect the risk/return characteristics of the large-cap companies (p. 301)

stock exchange a market in which shares of stock and common stock equivalents are bought and sold (p. 325)

stock market a public market for trading ownership shares (stock) of a company among investors (p. 298)

stock equal parts or shares of a company's capital; a method of sharing ownership of a company with other investors (p. 324)

stop order a trade request that automatically converts to a market order when a predetermined price (a stop price) is reached (p. 338)

sublease the transfer of a lease agreement to a new tenant (p. 170)

T

tax credits credits that reduce your tax liability, dollar-for-dollar (p. 228)

tax-deferred taxes are not paid on the money or interest earned until the year it is withdrawn; a delay in taxation, meaning that funds are taxed at the time of withdrawal; IRA and 401(k)s grow tax-deferred, but they are taxed when the retiree taps them (pp. 83, 237)

taxable income adjusted gross income minus deductions and exemptions (p. 228)

taxes fees charged by the government on a product, income, or activity (p. 222)

term life insurance insurance that covers you for a fixed amount over a certain time period at a relatively low cost; when the term is over, payments to the insurance company stop and the insurance goes away (p. 263)

testate having made a legally valid will (p. 404)

time value of money where a dollar now is worth more than a dollar in the future, even after adjusting for inflation, because a dollar now can earn interest (p. 32)

times interest earned ratio an indicator of financial leverage; calculated as earnings before interest and taxes (EBIT)/total interest payments (p. 335)

trailing-stop order a stock trade request that depends on a predetermined price (p. 338)

trustee a person who manages the money in a trust (p. 406)

trustor a person who puts money into a trust (p. 406)

turnover rate percentage of stocks turned over (bought and sold) every year (p. 308)

12b-1 fee an extra fee charged by some mutual funds to cover promotion, distributions, marketing expenses, and sometimes commissions to brokers (p. 299)

U

umbrella liability insurance a supplemental policy that provides high limits of additional liability coverage above the limits of a homeowner's and auto policy (p. 254)

universal life insurance insurance that is similar to whole life insurance, except it does not have a guaranteed minimum return (p. 263)

unsecured credit card a credit card without collateral, where repayment is based on your promise to repay the borrowed amount (p. 111)

usury laws state laws specifying the maximum legal interest rate at which loans can be made (p. 125)

V

value stocks underappreciated stocks in the market, typically with single-digit P/E ratios (p. 332)

variable-rate mortgage loan in which the interest rate varies based on a benchmark plus an additional spread, called an ARM margin; also known as an *adjustable-rate mortgage* or a *floating-rate mortgage* (p. 176)

vested when one has satisfied the terms of employment and thereby has access to pension benefits contributed by the employer (p. 397)

voluntary simplicity a simplified lifestyle, where unvalued consumption and clutter are reduced (p. 6)

W

W-2 form form your employer sends to you and the IRS every year showing your earnings and the amount withheld for taxes (p. 228)

W-4 form form filled out when starting a new job that determines how much of one's pay is withheld for income taxes (p. 224)

wage earner bankruptcy Chapter 13 bankruptcy for individuals with a regular source of income (p. 208)

weighted-average maturity (WAM) the length of time until the average security in a fund will mature or be redeemed by its issuer (p. 303)

whole life insurance insurance that provides a fixed amount of life insurance and also a cash value as long as you pay the premiums (p. 263)

will a legal declaration of your decision as to the dispersion of your assets and the caring for your dependents following your death (p. 404)

withholdings taxes taken out of your paycheck before you actually get your paycheck (p. 224)

Y

yield the interest rate of a bond (p. 359)

yield to call the interest rate you receive between now and the early repayment date (p. 359)

yield to maturity the interest rate you receive between the date you buy the bond and the date it is repaid, including all payouts, coupons, and capital gains/losses (p. 359)

photo credits

TABLE OF CONTENTS

viii Meghann Woods Photography; **xxii** © WendellandCarolyn/iStockphoto; **xxiii** ballyscanion/PhotoDisc/Getty Images; **xxiv** (l) Photographer's Choice/Getty Images, (r) Comstock Images/Jupiterimages; **xxv** © Henrik Jonsson/iStockphoto; **xxvi** (l) © Dynamic Graphics Group/PunchStock, (r) Don Farrall/Getty Images; **xxvii** © Troels Graugaard/iStockphoto

CHAPTER 1

2 BananaStock/PunchStock; **4** (l) Author provided photo, (r) Tim Pannell/Corbis; **8** Rubberball/Getty Images; **12** BananaStock/PunchStock; **27** Author provided photo

CHAPTER 2

28 © Dynamic Graphics Group/PunchStock; **30** (l) Author provided photo, (r) Artville/Getty Images; **31** Author provided photo; **33** Author provided photos, Source: University of Iowa; **35** Stockbyte/Getty Images; **42** Comstock/PunchStock; **51** Author provided photo

CHAPTER 3

52 David Roth/Lifesize/Getty Images; **54** (l) Author provided photo, (r) Jessica Peterson/Rubberball/Getty Images; **59** David Roth/Lifesize/Getty Images; **61** Ingram Publishing/SuperStock; **76** Author provided photo

CHAPTER 4

78 Ocean/Corbis; **80** Image Source/Getty Images; **83** Ariel Skelley/Blend Images/Getty Images; **87** PhotoLink/Photodisc/Getty Images; **95** Ocean/Corbis; **106** Author provided photo

CHAPTER 5

108 Ryan McVay/Getty Images; **110** (l) © Jose Luis Pelaez Inc/Blend Images LLC, (r) ballyscanion/Photodisc/Getty Images; **114** Ryan McVay/Getty Images; **117** CMCD/Getty Images; **118** Corbis - All Rights Reserved; **120** Image Source/PunchStock; **122** image100/Corbis; **126** Comstock Images/Jupiterimages; **134** Author provided photo

CHAPTER 6

136 Adam Crowley/Getty Images; **138** Author provided photo; **139** Logo reprinted with permission of Equifax; **143** Chuan Khoo/Getty Images; **149** Adam Crowley/Getty Images; **160** Author provided photo

CHAPTER 7

162 Fuse/Getty Images; **164** BananaStock; **165** (l) Author provided photo, (r) PhotoLink/Getty Images; **169** (l) Fuse/Getty Images, (r) Author provided photo; **170** Author provided photo; **173** Thinkstock/Masterfile; **174** Author provided photo; **190** Author provided photo

CHAPTER 8

192 Photographer's Choice/Getty Images; **194** (l) Author provided photo, (r) Design Pics/PunchStock; **201** Photographer's Choice/Getty Images; **204** Stockbyte/Getty Images; **218** Author provided photo

CHAPTER 9

220 Photodisc/Getty Images; **222** Thinkstock/Jupiterimages; **229** Comstock Images/Jupiterimages; **236** Ingram Publishing; **237** Photodisc/Getty Images; **245** Author provided photo

CHAPTER 10

246 Blend Images/Getty Images; **248** Author provided photo; **253** Digital Vision/Getty Images; **254** Onoky/Getty Images; **261** (t) Tetra Images/Getty Images, (b) Author provided photo; **265** Blend Images/Getty Images; **274** Author provided photo

CHAPTER 11

276 Imagestate Media (John Foxx); **278** (l) Design Pics/Kristy-Anne Glubish, (r) The McGraw-Hill Companies, Inc./Jill Braaten, photographer; **280** Imagestate Media (John Foxx); **286** BananaStock/PictureQuest; **294** Author provided photo

CHAPTER 12

296 Royalty-Free/CORBIS; **298** (t) Author provided photo, (b) Royalty-Free/CORBIS; **311** OJO Images/Getty Images; **321** Author provided photo

CHAPTER 13

322 Jacobs Stock Photography/Jupiterimages; **324** (t) Fancy/Veer, (b) Courtesy of Lego Corporation; **337** Digital Vision/Getty Images; **339** Jacobs Stock Photography/Jupiterimages; **347** Author provided photo

CHAPTER 14

348 Ingram Publishing/AGE Fotostock; **350** Author provided photo; **351** Author provided photo; **353** Author provided photo; **355** David Zurick; **364** Ingram Publishing/AGE Fotostock; **365** Royalty Free/CORBIS; **372** Author provided photo

CHAPTER 15

374 The McGraw-Hill Companies/Maggie Mills; **376** Author provided photo; **380** The McGraw-Hill Companies/Maggie Mills; **393** Author provided photo

CHAPTER 16

394 Rolf Bruderer/Blend Images LLC; **396** Design Pics/Kristy-Anne Glubish; **409** Photodisc/Getty Images; **409** Ingram Publishing/SuperStock; **418** Author provided photo

CHAPTER 17

420 Author provided photo; **422** (t) Author provided photo; **422** (b) Author provided photo; **424** Author provided photo; **425** Author provided photo; **428** Author provided photo

index

A

Acceleration clause, 206–207
Actively managed mutual funds, 301
Adams, James Truslow, 423
Adams, Scott, 164
Adjustable-rate mortgages (ARMs), 85, 176–178
  properties of, 177
Adjusted balance method, 118
Adjusted gross income (AGI), 228, 235
Advance directives, 259, 261, 407–408
All-or-nothing order, 337–338
Allen, Woody, 284
Allocations, 7
Alternate payment options, 123–124
Alternative minimum tax (AMT), 232–234
  avoiding the, 233
  calculating and reporting, 233
American Express, 116
American Recovery and Reinvestment Act, 224
American Recovery and Reinvestment Bill, 235
American Stock Exchange (AMEX), 326
America's Cheapest Family (Economides and
  Economides), 423
Amortization, 124
Amortization tables, 125
Annual budget review, 425–426
Annual credit report, 145, 153
Annual payment example, 44–45
Annual percentage rates (APRs), 31–33,
  119, 125, 179
Annual percentage yields (APYs), 31–33
Annual report, 334
Annuities, 35, 399
Annuity due, 39–40
Appraisal fee, 177
APR (annual percentage rates), 31–33, 119,
  125, 179
Arbitration, 116
Armour, Richard, 136
Asset(s), 56
  appreciation of rental property, 379
  diversification of, 284–285
Asset allocation, 284
Assumption of loan, 206
ATM (automated teller machines)/debit cards, 82,
  93, 97–98
Attorney-in-fact, 259, 407
Augmenting income, 12
Auto insurance, 249–252
  collision, 251

comprehensive coverage, 250–251
full coverage insurance, 250
liability insurance, 250
lowering costs of, 252
roadside assistance, 251
SR-22 liability insurance, 251
uninsured/underinsured motorists, 251
Auto loans, 83
  leasing vs. buying, 167
Auto purchase, 164–170
  after-sale activities, 169–170
  banks and credit unions, 168
  car dealerships, 168
  closing the deal, 168–169
  comparison shopping, 168
  dealer financing, 168
  determining affordability, 165–166
  doing your homework, 165–169
  financing options, 168
  insurance cost, 168
  leasing vs. buying, 166–167
  needs vs. wants, 164
  negotiating the deal, 168
  new cars, 165–166
  price, 166–167
  private sales, 168
  process of, 165
  reliability and service records, 167–168
  test drive, 168
  trade-ins, 168
  used cars, 165
Automated teller machines (ATMs), 82, 93, 97–98
Automatic bill payments, 116
Automatic investments, 306
Average daily balance method, 118
Average tax rate, 232, 234
Axten, Simon, 152

B

Back-end load, 299, 310
Balance sheet, 56
Balanced mutual funds, 304
Balloon mortgage, 85
Balloon payment, 128
Balloon-payment loan, 182
Balloon-payment mortgages, 176–177, 178
Bank of America, 94, 116
Bank cards, 93
Bankrate Student Loans, 123

Bankrate.com, 33
Bankruptcy, 193, 208–211
    Chapter 7, 208
    Chapter 13, 208
    consequences of, 208–209
    counseling and education requirements, 208
    life after, 211
    means test, 208
    moral and social consequences of, 209–211
    resources, 209
    student loans, 210
    types of, 208
Barber, B. M., 340
Basic checking account, 92
Bear market, 328–329
Bearer bonds, 350
Behn, Aphra, 78
Being in the red/black, 59
Beneficiary, 406
Better Business Bureau, 203
Beverage costs, 65
Bill payment services, 83
Black Friday, 69
Bogle, John C., 98
Bok, Derek, 122
Bond(s), 349, 351
    basics of, 350–353
    benefits and risks of, 361–364
    buying bonds, 364–365
    call features of, 352
    convertible bonds, 355
    corporate bonds, 355–356
    high-yield (junk) bonds, 356
    how they work, 350–351
    municipal bonds, 353–355
    premium/discount, 351–352
    strategy for, 364–365
    Treasury bonds, bills, notes, and TIPS, 353
    types of, 353–356
    U.S. savings bonds, 353
Bond evaluation, 356–361
    bond value, 359–361
    ratings, 357
    researching bonds, 357–359
Bond ladder, 362
Bond mutual funds, 303
Bond ratings/rating agencies, 357
Bond value, 359–361
    calculation of, 380
    taxes and, 380–381
Book exchanges, 198
Bracketed order, 337–338
Brokers, 326, 336
Browne, Sir Thomas, 10
Budget, 66–67, 199

realistic budgeting, 66–70
reviewing and revising, 67–69
spreadsheet template, 68
steps in building of, 67
Budget plan, 4
Budget variances, 67
Budgeted buckets, 63–64
Buffett, Warren, 7, 311, 315, 324, 339–340, 356
Bull market, 328–329
Bull run, 298–299
Buy-to-close order, 337–338
Buying a home
    closing costs, 177
    finance shopping, 179
    mortgages, 175–176
    purchase price, 175
    real estate agents, 174–175
    selection criteria, 174
Bypass trust, 405–406

C

Cafeteria plan, 237
Call feature, 352–353
Call risk, 362
Capacity, 113–114
Capital, 115
Capital gain or loss, 233
Capital gains reinvestment, 307
Car dealerships, 168
Career choices, 17–18
    information on, 18–19
Career goal, 4
CarFax, 167–168
Carnegie, Andrew, 379
Carpenter, Dave, 363
Cash, 56
Cash advance loans, 125
Cash allocations, to budgeted buckets, 63–64
Cash cards, 93
Cash dividend, 330
Cash flow, 12
Cash inflows/outflows, 59
Cash purchase discounts, 120
Cash value (of life insurance), 56
Cashier checks, 98
Central Source Annual Credit Report Request
    Service, 146
Certificates of deposit (CDs), 81–82, 303
Chapter 7 bankruptcy, 208
Chapter 13 bankruptcy, 208
Character, 113
Charitable giving, 408–410
    impact on taxes, 408–409

lifetime gifting, 410
   selections, 408
Charitable remainder trust, 406–407
Check advance loans, 125
Checking accounts, 82, 88–94
   account register (sample), 91
   account statement (sample), 90
   balancing of, 89–92
   basic checking, 92
   free checking, 92
   interest-bearing checking, 92–93
   keeping track of transactions, 90
   overdraft protection, 93–94
   reconciling account, 90–92
   types of, 92–93
   written check (example), 89
ChexSystems, 94
Chrysler bankruptcy, 280
Churchill, Winston, 348
Cicero, 374
Citi Private Bank, 10
Citibank, 94
Class C shares, 311
Clipping coupons, 350
Closed-end mutual funds, 298, 300
Closing, 176
Closing costs, 177, 179
COBRA (Consolidated Omnibus Budget
   Reconciliation Act), 258
Coin counting fee, 98
Coinsurance, 255–256
Collateral, 82–83, 114–115
College savings, 287
College savings plans, 80–81
Collision insurance, 251
Commercial banks, 88–89, 94
Commercial paper, 303, 355
Commissions, mutual funds, 311
Common stock, 325
Commonwealth Fund Biennial Health Insurance
   Survey, 247
Community credit unions, 95
Company evaluation, 334–335
  evaluation criteria, 334–335
  financial reports/statements, 334
  research, 334
Company pension plans, 400
  job transitions and, 401
Company savings plans, 396–399
   401(k) plans, 397
   individual retirement accounts, 398–399
   Roth 401(k) plans, 397
   simplified employee pension (SEP) plans, 398
Compounding, 30–31
  power of, 30–34

Compounding interest, 31–32, 402
Comprehensive insurance, 250–251
Computer security, 150–151
Conditions, 115
Congressional Budget Office, 126
Consolidated Omnibus Budget Reconciliation Act
   (COBRA), 258
Consumer credit, 109
Consumer Credit Protection Act, 202–203
Consumer Federation of America, 129
Consumer fulfillment, 6
Consumer protection, debt collection and, 202–203
Consumer purchasing, 6
Consumer Reports, 146, 166–168
Contingent deferred sales load (CDSL), 312
Continuous automatic investing, 306
Control, 8
Convenience in banking, 95–96
Convertible bonds, 355–356
Convertible preferred, 325
Copayment, 255–256
Corporate bonds, 355–356
Cosigner, 113
Cost basis, 308
Cost-of-living comparisons, 403
Coupon, 350–351
Coupon rate, 359
Coupon yield (coupon rate), 359
Coverdell Education Savings Account (ESAs),
   287–288
Cramdown, 205
Credit, 109–111
   applying for, 112–113
   basics of, 110–116
   costly alternatives to, 125–129
   establishing credit, 138–139
   five Cs of credit decision, 113–115
   making payments on time, 201
Credit accounts, limiting number of, 146
Credit application, 113
Credit builder, 117
Credit card(s), 84, 110–111, 120
   advantages/disadvantages of, 116–117
   automating payments, 121
   charges and fees, 118–119
   choosing a card, 120–121
   credit limits, 117
   debt management for, 201–203
   errors on your statement, 119–120
   fees, 119
   finance charges, 118–119
   grace periods, 117
   interest rates, 117–120
   items to avoid charging, 142
   stop using of, 199

Credit card(s)—*Cont.*
   tips on managing, 120–121
   understanding of, 116–121
   zero percent deals, 119
Credit Card Act of 2009, 138
Credit card fees, 119
Credit card penalties, 119
Credit card purchases, 140–141
Credit card statement, 119–120
Credit costs, 119
Credit counseling, 146–147, 201–202, 209
Credit history, 140
Credit limits, 117
Credit options, 111–112
   depository institutions, 112
   finance companies, 112
   general purpose credit cards, 111
   revolving lines of credit, 111
   signature loans, 111
   store credit cards, 111–112
   unsecured credit card, 111
Credit-rating agencies, 355
Credit report
   accessing of, 144–145
   account detail (sample), 141
   annual report request, 145, 153
   correcting errors on, 147–149
   dispute letter (sample), 148
   expunging negative information, 148–149
   freezing of, 151
   identifying missing accounts, 147–148
   monitoring of, 150
   reading of, 139–141
   reporting errors on, 147
   strengthening of, 145–147
   websites for, 149
Credit reporting agencies, 139–140
Credit risk, 280
Credit score, 137–138
   deriving the score, 141–144
   improving your score, 144–147
   mortgage interest rate, 145, 177
Credit unions, 88–89, 95, 235
   auto financing, 168
Creditor, 350
Cummings, E. E., 69
Current ratio, 334–335

D

Day order, 337–338
Dealer financing, 168
Debit card, 82, 93, 97
Debit card replacement fee, 98

Debt
   making payments on time, 201
   methods to pay down, 147
   paying off of, 200
   paying off vs. transferring balance, 146
   steps to get out of, 199–201
Debt collection, consumer protection and, 202–203
Debt consolidation, 201–202
Debt management, financial life stages of,
     152–153
Debt ratio, 335
Debt ratio limits, 114
Debt-settlement companies, 202
Debt-to-income ratio, 113–114
Debt-to-income ratio calculator, 115
Declaration page, 248–249
Deductible, 250–251, 256
Deductions, 228, 235–236
Deed-in-lieu of foreclosure, 206
Default, 280
Default interest rates, 124
Default risk, 280, 362
Deferment, 123
Deferred deposit loans, 125
Demand deposit account, 88–89
Dependent care account, 238
Dependent life stage, 12–13
   debt management, 152–153
   financial instruments for, 80–82
   life insurance, 264
   retirement planning and, 401
   stocks and, 340
Deposited item returned, 98
Depository institutions, 112
Depreciation risk, 379
Diener, E., 18
Diners Card, 116
Direct stock-purchase plans, 339
Direct tax, 222–223
Dirksen, Everett, 410
Disability insurance, 259–261
   lowering costs of, 252
Disability and long-term care, 259–262
Discount, 353
Discount bond, 352, 355
Discount brokers, 336
Discounting, 36–37
Discover, 116
Disney, Walt, 14
Diversification, 284–285
   automatic asset-allocation funds, 284–285
   mutual funds, 304–305
   reasons for, 284
   targeted funds, 284–285
Dividend reinvestment plans (DRIPs), 339

Dividend(s), 325, 331
  mutual funds and, 307
  stocks and, 330
Dividend yield, 331
Dollar-cost averaging, 12, 306–307
Domicile, 406
Dominquez, Joe, 6–7
Donaldson, John, 363
Dow, Charles, 328
Dow Jones Industrial Average (DJIA), 328–329
Downshifting, 11–12
Dunn and Bradstreet, 120
Durable power of attorney for health care, 408
Dylan, Bob, 2

E

E*Trade, 332, 336
Early family life stage, 13
  debt management, 153
  financial instruments for, 84–85
  home ownership, 172
  life insurance, 265–266
  portfolio evaluation and, 286–288
  retirement planning and, 401
  stocks and, 340
Earned income tax credit (EITX), 239–240
Earnings before interest and taxes (EBIT), 335
Earthquake insurance, 253
Economides, Annette, 423
Economides, Steve, 423
Education choices, 18
Education deductions/credits, 238–239
Education savings account (ESA), 80–82, 86, 286–288
Efficient markets, 327
80-10-10 rule, 7
Einstein, Albert, 32, 35–36
Electronic (Internet) banking and bill payment services, 82–83
Electronic and professional filing, 230
Emergency Economic Stabilization Act of 2008, 95
Emergency fund, 194, 196, 198
Emmonds, R. A., 18
Empty nest life stage, 13
  debt management, 163
  financial instruments for, 85–86
  home ownership, 173
  life insurance, 266
  portfolio evaluation and, 288–289
  retirement planning, 401
  stocks and, 340–341
Encore careers, 86

Energy star savings, 64
Enough, 6–7
Epictetus, 322
Equifax, 139
Equity, 171
Equity mutual funds, 301–303
Equity REITs, 384
Estate and inheritance taxes, 404–405
Estate planning, 4, 404–408
  advance directives, 407–408
  important papers checklist, 404
  legal documents of the estate, 404
  power of attorney, 407
  trusts, 406–407
  wills, 404–406
Estate taxes, 223, 404–405
Event study, 327
Every Penny Counts journal, 199
Exchange-traded funds (ETFs), 301, 303
Excise taxes, 223
Exclusions, 256
Executor, 404
Exemptions, 228–229, 235–236
Expense ratio (of a mutual fund), 299, 301
Expenses, trimming of, 197–199
Experian, 139
Extended-hours order, 337–338
Extended warranties, 117

F

Face value (of life insurance), 56
Facebook, 152
Fair, Bill, 141
Fair Credit Billing Act, 120
Fair Credit Reporting Act, 147
Fair Debt Collection Practices Act (FDCPA), 202–203
Fair Housing Act, 382
Fair Isaac Corporation; see FICO (Fair Isaac Corporation) credit score
Family codes of conduct, 10
Family mission statements/constitutions, 10
Federal Deposit Insurance Corporation (FDIC), 95–96, 278–280, 303
Federal Direct Student Loan Program, 122–123
Federal Family Education Loans, 122
Federal Home Loan Mortgage Corporation (FHLMC) (Freddie Mac), 176
Federal Housing Administration (FHA), 114
Federal National Mortgage Association (FNMA) (Fannie Mae), 176
Federal Reserve Bank, 30, 110, 114
Federal Student Aid, 122–123

Federal student loans, 126
　subsidized vs. unsubsidized, 123
　to parents, 122
　to students, 122
Federal Trade Commission (FTC), 128, 148–149,
　　151, 203
　Foreclosure Rescue Scams, 206
Fee(s), 119
Fee-for service, 257
FICO (Fair Isaac Corporation) credit score, 140–143
　activities that drive score, 144
　amount owed, 142
　applications for new credit, 143
　length of credit history, 143
　payment history, 142
　types of credit in use, 143
FICO score range, 142
FICO score variables, 142–144
Filing status, 227
　head of household, 227
　married filing jointly, 227
　married filing separately, 227
　qualified widow(er), 227
　single, 227
Finance charges, 118
　adjusted balance method, 118
　average daily balance method, 118
　minimum finance charge, 118–119
Finance companies, 112
Financial calculator keys, 37
Financial crisis of 2008, 9
Financial goals, focus on, 424–425
Financial independence, 8–14
　options to, 11–12
Financial institutions, 94–98
　commercial banks, 94–95
　convenience, 95–96
　costs, 96–98
　credit unions, 95
　insured savings, 95
　minimum balance, 97
　overdraft fees, 97–98
　products and service, 96–97
　savings institutions, 95
　transaction costs, 97
Financial instruments, life stages, 80–88
Financial intermediaries, 94–95
Financial leverage, 334
Financial life stages, 12–14; see also
　　specific stage
　aligning financial instruments with, 80–88
　debt management, 152–153
　dependent stage, 12–13, 152–153
　early family stage, 13
　empty nest stage, 13

financial instruments for, 80–88
　home ownership and, 172–173
　independent stage, 13
　retirement stage, 13–14
Financial literacy, 9–11
Financial plan, 4–5, 12, 15–16
　foundation for, 5–8
　goal setting, 15–18
　identifying values, 5–6
　methods to achieve goals, 8–12
　mission statement, 14–15
　perception of financials, 5
　relationship with money, 5–8
　vision for future, 14–15
Financial reassessments, 425–426
Financial reports, 334
Financial statements, checking for accuracy, 150
Financial trouble
　early warning signs of, 194–196
　forewarnings of, 194–196
　necessary vs. nonessential spending, 196–199
　red-flag warnings, 195
　trimming expenses, 197–199
　yellow-flag warnings, 195
Fitch, 357–358
529 college savings plans, 80–82, 86, 286–288
Five Cs of credit decision, 113–115
　capacity, 113–114
　capital, 115
　character, 113
　collateral, 114–115
　conditions, 115
Fixed-income securities, 362
Fixed interest rate, 117
Fixed-rate/fixed-term mortgages, 85, 176, 178
Fixed tax, 223
Flipping properties, 377–378
Flipping real estate, 377–378, 386–389
　finding property, 386
　fixing up and adding value, 387
　flipping land, 389
　mistakes to avoid, 388
　reselling property, 387
　ROI on flipping, 386
　steps to success, 386–387
Flood insurance, 252–253
Flynn, Errol, 30, 138
Food savings, 197
Forbearance, 123, 205
Forbes, Malcolm, 406
Ford Federal Direct Student Loans, 122
Ford Motor Credit, 112
Foreclosure, 85, 170, 203–207
　avoiding of, 204–206
　mortgage problems, 204–205

preforeclosure process, 206
process of, 206–207
reinstatement, 205
resources for, 207
selling a home, 206
short sale, 206
temporary solutions to, 205
Foreign stock exchanges, 326
Form 1040, 229–230
Form 1040A, 229
Form 1040EZ, 229
Form 1099-Div, 307
401(k) plans, 11, 84, 235, 239, 287, 302, 315,
    397, 400
Francis, Brendon, 394
Frank, Robert, 10
Franklin, Benjamin, 4, 6, 55, 81, 144, 146, 194,
    222, 278, 423
Free checking, 92
Front-end load, 299, 310
Frugal living/frugality, 6, 12, 424
Full coverage auto insurance, 250–251
Full-service brokerage houses, 336
Fund manager, 298–299
Future value (FV), 35
    example, 37
    financial calculator method, 36
    long-hand method, 36, 39
    of lump sum, 35–36
    reference table method, 36
Future value of an annuity (FVA), 39–41
    financial calculator method, 40–41
    reference table method, 40
Future value interest factor (FVIF), 36
Future value interest factor (FVIF) table, 37
Future value interest factor of an annuity (FVIFA),
    40–41
Future value interest factor of an annuity (FVIFA)
    table, 40

G

Gas savings, 197
Gates, Bill, 7
General Motors Acceptance Corporation
    (GMAC), 112
General obligation bonds, 355
General purpose credit cards, 111
Genspring Family Offices, 10
Getty, J. Paul, 403
Gift taxes, 223
Giving goals, 4
Glickman, Louis J., 376
Global funds, 304

Goal setting, 4, 15–17
Goals, as SMART, 16–17
Goldbart, Stephen, 10
Good faith estimate, 179
Good-til-canceled order (GTC), 337–338
Google, 325
Government health care plans, 257–258
Grace period, 117
Grocer, Stephen, 327
Gross income, 227–228
Growth stocks, 332

H

Hale, Sarah J., 173
Halliburton, Thomas, 197, 367
Happiness, 17–18
Hausner, Lee, 10
Havner, Vance, 20
Head of household, 227
Health insurance, 255–259
    basics of, 255–256
    COBRA, 258
    government health care plans, 257–258
    lowering costs of, 258
    managed care plans, 256–257
    options for, 256–258
    system overhaul of, 260
    terms and costs, 256
    types of plans, 257
Health maintenance organization (HMO), 256–257
Health savings accounts, 238
Herszenhorn, David M., 126
Hertzburg, Frederick, 18
Hesiod, 286
Hewitt Associates, 302
High deductible plan, 257
High-risk, high-potential return, 284
High-yield (junk) bonds, 356, 363
Holiday Club accounts, 69
Holmes, Oliver Wendell, 385
Home equity, 85
Home equity line of credit (HELOC), 85, 88, 181
Home equity loans, 85, 181–183
    balloon-payment loan, 182
    comparison shopping, 182
    disadvantages of second mortgage, 182–183
    fixed-rate/fixed-term loan, 181–182
    types of, 181–182
Home inspection, 177
Home inventory, 254
Home ownership, 170–173; see also Buying a home
    advantages/disadvantages of, 171
    increase in equity, 171

Home ownership—*Cont.*
  life stages and, 172–173
  personal ownership, 171
  refinancing, 179–180
  rent vs. buy, 170–172
  tax advantages, 171
Home sale, 206
Homeowners' associations, 174
Homeowner's insurance, 252–255
  home inventory, 254
  liability insurance, 254
  lowering cost of, 255
  umbrella liability insurance, 254–255
Hope, Bob, 95
Hope credit, 239
Horwitz, J., 18
Housing price index (HPI), 377
Houssain, Farhana, 260
Howard, Rick, 152
Howard, Sidney, 169
Hubbard, Kin, 18, 285

I

Ibsen, Henrik, 426
Identity theft, 149
  defined, 149
  protection/safeguards, 117, 151
  safeguarding against, 149–152
  steps for victims, 151
  strategies to protect against, 150–151
IFF Advisors, 10
Inactive account fee, 98
Incentive stock options (ISOs), 233
Income
  augmenting of, 12
  increasing of, 201
Income plan, 4
Independent life stage, 13
  debt management, 153
  financial instruments for, 82–84
  life insurance, 264
  portfolio evaluation and, 286
  retirement planning and, 401
  stocks and, 340
Index market funds, 301
Indirect tax, 222–223
Individual retirement accounts (IRAs), 82–84, 239,
    299, 398–400
  annuities, 399
  Roth IRAs, 399
  spousal IRAs, 399
  traditional IRAs, 398–399
Inflation, 279, 285

impact on savings, 278–279
Inflation risk, 362
Inheritance tax, 405
Initial public offerings (IPOs), 298, 300, 324–325
Institutional share class, 311
Insurance, 247; *see also* Auto insurance; Health
    insurance
  auto insurance, 168, 249–252
  basics of, 248
  disability and long-term care, 259–262
  health insurance, 255–259
  home ownership, 174
  homeowner's and renter's insurance, 252–255
  importance of, 248
  knowing policy terms, 248–249
  landlordship, 381
  life insurance, 262–266
  reassessment of, 426
  selecting a company for, 248–249
Insurance claim, how to file, 254
Insurance company, 248–249
Insurance plan, 4
Insurance rider, 253
Insured savings, 95
Interest-bearing checking, 92–93
Interest-free loans, 117
Interest rate(s), 117
  basics of, 110–116
  risk and, 116, 280–281, 362
Interest rate risk, 116, 280–281, 362
Interest rate spread, 112–113
Intermediate goals, 15
Intermediate-risk, intermediate-return investments,
    284
Internal Revenue Service (IRS), 8, 83, 227,
    229–230, 379
  Form 6251, 233
International funds, 304
International Student Travel Confederation (ISTC), 67
Internship, 58
Intestate, 404
Investment(s), 85, 279
  basics of, 277
  for passive income, 12
  reassessment of, 426
  risk of, 279
  savings vs., 278–279
  timing income from, 238
Investment account, 12
Investment clubs, 338–339
Investment plan, 4
Investment pyramid, 283–284
  high-risk, high-potential return, 284
  intermediate-risk, intermediate-return, 284

low-risk, low-return, 284
no-risk, known-return, 283
Investment seed money, 298
Investment strategies, 278
mutual funds, 312–315
IRAs; *see* Individual retirement accounts (IRAs)
Irrevocable trusts, 406–407
Isaac, Earl, 141
Itemized deductions, 228
Itemizing, 237

J

J.D. Power and Associates, 167
Jefferson, Thomas, 181
Jesperson, Mark, 210
JPMorgan Chase, 94
Junk bonds, 356, 363

K

Kay, Michael, 363
Kelley Blue Book, 167–168
Knauerhase, Rob, 228
Knittel, Christopher, 327
Knox, Noelle, 388
Kudla, David, 302
Kurlander, Glen, 10

L

Lagomasino, Maria Elena, 10
Landlordship, 380–382
advertising, 381
budgeting expenses, 380–381
communication, 381
dispute resolution, 381
home checklist, 381
insurance, 381
maintenance and repairs, 381
rules for tenants, 381–382
tenant screening, 380
written terms, 382
Larson, Doug, 174
Last will and testament, 404
Lauricella, Tom, 88
Lease(s), 166, 376–377
Leasing vs. buying auto, 167
Lee, Dina, 363
Leisure, 1
Lending counseling, 205
Letter of intent, 404

Leverage, 386
Lewin, Tamar, 126
Liabilities, 12, 56, 58
Liability insurance, 250, 254
Life insurance, 262–266
comparison of, 265
dependent life stage, 264
early family life stage, 265–266
empty nest life stage, 266
independent life stage, 264
lowering costs of, 266
personal finance life stages, 264–266
recommended amount of, 264
retirement life stage, 266
types of, 263–264
Life stages; *see also* Financial life stages
portfolio evaluation and, 286–287
retirement planning and, 401–403
stock ownership, 340–341
Lifetime learning credit, 239
Limit order, 336–337
Limited liability company (LLC), 382–383
Liquidation, 208
Liquidity, 56
mutual funds, 308
Liquidity risk, 282, 362
Listing agent, 174
Livermore, Jesse, 302, 341
Living will, 259, 408
Load share classes, 312
Loan application fee, 177
Loan modifications, 205–206
Loan origination fee, 177
Loan payments, calculation of, 44–45
Loan-to-value (LTV) ratio, 175
Loans, as costly cash, 125–129
Locke, John, 425
Long-term care insurance, 261–262
lowering costs of, 262
Long-term goals, 15
Loonin, Deanne, 210
Loss payee, 250
Low-risk, low-return investments, 283
Lubbock, John, 52
Lump sum, 35
Lyubomirsky, Sonja, 17–18

M

Madoff, Bernie, 11
Managed care plans, 256–257
Manufacturer Suggested Retail Price (MSRP), 166–168
Margin loan, 114–115
Marginal income tax rates, 232, 234

Market makers, 326
Market order, 336–337
Market risk, 280–282
Married filing jointly, 227
Married filing separately, 227
Marx, Groucho, 289
MasterCard, 116
Maturity, 350–351
Means test, 208
Medicaid, 257
Medicare, 257
Medicare taxes, 223
Medigap/Medigap policies, 256–257
Minimum balance, 97
Minimum finance charge, 118–119
Mission/mission statements, 10, 14–15
Money, 17
  personal relationships with, 4–7
  stress and, 70
  value and, 30
Money market mutual funds, 303
Money, Meaning and Choices Institute, 10
Money order/cashier checks, 98
Money personality, 3, 5
Money relationship quiz, 6
Monthly budget review, 425
Moody's, 357–358
Morningstar, 308
Morningstar Style Box, 301, 313
Mortgage(s), 85, 170–171, 178
  avoiding foreclosure, 204–206
  disadvantages of second mortgages, 182–183
  forbearance, 205
  interest rate and credit score, 145
  loan modifications, 205–206
  long-term solutions, 205–206
  preforeclosure process, 206
  reinstatement, 205
  repayment plan, 205
Mortgage credit certificate (MCC), 237
Mortgage interest credit, 237
Mortgage problems, 204–205
Mortgage REITs, 384
Motivation to Work, The (Hertzburg), 18
Motley Fool website, 227
Multiple Listing Service (MLS), 387
Municipal bonds, 237, 353–354, 356
Mutual funds, 297, 299
  actively managed funds, 301
  automatic investment, 306
  back-end load, 310
  balanced funds, 304
  basics of, 298–299
  benefits and risks of, 304–308
  bond funds, 303

capital gains reinvestment, 307
characteristics of investors, 300
choosing and buying of, 312–315
commissions, 311
cost basis of, 308
costs and fees of, 299, 309–310
diversification and, 304–305
dividends and, 307
ease of recordkeeping, 307–308
ease of researching, 305
ease of understanding, 305
equity mutual funds, 301–303
exchange-traded funds (ETFs), 301
fees, 310
finding price of, 309
front-end load, 310
global and international funds, 304
history of, 298–299
index funds, 301
investment strategies, 312–315
liquidity of, 308
low initial investment, 306
money market funds, 303–304
no-load share classes, 312
other specialized funds, 304
professional fund manager, 304
regulation of, 299
research websites for, 306
risks and, 308
sector funds, 304
share classes, 311–312
types of, 299–304
variety of, 305
where to buy, 315

N

National Association of Insurance Commissioners
    (NAIC), 248
National Association of Real Estate Investment
    Trusts, 385
National Association of Securities Dealers Automated
    Quotation Stock Market (NASDAQ), 326
National Auto Dealers Association, 167–168
National Credit Union Administration (NCUA), 95
National Credit Union Association (NCUA), 278–280
National Credit Union Share Insurance Fund
    (NCUSIF), 95
National Federation for Credit Counseling (NFCC), 202
National Flood Insurance Program, 253
National foundation of Credit Counseling, 146
Necessary vs. nonessential spending, 196–199
Negative net cash flow, 59
Negotiable instruments, 82, 88–89

Neighbor Works, 205
Net asset value (NAV), 299, 301, 308
Net cash flow, 59
Net worth, 58
Networks, 256
New cars, 165–166
New York Stock Exchange (NYSE), 326
Nielson Report, 110
90-10 rule, 7
No-load mutual fund, 299, 301
No-load share classes, 312
No-risk, known-return investments, 283
Non-earned income, 8
Nonrefundable credits, 228

O

Obama, Barack, 126, 255
Odd lot, 336
Odean, T., 340
Offerings, 324
One Share, 339–340
Open-end mutual funds, 298, 300
Open outcry, 326
Opportunity cost, 60–63
Ordinary annuity, 39
Orman, Suze, 235
Out-of-pocket expense, 256
Over-the-counter Bulletin Board (OTCVV), 326
Over-the-counter (OTC) market, 326
Overdraft fees, 97–98
Overdraft protection, 93–94

P

Paper money, 30
Par (face value), 353, 355
Partnership, 382–383
Passive income, 8
    investing for, 12
    rental property, 379
Pay yourself first, 35, 63
Payday loans, 125–127
    loan cost, 127
Pell grants, 126
Penny-pinching, 66
Penny stock, 326
Pension plans, 238
Perkins Loans, 122
Perma-debt, 138–139
Permanent life insurance, 263
Person of record, 307
Personal balance sheet, sample, 58

Personal cash flow statement, 55, 59–60
Personal financial management
    balance in, 422–423
    reassessments, 425–426
    sustainability, 423–425
Personal financial plan, 4, 12
Personal financial statements, 55–58
Personal financial success, 7
Personal identification number (PIN), 93
Personal life stages, 13
    stocks and, 340–341
Personal mission statement, 14–15
Personal ownership, 171
Personal property insurance, 253–254
Personal relationship with money
    identifying values, 5–7
    perception of financials, 5
Personal values, 5
Phishing, 150, 152
Picasso, Pablo, 65
Pink sheets, 326
PINs, protection of, 151
PLUS loans (Parent Loan for Undergraduate
    Students), 122
Point-of-service (POS) plans, 256–257
Points, 176–177
Pope, Alexander, 10
Portfolio, 284
Portfolio evaluation, 285–289
    early family life stage, 286–288
    empty nest life stage, 288–289
    independent life stage, 286
    life stages and, 286–289
    maintaining balance, 285–286
    retirement life stage, 289
Positive net cash flow, 59
Post-dated check loans, 125
Power of attorney, 259, 407
Predatory lending, 124–125, 128
Preference shares, 325
Preferred provider organization (PPO), 256–257
Preferred shares/stocks, 325
Preforeclosure process, 206
Prelec, Drazen, 199
Premium, 248–249, 256, 351
Premium bond, 351, 355
Prepaid tuition plan, 81
Present value (PV), 35
    financial calculator method, 38–39
    long-hand method, 38
    of lump sum, 37–40
    reference table method, 38
Present value of an annuity (PVA), 41–43
    example, 44
    financial calculator method, 44

Present value of an annuity (PVA)—*Cont.*
  long-hand method, 41–42
  reference table method, 42–43
Present value interest factor (PVIF), 38–39
Present value interest factor of an annuity (PVIFA), 42–43
Pretax contributions, 83
Price-to-earnings (P/E) ratio, 331–332
Price-to-earnings (P/E) valuation process, 332
Primary care physician, 256
Private banker, 96
Private companies, 324–325
Private mortgage insurance (PMI), 175
Private sales, 168
Private student loans, 122–123
Probate, 407
Professional fund manager, 304
Progressive taxes, 222–224
Promissory note, 112
Property taxes, 223
Prospectus, 298, 300, 384
Protection goals, 4
Public companies, 324–325
Public goods and services, 222–223
Purchase protection, 117

Q

Qualified tuition plan, 80
Qualified widow(er), 227
Quealy, Kevin, 260
Quinn, Jane Bryant, 278, 280

R

Ramsey, Dave, 203
Real estate, 377
Real estate brokers, 174–175
Real estate investment(s), 375
  basics of, 376–378
  flipping real estate, 377, 386–389
  measuring return on investment (ROI), 377–378
  real estate investment trusts (REITs), 377, 384–385
  rental property, 376–383
  shared ownership, 382–383
  types of, 376–378
Real estate investment trusts (REITs), 377, 384–385
  avoiding scams, 385
  how to invest in, 384
Real Estate Settlement Procedures Act (RESPA), 179

Real property, 85
Recordkeeping, 307–308
Redemption fee, 299
Refinancing your home, 179–180
Refundable credits, 228
Regressive taxes, 222–224
  examples of, 223
Reinstatement, 205
Reinvestments, 238
Relative Solutions, 10
Rent, 377
Rent vs. buy, 170–172
Rent payments, 379–380
Rent-to-own, 128
Rental car coverage, 117
Rental property, 376–383; *see also* Landlordship
  advantages of, 378–379
  asset appreciation, 379
  depreciation risk, 379
  disadvantages of, 379–380
  failure to receive rent payments, 379–380
  landlordship, 380–382
  passive income, 379
  rental ROI, 376–377
  tax advantages of, 379
  temporary rentals, 383
  unoccupied property, 380
Rental reimbursement, 251
Renter's insurance, 253
Renting, advantages/disadvantages of, 170
Repossession, 114
Repurchase agreements, 304
Research, company evaluation, 334–335
Responses, 115
Retirement funds, comparison of, 400
Retirement life stage, 13–14
  financial instruments for, 86–88
  homeownership, 173
  life insurance, 266
  portfolio evaluation and, 289
  retirement planning, 402–403
  stocks and, 341
Retirement planning, 396–403
  company savings plans, 396–399
  early family life stage, 401
  empty nest life stage, 401–402
  late dependent/independent life stages, 401
  life stages and, 401–403
  reasons for savings, 397
  retirement life stage, 403–403
  Social Security, 399–401
Retirement savings calculators, 402
Retirement savings contributions credit, 236–237
Retirement savings estimator, 402

Return on investment (ROI), 376, 378
    on flipping, 386
    measurement of, 377
    rental property, 377
Revenue bonds, 355
Reverse mortgage, 86, 88
Revocable living trusts, 406–407
Revolving lines of credit, 84, 111–112, 114
Rewards, 117
Richmond, Riva, 152
Right-sizing, 85
Riney, Earl, 362
Risk
    default or credit risk, 280
    interest rate risk, 280–281
    interest rates and, 116, 280
    liquidity risk, 282
    market risk, 281–282
    of mutual funds, 304–308
    return and, 280–282
Risk premium, 279
Risk tolerance, 282
Roadside assistance, 251
"Robin Hood" tax, 224
Robin, Vicki, 6–7
Rockefeller, John D., 10, 390
Rogers, Will, 220
Roll over, 127
Roosevelt, Franklin D., 353
Ross, Jenna, 210
Rosten, Leo, 286
Roth 401(k) plans, 397, 400
Roth IRAs, 83, 235, 286, 399–400
Round lot, 336
Russell 2000 funds, 301, 303

S

S corporation, 382–383
Sales tax, 223
Sallie Mae Student Loans, 123
Salvage value, 251
Samuelson, Paul, 364
Savings, 278–279
    compound interest, 402
    impact of inflation on, 278–279
    investments vs., 278–279
    pay yourself first, 63
Savings accounts, 80
Savings banks, 95
Savings institutions, 95
Savings and loan associations (S&L), 95
Second mortgage, 85, 182–183
Sector funds, 304

Secured credit card, 111
Securities, 326
Securities Act of 1933, 299
Securities Exchange Act of 1934, 299
Securities and Exchange Commission (SEC),
        299–300, 325, 334
    Investment Company Act, 303
Sell-limit order, 338
Sell-stop order, 338
Selling agent, 174
Senior debt obligations, 357
Series E bond, 353
Serin, Casey, 388
Service records, 167
Shakespeare, William, 62
Shapiro, A., 199
Share(s), 298–299
Share classes, 311–312
Share draft accounts, 88–94
Share price, 299
Shaw, George Bernard, 266, 408
Short sale, 206
Short-sell order, 337–338
Short-term capital gain, 233
Short-term goals, 15, 17
Shortages, 386
Signature loans, 111
Simester, Duncan, 199
Simple interest, 31
Simplified employee pension (SEP) plans,
        397–398
Single filing status, 227
Skimming, 150–151
SMART (specific, measurable, attainable, realistic,
        time-bound) goals, 16–17
Social Security, 86, 260–261, 399–401
Social Security Act, 288
Social Security taxes, 223
Sowell, Thomas, 250
Specialist/market marker, 326
Specialized mutual funds, 304
Spending goals, 4
Spending habits
    analysis of, 54–60
    budgeted buckets, 63–64
    daily spending, 55
    necessary vs. nonessential, 196–199
    pay yourself first, 63
    stopping leaks/adjustments, 64–65
    sustainable consumption, 65
Spending journal, 55–56
Spending money, 70
Spousal IRAs, 399
SR-22 liability insurance, 251
STA Travel, 67

Stafford Loan, 122
Standard & Poor's, 357–358
Standard & Poor's 500 (S&P 500), 303, 328
Standard & Poor's 500 funds, 301
Stango, Victor, 327
State Children's Health Insurance Program
    (SCHIP), 258
Statutory prospectus, 313
    summary prospectus, 313
Steinbrenner, George, 409
Stock(s), 298, 323–325
    basics of, 324–326
    buying directly, 339–340
    buying and selling, 336–341
    buying single shares, 339–338
    common stock, 325
    dependent life stage, 340
    direct stock-purchase plans, 339
    dividend reinvestment plans (DRIPs), 339
    early family life stage, 340
    empty nest life stage, 340–341
    independent life stage, 340
    investment clubs, 338–339
    personal life stages and, 340–341
    preferred stock, 325
    private and public companies, 324–325
    retirement life stage, 341
    types of brokers, 336
    types of, 325
Stock dividend, 330
Stock evaluation, 327–334
    company evaluation, 334–335
    comparison of indexes, 329
    dividend yield, 331
    dividends, 330
    expectations, 327–328
    market and indexes, 328–329
    price, 329–330
    price-to-earnings (P/E) ratio, 331–332
    stock quotes, 329–330
Stock exchanges, 325–326
    American Stock Exchange (AMEX), 326
    foreign stock exchanges, 326
    National Association of Securities Dealers Auto-
        mated Quotation Stock Market (NASDAQ), 326
    New York Stock Exchange (NYSE), 326
    over-the-counter (OTC) market, 326
Stock funds, 301–303
Stock market, 298–299
Stock quotes, 329–330
    types of trades, 336–338
Stop-limit order, 337–338
Stop-loss orders, 338
Stop order, 337–338
Stop payment fee, 98

Stop price, 338
Store credit cards, 111
Straight bankruptcy, 208
Strategic allocation funds (SAFs), 315
Strategic plans, 10
Stress, 70
Stress management, 7
Student loans, 83, 122–126, 210
    alternate payment options, 123–124
    amortization tables, 125
    calculating payments, 124
    consolidation and refinancing, 123
    deferment, 123
    federal loans, 122
    forbearance, 123
    payment example, 124
    private loans, 122–123
    repaying loans, 123–124
    repayment of, 123
    restructuring of, 126
Sublease, 171
Subordinate debt, 357
Subprime mortgages, 281
Sustainability, 423–426
Sustainable consumption, 65

T

Target strategy, 365
Tax advantages, rental property, 379
Tax audits, 230–231
Tax credits, 229, 238–240
    education deductions/credits, 238–239
    family values credits, 238
    other credits, 240
Tax-deferred, 82
Tax-deferred accounts, 299
Tax-deferred investments, 83, 237–238
Tax filing, 227–231
    basics of, 227–228
    filing status, 227
    gross income, 227–228
Tax forms
    electronic and professional filing, 230
    use of, 229–230
Tax-friendly states, 222
Tax liabilities
    exemptions and deductions, 235–236
    itemizing, 237
    mortgage interest credit, 237
    retirement savings contributions credit, 236–237
    strategies to minimize, 235–239
Tax management, 221
Tax preparers, 231

Tax rates, 232–234
    alternative minimum tax (AMT), 232–234
    average tax rate, 232, 234
    marginal income tax rates, 232, 234
Tax software packages, 230
Taxable income, 228–229
    lowering of, 237–238
Taxes, 223
    bonds and, 380–381
    charitable giving, 408–409
    estate and inheritance taxes, 404–405
    fulfilling liabilities, 224
    home ownership, 174
    progressive/regressive taxes, 222–224
    types of, 222–226
Teaser rates, 97
Telephone costs, 64
Teller fee, 98
Temporary rentals, 383
10K report, 334
10Q report, 334
Term life insurance, 263, 265
Terra Cycle website, 65
Test drive, 168
Testate, 404
Thrift institutions, 95
Time deposits, 81–82
Time value of money, 32–33, 35–42
Times interest earned ratio, 335
Title loans, 127–128
Title search, 177
Todd, Mike, 276
Toyota Motor Credit, 112
Trade-offs, 6, 8
Traditional IRAs, 83, 398
Trailing-stop order, 337–338
Transaction costs, 97
TransUnion, 139
Travel discounts, 67
Treasury bills, 282, 353–354
Treasury bonds, 353–354
Treasury Direct, 364–365
Treasury Inflated-Protected Securities (TIPS),
    353–354
Treasury notes (T-notes), 353–354
Trump, Donald, 7
Trustee, 406
Trustor, 406
Trusts, 406–407
Truth-in-Lending Act, 119, 127
Truth in Savings Act, 32
Tucker, Sophie, 70
Tugend, Alina, 66
Turnover, 313
Turnover rate, 308

Twain, Mark, 331
12b-1 fee, 299, 301, 312
28/36 rule, 113

U

Ultimate Cheapskate's Road Map to True Riches,
    The (Yeager), 66
Umbrella liability insurance, 254–255
Unearned income, 228
Uniform Commercial Code, Article 3, 89
Uninsured/underinsured motorist
    insurance, 251
U.S. Bureau of Labor Statistics, Occupational Outlook
    Handbook (OOH), 18–19
U.S. Department of Education, 122
U.S. Department of Housing and Urban Development
    (HUD), 205, 207, 382
U.S. Living Will registry, 261
U.S. Mint, 30
U.S. savings bonds, 353–354
U.S. Treasury bonds, 280, 365
Universal life insurance, 263–265
University of Iowa Community Credit Union, 95
Unlisted stock, 326
Unoccupied property, 380
Unsecured credit card, 111
Upcycling, 65
Used cars, 165, 167
Usury laws, 124–125

V

Value stocks, 332
Values driven financial planning, 5–6
Vanguard Group, 98
Variable interest rate, 117
Variable life insurance, 265
Vaughan, Bill, 420
Vehicle identification numbers (VINs), 167
VeriSign iDefense, 152
Vested, 397
Visa, 116
Vision/vision statement, 14
Voluntary simplicity, 6

W

W-2 form, 228
W-4 Deductions and adjustments worksheet, 226
W-4 form (Employee's Withholding Allowance
    Certificate), 224–225

W-4 Personal allowances worksheet, 224–225
W-4 Two-earners/multiple jobs worksheet, 226
Wage earner bankruptcy, 208
Wall Street Journal Online, 329, 332–333
Wealth accumulation, pay yourself first, 35
Weighted-average maturity (WAM), 303
Weir, Tom, 409
Wells Fargo, 94
Whole life insurance, 263, 265
Williams, Rich, 126
Wills, 404, 408
Wilson, Earl, 140
Withholdings, 224
Woods, Tiger, 327
Workers' compensation, 261

Y

Yahoo! Finance, 358
Yeager, Jeff, 66
Yield, 359
Yield to call, 359
Yield to maturity, 359
Young, Henry, 28
Your Money or Your Life (Dominquez and Robin), 6–7

Z

Zero percent deals, 119